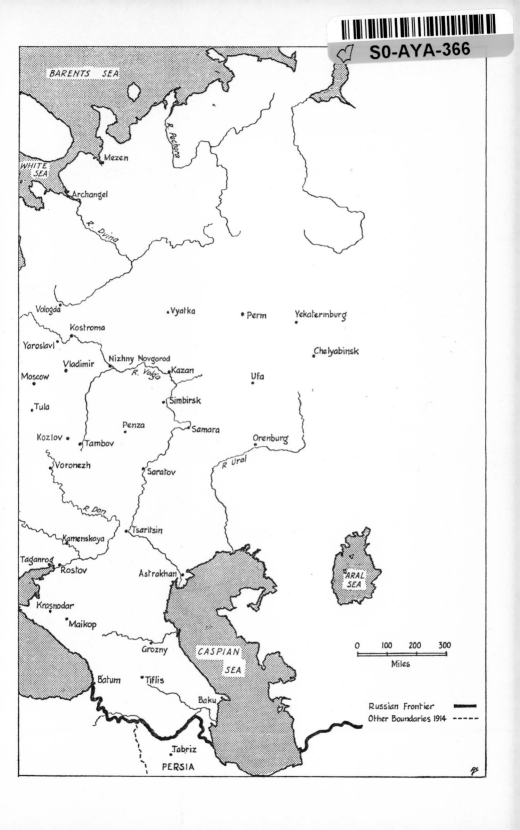

SO-AYA-366

BARENTS   SEA

WHITE
SEA

Mezen

R. Pechora

Archangel

R. Dvina

Vologda

Vyatka

Perm

Yekaterinburg

Kostroma

Yaroslavl

Chelyabinsk

Vladimir

Nizhny Novgorod

Kazan

Ufa

Moscow

R. Volga

Tula

Simbirsk

Penza

Samara

Kozlov

Tambov

Orenburg

Voronezh

R Ural

Saratov

R. Don

Kamenskaya

Tsaritsin

Taganrog

Rostov

Astrakhan

ARAL
SEA

Krasnodar

Maikop

Grozny

CASPIAN

SEA

0   100   200   300

Batum

Tiflis

Miles

Baku

Russian Frontier

Other Boundaries 1914 - - - - -

Tabriz

PERSIA

THE FIRST FIFTY YEARS

THE FIRST
FIFTY YEARS
SOVIET RUSSIA 1917–67

BY

IAN GREY

COWARD-McCANN, INC.
NEW YORK

For
WINSOME
SONYA
DAVID
CATHERINE

Preface

THE history of Russia in the fifty years since 1917 is the story of the survival and the transformation of a vast, backward nation into a great modern power. In scale, suffering, and achievement it is an epic of which the Russian people, who have displayed extraordinary fortitude, dynamism, and power of survival, is the hero.

The first world war and the collapse of the tsarist regime had led to the October revolution and the civil war, one of the most savage conflicts in history, when inhumanity and exalted idealism existed side by side. In the course of three-and-a-half years of war against Germany and then the civil war, some twenty-seven million Russians perished. Lenin's New Economic Policy provided a brief respite, but then the nation was plunged into a concentrated industrial and agricultural revolution. This was the beginning of Stalin's iron age. Terrible excesses marred this period, but he imposed a discipline and gave an impetus without which the industrialization of Russia would not have been carried through so rapidly.

After this hard but massively productive period, Russia was engulfed by the second world war in which some twenty-five million Russians lost their lives and almost the whole of European Russia was devastated. Emerging as victors the Russians at once tackled the immense task of reconstruction.

The early history of the Soviet regime witnessed conflicts of personalities and, after the death of Lenin, savage struggles for power as Stalin eliminated his rivals and asserted his supremacy. An important outcome of this struggle was the fundamental change in the outlook of the bolshevik party. Lenin, Trotsky, Bukharin, and other old bolsheviks had stood for the international communist movement. Stalin was the nationalist who stood for Russia first. In fact, without his dedicated nationalism and his leadership, Russia might well not have survived as a nation.

Stalin has been the dominant figure for most of this period. He was the great national leader in the Russian historical tradition. Ivan the Terrible and Peter the Great were his progenitors. Like them he was concerned not with the individual but with the nation. Like Peter he was obsessed with Russia's backwardness and her consequent vulnerability to attack. His overriding concern was to ensure that Russia should catch up with the advanced nations of the world. Like Peter he recognized that delay might be fatal. Indeed, the headlong industrialization of Soviet Russia in the 1930s recalls Peter's drive to modernize Russia in the early eighteenth century. Both men also made frantic efforts to develop Russia's military and naval might. Both made serious mistakes, but by their drive and singlemindedness both achieved their objective of establishing Russia as a strong power.

Peter was, however, tsar by the grace of God and none among his subjects had dared to challenge his position or authority. Stalin was supreme ruler by reason of his superior ability, foresight, and ruthlessness. He eliminated all opponents and even thousands of citizens whom he believed to be antipathetic to his policies. His monstrous inhumanity has stained his name indelibly, so that, like Ivan, he may be remembered only as 'the Terrible'. In writing of him and his rule I have been at pains not to extenuate his misdeeds, but I have sought to place him in the context of Russia and her history and to record his achievements.

Understanding of this momentous period in Russia's history has often been overcast by politics. Western historians have tended to write as protagonists in the cold war. Soviet historians shackled by the demands of the communist party are prone to suppress and distort. Many decades will doubtless pass before historians are able to write dispassionately. In this account I have sought to describe the first fifty years of the Soviet regime as the most recent chapter in the history of a nation which has since the foundation of Kievan Rus endured for nearly a thousand years. I have sought also to interpret Russia, her story, outlook, and policies in this century with all the impartiality that I am able to command.

A nation so frequently invaded and devastated throughout her history inevitably develops an outlook on defence and other matters different from that of a nation like the United States which has always known security. War and invasion, the needs of defence, the habit of obedience to authority, and the general demand for a strong central authority in a country so vast and comparatively sparsely populated have contributed towards an attitude which lays emphasis on the community and the nation rather than on the individual. This has been an ingredient in the Russian approach to communism, which has not always been readily understood.

In general Marxism–Leninism has impressed the vast majority of people in the West as an unrealistic and impractical theory and, in its militant form, as a menace. But communism ceased to be of major importance as a factor in Soviet foreign policy under Stalin's rule. He was concerned with Russia's interests and defence. He pursued a national policy, similar to the policies of the tsars, and invoked communism only if and so far as it served those interests. His foreign policy was, in fact, geared in the first instance to meet the threat of German aggression and, since 1945, the threats of U.S. aggression, of the revival of German militarism, and of the chauvinistic communism of the Chinese.

Internally the Soviet regime has pursued the vast experiment of state ownership and control and a planned economy. Experts conflict in evaluating the degree of success achieved by the system, especially in agriculture. It seems clear, however, that without the momentum which Stalin was able to give or the stimulus of war or other national crisis, the socialist system leads to stagnation by destroying individual initiative. The Soviet experiment had undoubtedly had an important influence in many countries of the world, especially in promoting attempts to plan their economies. In the Soviet Union, however, the interesting development, since the death of Stalin, has been the realization, not openly acknowledged, that socialism must be tempered in some degree to encourage enterprise among Soviet citizens in industry and agriculture.

Since it is fundamental to my approach to Russia and her history, it is necessary to state that Russia must be regarded as part of Europe and the West and, further, that world peace and a reasonable way of life for the Russian people depend ultimately on the advance of the Soviet regime towards a genuine liberalism and the reunion of Russia with the Western community of nations.

It is no part of the historian's function to probe into the future, but he would not be human if he did not wonder what the next fifty years will bring. Certain Western historians confidently expect the emergence of a new autocrat, whether Shelepin, Polyansky, or some *apparatchik* still not prominent. Such a development is, they maintain, inevitable in a country which has known only autocratic rule. But, while it is true that bolshevism is a natural continuation of the tsarist system, it is false to assume that Russia is doomed by factors of national character to such rule. The Russian people have rallied to their autocrat throughout their history primarily for reasons of defence. If the Russian fear of aggression from the West, especially by the U.S.A., were abated, the sense of being beleaguered and of needing a tsar or a Stalin would diminish. Subject mainly to the relaxation of this pressure from outside, Soviet Russia will, I believe, evolve rapidly towards the more liberal regime for which the demand among the Russian people is already mounting.

The task of condensing this account of a period so important and eventful into one volume has presented many difficulties. It has resulted in omissions which I regret. The Jews, their contribution to the revolution and their subsequent disappointment, the Orthodox Church and its fate under the bolsheviks, art and literature and Soviet nationalities policy are aspects of the period which I had planned to cover. In condensing severely, however, I hope that I may have succeeded in bringing out more strongly the main flow of events and at the same time in conveying something of the essence of Russia in this period.

The chief sources on which I have drawn are listed in the bibliography and in the notes to each chapter. I would like, however, to pay tribute to Leonard Schapiro's *The Communist Party of the Soviet Union*, Merle Fainsod's *How Russia is Ruled*, and the eight volumes of E. H. Carr's *History of Soviet Russia*, which I have found especially helpful. Alexander

Werth's *Russia at War* was of great value to me in writing Part V. I was myself in North Russia in 1942–4, part of the time at sea with the Soviet Northern Fleet as a British liaison officer, and later in Moscow and Leningrad. My memories of these months confirm the impressions reported by Alexander Werth who travelled so widely and witnessed so much more than I was able to see.

A problem has been to fit very recent events, such as the Vietnam war, the visit of Kosygin to Britain in February 1967, and similar items, into the perspective of this history. The Vietnam war, if it does not escalate further, will drag to a stalemate and in a decade it will have the significance that the Korean war has today. Other developments which have loomed large in the press in 1966–7 will also fall into place as the years pass. I have therefore not taken it upon myself to anticipate or forecast, but in my closing pages have sought to indicate trends and the directions in which they were evidently pointing.

In transliterating Russian names I have broadly followed the system adopted by the British Academy. Usually I have preferred the Russian plural form, unless the word, like kulaks, seemed more acceptable in its English form.

I should like to record my appreciation of the help and facilities which I have enjoyed, and without which I could not have written this book, in Chatham House (The Royal Institute of International Affairs), the London Library, and the British Museum. To Miss Helen Roy for making the index I express my gratitude. I have also had help from several friends in tracking down references, corroborating impressions, elucidating points of translation, and in other ways; although they remain nameless, they know that they have my thanks.

My family deserves special mention for its patience with a father absorbed by his task, and I acknowledge with love and gratitude the constant support of my wife.

London
March 1967.

And you, Russia of mine—are you also not speeding like a troika which nought can overtake? Is not the road smoking beneath your wheels, and the bridges thundering as you cross them, and everything being left in the rear, and the spectators, struck with the portent, halting to wonder whether you be not a thunderbolt launched from heaven? What does that awe-inspiring progress of yours foretell? What is the unknown force which lies within your mysterious steeds? Surely the winds themselves must abide in their manes, and every vein in their bodies be an ear stretched to catch the celestial message which bids them, with iron-girded breasts, and hooves which barely touch the earth as they gallop, fly forward on a mission of God? Whither, then, are you speeding, O Russia of mine? Whither? Answer me! But no answer comes—only the weird sound of your collar-bells. Rent into a thousand shreds, the air roars past you, for you are overtaking the whole world, and shall one day force all nations, all empires to stand aside, to give you way!

Nikolai Vasilievich Gogol, *Dead Souls*
Trans. D. J. Hogarth

Contents

List of Illustrations

Key to Acknowledgements

[1] Keystone Press
[2] Mansell Collection
[3] Press Association Ltd.
[4] Radio Times Hulton Picture Library
[5] Novosti Press Agency
[6] Camera Press Agency

Maps

THE FIRST FIFTY YEARS

Prelude

March 1917

BY the beginning of 1917 unrest in Petrograd was acute. But no one realized that one of the most momentous revolutions in history was about to break over Russia.

The third winter of the war against Germany and Austro-Hungary had been exceptionally severe and the savage cold had aggravated the hardships in the city. The people had no fuel for heating and queued for hours for their small bread ration. The workers, enduring harsh conditions and in the munition industry working a minimum ten-and-a-half-hour day, were weary and rebellious.

Petrograd was, however, still a city of order and elegance. The ballet with Karsavina as *prima ballerina* was at its most brilliant. Feodor Chaliapin was singing at the Narodny Dom. The nobility and wealthy merchant families sought distraction in theatres, restaurants, and other fashionable places or entertained in their homes. But the gaiety was forced and the appearance of normality unreal.

The court no longer led the social life of the capital. The imperial family had retired to Tsarskoe Selo, fourteen miles away, after the revolutionary outbreak which had followed the war against Japan in 1905. The Winter Palace, formerly the scene of magnificent balls and receptions, was quiet. Only once during this period of more than ten years had the palace come to life with its old splendour. This had been for the celebration of the tercentenary of the Romanov dynasty, the last of the great imperial occasions. But, more than the withdrawal of the court and the wartime austerities, the war itself cast dark shadows over the city. Most families had suffered bereavements or were waiting anxiously for news of their menfolk, serving on one of the fronts.

During 1917, however, the mood of Petrograd had turned to anger. People of all classes were exasperated by food and other shortages, and for the great majority the almost daily rises in the cost of living brought new hardships. The defeats and withdrawals of the army, the pride of the nation, added to the general distress. In fact, the army had fought magnificently, but defeat in East Prussia had overshadowed victories elsewhere, and war-weariness had spread among the people like a paralysis. Moreover, victories and defeats alike had been accompanied by terrible casualties, and by mid-1917 more than five-and-a-half million Russians had lost their lives. Reports of troops suffering frostbite because they had

3

no boots or warm clothing, of men being sent into action without rifles or ammunition, of wounded men dying untended, and of the carnage on all fronts appalled everyone.

In every century of their history, however, the Russian people have endured far more gruelling trials and, indeed, they have usually been capable of extraordinary endurance. But now the feeling that the nation was drifting leaderless troubled and angered them.

Since 1905 the throne had been declining in power and authority. Tsar Nicholas for all his conscientious efforts had proved hopelessly inadequate. He had taken important steps towards constitutional government, but then under the influence of the Empress and other reactionaries he had tried to draw back and to maintain the old autocracy. The war had rallied the nation to him and his people would have accepted his reactionary measures, if he had been a real autocrat. But he was no leader and by 1917 he had lost the last shred of popular confidence.

Strikes and demonstrations became more frequent in the capital. Revolutionaries were active among the workers, but their influence was insignificant. The disorders were almost wholly spontaneous outbursts of popular anger. In spite of frequent warnings and reports, however, Nicholas seemed unaware of the mounting crisis. When at last he realized the gravity of the situation in the rear, it was too late.

Early in March, distressed by the illness of his children at Tsarskoe Selo and by the reported unrest, Nicholas decided to leave the Supreme Headquarters at Mogilev and to return to Petrograd. He set out between 4 and 5 p.m. on 13 March, his personal train preceded by another for security. Insurgents had seized control of the railways at certain points but the train made good progress as far as Malaya Vishera. Here, to avoid possible capture at the approaches to the capital, it was diverted to a line running due west to Pskov, the headquarters of General Ruzsky, commanding the northern front. The imperial train arrived there on the evening of 14 March.

Nicholas now informed Ruzsky that he would make the concessions tirelessly urged by the president of the Duma, Count Mikhail Rodzyanko, and others. He would appoint a prime minister, commanding the confidence of the country, and give him full authority over his colleagues and over general policy; only foreign policy and the armed forces would remain imperial prerogatives.

Ruzsky at once spoke by telephone with Rodzyanko. By this time, however, revolution had erupted in the capital. The Soviet of Workers' and Soldiers' Deputies had been formed and the Duma committee in the midst of the turbulence of the Tauride Palace was struggling to hold back the threatening anarchy. Rodzyanko told Ruzsky bluntly that the tsar's concessions had come too late.

Rodzyanko communicated with the chief of staff, General Alekseev, in Mogilev. Alekseev and the quartermaster-general, Lukomsky, were already of the opinion that Nicholas must abdicate. Without delay Alekseev got into touch with the generals in command on all fronts. The Grand Duke Nicholas, commanding the Caucasus, General Sakharov, chief of staff, Rumania, General Brusilov, commanding the south-west front, General Evert on the western front, and General Ruzsky were unanimous that abdication was inevitable.

Alekseev reported to Ruzsky on the morning of 15 March. Ruzsky at once informed the tsar that in the opinion of his generals his abdication was the one course that might unite the nation and prevent civil war.

Nicholas was taken by surprise. Until this moment he had never dreamt that he might face such a demand, least of all from his uncle, and his generals whom he considered as brother-officers. But he made his decision without delay. To Alekseev he sent a telegram which read:

'In the name of the welfare, tranquillity and salvation of my dearly beloved Russia I am ready to abdicate from the throne in favour of my son. I request all to serve him truly and faithfully.'[1]

This telegram was to have been telephoned to Rodzyanko in Petrograd. Ruzsky held it back, because the news had reached Pskov that two representatives of the Duma committee were already on their way to negotiate the tsar's abdication.

Vasily Shulgin, a leading member of the Duma, and Alexander Guchkov, chairman of the Octobrist party, had been chosen to carry out this fateful task. Their special train, drawing a single carriage, travelled slowly all day through the bleak frozen country of north-west Russia and reached Pskov at ten in the evening of 15 March. Guchkov and Shulgin at once made their way across the station to the platform where the imperial train was standing. Both were profoundly moved by their mission, but convinced that it was the only way to save the country and the dynasty and, indeed, the life of Nicholas himself.

In the imperial carriage, its walls lined with green silk and furnished with a few tables and chairs, Nicholas received the two men kindly, taking pains to put them at ease and to help them in their task. He was calmer, far calmer than they were. Guchkov, unaware that the tsar had already taken the decision to abdicate, spoke forcefully of conditions in the capital and explained why he and his colleagues considered abdication unavoidable.

During this speech Nicholas looked to the front, quite withdrawn. All his life he had been overburdened by the responsibilities of the throne and of the coronation oath to preserve the imperial heritage as he had received it from his father. A small man, soldierly in bearing, austere in his way of life, and gentle in his feelings, he had tried, often mistakenly, but always sincerely and with all his might to meet the demands which a cruel fate had imposed on him. Increasingly he had become aware that the task was beyond him. His face revealed the strain in the sunken hollows beneath his cheek bones. He had begun to take refuge in an impenetrable reserve which was rooted in his piety and in his personal fatalism. He was always a very humble man and now he submitted quietly to the demand for his abdication. Some felt that this fateful step was even welcome to him; it was a release, allowing him a freedom, such as he had never known; it held promise of days to be spent with his wife and children whom he adored.

Nicholas listened to Guchkov's speech. He then indicated his acceptance of the proposals, but explained one change he wished to make. He had at first agreed that his son should succeed him, but during the afternoon he had changed his mind. The thirteen-year-old tsarevich Aleksei was haemophilic. Nicholas, who loved his son even more than his four daughters, had asked his personal physician, Dr Fedorov, if the condition was incurable. Faced with this direct question, Fedorov had sadly replied that he knew of no cure. Accepting then, what he had probably always known, that the boy would not long survive, Nicholas had decided to keep him under his own care. He therefore told Shulgin and Guchkov that he would abdicate in favour of his brother, Mikhail. He added quietly, simply, 'You will understand a father's feelings.'

This change was, in fact, unconstitutional, but Shulgin and Guchkov felt that they could not raise objection. The deed of abdication was signed, and the two men took leave of their former sovereign.[2]

Returning across the station, dimly lit by blue lamps, Shulgin and Guchkov found that a crowd, stirred by rumours and possibly by some sense of foreboding, gathered around them, asking in whispers, 'What is it? . . . What has happened?'

Guchkov told them of the tsar's abdication. 'Russian people,' he continued, 'bare your heads, cross yourselves, give prayer to God . . . Russia is entering on a new road. Let us ask God to show us his mercy.'

The people in the crowd crossed themselves and, kneeling in the snow, prayed for Russia and for themselves. In Petrograd all was anarchy and feverish planning and plotting; the people of Pskov were closer to Russia at this point and, as they prayed, all was, in Shulgin's words, 'deadly quiet'.[3]

PART I

THE COLLAPSE
OF THE TSARIST REGIME

CHAPTER ONE

Tsarist Russia

THE abdication of Nicholas II marked the end of the Romanov dynasty and the collapse of tsarist rule. The autocratic regime which had during more than four centuries forged a strong and united nation had suddenly and undramatically fallen. It had happened not as a result of the volcanic eruption of popular discontent, but because the tsar and the nobility had failed. By the end of the nineteenth century they had become an insufferable burden and brake on the nation, as it strained to develop in every field and to become a modern power.

The revolution that followed brought a tidal wave of change. It swept away the institutions, policies, and outlook which had been built up through centuries. The men who rose to power out of the revolutionary chaos threw up a façade of new ideologies, new titles, and institutions, and they proclaimed a new era.

Bewildered and overwhelmed, the people struggled to survive, and with the century-old habit of obedience they followed anyone who now offered effective leadership. Some among them were inspired by the novel doctrine of Marxism, which they heard from the lips of professional agitators and propagandists; the great majority were untouched by revolutionary ideas. But, as they laboured to repair the ravages of revolution and civil war, they found that the needs of the nation were basically the same as in previous centuries, and the methods developed to meet them were also strikingly similar. To many it seemed that Russia in the twentieth century was living through an era of change, greater in scope, but in essence the same as that which Peter the Great had instituted two hundred years earlier.

The society which had vanished dramatically and suddenly was so rooted in privilege and order that it had seemed indestructible. It centred on the tsar and his court, and on the Orthodox Church which upheld the regime and played an essential part in every state activity. The nobility was a numerous highly privileged caste. Many nobles served the state honourably, but the majority spent their lives alternating between their estates and the capital in a cultured, sociable idleness. Their world was portrayed in Pushkin's *Evgenii Onegin* and in Tolstoy's *War and Peace* and *Anna Karenina* in which devotion to service, endless social life, and ennui, especially in the young, made up daily life.

The massive base on which the whole society rested was the peasantry.

9

The Russian peasants were remote from the nobility and gentry, from the priesthood and state officials who dictated their way of life. Usually short, broad-shouldered, heavily bearded, poorly fed and clad, the peasant in most provinces led a life of intolerable hardship. His only outlets were church-going and getting drunk on holy days and whenever opportunity offered. But he was capable of extraordinary physical endurance and possessed a shrewd intelligence.

The institutions which had kept these divided classes united in one society were the absolute monarchy, the Orthodox Church and the highly centralized system of government and the bureaucracy. The absolute monarchy in Russia was more extreme than the European monarchies which had proclaimed the divine right of kings. Ivan the Terrible, the first crowned tsar of Russia, had in the sixteenth century established the elevated conception of the tsar as divinely appointed, absolute in authority, and answerable only to God. The people had accepted this image of their sovereign and had submitted to his power. Long after western Europe had discarded all theories of the divinity of kings, the Russians continued to show the same subservience to their autocrat. In part this was a reflection of a sturdy passivity and indifference to political rights. In part it was due to the absence of any class of people in Russia able to challenge or restrain the autocracy. But of all the factors which had kept the absolute monarchs enthroned in Russia the most important was defence.

Lacking natural frontiers, Russia was exposed on all sides to enemies. During the first three centuries of its history incessant raiding and invasions by the Tatars in the east and south and by Germans, Lithuanians, Swedes, and Poles from the west had kept the nation in a state of almost permanent mobilization and had consumed the greatest part of the national revenues. In the nineteenth and twentieth centuries Russia suffered major invasions which had penetrated deep into the country, inflicting terrible devastation.

The cruel experience of enemy invasion was a part of Russian life. The people had rallied to the Grand Prince of Moscow for protection and they had continued to support their tsars, for it was only by the creation and maintenance of a strong, united nation with power centralized in his hands that they could defend themselves.

The Russian Orthodox Church was of immense importance in forging the national character and outlook of the people. It had played a momentous part in the founding of the nation under the rule of Moscow and in maintaining the power of the throne. It ordered the lives of the people with a calendar of feasts, fasts, and holy days. In no Christian country has the life of the nation and the everyday life of the people been so closely identified with their religion.

The Russian church also contributed to the stagnation of the nation. In stressing the importance of the community, it discounted the individual so that individual initiative and will remained weak. It encouraged the attitude of absoluteness which admits no compromise; the community was all-important and it had no room for independence of thought or deed; he who was not with them was against them. It taught men to embrace suffering and injustice willingly as part of the price of salvation. It was a stronghold of ultra-conservatism. Change was abhorrent, evil, sinful. This religious conservatism carried into the secular field, discouraging reform and entrenching the backwardness of Russia.

Beneath the tsar in the sharply defined social hierarchy came the land-owning nobility. This class might have acted as a restraint on the absolute power of the autocrat, but it failed to develop strength and cohesion and became increasingly subordinate. The majority of the nobility had held their estates from the tsar in return for their services. A new class of serving gentry, developed to meet the growing military and civil needs of the state, also held land on service tenure. Peter the Great in the course of his tempestuous reign had enforced this principle of service. All, from himself as tsar down to the humble serf, owed service to the state either in the army or navy or in the ministries. He established ranks of service which took the place of the hierarchy of birth in conferring seniority and the patents of nobility.[1] Gradually, however, the service estates came to be regarded as hereditary and the liability to serve was relaxed, until in 1762 it was abolished, except in time of national emergency. Also, the nobility as a whole had failed to become rooted in their estates and few took any interest in agriculture. The land was no more than a source of income, and most nobles regarded living on their estates as being buried alive.

The urban and merchant class, which had played a significant role in the political development of western Europe, was small in Russia, and indeed virtually non-existent in the earlier decades. The cities and towns, established in Muscovy, were primarily military and administrative centres, which never acquired the economic power and independence of the cities in the West. Novgorod and Pskov were for a time exceptions. But Ivan the Terrible had crushed the last embers of independence in Novgorod which was later completely overshadowed by Peter the Great's new city at the mouth of the Neva.[2]

All power and responsibility were centred on the tsar. In a country of Russia's immensity such extreme centralization led to endless delays and frequent chaos. Peter the Great was the first to attempt sweeping reform of the administration. At first he attempted to decentralize by dividing the country into eight vast governments. When this failed he concentrated on creating a strong central executive. The Senate and the system of collegial boards which he adapted from Swedish practice gave promise of more efficient administration and even of sharing power with the tsar. But the new institutions failed to develop. Educated and competent officials were few in a country where illiteracy was widespread and education even among the upper classes was limited. Peter enlisted foreigners to instruct his people and he took steps to introduce wider education. But his successors lacked the energy and vision to pursue his reforms.

The system of government as it functioned in Russia in the nineteenth century and until the revolution was clumsy and inefficient. The tsar appointed ministers who did not form a cabinet, but answered directly and individually to him. He was his own prime minister and the additional burden of co-ordinating policy in a country in which delegation of authority was discouraged and minor matters continued to be referred to the tsar for decision, made his duties exceedingly heavy. Under a tsar like Nicholas II who was intelligent, quick, and industrious, but indecisive and unable to co-ordinate policies, confusion and inefficiency resulted on a massive scale. At a time of national crisis, like the first world war, the country was reduced to chaos.

One of the most important arms of the administration was the 'Personal Chancellery of His Imperial Majesty' which answered immediately to the tsar himself.[3] It was divided into sections of which the third section was notorious. The powers of this section were wide, but in practice it concentrated mainly on political offences. For this purpose it called on the *gendarmerie*, who carried out its orders in making political arrests. Persons accused of political crimes could be brought before the ordinary courts. More often the head of the third section would exercise his authority to order 'administrative arrest' of persons considered a danger to state security. No appeal lay from such arrest and many, falsely accused or mistakenly taken into custody, were condemned to 'administrative exile' without trial.

Exile to Siberia or distant parts of European Russia was not then such a harsh punishment. The exiled person could take his family, buy food and clothing, and correspond with friends. As most of those condemned to this form of exile belonged to the upper classes and, like Lenin himself, had sufficient means to buy all that they needed, their lives were not unpleasant. Imprisonment in a penal settlement or a fortress was by contrast extremely severe. But, as has been noted, tsarist prisons were 'mild, almost humanitarian' compared with the concentration camps of totalitarian regimes in the twentieth century.[4]

Throughout the country the police were ubiquitous. They were organized in three forces, independent of each other—the ordinary police, the *gendarmerie*, and the numerous agents of the third section—and, enjoying special protection, they were often an arrogant and oppressive force in the lives of the people.

Russia was an agricultural country. Of her total population in 1850 of some sixty million about 250,000 were landowning nobility, a further three-and-a-half million people were in the towns, while the peasants made up the remaining fifty-six million. This great peasant mass tilled the soil, provided the troops, paid the taxes, and humbly obeyed tsar and landowner. With incredible patience and stamina the peasants accepted the slavery of serfdom, poverty, and hunger.

The great revolts, led by Stenka Razin in the reign of Tsar Alexei, by Bulavin, in the reign of Peter the Great, and by Pugachev in Catherine the Great's reign, had come only when the peasants, driven beyond all endurance by the hardships of their lives, had given way to a dark destructive fury. Then, like the blinded Samson, they had sought to destroy their world and themselves with it. But they had not denied their loyalty to their autocrat.

Serfdom, which lay at the root of the stagnation of their lives, had been introduced gradually to meet the needs of the state, especially for defence. It had first tied the peasant to the land and then, as the privileges of the landowning nobility increased, the peasant had become a chattel. The sole obligation of the landowner was to ensure that his peasants paid taxes and were available to serve in the army; in all other respects they were at his disposal. He could forbid their marriage, have them flogged, or sentenced to hard labour in Siberia. He could sell a serf with his family or alone, tearing children from parents, with or without the land, to another landowner.

Even before serfdom had become established, the peasants had evolved the village commune (*mir* or *obshchina*), the members of which owned nearly all things in common. This primitive institution was responsible for the payment of taxes on the basis of the number of 'revision souls' ascribed to it in the census lists. It decided the crops to be grown and the distribution of land among its members. It was also responsible for issuing the passport, required by a peasant wishing to work away from his village. The landlord's permission was also needed before he departed, but since the commune was responsible for collecting and paying the village taxes and for ensuring that the cash or labour due to the landowner was paid, the latter was less likely to raise objections. Indeed in the less fertile northern provinces the landowners had begun to draw most of their revenue, not from agriculture, but from dues paid by their peasants who were allowed to work in the new industries. The peasant, in fact, suffered the double slavery of serfdom and the commune.

A group of patriotic intellectuals in nineteenth-century Russia, known as the Slavophiles, proclaimed the commune as an example of genuine self-government at village level. They saw in the natural sharing of labour and profits of the commune a genuine socialism, innocent of the crude competitive individualism of the West. The commune was, they held, an institution to be cherished by all Russians as peculiarly their own creation, which had mitigated the evils of serfdom in the past and would bring new benefits to the peasants and the nation in the future. In fact, the commune lay upon the peasant like a dead weight. He could take no special interest or pride in his land not only because it was allocated to him in strips, often widely separated from each other, but also because he could never be sure of cultivating the same land, for the commune was always liable to re-allocate the land in accordance with the needs of the community. The system thus gave no security of tenure and its standard was the interests of the commune as a whole. Agriculture remained backward and serfdom, holding more than three-quarters of the population in its dead grasp, was abetted by the primitive commune which killed any remaining interest in the land that the peasant worked. Serfdom and the commune lay, like gangrenous growths, at the heart of the stagnation and corruption of the tsarist regime.

Not only in agriculture but in every field of national life Russia was backward, compared with the other nations of Europe. Geography and history had isolated her. Colonization of the immense Eurasian plain and the unending struggle against enemies on every frontier had absorbed the energies and dominated the thoughts of the people.

In the fifteenth century, when the nation was coming to birth, the Russians had known little of the Renaissance and the Reformation, the expanding trade and the new horizons unfolding in the West. As soon as the Great Russian principalities had been united under the rule of Moscow, Ivan III and Ivan the Terrible had sought to revive the trade and intercourse which had been part of the heritage of Kiev and Novgorod. They had found their efforts actively thwarted by the Germans, Swedes, Poles, and Lithuanians. These western neighbours, anxious to keep the Russians backward and isolated, raised barriers against this potentially powerful neighbour.

The process of reviving trade and introducing Western ideas and techniques into Russia had advanced very slowly in the sixteenth and seventeenth centuries. The policy of Westernization had gained a new dramatic impetus in the reign of Peter the Great. He had bludgeoned his people into embracing new ideas. He established Russia's free access to the Baltic, and revived trade and intercourse with the rest of Europe on a new scale. The stubborn resistance of the mass of his subjects and the apathy of his successors limited the effectiveness of many of his reforms. But he succeeded in launching Russia on the path of development and the impetus of his work was never entirely lost.[5] In the following century Russia began to stir, as though with some deep instinctive urgency, and by the end of the nineteenth century Russia was beginning to catch up with the West in every sphere.

The policy of reform and modernization nevertheless continued to meet opposition. The ideas aroused by the French revolution had put all Russian reactionaries on their guard. Catherine the Great and Alexander I, despite their liberal pretensions, were stubborn in their defence of the old regime. But the demand for change could not be suppressed, even by the thirty years of Nicholas I's reactionary rule. The defeat of Russia in the Crimean War revealed to all the bankruptcy of his repressive paternalistic system of government. On his death the whole nation breathed a sigh of relief and their relief was mingled with a gathering faith that out of the ruins of the Crimean War a new Russia would rise.

Alexander II succeeded to the daunting heritage of Russia's age-old problems, which had been exacerbated to explosion point during his father's reign. He had the courage and determination to face the bitter opposition of the reactionary nobility and gentry, and to enforce many reforms. His reign, opening with the promise of a golden age, nevertheless drifted into apathy and the terrorism which resulted in his assassination in March 1881. But he deserves credit for the reforms he carried out and especially for the emancipation of the serfs.[6]

Nicholas I had freed all state peasants from personal serfdom, but the liberation of all serfs was needed and this raised major problems. Liberation without land would merely condemn the peasants to starvation. The landowning nobles were unwilling to grant land to their liberated serfs, and not even Nicholas I was prepared to dispossess them compulsorily. Meanwhile outbreaks of peasant violence became more frequent. At least 400 cases occurred in the last ten years of Nicholas I's reign and in the following six years (1855–60) a further 400 outbursts occurred. But still the great majority of the landowners remained opposed to the abolition of serfdom, advocating sterner repression to keep the peasants in their places. The tsar and a few of his advisers recognized the growing danger. Alexander himself expressed their fears when, addressing the Moscow nobility, he said, 'It is better to abolish serfdom from above than to wait until the serfs begin to liberate themselves from below.'

The Act of Emancipation, as finally promulgated on 3 March 1861, was a reform of the greatest importance. Serfdom was abolished. Land from landowners' estates was assigned to the peasants for which they paid small annual redemption dues to the government, and the landowner received compensation from the government in respect of the land taken from him. But the landowners succeeded in thwarting to some degree the purpose of the emancipation and protected their own interests at the expense of the peasants.

Moreover, in spite of the good intentions of the act of emancipation, the unfortunate peasants were still denied real freedom. Although released from the arbitrary authority of the private landowner, they remained shackled to the commune. The land, assigned to them in perpetuity and on which through the commune they paid redemption dues, continued to be to a large extent under the direct control of the commune.

The peasants had expected both freedom from serfdom and possession of the lands. They found now that their conditions were much the same and that they had the additional burden of paying redemption dues. Feeling that they had again been cheated, many gave way to violence, and unrest among them continued, until the Stolypin reforms early in the twentieth century.

Alexander had also recognized the need for major reforms in local

B

government, in the legal system, in the army, and in education. The local government reform gave rise to urban councils and to the zemstva, the district or provincial assemblies, in European Russia, representative of all classes. Disputes between liberal and reactionary forces led to some reduction in their powers, but they had wide responsibilities and they demonstrated that in local and provincial government the Russian people could work effectively together. The zemstva in particular fostered the growth of liberal ideas. They employed members of the intelligentsia in increasing numbers, as teachers, doctors, and engineers who, mingling with the nobility and gentry, infected them with the new political theories.

In 1864, the same year as the zemstva reform, important changes were introduced into the judicial system. Their effect was to give Russia a legal system comparable with the most efficient in the West. One important result of these reforms was the organization of lawyers for the first time, amounting to the creation of a new profession. This legal profession attracted Russian intellectuals who made it one of the most brilliant and learned bars in Europe. Moreover, in the absence of a parliament and an unrestricted press, the freedom of speech in the courts and the publicity received by trials gave the courts and the legal profession a special influence in the formation of public opinion.

Of similar importance were the reforms introduced in the army by Milyutin, Alexander II's minister of war. Formerly all serfs and certain classes of townsmen could be torn from village and family, and made to serve for twenty-five years. Milyutin reduced the period of service to sixteen years. He also reorganized the military system, paying special attention to training which had in the past been subordinated to parade ground drill. His most important reform, however, was the introduction of general conscription on an equitable basis. The law of January 1874 made military service compulsory for all Russian men, aged twenty and fit, but subject to certain exemptions. The only son or grandson or the sole supporter of a family was exempt from service. The term of service was six years, to be followed by nine in the reserve, and another five years in the militia. It might also be reduced in accordance with the education of the recruit, those with university education serving for only six months. But, except for the traditional selection of the guards from the nobility, class and privilege no longer played any part in recruitment for the army.

Education, subjected to some restrictive measures during Alexander II's reign, was greatly expanded with increases in the numbers of teachers and of schools open to all classes. In some fields of education Russia was well ahead of other European countries, especially in the education of women; in 1881, for example, some 2,000 women were attending higher courses at the universities.

This development of education in Alexander II's reign was to have special importance for the revolutionary movement. It fostered the growth of the intelligentsia who provided a new, restless element in Russian society. This new class was made up of the children of impoverished nobles, of the clergy, of merchants, and even of peasants who with the greatly increased opportunities for education had attended secondary schools, and had even graduated from universities. They were the *pazno-chintsi*, who belonged to no specific class, the outsiders who fretted because they were intelligent and educated, but could find no outlet for their talents and energies in a society which, in fact, needed them. From this new class came most of the radicals and revolutionary leaders. Many were embittered by direct experience of the hardships and sufferings of the people. To them improvement of material well-being was more urgent than constitutional reform. The tolerance and objectivity of the radicals of noble origin formed no part of their outlook. They were filled with a savage indignation which bred extremes and terrorism.

A French diplomat said of Alexander II: 'His was not a great intellect, but he had a generous soul, very upright and very lofty. He loved his people and his solicitude for the humble and the suffering was unbounded.'[7] He had abolished serfdom and had introduced far-reaching social and administrative reforms. But he had never been popular. From the nobility he met with constant opposition and the new revolutionary movement with its active terrorist element hounded him. In the last years of his reign terrorists made repeated attempts to murder him; he became the quarry in a man-hunt. In March 1881 he signed a statement, announcing the first steps towards an elective body with legislative powers. It was a proposal holding promise of a major constitutional advance which might have laid the foundations of parliamentary and democratic government in Russia.

On 14 March, however, as he rode through St Petersburg, a terrorist threw a bomb which shattered his carriage. He was unhurt and, against the advice of those near him, insisted on going to the aid of one of those injured. At this moment another terrorist threw a bomb, which shattered both his legs. He whispered to his brother, 'Home to the palace to die there.' The same French diplomat said of him, 'He was a great Tsar and deserved a kinder fate.'[8]

The assassination of his father made an enduring impression on Alexander III who succeeded to the throne. To him it was a vivid demonstration of the perils of all liberal and revolutionary ideas. He discarded his father's plans for further reforms. A powerful giant of a man, who could bend iron bars in his naked hands, Alexander had an imperious will and decisive mind. He was a natural autocrat. He expected to be and was obeyed. For the thirteen years of his rule any signs of liberal or revolutionary activity were summarily suppressed.

Alexander III's reign was a time of unrelieved repression, but it was also a time of intensive economic, industrial, and even agricultural development. This expansion was directed chiefly by Sergei Witte, a man of humble origin who had risen by sheer ability to be minister of finance. A convinced believer in the autocracy, as embodied in his master, whose special trust he held, Witte was to despise Alexander III's son and successor, Nicholas II, for his failure to live up to his father's example.

In this period of great economic and industrial activity one of the basic factors was the rapid growth in population. Between 1850 and 1900 the population of Russia doubled. It increased by thirty per cent in the next fifteen years and in 1914 the total population, excluding Finland, was 170 million. This rate of increase seriously aggravated the problem of rural overpopulation. In great numbers people moved to the cities and towns. In 1851 only some three-and-a-half million were to be found in cities and towns: by 1914 the figure had risen to twenty-five million.

The industrial expansion in the early stages had depended primarily on seasonal labour by peasants. The workers, growing rapidly in number, were still peasants, rooted in the villages and lands to which they could return. Rapidly during the second half of the nineteenth century a new industrial working class evolved, distinct from the peasantry from which it came. The rate of growth of this class has been exaggerated by Marxists, for this industrial proletariat was fundamental to their theory of revolution. By 1914, however, there were possibly three million factory workers, about one million miners, and some 800,000 railway workers, all of whom were to play a dominant part in the revolutions of the twentieth century.

Notwithstanding this flood of people to the cities and towns, eighty-five per cent of the population was still on the land. The problems of the peasant and of agricultural production remained the most fundamental, and apparently insoluble in Russia, although mainly as a result of Alexander II's reforms the country was moving swiftly from the old patriarchal and feudal system towards a new state capitalism.

Agriculture was, in fact, not stagnant during this period. The area under cultivation expanded and the yield increased. But the growth in the size of the harvests was chiefly due to application of modern methods and large-scale farming in the black soil regions in the south. The mass of the peasants, especially in the north, still lived in degrading poverty. Crop failures led to famine, especially in 1891–2, when the zemstva carried out remarkable feats in famine relief.

The peasants fell into arrears with their poll tax and redemption dues, and the government finally abolished both payments. Moreover, efforts were now made to assist the peasants to buy or rent land through the land bank. By 1905 with this help the peasants had acquired nearly a third of all the lands which had remained in the ownership of the nobles at the time of the emancipation. This eased, but was far from solving, the problem of rural overpopulation. Many peasants migrated into the Siberian expanses. The government had sternly discouraged this movement until the 1880s, when a new expansionist policy in the Far East led them to support it. Towards the end of the century the migration was running at 100,000 people annually. But this, too, merely eased the problem, and thousands of peasants were forced to seek employment away from their villages.

Only after Stolypin's reforms, first introduced in November 1906, were the peasants freed from the commune and encouraged to work the soil as individual yeomen farmers. Marxists insisted that this reform exacerbated the process, which had been at work since the emancipation, of dividing the peasants into a small minority of prosperous farmers, or kulaks, and the great majority living at bare subsistence level. While it was true, as Marxists alleged, that a number of rich peasants quickly emerged after the reform, the peasants of medium prosperity were as late as 1917 the most numerous category.

Indeed, the peasant reaction to Stolypin's legislation left no doubt that this was the incentive that they had needed. Between 1906 and 1915 $2\frac{1}{2}$ million peasant householders applied to secede from their communes, and by 1915 7 million peasant families possessed hereditary private holdings. Had this legislation remained in force for even another decade, it might have proved to be the basic solution to the problem of the peasant and of agricultural production, which has plagued Russia for centuries. The bolshevik revolution put the clock back so far as the peasants were concerned. Under new names the commune was to be revived, but in an even more stringent and repressive form.

The boom in railway building in the last decades of the nineteenth century gave impetus to industrial development. In 1850 Russia had no more than 660 miles of railways: by 1912 the railways covered 40,194 miles. The new railways were of particular importance in the rapid growth of heavy industry. A new industrial area grew up around the coal mines of the Donets Basin and the iron ore of Krivoi Rog. Pig iron output of $1\frac{1}{2}$ million tons in 1900 increased to $3\frac{1}{2}$ million tons by 1914. Towns became cities. Ekaterinoslav's population grew from 47,000 to 120,000 and that of Rostov-on-Don from 80,000 to some 150,000 in a few years. The Caucasian oil wells, centred on Baku, produced some 160,000 tons of crude oil in 1860, 7 million tons in 1905, and 9 million tons in 1913. The textile industry showed a similar growth.

The government's policy in the economic and industrial fields during the reign of Alexander II was one of *laissez faire*. It granted concessions to private companies for the construction of railways, and sold or leased government-owned factories and mines to private individuals and companies. It also pursued a policy of free trade. But these policies were soon reversed. Many Russian merchants and private directors were inexperienced; the railways were reduced to chaos; many privately managed enterprises foundered.

From the 1870s the government followed a strict protectionist policy and actively participated in the railways and the metallurgical industries of which it was by far the most important customer. Witte on becoming minister of finance increased government support for industry and its protection by means of tariffs. He gave special attention to exports in order to create a favourable trade balance.

In 1897 Russia's gold reserves were so substantial that Witte was able to adopt the gold standard. His main purpose in doing so was to attract foreign capital into Russia and in this he was highly successful. In 1900 as many as 269 foreign companies were operating in Russia (of them there were 162 Belgian, 54 French, 30 German, and 19 British). Foreign capital flowed in growing amounts and added to the stupendous expansion of Russian industry. Witte's vision of a modernized and industrialized Russia, standing as an equal among the other nations of Europe, was approaching realization.

The dark side of these achievements was that the peasants and workers bore most of the burden and few of them shared in the benefits. They were the chief source of direct and indirect taxes. Moreover, the favourable balance of trade, needed to service foreign loans and support the currency, was secured primarily by exports of grain which could well have been consumed by the poorer peasants and workers. Thus it has been said that Russian military power and industrial development were financed directly by grain exports, foreign loans and investments, and indirectly by the over-taxation and the undernourishment of the peasants and workers.

Rapid industrialization has, however, in every country given rise to inequities and imbalances. In Russia through labour legislation and the reforms of Stolypin much was being done to spread the burdens more fairly, as indeed had been done by Milyutin's military reforms. A balance might well have been achieved early in the twentieth century.

Tsarist Russia was thus far from being a nation stagnating and incapable of change without some dramatic stimulus such as the revolution provided. Despite the inadequacies of the tsarist regime, the nation had begun to move in the nineteenth century and its advance was gathering momentum. By the end of the century Russia was overtaking the West in many fields. But the war intervened, the tsarist regime collapsed, and the revolution introduced new ideas.

CHAPTER TWO

The Revolutionary Movement

THE Russians have throughout their history shown a facility for adapting ideas from other countries and imprinting them so deeply with their own character that the original idea has been transformed and re-created as something new. This is apparent in Russian architecture. It applies equally to religious and political ideas, and especially to the revolutionary movement of the nineteenth and twentieth centuries.

The Decembrist rising in 1825 was the beginning of the revolutionary movement in Russia. Direct contact with western Europe, particularly during the Napoleonic wars, had fired many army officers with liberal ideas. The rebellion of the group of young officers in 1825 was, however, little more than the outburst of a few individuals against the autocracy. The conspirators had no popular support in the country, and Nicholas I crushed them without mercy. All liberal ideas were suppressed, but during the thirty years of his reign they fermented underground.

At this time the intelligentsia was splitting into two camps, the Slavophiles and the Westernizers. Their conflicting views influenced the revolutionary movement, and the division between them reflected the division in outlook which has persisted in Russia's history and continued since the revolution in the Soviet Union.

The Slavophiles were deeply religious and conservative. They believed fervently in the great mission of Russia to give the world a new civilization or to purify and revitalize Western civilization which in its existing state they abhorred. Holy Russia with her unique culture and traditional institutions, like the peasant commune, would, they argued, transform the rest of Europe where rationalism and individualism had perverted the Graeco-Roman heritage. Within Russia, the Slavophiles held, the first necessity was to purge the autocracy and the government of the corrupting innovations made by Peter the Great and to return to the old Muscovite methods of the *Zemsky Sobor* (Assembly of the Land), the Boyar Council, and the commune. To them Peter the Great was the antichrist who had turned Russia from her heritage. His city, St Petersburg, was the symbol of all the damage he had wrought: Moscow was their capital.

This creed, passionately held by many Russians, was clearly utopian and unrealistic. It belonged to the early sixteenth century when a monk in Pskov had written of the 'blessed city of Moscow' as the third Rome.[1]

Nevertheless, it represented a deep-rooted popular belief in Russia's messianic mission in the world and specifically in western Europe.

The Westernizers denounced Russia's past and traditions. They held that Russia was stagnating and that her future would depend on revival of the policies of Peter the Great, whose memory they venerated. The most outspoken of the Westernizers, Peter Chaadayev, even criticized Orthodoxy as a sterile cult and expressed the view that Russia would have fared better as a Roman Catholic or Protestant country. St Petersburg was scandalized by such heterodoxy. Nicholas I declared him to be a lunatic and placed him under medical supervision. Chaadayev was, however, simply a brilliant intellectual who loved his country and lamented its backwardness which could, he believed, be remedied by following the progressive examples of the West.[2]

Many Westernizers, like Alexander Herzen, visited western Europe for the first time 'with reverence, as men used to enter Jerusalem and Rome', but were soon revolted by bourgeois behaviour and standards. They returned to Russia with the outlook of the Slavophiles. Herzen himself developed a mystic faith in the peasant commune as the means through which Russia would achieve socialism and salvation.[3]

The Populists (*Narodniki*) who emerged as the leading socialist group in the 1870s were inspired chiefly by the writings of Herzen, Chernyshevsky, and Lavrov. All three political thinkers idealized the commune as the means by which Russia, avoiding the evils of Western capitalism, would evolve her own socialist society. During the ferment of ideas that followed the emancipation of the serfs in 1861, Peter Lavrov, a professor of mathematics, was particularly influential. He shared the view of Marx that capitalism, the growth of which could already be observed in Russia, would pave the way for socialism. Since, however, the Russian workers were still peasants and there was no proletariat, the revolution would stem from the peasantry and the natural socialism of the commune. He therefore urged that groups of revolutionaries should educate the people politically so that they could consciously develop the commune towards this goal.

The populists enthusiastically embraced their mission of 'going to the people'. In 1874 young men and women went in hundreds among the peasants, some under Lavrov's influence to teach, and others, stirred by Mikhail Bakunin's anarchistic doctrine of destruction, to instigate rebellion. They met only with suspicion, hostility, and rejection. Often peasants attacked the young populists or handed them over to the police. Many were arrested and imprisoned or banished to distant parts. But, although harshly disappointed, they were not completely disillusioned. In 1876, they formed the first Russian revolutionary party or secret society, known as *Zemlya i Volya* (Land and Liberty) with the object of bringing about social revolution. Terrorism was to be one of their chief weapons against the authorities. A new movement to the people was also organized. This time the populists did not go as itinerant preachers, but settled among the peasants, seeking to win their confidence. This movement, while far from breaking down the suspicion of the peasants, had some small success.

Among the intelligentsia and, indeed, all progressive elements of Russian society, the populists enjoyed sympathy in their struggle against autocracy. This was demonstrated in February 1878 at the trial of Vera Zasulich, a student and an ardent revolutionary. She had shot and wounded the governor of St Petersburg. The evidence against her was conclusive, but the jury acquitted her and voices rose in excited approval of the verdict throughout Russia.[4]

Within the revolutionary party, however, an impatient demand for action was growing. The overthrow of the autocracy was urgent. Capitalism was gathering impetus and, it was feared, would destroy the commune on which their socialism was to be based. A congress of the party, held on 24 June 1879, at which it was renamed *Narodnaya Volya* (People's Will) acknowledged the need for immediate political action. This resulted, after two attempts, in the assassination of Alexander II in 1881, one of the most destructive and tragic acts in Russia's history. It sent a wave of revulsion through the country. It destroyed the sympathy which all progressive elements of the population felt for the idealism of the populists. It wiped out the support which the intelligentsia was giving to revolutionary and liberal ideas. A period of stern reaction followed. The constitutional reforms, which Alexander II was about to promulgate and which might have brought to Russia the beginnings of the political freedom and social justice that the populists and the intelligentsia as a whole craved, were forgotten. When, more than twenty years later, these reforms came, they came too late.

One of the most prominent members of the Land and Liberty party had been G. V. Plekhanov, the father of Russian Marxism. He had become dissatisfied with the party and had set up a new group with P. B. Axelrod, Vera Zasulich, and a few others. To escape the repressive regime of Alexander III he soon afterwards went to live in Switzerland, where he became converted to Marxism. In Russia he had witnessed the failure of populist attempts to awaken peasants politically. Marxism with its scientific argument of the growth of capital, followed by the bourgeois democratic stage and finally erupting in the socialist revolution, brought about by the politically mature working class, appealed to him far more strongly. In September 1883 in Geneva he founded the first Russian Marxist party, known as the Group for the Liberation of Labour.

With his small, tidy beard and *pince-nez*, Georgii Plekhanov looked like a character from one of Chekhov's plays, but, possessing a powerful intellect and great learning, he was not ineffectual. Although the son of a wealthy landowner, who had grown up in the opulent comfort of his class, he had become a doctrinaire revolutionary at an early age. He was neither an original thinker, nor a man of inflexible beliefs or principles, but he had a keen analytical mind and in Switzerland soon asserted himself as a leading Marxist theorist. By nature, however, he was cold, arrogant, and intolerant of criticism. The appeal of Marxism was for him wholly intellectual and in this he contrasted with his two closest associates, Axelrod and Vera Zasulich, who had embraced Marxism only because they believed that it would enable the oppressed to find a better life.

During the first ten years Plekhanov and the other Marxists in exile had little contact with Russia. But several small circles, calling themselves social democrat or Marxist, formed inside Russia. The first volume of *Das Kapital* had appeared in Russian translation in 1872, passed by the imperial censor as a work too heavy and academic to interest any but a few scholars and certainly unlikely to provoke revolution or endanger the regime. Intellectuals gathered in eager groups to discuss the new theory. Controversy centred on the question whether capitalism on Western lines could develop in Russia. The populists argued that the Russian people were peasants who would evolve their own socialism without being influenced by the capitalism and democracy of the urban, industrialized West. The Marxists held that capitalism already existed in Russia.

Among the Marxists themselves, however, disagreements broke out even at this early stage. Some, like Plekhanov and Axelrod, became fanatic Marxists; others, like Berdyaev and Struve, merely saw in Marxism a new political theory, meriting close examination, and both the two latter men, in fact, were to move on to liberalism. Many lukewarm Marxists were influenced by Eduard Bernstein's *Evolutionary Socialism: A Criticism and an Affirmation*, published in 1899. Bernstein argued that the workers would achieve far more by democratic reform than by revolution. He held that, when the workers were fit to govern, they would achieve power without revolution. It was not democracy when a majority dictated to a minority, but when 'no single class enjoyed special privileges in the light of the aims of Society as a whole'.[5] Bernstein's arguments infuriated German and Russian Marxists. They damned them as 'reformism' and 'revisionism', which with 'economism' have remained terms of strongest communist censure.

Early in the 1890s unrest in the towns and in the country developed acutely. Industry was expanding and this expansion gained further momentum when Witte became finance minister in 1891. But strikes became more frequent and factory workers demonstrated against the harsh conditions and intolerably long hours. Moreover, the famine in 1891 brought thousands of starving peasants into the towns in search of food. Many found their way into factories and, desperate for work, they were ready to put up with the inhuman conditions. This flow of peasants aggravated industrial unrest and added new bitterness to the general criticism of the government's inaction and incompetence. Intellectuals turned more to revolutionary activity as the only possible action remaining against the autocracy and police repression. Social democratic and social revolutionary groups multiplied throughout the country and especially in the western non-Russian provinces of the empire.

During these years of ferment in Russia, a young man, named Vladimir Ilyich Ulyanov, was half-heartedly practising law in the provincial town of Samara on the Volga River and actively studying Marx, Engels, and Plekhanov. Under the pseudonym of 'Lenin' he was to dominate the revolutionary movement and to prove one of the great political leaders in history.[6]

Lenin was born on 22 April 1870 in Simbirsk (now Ulyanovsk). His father, Ilya Nikolaevich Ulyanov, came from Astrakhan, and may have been of mixed Russian and Kalmuck blood. If true, this would help explain the high cheek bones and slant eyes, and the touch of the Asiatic which marked the appearance of both father and son. Ilya Nikolaevich was a stern man with high principles and dedicated to his work as schoolmaster. By his own industry he rose to be an inspector of schools with seniority in the state service that gained him the patent of hereditary nobility and the right to be addressed as 'Your Excellency'. Lenin's mother, Maria Alexandrovna, was the daughter of a military surgeon, named Blank, probably of German origin. She was a remarkable woman, strong in character, energetic, and devoted to her family. Both father and mother were thus hard-working, austere, and disciplined. Their way of life contrasted with the gross indolence of local Russian society, which was portrayed so effectively by Goncharov, also born in Simbirsk, in his novel *Oblomov*. Lenin was to resemble his parents in his energy and austerity, his self-discipline and his love of work.

Lenin's parents were not active in politics, but were by inclination liberal-conservatives. All of their six children, however, became revolutionaries. Alexander, the eldest, and Lenin, the second son, were both highly intelligent. From the Simbirsk Classical High School, Alexander went on to St Petersburg University to study science and there became an ardent revolutionary. He took part in a terrorist plot to assassinate Tsar Alexander III, and was arrested, tried, and condemned to death. The sentence would probably have been commuted to imprisonment and exile if he had petitioned for mercy. He refused to do so, despite his mother's pleas, and on 20 May 1887, displaying the fervour of a martyr, he was hanged.

In this tragic period Maria Alexandrovna needed her courage and energy. Her husband had died the previous year of a cerebral haemorrhage, probably brought on by overwork. She had sat through the trial and taken leave of her son shortly before his death or, according to some accounts, at the scaffold. But then she and her children were placed under police supervision and ostracized by the provincial society of which they had been respected members. The tsarist regime was, however, neither vindictive, nor so ruthless as its successor was to be. Maria Alexandrovna received her government pension after her husband's death. In addition, she had money from her father's estate and she was a good manager. She applied herself now to the care of her children.

Lenin had not been close to his brother, Alexander, and, although the execution may well have come as a shock and a deeply felt family tragedy, it is far from certain that the event fired him with thoughts of vengeance or made him embrace the revolutionary cause. He could be cold, detached, and ruthless, and the death of his brother may have made little impression on him. Certainly within a month of the execution he sat his examinations and matriculated with distinction and a gold medal from his school.[7] The family then moved to Kazan and he was admitted to the Law School of Kazan University.

Before the end of the year, however, Lenin had been expelled for taking part in a student demonstration. He was refused permission to continue his studies and during the next three years he lived in Kazan or in Samara, spending the summers on his mother's estate. She made repeated applications for him to be allowed to complete his law studies as an external student, and finally the minister of public education relented. In March 1891 Lenin went to St Petersburg and by November of the same year he had passed all his examinations, having crammed the four-year course into eight months. In possession of a certificate entitling him to practise as an assistant attorney he returned to Samara, but he now had little thought of the law.

At some stage, whether at the time of his brother's execution or later, Marxism had burst upon him as the truth, the only philosophy of life, providing the answer to the problems not only of Russia but of the world. He had embraced this new ideology with a total dedication. which was one of the sources of his strength. Now in Samara he gave every minute to the study of Marxism and he was to devote the rest of his life entirely to its application.

In August 1893 Lenin returned to St Petersburg, this time to be at the centre of the Marxist movement in Russia. Here in the following year he published his first important pamphlet, which was a strong attack on the populists. Already he was using his great talent for polemical writing. He was now playing an active part in the social democratic groups in the city. Here for the first time, moreover, he had direct contact with industrial workers. He saw the intolerable conditions of their lives and was surprised that they were so slow to organize and to take part in revolutionary activity, but he did not doubt that he could mould them into a truly Marxist proletariat. His attention shifted almost exclusively to them and away from the peasants who, in their attachment to the land they worked, were naturally conservative and resistant to revolutionary ideas.

At this time the leading Russian Marxists were Plekhanov and the other members of the Liberation of Labour group, living in Geneva. In 1895 Lenin applied for a passport to go abroad and for four months he travelled in Germany, France, and Switzerland. Plekhanov made a deep impression on him. After months of talking with simple, uneducated workers and with ardent provincial revolutionaries, he found himself in the presence of a man of great intellectual stature and, moreover, one with a profound understanding of Marxism, such as he had never before met in one of his own countrymen. He conceived a deep respect, touching on veneration, for this austere intellectual, and looked on him as his guide and superior. But he was incapable of accepting anyone as his leader for long and was soon to supplant Plekhanov.

The twenty-five-year-old Lenin himself made an impact upon the exiles. Pavel Axelrod, a populist converted to Marxism, who was to hate Lenin in the years to come, commented after these first meetings: 'I felt then that I was dealing with the man who would be the leader of the Russian revolution. He was not only an educated Marxist—there were very many of them—but he knew what he wanted to do and how it had to be done. He smelt of the Russian land.'[8] It was a remarkably perceptive comment, for Lenin did not always make a strong impact on people in first meetings. 'He was,' Gorky noted, 'somehow too ordinary and did not give the impression of being a leader.'[9] Short and squat in build, with thick neck, round red face, high cheek bones and slant Mongol eyes, slightly turned-up nose and high, domed forehead, and wearing untidy, ill-fitting clothes and cloth cap, he merged in the crowd.[10]

On closer acquaintance, however, friends and enemies alike came to appreciate the tremendous strength of his determination and his dynamism, his powers of work, and his ruthlessness. He was indeed a supreme example of the elemental force that a man, able to concentrate his whole being effectively and absolutely on a single objective, can become. He was not like a volcano, dramatic and suddenly explosive, but like the sea, remorseless, battering down all obstacles lying before it.

Axelrod's feeling that Lenin smelt of the Russian land probably arose from the homesickness which he, like all Russians, felt acutely when away from his country. Lenin fresh from St Petersburg and the Volga lands came to them like a breath of home air. Axelrod can hardly have thought that Lenin was a son of the soil. Brought up in a strict but comfortable middle class home, he had had little contact with the peasantry. Similarly his knowledge of the industrial workers was limited to the few months spent in St Petersburg before going abroad.

In his basic character, as in his appearance, however, Lenin was unmistakably Russian and part of the Russian revolutionary tradition. He was extreme in his ideas and actions. Like the anarchists and the socialist revolutionary terrorists, he was contemptuous of half-measures and of compromise. His conviction that his objectives were right and that he personally had a mission to accomplish them, was unshakable. He had no doubts and he did not tolerate opposition. He did not respect opponents or concede that their views might have merit of any kind. Opponents should be reduced to impotence or exterminated. In short, his outlook was absolute in its ruthless determination, its arrogant confidence, and in its in-humanity towards all who did not support him.

Lenin was, nevertheless, capable of tenderness and affection, as he showed in his letters to his mother[11] and in his relations with Krupskaya, his wife. Krupskaya was so much part of him and his work that she seems to have no separate existence or personality. One suspects that children, if they had had a family, would have been a trespass on their partnership. But the more important influence in his life was his mother, Maria Alexandrovna. He revered her for her devotion, her unquestioning love and practical support. Krupskaya wrote of her: 'I loved Maria Alexandrovna very much. She was so sensitive and attentive. Vladimir Ilyich (Lenin) inherited his mother's will-power, and also her sensitivity and attentiveness to people.'[12] But the impression made by Lenin of inhuman dedication to his mission remains starkly irresistible. It was part of his strength that his feelings for others, even for these two women,[13] and indeed for any human being, could never interfere with his plans or his basic pursuit of power.

In September 1895 Lenin returned to St Petersburg. He was laden with illegal revolutionary papers, hidden in false bottoms of his cases. His im-mediate purpose was to weld the numerous small Marxist groups in Russia into a single social democratic party. As a step in this direction he joined with Julius Martov, a Jewish Marxist who had been active in organizing Jewish workers in Vilna and who was now devoting his energies to the Russian movement. With Martov he founded the Petersburg Union of Struggle for the Liberation of the Working Class. But he regarded this party only as an expedient. Martov noted that he was 'cold, if not con-temptuous' towards it.[14] In fact, Lenin's plans were soon to bring him into conflict with Martov, Plekhanov, and others. Their idea was to educate the workers and to awaken their social consciousness so that the revolution would be a mass movement. But already Lenin was thinking in terms of a small disciplined group of professional revolutionaries who would lead the workers into revolution. He was at this time preparing to publish a new revolutionary periodical, called *The Workers' Cause*. But on 22 December 1895 police raided his rooms and found ample evidence of his activities, including all the copy, ready for press, of the first issue of the paper.

Lenin spent the whole of 1896 imprisoned in the House of Preliminary Detention in St Petersburg. Conditions in the prison were not especially restrictive, however, and he managed to keep up illegal correspondence with revolutionaries outside. He made good use of the prison library and of books sent in to him to prepare for his major work, *The Development of Capitalism in Russia*. Indeed, the quiet routine suited him and he even expressed 'a kind of regret that he was released too early. "If I had been in prison longer I would have finished the book." '[15]

In February 1897 he learnt that he had been sentenced to three years' exile in Siberia. He was released from prison and allowed several days of freedom to prepare for his journey. Then, at the request of his mother, he was granted permission to travel independently without guards and at his own expense to Siberia. Leaving St Petersburg on 1 March he broke his journey in Moscow to spend some days with his mother. He then went to Krasnoyarsk by train and from there by boat along the great Yenisei River to the village of Shushenskoe in the sparsely settled southern region of Central Siberia. Here he remained in exile until February 1900.

Shushenskoe, which Lenin called 'not a bad place', was, in fact, set in beautiful surroundings which at one stage moved him to try to write poetry. He swam in the Yenisei in summer and skated in winter. A keen hunter, he made frequent visits to the river swamps to shoot wild fowl. Food was plentiful, plain, and good. He rented a room in a peasant's hut and had the basic comforts and necessities he required. At first he sent a stream of requests to his family for socks, a mackintosh cape, a suit, for books and writing materials and for money. He corresponded widely with revolutionaries in European Russia and abroad. He received masses of mail. On 24 February 1898 he wrote to his mother, 'I have received a pile of letters today from every corner of Russia and Siberia and therefore felt in a holiday mood all day.'[16] For him it was a healthy, ordered way of life, free of all distractions, in which he could work, and he worked intensively. While there he finished *The Development of Capitalism in Russia* which was published legally in St Petersburg in 1899 under the pseudonym of Vladimir Ilin. It established his reputation as a leading Marxist theoretician.

In May 1898 Nadezhda Krupskaya, a tall, grave schoolteacher and a convinced Marxist, who had conceived an adulation for Lenin, arrived in Shushenskoe to begin her three-year exile. She had been destined to go to another part of Siberia, but her plea to be sent to the same place as Lenin had been granted. In July they were married and it was a perfect union of leader and lieutenant. Krupskaya was earnest, self-effacing, and wholehearted in her devotion to the cause which she now served through Lenin. Her honeymoon was typical of the whole of her married life. She spent the mornings with him working on a translation of Sidney and Beatrice Webb's *Theory and Practice of Trade Unionism*, and the afternoons copying the text of *The Development of Capitalism in Russia*. It was a strange marriage, held together not by love, affection or companionship, but by devotion to the Marxist cause.

During the years of Lenin's exile, the social democratic movement had gathered strength. In March 1898 a small, illegal meeting, calling itself the first congress of the All-Russian Social Democratic (Labour) Party, was held in Minsk. Delegates attended from the Unions for the Liberation of Labour in St Petersburg, Moscow, Kiev, Ekaterinoslav, together with a group from the Bund. This was the name given to the General Jewish Workers' Union in Lithuania, Poland, and Russia, which had been founded at a congress in Vilna in 1897. The social democratic movement had grown more rapidly among the Jews of west and south-western Russia than among the Russians or any of the national minorities in the Russian empire. The Jews were on the whole better educated and more ready to organize in such a movement, especially in the face of the sporadic anti-Semitism of the tsarist regime which had wide popular support among the Great Russians.

The first all-Russian congress proclaimed the birth of the Russian Social Democratic Party, published a manifesto of its aims, and elected a three-man central committee. Within a few weeks, however, most of the delegates had been arrested and exiled. The central committee ceased to exist and the movement was riven by internal disputes.

'Economism' was the name given to the chief heresy at this time. The economists held that the workers should struggle for higher wages, shorter hours, better factory conditions, leaving the fight for political power to the liberal intellectuals. Two factors underlay the arguments of the 'economists'; first, they held that it was more sensible to pursue power by stages rather than to concentrate on seizing supreme power; second, they recognized that workers were still loyal to the tsar and unwilling to listen to attacks on him and his regime.[17]

Conflict over this heresy spread to the exiles in the West where Plekhanov and Axelrod, who believed that they alone could lead the Russian revolutionary movement, were pained when the younger men did not follow their lead. Plekhanov refused to sponsor the publications of the union of Russian social democrats, and *Rabochee Delo (The Workers' Cause)*, first published in 1899, was condemned as 'economist' in its policy. Plekhanov, Axelrod and from exile, Lenin, wrote attacks on the paper. Support for 'economism' nevertheless grew. In 1899 Kuskova, one of the adherents of the heresy living abroad, published a pamphlet known as *The Credo* in which she argued the 'economist' case forcefully. This pamphlet drew violent replies from Plekhanov and Lenin. Yet a third group, known as the 'Legal Marxists' emerged. They were in the eyes of the orthodox Marxists even worse heretics than the 'economists', for they were 'revisionists' who virtually denied violent revolution and favoured parliamentary evolution on the lines proposed by Eduard Bernstein.

Many of the disputes among the Marxists at this time and later concerned fine distinctions, devoid of practical relevance. Often clashes over doctrine merely veiled conflict of personalities and the struggle for leadership of the movement. But the violent arguments were also part of the process of assimilating and applying to Russia a Western doctrine, conceived and rooted in Western conditions.

Russia with her peasant masses, her primitive agriculture, and her undeveloped industries lagged far behind the industrial economy of the West. But she had to catch up and to reach the same stage of industrialization before she was ripe for the application of Marxism. This meant carefully following in the steps of the West. The Westernizers had always argued that this was the only path of progress, and all of the Russian social democrats were ardent Westernizers. But Lenin had begun to recognize that a Western system could not be simply transplanted to Russian soil. Thus the issue, underlying many of the disputes and struggles, was whether the party should slavishly apply the Western doctrine or whether it should be adapted to fit Russian conditions.

In February 1900 Lenin's special period of exile came to an end. Leaving Krupskaya in Siberia to serve the rest of her time, he returned to European Russia. He settled in Pskov which was near to St Petersburg and to the frontier, but soon he moved to Munich. His immediate plans were to convene a new congress at which the heresies could be condemned and unity restored to the movement. His other urgent project was to produce a paper, called *Iskra* (*The Spark*) in which he could condemn deviation and establish orthodox Marxist doctrine, while rallying all social democrats in Russia.

From the earliest days the propaganda and arguments of Russian social democrats were loud and furious. Many revolutionaries seemed to feel that they had to shout to gain attention. Both the tone and invective of their polemics were aspects of the extremism which was part of the movement. But it was Lenin who introduced the strident, biting mockery and abuse, which was repeated remorselessly until the victim was permanently labelled. His language in attacks on those he considered heretics was violent and offensive, lacking all restraint and dignity. At times his own comrades remonstrated with him, but without effect. When Struve, who had been a friend and colleague, cast aside Marxism and joined the liberals, Lenin damned him in the columns of *Iskra* as a 'renegade and traitor'. A friend complained against such language, pointing out that workers might feel it their duty to kill Struve. 'He deserves to die!' was Lenin's only response.[18] Lenin, in fact, set the tone which Soviet spokesmen have continued to use in propaganda and the press and which has constantly antagonized and confused people in the West, acting as an obstacle to understanding.

The first issue of *Iskra* appeared on 24 December 1900, printed in Leipzig with the help of the German Social Democratic Party. The editorial board consisted of Plekhanov, Lenin, Martov, Axelrod, Potresov, and Vera Zasulich. Copies of the paper were smuggled into Russia and circulated by agents living underground. It quickly gained influence and became the mouthpiece of the Marxist movement. In its fourth issue Lenin was already maintaining that *Iskra* should be not only the propaganda and ideological organ of the party, but also the organizational centre, directing a network of secret agents in Russia.

Industrial unrest mounted in the first years of the century. Strikes were more frequent and the number of workers involved in them more than doubled between 1900 and 1903. On occasions workers even supported student demonstrations. In part the increased unrest was a reaction to the general economic crisis, affecting the whole of Europe. The main reason, however, was the growing impatience of all classes of Russian society with autocracy, its repression, its continued denial of the most elementary political rights, but even this would have been accepted had the regime been efficient in dealing with the problems facing Russia. Progressive elements among the middle class were increasingly antagonistic towards the tsar and his government and, unable to form political parties themselves, they supported the revolutionaries. In these conditions *Iskra* gained new and wider influence. Its agents managed, often by dubious tactics, to win over revolutionary committees and to eliminate heretical elements.

It is nevertheless important to note that the mounting revolutionary mood in Russia at this time was a spontaneous growth. *Iskra* and the social democrats did not create it, but battened on it, like a remora attached to a shark. The social democrats were still only a small minority in the workers' movement. They agitated and often triggered off strikes and demonstrations, but they were far from representing or controlling the workers, and among the peasants they had no influence whatsoever.

In the ferment of the 1890s the populist groups had revived. Many who had been exiled after the murder of Alexander II returned to European Russia at this time and they banded together with others, taking the name of Socialist Revolutionaries. In 1902, all of these forty-nine groups formally joined in the Socialist Revolutionary Party. As heirs of the populists they disagreed fundamentally with the social democrats, and they rejected Marxism. They gave priority to agriculture and the peasantry as the natural foundations upon which to build socialism in Russia, and set up a special branch, known as the Peasants' Union, to organize the peasants on the land.

Terrorism remained part of their programme. Terror would, they still believed, help to intimidate the government and to further the revolutionary struggle. They recognized that the assassination of Alexander II had been a serious mistake, and they excluded the tsar from their lists of victims, which now comprised the most hated officials and ministers. A special section, known as the fighting organization, was responsible for acts of terrorism, and under its first leader, Grigori Gershuni, a young chemist, and then under Azef, an incredible creature who was both a secret agent of the tsarist police and the leader of this terrorist group, it was an effective murder squad.

The socialist revolutionary party attracted immediate support especially among teachers, students, and the progressive members of all classes. The party and its policy appealed far more widely than the social democrat party and doctrinaire Marxism. It called for a great act of faith to accept at this time in Russia the Marxist theory of a mass proletariat, rising in revolution, when, despite the tremendous development of industry in Russia, the peasants still made up well over a hundred millions of the total population, excluding Finland, of 170 millions. The socialist revolutionary policy was evidently closer to the facts of life in Russia at this time. The party's official newspaper, *Revolutionary Russia*, printed abroad and smuggled over the frontier, gathered more supporters. Widespread revolts among the peasants in 1902 were used by party agents to stir up greater unrest on the land, and their appeals to the peasantry were more and more successful.

The socialist revolutionary party suffered, however, from two defects which were to prove fatal in the struggle for power: first, it lacked organization; second, and most important of all, it lacked leaders, or more specifically, it lacked a leader of the calibre and determination of Lenin.

During these years Lenin was working out his tactics for achieving revolution and seizing power. He set out his ideas in a pamphlet, published in 1902, under the title *Chto delat?* (*What is to be done?*) In it he argued strongly for a highly centralized party of professional revolutionaries, chosen and strictly disciplined, who would act as the vanguard, leading the working class into revolution. This was an innovation. It swept aside the basic Marxist conception of a proletariat, embracing the great majority of the people in a mature capitalist society, which would seize power. In this departure from orthodoxy lay the beginnings of the split in the Russian Marxist movement which came in 1903, but it was also to prove the source of social democrat strength and to make possible Lenin's seizure of power.

The second congress of the Russian social democratic party, for which Lenin had been working since his return from exile, took place in July 1903 in Brussels whence it was forced by police action to move to London. Conflicts between the members of the editorial board had been frequent during 1902. Plekhanov readily took umbrage but neither he nor Axelrod nor Martov realized that Lenin was already working secretly among them to create a small group of professional revolutionaries, obedient to his command. But, although he was now beginning to emerge as the leader of the movement, he was not yet in a position to displace Plekhanov.

In April 1902, partly because of difficulty in printing *Iskra*, but partly, too, to get away from Plekhanov's supervision, Lenin and Krupskaya moved to London. Here for the first time Lenin met Trotsky. Lev Davidovich Bronstein, but known to all as Trotsky even in these early days, was the son of a Jewish landowner in the Ukraine. He had become a revolutionary while still a student, and had attracted attention by his wit, his fiery eloquence, and his agile brain. Exiled to Siberia he had escaped and although penniless had made his way to London. Lenin had heard glowing reports of the young Trotsky, who was known for his prolific writings and had in fact been nicknamed 'The Pen', and at once sought to engage him in the movement. From the start, however, Plekhanov felt a strong antagonism towards Trotsky, and the harmony of the editorial board was further disrupted when Lenin insisted on the new arrival helping in the production of *Iskra*.

In April 1903 Lenin and Krupskaya moved to Geneva and the disputes, instigated mainly by Lenin, became sharper. A draft programme for the party had to be agreed for submission to the second congress. This led to an immediate conflict between Lenin and Plekhanov on matters of theory, but a compromise draft avoided an open split between them. Lenin was now biding his time, until he could appeal for the support of the congress. A practical politician who was prepared to compromise in disagreements on theory, he was far more concerned about party organization, for through organization he could gather power into his own hands and then he could dispose of the theoretical questions.

Delegates from Russia assembled in Geneva early in the summer of 1903 and then moved to Brussels where the congress opened on 30 July 1903. Of the 57 delegates, 43 had a vote and of them 8 had a second vote, giving a total of 51 votes to be cast. On paper the *Iskra* group could command a majority of at least 41 votes. The early meetings were given over to trivial matters, but as the proceedings continued disunity began to appear in the *Iskra* group. The most probable reason was the growing antagonism towards Lenin whose ruthless power-seeking and incessant lobbying angered many delegates. He was alarmed to find a clear split growing in the group between those whom he called 'hard' members, who supported him, and 'soft' members, on whom he could not rely.

This division became important in the twenty-second session, when the draft party rules were before the congress. Martov, who had so far supported Lenin, now opposed him over the definition of party membership. Martov proposed to extend membership to anyone 'who gives the party his regular personal co-operation under the direction of one of the party organizations'. Lenin wanted to restrict membership to one who 'supports the party both materially and by personal participation in one of the party organizations'.[19] Bearing in mind the rudimentary state of the party in Russia at this time the difference between the two drafts was of trivial importance. But Lenin was inflexible in his determination that the party should be a small, centralized, disciplined group of professional revolutionaries, and he sought in his draft to exclude from membership all who did not actively participate in its work. In the voting Martov obtained 28 against Lenin's 23 votes, but he made no attempt to entrench this majority. Indeed, Martov, eager to serve the party and the revolutionary cause, had no thought of using his majority to secure power for himself. He was content to rely on democratic processes within the party and so fell victim to Lenin's tactics.

In the twenty-fifth session the congress considered the status of the Bund and its claim to sole authority in matters concerning the Jewish proletariat. This claim was rejected by a large majority and the delegates of the Bund walked out. Another dispute caused the 'economist' delegates to walk out too. This left a total of 44 votes of which Lenin could count on

24. Martov had lost his majority and Lenin moved in to seize control of the party.

The party machinery, as already approved by the congress, comprised the supreme party council of five members, two appointed by the central committee of three, operating inside Russia, two appointed by the central organ, which was *Iskra*, responsible for ideological leadership, and the fifth elected directly by the congress. Lenin now threw himself into the task of ensuring that his supporters formed a majority on both the central committee and the editorial board. He intrigued and he lied in his endeavours to secure this control and his blatantly obvious tactics again antagonized delegates.

In protest Martov and his supporters abstained from the elections to the central committee and the central organ, and Lenin's men were elected. It was on this basis that Lenin took the name of 'bolsheviks' (majority-ites) for his group and called Martov and the others 'mensheviks' (minority-ites). With his keen sense of propaganda he hammered these names into general usage. Strangely enough, Martov accepted the title of mensheviks, even though at times they were to hold the majority in party committees. Thus Lenin had won a major victory and with the principle of dictatorship accepted by many he was already in a strong position to lead the revolutionary forces. But in the process he had made enemies, and he had achieved his advantage at the price of splitting the party. He attempted to blame this split on Martov, accusing him and his supporters of crudely scrambling for seats and power in the councils of the party. This was effrontery, but typical of the aggressive stand which Lenin usually took in anticipation of criticism. The immediate cause of the split was, as Martov himself stated, Lenin's insatiable lust for personal power.[20]

The division of the party between bolsheviks and mensheviks was not, however, merely the result of Lenin's tactics and determination to lead. It was fundamental to Marxism in Russia, bringing into the open the two different approaches to its application. The mensheviks held to the Western view that they must await the growth of political understanding among the masses and only then could they move forward as a broadly based party. The bolsheviks held to the practical and urgent conception of a small, disciplined vanguard of dedicated revolutionaries who would lead and drive the masses along the Marxist path. The mensheviks were closer to the original doctrine of Marxism, but the bolsheviks were to prove more in harmony with Russian national tradition.

The congress had been a wearisome struggle, especially for Lenin. He had thrown himself into it whole-heartedly; he was ready to fight to the end for his principle that the party should be controlled by a small central committee, obeying the leadership of one man, and not by a large democratic group. He saw clearly that the *Iskra* board was the instrument of control which he must dominate. At the congress he had partially achieved this aim, by reducing the size of the board from six to three and by the election of Plekhanov, Martov, and himself to the board. Martov had refused to serve and this had left Plekhanov and himself in charge. But this victory was shortlived. Feeling in the party was running strongly against him. Former comrades openly criticized and attacked him. Trotsky launched the most vigorous attack, describing him as a 'despot and terrorist who sought to turn the central committee of the party into a committee of public safety—in order to be able to play the role of Robespierre.'[21] Bowing to the general mood, Plekhanov now insisted on bringing Axelrod, Potresov, Vera Zasulich, and Martov on to the editorial board again. This gave the mensheviks a majority and Lenin resigned from *Iskra*.

Exhausted by the long struggle and near to a nervous breakdown, Lenin was taken away by Krupskaya to tramp through the Swiss countryside. They carried knapsacks and slept in the open. On 2 July 1904 Krupskaya wrote to Lenin's mother, 'Volodya (a diminutive of Vladimir) and I have made a pact not to discuss business matters. We sleep ten hours a day, swim and walk. Volodya does not even read the papers properly.'[22] This was the kind of rest he desperately needed. He returned to Geneva, ready to renew the struggle, and in December 1904 he published the first issue of a new paper, called *Vperiod (Forward)*. But, while he talked of revolution and the need to organize revolts in Russia, his main concern was the struggle against the mensheviks. It was a striking example of his capacity to concentrate on the immediate problems and, as though he had put on blinkers, virtually to ignore other far greater matters, such as the war with Japan and the new mood of anger which it aroused in Russia.

CHAPTER THREE

The Revolution of 1905

RUSSIA had long been seeking outlets to the Pacific. In 1858 China had ceded the Amur and the Maritime Provinces, and for some years Russia was content to consolidate these gains. Interest in the Far East had revived in the reign of Alexander III. In 1891 he had sent his tsarevich, soon to reign as Nicholas II, on an eastern tour and in this year work had begun on the Trans-Siberian Railway. The Sino-Japanese War of 1894–5, revealing the weakness of China and the emergence of Japan as a new power, had quickened Russian ambitions.

Under the peace treaty with Japan, China agreed to cede the Liaotung Peninsula together with Formosa (Taiwan) and the Pescadores Islands. But then China appealed to Russia who, supported by France and Germany, brought pressure to bear on Japan to restore Liaotung to China in return for a larger indemnity.

Within a year China paid the price for Russian intercession. Witte took advantage of the presence of the Chinese chief minister at the coronation of Nicholas II in 1896 to negotiate an alliance against Japan and to obtain rights to continue the Trans-Siberian railway across northern Manchuria to Vladivostok with a branch line from Harbin to Mukden and Dalny. This was an important concession, for the alternative route north of the Amur River would have doubled the length of the final leg of the railway. Two years later Russia secured a twenty-five-year lease of the southern tip of the Liaotung Peninsula with the right to construct a military and naval base at Port Arthur and a commercial port at Dalny, both of which were ice-free.

Manchuria was now within Russia's grasp, but Nicholas II's grandiose visions of dominating the Far East alarmed other powers. The Japanese became convinced that the Russians threatened them directly, and in 1902 signed a treaty of alliance with Britain. This alliance, together with the opposition of the U.S. Government and the reserved support conceded by France to Russia's Far Eastern policy, disturbed Nicholas and his advisers. But Witte who counselled restraint was dismissed and Plehve, the minister of the interior, who now had the ear of the tsar, poured scorn on the idea that a small emerging country like Japan would dare to attack the greatest land power in the world. This kind of argument appealed to Nicholas who had small understanding of foreign or military affairs, and was pathetically eager to prove himself able to follow in the steps of his father and grandfather. Moreover, at this time of growing internal discontent, Nicholas hoped that a great national gain, such as the annexation of Manchuria or Korea, would prove a distraction. Indeed, it seemed the only possible solution, for vacillating between repression and concession he was bewildered by the persistent unrest of his people. Plehve, equally barren of constructive policies, expressed the view to the tsar that 'a small victorious war' would certainly ward off the revolution that was threatening. Nevertheless, while most governments recognized that war between Russia and Japan was imminent, Nicholas seemed unaware of the danger.

On the night of 8–9 February 1904 the Japanese attacked without warning. By April they had virtually immobilized the Russian naval squadrons in Port Arthur and Vladivostok, although they were never able to hold complete command of the seas. The Japanese high command was counting on a swift victory, while they had a clear superiority of forces in the Far East. In April a Japanese army, 40,000 strong, crossed to Korea and on 1 May attacked the Russian force of 7,000 holding the line of the Yalu River. The Japanese won a complete victory which was of more than local importance; the whole of Asia was excited by this first defeat in modern times of a European by an Asiatic power. Towards the end of May the Japanese at Nanshan again defeated the Russians, whom they outnumbered ten to one, and cut off the Russian garrison in Port Arthur from the main forces in Manchuria.

At Liaoyang the main Russian force under its commander-in-chief, Kuropatkin, was engaged on 25 August by the Japanese, who intended this to be the decisive battle of the war. The Russians were defeated, but withdrew in good order. Kuropatkin now realized that the Japanese were nearing the end of their resources and he took the offensive. The resulting battles, fought on the Sha-ho River in October and at Sandepu in January 1905, were, however, costly and indecisive.

During these months the small Russian garrison at Port Arthur had shown great courage and endurance in repelling the attacks. But on the death of their commander, Kondratenko, who had inspired their resistance, his successor, Stoessel, in circumstances suggesting cowardice or treachery surrendered the fort to the Japanese. In the battle of Mukden (19 February–10 March) the Russians were again defeated, but both sides suffered severe losses. The Russians then retreated to the north.

Russian prestige suffered a further devastating blow in the Straits of Tsushima on 27 May. Admiral Rozhestvensky had sailed the Baltic Fleet half way around the world to restore Russian naval supremacy in the Far East. After innumerable mishaps, he reached the Sea of China at the beginning of May. But off Tsushima his fleet was annihilated by the Japanese, commanded by Admiral Togo.

Russia and Japan had now fought to a standstill. Japan had failed to win the swift decisive victory on which she had counted and now, financially strained, she faced the growing might of Russia whose reinforcements were massing in Manchuria. But in Russia the war was bitterly resented. Nicholas II, realizing that it could not end as 'the small victorious war' which Plehve had promised and that it was so seriously aggravating unrest as to threaten his regime, grasped at the offer of mediation from President Theodore Roosevelt. He was compelled now to call on Witte to conduct the negotiations. The resulting Treaty of Portsmouth, signed on 5 September 1905, bound Russia to surrender to Japan the Liaotung Peninsula with Dalny and Port Arthur and half of Sakhalin, to evacuate Manchuria, and to acknowledge Korea as a sphere of Japanese interest. In the circumstances Witte had handled the negotiations with skill, yielding only so much as was inevitable and saving intact the Amur and Maritime Provinces. His reward was the title of 'Count', but while he was honoured grudgingly at court the peace gained him no popular acclaim, and for some years he was known mockingly as 'Count Portsmouth' or 'Count Half-Sakhalin'. The war with its defeats and damage to Russian prestige had been to the people an unnecessary and costly adventure. It had, moreover, uncovered the gross inadequacy of the tsar and his government.

While Russia was drifting into war with Japan, internal discontent had been mounting dangerously. The number of people charged with political crimes rose from 1,580 in 1900 to 5,590 in 1903, and these figures did not include the numerous cases of administrative arrest and exile. Strikes were more frequent. They were still largely unorganized and, despite the efforts of social democrats and socialist revolutionaries, concerned more with immediate economic demands than with revolution and political gains. But workers were slowly recognizing the need to act together and not in isolated factory units. Thus in 1903 violent strikes broke out in Rostov and spread like a forest fire west and east across southern Russia from Odessa to Baku, and the workers' slogans contained political as well as economic demands. More than 500 factories and 225,000 workers were involved but, kept in the perspective of Russia's massive size and great population, these figures amounted only to three per cent and five per cent respectively of the totals. Cossacks were called in to disperse the strikers, many of whom were summarily punished.

The peasants were increasingly restless and always unpredictable. *Revolutionary Russia*, the paper of the socialist revolutionaries, had increased its circulation from 1,000 copies in 1900, when it was first published, to over 10,000 in 1903, and in addition they distributed more than 395,000 leaflets. But this propaganda was but a small drop, hardly breaking the surface of the ocean of over a hundred million peasants in Russia.

Barely touched by revolutionary propaganda the peasants would suddenly and dramatically rebel, like a force of nature. Arson, murder, and blind destruction marked the numerous local outbreaks which took place all over the country. In May 1902 revolts spread through the provinces of Kharkov and Poltava on such a scale that troops had to be called in. But repression was no remedy. Once he felt pushed to breaking point, the peasant was always liable to give way to a destructive fury in which he gave no heed to punishments to come. He was thus a dangerous force in the country and one which inspired fear.

Unrest among the subject nationalities of the Empire intensified as the rigidity of Russian policy and the incompetence of the tsar and his officials became more intolerable. The Finns had ample ground for complaint. Although Nicholas had on his accession sworn to honour their historic rights, Finland was forcibly converted into a Russian military district and the Finnish Diet was restricted in its powers. The Finns were also subjected to an intensive campaign of Russification which they met with passive resistance. In the Baltic provinces the policy of Russification further antagonized the Letts, Lithuanians, and Esthonians who were now eager to establish their own national identities.

In Poland the unrest was most acute. The drive for Russification had gone to such stupid lengths that instruction on Polish literature was permitted only in the Russian language. Poles were excluded from government posts in their own country. Other restrictions angered the Poles among whom rapid industrialization, especially in such new centres as Lodz, added force to the revolutionary movement. At the same time a strong middle class was developing, in part taking the place of the landed nobility, and a new national democratic party was organized.

In the Ukraine and in White Russia movements among the people to assert their identities, distinct from the Great Russian, gained strength. A deplorable development at this time was the growth of anti-Semitism, which was always latent in these regions. New large-scale *pogroms* had the active, or at least tacit, support of ministers and officials. The anti-Jewish movement reached a climax with a massacre of the Jews in Kishenev, the chief city of Bessarabia, in April 1903, and in the *pogrom* in August of the same year in Gomel in the province of Mogilev.

The ferment in the Ukraine was especially aggravated by the rapid growth of industries in the Donets coal basin. In White Russia strenuous efforts to re-establish the Uniate Church[1] sharpened popular discontent. In central Asia and the Caucasus the same restlessness, arising especially from resentment of Russification, was apparent. Baku, the centre of the rapidly expanding oil industry, had already become one of the most turbulent industrial towns in the whole country.

For all the unrest and popular discontent throughout the vast expanse of Russian empire two men—Nicholas II and Vyacheslav Plehve—were in large measure directly to blame. Nicholas was so inadequate an autocrat as to be an instrument of revolution. A small, tidy, almost saintly man, he had inherited a role and a responsibility which were beyond his strength and capacity, but he believed with his whole being that, like his father, he had to maintain the principle of autocracy. Had he granted even limited political rights to his people, he might well have kept his throne, and Russia might have been spared a bloody and cruel revolution. But he was never able to understand the mood or the demands of his people. He was indeed pathetic, and yet he embodied in himself most of the cardinal Christian virtues. He was truly pure in heart, but, if he saw God, it was small comfort to the millions of his people who suffered and died as a result, partially at least, of his failure.

A further disastrous factor was that, being weak and readily influenced by others, Nicholas should have married Alexandra, Princess of Hesse-Darmstadt and a grand-daughter of Queen Victoria of England. She has been described as 'in the deepest sense a Victorian gentlewoman'.[2] She was stately, beautiful, a devoted wife and mother, but in everything she was inflexible and fanatic. When after deep searching of heart and conscience, she embraced Orthodoxy, the church of her husband, she showed the extreme fervour of the convert. She had no understanding of Russia or of the court, where her great reserve had made her unpopular from the start, but having married Nicholas whom she adored she became a chauvinistic Russian patriot, and she elevated his role as autocrat into an article of faith. Nicholas loved Alexandra tenderly and whole-heartedly, and even when her advice seemed to him extreme he was reluctant to hurt her feelings by disregarding it. She was to exercise a dire influence on him during these fateful years.

In his choice of advisers Nicholas was unpredictable and lacked the sure instinct of his father, Alexander III. Not only was Nicholas haphazard in making appointments, but increasingly the influence of his wife made him choose the most conservative and reactionary men. Such a man was Vyacheslav Plehve. A narrow police bureaucrat, he had gained some prominence by bringing to justice all who had been involved in the assassination of Alexander II. When in April 1902 Sipyagin, the minister of the interior, was assassinated, Nicholas appointed Plehve in his place.

Plehve pursued his new duties with energy. He was mainly responsible for the increased persecution of national minorities, especially the Finns and Armenians. He was virulently anti-Semitic. In his ministry were forged *The Protocols of the Elders of Zion*, which purported to be the plans of the Zionist Congress of 1897 for a Jewish conspiracy to dominate the world. But he was most active in promoting police action.

Antagonism towards the tsar and his ministers had become so strong and widespread as to defy suppression. In increasing numbers Russians took part in illegal political meetings and secretly worked for reforms. Only a small proportion were revolutionaries, but few among the moderates would co-operate with the police or with government officials. Witte, although a reactionary, was primarily a politician, who tempered repression with concession when opposition grew too strong. Plehve lacked such commonsense. He intensified police activities. Spies even reported on Russian *émigré* circles and on students at universities abroad. Agents were infiltrated into every political group in Russia. The police had full reports on Lenin and the bolsheviks among whose most respected members were agents, like Rodion Malinovsky, whom Lenin had trusted implicitly.[3]

The most remarkable and notorious of these police agents was Yevno Azef, the son of a Russian Jewish tailor. He was a member of a Russian socialist student group at a German engineering school when he was enlisted as a secret agent. On his return to Russia he worked as an engineer and became an active member of the socialist revolutionary party, on which he reported regularly to his police masters. But then he succeeded Gershuni as head of the terrorist section of the party and during the years 1903–8 he was directly responsible for organizing its chief assassinations. His amazing double career as police agent and revolutionary terrorist remained undetected for five years. When unmasked it caused a public outcry. Confidence in the socialist revolutionary party was undermined. Azef himself, however, escaped to Berlin where he lived under another name.[4]

Among the police, however, were some who realized that repression could not eliminate discontent or opposition and that the great majority of the people were not revolutionaries. They argued that the popular demands for better conditions should be channelled into legal organizations. Not only would this relieve the growing pressure of anger and impatience, but it might lead to moderate reform.

The remarkable police scheme, devised for this purpose, was the work of Sergei Zubatov, Director of the Department of the Political Police in Moscow. Known as 'police socialism', Zubatov's plan provided for labour associations, run under police supervision, which would avoid political activity and concentrate on economic demands. The chief of the Moscow police, General Dmitri Trepov, was enthusiastic about the project, and obtained the approval of the minister of the interior and of Grand Duke Sergei, Governor-General of Moscow. The scheme was first launched in Moscow in 1900, and at once proved popular and successful. Similar labour organizations were set up in St Petersburg, Odessa, and other cities. Soon, however, the police were finding it difficult to keep them under control. In Odessa the labour organization planned a mass strike in the summer of 1903, which got so far out of hand that troops had to be called in to restore order. Zubatov was officially rebuked and removed from office. His scheme was then suppressed, but his idea lingered and it was to give rise to a tragedy which shook the foundations of the tsarist regime.

An Orthodox priest, named Father Georgii Gapon, had while serving as chaplain in a St Petersburg prison become enthusiastic about Zubatov's plan. He was himself in touch with the police and may well have been an agent when he organized the St Petersburg Society of Russian Factory and Workshop Workers. This society enjoyed police protection even after Zubatov's scheme had been abandoned. As its president, Gapon developed it until by the end of 1904 its membership was over 8,000 and it had branches throughout the capital. Its activities were social and educational and apparently non-political, but within it Gapon had set up a secret revolutionary committee.

Late in December 1904 the dismissal of four men from the Putilov works had led to a strike and by 20 January strikers numbered over 150,000. Their demands were limited to immediate economic needs, and they did not heed the slogans of the social democrats and the socialist revolutionaries, working among them. All the strikers looked to Gapon as their leader. On 20 January he proposed to a mass meeting that they must all march in procession to the Winter Palace and humbly present to the tsar a petition for the granting of their demands. But Gapon, a devious and excitable man, had in mind something more than the peaceful procession of loyal subjects which has become the general legend. In his harangue to the massed strikers he said that face to face with the tsar they would say: 'Your Majesty, we cannot go on like this; it is time to give the people their freedom.' If the tsar agreed, he must swear an oath. If they were kept outside the palace gates, 'We will,' he said, 'force our way through. If the troops fire on us, we will defend ourselves. Part of the troops will then come over to us. We will then make a revolution, we will build barricades, sack the stores of arms and ammunition, storm the prison . . . The Socialist Revolutionaries have promised us bombs . . . we will win through!'[5]

Gapon notified the minister of the interior that the march would take place next day and assured him that it would be peaceful. He also sent a note of the demands to be presented to the tsar, which included full civil and political freedom for all and the setting-up of a constituent assembly. Police agents who had been present at the mass meetings had, however, reported on Gapon's inflammatory speeches, and his assurances that the march would be peaceful did not calm the government's fears that they were about to face a dangerous revolutionary demonstration. The tsar and his family were at Tsarskoe Selo, not the Winter Palace, but officials were alarmed that Gapon's mob would take over the city by force.

On the morning of Sunday, 22 January, 'Bloody Sunday' as it was to be known, thousands of workers, many accompanied by their wives and children, moved from all parts of the city towards the Winter Palace. Gapon was at their head, resplendent in his Orthodox robes and flanked by holy ikons. The crowd was, in fact, unarmed, for the socialist revolutionaries had failed to deliver their promised bombs. But the police and officials presumably did not know this and they were uneasy. As the vast crowd approached the palace, military and police detachments called on them to halt. The crowd moved steadily forward. In the square before the palace, the troops and police, faced by the seemingly relentless march, lost their heads and began firing into the mass of people. Many fell dead and hundreds were wounded. At the first shots Gapon fell to the ground unhurt, and then quickly made his escape. The crowd scattered, while the cries of the wounded and dying and the shrieks of women and children echoed through the city. By nightfall order had been restored.

News of this massacre spread rapidly and it horrified the nation. All were ready to believe that the tsar had coldly and deliberately shot down helpless men, women, and children, his own subjects who were seeking merely to present a loyal and humble petition. Nicholas, like his predecessors, had always been cherished as the 'Little Father' of his people; even in the midst of the mounting discontent of the nineteenth century all Russians, except for the few extremists, had continued to venerate him as the protector of his people. Suddenly this massacre on 'Bloody Sunday' had destroyed their traditional image of their sovereign. Gapon told Lenin subsequently: 'We have no Tsar any more. Rivers of blood separate the Tsar from the people.'[6]

Nicholas himself was shaken and bewildered by the events of this day and by the tempest of hostility that swept the country. It was indeed a cruel stroke of fate that he who sincerely loved his people should find himself hated by them as a tyrant. He tried to make amends by ordering the payment of compensation to families of the dead and wounded, and by appointing a commission to consider workers' complaints. It was too late. The people no longer saw in him their divinely appointed sovereign and 'Little Father', but regarded him as a monster.[7] This change in the popular attitude removed one of the main foundations on which the whole regime rested: it was a major factor in preparing the way for revolution.

Plehve, the hated minister of the interior, had been assassinated on 28 July 1904. A young socialist revolutionary, named Sazanov, had thrown a bomb into his carriage as he rode through St Petersburg. Sazanov was acting on the orders of the fighting organization of which Azef, the police agent, was the director; on this occasion as on others he had neglected to report the terrorist plans to his police superiors.

News of Plehve's death was received with general relief and even rejoicing, except at court. Nicholas was unsure whether to hunt down the revolutionaries and pursue with even greater vigour Plehve's repressive policies, or to bow to the growing tide of opposition. Finally, as though pushed into it by the force of public opinion, he chose the latter course, appointing as the new minister Prince Svyatopolk-Mirsky, a moderate liberal and a man of integrity who was widely respected. His appointment, indicating that the government was retreating from its policy of repression, aroused general optimism. It marked the beginning of a new period, known as the 'Russian spring', during which the middle-class liberals emerged on to the political stage. This factor, rather than the dramatic and highly publicized tragedy of 'Bloody Sunday', marked the real beginning of the revolution of 1905.

From their foundation in 1865 the elective district and provincial councils, known as the zemstva, had attracted men of liberal outlook. Many progressive landowners and professional men, who scorned service in the corrupt and reactionary bureaucracy, devoted themselves to the zemstva which enjoyed popular support and achieved remarkable results. The Saratov zemstvo, for instance, set up a bacteriological station and effectively halted the epidemics which had for decades come into the province from the east. The zemstvo of Vyatka, run by elected peasant farmers, was renowned for its efficiency. The Tver zemstvo developed cottage industries and, like other zemstva, maintained a team of agricultural experts who advised peasants on increasing the productivity of their lands. In education and health services the zemstva were particularly effective; many rural districts of the vast province of Moscow were developed, until a school existed within two miles and a hospital within three miles of every village.

The zemstva had flourished while they concerned themselves with social developments. Attempts to extend their activities to national politics had at once faced them with official obstruction. But the zemstva had drawn new strength from working together. The terrible famines of 1891–3 in particular had made them co-ordinate their work. The provincial zemstvo of Moscow was generally accepted as the leader, especially as its chairman during the years 1895–1902 was Dmitri Shipov, an able and dedicated man. He organized private meetings of zemstva chairmen to concert action not only in the social and economic fields but also to formulate political demands. This provoked a strong reaction from the government. Plehve was already exercising greater control over the zemstva and deliberately hampering their work. In 1902 he had refused to confirm the re-election of Shipov as chairman of the Moscow zemstvo, an action which aroused general indignation.

During the 'Russian spring' which followed the appointment of Svyatopolk-Mirsky, the liberal zemstvo organizations sprang into action. Shipov convened a zemstvo conference in St Petersburg from 19 to 22 November 1904 which unanimously approved a petition to the tsar, requesting the grant of full civil liberties for all classes and nationalities, and the setting-up of a national assembly. The question whether this assembly should be consultative or legislative was the only point on which the zemstvo representatives were divided. The tsar's response was simply to direct the zemstva to desist from discussing political affairs. He nevertheless announced his intention of granting reforms, but not a national assembly.

The proposals of the zemstva congress received strong support from all progressive sections of Russian society. The legal profession, followed by the engineers, academic teachers, doctors, authors, and similar groups formed themselves into unions, all of which pledged themselves to work for the fulfilment of the zemstva proposals.[8] The more radical liberals of the zemstva and of the professional class, led by Peter Struve and other converts from Marxism, joined in the League of Liberation, which was almost as strongly opposed to socialism as autocracy. It now worked to increase the pressure on the tsar and his government to grant civil liberties and a representative assembly.

On 25 December 1904 Nicholas issued a decree, stating that reforms would be considered, but that he would not amend the fundamental laws of the empire. This satisfied no one. The liberals of the League of Liberation now joined in a united front with the socialist revolutionaries, who had temporarily halted their terrorist activities, and with the mensheviks, the dominant element in the social democratic party. The united front thus included all shades of radical opinion except only the very small bolshevik group.

At this point the whole nation had been shaken by the massacre on 'Bloody Sunday' and then by the news of the shameful surrender of Port Arthur to the Japanese. These disasters exhausted the patience of the people who erupted in revolts all over the country. The socialist revolutionary fighting organization revived its terrorist campaign and on 17 February 1905 Grand Duke Sergei, an uncle of Nicholas II, was assassinated in broad daylight in the Kremlin by a young socialist revolutionary, Ivan Kaliayev. The Grand Duke was a harsh, bigoted man of whom his own cousin wrote: 'Try as I will, I cannot find a single redeeming feature in his character.'[9] His death was no loss, but he was a member of the imperial family and this fact, together with the demeanour of the assassin, undoubtedly impressed Nicholas. Kaliayev had made no attempt to escape after the assassination, and had borne himself with dignity and courage during the police investigation. Grand Duchess Elizabeth, the widow, a beautiful and deeply religious woman, had visited him in prison and had offered to plead for his life if he would merely express sorrow for his deed. He refused, saying that his own death might help the revolutionary cause; he showed the same courage at his execution.[10]

To maintain stricter order Nicholas now appointed General Dmitri Trepov, known for his energetic repression of revolutionaries, as governor-general of St Petersburg. He also replaced Svyatopolk-Mirsky by Alexander Bulygin at the ministry of the interior. He realized, nevertheless, that some concessions to popular demand were unavoidable and on 3 March he publicly announced his instruction to Bulygin to prepare a plan under which 'the most worthy persons should be elected to share in the drafting and discussion of laws'.[11]

The terms of the rescript to Bulygin aroused no great hopes and did little to calm the general unrest. Strikes and peasant outbreaks, usually with pillaging and burning down of landowners' homesteads and at times with greater violence, continued. But the pronouncement was taken as giving permission for the formation of political parties, and it stimulated the organization of the liberals.

A notable development at this time was the uniting of all the professional unions in the Union of Unions under the chairmanship of P. N. Milyukov, an able historian and the outstanding liberal of the day. Moreover workers, peasants, and liberals of the zemstva and the professional unions were beginning to work more closely together. The socialist revolutionaries were gaining wider support in the countryside with their slogan 'All land to the peasants'. In July a conference of peasant representatives in Moscow, promoted by liberals and socialist revolutionaries, formed the

The former Emperor Nicholas II at Tsarskoe Selo, 1917

Vladimir Ilyich Lenin, Red Square, 1 May 1919

All-Russian Peasants' Union on the lines of the professional unions and, indeed, the Peasants' union promptly joined the Union of Unions.

The news of the annihilation of the Baltic Fleet at Tsushima on 27–28 May staggered the nation, inured though it was to disasters. This humiliating defeat put a halt to any lingering hopes that the war against Japan might end in victory. It gave rise to a general demand to stop hostilities and to summon a national assembly. Shipov convened a coalition congress of leaders of all groups of zemstvo and other liberals, which agreed to ask the tsar to receive a delegation, representing the people as a whole. Nicholas, himself deeply shaken by the defeat of his navy, agreed and on 19 June a deputation from the zemstva and town councils, headed by Prince Sergei Trubetskoy, chosen because he was a non-party man, respected for his personal integrity and the great ancestry of his family, had audience at the palace. Trubetskoy spoke earnestly of the need to regain the confidence of the people and to share the responsibilities of government with them. Nicholas in the same spirit assured him that he intended to summon a national assembly and with the co-operation of his people to launch a new era.

On 19 August an imperial decree was proclaimed, setting out the terms of the Bulygin law on the Duma. But as many had feared, despite the tsar's assurances, it contained only half-hearted provisions for a consultative body. Public agitation for a constituent assembly with real powers increased. To all it seemed that a long struggle lay ahead before this demand would be met. No one expected the sudden development, which now forced the hand of Nicholas.

Late in September a printers' strike in Moscow spread to other trades. Printers in St Petersburg came out in sympathy. These strikes continued until in October a general strike of railway workers acted as a stranglehold on the nation. Factories in St Petersburg and Moscow were forced to close. Teachers and members of all professions stopped work. Within a week the whole country was in a state of paralysis. This crisis had developed without organization or leadership of any kind. It was a dramatic and spontaneous explosion of popular discontent.

Later in October the mensheviks, supported by the socialist revolutionaries and others, took the initiative in improvising the St Petersburg Soviet of Workers' Deputies, elected on the basis of one deputy for every thousand workers. Its president was an able lawyer, named Nosar, known by his pseudonym of Khrustalev, but the vice-president, Leon Trotsky, was its driving force. On this occasion the soviet played no decisive role, but it was to be the forerunner of the vastly more important revolutionary soviet.

During 1904 Lenin's overriding concern had been not the war with Japan, not even the revolutionary movement, but his own control over the party. He had broken with Plekhanov and had antagonized others in the movement. He was now working furiously to gain sufficient support for the

C

convening of another party congress through which he could gain control. By persistence and manipulation he secured the meeting of a third congress which opened in London on 25 April 1905. This congress was, in fact, illegal. The supreme authority of the party, the party council, had refused to authorize it. The mensheviks would not recognize it and held a simultaneous congress of their own in Geneva. At his London congress Lenin nevertheless moved a step closer to his objective of a centralized party of disciplined professionals, owing personal allegiance to him as leader.

Absorbed by party affairs, Lenin was detached from events in Russia and even viewed with suspicion the activities of party members there. In particular he regarded the new Soviet of Workers' Deputies with hostility. He had no use for any organization not wholly under his control and his antagonism towards the soviet was undoubtedly increased by the ascendancy of Trotsky who had not only become a menshevik at this stage but now lost no opportunity to attack him and his plans.

Aged twenty-six, of striking presence, brilliantly clever, and an eloquent speaker who could stir any mob by his oratory, Trotsky was at this time the outstanding social democrat. Lenin himself, although a greater, more powerful leader, could not have disputed place with Trotsky in this particular kind of crisis. Perhaps because he realized this, Lenin made no attempt to take over the leadership of the soviet or to support it in any way. He may also have realized that it would be shortlived. Indeed, on 29 December, troops dissolved the soviet, arresting 190 of its members. Improvised to take advantage of the strike, the soviet had never commanded real support among the workers. Its final appeal to them and to all social democrat organizations to strike met with response only in Rostov-on-Don and in Moscow. In Rostov armed strikers and police clashed during the period from 21 to 29 December, but order was soon restored.

The rising in Moscow, which has become distorted by legend, was more serious. There the general strike developed into an armed rebellion with fighting in the streets and at barricades, lasting from 21 December until 2 January 1906. Casualties totalled more than 1,000 dead. But troops, especially the Semyonovsky Guards sent from St Petersburg, restored order. The strikers had hoped that the troops would support them, but except for small groups of disaffected men the army was loyal and the rising failed.

The general strike had faced Nicholas with a challenge. In desperation he had turned to Witte who had just returned from negotiating peace with Japan. Witte offered him two alternatives: a military dictatorship or the grant of civil rights and of a legislative Duma or council, and an undertaking that no law would come into force without its consent. Nicholas hesitated, but he knew that, in fact, he had no alternative but to grant civil rights and the Duma.

For two days he could not bring himself to sign the manifesto, drafted by Witte, containing the necessary concessions. He and the empress prayed together seeking guidance in this decision. He felt that he was being forced to sign away the heritage of the son born to him and the empress earlier in the year. He feared, too, that he would be breaking his solemn coronation oath. But finally, on 30 October, recoiling from the prospect of plunging his people into a bloody civil war, he signed.

The October Manifesto was greeted excitedly throughout the country. Crowds gathered in the cities and towns, some singing the *Marseillaise,* to celebrate the end of autocracy and the beginning of democracy. The manifesto granted them: (i) civil liberty based on the principles of the inviolability of the person and freedom of conscience, speech, assembly, and union; (ii) the right for all classes to participate in elections to the Duma; (iii) guarantee that no law would be enacted without the consent of the Duma; and (iv) that the Duma would have power to pronounce on the legality of acts, decreed by the autocrat himself.

The jubilation of the people, like the heart-searchings of the tsar, was real, for the manifesto established the beginnings of a parliamentary democracy and a constitutional monarchy.

CHAPTER FOUR

Experiment in Democracy

THE October Manifesto excited hopes that at long last constitutional government would be granted, but strong suspicion underlay these hopes. Mistrust of the tsar and the reactionaries at court was widespread. Unrest continued among the peasants and a revolt in central Russia was on such a scale as to recall the Pugachev rebellion in the reign of Catherine the Great. Among the Poles and Baltic peoples strikes and uprisings became more frequent. Discontent in the armed forces erupted in open mutiny. Early in November sailors mutinied at the Kronstadt naval base in the approaches to St Petersburg. Guards regiments restored order and arrested some 3,000 mutineers. Then sailors in the Black Sea naval base at Sevastopol rebelled. Their leader, Lieut. Peter Schmidt, planned to spread the mutiny through the Black Sea Fleet, but his plans failed.

The furious reactions of the extreme right to the manifesto aggravated the general unrest. Clinging to the old ideals of autocracy, Orthodoxy, and Russian nationalism, the right wing of the nobility, the Orthodox hierarchy, and the bureaucracy denounced the manifesto as a treacherous surrender to the revolutionaries. They raged against the intellectuals and the national minorities, especially the Jews, as traitors to Holy Russia.

Many of these reactionaries formed or supported the Black Hundreds which were gangs of thugs, some led by landowners, and tolerated by the police who at times actively helped them. The Black Hundreds attacked Jews and intellectuals, including school teachers, students, and even school children. One of the most powerful of the reactionary societies, formed at this time, was the Union of the Russian People under the presidency of Dr Alexander Dubrovin. It had a distinguished membership and the highest patronage. Grand Duke Nikolai Nikolaevich, Peter Durnovo, the new minister of the interior, and even the tsar himself supported it. Behind its respectable façade, however, the union with finance and assistance from the police conducted vicious propaganda campaigns against the Jews and national minorities, as well as against the revolutionaries, liberals, and intellectuals generally. It also operated a secret fighting organization, similiar to the terrorist section of the socialist revolutionaries, which promoted murders and violent attacks on those whom they regarded as their enemies. Other reactionary groups were formed and all bore witness to the alarm felt by supporters of the old autocratic regime.

In the turmoil of these days the cities and towns of Russia possessed a sinister and growing underworld. Terrorists and criminals, revolutionaries and police agents, anarchists and outcasts from the intelligentsia and other classes mingled in these dark fringes of society. Misguided idealism, vicious crime, and despair driven to violence and self-destruction seethed together in these cauldrons which recall the underworld of Rome at the time of the Catiline conspiracy.

During these months, nevertheless, the main political parties which were to contest the elections to the state Duma were forming. The constitutional democrats, known as the Kadets, were the leading liberal party, drawing their support from the landed gentry, the professional classes, and the zemstvo liberals.[1] A foundation congress, actually in session when the tsar's manifesto was proclaimed, united the members of the League of Liberation, the Union of Unions, and the zemstvo constitutionalists. The two main attitudes of the party were reflected in its names. The constitutionalists, who included V. Maklakov, accepted autocratic rule, not arbitrarily and capriciously exercised as in the past, but limited by a constitution or fundamental law. The democrats, to whom Milyukov belonged, took their models from the West and wanted a full parliamentary democracy, and even a republic. The October Manifesto had faced them with the need for a decision. Maklakov and the constitutionalists found that most of their demands had been met in the manifesto. But the democrats accepted the manifesto merely as a beginning. This basic division between them was never healed and contributed to the doom of the party.

The Kadet programme for the elections was one of radical reform. It included expropriation of the land for the benefit of the peasants with compensation to the landlords, universal suffrage and full civil liberties, and progressive reforms in labour legislation. Less radical than the Kadets were the Octobrists, who belonged to the Union of 17th October, the date of the manifesto, which was formed at this time under the leadership of Alexander and Nicholas Guchkov, Mikhail Rodzyanko, and Dmitri Shipov. The union's members were drawn in the main from the right wing of the zemstvo liberals, but they had support from the business class in St Petersburg and Moscow, and from the more liberal element of the bureaucracy.

The extreme left, comprising the socialist revolutionaries and the social democrats, was confused by these new developments. All were hostile to the new liberal parties, to the projected Duma, and to the October Manifesto itself. Leon Trotsky went to the lengths of tearing up a copy of the manifesto before the eyes of a large crowd, celebrating its proclamation. Dramatic and reckless, it was a gesture typical of Trotsky.

The 1905 revolution made a strong impact on the social democrats. They recognized that a spontaneous popular movement had developed and that they had neither led nor influenced it; far from being in the van of the general upheaval, they had merely followed, trying wherever possible and without success to steer unrest towards large-scale class revolution.

During 1905 and 1906 the social democrats argued among themselves in search of a policy. But they were clear that the first step must be to heal the split between the mensheviks and the bolsheviks. The two groups had been drawing more widely apart and working as separate parties. Many menshevik and bolshevik groups now merged spontaneously. In November 1905, without reference to the central committee of the party, the bolshevik committee and the menshevik group in St Petersburg decided to unite. Lenin found that he could not stand out against this pressure of the rank and file for reunion, but he was determined that the merger should not take the form of simple fusion of groups on the spot. He insisted that a congress must be convened to effect the union. In December 1905 the bolsheviks held a conference at Tammerfors in Finland and agreed to call a congress for this purpose.

Known by the bolsheviks as the fourth party congress and by the mensheviks as the unification congress, it met in Stockholm from 23 April to 8 May 1906. From the start it became clear that the bolsheviks would not have a majority. Lenin, realizing that he could not dominate the congress, showed an unusually conciliatory spirit during the proceedings. He assured delegates that he certainly did not hold the view that bolsheviks and mensheviks could not work together. He went out of his way to show himself to be a most reasonable man, concerned only for the success of the Marxist cause. At the conclusion of the congress, however, he and certain other bolsheviks listed in a declaration the decisions of the congress which they considered mistaken and claimed the right to struggle in 'comradely' debate to have their views accepted.[2] He was soon to demonstrate that his ideas and objectives and his methods were unchanged.

In all 111 voting delegates attended the congress, and the mensheviks had a majority of sixty-two delegates as against forty-four or forty-six bolsheviks. The Georgians sent a large delegation which included a young bolshevik, named Josef Dzhugashvili, who used the name Koba and was later to be known as Stalin. Aged twenty-seven at the time, he had long been an active revolutionary in Tiflis where he was then joint editor of the *Kavkazsky Rabochy Listok* (The Caucasian Workers' News Sheet). The Tammerfors conference had been the first time that he had left his Caucasian homeland to visit European Russia. He had gone in a mood of excitement and wonder, particularly because he would have the opportunity of meeting Lenin, 'the mountain eagle of our party', as he called him.[3] His first glimpses of Lenin proved disappointing, but as the conference had continued he had been increasingly impressed by his master.

The Stockholm congress agreed that the merger of the two groups should take place at once without formality. Lenin then had the satisfaction of having his Paragraph I of the party constitution, dealing with membership, which had caused the split in the party, adopted. Some mensheviks still argued that the immediate task was to organize a mass party, but the great majority, including Martov, were now convinced that a strongly centralized party machine was needed to lead the proletariat in the final victorious revolution.

Land reform was debated at length. The social democrats had so far paid little attention to the peasants, taking it more or less for granted that they would docilely follow in the wake of the proletariat. The socialist revolutionaries, primarily concerned with the peasants, had made a strong appeal to them by promising them the land. Now the 1905 revolution made Lenin realize that the peasants must inevitably play a major part in the revolutionary movement. At the congress in Stockholm the mensheviks proposed a municipalization of the land, which meant transferring it to locally elected councils to be administered for the benefit of the peasants. This policy, in some degree perpetuating the commune, can have had little appeal for the peasants. Lenin and the bolsheviks advocated nationalization of the land by vesting it in the central government, a policy with even less appeal. But Lenin was quick to appreciate this defect. He made it clear soon after the congress that 'we must call upon the peasants to seize the land' and later, when firmly in power, they could confiscate the holdings of the unfortunate peasants and vest them in the central government.[4]

The young Georgian, Dzhugashvili, with great boldness, spoke against both proposals. He argued for 'distributism' as it was called, which was no less than the direct sharing out of the land among the peasants. He pointed out that this was what the peasants wanted and this alone would secure their support. When his proposal was attacked, even by Lenin, he stood his ground, emphasizing that in fostering rural capitalism it was in accordance with Marxist doctrine and would be a logical advance towards the socialist revolution.[5]

The immediate problem facing the party was the practical policy to be adopted towards the Duma. The bolsheviks had already decided at their conference in Tammerfors that, since the Duma would be reactionary and would inevitably come to terms with the autocracy—a prognosis that was to prove completely wrong—they should oppose it by every means in their power. This meant boycotting the elections. They were particularly disturbed by the possibility that their participation in the elections might encourage the workers to think that they could gain their objectives by parliamentary methods, and without resorting to violent revolution.

Lenin had been less convinced about the need to boycott the elections and all participation in the Duma. He could see the possibilities of exploiting it to the advantage of the Marxist cause. In his then conciliatory mood, however, he bowed to the strong demand for boycott. By the time of the Stockholm congress, the Duma elections were already well advanced, and the victory of the Kadets was clear.

The mensheviks had on the whole been less strongly opposed to participation in the elections. They had left the decision to local committees, many of which nominated candidates. Finally in Stockholm the mensheviks urged that the boycott should be abandoned, and proposed that the social democrats should organize a special group in the Duma under the control of the central committee of the party. By this time, however, they were already too late to take part in most of the elections.

The socialist revolutionaries, too, were divided on this question. Their objective was still a constituent assembly to be achieved by revolution. But this lay in the future and on the immediate practical question of the elections their party congress, held in January 1906, decided on boycott. In practice, however, this proved impossible to implement. The peasants voted in large numbers. Many supported the Kadets, but many cast their votes for candidates who proclaimed socialist revolutionary policies. The successful candidates in this category formed an important block in the First Duma, known as the Trudovik, or Labour, group.

The elections took place in March and April, and although the first national elections to be held in Russia's history, they were orderly, the peasants and workers in particular showing care and intelligence in casting their votes. The franchise was complex with indirect voting based on wealth and social classes through electoral colleges, but it was broad and allowed considerable representation of public opinion. The Kadets won 179 seats; the Trudovik group, comprising the unofficial socialist revolutionaries, gained 94 seats; the social democrats, who had belatedly contested the elections in certain regions, won 18 seats. The right-wing parties won only 32 seats of which 17 were held by Octobrists. The remaining seats were held by deputies representing the national minorities and small groups.

The new constitution, provided by the October Manifesto, had many interesting features. It introduced the cabinet system with a prime minister, as president of the council of ministers, who had control over and responsibility for his colleagues. This in itself was a major innovation, for the council now took the place of the committee of ministers, appointed by the tsar and answering individually to him, which had caused confusion and inefficiency. The new legislature was bicameral. The upper house was an enlarged version of the council of state, set up by Alexander I in 1810 to prepare and revise legislation, but which had never become an effective body. The new state council had 196 members, half nominated by the tsar from the existing state councillors, half elected by public bodies, such as the church, the zemstva, the Academy of Sciences. But this council was so reactionary and unrepresentative that its sessions, held at the same time as those of the Duma, attracted little attention.

The Duma or lower house suffered from many limits on its powers. Ministers, appointed by the tsar on the recommendation of the Prime minister, were not responsible to the Duma. Each house had power to initiate legislation, but the state council could reject any bill passed by the Duma, and legislation after passing through both houses still required the assent of the tsar who could exercise an absolute veto.

The legislature had no power to amend the fundamental laws which had been revised in anticipation of the convening of the first Duma. One new provision in the fundamental laws which was to give rise to angry conflicts was Article 87. This article empowered the government to make any law it considered necessary to deal with an emergency arising when the Duma was not in session, subject to the law being presented for the Duma's approval within two months of its next meeting.

The tsar retained wide powers. The government answered to him and he could dismiss it at any time. He could dissolve the Duma at will. He held the sole command over the army and the navy. He could proclaim a state of emergency in any part of the empire and this had the effect of suspending all legal guarantees. His executive authority, including the power to appoint or remove all administrative officers, remained. Despite the fears of reactionaries at court, and the empress in particular, his position was still that of a constitutional monarch.

The restraints on the Duma were thus formidable, but it nevertheless occupied an important position in the state. It could publicly criticize and arraign the government or individual ministers; it could examine budget estimates, and its approval was needed for all new legislation. Most important of all, the Duma could concentrate the full weight of public opinion against policies which were unpopular and unacceptable. In a country where discontent had always been suppressed until it exploded in rebellion and in which the autocrat and his ministers had been above criticism, this was a significant advance.

The Duma opened on 10 May 1906, but five days earlier Witte had ceased to be prime minister under the new constitution of which he was chief architect. Nicholas recognized his ability and had turned to him in such crises as negotiating the peace with Japan, organizing the return of troops from the Far East, and in the general strike of October 1905. Just over a month before the Duma met, Witte had deserved his special gratitude for negotiating with France the enormous loan of 2,250 million francs, with the purpose of securing the government's financial position and of making it independent to a large degree of the interference of the Duma. But Nicholas had never liked or trusted Witte, and he may perhaps have been aware of the contempt which Witte in his heart felt for him. A few months later he was to write: 'As long as I live I will never trust that man again with the smallest thing. I had quite enough of last year's experiment. It is still like a nightmare to me.'[6]

Nicholas's feelings were not without basis. Witte for all his ability and his practical sense as a politician was a man without principle, concerned with power and honours for himself, and by turn subservient, arrogant, crude, and vindictive. At court he had many enemies and none more ardent than the empress who blamed him for the October Manifesto. She also hated him because she believed that he was carefully building up his position as president of the council of ministers, so that, like the British prime minister, he would be able to relegate the Russian autocrat to the impotence of a constitutional monarch. Other powerful enemies were Trepov, the governor-general of St Petersburg, a widely hated man who nevertheless had the tsar's confidence, and P. N. Durnovo, who had been appointed minister of the interior by Witte and who now intrigued against him. Among the liberals and revolutionaries he was also mistrusted. Witte was nevertheless one of the few men with experience and acute political sense who might have rescued the tsarist regime from the tidal wave of revolution which was to engulf it.

Weak and vacillating, Nicholas was now almost completely under the influence of reactionaries at court. At the time of signing the manifesto he had believed that these great constitutional concessions were inevitable and he had sincerely intended to carry them out. His second thoughts had come later when he was persuaded that he must salvage more of the autocratic powers which he had inherited. Dominated by the implacable faith of the empress in the principle of autocracy, he became at times like a man blindly following his fate, as he set foot on the road that was to end in the destruction of himself, his family, and all that he valued in life.

The new prime minister was Goremykin, a wily old man who clung to office as he clung to life itself. He was a bureaucrat who hated all change and who held loudly to the principle that the tsar was in all things absolute and that ministers were merely his servants. The empress referred to him affectionately as 'the old man'. Other members of the cabinet, some chosen by Nicholas and others by Witte, were, however, of a different calibre. Count Kokovtsov, the minister of finance, was intelligent, able, and widely respected. Izvolsky, the foreign minister, was a devoted public servant. But the dominant minister, and, indeed, one of the most remarkable men of the day, was Peter Stolypin. He had been a provincial governor and had carried out his duties with wisdom and efficiency. He had attracted attention especially during the unrest of the previous year when he had by his presence and courage restored order in the Saratov province, one of the most turbulent in the country. In one village which was in open rebellion he had walked alone, ignoring the rifle fire directed at him, and had implored the insurgents not to force him to order troops against them. His plea was heard and peace was restored without the destruction of the village, which was the normal method of eliminating such centres of trouble. But Stolypin could be ruthless in putting down insurrection. On 14 September 1906, making use of Article 87, he set up field courts-martial which dealt promptly with acts of terrorism. In eight months these courts sentenced 683 rebels and terrorists to death. An attempt made to assassinate him at his country house outside St Petersburg failed, but his daughter was maimed for life. He was not, however, a man to be deterred by such dangers and he did not hesitate to deal firmly with terrorism.

Peter Stolypin was a big man with a fine forehead, piercing eyes, and heavy beard and moustache. In any gathering his presence was felt, and his courage, honesty, and integrity made him a natural leader. Contemporaries wrote of his 'unquestionable personal nobility'.[7] He was not a reactionary, but a constitutionalist who wanted a fundamental law to regulate the exercise of the autocratic power. He was ready to work with the Duma, and declared that he wanted 'to show the country that it had parted company forever with the old police order of things'.[8] He boldly introduced reforms that were overdue and sought to deal with the demands of the people, rather than to suppress them.

The Duma sought from its first meeting to follow the procedure at Westminster. In reply to the speech, made to the deputies by the tsar, when he received them at the Winter Palace, they submitted an address to the throne, setting out their main proposals. Goremykin with his ministers then came before the Duma, but instead of dealing with proposals constructively, he ranted, telling the deputies that their demands, including land for the peasants, were 'inadmissible'. A young liberal, Vladimir Nabokov, who had drafted the address, then moved a vote of censure on the government. In the debate that followed, one deputy after another spoke on the abuses and incompetence of the government. Their criticism was so vehement that it seemed that the liberal majority in the Duma was more concerned to condemn the government than to embark on a programme of reforms. Duma and government now reached deadlock. Each side wondered what step to take next. The Kadets and the Trudoviks brought forward two bills to effect compulsory expropriation of the land for the peasants, and only the Kadet bill provided compensation for the landlords. Neither bill had any chance of becoming law, but the fact of tabling them won further popular support for the Duma.

The tsar and several of his ministers now wanted to dissolve the Duma before it became more provocative. They hesitated, fearing a public outcry. Izvolsky counselled strongly against dissolution, because it would antagonize opinion in England and France, and in particular might prejudice Russia's *rapprochement* with England. Trepov advised the tsar to call on the liberals to form a government, for he was convinced that they would fail so completely that a military dictatorship would be necessary to restore order and normal services. Nicholas hesitated. Informal approaches were made to several leading men in the Duma. Milyukov was again sounded as to his readiness to form a government, but he made conditions which were quite unacceptable to the government.

For all his belief in parliamentary government, Milyukov was inflexible and doctrinaire. With other members of the Kadet party he suffered from the almost arrogant belief that they represented the will of the people and that they had a mandate to introduce parliamentary government. They did not ask or petition, but demanded or imposed conditions which were excessive. They were, in fact, victims of their own inexperience and they squandered their opportunities. Milyukov and the Kadets should have co-operated with the government in this and the later Dumas. They were closer to public opinion and representative of the progressive elements among the Russian people at the time. But they lacked experience of governing. The government and bureaucracy had the direct knowledge of how to run the vast complex machinery of state, but was remote from the people. In harness the Duma liberals and the government might have entrenched the constitutional gains of the 1905 revolution.

On 20 July Nicholas formally dissolved the Duma and appointed Stolypin as prime minister. It was noteworthy that he did not entertain any ideas of suspending it permanently. But the deputies were incensed. Members of the Kadet and Trudovik parties hastened to Vyborg in Finland, where they had greater freedom from police interference. From there they issued an appeal to the country to demand that the dissolution be cancelled and, pending the recall of the Duma, the people were asked to withhold payment of their taxes and to refuse recruits for the army. It was a stupid appeal. It was unconstitutional, for the tsar, like the monarch in the British constitution which they had made their model, clearly had the right of dissolution. Furthermore the Kadets had no party organization in the country to implement such an appeal, and it went unanswered, but it had the unforeseen result that all who had signed it in Vyborg were charged under Russian law, which precluded them from standing for re-election, a fact which deprived the second Duma of many able men.

In the period until the new Duma was elected, Stolypin ruled. It was, he explained to Sir Bernard Pares, the British observer and the leading British historian of the period, a time of great difficulty for him. Opposed to revolution and eager for reform, he needed the support of the Duma.[9] He did not, however, delay for this reason, for he maintained that the government had already evaded facing essential reforms for too long. Relying on the controversial Article 87, which had never been intended to cover fundamental legislation, he introduced major reforms on land tenure and the rights of the peasants.

The abolition of serfdom in 1861 had been a first step towards liberating the peasants from the slavery of their lives. But the village communes in their close control over the land and the persons of each peasant household had perpetuated many of the evils of serfdom. Impoverished and thwarted the peasants had stagnated as an inferior class and their condition had, like a mighty ulcer, continued to suppurate and poison the nation.

Stolypin, in a series of *ukazi*, now began a transformation in the position of the peasants. For the first time in Russia's history the peasants were granted the full rights and status of other classes. In his *ukaz* of 22 November he gave every peasant the right to secede from his commune, claiming his share of the commune lands, the strips gathered together into one holding, as his personal property which he could pass to his heirs. This was a revolutionary change which dealt with the two age-old grievances of the peasants; first, that they were allocated land in strips, often widely separated, and, second, that the land they worked, and which they felt to be their land for this reason, could never become their personal property. For peasants with determination and a sense of independence, this *ukaz* opened new horizons. Many were quick to take advantage of it, as was shown by the fact that between 1906 and 1915 more than two-and-a-half million peasant householders applied to secede from their communes.

The land reforms were challenged when the Duma met. Some deputies opposed all government legislation; many deputies resented the fact that Article 87 had been used for such important measures. The strongest opposition came, however, from the reactionaries who cherished the patriarchal system, despite the ample evidence of its failure, and who continued to regard the commune as a bulwark against revolution. But Stolypin pressed ahead with these reforms, directed towards the creation of a broad class of independent yeomen farmers who, like the farmers of England and France, would serve as a responsible, stabilizing force. In this he had wide support among the liberals and from the peasants themselves.

In 1910 and 1911 Stolypin brought in further laws to deal with problems which had not been foreseen. The Land Organization Commissions, set up in 1906, were given wider authority to ensure effective execution of the reforms. The Peasant Land Bank was given increased powers to enable peasants to acquire new lands. The results were impressive; by 1915 the number of peasant families with hereditary private holdings was probably more than seven million.

The land reforms also led to an overall improvement in efficiency. Many landowners began to take a direct interest in managing their estates and in applying modern methods. A new class of prosperous yeoman farmers, known as kulaks, emerged and they added considerably to the greater output of the land. But these reforms, momentous in many respects, were only a beginning. They did not solve the terrible problems of over-population and poverty on the land. Migration to Siberia and other Asiatic regions, which was never less than 20,000 in any year between 1907 and 1913 and which reached 650,000 in 1907, gave some slight relief from the pressure. What was needed, however, was time to allow the land reforms and the new agricultural methods to develop.

'Give us ten years and we are safe!' exclaimed S. I. Shidlovsky and, as a liberal landowner and Chairman of the Land Commission of the third Duma, who had devoted his life to land reform, he was voicing the prayer of the majority of the deputies.

Lenin, too, understood the significance of Stolypin's land reforms. He saw the danger that, given time to consolidate the new position of the peasants, a radical socialist revolution might become impossible or would at least be delayed indefinitely. In an article, published on 29 April 1908, he warned the mensheviks that Stolypin's policy might well succeed in achieving a complete bourgeois revolution. The agricultural system would then acquire a solidarity which would remove the existing chances of the revolution by a radical peasantry and proletariat for which he was then agitating. But time was running not in favour of Stolypin's reforms but in favour of Lenin's revolutionary upheaval.[10]

On the dissolution of the first Duma, the dates for new elections had been announced. Stolypin had intended that these elections would be conducted on the same basis as before, and agreed only with reluctance to a revised franchise.[11] This revision, by eliminating whole categories of electors and restricting others, was intended to ensure the election of a conservative Duma, which would support the government. It was clearly unconstitutional and provoked a storm of protest. But the government's hopes were disappointed. The Kadets gained 123 seats, the Trudovik group 97, the Polish nationalists 39, and the socialists, who had this time entered whole-heartedly into the election campaign, won 83 seats.

The second Duma, which met on 5 March 1907, was thus almost as strongly in opposition as its predecessor. The Kadets, weakened by the loss of those members who had signed the Vyborg Manifesto, nevertheless had several able men, like Andrei Shingarev and, in particular, Vasily Maklakov, a brilliant lawyer and orator. But there were also disruptive elements. The reactionaries were bent on destroying the Duma by involving it in debates on terrorism and matters likely to damage its prestige in the public mind. The revolutionaries also pursued disruptive tactics. Stolypin, unable to secure the co-operation even of the Kadet liberals, resigned himself to working with a hostile Duma. He was prepared, however, to face the unending debates if he could avoid dissolution, for he appreciated the significance which the Duma was acquiring in the life of the nation.

At court, agitation for dissolution began to gain strength. The landowning nobles were now disturbed by Stolypin's agrarian legislation, fearing that it would lead to further peasant revolts. In April a congress of the nobility and patriotic societies petitioned the tsar to disband the Duma. Nicholas himself was eager for dissolution. Outspoken criticisms in the Duma, especially involving the armed forces, had angered him. Meanwhile, two plots, implicating the social democrats and the socialist revolutionaries, had been uncovered. Both parties had, in fact, suspended terrorist activities for the duration of the Duma's sittings, and the plots may well have been the inventions of the police. On 14 June Stolypin faced the Duma with the demand for the expulsion of the social democrat deputies, so that, deprived of their parliamentary immunity, they could be brought to trial. The Duma insisted on first investigating the charges. This was unacceptable to the government. On 16 June 1907 an imperial manifesto declared that, since the Duma no longer represented the people and since it harboured enemies of the nation, it was dissolved.

The fifth congress of the social democrat party, held in London in May 1907, had, in fact, strongly condemned violence. It had forbidden 'partisan actions' and, in particular, 'expropriations', the euphemistic name given to robbery, often with violence, of state and private institutions to obtain funds for the party. The London congress, in which the bolsheviks had a majority, was also critical of its deputies in the Duma. The deputies had shown signs of independence and were reminded that they were in the Duma to make revolutionary propaganda, and not to legislate.

The congress had adopted Lenin's proposals for closer co-operation with the socialist revolutionaries. This was, Lenin considered, expedient because their agrarian policy was akin to his own in its immediate aims. The mensheviks would have preferred to co-operate with the Kadets, because their respective agrarian policies were not incompatible. Such disputes were typical and at that time were conducted as though in a vacuum, for they had no direct bearing on events inside Russia.

While the fires of revolution were all but extinguished in Russia and the revolutionaries abroad squabbled and fretted, Lenin never ceased to struggle for a centralized, conspiratorial, rigidly disciplined party organization under his leadership. The unity of the party, forged at the Stockholm congress and confirmed at the London congress, was no more than a façade. Lenin had maintained his bolshevik centre, comprising the members absolutely loyal to him. For him this centre was the party, and the mensheviks and others outside it were not comrades but enemies. The decisions of the party, taken in congress, were binding on all when he agreed with them, but never binding on him and the centre, if he disagreed. He saw himself as ultimately the sole source of authority, and he did not hesitate to disregard party rulings.

Lenin demonstrated this immediately after the London congress when, on 26 June 1907, an act of expropriation took place in Tiflis. It took the form of a dramatic bank robbery, engineered by the Georgian bolshevik, Dzhugashvili-Stalin. The haul of 341,000 rubles, mainly in 500-ruble notes, was smuggled out of Russia to the bolsheviks in exile. Lenin had detailed one of his most trusted supporters, Dr Jacob Zhitomirsky, to pass on the money, little suspecting that he was a police agent. Zhitomirsky informed and the others involved in handling the money were arrested. The responsibility for the robbery became public and not only the Russian social democrats but the Second International was shaken by this flagrant disregard for party policy. The mensheviks were even more shocked when they discovered that Lenin had given his approval to a partisan band, led by a certain Lbov, operating in the Urals. Other examples of Lenin's scorn for party decisions and for normal morality came to light.

In 1909 the central committee, still nominally united, considered the expulsion of Lenin from the party. But Plekhanov, Trotsky, the Bund, and others feared that many bolsheviks would then rally to him and the party would be greatly weakened. A compromise decision was reached, one condition of which was that the bolshevik centre would be dissolved. Lenin accepted this condition, but the centre was never disbanded.

At this time Lenin moved steadily towards the final split in the party. It had existed for some years, rooted in the two different conceptions of party organization. The mensheviks stood for the broadly based party, and the bolsheviks held that a small centralized vanguard of disciplined professional revolutionaries under Lenin's leadership was the essential organ of revolution. Conditions in Russia during the years 1906–14 strongly favoured the menshevik conception, but conditions in 1917 were to favour Lenin.

Fundamental to this split and more important than differences of policy, however, were the clash of personalities and one man's struggle to dominate. Lenin was driven by his own sense of infallibility as a revolutionary leader and by his will to power. He now made an important advance towards personal victory.

In January 1912 at the headquarters of the Czech social democrats in Prague the bolsheviks formally proclaimed that they were the party. The mensheviks and all others who did not accept Lenin's leadership were condemned as renegades. The new central committee, then elected, included Ordzhonikidze, Sverdlov, and Zinoviev. Among the delegates was a young man, named Scriabin, later known as Molotov. Soon afterwards Lenin co-opted to the central committee the Georgian, Dzhugashvili/ Stalin, who had first caught his attention as a result of the Tiflis expropriation, but who was then in exile in Siberia. At last Lenin had the hard core of a bolshevik party under his sole direction and he was ready to take advantage of the new unrest.

The socialist revolutionary party had passed through similar trials during these years. Its fortunes were more difficult to follow, however, because as the party of the peasants it was less concentrated and organized than the party of the workers. Moreover, it lacked the able leaders that the social democrats had. The party was also at this time severely shaken and demoralized by the public accusations against Yevno Azef who had been leader of its fighting organization and one of the party's key men.[12] The socialist revolutionaries survived this storm, just as the social democrats survived the storm over the Tiflis robbery and the scandal of Rodion Malinovsky, and they continued to hold the support of many among the peasants.

The imperial manifesto, dissolving the second Duma, announced that elections would be held on 14 September for a new Duma which would meet on 14 November. At the same time, in direct violation of the fundamental laws, a new franchise was proclaimed, reducing even more severely the representation of workers, peasants, and non-Russian peoples. The landowning class was favoured, and in towns a sharp division was made between the wealthy upper class and the rest, which included the professional class, the two unequal parts having the same number of votes. In the non-Russian regions of the Empire, the Russian minorities were favoured. The Poles, for instance, had had thirty-six Deputies in the second Duma, to which they had made a valuable contribution, but their representation was now cut to fourteen. Many categories, such as migratory peasants, were arbitrarily excluded from the franchise. The result was that under the indirect voting system one elector was chosen by every 230 landowners, 1,000 wealthy merchants, 15,000 middle class towns-men, 60,000 peasants, and 125,000 workers.[13]

The new electoral law aroused a public outcry. But the government felt now that it had recovered its authority and waited for the storm to die down. The parties began preparing for the new elections. It was widely realized that, despite the limited franchise, the Duma was still a valuable forum. Its proceedings were not subject to censorship and through the full reports of debates, matters of public concern were ventilated. The Duma still had power to examine in detail the annual budget, and this gave scope for criticism of the government. Finally, it was clear that any national assembly, elected at this time in Russia, even on a franchise so grossly selective, would oppose the government.

The third Duma which met in November 1907 and was to continue for its full term of five years, was more conservative than its predecessors. The Octobrists with 153 seats were the dominant party. The nationalist and reactionary groups to the right of the Octobrists had some 140 seats. The social democrats, led by a fiery little Georgian named Chkheidze, had 20 seats. The Kadets, who had failed in the two preceding Dumas, now had only 54 deputies, owing partly to the operation of the new electoral law. The Trudovik group had 13 deputies. This Duma by co-operating with the government was to achieve significant results.

The leader of the Octobrist party was Alexander Guchkov. The grandson of a serf and son of a Moscow merchant, he had had an adventurous career. He had ridden along the Great Wall of China during the Boxer Rebellion when the infuriated Chinese were killing all foreigners on sight, and had fought for the Boers against England in South Africa. During the Russo-Japanese War he had stayed behind at Mukden to hand the wounded into the care of the advancing Japanese. In the crisis of 1905 he had spoken out for enlightened conservatism. The emperor and empress had invited him to the Winter Palace and he had urged Nicholas to revive the links between the throne and the people by convening an Assembly of the Land on the lines of the *Zemsky Sobor*, first summoned by Ivan the Terrible in the sixteenth century. With his panache, courage, and intelligence, Guchkov was a man who could not help attracting public attention. But he did not seek it and, in fact, was a politician of integrity, anxious to serve his country. He believed in parliamentary government on the English model, and under his leadership the Octobrist party of patriotic reform was far closer to the Kadets than to the parties of the right.

The Duma, as originally envisaged by Nicholas and others, had been intended to function rather through commissions than as a single chamber. The first and second Duma had made little use of these commissions. It was, however, a useful system, for the Duma could examine ministers and a commission, with an able chairman and reporter, could expose incompetence, waste, or wrong policies. Ministers, who failed to satisfy commissions or who showed an arrogant or casual attitude, could find their estimates rejected by the Duma or their policies exposed to public criticism.

Guchkov made full use of these commissions. The Duma commission on imperial defence achieved striking results. The army and the navy belonged to the tsar's sole prerogative under the fundamental laws and were therefore outside the Duma's jurisdiction. Moreover, Nicholas had been deeply antagonized by the furious criticisms of the fighting services made in the second Duma. Guchkov had to act with great care in examining the army and navy estimates. But, like the best officers of both services with whom he was in close contact, he was deeply conscious of the weakness, exposed by the defeats inflicted by the Japanese, and aware of the urgent need to reform and revitalize the fighting services. Kolchak, who with a number of young naval officers, was anxious to set up a regular naval staff and to modernize the Admiralty, obtained the Duma's support through Guchkov and in due course his plans received the tsar's approval. Similar plans for major reforms in the army were also adopted. Nicholas's heart was in his army and he was delighted with the constructive attitude now displayed by the Duma. The commission on education also produced outstanding results. But most important of all was the work of the Duma in revising and promoting Stolypin's agrarian reforms.

The close understanding between Guchkov and Stolypin facilitated the working relations of the government with the Duma. They had made no agreement, but co-operated on a basis of mutual respect. Guchkov realized that Stolypin could only be replaced by some reactionary who would make greater difficulties for the Duma. Witte was trying to regain the tsar's confidence and to win the support of the extreme right, but no one trusted him. The Duma greatly preferred Stolypin who, moreover, had several able ministers in his cabinet. But relations between the government and the Duma were not unclouded.

Stolypin had made many enemies among the bureaucrats and reactionaries, and certain bills which he presented cost him the goodwill of the Duma. Like Guchkov, too, he had incurred the hatred of the empress who believed that he had deliberately 'overshadowed his sovereign'. Right-wing antagonism towards him was running so high that Stolypin even told Guchkov that he felt sure that he would be assassinated by a police agent.[14]

In September 1911 he and Kokovtsov, the finance minister, attended the tsar on a ceremonial visit to Kiev. In the opera house as the final act of the gala performance was about to start, Stolypin was shot at point blank range. The tsar in his box, hearing the commotion, looked down to see Stolypin in the stalls turn slowly and make the sign of the cross in the air towards him, and then sink down on to his seat. The assassin, a certain Bagrov, who apparently worked both for a revolutionary organization and for the police, was saved from lynching by being hustled away under arrest.[15]

The murder of Stolypin aroused indignant protests, especially over the inadequate police precautions. An official enquiry recommended the public trial of those responsible, including the assistant minister of the interior. But Nicholas, to whom Kokovtsov brought the report of the enquiry, was at the time giving thanks that his only son had just been spared from death, and he refused to sanction the punishment of anyone. It was a genuine gesture on his part, but it encouraged rumours that Stolypin had met his death through foul play in which senior officials were implicated.[16]

Kokovtsov succeeded as prime minister, but despite his ability, integrity, and the great respect in which he was held, he did not possess the dominating personality and presence which had marked Stolypin as the leader. At this time Russia desperately needed a leader. A new, sinister, influence had appeared at court, the peasant, Grigori Rasputin, whose rise to power Kokovtsov and the Duma were powerless to prevent.

Grigori, son of Efim, was born in the village of Pokrovskoe in the Tobolsk province, just to the east of the Ural mountains. Like many Russian peasants he had no surname, but from an early age he was apparently known as Rasputin, meaning 'the debauchee' or 'the libertine'. His conduct so shocked the whole province that the Bishop of Tobolsk ordered an enquiry and the civil authorities were about to act, when he vanished into the vast spaces of Russia.

For some years Rasputin roamed through Russia as a penitent, or one of the *stranniki*, the ascetic wanderers who scorned even the barest comforts as they searched for truth and salvation. The *stranniki* were not unusual figures in tsarist Russia and, revered as holy men, they lived by charity. The harsh simplicity and dedication of their lives even lent them a certain authority and freedom, and they spoke to all, even on occasions to tsars, with a sturdy peasant bluntness.

In his wanderings Rasputin visited the Balkans and at least twice made the pilgrimage to Jerusalem. At the end of 1903 he turned up at the religious academy of St Petersburg. He had in his wanderings learnt to read and write and had acquired some theological knowledge. He was credited with the ability to heal and to prophesy, and he possessed undoubted hypnotic powers. Feofan, the inspector of the academy, and Hermogen, the Bishop of Saratov, two able and saintly men, were impressed and gave him their blessings and support.

Rasputin was described at this time as a thickset peasant of medium height with long greasy hair and beard, bushy eyebrows overhanging piercing grey eyes, and having a strange, unpleasant body smell. Not only in appearance but also in character he was in many ways a typical Russian peasant. He was a mixture of good and evil, kindness and cruelty, innocence and cunning, piety and viciousness, but in him these qualities were present in extreme form. He was a drunkard and an insatiable sensualist, but he also had a capacity for religious devotion and mystic feeling. He passed from one extreme to the other until they seemed to blend in the dangerous belief that, since repentence alone could secure salvation, it was necessary to sin in order to repent.[17]

Spiritualism, hypnotism, and the occult were then in high fashion in St Petersburg, and Rasputin was taken up by a Grand Duchess who introduced him to Anna Vyrubova, an impressionable light-headed woman on whom the imperial couple had taken pity. Vyrubova had become the constant companion of the empress and she brought Rasputin to Tsarskoe Selo where the imperial family lived a simple, isolated family life.

Empress Alexandra herself had strong occult leanings. She had, when desperate for a son, consulted a certain 'Dr Phillipe' from Lyons, and other charlatans had attracted her interest. Being obsessively devout and given to superstition, she was a ready prey to religious cranks. But another factor, the birth of her son, Alexei, on 12 August 1904, brought her under the spell of Rasputin. She had borne four daughters and had prayed earnestly that she might produce an heir to the throne of her beloved Nicholas. Soon after the birth of the tsarevich, however, it was found that he suffered from the horrifying disease of haemophilia.[18] The effect of this upon the fanatic, narrow mind of the Empress was devastating. She had on her conscience the fact that she had introduced this dread hereditary disease into the Romanov dynasty. But her first concern was to protect this son, whom she adored, so that he would succeed his father. With all the fervour of her nature, she turned to God for help, finding in Rasputin her intermediary. From this time her son was never absent from her thoughts and she watched over him with loving solicitude. He was a delightful, high-spirited boy, but every fall or cut brought on bleeding that threatened death, and his mother lived in an agony of anxiety.

Rasputin was not wholly a charlatan, and he seems to have possessed powers of healing. On several occasions, by touching the tsarevich or speaking to him by telephone, he brought him out of danger, when the doctors seemed powerless. This was the source of Rasputin's influence. He promised the Empress that the boy's life was safe, while he lived. With her fanaticism she began to revere him as a holy man, almost a Christ, and she refused to believe any reports, no matter how irrefutable, about his behaviour.

Nicholas was far less carried away by Rasputin, but he, too, had witnessed his power to relieve the suffering of the tsarevich, and he was both unwilling and unable to check his wife in her extremes. Also he felt that in Rasputin he had found a man of God, a true *strannik* and *starets*, and at the same time a peasant through whom he had contact with the Russian masses, and he welcomed Rasputin's assurances of their loyalty.

From 1906 Rasputin's influence steadily increased, reaching a peak in 1915 when with the empress he virtually ruled Russia. But his drunken sexual orgies gave rise to constant scandal. He possessed an extraordinary fascination for women and took delight in humiliating ladies of the nobility whom he detested. But women put up with his ill-treatment, amounting at times almost to rape; only one woman turned on him and stabbed him in the abdomen, but, although the wound was severe, he quickly recovered.

At the beginning of 1911 Stolypin ordered Rasputin to leave St Petersburg. The order was obeyed, but it intensified the determination of the empress to secure his dismissal. In 1912 the press began a campaign against Rasputin's monstrous behaviour. Nicholas imposed a ban on reference to him in the press, which was a violation of the law abolishing censorship, and which further antagonized the liberals. But he could not suppress talk among the people, and rumours had begun to besmirch the empress herself and the whole imperial family.

The third Duma came to the end of its five-year term and was dissolved in June 1912. The fourth Duma, which was to continue until 1917, was similar in composition. Kokovtsov had no real confidence in the Octobrists and had sought the election of a majority more to the right of Guchkov and his party. He was not successful and found himself still dependent on the Octobrists to secure the passage of government legislation. Guchkov himself, probably through police manipulation, failed to secure re-election and his presence was greatly missed. His successor as President of the Duma was Mikhail Rodzyanko who, although commanding in his massive personality, lacked the ability and political sense of Guchkov. The Duma became more unruly and ineffective in checking the government which now included several arch-reactionaries like Nicholas Maklakov, the minister of the interior, who was the complete opposite of his liberal brother, Vasily, and they were determined to disrupt the Duma.

Reaction was growing in strength. The tercentenary of the Romanov dynasty, celebrated in 1913, rallied monarchists. Empress Alexandra was now even more hostile towards the Duma and Kokovtsov, Guchkov, and others because of their opposition to Rasputin. She harassed the unfortunate Nicholas with demands that he dismiss the Duma and all who presumed to encroach on his autocratic powers. He was under similar pressure from others at court. The most that he ever brought himself to suggest, however, was that the Duma might be reduced to a consultative body and, when he met with strong opposition from his minister of justice, he did not press this proposal.

Stolypin's ministry, lasting only five years (1906–11) had been a period of rapid political, economic, and industrial development. Agriculture had benefited from his reforms and a succession of good harvests had brought widespread prosperity. Industry was expanding with a new momentum. Indeed, it has been stated that the seven years from 1907 to 1914 were the most prosperous in Russia's history.[19]

Education, neglected through the years by church and state with the result that only thirty-seven per cent of children of school age were attending schools, now received attention. In 1908 Stolypin's government introduced a bill to provide free primary education for all children. Funds were allocated and it was planned that by 1920 all children would have schooling. By 1914 the number of primary schools had increased by fifty per cent over the figure of six years earlier. In secondary schools and higher education the rate of expansion was slower, but still impressive. Russia was at last tackling her grave problems of illiteracy.

The growth of political consciousness was, however, the most significant factor of the period. Stolypin himself had been keenly aware of this development and anxious that nothing, and especially war, should halt it. In July 1911 he had written to Izvolsky, the Russian ambassador in Paris, that 'Every year of peace fortifies Russia not only from the military and naval point of view, but also from the economic and financial. Besides, and this is the most important, Russia is growing from year to year: self-knowledge and public opinion are developing in our land. One must not scoff at our parliamentary institutions. However imperfect, their influence has brought about a radical change in Russia . . .'[20]

During the period of the first three Dumas unrest in industry and on the land had sharply declined. In 1910 industrial strikes involved only 46,000 workers, compared with two-and-three-quarter million in 1905 and one million in 1906. The revolutionary movement had faded until only small pockets of the staunchest revolutionaries remained. In the period of the fourth Duma, unrest revived. The new strikes were mainly economic in character, but after April 1912 they became increasingly political. In that month strikers on the Lena goldfields, which were British-owned, were fired on by troops and over one hundred were killed or wounded. This caused a series of sympathy strikes in other parts of the country and was the beginning of a rapid growth of political strikes.

The social democrats and the socialist revolutionaries were a negligible influence in the events of the years 1906–14. Both were in eclipse for most of the period, and consumed their energies and frustrations in internecine quarrels. Only in the years 1912–14 did they revive and then because they were able to take advantage of the spontaneous general unrest, provoked in part by the restoration of the authority of the tsar and his government.

In 1912 it seemed that the growing discontent might presage a repetition of the 1905 revolution. Much had happened, however, in the intervening years to prevent such a repetition. The parties in opposition were now sharply divided and no longer had the same basic unity of purpose. But the important factor was that Russia was on the move and gaining momentum. In industry, agriculture, education, and trade the developments were striking. Politically, too, as Stolypin appreciated, the Duma and the public attitude towards it represented a major advance. The momentum of the advance frightened the reactionary and conservative elements. But, like Gogol's troika, flying through the snow, the nation was straining to advance into the twentieth century and already was overtaking the West in every field. Only war could have brought this advance to a halt.

CHAPTER FIVE

War

On 2 August 1914, the day after the German declaration of war, Nicholas II stood on the balcony of the Winter Palace before the people, crowding in their thousands into the vast space below. They had gathered from all parts of St Petersburg to demonstrate their loyalty to the throne. They now listened with patriotic fervour as their emperor publicly swore the oath, word for word, which Alexander I had sworn at the time of Napoleon's invasion, that he would not make peace while an enemy soldier remained on Russian soil. In a mood of exaltation the great crowd then knelt on the cobble-stones and sang 'God save the tsar'.

Suddenly and completely Germany's declaration of war had united the Russian people. Workers, who had massed in the streets of St Petersburg with placards and shouts of 'Down with the tsar!', now bore loyal slogans. Not for over a century had the nation rallied in this spirit of dedication and sacrifice. The war against Japan had been resented as an irresponsible adventure and one which, because it involved them in primitive, despotic Asia, had seemed to encourage all that was backward in Russia. By contrast the war against the Central Powers had full popular support, because Germany was the aggressor, because both Germany and Austro-Hungary represented the reactionary, monarchal, principle, and because this war had brought Russia into alliance with republican France and constitutional England. Many Russians even welcomed the German challenge because it had inspired the reunion with western Europe with which, they felt, Russia's true destiny lay.

Alliance with France had become the cornerstone of Russian foreign policy. The minister of war, Sukhomlinov, and certain other ministers and people at court were in favour of reviving Russia's traditional friendship with Germany. But this policy had made no headway, especially as Germany had been supporting Austro-Hungary in the Balkans and had, moreover, so developed her own influence in the Balkans since 1903 as to cause Russia real anxiety. In fact, no proposal for closer relations with Germany could have gained acceptance at this time when general hostility towards the Germans had, as though suppressed for too long, gripped the nation. Even the Germanic name of the capital, St Petersburg, had had to be changed in response to public demand to the Slav name, Petrograd.

At the outbreak of the war the conviction among the Russians, as among all the participants, was that the struggle would be short and

70

victorious. For Russia, after defeats in the Crimea and against Japan, victory was essential to restore national pride and prestige. It was important, too, for national morale to defeat the Germans who for more than two centuries had usually held key positions in government offices, industry, and even on private estates, and had by their energy, ability, and discipline made the Russians feel incompetent and inferior. Thus, while Austro-Hungary was responsible for instigating the war, Russians were never in doubt that Germany was the real enemy.

In the midst of the patriotic fervour a few voices were raised in warning. Kokovtsov, as finance minister, like his predecessors in this office, had consistently warned the tsar that Russia, even supported by foreign loans, could not afford a major war. Stolypin, before his assassination, had stressed that war would spell disaster for the nation. In July 1911 when trouble threatened in the Balkans, he had written, 'We need peace: a war during the coming year and especially in the name of a cause the people would not understand would be fatal for Russia and the dynasty.'[1]

Finally, Rasputin in 1914, when in Pokrovskoe recovering from a knife wound inflicted by a woman whom he had degraded, sent a cable: 'Let Papa not plan war, for with war will come the end of Russia and of yourselves.' This prophecy angered Nicholas who cast it aside as he cast aside the other warnings.[2]

On 8 August 1914 the Duma met in a special one-day session to vote the huge war budget. It was a stirring occasion. Nicholas transported by the upsurge of popular loyalty, the 'sacred union', as he called it, of the tsar with his people had earlier greeted Rodzyanko, the president of the Duma, with the words, 'I am your friend until death. I will do anything for the Duma. Tell me what you want.'[3] In the Duma session the spokesmen of the Lithuanians, Jews, Volga and Baltic Germans, and of the Moslems all pledged support in defence of the nation. The Russian deputies also spoke strongly in support of the war effort, but Milyukov, the Kadet leader, and Kerensky, leader of the Trudovik party, also placed on record their demands to be made after the war for freedom and democracy.

The outbreak of war had plunged the Socialist International into confusion. At its congress in Stuttgart in 1907 the resolution had been adopted to work to prevent war, but in the event of war socialists were duty-bound to take advantage of the resulting political and economic chaos to hasten the destruction of capitalist class rule. When the war came, however, all socialist parties except in Russia and Serbia readily voted in support of the war budgets. The leaders of the Socialist International, justifying the actions of these socialists, argued that socialist policies must be postponed while one's country was threatened. The second Socialist International never recovered from the divisions opened within it by the war.

In Russia the response of the thirteen social democrat deputies to the

war was confused. The leader of the bolshevik deputies, Rodion Malinovsky, whom Lenin trusted implicitly and had made his spokesman in
the Duma, had resigned his seat in the previous May to avoid being
exposed as a police agent. He had, in fact, reported regularly to the secret
police on the activities of Lenin and his group so that the police knew in
detail their ideas and plans and the persons involved.[4] With Malinovsky
out of the way and freed from the close control of Lenin who was then in
Austrian Galicia, the bolshevik deputies instinctively joined with the
menshevik deputies. They made a combined declaration, deploring the
horrors of war and proclaiming the need to defend 'the cultural treasures
of the people from all attacks ...' In the fervent mood of the Duma and
the eloquent patriotism of the speeches, the declaration was ludicrous.
Kerensky, speaking for the Trudoviks, was more in harmony with the
general mood when he acclaimed the need 'to defend the native land and
culture, created in the sweat of generations'.[5] When the time came to
vote, the social democrats and Kerensky and the Trudoviks were unwilling to vote for the budget or to incur unpopularity by voting publicly
against it, and they simply walked from the chamber without voting at
all.

In the impotence of exile in Switzerland Lenin fumed against the joint
declaration that his followers had supported. It contained sentiments and
statements which he abhorred, and he made haste to send them his *Theses
on the War* with the demand that they should be obeyed. The essence of
the war theses was a call for the defeat of Russia 'as the lesser evil' and
for 'the conversion of the imperialist war into a civil war'.[6]

The *Theses* also denounced the Socialist International for its failure to
unite socialists against the war. At Zimmerwald in the following year,
socialists gathered from several countries to concert action. Lenin and
Zinoviev and the mensheviks, Martov and Axelrod, led the 'Zimmerwald
Left', as it came to be called, which demanded civil war as the only way
to end the imperialist war. But the majority agreed a manifesto calling on
the working class to struggle for peace. The conference then formed the
Zimmerwald Union, as an informal organization to provide co-ordination
among left-wing, anti-war groups.

In Russia Kamenev, Lenin's representative on the central committee
of the party, and the five bolshevik deputies were far from accepting their
leader's *Theses*. They considered that Lenin, living in exile, was wholly
out of touch with the country and simply did not understand that such a
policy would bring down upon the party the hostility of workers and
peasants.

On the night of 14 November Kamenev, the bolshevik deputies, and
five representatives of local bolshevik organizations met to discuss Lenin's
demands. The police knew about this meeting well in advance and in a
raid not only arrested all taking part, but also took copies of the *Theses*
and found in the possession of Muranov, one of the deputies, a list of the

names and addresses of all local bolshevik leaders. Since the meeting had taken place in a designated martial zone, the police ignored the parliamentary immunity of the deputies and arranged a secret trial. Kerensky, the Trudovik leader and noted advocate, defended them and proposed to the court that Lenin himself should really be tried in his absence and his defeatist views made widely known. At the trial, moreover, the deputies strongly repudiated Lenin's *Theses*. They were nevertheless found guilty of disseminating defeatist propaganda and exiled to Siberia.[7]

In the high drama of these days the dissent of this tiny minority went unnoticed. The nation was feverishly preparing for war and mobilizing the largest army in history. Full mobilization needed three months, but despite the vast distances, the inadequate roads and railways, and the slow river transport, 4,215,000 men had answered the call-up by 30 September.[8] The fact that ninety-six per cent of the men called up reported within time was a demonstration of the earnest mood of the whole nation.

The Russian armies which had massed by the end of 1914 were well led, disciplined, and their morale was high. The British liaison officer, General Sir A. Knox, himself an able professional soldier who constantly visited the various Russian fronts in this period, paid repeated tributes to the fighting spirit and chivalry of officers and men.[9] But it was an army belonging to the previous century. Its equipment and transport were pitifully inadequate by comparison with the German war machine.

Nicholas threw himself whole-heartedly into this war against Russia's ancient enemy, and his family ties with Germany in no way diminished his determination to fight to the end. He was, moreover, as Sir Bernard Pares has described him, 'the simple, impressionable tsar ... conspicuous in his chivalry to his country's allies'.[10] When within five days of the German ultimatum the French government began demanding through their ambassador, Paléologue, that the Russian armies should invade Germany, thus relieving the drive on Paris, Nicholas responded gallantly. The French continued throughout the war to demand Russian action, and he never failed to go to their aid.

In August 1914, before his forces were nearly mobilized and ready, Nicholas ordered three armies into East Prussia. It was a major error. If he had remained on the defensive, ready to withdraw into the depths of Russia, compelling his enemies to lengthen their lines of communication, he would surely have been victorious. Peter the Great had proved this strategy against Charles XII of Sweden in the eighteenth century and Kutuzov against Napoleon's army in the nineteenth century. Moreover, the Russian soldier, a magnificent fighter when properly led, was at his best when fighting on his own soil.

Early in August the 1st Russian Army, commanded by General Paul Rennenkampf, advanced into East Prussia to positions north of the Masurian Lakes. The 2nd Army under General Alexander Samsonov, moved south of the lakes. The 10th Army was to advance, when ready, to link them. The 1st and 2nd Armies each separately outnumbered the German defending forces, but in all else they were at a severe disadvantage.

On the approach of the 1st and 2nd Russian Armies, the German commander, Prittwitz, took fright and ordered a complete withdrawal from East Prussia. But Moltke at the German headquarters at once removed him from this command, replacing him with General von Hindenburg, then on the retired list, and giving him General Ludendorf as his chief of staff. At the same time two army corps were detached from the Western Front and hurriedly sent to the East.

Hindenburg and Ludendorf recognized that, despite their superiority in transport, artillery, and equipment their position in East Prussia was precarious. They expected Rennenkampf to advance in co-operation with Samsonov and then, as Ludendorf wrote, 'He need only have closed with us and we should have been beaten.'[11] For a full week the battle was in the balance. Fighting was fierce. The Russians were clearly superior in hand-to-hand engagements, but suffering terrible casualties from German artillery and machine-gun fire. Meanwhile the Russian 1st and 2nd Armies had been drawing not closer together but farther apart, and the 10th Army which was to fill this gap was still forming and far behind.

At this point the German commanders embarked on a bold scheme. They withdrew the whole of their forces, except two cavalry brigades and the Koenigsberg garrison facing Rennenkampf, and transported them swiftly by rail over the distance of 130 miles to attack Samsonov. In this sudden massed assault the Russian 2nd Army was destroyed.[12] The German army was then moved back with the same speed and efficiency to attack Rennenkampf. Again, so slow were Russian communications and intelligence services, the Germans were able to mount a surprise attack. But Rennenkampf, who had something of the obstinate endurance of Kutuzov, withdrew his army intact and once on Russian soil his lines held firm.

The battle of Tannenberg, as it was called by the Germans,[13] was hardly over when the Austro-Hungarian armies, a million men strong, invaded Russian Poland. Grand Duke Nicholas as the Russian commander-in-chief had appealed to the Poles as Slavs to fight alongside the Russians against the Central Powers, and had promised them autonomy at the end of the war. Nicholas II had endorsed this promise, despite the opposition of the empress and of reactionaries in the government and at court. The Poles gave their full support, feeling that the alliance with France and England was a guarantee that the tsar would honour his promise. They were, moreover, strongly anti-German and they knew that the Central Powers, if victorious, would certainly redivide their country.

The four Russian armies opposed to the Austro-Hungarians won a decisive victory. They took Lemberg and occupied much of Galicia. The Austrians lost more than a quarter of a million men in casualties and over

100,000 prisoners as well as massive quantities of materials. Hindenburg had to rush reinforcements and equipment to them to revive their morale and hold them from suing for a separate peace.

Meanwhile the French through their ambassador were pressing with 'mischievous importunity'[14] for the Russians to launch a new invasion of Germany. Nicholas, although his northern armies were still recovering from their defeat at Tannenberg, ordered a new advance. Meanwhile Hindenburg had moved on Warsaw, seeking to relieve the Austro-Hungarians in Galicia. The Russians held firm and the Germans were forced to retreat. Regrouping, they then attacked Lodz. Again their attack failed and the year closed with the Russians driven from East Prussia but in possession of most of Galicia.

Russia's casualties in these first months of the war were, however, appalling. In East Prussia alone her losses were estimated at 300,000 men as well as 650 guns and a great quantity of equipment. The quartermaster-general, Danilov, wrote that 'The effectives of the army were melting, the lack of officers was taking on alarming proportions.'[15] He estimated that the wastage of men was 300,000 a month. Brusilov, commanding the 8th Army, complained with justification that the new drafts were 'disgustingly untrained ... such men could not be called soldiers'.[16] But most serious was the terrible casualty rate among officers. The renowned Preobrazhensky regiment of guards in one battle lost forty-eight of its seventy officers. The 18th Division had only forty officers left from its complement of 370. General Sir A. Knox, who reported critically on the failures in co-ordination, planning, and supplies, repeatedly paid tribute to the magnificent courage and even gaiety of the troops in heart-rending conditions. He acknowledged, too, the courage and chivalry of the officers who ordered their men to take cover, but themselves, scorning to crawl forward under fire, fought standing, and against German machine-guns they could not survive. Knox noted sadly that 'these people play at war'.[17] The officers who sacrificed their lives in the first year of the war were the regulars who knew their men, and their loss was to be felt in February 1917 when raw recruits fired on their officers and discipline broke down in the army, opening the floodgates to revolution.

The Russians also faced a desperate shortage of munitions and equipment. Troops in training had to share one rifle between three men. Many were moved up to the front without rifles and had to wait for a comrade to fall to seize his equipment. All batteries were reduced from eight guns to six and were severely restricted in the number of rounds they could fire in a day. In part this was due to the inefficiency of the War Office under Sukhomlinov, who was later impeached. The fact that the army had been as well equipped as it was at the outbreak of war was the result of the reforms instigated or pressed through by the Duma. But the shortages of munitions were a result primarily of Russia's industrial backwardness which could not be overcome in a decade.

In spite of the fearful casualties and the shortage of supplies, morale among the Russian troops remained remarkably firm. In Petrograd and Moscow, however, expectations of victory had been so high and feeling against Germany so strong that the defeat in East Prussia had in Russian minds completely overshadowed the great victory against the Austro-Hungarian armies. Moreover, the Russian High Command now realized that in training, equipment, and transport the Germany army was vastly superior and that the Russians must pay for their deficiencies by sacrifices of men. Defeatism was, however, virtually non-existent at the fronts and in the rear, except for Lenin and the small group of his followers. But a few opponents of the war remained, two of whom were influential. Count Witte had consistently opposed Russia's participation in the war. In March 1915, however, he suddenly died.[18]

Witte's ally was Rasputin. He was apparently a sincere pacifist who believed in peace and co-operation between all nations and religions, and had shown political courage in championing the Jews. He also appreciated that the war might result in the political and economic collapse of Russia. His influence with the Empress was now stronger but since the Duma debates on his scandalous conduct his meetings with the imperial family, arranged discreetly at the house of Anna Vyrubova, had become less frequent. But even the public outcry against him over his drunken, indecent behaviour during a visit to Moscow in April 1915 did not result in his dismissal.

The tsar himself, his government, and his armies were still absolutely confident that Germany would be defeated. Russia, England, and France were each committed not to make a separate peace, but with the failure of Russia's invasion of East Prussia the need for mutual assistance and especially for aid to Russia had become urgent. Access to Russia in the south had been blocked by the Turks and the Gallipoli campaign was mounted with the purpose of ejecting the Turks from the Dardanelles and establishing supply lines with Russia by this route. The campaign against the Turks would also, Russians hoped, win for them permanent control of the straits and possession of Constantinople where the Slavophile dream of restoring the Orthodox Cross to the dome of St Sophia could be realized.

The other route to Russia was northwards by sea to Archangel, which the English sea captain, Richard Chancellor, had discovered in the reign of Ivan the Terrible when seeking the north-east passage to Cathay. The White Sea was, however, icebound in winter and the subsidiary port of Murmansk on the Kola Inlet was therefore developed. A cable was laid. connecting the port with Scotland, but the railway from Murmansk to Moscow was only completed towards the end of the war.

In the first months of 1915 the Russians continued their advance, crossing the Carpathian Mountains at certain points and capturing the fortress of Przemysl with its garrison of 120,000 men. Hopes ran high at this stage of the war, for Italy was about to take up arms on the side of the Allies and to attack Austro-Hungary in the south. But 1915 was to be a year of retreat. In May under General von Mackensen and with tremendous superiority in artillery the Germans began to move forward. The Russians fought with amazing courage but at a terrible price. The 3rd and 8th Armies, commanded by Brusilov, suffered severely. By the end of the first ten months of the war Russia had lost 3,800,000 men. On no other front had human life been sacrificed on such a vast, tragic scale. Ludendorf wrote of the fighting near Warsaw, 'I shall never forget it . . . I look back with horror,'[19] and later referred to the 'supreme contempt for death' shown by the Russian troops.[20]

By the end of August the Russians had been driven from Poland and part of Lithuania. The new German lines ran north and south centred on the Pinsk Marches, and represented a major advance to the East. The Turks, too, had won initial successes. In November 1914 they had attacked in Transcaucasia, but the Russians, after calling on their Allies for a diversionary attack on Constantinople, found that they could repel the Turks alone. In the Black Sea, however, Turkish ships, supported by two German cruisers, kept the Russian Black Sea Fleet at bay. In March 1915, the Allies launched their attack on the Dardanelles, but it failed and in the autumn of 1915 England and France withdrew their forces. Further, the Serbian army suffered defeat in September 1915, so that the straits and most of the Balkans remained under the control of the Central Powers.

Despite these reverses, the Russian troops remained in good heart. In the rear, however, and especially in Petrograd, indignation over munition scandals and government bungling was growing. Early in 1915 public opinion was deeply shocked by the treachery of Colonel Sergei Myasoedov. A friend of the war minister, Sukhomlinov, he had held high military office while serving as a German spy and sending secret information to the enemy by aeroplane. He was tried and hanged as a traitor on 10 March.

Nicholas II fretted over the sacrifices and hardships of his soldiers, and shared in the public resentment of the failures in the organization of equipment and supplies. In June on the instigation of Rodzyanko, president of the Duma, he dismissed Sukhomlinov from the war ministry, together with three other ministers who were not whole-hearted in their war effort. Soon afterwards, the Duma by 345 votes to 30 decided to impeach Sukhomlinov for criminal negligence, and the tsar gave his approval. He appointed General Alexei Polivanov, an honest, well-informed, and extremely able administrator as war minister, and men equally respected by the public to the other vacant ministries. He also adopted Rodzyanko's proposals for a special defence council to co-ordinate and speed up supplies of every kind to the army. This council, comprising members of the government, the Duma, of industry and public organizations, proved effective, and was followed by other similar councils with responsibility for food, transport, fuel, and refugees.

A general demand began for the recall of the Duma, and it was significant that in these days of crisis the people should already look to the Duma to voice their discontent and to arraign the government. Nicholas called the new session to open on 1 August 1915.

The Duma despite its right-wing majority was strongly critical of the government, and especially of Goremykin, the inept old man, whom Nicholas had appointed prime minister in January 1914. The parties were drawing closer together and many deputies who had served at the front with the Red Cross and had witnessed the carnage gave a new urgency to the debates. At the first meeting the nationalist, Count Vladimir Bobrinskoy, submitted a demand which had the support of most parties for a 'Ministry of Confidence' headed by a prime minister who had the confidence of the nation. At this time Milyukov and leaders of certain other parties in the Duma and the council of state formed a new political coalition under the name of the Progressive Block. Its programme, in the main drafted by Milyukov, was broad in its demands, but not immoderate. It was less radical than the Kadets and other parties wanted. But it had considerable support from the right-wing. It demonstrated, in fact, that under the pressure of the war and the failure of the government and the bureaucracy, the political parties had learnt to compromise. The majority of the ministers in the cabinet were anxious to reach some agreement with the coalition. This, too, was an important advance, holding promise of a constitutional government. But Goremykin opposed negotiations. The empress was furiously antagonistic to the block and its programme. Nicholas himself realized that he was committed to the constitutional reform, initiated by the October Manifesto of 1905. He was not now opposed to the programme of the progressive block, but he insisted that it could only be discussed after the war had been won.

The reactionaries, led by Goremykin in the government, and by the Empress at court, had their way and on 16 September the Duma was adjourned until November. The deputies dispersed quietly, but they bitterly resented their impotence and the tragedy of the nation which at this time continued to drift leaderless. In their sense of hopelessness they reflected the new and growing mood of defeatism among the people, which contrasted sharply with the fervent spirit of only a year ago.

At this time another event had distressed the government, most of whom resigned, and had destroyed the Duma's faith in ultimate victory. This was Nicholas's decision to assume the supreme command of the army. Grand Duke Nicholas had been the commander-in-chief since the beginning of the war. He had impressed everyone with his ability and his courage, and had the confidence not only of the Russian nation but also of the Allies, and he was respected by the enemy. Ludendorf paid him the tribute that he 'was a really great soldier and strategist'.[21] It was unthinkable that he should be displaced at this critical stage of the war by Nicholas himself. But there were other serious dangers in this change. It would remove the tsar from the capital, leaving the empress and Rasputin to rule in his name; it would make the tsar directly responsible for military reverses; it would, as eight ministers of the cabinet stated in a letter addressed to him, 'threaten with serious consequences Russia, your dynasty and your person'.[22] Even Goremykin and other reactionaries expressed their strong opposition to this change. On 2 September the whole cabinet met at Tsarskoe Selo and begged him to reverse his decision but Nicholas, clutching in his hands a small ikon given to him by the empress, stood firm.

Since the beginning of the war Nicholas had wanted desperately to take over the high command. He sincerely wished to be with his army, sharing in its fortunes and misfortunes, and demonstrating that he was personally committed to the war. He had wanted to assume command of his forces in the Japanese War in 1904 for the same reasons, but had been dissuaded. But now in the face of strong pressure he stubbornly refused to yield, because the empress and Rasputin were behind him.

Kokovtsov had, when prime minister, once remarked that Nicholas would have been an excellent constitutional monarch, if he had not been married to Alexandra. He believed fervently in the autocratic ideal, but had shown in his October Manifesto and in other acts that he could compromise. But his wife conceived it to be her duty to save the autocracy for him and their son. She saw clearly his goodness of character and his weakness. She devoted herself to the task of strengthening him with her firmness and courage. 'Be firm, remember that you are Emperor,' she wrote repeatedly to him.[23] Her influence became dominant, cancelling out the advice of his ministers. She was dauntless and although she acted from the most wholesome motives of love for her husband, her family, and her adopted country, no woman could have exercised a more dire influence. But her struggle although utterly misguided was so courageous and whole-hearted that it attained a certain grandeur.

During the first year of the war the empress had not interfered in politics. She suffered from poor health and like Florence Nightingale, whom she resembled in some respects, she was for a time confined to a wheelchair. She nevertheless tended the wounded in hospitals, undertaking the most menial and harrowing duties with the cheerfulness of one who finds fulfilment in humble service. But she worried about the position of Nicholas, feeling more and more that he was being pushed aside. She had become bitterly hostile to Grand Duke Nicholas, because, so she believed, he deliberately overshadowed his sovereign. The Grand Duke was, in fact, a loyal subject who accorded every respect and obedience to his tsar. But the empress hated him also because he had rejected her man of God. Evidently Rasputin had proposed visiting the Headquarters to present a new ikon to the commander-in-chief who was a deeply religious

D

man. The Grand Duke's response to this proposal was brusque; he telegraphed to Rasputin, 'Come and I'll hang (you)'.[24] The empress began to blame the grand duke for the bloodshed on all fronts and she readily believed any rumour against him. She became more convinced that the tsar himself must assume the supreme command and lead the nation to victory.

From the time when Nicholas departed for Mogilev, the government in the rear passed into the hands of the empress, and Rasputin wielded great power. All who were unacceptable to him or to the empress were dismissed. Even Goremykin fell and in his place Rasputin's accomplice, Boris Sturmer, a crude reactionary, who was utterly incompetent, was appointed. The people watched powerless as the government became more debased. Rumours spread that the empress and Rasputin were spies in the service of the kaiser, that she was the mistress of Rasputin, and that the tsar himself had lost all faith in the war effort. All of these rumours were completely false, but they were believed. They showed, too, how the throne as the great symbol of national unity was being degraded and losing its power.

War preparations nevertheless went ahead with growing momentum. Voluntary organizations worked to remedy deficiencies. The civilian Red Cross under the chairmanship of Prince Georgi N. Lvov, had prepared a million beds within a few weeks of the outbreak of the war, and it had frantically extended its activities to provide food and transport for the troops. As the government departments proved incapable of meeting military needs, a network of war industry committees was developed to speed up supplies to the front. English and French technical advisers were also now helping with production. New equipment was arriving in quantity from England, France, Japan, and the U.S.A., but the two ports of Archangel and Vladivostok and the railways could not handle the increased volume of freight and much of it did not get through to the front. By early 1916, however, the critical shortages of munitions had largely been relieved. The call-up of further reserves had reinforced the army. In the last six months of 1915 some 2,680,000 men and in the first half of 1916 a further 1,475,000 men had been mobilized.[25] They received hasty training and were posted without delay to operational units.

The Allies at a conference in Chantilly in December 1915 had agreed to launch a combined offensive in the summer of 1916. But the Germans were also planning a summer offensive on Verdun and the Austro-Hungarians were preparing to attack Italy in Trentino. Launched in May 1916, the Austrian attack was so successful that the King of Italy appealed to the tsar to divert the Austrians by invading from the East. Yet again the Russians went to the aid of their allies. Early in June, General Alexei Brusilov attacked along a 300-mile line from Lutsk to the Carpathians. The Russian offensive was so successful that the plans for later in the month were cancelled and more troops were thrown into

Brusilov's advance. But again the Germans hurriedly reinforced the Austrians, transferring fifteen divisions from the Western Front. Gradually the Russian advance slowed down and although he had taken some 450,000 prisoners in the course of the campaign which lasted until September, Brusilov was unable to gain any more territory.

One effect of the early success of Brusilov's offensive was to make Rumania decide to join the side of the Allies. Since the start of hostilities Rumania had wavered between war and peace. The Russians had considered her more useful as a neutral, foreseeing that she would be a liability as a belligerent. But France, exerting every pressure insisted in the summer of 1916 that Rumania should take up arms to ease the pressure on the Allies along the Somme.

At once it became evident that French pressure had yet again added to Russian burdens. In August the Rumanians invaded Transylvania, where the Germans defeated them, gaining direct access to their Bulgarian and Turkish allies from whom Rumania had separated her. Soon more than a quarter of the whole Russian army had to be devoted to the defence of Rumania.

In Brusilov's campaign of the summer of 1916 the Russian losses were more than 1,200,000 men killed.[26] Conditions at the front were nightmarish. Supplies had become increasingly unreliable and food was at times reduced to one or two days' reserve. Transport and Red Cross services were disrupted and the wounded had small chance of survival. But morale remained high. Hindenburg, planning for the coming year, stated that, whereas the Austrian army was at breaking point, the Russian armies showed no signs of disintegrating. 'We had to anticipate,' he wrote, 'that in the winter of 1916–17, as in previous years, Russia would succeed in making good her losses and renewing the offensive powers of her armies.'[27]

Until the abdication of the tsar, the fighting spirit of the Russians at the front remained high. A meeting of Allied chiefs of staff at Chantilly in November 1916 had agreed a co-ordinated offensive on both the Eastern and Western Fronts early in the spring of 1917. Among the Russian troops there was a widespread confidence that this offensive would bring final victory.[28] In February 1917 an Allied mission had come to Petrograd to discuss preparations for this offensive. Its members also felt the contagious confidence that victory was at hand. But within two weeks of their departure the tsarist regime had collapsed and in the chaos the forces of revolution gathered.

The rot had started in the rear. The economy was under severe strain. The government had raised loans to cover the cost of the war and was now printing new money which quickly declined in value. As the national income declined, the proportion devoted to the war increased. The cost of living had by the end of 1916 risen by nearly three hundred per cent since 1914, but wages had risen less than one hundred per cent in the same period. Food shortages became more acute, aggravated by the inadequate transport system and the unwillingness of the peasants to sell grain to the government at fixed low prices.

None of these factors was, however, a major cause of the collapse of the regime; the Russians had survived far worse troubles in their history. The real cause was the general feeling of desperation and impotence, as they realized that the nation was foundering through lack of leadership. This mood was fully reflected in the angry speeches in the Duma which had begun a new session on 14 November. Milyukov, representing the progressive block, had attacked the government violently. He laid bare one by one its failures, ending each assault with the question, 'Is this stupidity or treason?' Other deputies had spoken with the same bitter feeling. Vasily Maklakov, the right-wing liberal, in a powerful speech asked where was 'the government of Great Russia in the Great War?'[29] The speeches, Milyukov's speech in particular, brought hearty applause from every part of the House, and it was echoed by the people outside. Stupidity amounting to treason had marked the acts of the government, and the tsar was a dim, feeble figure, far away in Mogilev, who allowed his autocratic power to fall into the hands of the empress and the sinister, debauched charlatan, Rasputin.

The denunciations of the Duma forced Sturmer to resign. But his place as prime minister was taken by Alexander Trepov, who was not equal to the task. He tried desperately to remove Alexander Protopopov, the most hated and despised minister in the government, who was known to be a creature of Rasputin. But Protopopov remained at the ministry of the interior, and Trepov was powerless.

On 2 December, in the Duma, Vladimir Purishkevich, an extreme conservative, brought the proceedings to a climax with an impassioned attack on Rasputin as a Judas and destroyer of the dynasty. This like the earlier speeches in this angry session was banned by the government, but was printed defiantly and thousands of copies were circulated. Hostility between the Duma and the government had come to a crisis and on 30 December the Duma was prorogued.

Two days later, on 1 January 1917, the body of Rasputin was found in the ice of the Malaya Neva River in Petrograd.[30] Many people had thought of killing Rasputin, hoping to rid the country of his influence and to dispose of a German spy.[31] The man who killed him was Prince Felix Yusupov, scion of an ancient Russian family, a member of the élite Corps of Pages, who had studied at Oxford before the war and had married the tsar's niece. Yusupov believed that within two weeks of Rasputin's death the empress would become mentally unhinged and that Nicholas would then be a constitutional monarch with power effectively in the hands of the Duma.

Yusupov had invited Rasputin to visit him and the cellar of his mansion had been luxuriously prepared for the occasion. The food included chocolate and almond cakes, of which some contained lethal doses of cyanide and certain glasses of wine were also poisoned. Yusupov himself was deeply afraid of Rasputin's supernatural powers and near to collapse during this evening. His fears increased when Rasputin ate two of the poisoned cakes and drank freely of the wine without showing any ill-effects. Rasputin even asked the prince to play his guitar and then suggested that they should visit the gipsies, 'With God in thought but with mankind in the flesh', one of his favourite sayings.

While Yusupov entertained Rasputin in the cellar, his accomplices waited anxiously upstairs. Finally, making an excuse, Yusupov went upstairs, told of the victim's apparent immunity from poison, and returned to the cellar holding a revolver behind his back. He asked Rasputin to say a prayer before a crystal crucifix and, as he prayed, Yusupov shot him near the heart. Rasputin fell backwards on to a bearskin rug. The conspirators rushed down to the cellar, examined the body and declared him dead.

All then went upstairs to prepare for the next move. Some minutes later Yusupov went down to the cellar again and was transfixed with horror when Rasputin, his eyes and face twitching, rose to his feet and grasped him. Tearing free, Yusupov dashed upstairs. Rasputin like an enraged animal clambered after him and bursting through an outside door stumbled into the courtyard. Purishkevich followed, firing his revolver and Rasputin fell into the snow. By this time Yusupov was vomiting violently, but he threw himself on to the body and in a state of hysteria battered the head with a piece of steel. But Rasputin was still not dead. They threw his body into a hole in the ice of the river, and he died by drowning.[32]

The death of Rasputin brought none of the dramatic changes expected by the conspirators. The empress did not collapse. The death of her holy man was for her a terrible tragedy, since she believed that he was the protector of the tsar and her children and the saviour of the ailing tsarevich. But she drew strength from her faith and she had great courage. Now completely estranged from the rest of the imperial family, she retired with Nicholas and the family into a little world of their own. Vyrubova wrote simply that, 'Never had the Emperor and Empress . . . seemed so lonely or so helpless.'[33] With almost saintly stoicism they awaited the fate that advanced upon them.

Meanwhile unrest was increasing. Strikes were more numerous. Food riots broke out, aggravated by the knowledge that the cities had adequate stocks, but that the authorities had failed to organize proper distribution. Revolution was on everyone's mind, but it was not clear whether army generals, high officials, groups close to the government or the Duma, or whether workers and peasants would overthrow the regime and seize power.

At the end of December, Trepov had resigned, but despite all the warning signs Nicholas appointed as prime minister Prince Nicholas Golitsyn, an old man, incapable of dealing with the explosive situation, who, moreover, owed his appointment to the empress. Her influence was again evident when Golitsyn postponed the next meeting of the Duma from 25 January to 27 February. This change aroused further resentment. The Duma, although the franchise for the elections was grossly restrictive, had become really representative in its bitter criticisms of the government. The new sitting of the Duma was keenly awaited throughout Petrograd.

Antagonism to the throne and the government mounted ominously. The council of state, always composed of arch-conservatives, now sided with the Duma in demanding the appointment of ministers, commanding the confidence of the people. All senior members of the imperial family in the course of these weeks warned Nicholas and his wife of the disaster towards which they were leading the country. The empress rejected their warnings and Nicholas himself seemed not to hear them. Hatred of the empress reached such a pitch that several people plotted to remove or to kill her. Grand Duchess Maria Pavlovna, widow of one of the tsar's uncles, proposed to Rodzyanko, president of the Duma, that she must be 'annihilated', and she clearly had it in mind that he would co-operate with her in the deed.[34]

The British ambassador, Sir George Buchanan, was so distressed by the rapid approach of revolution that, putting aside protocol, he earnestly warned Nicholas in a long audience on 12 January.[35] But the most dramatic and forthright warning came from Mikhail Rodzyanko a few days later. An enormous man of some twenty stone, he towered over Nicholas, who had in the past resented his loyal, respectful but outspoken reports. But on this occasion he listened as Rodzyanko spoke of the 'Indignation against and hatred of the Empress . . . growing throughout the country', and named the able and honest ministers, dismissed without reason and replaced by the nominees of the empress and Rasputin who were often despicable creatures like Protopopov.

' "Your Majesty [he continued], do not compel the people to choose between you and the good of the country. So far the ideas of Tsar and Motherland have been indissoluble, but lately they have begun to be separated."

'The Emperor pressed his head between his hands, then said: "Is it possible that for twenty-two years I have tried to act for the best, and that for twenty-two years it was all a mistake?"

'It was a hard moment. With a great effort at self-control I replied: "Yes, Your Majesty, for twenty-two years you have followed a wrong course." '[36]

Nicholas had reached a final stage of impotence and fatalism. He knew that the warnings of Rodzyanko and others were sincere and warranted, just as he knew that his wife was misguided, but he could not act to halt or deflect the wave of revolution, sweeping towards him, and passively he waited for it to overwhelm him.

CHAPTER SIX

The Collapse of the Tsarist Regime

IN the first months of 1917 the general unrest in Petrograd was at explosion point. None knew how or when it would erupt. Least of all did anyone anticipate that the existing order, like an imposing cathedral, grown rotten with time, would cave in, the cupola falling and then the walls, leaving the people bewildered in the midst of the ruins of all that had given order and stability in their lives.[1]

The March Revolution, like many of the great upheavals in history, began with a coincidence of insignificant events. On 8 March socialists celebrated Women's Day in the city with political meetings. Demonstrations against food shortages followed and developed into bread riots. Workers from many factories came out on strike, bringing some 90,000 people on to the streets. Crowds surged down the Nevsky Prospekt and into the main squares. Many carried red banners and placards, inscribed 'Bread!' and 'Down with the autocracy!'

The demonstrations were fairly orderly, but they coincided with a lockout, involving more than 20,000 workers from the Putilov munition works, which were notorious for industrial strife. By the following day the total number of strikers had multiplied almost tenfold. They attacked police with cobble stones and chunks of ice, but no shots were fired, and there were no serious incidents.

Despite these disorders and the angry mood of the people, the gravity of the crisis was still not apparent. Strikes and demonstrations had become commonplace in Petrograd. Sir George Buchanan, the British ambassador, who was well informed about Russian conditions, telegraphed to London that 'Some disorders occurred today, but nothing serious.'[2] The possibility that revolution would burst upon the city seemed remote.

The government had no fear of a major uprising. Protopopov, minister of the interior, had made special plans. The garrison of the capital had been brought to a strength of 160,000 troops. A military commander had been appointed in charge of each of the city's seven police districts. Also a special force, 12,000 strong, comprising soldiers, *gendarmes*, and police, waited in readiness. Finally Cossack cavalry units, usually relied on to suppress riots, were at hand. The measures were impressive, but they took no account of the fact that the troops were young, untrained, and undisciplined, and led by hastily promoted officers whom they hardly knew.

On 10 March the demonstrations spread and the garrison troops, while not going so far as to mutiny, were increasingly passive in their attitude to the strikers. Even the Cossacks merely sat their horses and held on their saddles their *nagaiki*, the dreaded short whips which they always carried, watching the crowds and refusing to disperse them. As the day wore on, the troops began siding openly with the demonstrators.

The tsar was at the Stavka, the supreme headquarters in Mogilev, where he received regular reports from Petrograd. Unrest was confined mainly to the city; on the fronts, apart from a trickle of desertions, the troops were loyal and disciplined. To Nicholas the strikes and disorders were no more than irresponsible sabotage of the war effort. He evidently had no inkling that these were the first tremblings of the earthquake that was to destroy him and his dynasty. His overriding concern was the prosecution of the war and he reacted sharply to the disruption of the munitions industry and to the unpatriotic demonstrations. He sent peremptory instructions to General Khabalov, commander of the Petrograd military district, to suppress all disorders, using such force as was necessary. Acting on these orders, Khabalov posted proclamations throughout the city that troops would fire on crowds refusing to disperse.

On 11 March troops of the Volynsky and certain other regiments on the orders of their officers fired on demonstrators. The training detachment of the Volynsky regiment even used machine-guns against the crowd in the Znamenskaya Square, at the eastern end of the Nevsky Prospekt, killing forty people and wounding many more.

Intimidated by this show of force, the crowds melted away. The government arrested a number of suspected revolutionaries, including five members of the Petrograd committee of the bolshevik party, and dispersed the few remaining demonstrators. But its rule over the city was precarious. The garrison troops were uneasy. An uprising in the Pavlovsk regiment was put down, but in other regiments troops were near to mutiny.

At this point Mikhail Rodzyanko, the president of the Duma, sent an appeal to the tsar at the Stavka. It read: 'The situation is serious. There is anarchy in the capital. The Government is paralyzed. It is necessary immediately to entrust a person who enjoys the confidence of the country with the formation of a government. Any delay is equivalent to death . . .'[3]

Nicholas did not reply. On the following morning Rodzyanko sent a more urgent warning. 'The situation is growing worse. Measures must be adopted immediately, for tomorrow will be too late. The last hour has come when the fate of the fatherland and the dynasty is being decided.'[4] Still Nicholas did not act.

Rodzyanko had not exaggerated. Mutiny was already spreading among the garrison troops. Men of the Volynsky regiment had during the night decided among themselves that they would not fire again on the crowds. On 12 March mutiny spread to the Preobrazhensky and Litovsky and other regiments. Pushing aside their officers and killing many who resisted, troops made their way on foot across the frozen Neva to the Vyborg district. There they made common cause with the workers. Together they attacked the police and raided stations and arsenals for weapons and ammunition.

The mutiny of the troops was the turning point. While they had obeyed the orders of their officers, the government was secure. But now revolution swept through the city. No person or party had organized or now led it. Workers had come out on strike and had demonstrated in the streets spontaneously, moved by discontent, war-weariness, and anger. For many months they had been in a turbulent mood, but always restrained by fear that the tsar would send his Cossacks to ride them down or soldiers to suppress their demonstrations with fire and sword. But the troops, stirred mainly by fear that they would be sent to the front, now made common cause with the workers. The firing on the crowds of the previous day had suddenly ignited the mutiny latent among them.

As they surged, often arm in arm, through the broad avenues of the city, workers and troops were in a mood of high excitement, almost good-natured. They drew confidence from their numbers. In great crowds they made their way to the Tauride Palace where the Duma met. All felt that the tsar no longer ruled, but they obeyed an instinctive need to gather around some centre of authority and the Duma was all that remained in the midst of anarchy. In their excitement the insurgents clamoured for the Duma leaders. They cheered the stirring patriotic speeches of Rodzyanko, Milyukov, and Shulgin as much as those of the new men of the soviet which was feverishly emerging. They were confused, bewildered, and noisy, like children released suddenly from all restraints.

Rodzyanko now made another frantic attempt to persuade the tsar to appoint a responsible ministry. Even at this last moment it was, he felt, possible that a government of able and honest men might bid for popular confidence. In this appeal he had the support of Grand Duke Mikhail, brother of the tsar. Mikhail reported on the anarchy in Petrograd and urged the appointment of Prince G. Lvov, chairman of the all-Russia union of zemstva, or of Rodzyanko himself, as prime minister, empowered to form a new government. Nicholas coldly rejected his brother's advice.

At the Stavka the unrest in the capital still seemed remote and unreal, not only to Nicholas, but to many on the staff of the high command. On 12 March General Ivanov was ordered to proceed to Petrograd with a detachment of Cavaliers of St George, men who had won high decorations for bravery in action and were considered the most loyal in the army. Believing that this force would readily deal with the unrest, the high command took no further action. General Ivanov was to find, however, that his cavaliers were not immune to subversion. On contact with garrison troops they began to desert and soon only a handful remained. Similarly, detachments sent by General Ruzsky from the northern front reached Luga, and, fraternizing with revolutionary troops, refused to go farther. The Stavka then gave orders that no further detachments of troops should be sent to the capital.

Petrograd was seething with excitement and activity. The Duma, faced with a dissolution order, presented by the prime minister, Golitsyn, agreed that it could not disperse, leaving the city and whole country without even the semblance of a government. The Duma, therefore, dissolved formally but the deputies merely moved to another part of the palace so that legally they would be meeting as private citizens. They then unanimously passed a resolution not to disband or to leave the capital. They elected a provisional committee, including representatives of all parties, except the extreme right and the bolsheviks on the extreme left, with the task of restoring order and co-operating with other representative bodies. They also appointed a military commission under Colonel Engelhardt to work for the restoration of discipline among troops of the Petrograd garrison and to guard against any attempt to restore the old regime.

The committee of the Duma assumed power, but was at once faced with a rival organization, the soviet of workers' and soldiers' deputies, which was to be more representative of the insurgents and which was to obstruct and finally supplant it.

The soviet had first come into existence during the revolution of 1905. It had existed then for only a few months, but now on the collapse of the regime it quickly revived. The workers' group of the war industry committee with the co-operation of the trade unions, left-wing parties in the Duma, and certain other groups, formed a temporary executive committee, known as Excom, of the soviet of workers' deputies. The soviet, already attended by some 250 delegates of the workers and troops, chosen hastily on the basis of one deputy for each thousand workers and one for each army company, met on the evening of 12 March in the Tauride Palace and formally constituted the Soviet of Workers' and Soldiers' Deputies.

The Tauride Palace, a building of great magnificence, erected by Catherine the Great for Prince Potemkin after his conquest of the Crimea, was now crowded with members of the Duma and of the soviet, all of whom were surrounded and harried by swarms of workers and troops. In the main the crowds were still good-natured and curious, but the sight of a police uniform or of one of the tsar's unpopular ministers could bring on an ugly murderous mood. So crowded was this vast palace that it seemed that the mob had taken over completely.

The soviet spoke with many voices. Of the men who were to dictate the character of the revolution, Lenin, Zinoviev, and Trotsky were still abroad, while Stalin, Dzerzhinsky, and Kamenev were in prison or in Siberia. Within the executive committee the small bolshevik minority strongly opposed any support for the bourgeois government of the Duma and urged the formation of a temporary revolutionary government until the constituent assembly could be elected. Another group of deputies argued that the soviet should join the Duma committee in forming a coalition government. The majority, however, held that the soviet should not assume power at this stage, nor should it share power with the Duma committee. This was in accordance with Marxist theory, as currently interpreted, that in Russia the bourgeois revolution must precede the seizure of power by the proletariat.

The soviet deputies feared also that, if they attempted to seize power at this early stage, they would rally the whole of the propertied class in defence of the tsarist regime. The soviet's decision was, therefore, that all responsibility should lie with the bourgeois government to which they would give minimal support. It was an attitude calculated to undermine any new government. In fact, the committee of the soviet took considerable powers to itself, while avoiding the opprobrium of responsibility.

Petrograd had given birth to the revolution, but within a few days it had spread over Russia with surprising ease and speed. The collapse of the tsarist order had been so sudden and complete that there was no resistance. Moscow, the old capital, the citadel of Holy Russia, was taken over by the revolutionaries without bloodshed. Other cities and towns elected their own soviets, and the old officials and officers seemed to melt away, offering no opposition. Only in Kronstadt and Helsingfors, where the sailors were turbulent and hated their officers, were there serious excesses.[5]

The most urgent task now facing the Duma committee and the soviet in Petrograd was to bring some order into the chaos. All knew that the armed soldiers and workers, wandering aimlessly and uncontrolled in all parts of the city, might be transformed by some small unexpected incident into a violent destructive force. 'The Tauride Palace,' wrote Sukhanov, an eyewitness of these events, 'the brain and heart of the revolution, ringed round by menacing unguarded guns and meagre little groups of soldiers without officers, awaited the will of God...'[6]

The soviet had won early popularity with the promulgation of its 'Order Number One', published in *Izvestiya* on 14 March which virtually gave control of the armed forces into the hands of committees elected by the soldiers and sailors themselves. Parts of this order introduced reasonable reforms in the traditionally harsh conditions of the army and navy. Other parts were, however, completely destructive of discipline and hastened the disintegration of the two services.[7] Nor was this famous order calculated to bring stability into the capital or the country as a whole. Members of the soviet executive committee therefore sought out the Duma committee to discuss the projected provisional government.

Sukhanov, who with Chkheidze, Sokolov, and Steklov represented the soviet committee in these negotiations, described the meeting which began some time after midnight on 15 March and lasted until the dawn hours. Kerensky, soon to hold the centre of the stage, was present. But he was exhausted from delivering countless speeches and the hectic activity of the last few days and he now took no part. Rodzyanko, also near exhaustion and distracted at this time by his communications with the tsar at the Stavka, was losing hope and was an onlooker rather than a participant. Shulgin, the writer and conservative member of the Duma, who had, like other members, watched the revolution approaching and had vainly urged the tsar to make concessions, wandered about the room and did not speak.

Paul Milyukov, the leader of the Kadet party, dominated the meeting. A professor who had studied under Vinogradov and Klyuchevsky, Milyukov belonged nevertheless to the world of political activity rather than the calm of academic life. He believed fervently in the constitutional democracy of western Europe, especially England, as the freest and most just form of government. He was also a staunch patriot who feared that revolution and the radical socialism of the social democrats would destroy all that was best in Russia. He was now fighting all the more desperately for a parliament and a constitutional monarchy, because he had seen this system come so near realization during the past ten years.

In the Duma committee room in the Tauride Palace, Milyukov faced the deputies of the soviet, knowing well that the real power in the city was in their hands. But he struggled tenaciously for the principles in which he believed. Sukhanov, a convinced Marxist, interpreted every word spoken in terms of class struggle. The disinterested love of country and the conviction that a particular form of government was best suited to Russia, which Milyukov sincerely felt, were to the revolutionaries merely façades to an all-consuming class interest or misguided ideas which were hangovers from the old regime.

The two parties, nevertheless, reached agreement on a wide range of subjects. On 16 March the new provisional government issued a declaration setting out the names of its cabinet and its guiding principles, based on this agreement. The committee of the soviet published its declaration in *Izvestiya* on the following day, promising support to the new government but only in so far as it fulfilled its obligations.[8]

The policy to which the provisional government committed itself embraced the grant of political amnesty, of full civil rights, and the elimination of caste, religious, and national discriminations. Of special importance to both Duma and soviet was the undertaking that immediate preparations would be made for convening a constituent assembly with responsibility for establishing the form of administration and the constitution of the country on the basis of general, equal, secret, and direct voting. Other provisions included the extension of political rights to soldiers, but the need to maintain military discipline was stressed. One item, insisted upon by the soviet deputies which was to prove fatal to the provisional government in the end was that the Petrograd garrison should not be moved or disarmed.

The declarations represented a considerable achievement for Milyukov. But it was a limited victory. The real power still lay with the soviet and its promise of support to the provisional government was grudging and conditional. Moreover, the declarations had passed over in silence the two most urgent and critical problems of the day, namely the problem of the peasants and the land, and the even more pressing question of Russia's further participation in the war.

Milyukov and the Duma committee were determined that Russia should continue fighting. Among the deputies of the soviet and, indeed, among workers and troops, feelings of patriotism were still strong. They believed that the war against Germany must continue since, if the kaiser were victorious, he would surely restore and maintain the tsarist regime in power. But none among the troops in the capital wanted to fight and discipline at the fronts was now beginning to break down rapidly.

Milyukov and the Duma committee were anxious to commit the soviet further to the provisional government. But the executive committee of the soviet had decided by thirteen votes to eight against deputies serving in the government. Chkheidze, when offered the ministry of labour, rejected it. But Kerensky accepted the ministry of justice, explaining his action in an emotional speech which won deafening applause from the members of the soviet, if not from its committee.

The problem of the future of the tsar and his dynasty remained. But before the provisional government formally assumed office on 16 March, this had been resolved by the abdication of Nicholas II.

For the members of the soviet and the people in Petrograd, the revolution had meant the end of the tsar and his regime. They were watchful against attempts to restore the monarchy. Among the liberals of the Duma, various opinions existed. The foundation congress of the Kadet party had left undecided the question whether the future state was to be a republic or a monarchy. But the members of the Duma committee now wanted to retain the monarchy in some form of constitutional government. All were agreed that Nicholas himself had failed and must go.

When on the afternoon of 15 March, Milyukov spoke to workers in the colonnaded hall of the Tauride Palace on the policy of the government and, not having heard yet the final terms of abdication, explained that Tsarevich Alexei would be heir to the throne and Grand Duke Mikhail regent under a constitutional monarchy, the crowd roared its disapproval. Popular opposition was so strong that he was forced to amend his statement and later to say that the retention of the monarchy had been his personal idea.[9]

The last scene before the curtain came down on the Russian monarchy was enacted in the house of Grand Duke Mikhail on the Millionnaya in Petrograd. Most of the members of the Duma committee were present to discuss whether Mikhail should accept the throne. Milyukov, his voice reduced to a croak by constant speech-making, implored him to accept. But Rodzyanko and Lvov, both strong monarchists, knew that already the monarchy belonged to the past. Kerensky made an impassioned appeal to him to reject the throne. Mikhail withdrew to another room and, returning half an hour later, he announced that he would not accept the throne, unless requested to do so by the constituent assembly when elected. The second deed of abdication was at once typed and signed.[10]

Nicholas himself had meanwhile retired from Pskov to Mogilev. He made several requests to the provisional government to be allowed to rejoin his family in Tsarskoe Selo and, when they were well enough, to travel to Port Romanov on the Murman coast. Prince Lvov sent a telegram on 19 March, granting this request and a few days later Nicholas was reunited with his family. The government was evidently anxious that the imperial family should find asylum abroad. In fact, Milyukov had on 21 March asked the British ambassador to obtain his government's approval for them to go to England, and King George V had invited them to make their home there until the end of the war.[11] But the soviet was now demanding the arrest of the imperial family and insisting that they should not be allowed to leave the country.[12] The government yielded to this pressure. The ex-tsar and his family remained under guard at Tsarskoe Selo until the summer when they were escorted to Tobolsk in Siberia. So long as they were together they did not greatly mind where they were sent, but in fact they were taken to Ekaterinburg.

The tumultuous events of March had swept away the organs of the central government and had created nothing in their place. Anarchy reigned and the provisional government was powerless to restore order. It had no legal basis and existed on the sufferance of the soviet. It could not even rely on the police and the army. The hated tsarist police had been replaced by an inexperienced and unreliable militia. The troops in Petrograd had already mutinied and, resentful of authority, were not inclined to obey any government.

The provisional government nevertheless existed as the sole authority and its impotence was not yet apparent. Abroad it was credited with being in control. Milyukov as foreign minister had sent telegrams to allied governments, which gave the impression that it was soundly based and would co-operate with the allies. Anxious to be the first to accept the new republican regime, David Frances, the U.S. ambassador, conveyed his government's recognition on 22 March. Two days later the ambassadors of Britain, France, and Italy, all eager to keep the Russian armies in the field against Germany, followed suit.

In these first weeks the provisional government also enacted several major reforms. It granted full autonomy to Finland and recognized the independence of Poland. Tsarist restrictions, based on religion and race, especially concerning the Jews, were abolished. On 25 March the death penalty and, on the following day, courts-martial, except at the front, were abolished. But these reforms, although acclaimed, did not win popular support for the government; indeed, they had little direct meaning for the people who in these hectic days of the revolution were intoxicated by their complete freedom from all restraints.

In the provinces the peasants were taking the law into their own hands and seizing the land. The government issued appeals and appointed a main land committee to collect facts in preparation for the legislation which the constituent assembly would have to consider. But in the isolation of distant villages, the peasant felt free to satisfy his age-old land hunger. In the cities the workers were also active. As they became increasingly aware of their power, they demanded an eight-hour day and other industrial reforms, and no one offered serious resistance to their claims.

The problem weighing most heavily on the provisional government, however, was the prosecution of the war. The Petrograd garrison had become an unruly mob. Among the troops at the front, discipline had only started to decline seriously after the tsar's abdication. Order No. 1 of the Petrograd soviet had speeded the process and publication in *Izvestiya* on 28 March of the Declaration of the Rights of Soldiers, liberalizing further the conditions of military service and striking away the bases of army discipline and efficiency, had added a new momentum. Men at the front no longer knew what they were fighting for, and, as peasants, their concern was to return to their villages to get their share of the landlord's estate. Deserters were soon flowing eastwards in a mighty flood, adding to the chaos in the rear.

The task of restoring and maintaining discipline in the army became impossible. The provisional government was, however, politically and emotionally committed to the war. To the Kadets, in particular, it was a matter of national honour not to fail the allies. The leaders of the soviet now denounced the war as an imperialist struggle which only the workers of all countries combining their efforts could halt. But they also proclaimed the strength of the new revolutionary army and they did not dare propose a separate peace. Apart from the bolsheviks, no one was prepared to go so far as to urge peace with Germany.

Meanwhile the Petrograd soviet remained an unwieldy inchoate body of nearly three thousand members. Its executive committee was responsible for policy, but this, too, had become so large that a bureau of twenty-four members took over most of its work. Leaders were lacking and the return from exile of Heracles Tseretelli, like Chkheidze, a Georgian, but of stronger personality and greater ability, made the Soviet more effective. He dominated the all-Russian conference of soviets which opened on 11 April in Petrograd. His policy towards the war, labelled 'defensist', was that until other peoples followed the Russians in overthrowing their governments the Russian revolution must fight resolutely against foreign enemies. Kamenev, speaking for the bolsheviks, urged that the national struggle must be transformed into a revolutionary struggle of 'the peoples of all the warring countries against the Moloch of war, the Moloch of imperialism'.[13] But in the voting Kamenev received only 57 votes, while 325 votes were cast for Tseretelli's resolution.

This all-Russian conference was an impressive demonstration of the growth of the soviets in the brief period since the collapse of the old regime. Seven armies, thirteen reserve units, twenty-six front line units, and 138 soviets sent their delegates to it. The Petrograd soviet was acknowledged as the senior and its lead was generally followed. Indeed, at the end of the conference the Petrograd executive committee expanded to include provincial representatives and so became the all-Russian executive committee. But several of the local and provincial soviets, as in Kronstadt, Tsaritsyn, and Krasnoyarsk, were extremely active and independent.

The Bolsheviks were still a minority party. The first all-Russian congress of soviets, which met on 16 June, was attended by 1,090 delegates, of whom 777 declared their party affiliations, and of them only 105 were members of the bolshevik party. As yet the simple but extreme line taken by many of them, and advocated by Lenin, was not acceptable and even offended the people. Also the bolsheviks lacked leadership in Russia at this stage. On 25 March, Stalin, Kamenev, and Muranov returned from exile and at once took over the editorial office of *Pravda*. But their pronouncements on the war and other matters were confused and contained nothing to set the bolsheviks apart or to mark them as the leaders.

As one bolshevik, Ludmilla Stal, noted: 'All the comrades groped about in darkness until the arrival of Lenin.'[14]

PART II

REVOLUTION AND
CIVIL WAR

CHAPTER SEVEN

The October Revolution 1917

LATE in the evening of 16 April Lenin arrived at the Finland Station in Petrograd. A great crowd gave him a thunderous welcome. The station was festooned with red banners. Guards of honour presented arms and a military band struck up the *Marseillaise* as he stepped from his carriage. Someone thrust a large bouquet of flowers in his arms. The shouting, the military music, and the excitement marked it as an exceptional occasion.

Sukhanov describing the scene noted that 'the Bolsheviks, who shone at organization and always aimed at emphasizing externals and putting on a good show, had dispensed with any superfluous modesty and were plainly preparing a real triumphal entry.'[1] But now they had an additional reason for presenting Lenin to the masses as a hero. This was the need to offset the unfavourable impression created by the fact that Lenin and his party had travelled from Switzerland through Germany in a special 'sealed' carriage by courtesy of the enemy government.[2] Lenin himself feared that he would be arrested on arrival. Patriotic and anti-German feelings were still strong among the Russians and in the days ahead the bolsheviks were to be acutely embarrassed by charges that their leader was a German agent.[3]

Wearing a round winter hat, his head thrust forward aggressively, Lenin walked along the crowded platform to the imperial waiting room. The local bolshevik leaders had already met him in Finland, but the president of the soviet, Chkheidze, and members of the Excom were there to welcome him formally. Chkheidze looked gloomy as though filled with the foreboding that here was the man who would displace him and his fellow mensheviks, and, indeed, Lenin had at one time or another denounced him as a scoundrel and a traitor, although he was neither, and merely a political opponent. He delivered his speech of welcome 'with not only the spirit and wording but also the tone of a sermon'.[4] He even coupled his morose welcome with an astonishing appeal to Lenin to co-operate in the defence of the revolution.

Standing in the imperial waiting room, holding the bouquet of flowers, Lenin looked around him, ignoring Chkheidze and the welcoming committee. When he came to reply to the speech, he continued to ignore the Excom delegation and proclaimed the revolution as the beginning of a new epoch, making it clear by word and manner that they did not belong to it.

Coming out of the main entrance Lenin went to get into a closed car, but the crowd demanded to see this strange, powerful little man, whom they knew by name and not by sight. He climbed on to the bonnet of the car and made another speech. He then transferred to an armoured car and, preceded by a mobile searchlight, like a one-eyed monster, he made a hero's progress through the city. At nearly every street crossing he stopped to speak until he arrived at the palace of Kshesinskaya, the famed ballerina, which the bolsheviks had made their headquarters. Even from the balcony of the palace he harangued the crowd in the court-yard.

It had indeed been a triumphal return, but Lenin's speeches had disturbed many of his listeners. Intent on ramming home his message, he was often grossly insensitive to the feelings of his audiences. Returning after a long absence he might well have shown more caution. But he angered many by decrying defence of the fatherland as nothing more than a defence of capitalism and by demanding immediate peace negotiations. 'Ought to stick our bayonets into a fellow like that,' Sukhanov overheard one irate soldier say to another. 'Must be a German ... Eh, he ought to be ...'[5] But within a few days, as he realized that his speeches were antagonizing many of his listeners, he moderated his language.

Lenin now worked furiously to impose his ideas and tactics on the party. Within a few days of his return, he presented his *April Theses* to the seventh all-Russian conference, which was then meeting. The ten points of his programme stressed that the immediate goal was control by soviets of workers' deputies over production and distribution; the party should oppose the provisional government and reject unification with the mensheviks; all land must be nationalized and administered by soviets of agricultural labourers' deputies; banks must be fused into the one state bank; genuine peace was impossible until capitalism had been overthrown, and this must be explained to the armies in the field by propaganda which should encourage the troops to fraternize with the enemy.

The *Theses* staggered the bolsheviks, especially the demand for immediate revolution. At an earlier session the conference had unanimously approved a resolution, moved by Stalin, calling for 'vigilant control' over the activities of the government and support for the Petrograd soviet as the 'beginning of a revolutionary power'.[6] Stalin, like other party members, took for granted that the provisional government marked the beginning of a term of bourgeois democratic government which at some future time would be displaced by the dictatorship of the proletariat. The possibility of an immediate transfer of power to a revolutionary government was far from their minds.

The party did not at once tamely adopt Lenin's dogmas; he usually had to struggle to win support for his ideas. Kamenev, Zinoviev, and many others strongly opposed this new policy of immediate revolution, but Stalin quickly lined up behind him. The conference nevertheless adopted several resolutions in direct conflict with the *April Theses*, especially in seeking union with the mensheviks.

Early in May the provisional government faced a crisis. Milyukov as foreign minister sent a note to allied governments, confirming Russia's determination to continue fighting and to observe its treaty agreements. Members of the soviet and many others took the note to imply that the government was still pursuing tsarist policies and was ignoring the soviet's formula of peace without annexations and indemnities. On 3 May troops and demonstrators, some 30,000 strong, appeared at the Marinsky Palace, now the seat of the government, demanding Milyukov's resignation. The soviet Excom held urgent discussions during the night and finally agreed to continue its support for the government, subject to explanations to certain parts of the offending note being issued.[7] But this did not prevent more serious popular disturbances on the following day, when several people were killed and many were wounded. General Kornilov, commander of the Petrograd garrison, ordered troop units to take up positions ready to deal with the demonstrators. But the troops turned for confirmation of these orders to the soviet which directed that no military unit should come on to the streets except on instructions issued under the seal of the Excom and signed by at least two of the soviet leaders. Kornilov, disgruntled at finding himself subordinate to the soviet instead of the government and by the decline in the latter's authority, resigned and was given command of an army on the south-western front.

This May outburst showed that the soviet, not the provisional government, wielded the authority over troops and workers in the city. But it was a tenuous authority and members of both the Excom and the government, alarmed by the threats of violent upheaval which would lead inevitably to bloodshed and to greater anarchy, reluctantly came together in a coalition. Milyukov and Guchkov opposed this move, but Milyukov, after the storm over his note to the Allied governments, and Guchkov, the minister of war, now broken in health and spirit, both resigned. Among the members of the Excom, too, many had strong misgivings, but Kerensky's passionate advocacy finally won a majority of forty-four votes to nineteen in favour of coalition. Negotiations over the policy to be pursued were prolonged and involved compromise on many points, but it was agreed that the army must be brought to a state of readiness for further offensive operations.

Outstanding among the members of the new coalition government was undoubtedly Alexander Kerensky. Born in Simbirsk, the son of a headmaster, he had studied law at St Petersburg University and had practised in Saratov, winning popular acclaim there for his defence of political offenders. He possessed great intelligence and ability and a restless, driving energy. He was a natural orator, exuberant, dramatic, and able to arouse his audience. In politics he was a revolutionary socialist but moderate and humane and lacking the implacable fanaticism of Lenin, or of

Trotsky whom, of the leading men of this time, he most resembled. His weakness was that he became carried away by his emotions and enthusiasms, losing sight of the realities and dangers facing him.

As minister of war, Kerensky at once threw himself into the task of preparing the army for an offensive. He recognized the difficulties, but believed that the troops would respond to his appeals and to the new liberal charter of soldiers' rights. One of his first actions was to appoint as commander-in-chief General Brusilov, who had led the brilliant Russian offensive of 1916. He also attached commissars to the army with the primary duties of raising morale and discipline among the troops and acting as liaison officers between commanders and the newly elected soldiers' committees. Kerensky himself made an extensive tour of the front, appealing to the patriotism and the revolutionary spirit of the men, and his sincere emotional speeches evoked enthusiastic responses. 'Our army under the monarchy accomplished heroic deeds, will it be a flock of sheep under the republic? ... We, revolutionaries, have the right to death.'[8] He was 'carried shoulder-high and pelted with flowers. Everywhere scenes of unprecedented enthusiasm took place ... Men flung their Crosses of St George at the feet of Kerensky, who was calling on them to die ...'[9] But the anarchy in the rear, the weakness of the government, and the breakdown of discipline in many regiments could not be cured by the words of one man, and the propaganda of Germans and bolsheviks alike further countered the effect of his appeals.

Meanwhile unrest and lawlessness were raging unchecked throughout the country. 'Lynch-law, the destruction of houses and shops, jeering at and attack on officers, on provincial authorities or private persons, unauthorized arrests, seizures, and beatings-up were recorded every day by tens and hundreds. In the country burnings and destruction of country-houses became more frequent ... Quite a few excesses were observed among the workers—against factory administration, owners, and foremen. But more than anything else, of course, it was the unbridled rioting soldiers who were destroying law and order.'[10]

In these conditions the bolsheviks were gradually gaining wider influence and support. But the mensheviks and the social revolutionaries still had a massive overall majority in the soviet. The return of Trotsky on 17 May was in due course to give a new impetus to the bolshevik cause. A small man of boundless energy, electric vitality, high intelligence, great executive ability, and mercurial temperament, Trotsky was the complement of Lenin and second only to him as the leader of the bolshevik revolution. At the time of his return to Russia, Trotsky was not a member of the party. He was too independent and self-willed to accept the rigid party discipline demanded by Lenin, and was actively reviving a small group known as the Mezhraiontsy who held a position between the bolsheviks and the mensheviks. But fundamentally Trotsky and Lenin were in agreement, especially since Lenin had now embraced the policy of passing directly from the bourgeois to the socialist revolution, a policy which Trotsky had been advocating since 1905. Trotsky had in one of his first speeches in May summed up his position, using almost the same words as Lenin—'All power to the Soviets: no support to the Provisional Government.' He was soon to be warmly welcomed into the party and elected by a great majority to its central committee.

Under the leadership of Lenin and Trotsky, the party continued to gain support. The soviet still wielded the chief authority, as was demonstrated when a rally of rank and file party members, planned to take place on 23 June, was effectively banned by the all-Russian congress, then in session. But a week later a rally authorized by the congress as a peaceful display of confidence in the soviets turned into a bolshevik demonstration with slogans demanding an end to the war.

On the following day the Nevsky Prospekt and the other main streets of the city resounded with the cheers of crowds, celebrating the opening of an offensive on the Galician front. The people sang patriotic songs and bore portraits of Kerensky, the hero of the day. In this there was some justice. His burning faith and incredible energies had breathed life into the army and had made the offensive possible. But it was to prove disastrous for the policy and the regime in which he fervently believed. Moreover, it revealed even more starkly how this policy ran contrary to the whole flow of events in Russia.

The attack began on 1 July near the Dniester River and against the Austrians it swept ahead victoriously. The Russians captured more than 18,000 prisoners in the first two days and the 8th Army, commanded by Kornilov, completely broke Austrian resistance, occupying the towns of Galich and Kalusz and taking some 20,000 prisoners. But then German troops, rushed up to support the Austrians, halted the advance and turned it into a retreat. The Russian armies dissolved into a fugitive mass of desperate, undisciplined men fleeing eastward. For Kerensky and other moderate revolutionaries this rout spelt the end of all hopes that the new government would be able to negotiate peace from a position of strength. For the conservatives and liberals it destroyed the last chance of restoring order and what they considered sound government. The bolsheviks who had consistently demanded an end to the war could rejoice, but they too were promptly engulfed in the tide of anarchy.

The 'July Days', as the outbreak which followed the rout of the army was called, was a period of mass madness. On 16 July armed troops and workers poured into the broad streets of Petrograd and made for the Tauride Palace. The city rang with shouts of 'All power to the Soviets,' and the demonstrators evidently sought to compel the Petrograd soviet to assume power. Troops and workers were in a state of angry excitement. They gave way readily to panic. Soldiers fired rifles and machine-guns at random and casualties were numerous. But on the following day the demonstration reached an ugly climax. Armed Kronstadt sailors, 20,000 strong and a raging mass of 30,000 workers from the Putilov plant swarmed into the city to join in the demonstration.

The Kronstadt sailors were especially nervous. Thinking they had been fired on as they marched through the streets, they fired back, broke into buildings where they thought they had seen snipers, and killed all who aroused their suspicions. Hysteria mounted among them. They surrounded the Tauride Palace and demanded certain unpopular leaders of the soviet. They nearly lynched the socialist revolutionary minister of agriculture, Chernov. He was saved by Trotsky who was popular with the sailors and subdued them with angry eloquence. In other parts of the city excesses of every kind were taking place. Casualties numbered four hundred or more as a result of the violence of these two days. But as Sukhanov wrote, referring to the second day, 'The blood and filth of this senseless day had had a sobering effect by evening and evidently evoked a swift reaction.'[11]

The outburst seemed to have started spontaneously but it had, in fact, been encouraged by individual bolshevik leaders in Petrograd and Kronstadt. On 17 July the party central committee had called for a 'peaceful organized demonstration' in support of the soviets. It was an irresponsible action, for the bolsheviks were not in control and the angry troops and workers were beyond organization. Sukhanov who wrote an eyewitness account of the anarchy of these two days, when the city was at the mercy of panic-stricken armed mobs, recorded that Lenin himself was confused and uncertain how to handle this runaway movement. His quandary was whether to repudiate it and risk alienating supporters or whether to try to harness it to an attempt to seize power. In fact, no plan had been made to capture the capital or to depose the provisional government and the bolsheviks were in no position to take advantage of the mass rising.[12]

On the following day, 18 July, reaction set in sharply. The provisional government, supported by nearly all the members of the Petrograd soviet, took action against the bolsheviks, accusing them of instigating rebellion against the revolution. But far more effective in destroying bolshevik prestige was the release by the ministry of justice of documents, allegedly proving that Lenin and other party leaders were German agents.[13] The accusation had an immediate impact. The Preobrazhensky regiment, which had taken a neutral stand, at once gave its support to the government. The Kshesinskaya palace and the Petropavlovsky fortress, two bolshevik centres, were occupied by government troops. *Pravda* was closed down. Certain of the more rebellious regiments were disbanded. A wave of arrests followed and many suspected of bolshevik sympathies were taken into custody. The bolshevik party became an object of popular hatred and was driven underground. But the government failed to deal thoroughly with the bolsheviks, as they might have done at this time. Party agitators remained free to continue their work, and in particular no attempt was made to disarm or disband the Red Guard, which the bolsheviks had begun to organize in late June through factory committees and which was to develop into a decisive force.

On the evening of 19 July Kerensky returned to Petrograd from the front. He at once demanded stronger measures against the bolsheviks, especially their leaders. Warrants were promptly issued and Trotsky, Kamenev, Lunarcharsky, and others were arrested. But the militiamen who went at 2 a.m. to Lenin's flat to take him into custody found that both he and Zinoviev had gone into hiding. Not only the bolsheviks but other revolutionaries were staggered by this flight. General opinion was highly critical of Lenin on political and moral grounds. Sukhanov was bitterly disappointed in this man with whom he often disagreed but whom he revered as 'Lenin the genius'.[14] 'The masses mobilized by Lenin, after all, were bearing the whole burden of responsibility for the July Days ... Some remained in their factories or in their districts—isolated, slandered, in sick depression and unspeakable confusion of mind. Others were under arrest and waiting retribution for having done their political duty according to their feeble lights. And the "real author" abandoned his army and his comrades and sought personal salvation in flight.'[15] Lenin was, in fact, in danger only of imprisonment which might have rallied public support to him. The possibility that he might be murdered by government agents, as he evidently feared, was remote. But he clearly preferred to keep his personal liberty and freedom of political action.[16]

Lenin now abandoned the slogan and policy of 'All power to the Soviets'. They had, he considered, shown themselves to be organs of reaction. He had accepted them as vehicles through which he would achieve absolute power and they had proved unsuitable. He argued now that only 'the revolutionary proletariat ... supported by the poorest peasantry' could attain power.[17] On 8 August the sixth bolshevik party congress took place in Petrograd. Lenin was still in hiding in Finland, but evidently dominated the proceedings from there. Stalin had the task of explaining the new policy which was troubling many party members. They felt reluctant to cast aside the soviets, but the congress finally adopted by unanimous vote the resolution defining the new policy.

This congress not only raised morale among the rank and file of the party but also agreed its future strategy. This was based on the assumptions that power would be seized by armed workers and peasants properly organized and led, and that the revolution to be successful must be accompanied, or at least followed promptly, by socialist revolutions in western Europe. Stalin and others argued that the revolution could be successful in Russia even though not accompanied by similar upheavals elsewhere. Some believed that a socialist revolution could not succeed in Russia alone. But all were confident that socialism would eventually sweep over the whole of Europe.

On 21 July Kerensky became prime minister on the resignation of the elderly Prince Lvov. He had difficulty in choosing a new cabinet and when formed on 8 August, it contained a socialist majority, but they were right-wing mensheviks and socialist revolutionaries who favoured moderation. The Excom of the soviet gave its support to the new government, subject to the undertakings that it would hold elections for a constituent assembly within two months, take action to deal with the land question, and convene an inter-Allied conference to discuss peace terms.

With this support, with the bolsheviks in disfavour, and Lenin in hiding, Kerensky and his government felt themselves to be in a strong position. They dealt firmly with both Finnish and Ukranian nationalists. Factory-owners, landowners, and army officers emerged from the revolutionary flood which had swept over them, and began to see hopes for the restoration of order and for their own survival. But all depended on the government finding solutions to the two root problems of peace and land. In this they could expect no understanding or support from the upper, professional, and middle classes. To them it was still dishonour not to be contemplated to desert their Allies and make peace with the Germans, and impossible to surrender land to the peasants. In their inflexibility and incapacity for facing realities, these classes condemned themselves to destruction.

Kerensky, although buoyant with confidence, also faced the difficult problem of retaining the support of the menshevik and socialist revolutionary leaders. They had a constant struggle to control their members and the government had to make concessions. At the same time the non-socialist supporters of the government were demanding firm measures to restore discipline in the army and in industry and to put an end to the general anarchy. The task of reconciling such opposed demands was beyond the powers of Kerensky and probably of any man at this time.

In an attempt at conciliation Kerensky convened a state conference in Moscow from 25 to 28 August. This brought together 2,414 delegates, representing every class and section of the population, except the bolsheviks. The conference was intended as a consultative body in which right and left would be balanced and able to work out some compromise programme. It was a bold conception but in spite of his impassioned speeches calling for unity, it failed to achieve any result.

From the outset the delegates divided into irreconcilable camps. The left-wing delegates were uneasy that, held in Moscow, the ancient capital and the enduring symbol of Russian conservatism, the conference would serve the reactionary groups. Rumours of monarchist conspiracies and of a reactionary coup unsettled the conference sessions. The left-wing delegates were, however, able to draw comfort from an effective one-day strike of workers in Moscow, organized by the bolsheviks. Kerensky tried desperately to mediate between right and left. He succeeded in winning the support of the left-wing delegates, but increasingly became the object of right-wing suspicion. Delegates on the right were now looking upon General Kornilov as their champion, especially after his powerful speech condemning the indiscipline at the front and the anarchy in the rear.

Kornilov was a Cossack of proven bravery, a strict disciplinarian and a sincere patriot. He was a colourful figure, small and slight in build, erect and with great vitality. He probably had Asiatic blood, for his eyes were slanting and he had a Mongolian cast of feature. He had served for long periods in Asia, preferred the company of Asiatics and spoke many of their languages. He was accompanied everywhere by his personal guard of Turcomen who were devoted to him and who in their Cossack tunics and tall black sheepskin hats provided a severe and exotic background to his presence.

A man of action and an able soldier, Kornilov had little experience of politics and politicians but he was not a reactionary. He accepted the March revolution and had no interest in seeking to restore the monarchy. His basic purpose was to strengthen the provisional government so that it was independent of the soviet and able to restore order, to revive the munitions industry and to continue the war vigorously. But he was bitterly opposed to the extreme left. 'It's time to hang the German supporters and spies, with Lenin at their head,' he burst out on one occasion.[18] Inevitably, however, he attracted many who saw in him the dictator who would replace the provisional government with strong right-wing rule.

In their basic aims Kerensky and Kornilov were broadly in agreement but they were to come increasingly into conflict. On 31 July Kerensky appointed Kornilov to be commander-in-chief in place of Brusilov. He needed a younger, more active commander after the failure of the July offensive and he also made the gesture to win approval from the right-wing. Moreover, unlike the generals of the old school who condemned the new system of commissars and deplored the decline of army discipline without seeking remedies, Kornilov welcomed the commissars and troop committees and was active in seeking to restore military discipline. But soon Kornilov lost patience with what he considered the government's weakness and vacillation and, influenced by reactionaries close to him, he began to take the law into his own hands and to plan a military coup.

In August Kornilov sent orders to his chief of staff, General Lukomsky, to station a Cossack cavalry corps and the Savage division, composed of Moslem horsemen from the Caucasus, in the vicinity of Velikie Luki which was within striking distance of Moscow and Petrograd by rail. It was an ominous command, indicating that he was planning to attack one or both of the cities. His relations with Kerensky were already strained and the possibility that Kerensky would order his arrest was widely rumoured. In fact, when Kornilov visited the capital at the end of August to discuss future military operations against the Germans, he armed his Turcoman bodyguard with machine-guns and, while he was making an official visit on Kerensky, this guard mounted their guns in the corridor of the Winter Palace ready to answer their master's first call for help.[19]

Early in September Kornilov's preparations were complete. Three cavalry divisions had been issued with hand-grenades and a ten-day supply of food and forage. Petrograd was to be occupied, assisted by two right-wing patriotic associations and some 2,000 men within the city. The cavalrymen were to advance on receiving news of an uprising in the city and in any case not later than 14 September.

Kornilov's military plans had been carefully laid, but his political intentions remained extremely vague. Apart from hanging bolshevik leaders and dispersing the soviet, he apparently planned to re-form the provisional government with himself at its head and Kerensky as minister of justice. Naïvely he thought that Kerensky would acquiesce in such a plan and when on 8 September he spoke by telephone with Kerensky he believed, rightly or wrongly, that he had been given this support. He was astonished next morning to receive a peremptory telegram, ordering him to hand over his command to Lukomsky and to return to Petrograd forthwith. Kornilov and Lukomsky both refused to obey the order. Kerensky then gave instructions that all movements of troops in the direction of Petrograd must be halted. Kornilov promptly countermanded the order and directed his cavalry divisions to advance according to plan.

This was civil war. At the Stavka in Mogilev, Kornilov and his commanders were confident. They had the support of the Cossacks, the Moslem troops, and the best of the remaining army units, and they did not believe that the unruly garrison and the armed workers in the capital were capable of real resistance. This was their great mistake. The military challenge to the provisional government and the threat of a reactionary dictatorship rallied the whole city behind Kerensky. In the soviet, the mensheviks, socialist revolutionaries, and the bolsheviks formed a united front. The Committee for Struggle against counter-revolution, representative of all groups, was set up and launched a national campaign of resistance to Kornilov.

The bolsheviks were particularly active in organizing defences. Moreover, they obtained the committee's approval for enlisting an armed workers' militia, which enabled them to rearm and expand the Red Guard, and within a few days it had recruited some 25,000 troops. Railwaymen and telegraph operators obeyed the committee's orders to sabotage all services on Kornilov's route from Mogilev to the capital. But the decisive factor in the failure of Kornilov's coup was the collapse of the morale of his own troops. The Savage division was on 10 September within forty miles of the capital when it was forced to halt because the railway lines had been torn up. Here a delegation of Moslems sent by the soviet mingled among them and soon persuaded them not to fight against the revolution. At every halt the Cossack divisions found themselves surrounded by propagandists and they, too, were soon denuded of the will to fight.

Kornilov's force became more and more disorganized as desertion and insubordination increased. By 12 September the attempted coup had collapsed without a shot fired. Kerensky himself assumed the title of commander-in-chief with General Alekseev as his chief of staff. Kornilov, Lukomsky, Denikin and other officers who had supported the plot were arrested and held in custody in a monastery in the nearby town of Bykhov.

This attempted coup had been an utter failure but it had serious repercussions. Instead of strengthening, it had the immediate effect of undermining Kerensky's position. He had tried to bridge the gap between left and right but the division had become deeper and wider. The provisional government had lost the confidence of the workers and soldiers who were now antagonistic and mistrustful. It had depended on the formal support of the soviet, but the moderate mensheviks and socialist revolutionaries who had controlled the soviet had been displaced by the bolsheviks, and on 8 October Trotsky was elected president of the Petrograd soviet.

In an effort to regain left-wing support and to continue the coalition government, which he saw as the one hope of preventing anarchy, Kerensky convened a democratic conference. It met in Petrograd on 27 September. Some 1,200 delegates attended, representing primarily the soviets, trade-unions, and local bodies. The propertied classes and the right-wing generally were excluded. The sessions were disrupted by bolshevik hectoring and barracking and several times Kerensky himself was shouted down. Most of the delegates recognized the dangers facing the country, but all trust and readiness to co-operate between the groups had vanished, and they could reach no clear decision concerning a coalition government. Kerensky nevertheless appointed a cabinet which the Petrograd soviet refused to recognize but which carried on for the time being.

The conference achieved one positive result in agreeing to set up a pre-parliament, called the Provisional Council of the Russian Republic or, as it was known, the council of the republic. It had 550 members of whom some 150, including 75 Kadets, were bourgeois representatives. It was to be a consultative body which would guide the government until the constituent assembly was finally convened. The parties chose their representatives with care to serve on the council. Sukhanov wrote that it was 'officially powerless, a concoction unworthy of the revolution and pathetic as an institution. But . . . its composition was exceptionally brilliant. It concentrated within itself, indeed, the flower of the nation.'[20]

The bolsheviks decided, much to the disgust of Lenin, to participate in this council and they were extremely active. Trotsky led the party in the council and of him Sukhanov wrote, 'He was quite different (from Lenin) and speaking generally quite unfitted to replace Lenin, but, I'm inclined to think, he was no less important a man, whom Lenin could not have replaced either, and without whom the forthcoming events could not have come about.'[21] But Trotsky was soon to lead the bolsheviks out of the council, and the remaining delegates lapsed into barren discussions, instead of considering the immediate practical problems facing the nation.

Throughout 1917 the bolshevik party had been growing in strength.

The 'July Days' and the denunciation of Lenin as a German agent had resulted in no more than a temporary set-back. Kornilov's abortive plot had brought a surge of support for the socialists and in particular for the bolsheviks. In May the party had some 80,000 members; in the following August Sverdlov reported to the sixth party congress that the number of party organizations had increased from 78 to 162 and that the total membership was estimated at 200,000. Most of the members were in the factories and among the troops. But even these figures showed how desperately small the party was in the country. Its membership represented only 5·4 per cent of the factory workers, averaged over 25 towns, and was but a small fraction of the total population.[22] They were still, compared with the mensheviks and the socialist revolutionaries, a minority but they were far better organized and, most important of all, they had exceptional leaders among whom Lenin was outstanding.

In hiding in Helsinki and then in Vyborg, Lenin had still made his influence felt. His views had dominated during the sixth party congress, held secretly in Petrograd from 26 July to 3 August, which had agreed that the revolutionary classes must seize power, but had not specified how and when this would happen. A number of delegates although they had voted for Lenin's new policy were still unwilling to discard the soviets. Many more believed that in accordance with orthodox Marxism they must accept a long spell of bourgeois government before the time could come for the socialist revolution. They had nevertheless voted unanimously for the new policy, expounded to the congress by Stalin, that the party must take on the role of 'front rank fighters against counter-revolution' and prepare, without being premature, for the ultimate seizure of power. They certainly did not realize that Lenin intended that the party should seize power and govern in the name of the revolutionary masses, or that he believed that the time was already ripe for insurrection.[23]

Still in hiding, Lenin was in a frenzy of impatience for action. He believed that the collapse of Kornilov's coup, amounting to the failure to create a dictatorship of the right, made a dictatorship of the left an immediate possibility. He wrote numerous pamphlets—'The Bolsheviks Must Take Power', 'The Crisis is Ripe', and 'Can the Bolsheviks Hold State Power?' and so on, and their titles reflected his urgent outlook at this time. He pressed tirelessly for immediate uprising. The party central committee, meeting on 28 September, had before it a demand from Lenin for the arrest of the government and the prompt seizure of power. But at this time the central committee and the party as a whole considered that they should aid the soviets to take power by taking part in the council of the republic. Lenin bitterly condemned this decision. The second all-Russian congress of soviets was to meet on 2 November and, fearing an upsurge of support for the old slogan 'All power to the Soviets', Lenin with all the polemical power and vehemence at his command fought for immediate insurrection independently of the soviets. In due course new elections would be held in which the bolsheviks would secure a majority, and then the new proletarian government would be responsible to the bolshevik-dominated soviets. But his demand now was that the party should grasp power and under his direction power once grasped could never be shared or surrendered.

Lenin did not sweep his own party, and still less others, off their feet so that they at once followed his lead. He had to struggle at every stage. He hammered home his arguments, repeating them tirelessly and wearing down opposition. On 20 October he slipped into Petrograd and was able to bring direct personal pressure to bear on the unconvinced party leaders. At a secret meeting on 23 October he won the support of the majority of the central committee for his resolution that 'an armed rising is inevitable and the time is perfectly ripe'.[24] Nine of the twenty-two members of this committee were absent from the meeting and of those present Zinoviev and Kamenev opposed the resolution. They incurred Lenin's scathing sarcasm and anger but they held to their views and even publicized them.[25]

Zinoviev and Kamenev both argued that the party should extend its influence by peaceful methods and that decisive action should wait until the constituent assembly had been convened. Many among even the senior members of the party shared the misgivings of Zinoviev and Kamenev. Lenin's demand for immediate insurrection seemed foolhardy. The July revolt had been chaotic. The Red Guard, although its strength had increased dramatically, consisted of armed but untrained workers. The Petrograd garrison was unruly and unpredictable. Even in organizations in which bolshevik influence was strong, there was no support for an uprising.

Lenin's plan involved a tremendous gamble, but it prevailed. He appealed to the masses by offering simple direct solutions to the three overriding questions of peace, bread, and land. But his real strength came from his fanaticism and his leadership, which contrasted with the inertia and muddle of the provisional government. He was positive and convincing as a leader and, while he did not succeed in rallying the masses about him, he won their sympathy to the extent that they would not fight against him and, least of all, on behalf of the government.

On 25 October the military revolutionary committee of the Petrograd soviet was set up under the chairmanship of Trotsky. This committee, which included representatives of the workers, soldiers, and sailors, was to co-ordinate and maintain control over all forces in the city and plan its defence. Operating through commissars and working under the supervision of individual bolsheviks, it more or less openly planned the insurrection.

Challenges to the authority of the provisional government became more blatant in the first days of November. The military revolutionary committee organized on 4 November the Day of the Petrograd Soviet. It brought on to the streets in a peaceful display the workers and soldiers of the city with the purpose both of giving them confidence in their numbers and of intimidating the government forces. It was a highly successful demonstration and Trotsky with his fiery eloquence inspired the masses with a new desperate enthusiasm.

Kerensky and his government were now provoked to action. On 5 November orders were given to close down the bolshevik newspapers, to arrest the bolshevik leaders who had participated in the 'July Days', and to charge members of the military revolutionary committee with criminal sedition. On the following morning the cruiser *Aurora*, anchored in the Neva River, her guns within range of the Winter Palace, was ordered to sea. The junkers, or military cadets, who together with small Cossack detachments formed the government's main military force, were joined at the Winter Palace by a newly formed battalion of women. Faced with these measures the military revolutionary committee acted immediately. It countermanded the orders to the *Aurora*, which remained at its Neva anchorage. It placed guards on the print-shops and the bolshevik newspapers were published after only a few hours delay.

Kerensky now appealed to the council of the republic for a vote of unconditional confidence. But while the council passed a resolution strongly critical of the bolsheviks it also demanded immediate action by the government to open peace negotiations and to announce land reforms. It passed no vote of confidence in Kerensky. And while the council of the republic debated resolutions, the bolshevik leaders at meetings in their headquarters from which Lenin himself was unaccountably absent were making the final plans for their uprising.

Early on the morning of 7 November the revolution began. Two main railway stations, the Nikolai and the Baltic, were occupied. The *Aurora* landed sailors who at once ejected the junkers guarding the Nikolai bridge. Action followed swiftly and smoothly. Detachments of its troops occupied the State Bank and the telephone exchanges, disconnecting all normal lines to the Winter Palace and the military staff. Patrols appeared at central points from which they covered prescribed areas. Troops surrounded the Marinsky Palace early in the afternoon and ejected the council of the republic, who recorded a protest but hurriedly dispersed.

Kerensky made frantic efforts to rally forces in defence of the provisional government. He had discussions with socialist revolutionary leaders and with the military staff, but it was clear that he could count on very little active support. Even the three Cossack regiments, opposed to the bolsheviks, were unwilling to risk their lives in defence of the government. Finally, in the hope that he might be able to rally loyal troops from the front, Kerensky requisitioned an American embassy car and slipping past the revolutionary patrols escaped from the city.

By afternoon the insurgents were in control of the whole of Petrograd, except for the Winter Palace. All had happened in an orderly, efficient manner and with few casualties, contrasting sharply with the confusion of the March revolution and the chaos of the 'July Days'. The military revolutionary committee had laid its plans carefully and, in fact, they had nothing to fear, for apart from a handful of junkers no one was prepared to fight for the government. Nevertheless the committee acted cautiously and did not order an assault on the Winter Palace until later in the afternoon.

At 6.30 p.m. an ultimatum was delivered to the staff of the Petrograd military district, demanding the surrender of the Winter Palace and threatening bombardment by the *Aurora* and other ships, if the demand was not met within twenty minutes. Hurried discussions took place among the ministers at the palace and in the staff. But then Red Guards occupied the staff building. Meanwhile the Winter Palace had not surrendered and the government by means of two direct telephones, unaffected by the seizure of the telephone exchange, anxiously contacted the city Duma and other anti-bolshevik bodies but no help resulted.

The military revolutionary committee then ordered armoured cars and troops to besiege the palace. The *Aurora* fired a blank round at 9 p.m. and this led to wild rifle and machine-gun fire, lasting for about half an hour. Then the women's battalion made a sortie in an attempt to rescue General Alekseev, who was rumoured to be still at the staff building. They were at once captured by the siege force. Several of the women were raped but none was badly injured.[26]

The guns of the Petropavlovsky fortress opened fire on the palace, but the gun crews were untrained and inexperienced and their erratic fire caused little damage. During the evening, however, Red Guards and soldiers entered the palace through the many side doors and special passages, seeking to disarm the junkers or to persuade them to give up their resistance, and they had some success. The capture of the palace had, in fact, become inevitable unless Kerensky by some miracle could bring up loyal troops from the front in time to defend it. Finally the ministers were cornered in one of the inner rooms of the vast palace and here they were arrested and taken to the Petropavlovsky dungeons. The capture of the Winter Palace had taken only a few hours and had cost the lives of five sailors and one soldier, and a few minor casualties.

Late on the same evening the second all-Russian congress of workers' and soldiers' deputies opened at the Smolny Institute. It was at once faced with the fact of the overthrow of the provisional government which the military revolutionary committee had already announced in a proclamation. In the congress the bolsheviks had some 390 deputies out of the total of 650 and the support of about 100 left socialist revolutionaries and so were in a dominant position. The congress gave formal approval to the bolshevik seizure of power, thus providing a legal authority for the creation of a new government and a new regime. Soon afterwards the mensheviks and the moderate socialist revolutionaries walked out, to be taunted by Trotsky as 'miserable bankrupts, your role is played out; go where you ought to be—into the dust-bin of history'.[27]

The deputies who had withdrawn from the congress had at once joined

E

with the members of the city Duma and other anti-bolshevik groups. They formed the committee for the Salvation of the Country and the Revolution, which became the main centre of opposition to the bolsheviks. They still enjoyed considerable freedom and they loudly condemned the uprising. From Kiev Kerensky sent an order which was published in the newspaper *Volya Naroda* (*The Will of the People*) that servants of the state must remain at their posts until the provisional government issued further instructions. But such orders and condemnations were futile while power vested more and more securely in the hands of the bolsheviks.

The committee for salvation was, however, able to obstruct the seizure and final transfer of power in some small degree. It proclaimed itself to be the successor to the provisional government, and instituted a campaign of passive resistance by officials. But shops, restaurants, and theatres remained open and trams ran. The people of Petrograd were unsure what was happening. Rumours spread, adding to the confusion. Many believed that Kerensky was advancing on the city with an army from the front. The bolshevik venture seemed unlikely to last. But the military revolutionary committee, still operating with speed and efficiency, was spreading its control over the city.

Lenin had remained out of sight on 7 November and, indeed, throughout the days leading up to the uprising. He had been the grand strategist, but had apparently taken little, if any, part in organizing and leading the insurrection. When on 8 November, however, he appeared at the session of the soviet congress, he was acknowledged as leader in a cheering ovation.

Meanwhile Petrograd was far from secure in the hands of the bolsheviks. Kerensky had managed to muster from the front only a force of 700 Cossacks. Led by General Peter Krasnov, however, they captured Tsarskoe Selo on 10 November, while the garrison of 16,000 looked on passively, unwilling to fight for either side. Krasnov and his Cossacks now threatened the capital. On the evening of the same day the committee of salvation and the junkers started an anti-bolshevik uprising within the city. At this point a few units from the front, advancing in support of Krasnov and the junkers would have enabled them to take the city and to displace the bolsheviks. But no reinforcements came. The junkers' uprising in the city collapsed. On 12 November Krasnov launched his small force against the Red Guards on Pulkovo heights, just outside the city. This time the Red troops fought with a will and the Cossacks, hopelessly outnumbered, running low in ammunition, and threatened with encirclement, retreated to Gatchina. There, isolated and subjected to bolshevik propaganda, the Cossacks quickly lost the will to fight on and the unit disintegrated.

In Petrograd at this same time a strong movement had developed in support of the creation of an all-socialist government. Many people, especially in the trade union movement, had long favoured such a solution. Several members of the bolshevik party, who had opposed Lenin in this seizure of power, also welcomed the proposals for a broadly based socialist regime. On 11 November the railways workers' union, Vikzhel, convened a conference of representatives of all socialist parties, of the committee of salvation, and of certain other trade unions to discuss this proposition. But hopes of a practical result faded as the long-winded discussions dragged on, and they were further depressed by bolshevik successes elsewhere in the country.

Kerensky had accompanied Krasnov in these operations and the bolsheviks were eager to capture him. At Gatchina one of the three directors of the bolshevik war commissariat, ostensibly there to negotiate an armistice, made a deal with the Cossacks, promising as a ruse that, if they would surrender Kerensky, neither Lenin nor Trotsky would be allowed to serve in the new government. Warned of the danger of capture, Kerensky managed to disguise himself in the uniform of a sailor or a Serbian soldier and with a false passport and visa issued by Bruce Lockhart, a young British agent, he made his way to Murmansk and escaped.[28] He had tried to lead the nation back from the abyss of revolution and violence and had failed, but he had tried boldly, courageously, and humanely.

The bolshevik capture of Petrograd had been swift and almost bloodless, and this pattern was followed throughout most of the country. Bolshevik-dominated soviets took over other cities. Cossacks of the Don, the Kuban, and Orenburg regions, the mensheviks in Georgia, and Ukrainian nationalists in Kiev, effectively resisted bolshevik attempts to seize control. Elsewhere they succeeded almost without fighting.

Moscow was the exception. Lenin had expected that Moscow would succumb readily and that Petrograd would be the scene of a great and bloody struggle for power: the opposite happened. In Moscow the bolsheviks and other socialists had co-operated more readily than in Petrograd and support for a coalition administration had been very strong. But all hope of compromise had suddenly vanished when the Moscow soviet adopted a bolshevik resolution to appoint a military revolutionary committee. On the same day the city Duma created a committee of public safety.

During 8 and 9 November the two committees prepared for the impending crash. Bolshevik forces were estimated at fifty-thousand soldiers and armed workers, and the committee of public safety had some ten thousand junkers, officers, armed students, and volunteers, but they were better trained and more effectively led. The bolsheviks had won over the soldiers in the Kremlin which was the important strategic stronghold and of added value for its arsenal. But patrols of junkers guarded every entrance to the Kremlin preventing the supply of arms and ammunition from the arsenal to the Red Guards and other supporters.

On the evening of 9 November the commander of the Moscow district,

Colonel Ryabtsev, sent an ultimatum by telephone to the military revolutionary committee calling on it to disperse and demanding the evacuation of the Kremlin, the post office, and certain other public buildings. He threatened to destroy the soviet's headquarters in Tverskaya Street with artillery fire if they rejected or ignored his demands.

In the event Ryabtsev did not open fire on the soviet headquarters. His troops nevertheless went into action with considerable success on 9 and 10 November. Junkers captured the post office and the main telegraph and telephone exchanges and certain of the city's railway stations. Ryabtsev then spoke by phone with Berzin, the bolshevik commandant of the Kremlin, telling him that the uprising had been put down and demanding the surrender of the Kremlin. Berzin deprived of communications, knew nothing of the conditions in the city and the morale of his troops was low. He therefore agreed to surrender on the condition that the safety of his troops was guaranteed. But on occupying the Kremlin infuriated officers and junkers ignored their undertaking and shot a number of soldiers. It was an indication of the bitterness which both sides felt and it was to lead to worse violence.

Moscow was now divided between the two forces. Broadly the division was between the working class districts held by the military revolutionary committee, and the central parts containing the government offices, the university, and the main shops, held by the junkers. For a week sporadic fighting took place in the streets with neither side gaining any real advantage. The junkers patrolled in armoured cars while the Red Guards dug trenches and sent snipers into the rear of their enemy where they made effective use of their rifles and hand-grenades. But gradually the superior numbers of the Red Guards began to tell against the junkers. On 11 November the Red Guard drove them from Tverskaya Street. At this time, however, the two sides were still skirmishing and each confidently awaited the arrival of reinforcements from the front.

On 12 November the railways workers' union managed to arrange an armistice. The terms agreed by both sides were that the military revolutionary committee and the committee of public safety would dissolve, making way for the formation of a government of representatives of the soviet, the Duma, and other kindred organizations. This was the same demand for an all-socialist regime which the mass of the people had supported in Petrograd. But the time was past when moderate or compromise solutions were possible, the conflict was now between violent extremes.

The armistice was only partially observed. The military revolutionary committee felt the tide turning in its favour, especially after receiving news that Red Guard detachments were moving up to the city from nearby industrial towns, and even from Tula and Minsk, to support them. The bolsheviks then denounced the armistice and on 13 November fighting broke out afresh and with a new bitterness. The junkers were now beaten back and their feeling, that they were fighting alone in the vastness of Russia, added to their sense of the hopelessness of their position. The Reds brought up artillery and bombarded the Kremlin. Many bolsheviks distressed by this destruction of the heart of the ancient capital protested, and Lunarcharsky resigned as commissar of education, but the reports of damage were exaggerated. This artillery fire to which they were unable to reply further depressed junker morale.

On the morning of 15 November Red Guards stormed the Kremlin, blowing open its great gates and crushing the exhausted junker forces. Bolsheviks, held captive since Berzin's surrender to Ryabtsev, were now released and at once beat to death a colonel and several junkers whom they accused of shooting their comrades. Later on the same morning the committee of public safety sued for peace and the military revolutionary committee agreed to an armistice. It was an uneasy armistice. Violent fighting broke out during the afternoon, resulting in many casualties. But at 5 p.m. a treaty of peace was signed. The committee of public safety was disbanded and all officers and junkers surrendered their arms but their safety was guaranteed. This was followed by a solemn demonstration of workers and soldiers in the Red Square as the 500 Red Guards killed in the struggle were buried in a common grave by the Kremlin wall. The officers and junkers buried their dead privately and quietly elsewhere.

Of the few remaining centres of opposition the Stavka at Mogilev, which was near the capital, worried the bolsheviks most. General N. N. Dukhonin was, in fact, the commander-in-chief of the Russian army at this time, for Kerensky's assumption of this office had never been more than a formality. Dukhonin had refused to recognize the council of people's commissars. He had ordered troops to proceed to Petrograd in response to appeals from the provisional government, but his orders had not been obeyed. He had sent a telegram to the bolsheviks demanding their unconditional surrender to the government, but he now recognized that he could not enforce this demand by sending troops and, indeed, he gave orders that all troop movements to Petrograd should be stopped.

On the night of 20 November the new soviet government instructed Dukhonin to propose an armistice with the Central Powers for the discussion of peace terms. He was to keep the government informed about the negotiations and was to sign the armistice only with their express approval. Two days later Lenin, Trotsky, and Ensign Nicholas Krilenko, an active revolutionary and one of the committee of three in Sovnarkom responsible for military and naval affairs, each spoke by telephone with Dukhonin, demanding that he start peace discussions. He prevaricated but finally refused to carry out these instructions. He was summarily dismissed but ordered to remain at the Stavka until the government's representative arrived.

At this point Dukhonin might have made his escape, but he dutifully waited to hand over his office. The situation confused him. A patriot and a military man, he did not understand the political situation or where his loyalties lay. A number of socialist revolutionaries, mensheviks, and liberals had gathered in Mogilev and from them and others he received plentiful but useless advice. The Allied Military Missions, attached to the Stavka, addressed a note to him on the inter-Allied agreement by which each party had undertaken not to make a separate peace or armistice, and warning him of the serious consequences if Russia defaulted. Dukhonin reported the note to Petrograd, and Trotsky responded angrily with the charge that the military representatives of the Allies were interfering in Russian internal affairs and seeking to promote civil war; he declared, furthermore, that the council of people's commissars was not bound by tsarist treaties.

Meanwhile, on 23 November, Ensign Krilenko with an escort of sailors had set out from Petrograd for Mogilev. At Pskov and Dvinsk he halted to remove generals from their commands or receive their submission and to ensure that the troops supported the new regime. He had no great difficulty since the armies on the Northern and Western Fronts were already strongly pro-bolshevik. The Allied Military Missions left Mogilev on 1 December for Kiev. The few remaining anti-bolshevik units departed at about the same time. Dukhonin remained.

On 3 December Krilenko reached Mogilev. Dukhonin under arrest was taken to his carriage at the railway station to hand over his command. Soldiers, sailors, and peasants crowded on to the platform demanding his execution and they wanted to lynch him on the spot. Krilenko spoke out against such summary action. The mob dispersed but after Krilenko had departed for the Stavka the crowd, led by sailors, set upon Dukhonin and pulling him out of the carriage beat him to death.

In the few weeks since 7 November, the bolsheviks had gained control of the vast territory of European Russia, except for pockets of resistance in the Cossack lands, in western Ukraine, and in Georgia. Their control was weak and might easily have proved shortlived. The bolsheviks numbered only some 300,000 of the total population of 150 million. But the people had completely lost confidence in the provisional government and, although passively, they supported the bolsheviks, because they promised bread, peace, and land. Few understood the policies and objectives of the bolshevik party. They were concerned only with the immediate promises and having no real alternative they waited to see what this small body of active and purposeful men would achieve.

None realized more acutely than Lenin that the power he had grasped was precarious. On every side his regime was threatened and it seemed impossible that it could survive. Inspired by a driving purpose, however, he and his colleagues set about the tremendous task of destroying the old order and creating a new system which, they believed, would lead to communism in which even the most humble would find equality and justice.

CHAPTER EIGHT

The New Regime

FOR Lenin the seizure of power was merely the first step. The revolution had overthrown the bourgeois class and now the proletariat must 'destroy the machinery of government and the whole state apparatus, replacing it with new machinery, consisting of armed workers'.[1] Then the bolshevik party as the leading force in this period, known as 'the dictatorship of the proletariat', must set about transforming society until socialism was achieved.

This transformation would develop in stages. In the early stage the nationalization of factories, banks, and land, and the ending of all exploitation of labour would be introduced, but some private production might still be allowed. This would cease when all industrial and agricultural production had been socialized and true socialism achieved.

The advance from socialism to communism would spread over a far longer period. When men had learnt to govern themselves and to give of their best to society without thought of gain; when they had forged a productive economy which met the needs of all, communism would have been realized. The state which was nothing more than the organized coercive instrument of the ruling class would then be unnecessary and would 'atrophy' or 'wither away', and the dictatorship of the proletariat, having served its purpose, would end.

In *The State and Revolution* Lenin set out concisely the steps to be taken to overthrow capitalist society and to create the new order. This pamphlet, begun in Zürich early in 1917 and published in Russia in November of that year, was to prove the most influential of his writings and to become the Koran of the communists. But, while working on this blueprint, he had not lost sight of the practical problems. No man understood the realities of power better than Lenin. He knew that he must at once secure the position of the party by gaining stronger popular support for it especially among the peasant masses, and that to do this he must carry out his promises of land and peace.

In a fury of impatience Lenin began to tackle the tasks of destroying the old and creating the new, while simultaneously winning popular support. He was a man in a hurry, exulting in the opportunity that he had at last to put into practice the theories which he had for so long cherished as scientific facts. It was as though he had during the past twenty-five years of conspiring, thinking, and writing, stored up incredible energies, and now at the age of forty-seven he craved action.

The second all-Russian congress of soviets meeting late on the evening of 7 November had given majority approval to the bolshevik seizure of power and, taking this as the legal basis of the new regime, Lenin at once set about selecting a cabinet which was appointed by decree of the congress.[2] The council of people's commissars (*Soviet Narodnikh Komissarov*) or Sovnarkom for short, as the new cabinet was called, was composed exclusively of bolsheviks. The left socialist revolutionaries who now formed a separate party had refused to participate in it unless it represented a coalition of all socialist parties, and Lenin had rejected this condition. Of the fifteen commissars three—Lenin as president of the council, Trotsky as commissar for foreign affairs, and Lunacharsky as commissar for the people's education—received a hearty ovation from the assembled deputies. The others, including the Georgian, J. V. Dzhugashvili (Stalin), the commissar for nationalities, were little known and all, except for Stalin, were soon to fade from the scene.

After approving the cabinet, the congress elected a central executive committee to which it delegated legislative authority to be exercised when the congress itself was not in session. This executive committee was at first composed of 101 members, of whom 62 were bolsheviks, 29 were left socialist revolutionaries, and 10 represented other parties. Executive authority was vested in Sovnarkom but it was soon wielding both executive and legislative functions.

For his appearance before the congress on 8 November Lenin prepared himself carefully. Trotsky presented him to the deputies, who gave him 'a tumultuous welcome'.[3] Lenin then read a proclamation addressed to the peoples and governments of all nations at war, proposing immediate peace without annexations and without indemnities. He announced the end of secret diplomacy and the intention of the soviet government to publish all secret treaties entered into by the tsarist regime. He then proposed a three-month armistice. He concluded with an appeal to the workers of England, France, and Germany to join the struggle for peace and the liberation of the exploited working masses.[4]

Lenin next read a short decree abolishing private ownership of land 'immediately and without purchase'. The administration of all private and church lands was placed in the hands of land committees and soviets of peasants' deputies. This nakaz prohibited the purchase, sale, lease, and mortgage of land, and the hiring of labour, and provided for distribution of all land to those who cultivated it by their own labour.[5]

The bolsheviks had always called for 'nationalization' of the land, as distinct from 'municipalization' proposed by the mensheviks. In August 1917 at the sixth party congress they had confirmed this policy. Immediately on seizing power, however, Lenin had abandoned nationalization in favour of the policy of the socialist revolutionaries. He knew that nationalization would have no attraction for the peasants, and it was to gain their support that, as he later acknowledged freely,[6] he adopted the policy of his rivals. But this change of policy was not simply an act of expediency. He had come to recognize that the revolution could not survive without the support of the peasants who made up more than eighty per cent of the population. The goal of the first stage of the revolution must be a 'democratic dictatorship of workers and peasants'.

Lenin also wanted the formal support of the socialist revolutionaries who dominated the all-Russian congress of peasant's deputies, which was to meet later in November. The second congress of soviets, from which the new government derived its authority, represented only workers and soldiers, and Lenin was anxious to win the backing of the peasants' congress. In this he was successful. On 25 November after heated debate, the peasants' congress, from which the more conservative delegates withdrew, agreed to merge with the congress of workers' and soldiers' soviets. The peasants' congress elected 108 delegates to the central executive committee and subsequently the left socialist revolutionaries accepted three places in the Sovnarkom.[7]

Lenin had thus managed to base his government broadly on the three classes of the workers, the peasants, and the soldiers. But there was considerable uneasiness within both the government and the bolshevik party. A moderate element in the council of people's commissars and in the central committee of the party continued to support the idea of an all-socialist government and at the same time grew more and more critical of Lenin's ruthless tactics and cynical expedients. Finally, five of the twelve commissars and five members of the small party central committee resigned. Far from regarding this as a crisis, however, Lenin was pleased to be relieved of these 'soft' comrades, and they were quickly forgotten in the turmoil of the period.[8]

At this time cabinet meetings of the people's commissars took place almost daily under Lenin's chairmanship and usually lasted five or six hours. Projects were submitted without warning or preparation, and each speaker was allowed only ten minutes. Lenin himself usually drafted the essence of the decrees which deluged from these meetings. Some of these decrees were no more than declarations; some dealt with petty matters, such as the extension of the borders of certain minor towns, or the formal taking-over of the Petrograd telephone exchange; but many decrees summarily introduced major changes.

A decree signed on 15 November by Stalin and Lenin proclaimed the right of the peoples of Russia to free self-determination.[9] The principle of egalitarianism was enforced. All titles and legal class divisions were abolished in civil life and in the army. Decrees of 29 and 30 December proclaimed the 'eradication of every inequality in the army', and established the principle that soldiers should choose their own officers and commanders and should elect committees to exercise supervisory control.[10]

Two decrees annulled the strict marriage and divorce laws of tsarist days. The full legal equality of men and women was emphasized. Divorce was to be granted on the request of either party to a marriage. Only civil marriage had validity in law. Illegitimate children were to have the same rights as legitimate.

This legislation and the decrees that followed were a commendable attempt to break completely with the primitive and poverty-stricken past in Russia in which women had been maltreated inferiors and child labour had been exploited. For many, however, Marxist insistence on the complete equality of the sexes led to extremes. Some argued that the family was a bourgeois institution which could have no place in communist society. Others held that free love was a natural consequence of the equality of the sexes. But the bolsheviks on the whole and Lenin in particular rejected such extremes. In 1915 Inessa Armand, the fervent young bolshevik and friend of Lenin, wrote a pamphlet on the demands of women and included 'the demand for free love'. Lenin objected strongly that this was not a proletarian but a bourgeois idea. Any form of licence and especially sexual licence, was repugnant to the austere, disciplined, bolshevik leader, and his standards, often puritanical, were shared by the majority of the party leaders.[11]

Private property was the subject of numerous decrees. Large houses were transferred to the ownership of town soviets or councils. Industry was nationalized gradually at this stage. A supreme council of national economy, responsible for organizing the national economy and state finances, had the power to confiscate such industrial enterprises as it considered necessary, in particular any which refused to submit to workers' control were taken over by the state. The eight-hour day became law at once. The decree on workers' control followed, giving workers in all industries a major share in management through their elected committee. This was in accordance with the dictatorship of the proletariat and also, as explained in *The State and Revolution,* designed to enable members of the proletariat to become proficient in every branch of management and administration.[12] All banks were nationalized and absorbed by the state bank.[13] On 10 February 1918 all debts incurred by the tsarist government were repudiated with some compensation for the smaller investors, but in the case of foreign debts the repudiation was absolute.[14]

A decree of 7 December swept away the tsarist legal system. Two new types of courts—the ordinary local courts and the revolutionary tribunals —were created.[15] The ordinary courts dealt with civil and criminal cases; the revolutionary tribunals had special jurisdiction in matters of counter-revolution and sabotage. In fact, Lenin had already seen the need not only for such tribunals but also for a central police organization with extraordinary powers to deal with subversion and the enemies of the regime. In December he entrusted to Felix Dzerzhinsky, an idealistic Pole who saw it as his duty to be merciless in defence of the revolution, the task of developing the new all-Russian extraordinary commission to fight counter-revolution and sabotage.[16] Dzerzhinsky organized the commission effectively and under its shortened name of Cheka it became a ruthless and dreaded secret arm of the regime, more feared than the tsarist third chancellery had been.

No part of Russian life escaped from this flood of decrees and innovations. The Russian alphabet was pruned of several archaic letters, the first change in the alphabet since Peter the Great's reform more than 200 years earlier. As from 1 February, the Gregorian calendar in use in the West was introduced in place of the Julian calendar which was thirteen days behind in the twentieth century.[17] A decree, promulgated on 5 February, effected the complete separation of church and state. Every soviet citizen was to be free to profess any religion or to be an atheist. Religious instruction was eliminated from all schools, but citizens could give or receive religious instruction privately.[18]

This displacing of the church from its traditional position in the life of the nation did not cause widespread distress. Suddenly and effortlessly the Russian people as a whole had disburdened themselves of the accumulated paraphernalia of Orthodoxy. The church had been indissolubly bound up in their minds with the tsarist throne and, when the latter had collapsed, the hold of Orthodoxy was suddenly very frail. Large groups of devout Christians remained, numbering hundreds of thousands and even several millions, according to various estimates. Never again, however, was the church to be able to count the whole population, with the exception only of Jewish, Moslem, and certain other minorities, as its flock. The Orthodox had become a minority. Gradually Marxism was to become the faith of the majority. Its message, that men must work and struggle now to create paradise on earth rather than suffer meekly for a promised heaven after death, seemed to offer a more positive creed for men surrounded by the ruins of the old order. Marxism was, the bolsheviks argued, the faith of a new dynamic society and it became the new Orthodoxy.

The winter of 1917–18 was grim, especially in Moscow and Petrograd. Food and fuel shortages had become more acute. Inflation had galloped under the provisional government and continued under the new regime, cancelling out savings, and wages, the sole source of income, were inadequate. The soviet leaders were noted for their austere living, but the fact that Lenin and the commissars shared their hardships did not make them easier to endure. Violence and crime became commonplace and no police existed to combat them. The local units of the workers' militia and the patrols of Red Guards were unable to keep order. Gangs of soldiers from the Petrograd garrison took to breaking into wine cellars and drinking themselves into a stupor. So frequent were these incidents that a special commissar had to be appointed in Petrograd with detachments of troops, charged with destroying stocks of wine and clearing the city of hooligans and drunkenness. This measure had some success in the capital but elsewhere lawlessness of every kind continued.

Mingled with the brutality and bestiality of the people, especially in Petrograd, were a desperate faith and a vision of change. For them the revolution was the beginning of labour in the birth of a tremendous new world. Alexander Blok captured this furious spirit in his symbolical poem of the revolution, *The Twelve*. Written on one night in January 1918, this poem was at once acclaimed and repeatedly recited to wildly enthusiastic crowds who felt in it the expression of their own feverish hope.

Throughout these hectic days of change all but the bolsheviks pinned their hopes on the constituent assembly. Since the overthrow of the tsarist regime in March 1917 the people had accepted that their constitution would be finally decided by this freely elected assembly. But the bolsheviks who had clamoured loudest for the elections were now in power, and they did not propose to give way to any elected body. Lenin went so far as to claim that the soviets representing workers, peasants, and soldiers, were a form of democracy superior to any body elected by universal suffrage.[19]

Lenin was now opposed to holding the elections which the provisional government had before its fall appointed to take place on 25 November. His colleagues considered that in their precarious position they could not fly in the face of popular demand and overruled him. They agreed, that the elections should take place and that the assembly should meet, but they were determined to dissolve it with bayonets if it showed any sign of independence. In the event the bolshevik fears were more than justified for they polled just under twenty-five per cent of the votes cast. Half the country voted for socialism, but against bolshevism. The bolsheviks nevertheless had majorities in the industrial centres and polled about half the votes in the army, and these centres of support, backed by rifles, were conveniently close to Petrograd and Moscow.

On 18 January 1918 the constituent assembly met for the first time. Sverdlov, pushing aside the socialist revolutionary president, read a declaration inviting the assembly to endorse the decrees passed by the second soviet congress. But the assembly rejected this declaration by 237 votes to 136. The bolsheviks and socialist revolutionaries withdrew. When on the following day the deputies returned to resume the adjourned session they found Red Guards barring their entrance to the Tauride Palace. A demonstration, unarmed on the insistence of the socialist revolutionary leader, Chernov, against this outrageous dispersal of the elected assembly, was dispersed by the rifle-fire of Red Guards.

On the same day the soviet executive committee issued a decree, endorsing the bolshevik action on the ground that the assembly was of help 'only to the bourgeois counter-revolution in its efforts to crush the power of the Soviets'.[20] In the last week of January the third all-Russian congress of soviets, elected by a carefully rigged ballot, approved almost unanimously the policy of bolsheviks and left socialist revolutionaries towards the assembly.[21] It seemed that the greater the deception and mendacity the greater was the need for a cover of legality.

The major challenge facing Lenin and his party during these first weeks in power was, however, the need to negotiate peace. The future of the bolshevik regime depended upon it. Lenin in particular recognized that the support he had among the troops and among the people generally was passive and conditional upon his bringing them peace. But peace with the Central Powers raised complex problems.

Lenin had consistently spoken of a general European peace based on the dictatorship of the proletariat. His peace proposals, he argued, would provoke revolutions in the capitalist countries and a 'revolutionary war' would follow. The proclamation 'to all warring peoples and their governments'[22] which he had read out to the soviet congress on 8 November and which the deputies had adopted unanimously had been an expression of this policy. But his appeals were based on total misunderstanding of the peoples and conditions in the West, and met with no response whatsoever.

The German supreme command, who were concerned with facts rather than theories, welcomed bolshevik peace moves. They knew that the soviet government was in no position to wage a revolutionary war, and would have to accept German terms. They recognized, too, that they would gain most from a separate peace. Germany was feeling the strain of the war. The Kiel mutiny in July 1917 had been a symptom of exhaustion and general unrest. Ludendorf knew that Germany's only hope of victory now lay in a crushing advance in the West, and for this he needed the troops tied down on the Eastern front.

Discussions for the armistice began on 3 December at Brest-Litovsk, the Polish city, which the Russians had burnt to the ground at the time of their retreat in July 1916, and which served as the German general headquarters in the East. Adolf Joffe, a bearded revolutionary intellectual, led the bolshevik delegation. It was an ill-assorted group which included representatives of workers, peasants, soldiers, and sailors in whose name the revolution had been made and who were to find themselves utterly bewildered by the negotiations. The delegations of the Central Powers were led chiefly by the German foreign minister, von Kuhlmann, by the Austrian foreign minister, Count Ottokar Czernin, and by Major-General Max Hoffmann, the extremely able Prussian who was, in effect, the commander-in-chief in the East.

The bolshevik delegation had come to Brest-Litovsk not only to negotiate an armistice but also to make the fullest use of the occasion for propaganda. Lenin and other members still cherished the mistaken idea that the proletarian masses of all warring nations would respond to their peace appeals. Agreement on the armistice was readily reached, for the Germans did not seek at this stage to impose humiliating terms, and the armistice was signed on 15 December.

The first session of the peace conference opened in Brest-Litovsk on 22 December. It was to prove a strange, unreal conference which threatened to drag on interminably. The Germans observed a strict protocol, giving precedence to the representatives of the vanquished, eating their meals with them, and maintaining an elaborate façade of courtesy. The Russians were defenceless but played cleverly for time. The Germans were in a position to dictate terms, but Kuhlmann wanted an agreed, not an imposed peace. He realized that terms imposed by brute force would have a damaging impact on opinion among Germany's allies as well as on world opinion. But ranged against him were Hindenburg and Ludendorf who thought only of military might. They were, moreover, impatient for peace so that they could move the divisions on the Eastern Front into the great spring offensive in France.

Joffe, leading the Russian delegation, submitted six proposals as the basis for a treaty. The proposals included, of course, the formula of 'no annexations and no indemnities', as well as guarantees of self-determination for nationalities and the protection of minorities. Kuhlmann made a non-committal reply, stating that the Quadruple Alliance was ready to sign without delay a general peace without forcible annexations and without payments in respect of war expenditures. But he added that the Russian terms could only form the basis of a peace if all the powers engaged in war accepted them. Joffe then moved that the negotiations be suspended for ten days to allow other belligerents to participate.

At this point Joffe and his delegation believed that their proposals had been accepted. But on 26 December Hoffmann left Joffe in no doubt that Germany would not release the territories which she had conquered and still occupied. The Russians waxed indignant and even spoke of withdrawing from further discussions. Hoffmann was not disturbed by this threat, however, for he knew, as he recorded in his war diaries, that 'there was no question of negotiations being broken off; the only chance the Bolsheviks had of remaining in power was by signing peace. They were obliged to accept the conditions of the Central Powers, however hard they might be . . .'[23]

Negotiations were resumed on 9 January 1918, but now Trotsky headed the soviet delegation. He put an end to the charade of old-world courtesy which had been followed and kept his delegates apart from their opponents, forbidding them to eat together. He disciplined the bolsheviks and made it clear that the negotiations were but another stage in the struggle of the proletariat.

The Ukrainian Rada, set up by anti-bolshevik nationalists in the western Ukraine, was now represented at Brest-Litovsk. The Central Powers hoped to gain special advantages, political and economic, from a separate peace with the Rada. Trotsky argued forcibly for the withdrawal of German troops from occupied territories and proclaimed the rights of all peoples to free expression of their will by referendum. He condemned the use of armed force and the suppression of democratic choice so vehemently that Hoffmann, when he came to speak, was brutally frank, stating that the soviet government itself was 'based purely on violence, ruthlessly suppressing all who think differently'.[24] He bluntly refused to consider withdrawal of German troops from Courland, Lithuania, or other territories.

Trotsky was magnificent during these negotiations and often dominated them. His country in chaos, its army demoralized, and the new revolutionary government barely in power, he was negotiating from a position of desperate weakness against professional diplomats who had behind them a powerful and victorious army. But he consistently and successfully challenged his opponents. He was at his best in an impossible position. His eyes flashed and he seared his enemies with his bitter scorn, and his intellectual brilliance often reduced their arguments to shreds. He knew, as Kuhlmann and Hoffmann knew, however, that no argumentation could dispose of German armed might. Trotsky anxiously played for time. Like Lenin he, too, was apparently expecting at any minute to learn that proletarian revolutions had destroyed the Hapsburg and Hohenzollern empires, and indeed war-exhaustion and the threat of famine had produced crises in the countries of the Central Powers, especially Austro-Hungary.

Kuhlmann and Hoffmann knew that Trotsky would drag out the discussions as long as he could, and Hoffmann became more and more impatient as the time for the spring offensive on the Western Front drew closer. Suddenly on 18 January Hoffmann produced a map of eastern Europe which he laid on the table in front of Trotsky. He pointed to the new frontier marked by a blue line which deprived Russia of her Polish territories, of Lithuania and western Latvia, and of her Baltic islands. South of Brest-Litovsk, Hoffmann explained, the frontier would depend on the outcome of negotiations with the Ukrainian Rada.

This was an ultimatum. Trotsky threatened to break off negotiations but finally agreed to an adjournment until 29 January. He had received instructions in a telegram signed 'Lenin Stalin' to return to Petrograd to discuss the German proposals. Leaving Brest-Litovsk on 18 January, he reached the capital in time for the bolshevik dissolution of the constituent assembly. It was an act which damaged soviet prestige among socialists abroad, and it also weakened Trotsky's case in Brest-Litovsk. The Central Powers had believed that the assembly would rally Russian patriotic forces who would then attempt to continue the war. Dissolution of the assembly meant to them that this danger had passed and that the soviet government, having seized power by force, must now end the war on any terms. Moreover, the forcible dissolution had deprived the bolsheviks of any moral basis for their arguments; they could no longer hurl accusations that the Germans relied on brute force and denied the people in occupied territories their democratic rights.

At this time Trotsky adopted a new formula for winning an advantageous peace which would, he believed, appeal to the proletariat of Europe and embarrass the Germans. This was his formula of 'no peace—no war', whereby the soviet government would announce an end of the war and demobilization of the Russian armies, but would refuse to sign any peace with the Central Powers. He believed, moreover, that the Germans would have difficulty in attacking and that if they advanced the Russians could then sign peace at the bayonet point. He had explained this new approach in letters sent to Lenin from Brest-Litovsk and now in Petrograd he argued forcefully in support of it. But Lenin was far from convinced. Unlike Trotsky he no longer believed that revolution was imminent in Germany. 'We cannot put our trust in the German proletariat, he argued. 'Germany is only pregnant with revolution. The second month must not be mistaken for the ninth. But here in Russia we have a healthy lusty child. We may kill it, if we start a war.'[25] He knew that Russia could not fight and had to accept the German terms. He feared that Trotsky's formula would result in Hoffmann ordering his armies to march and that realizing how helpless the soviet government was, he would impose even harsher terms. This might end with the bolsheviks being ejected from power, and that danger was paramount in his mind.

In Petrograd arguments over the peace terms were bitter and intense at this time. Bukharin had some support for his demand to break off negotiations and wage 'revolutionary war'. Lenin and Trotsky both dismissed this as foolishness, since they knew that they had no troops or means of fighting. Lenin explained tirelessly and with a realistic grasp of the facts that they must accept the annexation peace. Trotsky propounded his formula of 'no peace—no war'. But in an informal debate on 21 January, Lenin's policy received only 15 votes, while Trotsky gained 16, and Bukharin 32 votes. On the following day, however, the central committee of the party voted by 12 to 1 in favour of Lenin's policy of prolonging the negotiations and finally accepting the German terms, by 11 votes to 2 against Bukharin's proposals, and by 9 votes to 7 accepted Trotsky's formula. The intention was that at Brest-Litovsk Trotsky should play for time and when faced with a showdown should apply his formula of 'no peace—no war'.

As he prepared to return to Brest-Litovsk, Trotsky was confident that he would win what he called 'an honest democratic peace' and that if he failed he would have derived important propaganda advantage from the negotiations.[26] On the night of 26 January he addressed the third congress of soviets, which met in Petrograd from 23 to 31 January, and again he expressed his belief that if the German high command ordered a new advance into Russia the German troops would refuse to obey.[27] He still clung irrationally to this idea that the German people were ready to revolt and to follow in the steps of the Russians. 'The Germans would not dare to advance on Petrograd,' he said in Brest-Litovsk. 'It would cause revolution in Germany.'[28] Strikes in Germany and Austro-Hungary and the setting-up of soviets in Berlin and other major German towns where they were ruthlessly suppressed, encouraged him in this belief.

The German delegation returned to Brest-Litovsk, determined to break the stalemate into which the negotiations had drifted. Kuhlmann, the German foreign minister, had to keep in mind the vehement demands of Hindenburg and Ludendorf for immediate peace and the annexation of the territories occupied by German troops. But he was even more anxious to gain these ends by negotiation and not by open brute force, which would antagonize opinion not only in the Entente countries but in Austro-Hungary, especially at this time when President Wilson's 'Fourteen Points' were being debated. Kuhlmann's tactics were to negotiate a separate peace with the Ukrainian Rada which would, he hoped, lead Trotsky to agree to break the stalemate.

The conference resumed in Brest-Litovsk on 29 January and Trotsky at once refused to recognize any separate Ukrainian peace. He informed Kuhlmann and his delegations of the advance of the Red Guard on Kiev where nearly all the garrison had already sworn allegiance to the soviet government. He questioned whether the delegation of the Rada could claim to represent territory greater than the rooms they occupied by Brest-Litovsk. The treaty of peace with the Ukraine was, however, of special importance not only as part of Kuhlmann's tactics but also because Germany needed Ukrainian grain and other foodstuffs. The treaty with the Rada, the first peace of the war, was signed with special ceremony on 9 February. The negotiations then developed into a debate between Trotsky and Kuhlmann on the application of self-determination in the territories under German occupation. It was a debate in which neither side was prepared to concede a point. Kuhlmann felt, however, that he was gradually bringing Trotsky nearer to agreement. But behind him Hoffmann, and at the supreme headquarters Hindenburg and Ludendorf fumed with impatience over this criminal waste of time.

The conference was now reaching a crisis, and at this point Trotsky decided to make his dramatic statement which would bring it to an end. It was the kind of statement, almost theatrical, which he enjoyed making and from which he derived the maximum effect. On the afternoon of 10 February he addressed the conference. He began with a scathing indictment of imperialism, which the delegates, having heard it several times before, took to be a face-saving preliminary to acceptance of the German terms. But then he continued:

'We are removing our armies and our people from the war. Our peasant soldiers must return to their land to cultivate in peace the fields which the Revolution has taken from the landlord and given to the peasants . . .

'We are going out of the war. We inform all peoples and their governments of this fact. We are giving the order for a general demobilization of all our armies opposed at the present to troops of Germany, Austria-

Hungary, Turkey, and Bulgaria. We are waiting in the strong belief that other peoples will soon follow our example . . .

'At the same time we declare that the conditions submitted to us by the governments of Germany and Austria-Hungary are opposed in principle to the interests of all peoples. These conditions are refused by the working masses of all countries, among them by those of Germany and Austria-Hungary . . . We cannot place the signature of the Russian Revolution under these conditions which bring with them oppression, misery, and hate to millions of human beings. The governments of Germany and Austria-Hungary are determined to possess lands and peoples by might. Let them do so openly. We cannot approve violence. We are going out of the war, but we feel ourselves compelled to refuse to sign the peace treaty . . .' [29]

The delegates of the Central Powers were staggered and incredulous as they listened to this wholly unexpected pronouncement. Trotsky, delighted by the impact he had made, especially on Hoffmann, then led his delegation triumphantly from the hushed conference room. Later in the evening they set out by train for Petrograd.

Believing that he had won a diplomatic victory, Trotsky returned to Petrograd in an elated mood. He was convinced that, because the soviet government had declared the war to be ended, the Germans could not attack. In Petrograd and also in Vienna, the people celebrated the peace joyfully. But Lenin remained unconvinced that the danger had passed and he was soon to be proved right.

Kuhlmann had returned to Berlin, content to accept the new position. The occupied regions remained in German hands and no ultimatum had been necessary; it was now a matter of quietly consolidating German gains. But the supreme command disliked this vague, unconventional peace. Hindenburg and Ludendorf insisted that the German lines must be advanced to include Livonia and Esthonia, and that the position on the Eastern Front should be stabilized so that no danger existed of troops needed in France being held there. Furthermore, since the Rada had lost control in the western Ukraine, German arms must ensure the supply of Ukrainian grain without which neither Germany nor Austro-Hungary could survive the winter of 1918–19. On 13 February at the small resort of Homburg, where the kaiser was taking the waters, the supreme command after an angry debate gained approval for a new campaign.

Trotsky's refusal to sign a peace treaty was, the Germans now held, a denunciation of the original armistice which had specified seven days' notice before the resumption of hostilities. Hoffmann announced on 16 February that the armistice would end on 18 February. Lenin, Trotsky, and other members of the central committee frantically debated what should be done. Lenin made it clear that they must at once resume negotiations for peace; the formula 'no peace—no war' had not only failed but, as he had feared all along, it had endangered the revolution. But

Trotsky still wanted to delay in the hope of an outbreak among the German proletariat, and Lenin had lost all patience with this fanciful argument. Nevertheless, Lenin had to fight bitterly and only later on the night of 18 February was his policy endorsed by seven votes to six.[30]

In the early hours of 19 February the central committee sent a message to Berlin that under protest the soviet of people's commissars accepted the German peace conditions. Four days passed during which the bolsheviks waited anxiously to learn whether their surrender had been accepted. The Germans had already captured Dvinsk and were advancing on a broad front without meeting serious opposition. It seemed that they might now demand unconditional surrender. In the anti-German fever which gripped Petrograd, many demanded a holy war against the German imperialists. At this time Trotsky even appealed through the Allied embassies for support against the Germans, and some assurances were given. But the Germans were advancing unchecked on Petrograd and it was clear that any Allied help that might be forthcoming could not reach them in time. Lenin opposed any attempt to resist the Germans, but agreed that if finally driven to fight, Allied help and, indeed, any help would have to be accepted. At this time Trotsky resigned as foreign commissar because, as he told Lenin, this would help persuade the German government that the bolsheviks really meant to sign the peace treaty. He was at once appointed commissar of war with special responsibility for developing soviet defences.

At last on 23 February the new German peace conditions were received. As Lenin had anticipated, they were far harsher than the terms proposed at Brest-Litovsk.[31] Not only did the Germans demand, as before, the territories occupied by their troops, but also the evacuation of Latvia and Esthonia, the withdrawal of Russian troops and Red Guards from the Ukraine and Finland, and the immediate signing of peace between Russia and the Ukrainian People's Republic. The German terms concluded with the requirement that Russian representatives must proceed immediately to Brest-Litovsk and sign the treaty within three days.

Sverdlov read out these conditions to the central committee. The members listened with growing rage and exploded in fury when he came to the end. Bukharin shouted hysterically that they must fight, wage a holy war to the bitter end. Others supported him. Lenin remained cold and calm. This was what he had expected and he cut across the emotional calls for resistance with a demand that the peace should be signed without further delay or else they would be signing the death sentence of the soviet regime. He added: 'If this is not done, I resign from the government.'[32]

In spite of this threat of resignation, the debate continued in a fury. Bukharin pressed his call for a holy war. Trotsky hesitated, attracted emotionally by Bukharin's appeal, but recognizing the realism of Lenin's policy. Finally he abstained and by seven votes to four with four abstentions Lenin won approval for immediate acceptance of the new peace

SOVIET RUSSIA

FRONTIER CHANGES
AFTER PEACE TREATIES 1919-21

Mezen

Archangel

R. Dvina

BALTIC SEA

L. Onega

Tallinn

L. Ladoga

Petrograd

Novgorod

Vologda

Riga

Pskov

Vyatka

Danzig

Königsberg

Yaroslavl

Nizhni Novgorod

R. Dvini

Moscow

R. Volga

Kazan

Vitebsk

Minsk

Smolensk

Warsaw

Mogilev

Tula

Brest Litovsk

Orel

Penza

Lvov

Kiev

Kursk

Tambov

Voronezh

R. Dnieper

Kharkov

R. Don

Odessa

Kherson

Bucharest

SEA of
AZOV

R. Danube

Sevastopol

Stavropol

CASPIAN
SEA

BLACK SEA

Constantinople

Tiflis

0   100   200   300
Miles

Western Frontier ——————
Frontier 1914   — — — —

terms. But this decision had to be ratified by the Petrograd soviet and by the central executive committee of the congress of soviets, both meeting at this time in the Tauride Palace.

Lenin and the other members of the central committee drove at once from Smolny to the palace and it was nearing midnight when he stood to address the Petrograd soviet. He faced an openly hostile audience and he had to wait for shouts of 'Traitor! German spy!' to die down before he could make himself heard. But Lenin was quick to dominate this hostility. He hurled facts at the peasants, soldiers, and sailors gathered in front of him. He made them understand that a revolutionary war was impossible and that to save the revolution the humiliating peace must be signed. Finally, he won the approval of a majority of the soviet.

Next he went to face the central executive committee of the congress of soviets. It was even more antagonistic. Again cries of 'Judas! German spy!' greeted him and again he managed to secure approval for signing the peace treaty, but only by a majority of 116 votes to 85 with 26 abstentions.

Lenin did not leave the Tauride Palace until six in the morning. Russian acceptance of the peace conditions was received in Berlin some two hours later on 24 February. The soviet delegation, led now by Sokolnikov, set out on the same evening for Brest-Litovsk, and delayed by a destroyed railway bridge, they only arrived on 28 February. They demanded at once that the Germans should halt their hostilities, but Hoffmann insisted now that only the signing of the peace treaty would put an end to active warfare. Sokolnikov found, too, that a new demand had been added to the terms. This was the Turkish demand for the regions of Batum, Kars, and Ardahan, which their troops had captured.[33]

At last on 3 March, protesting strongly, Sokolnikov signed the peace.[34] By its terms Russia lost 1,267,000 square miles of territory and a population of 62 million. The territory signed away included 32 per cent of Russia's arable lands, about 33 per cent of her factories, and 75 per cent of her coal and iron mines.

The revolution had made peace one of its chief aims. Lenin could now claim that peace had been achieved, but it was at this price and also at the price of two million dead, more than four million wounded, and some two-and-a-half million prisoners of war. Never under the tsars had the nation been so rent and humiliated.

CHAPTER NINE

The Civil War

THE revolution had not so far presented the kind of challenge and the heroic struggle that make legends and weld a national unity of purpose. Up to the end of January or March 1918 it had meant only the collapse of the tsarist regime followed by months of anarchy. Groups of men bore revolutionary banners, but no leader, party, or political creed yet commanded the support of the mass of the people. In a state of inertia and suspicion, the Russians waited for something to happen.

The civil war shook them from this apathy. The struggle was long and marked by extraordinary ferocity. The bitter class war promoted by the socialists and the constant threat, often a reality, of famine contributed to the horrors of the struggle. The basic factor, however, was the degradation and inhumanity bred by years of war on fronts where the killed were counted in hundreds of thousands, where suffering became commonplace and human life and dignity sank to insignificance. But in the fires of desperation and savagery of the civil war a new revolutionary spirit was forged.

Lenin had foreseen the time of trial lying ahead of the nation and of his regime. He had insisted on the signing of the treaty of Brest-Litovsk, because he needed the breathing-space in which to consolidate the revolution, raise the economic level of the country, and prepare against imperialist attacks.[1] He took it for granted that Germany would be victorious against the Entente Powers, and that Russia would be at the mercy of the German army, which already occupied the Ukraine, Lithuania, and the Baltic states. The one hope was that Karl Liebnecht, leading the German left-wing socialists, would bring about the long-awaited revolution. Soviet Russia would then fight side by side with Soviet Germany against the imperialists. But he was no longer sanguine about the early outbreak of revolution in Germany. In any case Russia would have to fight and needed a respite in which to restore order and to create an army.

Instead of a breathing space, however, Lenin found an angry sea of dangers, surrounding his regime and threatening to sweep it away. The spring and summer of 1918 were critical. The Allies attempted intervention from Archangel, Murmansk, and the eastern maritime provinces. The Czechoslovak legion was fighting its way across Russia to Vladivostok in one of the strangest adventures in modern times. White forces threatened from Siberia, the Baltic provinces, from the Cossack lands of the Don, the Kuban, and from the Crimea. Within the soviet state the right-wing groups intrigued and prepared to struggle against the regime. The left socialist revolutionaries and the left communists called for a holy war against the German and other imperialists, and broke completely from the bolsheviks. In this sea of dangers it seemed that the soviet regime must founder: it survived because the bolsheviks fought with desperate courage and determination, because they had in Lenin and Trotsky leaders of genius, and because they alone had a definite purpose for which they were fighting. The Whites, in so far as they had an objective, fought for the return of the old regime; the bolsheviks fought for a new dynamic ideal, not of the dead past, but of the living future.

March 1918 was a momentous month for Lenin. After fierce debate he had gained approval for the signing of the peace treaty, but he faced an even harder struggle in obtaining sanction to ratify the treaty from the seventh congress of the bolshevik party, convened on 6 March, and from the fourth all-Russian congress of soviets, convened on 12 March.

The terms of the Treaty of Brest-Litovsk had horrified the Russian people. The national disgrace had rallied the anti-bolsheviks and had made many more officers and NCOs seek service with the White forces. The severity of the German terms had wide repercussions, especially among the Allies and in the U.S.A. But the reactions of those close to him gave Lenin immediate trouble.

The left socialist revolutionaries and the left communists now joined forces against him. Bukharin was the most vehement in denouncing Lenin and his 'obscene' betrayal of the revolution. He was joined by Karl Radek, Alexandra Kollontai, and Dybenko, the savage bully who was now commissar of the navy, as well as by Uritsky and Pokrovsky. Together they launched a new paper, *Kommunist*, to fight against ratification, and they plotted to embroil the country in war again with the Germans.

Lenin remained calm, although deserted by so many comrades and isolated by a storm of vilification. He was still convinced that the treaty must be ratified to save the revolution. He had no intention of honouring its terms, except so far as forced to do so. In particular he was determined to ignore the undertaking to refrain from propaganda in territories occupied by the Central Powers, namely the Ukraine, Poland, the Baltic States, and Finland. The proletariat of those territories and of the Central Powers themselves would, Lenin believed, respond to communist propaganda. At the same time, as a realist, he recognized that the Germans, too, probably had no intention of abiding by the terms of the treaty. Their armies could advance unopposed through Russia and, indeed, they were still advancing in the south. Lenin was, therefore, anxious to obtain some guarantees of assistance from the Allies—making use, as he termed it, of 'the brigands of the Entente' against the 'brigands of the Central Powers'.[2] But he wanted to make sure that any help given by the Allies was confined to the west and the south. The Japanese were active in eastern Siberia and he was not prepared to pay for Allied help the price of surrendering Siberian territory to Japan.

For three days the debate raged among the delegates to the seventh party congress. Many made fiery appeals to revolutionary zeal and honour, and they were cheered heartily. Against this emotional clamour Lenin ranged the cold facts and logic, summed up in the opening paragraph of the resolution which, late on the afternoon of 8 March, he called on the congress to adopt:

'In view of the fact that we have no army, that our troops at the front are in a most demoralized condition, and that we must make use of every possible breathing space to retard imperialistic attacks on the Soviet Socialist Republic, the Congress resolves to accept the most onerous and humiliating peace treaty which the Soviet Government signed with Germany.' [3]

Again Lenin succeeded in cutting through the haze of revolutionary fervour and in imposing his stern commonsense. By thirty votes to twelve with four abstentions, including Trotsky, the congress adopted his resolution.

The fourth congress of soviets faced him with a greater ordeal. More than one thousand delegates made their way to Moscow for this congress, which in itself was a striking achievement for many had to improvise transport and travel through dangerous bandit-infested provinces. At this congress the left socialist revolutionaries and the left communists redoubled their efforts, opposing Lenin both on the floor and outside the sessions. It was noteworthy that Lenin made no attempts to suppress or silence his opponents at this stage although he despised their emotional arguments. He did not, like Stalin in the years to come, dispose of them by execution or exile to penal settlements. He allowed them full freedom to express their views and he answered them, commanding support by the strength of his arguments.

The debate on the ratification of the treaty continued from the morning of 15 March until late in the evening of 16 March. Six resolutions had been tabled calling for rejection of the treaty, and one for ratification. But when Lenin moved on to the platform his presence was felt by the whole assembly and without impassioned appeals or dramatic gestures he dominated the congress. Indeed, his cold, rasping voice and his relentless argument made the preceding speeches seem empty rhetoric. For an hour and twenty minutes he addressed the delegates. The resolution for ratification was put to the vote when he sat down, and it was carried by 784 votes to 261 with 115 abstentions which included 64 left communists.[4]

In March 1918 the name of the party was changed from the All-Russian Social Democratic Labour Party (Bolsheviks) to the All-Russian Communist Party (Bolsheviks), and members thereafter called themselves communists as well as bolsheviks. But the main effect of the change was to stress the complete break with the social democrats who had shown readiness to embrace a parliamentary system which was anathema to the hard core of the party.[5]

A change of far greater and more lasting significance was the transfer of the capital from Petrograd to Moscow. Kerensky had made this proposal in the previous year and the bolsheviks in the Petrograd soviet led by Trotsky had condemned it furiously as bourgeois cowardice. But Kerensky's arguments for the move had been greatly strengthened by the terms of the peace treaty. 'If the Germans at a single bound take possession of Petrograd with us in it, the revolution is lost.' Lenin now argued. 'If on the other hand the Government is in Moscow, then the fall of Petrograd would only mean a serious part-blow.'[6] On 11 March 1918, Sovnarkom and the party headquarters were settled in the Kremlin.

The move to Moscow, although made only as a temporary expedient, was a portentous event. The two capitals—Petrograd and Moscow—symbolized the schism within the nation between attraction to the wealthy, technically advanced Western way of life and to the traditional Muscovite and Orthodox values. Petrograd, the magnificent city created by Peter the Great in the first quarter of the eighteenth century, was the gateway for Western ideas and techniques, and represented Russia's kinship with the rest of Europe. Moscow, the ancient capital around which the nation had been brought to birth in the fifteenth century, was a mediaeval city, crowned with golden crosses and cupolas, and centred on the Kremlin, walled, secretive, and suspicious of the West. The people of Petrograd regarded themselves as the leaders and innovators in Russian life and scorned the Muscovites as conservative and backward. They were now proud that their city was the city of the revolution and they looked forward to union with the revolutionaries of the West. But Muscovites were more prone to reject the West and to insist that Russia should work out her salvation alone.

The removal of the capital from Petrograd to Moscow foreshadowed the fundamental changes in policy and outlook of the bolshevik leaders. Lenin and most of his colleagues belonged in spirit to Petrograd and were orientated towards the West; they thought in Marxist terms of an international revolutionary movement. But the policy of socialism in one country and the leadership of Stalin were rooted in Muscovite tradition and when they were enthroned the Soviet Union turned her back on the West and went into isolation.[7]

The first phase of the civil war began in January 1918 with the bolshevik offensives in the Ukraine and the Don region. In the Ukraine the Rada, or popular assembly, had proclaimed Ukrainian independence. In reply to a soviet ultimatum sent on 17 December, the general secretariat of the Rada had at once pointed out that 'The Declaration of the Rights of the Peoples of Russia' of 2 November of which Lenin and Stalin were the authors had acknowledged the equality and sovereignty of the peoples of

Russia and that Sovnarkom could not now seek to impose its authority. But it was soon evident that the right of self-determination was dependent on the newly sovereign people not installing an anti-bolshevik government, as they had done in the Ukraine. Indeed, in January 1918 Stalin as commissar of nationalities urged the third all-Russia congress of soviets to review the principle of self-determination, and the congress agreed that in its application it must be 'subordinated to the principles of socialism'.[8]

The offensive against the Ukrainian nationalists was led by a former tsarist captain, Muraviev, who had become a socialist revolutionary. He had only a small force of Red Guards, Baltic sailors, and a few volunteers from the old army. But the Ukrainian troops were also few in number and they were more reluctant to fight, for the nationalist movement commanded only limited support in the Ukraine. Muraviev advanced swiftly and on 9 February he captured Kiev. But soon afterwards the Rada signed a separate peace with the Germans at Brest-Litovsk by which the Ukraine virtually became a German satellite. The Germans dissolved the Rada and appointed Skoropadsky, a former tsarist general, as hetman. German and Austrian troops then began to occupy the whole of the Ukraine, and the small Red forces, no match for regular troops, could only withdraw.

Antonov-Ovseenko, also an ex-tsarist officer, to whom Lenin had entrusted the overall command of these offensives had despatched his main forces into the Don region. The Cossacks of the Don and the Kuban, like the Cossacks elsewhere in Russia, were anti-bolshevik. Originally the Cossacks had been freebooters, hunters, and robbers, often of mixed Russian and Turkish blood, who lived about the lower reaches of the Don, Volga, and Dnieper rivers, taking pride only in their buccaneering exploits and in their freedom. Long since, however, they had formed special regiments in the tsar's armies and had been rewarded with privileges and grants of land. Peasants in the Don and Kuban regions, where they were known as the *inogorodny* (the otherlanders or non-locals) did not enjoy the same rights and they resented the Cossacks. Moreover, the larger towns, partially industrialized, of south-eastern Russia, like Rostov and Taganrog, contained strong pro-bolshevik groups. Thus the Cossacks in engaging the Red forces could not count on the support of the people of their regions. Moreover, Ataman Kaledin, the head of the Don government, found that war-weariness and the mood of change which gripped the country had sapped the readiness of his Cossacks to fight, and he had difficulty in raising forces to oppose the Red units advancing under Antonov-Ovseenko.

General Alekseev, the former commander-in-chief, had slipped out of Petrograd soon after the bolshevik revolution. He had arrived in Novocherkassk on 15 November, and had at once begun building up the volunteer army to oppose the new regime. Kaledin, depressed by the apathy of his Cossacks, acquiesced in Alekseev's enterprise but stipulated that his army must be a private army, dissociated from the Don government.

Alekseev made slow progress in recruiting his force. But he was greatly encouraged in December when five generals, including Kornilov, Denikin, and Lukomsky, who had been at Bykhov under open arrest after Kornilov's abortive coup, escaped and joined him.

Kaledin, reluctant to be compromised by association with such well-known counter-revolutionaries as Kornilov and the others, was soon to be grateful for the support of the volunteer army. In December a military revolutionary committee formed in Rostov called on his government to resign. In support of this committee Red Guards and Black Sea sailors engaged and defeated Kaledin's Cossacks and on 10 December took Rostov. But units of the volunteer army from Novocherkassk then expelled the Red forces and on 15 December restored Kaledin's government to power.

Volunteers came forward very slowly still to serve in Alekseev's army. In the main they were veteran officers and members of landowning and other families who had suffered at the hands of city or peasant mobs or as a result of the revolution. But most members of the displaced classes were concerned only for their families and for their own survival, and were not ready to risk their lives in such a hopeless struggle. Volunteers for this army were, therefore, men who were desperately anti-bolshevik and thirsting for revenge. By the end of February the strength of Alekseev's army was not more than 4,000 men, but nearly all were trained and experienced soldiers. The Red forces were at this time still undisciplined and poorly led, and they suffered from the same shortages of food and munitions as the volunteer army.

In mid-January Alekseev moved his army into positions in defence of Rostov. Later in the month, however, Kaledin's government was undermined when several Cossack regiments, meeting at Kamenskoe, repudiated Kaledin and set up a military revolutionary committee supporting the Red forces. A workers' revolt then compelled Kaledin to evacuate Taganrog, and Red troops threatened Rostov. Kornilov tried to persuade Kaledin to withdraw with the volunteer army. But this to Kaledin meant deserting the Don and, on 11 February, after addressing the assembled Cossacks, he went into a private office and shot himself through the heart.[9]

The volunteer army withdrew from Rostov on 21–22 February and two days later Sivers' Red Guard entered the city. On the following day the insurgent or Red Cossacks took Novocherkassk without opposition. Orenburg which had been the headquarters of a Cossack force commanded by Ataman Dutov was captured by local workers. Sailors of the Black Sea Fleet had already set up a soviet in the Crimea, suppressing a Tatar attempt to create a national government. For several days the sailors, always the most violent of the revolutionaries, had terrorized Sevastopol, murdering all men, women, and children who looked like enemies of the revolution. It was a foretaste of the Red terror to come.

On withdrawing from Rostov, the volunteer army made its way south to the Kuban. It was now isolated, a pathetic but gallant little force, which suffered severe hardships in the expanse of the steppes in the bitter cold of winter. It skirted towns and railways, and most villagers avoided contact with the Whites, only very reluctantly selling them food and fodder because they feared Red reprisals. Finally they crossed the Kuban River. Reinforced here by Kuban troops, the volunteer army, commanded now by Kornilov, on 9 April attacked Ekaterinodar where Red forces were some 30,000 strong. After four days of savage fighting, Kornilov gave orders for the town to be stormed at dawn on 13 April. But just before the attack was to begin he himself was killed by a stray shell. The attack was abandoned. Denikin, who assumed command, then led the small army some 700 miles to a position south of Novocherkassk, which was comparatively safe. The volunteer army had lost 400 killed and 1,500 wounded, but the reinforcements from the Kuban had raised its strength to 5,000 men. As it settled in quarters to recuperate, morale remained high and the renown won by the army attracted to it all who burned to fight against the bolsheviks.

While not underestimating the dangers of the anti-bolshevik and White forces, Lenin and his comrades had not anticipated the sudden new phase upon which the civil war entered after March 1918. The new struggle was ignited by a spark struck by a small, irrelevant incident at the railway station of Chelyabinsk when Czechoslovak troops clashed with Austro-Hungarian prisoners-of-war.

Shortly after the outbreak of war in 1914, Czechoslovaks in Russia had formed a separate brigade attached to the Russian army. After the March revolution the Czech nationalist leader, Professor T. G. Masaryk, had been authorized to recruit Czechoslovak prisoners and deserters in Russia; by autumn 1917 some 30,000 volunteers had joined, bringing the force to the strength of a corps.

Recognizing even before the November revolution that Russia was already out of the war, Masaryk obtained permission to transport this force to France. The Czechoslovaks had kept their discipline and morale and in the chaos of Russia they were a formidable fighting unit. But Masaryk firmly rejected approaches by Alekseev and others and refused to allow the Czechoslovaks to be involved in the civil war.[10] He was determined that they should fight at the side of the Allies in the West.

At this time relations between the Czechoslovak and the soviet forces were fairly harmonious. The Czechs had retreated from Kiev where they had been stationed and had with the Red Guards done what they could to hinder the advancing Germans. But soon the Czechs were complaining that communist propagandists were seeking to undermine their discipline and to recruit them into their own units. On the soviet side strong exception was taken to the presence of anti-bolshevik tsarist officers serving in the corps. Nevertheless towards the end of March the soviet government gave approval for the Czechs to travel across Siberia, not as troops but as free citizens, and special restrictions were imposed on the weapons they could take with them. But the Czechs no longer trusted the communists and, while surrendering some, they retained most of their arms.

By May the Czechs were strung out in slow-moving trains along the 5,000 miles of the Trans-Siberian Railway. At Chelyabinsk, just to the east of the Ural Mountains, a trainload of Austrian and Hungarian prisoners-of-war, travelling westwards to be repatriated under the terms of the treaty of Brest-Litovsk, halted. A train bearing Czechoslovaks eastwards also pulled into the station. The Austrians and Hungarians scorned the Czechs as traitors and deserters; the Czechs detested the Austrians and Hungarians as their former oppressors. The inevitable clash ended in the Czechs lynching a Hungarian.

Local soviet officials arrested a few Czechs, but released them when the Czech commander marched two battalions into the town. The matter was then referred to Moscow, where the soviet government now had misgivings about the permission granted in March for the corps to travel eastwards. The situation had changed. Russian fears that the Japanese would seize Vladivostok had been intensified by British and Japanese action in landing detachments to protect their nationals. Moreover, on the borders of Siberia a Cossack leader, named Semenov, had raised an anti-bolshevik force. He was known to have Allied support and it was clearly dangerous to allow the Czech corps which, as part of the Czech Army in France was really under Allied command, to proceed freely to this region.[11]

From Moscow the commissariat of war sent a wave of telegrams at first ordering that the Czechoslovaks should be absorbed into labour battalions or into the Red Army, and next that they should be detained and disarmed. Then Trotsky sent orders that all eastward movement of the Czech trains must be halted. These telegrams to the local soviets were sent in clear and the Czechs intercepted them. Alone in the vast and hostile continent where law and authority had broken down they resolved to keep together and fight their way to the east. Using the telegraph lines which ran parallel with the railway, the separated Czech units agreed on action and, small, disciplined, and well-armed, they rapidly crushed such soviet opposition as they met. By the end of June they had captured all the main towns and stations along the railway, except in the Irkutsk region.[12]

Lenin, Trostky, and others were quick to recognize that the survival of the bolshevik regime depended on the rapid creation of a disciplined and properly led army. This was not, however, a project to which they had given previous thought. Lenin was to admit to the eighth party congress in March 1919 that 'the task of building up the Red Army had in no way been prepared, even in theory'.[13] Like all socialists the bolsheviks regarded regular armies as the instruments of autocratic and capitalist

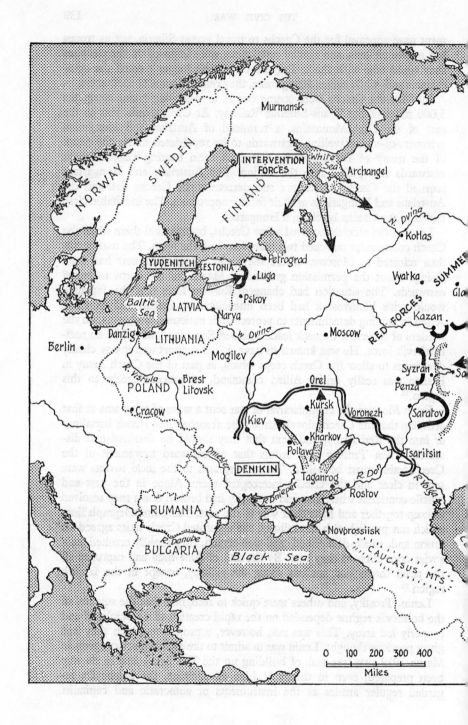

NORWAY

SWEDEN

FINLAND

INTERVENTION FORCES

White Sea

Murmansk

Archangel

N. Dvina

Kotlas

SUMMER

Vyatka

Gla

RED FORCES

Kazan

Sa

Moscow

Syzran

Penza

Saratov

Sa

Berlin

Danzig

ESTONIA

YUDENITCH

Baltic Sea

LATVIA

LITHUANIA

Petrograd

Luga

Pskov

W. Dvina

Narva

Mogilev

R. Vistula

POLAND

Brest Litovsk

Cracow

Kiev

Orel

Kursk

Voronezh

Kharkov

Poltava

DENIKIN

Taganrog

R. Don

R. Dniester

R. Dnieper

Rostov

Tsaritsin

R. Volga

RUMANIA

R. Danube

BULGARIA

Black Sea

Novorossiisk

CAUCASUS MTS

Ca

0   100   200   300   400

Miles

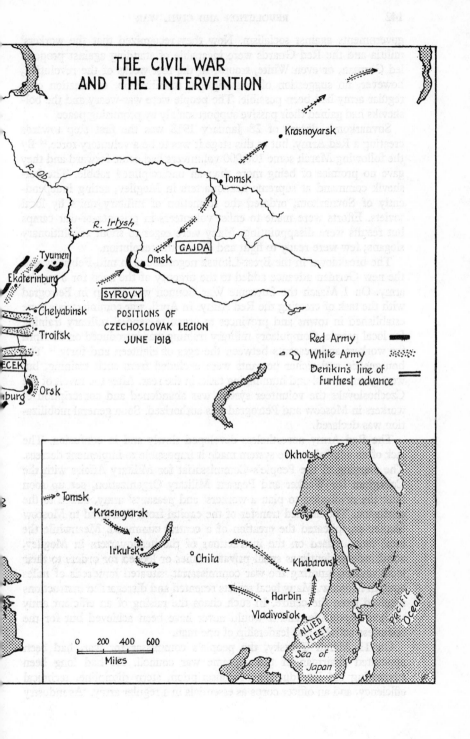

governments against socialism. Now they recognized that the workers' militia and the Red Guards were incapable of standing against properly led German, or even White, troops. In the first weeks of the revolution, however, no suggestion of conscription, mobilization, or creation of a regular army had been possible. The people were war-weary and the bolsheviks had gained their passive support mainly by promising peace.

Sovnarkom's decree of 28 January 1918 was the first step towards creating a Red Army, but at this stage it was to be a voluntary force.[14] By the following March some 100,000 volunteers had come forward and they gave no promise of being more than an undisciplined rabble. The bolshevik command at supreme headquarters in Mogilev, acting independently of Sovnarkom, ordered the formation of military units by local soviets. Efforts were made to enlist volunteers in prisoner-of-war camps but results were disappointing. Many were eager to shout revolutionary slogans; few were ready to fight and die for the revolution.

The breakdown in the Brest-Litovsk negotiations in mid-February and the new German advance added to the urgency of the need for a regular army. On 1 March the Supreme War Council was set up in Petrograd with the task of creating the Red Army. In April, war commissariats were established in towns and provinces to organize general military training for local people. Compulsory military training was introduced on 22 April for workers and peasants between the ages of eighteen and forty.[15] The bourgeoisie and richer peasants were excluded from such training, but were given menial and humiliating tasks in the rear. After the revolt of the Czechoslovaks the volunteer system was abandoned and conscription of workers in Moscow and Petrograd was authorized. Soon general mobilization was declared.

The Red Army nevertheless developed slowly and in confusion. The lack of an administrative system made it impossible to implement decrees. The merging of the People's Commissariat for Military Affairs with the Collegium for Worker and Peasant Military Organization, set up soon after the revolution to plan a workers' and peasants' army, added to the confusion. The hurried transfer of the capital from Petrograd to Moscow further complicated the creation of a central command. Meanwhile the local units, raised on the instructions of the headquarters in Mogilev, acted independently as small private armies or looked for orders to their local soviets, ignoring the war commissariat, situated hundreds of miles away in Moscow. Many local soviets resented and disregarded instructions received from the centre. In such chaos the raising of an efficient army seemed impossible, and it would never have been achieved but for the relentless activity and leadership of one man.

On 13 March Trotsky, the people's commissar for war, had been appointed chairman of the supreme war council. He had long been advocating the introduction of conscription, stern discipline, technical efficiency, and an officer corps as essentials in a regular army. 'As industry

Leon Davidovich Trotsky, 1924

Grigory Yevseyevich Zinoviev

needs engineers, as farming needs qualified agronomists, so military specialists are indispensable to defence,' he argued.[16] He had no patience with amateurism and had discarded the old romantic idea of a proletarian army, guided and disciplined only by revolutionary fervour. He insisted that the technical knowledge and experience of the displaced tsarist officers should be utilized. Opponents pointed to the danger that such officers would betray the Red Army and desert at the first opportunity. Lenin, too, reserved judgement on this highly controversial issue. But Trotsky got his way and ensured the loyalty of officers by a ruthless system of holding their families as hostages and by placing them under the permanent supervision of military commissars.

Between 12 June 1918 and 15 August 1920, 48,409 tsarist officers were recruited, and in 1918 they provided more than three-quarters of the commanding and administrative staffs of the Red Army. Many of these 'specialists', joined to save their familes or because, promoted from the ranks before the revolution they were ready now to embrace the new soviet regime. Many were influenced by Trotsky's pronouncement on 29 July 1918 that officers who refused to serve would go to special camps and, as all knew, they would there become victims of the Cheka and its terror. But, although the majority were coerced into service, these officers made a major contribution and, as Trotsky freely acknowledged, the Red Army would probably have suffered defeat in the civil war without them, especially in the early period, for by the end of the war two-thirds of the commanding officers had been promoted from the ranks.

Trotsky was at the same time determined to create a class army. He depended on the hard core of dedicated members of the communist party, and up to half of the total party membership served in the army. He insisted that the new army must never challenge or undermine the revolution.[17] A decree of 6 April, setting out the duties of the commissars for military affairs, made it their overriding duty to ensure that 'the Army does not become a thing apart from the entire Soviet system and that the various military establishments do not become foci of conspiracies or instruments against workers and peasants'.[18]

In the immensity of Russia the difficulties facing the new regime multiplied. Many of the early volunteers, their revolutionary zeal diminished by the experience of savage fighting, melted away, but the high desertion rate had the effect of purging the army of its unreliable elements. By 1 August 1918 the Red Army had 300,000 men and eighteen months later the figure was five million. It was, moreover, developing into a highly disciplined force with a strong fighting spirit.

At the end of September 1918 Trotsky set up the Revolutionary Military Council of the Republic under his own leadership with his trusted deputy E. M. Sklyansky and the commander-in-chief, Vatzetis, a former officer of the Russian general staff, as the two chief members. This council through the war councils of fourteen armies, each comprising the army

F

commander and two or three commissars, directed the soviet armed forces and gradually improved communications and established an overall command. But supplies raised constant problems. Industrial production had come almost to a standstill, rail transport was disorganized, and often the White forces prevented access to sources of essential materials. The soviet government was at first able to rely on stocks of ammunition and equipment, taken over from the tsarist and provisional governments, but shortages were soon felt. On 10 November 1918 an extraordinary commission for the supply of the Red Army was set up under the direction of Leonid Krassin and given responsibility for production and supply of war materials.[19]

In spite of the creation of this and other organizations and in spite of prodigies of improvisation, the soviet government and the Red Army were constantly facing crises of food and munition shortage, of poor discipline, and of falling morale, and were on the edge of collapse. They survived and were victorious because the White forces were plagued by similar problems, but mainly because the Whites became increasingly demoralized while the soviet regime, inspired by its leaders and the hard-core party members, grew in morale and in its determination to survive.

During the civil war several competent military leaders emerged, like Mikhail Frunze, M. N. Tukhachevsky, and Sergei Budyonny, but their contributions were as local commanders. The overall drive and direction came from Trotsky. Possessed by a demon of energy and a fanatic will to victory, he supervised the soviet conduct of the war. The special train from which he operated during this long period was a reflection of the man. This train was equipped with a printing press, an electrical generator, radio and telegraph station, and a garage for the cars in which he dashed to critical points away from the railway. The train was so heavy that two engines were needed to draw it. A machine-gun unit was also part of its complement, and all had to be on constant guard not only against White forces but also against attacks by the guerrilla bands which like private armies wandered the country, robbing and pillaging.

Trotsky made some thirty-six visits to the various fronts, which were separated by vast distances. In autumn 1919 the train crew and guards fought actively in defence of Petrograd, threatened by the assault of the White general, Yudenich. During the long train journeys Trotsky also wrote and published a small newspaper, called *On the Road*. In it he exhorted Red troops to greater efforts, threatened deserters and undisciplined units with dire punishments, and explained government policy. His mental and physical energy seemed inexhaustible. Indeed, through his dynamism and determination he contributed more than any other man to soviet victory in the civil war.

Faced with a stark struggle for survival, the communist leaders did not hesitate to apply extreme methods. The system known as war communism which they introduced hurriedly was a product of their desperation. This system involved complete centralized government control of the economic life of the nation. As Marxists the communists believed that all means of production should be vested in the state. But Lenin, always the realist, saw that the soviets and the workers as a whole were too inexperienced to take over management. He was prepared to move slowly in nationalizing industry, while encouraging the workers to gain knowledge and develop a sense of discipline and responsibility. He planned, moreover, to retain factory owners and managers under state supervision so that their technical and managerial skills would continue to benefit industry and the state.

The urgent demands of the war economy overruled Lenin's practical plans. By a decree of 28 June all major industries—iron, steel, textile, pottery, cement, and others were nationalized without compensation to the owners. This policy was applied more and more widely, until in November all plants with more than ten workers, or more than five workers if mechanical power was used, were taken over by the state.

With the increasing state control of the means of production, it also became necessary to regiment labour and to apply the principle that he who would eat must work. A decree in December 1918 made it compulsory for all between the ages of sixteen and fifty to work. The demands of war led soon to workers being mobilized in categories and directed to factories where they were needed. On 29 January 1920 a decree made all labour liable to mobilization.

Another important feature of war communism was the centralization of government and administration. An immense bureaucratic machine was hastily erected and came to wield tremendous power, usually with gross inefficiency. The supreme economic council with its forty or more departments, each responsible for a specific industry, became the central authority in charge of industrial production.

The most crucial and powerful of the new bureaucratic institutions at this time, however, was the food commissariat. As part of the policy of war communism, the state had nationalized internal trade and thus took over the functions of sole distributor as well as sole producer. The food commissariat in theory distributed the products of industry and of agriculture. In fact, industrial output had so declined in quality and in quantity and inflation had so debased the currency that food had to be requisitioned from the peasants. The commissariat was then responsible for distributing it among the urban population on the basis of ration cards. By 1920 some thirty-five million of these cards had been issued. Peasants were expected to provide for themselves and did not receive cards. But of the one hundred million and more who had no ration cards, many were in flight from the cities, the army, or simply had no food entitlement. Rations were allocated strictly on a class principle. Workers and soldiers were in the first category and received four times the ration of those in the fourth or lowest category who, if unable to supplement their rations, perished from malnutrition or starvation. Citizens in the fourth category were allowed one eighth of a Russian pound of bread every two days. Zinoviev, the head of the Petrograd soviet, commented that this category had been included simply 'to ensure that the bourgeoisie do not forget the smell of bread!'[20] His remark reflected something of the bitterness and spite encouraged by the prevailing class hatred.

The food commissariat functioned so slowly and inefficiently, however, that deaths from starvation would have been considerably higher had there not been alternative supplies. More than half the food consumed in the cities and towns was obtained by purchase or barter on the private market, or people by travelling into the country to buy food from peasants in the villages. Soviet officials accepted this free trade and even relaxed regulations in times of acute shortage; in the autumn of 1918, for instance, people were allowed to carry up to forty-eight pounds of foodstuffs on the railways.

Malnutrition and starvation nevertheless killed off thousands of people in cities and towns, especially during the long, bitterly cold winters when no fuel for heating could be obtained. Deaths were, of course, highest among the elderly and the displaced bourgeois who were unemployed and who survived while they were able to barter their jewellery and other valuables for food. But for all classes the hardships were indescribably severe.

In the years from 1916 to 1920 more than a third of the populations of the cities and towns in northern and central Russia fled from starvation to the country where they had more hope of finding food to keep them alive. This flight to the country had a disastrous effect on industry. Workers, despite threats of severe punishments, returned to their villages, and industrial man-power declined by as much as fifty per cent during the years of war communism. Many became black marketeers, some to make money, but most with the object of obtaining food for their starving families. All forms of private trading were unlawful. Special search detachments lay in wait at railway stations and markets, but goaded by hunger thousands braved the risks of capture and brutal punishments.

Barter and exchange were increasingly taking the place of money in legal as well as illegal trading. Inflation had reached monstrous proportions; the purchasing power of one ruble in 1913 was equal to that of 2,420 rubles in 1920. This decline in the use of money was, however, in accordance with soviet policy and communists even welcomed it as a move towards socialism. The government began paying wages in food and clothing. A decree of 4 December 1920 provided that food should be distributed free of charge. A further decree of 3 February 1921 abolished taxes, except in the form of requisitions in kind from peasants. The government nevertheless continued to print paper money and by the beginning of 1921 the notes in circulation were more than one hundred times as great as in 1917. Paper money had been useful at first in buying grain from the peasantry, but inflation soon reduced its value and to avoid such payment and forced requisitioning peasants both hid their surplus products and grew less.

Throughout the years of the civil war the spectre of famine pursued the soviet government and the Russian people. Food itself was not lacking in 1918 but the breakdown in transport and in distribution and the absence of means to buy grain from the peasants led to acute shortages. The greatest bread crisis came in the summer of 1918. Speaking on 9 June 1918 Trotsky said that 'How to live tomorrow is the concern that is uppermost in the minds of all ... Here is a telegram: "Give us bread or we perish" ... Here is another: "The death-rate is terrible. Hunger— typhus is raging".'[21] The soviet regime was fighting for its existence not only against the White armies, but also against famine and it took desperate measures.

A decree of 27 May 1918 vested in the food commissariat absolute power and responsibility for providing the people 'with articles of prime necessity and foodstuffs'.[22] It also provided for the setting-up of local food organizations, the formation of workers' detachments for collecting grain, the enforcement of the grain monopoly, and the distribution of consumer goods among the rural population. The detachments for collecting grain were mobilized mainly from the hungry regions of the centre and north, and by the end of July they had more than ten thousand members. Directed to wrest the grain from 'village bourgeoisie, the kulaks, and the speculators', alleged to have grain in abundance which they were holding back, the detachments of workers, usually with starving families, were whipped to a fury of class hatred by communist exhortations.[23]

The workers' detachments mounted their requisitioning operations on military lines. An ordinance of the food commissariat of 20 August 1918 laid down that each detachment must consist of not less than seventy-five men and two or three machine-guns, and be led by a commander and a political commissar. Detachments were to be so distributed that two or three detachments could be united speedily in case of emergency.[24]

Class hatreds were further intensified in June 1918 when a special decree, signed by Lenin and Sverdlov, set up committees of the village poor. The committees, known as the Kombedy, were responsible under the supervision of the food commissariat for distributing food, goods of prime necessity and farming implements, and for assisting local food organizations in requisitioning surplus grain from kulaks and the rich.[25] Poor peasants were encouraged in their work in the committees by special grants for themselves out of the produce they requisitioned.

Membership of the committees was allowed to peasants newly arrived in the villages and even to those who hired labour, provided that on such farms the consumption standard was not exceeded. Lenin had been careful to make the membership qualification broad to avoid a sharp division of the poorest peasants and farm labourers against other peasants. But most of the committees were composed of the poorest peasants, eager to despoil all who were better off than themselves. Like the workers' food detachments, the committees were authorized to use force to take food surpluses. They often took not only grain but livestock and implements which they divided among themselves.

The whole country was soon in the throes of the bread war which was as ferocious and pitiless as the civil war itself. Authority to requisition food was taken as licence to plunder. In countless villages in the provinces under soviet rule savage struggles erupted. Men were burnt alive, cut up with scythes, and beaten to death. Armed bands clashed and fought pitched battles. The committees gave rise to twenty-six major uprisings in July, forty-seven in August, and thirty-five in September.

Alarmed by this civil war which they had unleashed in the villages, Lenin on 18 August 1918 sent a circular letter to all the provincial soviets and food committees, drawing attention to the fact that the interests of the middle class peasants were being violated. He stressed that 'the Committees of the Poor must be revolutionary organizations of the whole peasantry against former landlords, kulaks, merchants, and priests, and not organizations only of the village proletarians against all the rest of the village population'.[26]

Once unloosed such savage hostilities, intensified by the continuing threat of starvation, could not be restrained or brought to order. Untold suffering and loss of life was caused throughout the country. The bitterness and bloodshed caused by these committees became so critical that in November they were abolished, at least in name, for a general re-election of village soviets was arranged at the same time and the most effective members of the committees then became members of the soviets. Moreover, the communists claimed that the committees of the poor and the workers' detachments had served the class struggle in the villages by dividing the people into two hostile groups and that this had also helped in the requisitioning of food.

The peasants had been ready to exchange their products for commodities and they hated the workers' food detachments which took their grain by force. They had no interest in the starving industrial centres. They used great cunning in hiding away their grain and in outwitting those who searched their farms and homes. As the detachments became more efficient and the regulations more stringent, they seethed with resentment against the soviet government and its officials. But although they often rebelled and fought against the armed detachments they made no serious attempt to launch a counter-revolution. The revolution had given them the land and they believed that the communist leaders intended to leave them in possession of their smallholdings. The Whites said they would return the land to the landlords and so the peasants understood that counter-revolution, if successful, would bring back the landlords. For this reason even though incensed by the violation of their rights and property, the peasants did not turn against the soviet government.

The communist leaders themselves recognized this as the basis of peasant support. In fact, their agrarian policy in the summer and autumn of 1918 aimed at merging the countless peasant smallholdings into collective farms as the first step towards a state-controlled agriculture. But the government was careful at this stage not to force the peasants into collective farming. Communists believed that propaganda and encouragement would bring the peasants to appreciate the benefits of agrarian socialism. They mounted a massive propaganda campaign, but their words passed over the heads of the peasants, who were concerned not with ideas but with the soil.

The socialist revolutionaries, the party of the peasants, were during these months strongly critical of the soviet government with whom they had so far co-operated. They were still opposed to the peace of Brest-Litovsk and pressed for renewal of the war against Germany and Austria. They were pro-war partly on ideological grounds, but they also denounced as servile the bolshevik attitude towards the Germans, because the Germans occupied vast areas of the fertile black soil regions from which they drew much of their support and loss of which was a major cause of food shortages. Now they held the government responsible for the civil war in the villages which, they argued, had been artificially created through the committees of the poor and the food requisitioning detachments. They also objected to the new soviet decree allowing courts to impose the death sentence in certain cases. Their furious opposition to the death penalty came strangely from a party which believed terrorism and murder to be justified on political grounds, as they were soon to demonstrate afresh, but this was typical of the grotesque and distorted idealism of the socialist revolutionary party.

The fifth all-Russian soviet congress met on 4 July in the Bolshoi Theatre in Moscow. The left socialist revolutionaries were now the sole remaining legal opposition party. In the previous month the all-Russian soviet executive committee had expelled right and centre socialist revolutionaries and mensheviks on the ground that they were plotting with counter-revolutionary leaders. In secret the left socialist revolutionaries made careful plans to challenge, and some even planned to overthrow, the government at this congress and to renew the war against Germany. They were now desperate and determined on a showdown.

In the Bolshoi Theatre the bolshevik delegates, composed mainly of soldiers in khaki, sat on the right facing the stage; the left socialist revolutionary delegates, mainly peasants in loose shirts, sat on the left. On the stage where Pavlova and Karsavina had danced and Chaliapin had sung sat the members of the central executive committee, some 150 in number, and in front of them on the stage was the presidium with Sverdlov, the president, in the centre. Minor delegates spoke on the first day. They were mainly socialist revolutionaries who attacked the government. The bolsheviks, accustomed to being the aggressors, were forced on to the defensive. The sessions threatened to be stormy.

On the second day the two parties joined battle. Sverdlov tried to explain and justify bolshevik policy towards Germany, the committees of the poor, and the death penalty, and was partially successful. But then Maria Spiridonova, the thirty-two-year-old leader of the left socialist revolutionaries, spoke. With dark hair pulled back into a knot at the back of her head, wearing *pince-nez* and dressed austerely, she looked like a school teacher. But her eyes glowered with fanaticism. Some thought that she was mentally unbalanced as a result of her tragic early life. In 1906 when a mere girl, she had assassinated a notorious official on the railway station of Borisoglebsk. Her attempt to turn the revolver on herself failed. She was carried away and repeatedly raped by Cossacks. After trial she was condemned to death but the tsar, on a strong plea of mercy for her youth, had commuted this sentence to penal servitude for life. She was a revolutionary of the emotional romantic kind, whom Lenin abhorred, but to her party she was a heroine.

Addressing the fifth congress, Spiridonova attacked the committees of the poor. She started quietly but was soon speaking with hysterical passion. She was vehement in her condemnation of Lenin. Turning to where he sat on the platform she shouted, 'I accuse you of betraying the peasants, of making use of them for your own ends. . . . Our other differences are only temporary. . . . When the peasants, the Bolshevik peasants, the Left Socialist Revolutionary peasants, and the non-party peasants, are alike humiliated, oppressed, and crushed as peasants—in my hand you will find the same pistol, the same bomb, which once forced me to defend . . .'[27] Her voice was then lost in the storm of cheers and applause. Sverdlov called for order and rang the chairman's bell. Trotsky came forward to speak but could get no hearing and, infuriated, had to return to his seat.

In the midst of this pandemonium Lenin walked calmly to the front of the stage. As he passed by Sverdlov he patted him on the shoulder and told him to put his bell away. Boos and jeers greeted him. Lenin stood silent, smiling and holding the lapels of his coat. Then he raised his hand and waited until gradually the tumult died down. Speaking firmly, his head thrust forward, he answered the socialist revolutionary criticisms one by one. The storms of interruption became fewer until this extraordinary leader of men dominated the vast theatre and his cold unemotional voice was heard in silence.

Other socialist revolutionary speakers who followed were able to arouse cheers of approval, but they could not destroy the ascendancy which Lenin had established. The communist majority passed resolutions approving the government's food policy and declaring that attempts to disrupt this policy in operation must be met with mass terror.

The sitting ended in the evening of 5 July and was to have been resumed on the afternoon of the following day. But the socialist revolutionaries had already decided on action outside the congress. Their central committee had made plans to assassinate the German ambassador, Count Mirbach, hoping thus to provoke the Germans to tear up the hated peace treaty and to renew the war. Most left socialist revolutionaries were content to support the government, provided that it carried on the war against Germany. But certain members of the party plotted an uprising against bolshevik rule.

In these two ill-conceived plans of action the left socialist revolutionaries demonstrated the fanaticism and idealism which were their striking qualities, but they revealed also the impractical and amateurish failings which made them incapable of carrying through a revolution or of challenging the bolsheviks under Lenin's leadership. They were most effective as exponents of terror.

On the afternoon of 6 July two men gained admission to the heavily guarded German embassy by means of a pass, issued by Alexandrovich, the vice-president of the Cheka, who was a socialist revolutionary. On being admitted to the office of Count Mirbach, the German ambassador, Blumkin, one of the two men, drew a Browning pistol and shot him dead. He then jumped through an open window, throwing a hand-grenade behind him, and made his escape.

Meanwhile the socialist revolutionaries had massed in the Pokrovsky barracks several thousand troops and units of sailors from the Black Sea Fleet. Their plan was to take over the city and arrest all bolshevik leaders. But excited by their numbers and apparent success they did nothing, apart from arresting Dzerzhinsky, the head of the Cheka, and a few others. When in the evening they advanced on the Bolshoi Theatre, they found strong bolshevik forces on guard, and they at once retreated to their headquarters.

On receiving first news of this uprising Trotsky had ordered two Lettish regiments into the city and had massed armoured cars. The socialist revolutionaries, intimidated by this show of force, made no attempt to fight and quietly surrendered. Their delegates in the Bolshoi Theatre were arrested. The counter-revolution was, in fact, suppressed so quietly and completely that the great majority of citizens of Moscow did not know that it had happened.

One other incident of the revolution was that Muraviev, the commander-in-chief of the Red forces on the Volga, who was himself a socialist revolutionary, tried to march his army on Moscow. His troops, however, learning of the attempted coup and its failure arrested him, and he shot himself. Of the socialist revolutionary leaders, Alexandrovich was caught, trying to escape, and was shot. Spiridonova and others were imprisoned in the Kremlin.

On learning of the assassination of the German ambassador, Lenin and

Sverdlov at once called in person at the German embassy to present their official condolences. Lenin in particular was alarmed that German troops would soon begin to surge into Russia, and he knew that, if this happened, his government could not survive. But his fears proved unnecessary. The Germans were now hard pressed on the Western Front and in no position to deploy troops against Russia. They were content in the end to accept the apologies of the soviet government and its assurances that a stronger guard would be posted at the embassy in future.

The left socialist revolutionaries had thus failed not only in their half-hearted efforts to overturn the soviet government, but even in their attempt to provoke a new war with Germany. During the stormy sessions of the congress, Trotsky and others had urged action to suppress this turbulent opposition. Lenin had hesitated considering, perhaps, that they would be more dangerous if forced underground, and also hoping through them to win greater peasant support. But now there could be no question of allowing socialist revolutionaries to hold responsible positions, especially in the Cheka. The party was outlawed. Many socialist revolutionaries then joined the communist party but those, like Maria Spiridonova, who were fanatic revolutionary idealists went underground. The soviet regime became a communist dictatorship which no longer tolerated opposition of any kind.

On 6 July, the day of the socialist revolutionary revolt in Moscow, the soviet government faced a further challenge when an anti-bolshevik group, led by Colonel Perkhurov, seized the ancient and important town of Yaroslavl, some 125 miles north of Moscow on the upper Volga. This coup was organized by Boris Savinkov, one of the many born conspirators who, like Azef and others, had few loyalties, but who by their cunning and unpredictable activities added to the confusion and fascination of Russia in this period. Savinkov had been a revolutionary terrorist and had planned the murder of Grand Duke Sergei, the tsar's uncle. He was for a time minister of war in Kerensky's provisional government; he had been an intermediary in the Kerensky–Kornilov affair, and he was now an active anti-bolshevik.[28] He was the main organizer of 'the Union for the Defence of the Motherland and Freedom', which had led the soviet government to declare martial law in Moscow towards the end of May. The Cheka had then arrested hundreds of ex-officers whom Savinkov was enlisting in his organization. He himself had escaped with his two chief assistants, Colonel Perkhurov and Dr Grigoriev, and was responsible for the capture of Yaroslavl and nearby Murom.

Savinkov claimed, probably rightly, that he had the active support of the French ambassador, Noulens, and that he was in constant touch with the French consul and military attaché in Moscow. The French plan was that Savinkov should seize Yaroslavl, Rybinsk, Kostroma, and Murom. Allied troops to be landed in Archangel as part of the intervention would then join with Savinkov's force in an advance on Moscow.[29]

The soviet government acted promptly. Yaroslavl was close to Moscow and strategically placed to serve as an anti-bolshevik centre for the whole upper Volga region. The government also feared the danger of Allied forces from Archangel supporting the Whites, although in the event these forces were only landed several weeks later and then in strengths too small to be a real danger. Other disturbing factors were the unreliability of the Red troops in the town and its neighbourhood and the antagonism of the local workers to the soviet government. Railway and factory workers had even promised Perkhurov their active support; in the event they took no part, but they refused to help the Red troops.

The battle for Yaroslavl lasted nearly two weeks and the soviet forces finally recaptured it on 19 July. Murom, taken by Perkhurov's forces on 8 July, was recaptured two days later. The attack on Rybinsk, a small town near Yaroslavl and important for its artillery stores, was repulsed by the Red garrison. But, although the soviet forces were numerically superior, their task was made far more difficult by the attitude of the local people, ranging from apathy to active hostility. This was the popular attitude in regions all over the country and the government met it with mass terror.

The extraordinary staff, responsible for putting down the uprising, issued warnings to local people that unless they obeyed instructions they would be treated 'as partisans of the rebels' and would receive no quarter as 'enemies of the revolution of the workers and poorest peasants'.[30] On recapturing Yaroslavl soviet officials at once shot 57 of the captured Whites. They then rounded up 350 people, said to have been active in the insurrection, and executed all of them. The 'Mass Red Terror' which was to be a deliberate policy of the soviet regime and an important instrument of victory, had begun.

At this time a grim tragedy perpetrated by the bolsheviks in Ekaterinburg, now called Sverdlovsk, epitomized the terror and inhumanity of the civil war and the struggle of Lenin and his party for power. After their removal from Tsarskoe Selo to Tobolsk, Nicholas and his family had continued to receive a certain courtesy and consideration but this began to change after the bolshevik revolution. In April a direct emissary from Sverdlov, named Yakovlev, arrived in Tobolsk to take the family elsewhere. Apparently he had instructions to escort them to Ekaterinburg, one of the strongest bolshevik centres. But Yakovlev, possibly in the hope of saving the imperial family from the death which he suspected awaited them there, tried to take them to Omsk. The local soviet intervened and in Ekaterinburg the ex-tsar and his family were lodged in the house of a merchant, named Ipatyev, which was now called ominously the House of Special Purpose. The tsarevich was too ill to travel at the time but was reunited with his father and mother in May.[31]

In Ekaterinburg Nicholas and his family were surrounded by crude hostility. Their new guards evidently found pleasure in demeaning not only him and his wife but also the children. Their daughters, the tsarevni, had to sleep on the floor and when they went to the lavatory the guards followed and, refusing to allow them to lock the door stood by making coarse remarks. Nicholas and each member of the family endured the hardships and humiliations of their daily lives with an almost saintly patience. They may well have entertained hopes of rescue, but as the weeks passed they became more resigned to the fate that seemed inevitable and, deeply religious, they found comfort in prayer.

Fighting was, in fact, going on in the vicinity of Ekaterinburg. By early July the Czechs and White forces had outflanked the city on two sides and on the morning of 25 July the Czechoslovaks were to capture it. The bolsheviks, fearing this possibility, had made their plans some weeks earlier. The military commissar of the Ural soviet, Goloshchekin, had gone to Moscow to consult with Sverdlov who presumably gave him instructions. On 12 July Goloshchekin returned to Ekaterinburg and was seen inspecting a deserted mine-shaft near the village of Koptyaki, fourteen miles from the city. On the day of his return Goloshchekin also reported to the Ural soviet, which took the decision that Nicholas and his family, their personal physician, Dr Botkin, and their three remaining servants should die.

Near midnight on 16 July Nicholas, his wife, the children, and staff were told to dress and go down to the cellar as fighting was expected to break out in the town during the night. Nicholas went down first carrying his sick son in his arms and the others followed. The head of the bolshevik guard, Yurovsky, a Siberian Jew, sinister in appearance, character, and in record, and a band of his men then entered the cellar. Yurovsky said that the local soviet had condemned them to death. He spoke indistinctly and the tsar did not hear him properly. But before he could ask him to repeat his words, Yurovsky shot him point blank with a revolver. He then shot the tsarevich, but did not kill him and had to despatch him with more shots. The other guards opened fire on the former empress, her daughters, and the servants. Blood poured over the floor. Revolver and rifle shots ricochetted from the cellar walls and the noise mingled with the shrieks and moans of the victims. Anastasia was only wounded and one of the guards killed her with his bayonet.[32]

The maid, Demidova, was missed by the shots and with a cushion parried frantic bayonet thrusts until finally she was cornered and transfixed. Yurovsky and his men had worked themselves into a frenzy, and went on shooting and bayoneting the bodies to make sure that no life was left in them. Then without delay they loaded their victims into a lorry which drove to Koptyaki, where in the course of several days they destroyed the bodies with acids and fire.

Nicholas, his wife and children had long ceased to matter in Russia. He had been so ineffectual as tsar that his abdication had caused only a passing shock and had hardly been mourned; the three-hundred-year rule of the Romanov dynasty which had achieved so much had closed on an abject note.

Anxious to dwell on other events and personalities of this period, historians have usually made only brief reference to this savage execution. But Nicholas was a saintly, but weak man, who paid heavily for the sins of his dynasty; his children were unspoilt and, like most children, lovable, while his wife, devout, foolish, and troublesome, was a real wife and mother. His doctor and three retainers were loyal servants who chose to serve until death. Nicholas and his family and their servants, divested of their imperial panoply became simple human beings, and that such people should be shot and brutally bayoneted to death must be a matter of deep sorrow. Moreover, in their final sufferings they had become representative of the thousands of victims of the Red terror which now began to grip the country.[33]

The council of people's commissars was discussing health regulations when Sverdlov interrupted to announce the death of the former tsar. The news was followed by silence until Lenin quietly moved the resumption of discussions. The official statement then released was a garbled account which even reported that the wife and son of the former tsar had been removed to a safe place. The soviet government was reluctant to admit to the killing of the children and feared some popular reaction to the news. But so much had happened since the abdication in March 1917 and the people were concerned with hunger and civil war. The news was received quietly and no one questioned it.

Another event which passed almost unnoticed at this time was the adoption by the fifth congress of soviets of the constitution or fundamental law of the Russian Socialist Federated Soviet Republic. A document of major importance, it defined the principles and ideals of the new regime. The communist credo had been set out in general idealistic terms in the Declaration of the Rights of the Working and Exploited People, generally ascribed to Lenin, Bukharin, and Stalin, which the third congress had adopted on 23 January 1918. This declaration formed the first part of the new fundamental law; the second part, describing the political organization and procedures of the regime, was drafted by a special committee under the chairmanship of Sverdlov appointed by the third congress.

One of the members of the drafting committee, Yu Steklov, introducing the law to the fifth congress on 10 July, said: 'The Declaration of Rights has made it clear that the great aim of Soviet Russia is to destroy the bourgeois and the exploitation of man by man, and to create in their stead a form of government under which all wealth produced by the workers and peasants shall belong to all the people, united in one fraternal labour collectivity ... When the socialist state finally comes into being ... we shall have true communism and the application of the principle ... "To each according to his need and from each according to his capacity".'[34]

The existing political organization was confirmed. The urban and rural soviets were held to be the source of all authority. All persons over eighteen years of age except churchmen, members of the Romanov family, former police agents, high officials, merchants, the insane and criminals, elected the delegates to the soviets. The law strongly favoured the urban against the rural inhabitant, the former having one delegate for every 25,000 electors and the latter one delegate for 125,000 inhabitants. This reflected the government's confidence in the support of the workers and its uncertainty about the peasants, and its determination behind a façade of high principle to retain power. The local soviets provided the base for a pyramid of congresses of soviets, comprising delegates indirectly elected at four separate levels with the all-Russian congress of soviets at the apex. When the all-Russian congress was not in session, the central executive committee exercised its functions and it elected the soviet of people's commissars (Sovnarkom) to direct the administration.[35]

The real power over the nation, however, which was not even mentioned in the constitution, was the communist party. It was becoming a well-organized, disciplined body of dedicated communists, numbering at this time some 270,000, and they were undergoing a constant process of proving and elimination in the furnace of the civil war. They held all the chief posts not only in the government but in the army and other key bodies. Austere in their way of life, shirking no responsibilities or dangers, the best of them were like members of a severe religious order. They were to ensure the supremacy of the party and the survival of its regime.

Although all other parties and groups had been outlawed and the communist party wielded supreme power, opposition was far from dormant. The socialist revolutionaries as the exponents of terrorism were a constant danger. In July and August, the period which Lenin called the most critical of the revolution when the civil war and the bread war were reaching a climax of savagery, the communist leaders were aroused to a frenzy by two acts of terrorism committed by them.

On 30 August M. S. Uritsky, the head of the Petrograd Cheka, was on his way to his office when a young socialist revolutionary, named Kenigiesser, shot him dead. On the evening of the same day Lenin addressed workers in the Mikhelsen factory across the Moskva River from the Kremlin. As he left the factory two socialist revolutionaries followed him. Near the exit one of them suddenly pushed aside several workers and the other, a young Jewish woman named Fanya Kaplan, drew a revolver and fired point blank. Lenin fell to the ground. One bullet had shattered his left shoulder and the other had penetrated his neck and lodged there. He behaved with cheerful fortitude as he was taken to the Kremlin. The injuries were severe, but within two days his sturdy constitution had carried him past the danger point and on the insistence of his doctors he went to recuperate at a rest house in Nizhni-Novgorod, now Gorky.[36] By 19 September although far from fully recovered he was again at work.

The two events of 30 August unleashed a fury of mass terror. In Petrograd more than five hundred people were shot dead as a reprisal for the killing of Uritsky. Fanya Kaplan was promptly executed.[37] On 2 September the all-Russian central executive committee (VTsIK) authorized mass terror as part of the official policy of the government. The commissar for internal affairs, Petrovsky, issued a proclamation to all soviets, stating that:

'The talk of mass terror against Socialist Revolutionaries, White Guards, and bourgeoisie has no basis in fact. It is time to put an end to this state of affairs. Local Soviets should arrest all Socialist Revolutionaries at once. A considerable number of hostages should be taken from the bourgeoisie and (former) officers. The least opposition, the least movement among the White Guards should be met with wholesale executions.

'Chekas and militia departments should make special efforts to locate and arrest all those living under assumed names and to shoot without formality everyone mixed up in White Guards and other dirty plotters against the government of the working class and the poorer peasantry. Show no hesitation whatsoever in carrying out mass terror . . .'[38]

Terrorism had erupted in all parts of the country since the beginning of the revolution and like a wave rolling towards the shore it had been increasing in magnitude. Red troops and in particular sailors of the Baltic and Black Sea Fleets, likewise White troops, had committed innumerable acts of violence and murder. One of the worst outbreaks had been in February 1918 when sailors had terrorized the people of Sevastopol, killing hundreds of men, women, and children. But in the main these incidents had been spontaneous independent acts of bloodshed.

Terrorism had, however, already been envisaged by the communists as an essential instrument of power. Felix Dzerzhinsky had declared in June that 'We stand for organized terror . . . Terror is an absolute necessity in times of revolution'.[39] Terrorism began to be enforced as the policy of the government in July after the socialist revolutionary insurrection in Moscow and the capture of Yaroslavl by Perkhurov's force. Its purpose was not only to intimidate and crush the enemies of the soviet regime, but also to coerce the great mass of the people who, as in Yaroslavl, were uncommitted, suspicious of the communists, and, unwilling to oppose the government openly, tried to stand aside. The fear and hatred inspired by the terror, as organized by the Cheka in every town and village, were the means not only of crushing the enemies of the regime but also the means of compelling workers and peasants to support the government. Long years of war, famine, and the complete breakdown of order had made most people, even those who were not anti-communist, reluctant to carry out obligations to the state except under compulsion and the terror provided it in an extreme form. Lenin and other communist leaders claimed that the regime could not have survived without the Red terror and during the years of the civil war the claim was probably justified.

The Cheka in conducting the terror wielded absolute power. It had grown rapidly and employed over thirty thousand agents. Many were criminals; many were brutalized and sadistic soldiers and 'uncouth illiterate peasant youths',[40] who were corrupted by licence to kill, torture, and confiscate property, and who made full use of their opportunities to enrich themselves by bribes and blackmail. They were far removed from the fanatic but idealistic Dzerzhinsky to whom the terror was a duty to the party and the revolution.

Disputes were frequent between units of the Cheka and local soviets. The two organizations were called upon to work closely together but the soviets, purporting to represent the people, resented the unchecked authority and the abuses of the Cheka agents. Complaints by the soviets became more and more numerous but this drew the ruling from Peters, a Lett who was prominent in the Cheka, that 'In its activity the Cheka is completely independent, carrying out searches, arrests, shootings, afterwards making a report to the Council of People's Commissars and the Soviet Central Executive Committee'.[41]

The terror was directed first against counter-revolutionaries and class enemies. Landlords and their families, former factory owners, and managers, merchants, and priests were summarily shot without trial or questioning. Women suffered the same fate as men and names of women figured frequently in the lists of victims. Cheka agents frequently arrested people without reason. One of their victims, Ivanov-Razumnik, wrote that 'Day after day "hostages" were arrested and shot, real and imaginary plots were constantly being "discovered".' In Moscow and Petrograd and every town and village in Russia the people lived through a fearful nightmare.[42]

The Red forces took no prisoners. Latsis, another Lett who was a senior official in the Cheka, declared in a statement on 'The Law of Civil War': 'Kill all wounded of the enemy camp . . . in civil war there is no place for judicial procedure. The struggle is one of life and death. If you do not kill, you will be killed'.[43]

In addition to class enemies and counter-revolutionaries, however, many peasants who fought against grain requisitions or abuses of local soviets, or who simply fell foul of soviet or Cheka officials, were executed. Numerically they were probably the main victims of the Cheka during the bread war. But it is impossible to estimate accurately the number of peasants or indeed the total of victims of the Red terror. Latsis stated that 12,733 people were shot in all Russia during the first three years of the Cheka's existence. But this figure falls far short of the true total. An estimate which is more reasonable, although possibly too moderate, is that the Red terror alone took the lives of fifty thousand people.[44]

The White forces conducted a terror no less ferocious. Like the bolsheviks, they took no prisoners. Leaders of private armies, like the Cossack, Semenov, in Siberia, committed atrocities comparable with those of the Cheka. Wrangel, who succeeded Denikin in the south late in 1919, recorded that he had 370 bolshevik officers and NCOs shot. But it is even more difficult to estimate the number of the victims of the White terror.

By July the soviet government found itself faced with increasing opposition on several fronts, largely inspired by the rapid success of the Czechoslovak corps. The eastern group of the corps, some 14,000 strong, commanded by General Dieterichs, a Russian of Czech descent, had on 29 June captured Vladivostok and had taken up positions around the city. The western group, commanded by General Chechek at Penza and by General Voitzekhovsky at Chelyabinsk, numbered some seventeen thousand men. The group under General Gajda in central Siberia was somewhat smaller. The original plan had been for the Czechoslovaks to travel as private citizens across Siberia to the Pacific coast. British ships were to embark and transport them nearly round the world to France where they would merge into the Czech army in France and fight on the Western Front. But then the Allied governments, impressed by the ease and scale of the Czech victories, revised their plans and towards the end of June ordered the Czechs to remain in Russia, consolidating their hold on the Trans-Siberian Railway and serving as the nucleus of a new Eastern Front.

The Czechs readily accepted the new policy. A law unto themselves, they had no intention of withdrawing and leaving their comrades behind. Also, encouraged by Allied, and especially French, promises of intervention on a massive scale, they were confident that they could conquer and restore order in Russia and then, instead of the long voyage to fight on the Western Front, they would be able to return by land through the Ukraine to a liberated Czechoslovakia.

Lenin and Trotsky were powerless against the Czechs in Siberia. Soviets were overthrown, often by the local populations, and the small bands of Red troops were dispersed without difficulty. In fact, the soviets had had at best the passive support of the people in Siberia. Untouched by violent class hatreds and even by the terror, by the famine and bread requisitions, which tormented European Russia, Siberia was detached. But the new Siberian government set up in Omsk in the wake of the Czech advance lost no time in antagonizing the people. It began with a moderate socialist policy and within a few weeks swung over to reaction, making its main purpose the restoration of private property of every kind.

Another government emerged in Samara on the Volga after the Czechs had at the request of the anti-communist elements occupied the town. Known as the Committee of Members of the Constituent Assembly, Komuch for short, it promptly made all soviets illegal and ruthlessly suppressed communist uprisings.[45] Red partisan bands were active in the vicinity of Samara, but the 'People's Army' as the force of White and Cossack troops was called, quickly put them to flight. This army had a number of daring commanders, foremost among them Colonel Kappel, who captured Ufa and Simbirsk in July, and on 6 August took Kazan, the capital of the ancient Khanate from which the Tartars had menaced Moscow until 1551, when Ivan the Terrible had conquered them and had established Russian power on the Volga.[46]

On the day following the capture of Kazan workers of the state munitions plants of Izhevsk to the north on the Kama River rebelled against their soviet. They had been antagonized by the communist requisitioning brigades and then by the peremptory methods of soviet officials in enforcing mobilization for the Red Army. They had killed or imprisoned all soviet officials and had given their support to Komuch which had proclaimed as its objective a 'united, free, and independent Russia' and the election of a democratic constituent assembly.[47] Other industrial towns in the region were staunchly anti-soviet and followed the example of Izhevsk. Within a few weeks the authority of the new anti-soviet governments extended over the vast territory from Perm in the north to Samara and Orenburg in the south. But Kazan was to prove the farthest extent of their westward advance.

The Siberian government at Omsk and the constituent assembly government at Samara, the two chief authorities to emerge, were both grossly incompetent and surrounded by corruption and they quarrelled incessantly. The former was right- and the latter left-wing in policy and not even the common purpose of ousting the communist government in Moscow could bridge this gulf.[48] Both governments, moreover, failed to win popular support and surprisingly the socialist revolutionaries were unable to attract the workers and the peasants of the region. A strong anti-soviet regime was set up in Ekaterinburg, but it sided with Omsk against Samara. In Ufa from 8 to 23 September representatives of the three governments and of other groups met to concert their political and military policies. But the differences between them were unbridgeable. The conference could only reach an unsatisfactory compromise in appointing a directorate of five with supreme authority. Thus on the middle Volga neither the threat of communist power extending over most of European Russia nor the new fighting spirit of the Red Army, dramatically demonstrated on 10 September while the Ufa conference was still in session by the recapture of Kazan, could bring the anti-soviet forces to united action.[49]

In the south-east, anti-soviet forces were also successful. Denikin and the volunteer army after calling off their attack on Ekaterinodar in April had taken up positions to the south of Novocherkassk. Two courses were open to Denikin. The first was to accept the plan urged upon him by General Krasnov, the Ataman of the Don, to advance against Tsaritsyn on the Volga and then moving up the river to join with the Czechs and the people's army on the middle Volga. The combined forces would then turn westwards and march on Moscow. Between Denikin and Krasnov, however, friction already existed. Krasnov, for instance, openly took help from the Germans in the Ukraine; Denikin remained loyal to the Allies although on occasion he accepted German munitions through Krasnov. But it was clear that the two commanders could only work together with strain and difficulty.

Denikin's second course of action, and the one which he took, was to turn south again and to capture Ekaterinodar, the Kuban capital. He considered this to be the more important objective, for he knew he would lose the support of the Kuban Cossacks who provided the rank and file of his army, if he failed to liberate the Kuban. The danger then would also be that the Germans would move into the region.

On 22 June Denikin marched the volunteer army, now numbering between 8,000 and 9,000 men, and with only limited supplies and munitions, into the Kuban. Waiting for them were Red forces some 10,000 strong and with ample supplies of every kind. But this army was no more than a collection of partisan bands, untrained and undisciplined. Moreover, the north Caucasian soviet had little authority over its commanders, who behaved as leaders of private armies and at times of crisis mutinied. In fact, soviet rule in the Kuban was precarious. Industrial workers and dependable communists were few in number and the *inogorodny*, or poor non-Cossack peasants, had been antagonized by Ukrainians, ex-sailors, and irresponsible groups who were no more than bandits, but who, calling themselves communists, terrorized the villages. As in the middle Volga region the weakness, indiscipline, and poor leadership of the Red forces contributed greatly to the success of the Whites.

Denikin's army captured Torgovaya on 25 June, severing communications between Tsaritsyn and Ekaterinodar. They next took the important railway junction of Tikhoretskaya, and on 16 August they occupied Ekaterinodar. Ten days later, with the capture of the Black Sea port of Novorossiisk, Denikin had gained access to supplies and had, moreover, secured his grip over the whole of the Kuban. But now the differences between Denikin and his officers and NCOs on the one hand and the Kuban Cossacks on the other became pronounced. The Whites of the volunteer army were fighting to restore Russia to her pre-war status of a united powerful nation, either as a monarchy or as a republic. The Kuban Cossacks were concerned with their region and once the soviet regime had been suppressed there they saw no point in fighting farther. They did not understand that the Kuban could not be kept apart from the challenges of the revolutionary movement. Other differences were to damage the union of the Whites and the Cossacks, but in August they were still together and in a position of strength.

Like the Kuban Cossacks, General P. N. Krasnov and his Cossacks were primarily concerned to clear the soviets from their region. Krasnov even appealed to the kaiser to support the independence of the Don. Any influence that the Germans might have wielded came to an end with their collapse on the Western Front. But Krasnov himself had never been merely a German puppet, like Skoropadsky in the Ukraine; he led the widespread popular movement among the Don Cossacks against the soviets and commanded an army of more than 30,000 men. He defeated the Red partisans and suppressed the soviets in the Don territory. He planned then to take Voronezh and Saratov and Tsaritsyn, and to form a link with the White forces on the middle Volga, thus ensuring the defences of the Don. But in this plan he failed. Bands of Red partisans who had retreated from the Ukraine, as the Germans advanced, had taken up positions on the Volga around Tsaritsyn. Further recruits had been enlisted from the workers in the Donbas mining region. Led by K. E. Voroshilov, later to be commissar for war and the navy, and by Stalin who had come to the south-east to organize grain requisitions, Tsaritsyn stubbornly held out against Krasnov and his Don Cossacks.

Throughout the summer months of 1918 the soviet leaders were preoccupied with these events on the Volga. When on 7 August Trotsky left Moscow in his special train for the front, he did not know that Kazan had fallen. He was shaken on receiving the news, for he knew that the Whites now threatened Moscow. But he was even more shaken by the state in which he found the Red Army. The troops had fallen back in disorder to Sviyazhsk and were demoralized. Many units were in a state of panic and were held together only by the leadership of officers like Mikhail Tukhachevsky.[50] At this point the Czechs and the Whites could have advanced to the walls of the Kremlin without meeting real resistance.

Within three weeks the Red Army had miraculously recovered as a fighting force. To Trotsky, always at his best when faced with a seemingly impossible situation, belonged most of the credit for reorganizing and inspiring the army with a new spirit. His methods were at times extreme. On 14 August he proclaimed that, if any unit retreated, its commissar and the commander would be summarily executed. Shortly afterwards he announced that 'twenty deserters were shot yesterday ... The first to go were the commissars and commanders who left their posts; next came the cowardly liars who played sick; and finally the Red Army soldiers who deserted ... Death to the coward! Death to the traitor-deserter!'[51]

This severity brought results and was effective in restoring discipline. The Red Army began to fight with a new desperate courage. An attempt by Colonel Kappel with White troops to take Sviyazhsk by surprise was fiercely repelled. Trotsky, supported by Tukhachevsky and others, was already planning to take the offensive. In August the 2nd and 5th Red Armies, operating with the Volga River Flotilla, began to advance and on 10 September they captured Kazan.

Trotsky was jubilant and was prompt to press home the propaganda advantage. His announcements raised the spirits of the Red troops and helped to demoralize the Whites. 'September 10 is a red-letter day in the history of the Socialist Revolution' he declared in one proclamation. 'On this day Kazan was torn ... from the White Guards and the Czechoslovaks. It is a turning point. The advance of the enemy has at last been stopped; his spirit is broken. After Kazan we shall recapture Ekaterin-burg, Simbirsk, Samara, and the other cities on the Volga in the Urals, and in Siberia . . .'[52]

The capture of Kazan was, in fact, a turning point. The representatives of the anti-soviet governments, meeting then in Ufa, and the People's Army lacked both the iron determination and the cohesion to withstand a major defeat. White troops, finding a new pugnacious enemy before them, took to their heels. Two days after the capture of Kazan, Tukhachevsky occupied Simbirsk. Along the Volga the White forces fell back and by the end of the year all the main towns, except Ekaterinburg, had fallen to the Red Army.

At the time when Trotsky rushed to Sviyazhsk to reorganize the Red forces, Stalin went to Tsaritsyn. He was still commissar of nationalities, but soviet territorial losses in 1918 had deprived his office of all real function. His mission to the Volga was to deal with a special emergency. Ataman Krasnov had severed the railway line between Tsaritsyn and Moscow and the capital depending wholly, after the loss of Siberia and the Ukraine, on grain supplies from the northern Caucasus was threatened with starvation. Stalin took prompt action, sacking inefficient and corrupt officials, and replacing revolutionary committees with individuals with direct responsibility for ensuring that trains ran and that supplies reached Moscow.

After attending to this task, however, Stalin remained in Tsaritsyn and to this period belongs the genesis of his personal struggle against Trotsky. It became a feud of such bitterness and violence as to influence the course of Russia's history. Years later it was to be a factor in Stalin's decision to fight the decisive battle of the second world war at Tsaritsyn, which had been renamed Stalingrad in 1925. This battle rather than the murder of Trotsky himself exorcised something of the intense hatred engendered in Stalin's mind by this rivalry.

The source of the vendetta was Stalin's personal jealousy. Lenin, Trotsky, and Stalin were the three dominant bolshevik leaders at this time but Stalin was very much the junior member of the trio. Lenin and Trotsky were enthusiastically acclaimed everywhere and the government was known as the government of Lenin–Trotsky. Stalin felt himself to be overlooked and held in obscurity. He accepted Lenin's ascendancy for Lenin had always been 'the master'. But with his pride and festering sense of inferiority he resented Trotsky and concentrated his hatred on him. For his part Trotsky underestimated Stalin, had no understanding of his morbid sensitivity, and constantly humiliated him.

As commissar of war, Trotsky was struggling to impose a centralized system of command and organization in the armed forces. But many leaders of partisan groups and detachments resented subordination to the central chain of command, especially as this often meant obeying the orders of Trotsky's 'specialists', the ex-tsarist officers. Tsaritsyn was one of the strongest centres of opposition to Trotsky's policy. Here Klim Voroshilov, the Donbas metal-worker, commanded the 10th Army which was the strongest Red force on the Volga. Stalin supported and probably instigated Voroshilov's insubordination.

Trotsky did not accept disobedience of his policies which had been endorsed by Lenin and the party central committee, and an open clash with the Tsaritsyn command became inevitable. It happened in July 1918 when Stalin cabled to Lenin, demanding that central military head-quarters should make no appointments to the northern Caucasus and the Don without the knowledge of Stalin himself and of Voroshilov. This demand accompanied by violent criticism of Trotsky's handling of the war in the south far exceeded Stalin's authority. Trotsky naturally pointed this out and insisted that Stalin, although a member of the government, must while in the south obey military orders.

Lenin, valuing the services of both men and adept at calming the jealousies which arose among his colleagues, was at pains to meet both claims. To Trotsky he fully endorsed his support for the policy of centralizing military command but he obtained Trotsky's agreement to granting Stalin's demands. The open clash was averted but Stalin's antagonism towards Trotsky, far from weakening, was intensified. He went out of his way to thwart Trotsky's leadership, even to the extent of writing on one of Trotsky's orders: 'To be disregarded'.[53]

After an initial success in September which Stalin at once reported to Moscow as a victory, White forces again surrounded Tsaritsyn. Trotsky was furious and cabled Lenin: 'I insist categorically on Stalin's recall. Things are going badly at the Tsaritsyn front in spite of super-abundant forces. Voroshilov is capable of commanding a regiment, not an army of 50,000 . . .'[54] Called before the revolutionary council of war, Stalin wisely refrained from defending Voroshilov and openly sought reconciliation with Trotsky. In October he returned to Tsaritsyn and a few days after-wards the White forces were finally repelled and the siege of Tsaritsyn lifted.[55] But, reporting on the military situation to a congress of soviets on the first anniversary of the revolution, Trotsky was strongly critical of the 10th Army and his public denunciation was yet another humiliation which Stalin could never forgive or forget.

The Red advance on the Volga was so swift and striking that Lenin and Trotsky seem to have felt that the struggle against the Whites was virtually over. Both were waiting on news of the outbreak of the socialist revolution in Germany. The collapse of Germany and Austria in Novem-ber had convinced them that not only the German but also the inter-national proletarian revolution was near at hand.[56] Lenin considered that the real danger now was attack by the victorious imperialists, England and France. As before, he showed how little he understood the international situation and the countries of Europe where he had lived. His mind was so concentrated on the tactics of revolution that he never achieved any real understanding of other societies and peoples and, indeed, his understanding of his own people, especially the peasants, was limited.

The collapse of Germany had immediate repercussions in the Ukraine. German and Austrian troops had occupied the vast steppelands after the signing of the peace of Brest-Litovsk, hoping to ensure a steady supply of grain for their famished peoples. They had gone in as supporters of the nationalist Rada, but had dissolved the Rada and had recognized General Skoropadsky as hetman of the Ukraine. The puppet hetman by his reactionary policies at once ranged against him the peasants and workers and, in fact, all but the small wealthy upper class. Strikes and outbreaks of violence increased in frequency and magnitude, despite the harsh punishments enforced by German and Austrian troops. Peasant bands waged guerrilla warfare against the government and the occupation forces. Robber gangs ranged over the countryside. Terrorist groups were active. White and nationalist Ukrainian agitators excited the people against the wealthy landlords, against the Jews, and against the occupation forces. The peasants, anarchists at heart, who resented all control and restraint which interfered with their occupation of the land, were always ready to be incited and once aroused caused havoc. Many Ukrainian communists had fled to Soviet Russia after the suppression of the Ukrainian Soviet Republic by the Germans, and these agitators were most effective in provoking uprisings. The Ukraine was soon in the grip of an anarchy even more savage than that which had followed the revolution in other parts of Russia.

As the realization spread among the German and Austrian troops that defeat was at hand in the West, and even more after the armistice, while they remained in the Ukraine they lost interest in suppressing uprisings and keeping order. Skoropadsky had increasing difficulty in maintaining his regime. He had only a very small and unreliable force, and the units of the volunteer army in Kiev were only just able to police the city. The hetman tried desperately but in vain to obtain outside support. In November Ukrainian nationalists meeting in Belaya Tserkov proclaimed a Ukrainian People's Republic headed by a directory. The leading member of this directory was Simon Petlura, formerly war minister in the Rada government. Support for the new directory and rebellion against Skoropadsky's regime developed into an overwhelming flood throughout the country. Only in Kiev where the Germans refused access to Petlurist troops did Skoropadsky's authority linger, but on 14 December disguised as a wounded German officer he fled.

Petlura's regime was, however, insecure. Among the peasants support for the communists, whom they thought of as having given them the land, was growing. They had not yet experienced such communist activities as forcible requisitioning of grain by workers' detachments and the ferocious struggles to which the committees of the poor had given rise. They wanted to be left alone and mistakenly they believed that the communists would leave them in peace.

Petlura's directory made strenuous efforts to appeal more widely to workers and peasants. It proclaimed a radical programme and convened a workers' congress from which landowners and bourgeoisie were excluded, but in which the peasants and intelligentsia supporting Ukrainian nationalism were well represented. But the directory made no headway, and it was clear that the cause of Ukrainian nationalism and separatism had no strong appeal among the people.

Rumours spread by communist agitators that the directory was negotiating with the Allied military authorities in Odessa aroused fears among the people that they were about to suffer a new occupation. With memories of the German occupation still vivid in their minds the peasants and workers were aroused further against the directory. Also the armed forces of the directory, made up of undisciplined peasants and workers divided into bands, each led by its own ataman, antagonized the people, especially the Jews in the towns, by their acts of violence and persecution. Moreover, the bands, disunited, inexperienced, and unruly could not stand against the advancing Red forces. On 5 February 1919 the Red Army took Kiev and the directory fled to the south.

Hanging over these events in the Ukraine, in the Caucasus, and on the Volga was the threat, which the soviet leaders actively feared, but which was never to materialize in any serious form, of Allied intervention.

Russia's withdrawal from the war had deeply disturbed the Allied governments. The war on the Western Front had then reached a desperate stage and the transfer of the German divisions from the east to the west threatened to be decisive. Many Allied ministers and military leaders urged a policy of immediate armed intervention to depose the soviet regime but troops in the strength needed could not be spared. Small detachments of British troops joined later by French and American detachments were landed in Murmansk in March and in Archangel in August, but their purpose was to guard the military supplies sent for use against the Germans.[57] Allied units had also been landed in Vladivostok to guard the military supplies there and to be ready to meet attacks by German and Austrian prisoners-of-war whom the soviet government were rumoured, falsely as it proved, to be releasing for the purpose of attacking the Allies. The small detachments landed were thus wholly defensive in purpose and not designed as interventions in Russia's internal affairs.

The swift successes of the Czechoslovak legion in the early summer of 1918 had made a strong impression on the Allied governments. The Czech victories suggested that the communist regime was weak and lacking the support of the Russian people, and that the Red Army was an undisciplined rabble. The presence of detachments of Allied troops with adequate supplies would, it was believed, encourage the people to rebel and displace the communists; they could then elect a new constituent assembly and renew the struggle against the Central Powers. This reasoning was quite false, but in the immensity of Russia and the confused complexity of the civil war such misconceptions were understandable.

The decision of the Allies towards the end of June to keep the Czechoslovaks in Russia so that they could consolidate their hold on the Trans-Siberian Railway and provide the spearhead of a new Russian attack on the Central Powers, was the first step towards real intervention. As part of this policy of armed intervention, the Japanese landed a force of 72,000 troops in Vladivostok, and the British, French, and Americans landed smaller forces, which were intended to move westwards in support of the Czechs.

The armistice of 11 November overtook this policy and led to confusion among the Allied leaders concerning further intervention. The objective of reviving the Eastern Front was no longer valid. Lloyd George and Woodrow Wilson wanted to reach some agreement with the communist regime. Winston Churchill, often in conflict with his own prime minister, urged armed intervention. George Clemenceau and the French government were determined to oppose the soviet regime by every means possible. Finally, intervention was adopted as the policy of England, France, the U.S.A., Japan, and Italy. But in action it was a muddled, hesitant policy, made more difficult by the extreme war-weariness and labour unrest in Britain and France.

As part of this policy, Britain and France signed a convention providing that Bessarabia, the Crimea, and the Ukraine would be the French zone of action while Britain would operate in Transcaucasia. Towards the end of November the British and French jointly sent ships to Novorossiisk with munitions and supplies for Denikin. Then a French division landed in Odessa, while British units took up positions in Batum on the Black Sea and Baku on the Caspian.[58]

Lenin was at this time making every effort to come to terms with the Allied governments. He believed that world capitalism would inevitably attack the new communist state, but that revolution was bound to come soon in the capitalist countries. Time was therefore on the side of the communists, and so soviet policy should be conciliatory and avoid provoking the capitalists. In the brief period from November 1918 to February 1919, the soviet government sent no less than seven peace proposals to the Allied governments. Woodrow Wilson and Lloyd George, both seeking peaceful relations with the new regime, were impressed by these approaches. On 5 January the British government proposed that the communist government and the anti-communist groups should declare a truce and send representatives to the Paris peace conference. The French government, however, firmly rejected the suggestion. Wilson and Lloyd George on 21 January 1919 persuaded the French to agree to invite representatives from all groups in Russia to a conference with the Allied powers on Prinkipo Island in the Sea of Marmora. The soviet government declared its readiness to take part in these discussions, but the White Russians refused to sit around any table with the communists.[59] Moreover, the French who had only agreed reluctantly to this proposal were now determined to go ahead with intervention. They had their way, for the Allied leaders then in Paris for the peace negotiations finally agreed to continue their support for the anti-communist forces. Their hope was that a unified White government would emerge to assume power as soon as the soviet regime had been overthrown.

At this time in Russia the prospect of a unified White government was extremely remote. In Trans-Baikalia the brutal Ataman Semenov, a half-Russian, half-Mongol freebooter, supported chiefly by Japanese money and arms, ruled as a dictator. Denikin and Krasnov commanded the two main anti-communist movements in the south. In Esthonia General Nicholas Yudenich had enlisted a small army and with British help planned to attack Petrograd. General Eugene Miller was the dominant leader of the anti-soviet government, backed by the Allies in the far north. But all these forces were on the borders of Russia and separated by vast distances which made unity physically impossible.

In Siberia, however, the directory, set up by the Samara government and other White organizations, occupied a more central position and seemed better placed to provide an alternative government after the overthrow of the soviet regime. But the directory was based on an uneasy compromise between the left- and right-wing representatives whose only point of agreement was their anti-communism. The former tsarist officers in particular wanted a strong conservative leadership, and they were responsible for the revolt on the night of 17–18 November which overthrew the directory and appointed Admiral Kolchak to be supreme ruler and commander-in-chief.

A distinguished naval officer, highly efficient, gallant, with a keen sense of duty and of personal honour, Kolchak was known and respected in the Allied countries. He had as a young officer taken a notable part in Arctic exploration. He had fought with great bravery in the defence of Port Arthur during the Russo-Japanese War. He had been a leading member of the small group of officers who, spurred by the humiliation of Russia's naval defeats at the hands of the Japanese, had reorganized the admiralty and his abilities had been recognized by promotion to rear-admiral at the early age of forty-three. In the following year (June 1916) he had been appointed vice-admiral in command of the Black Sea Fleet, and he had been acclaimed for his daring and efficiency in laying mine-fields close to Turkish shores.

The abdication of the tsar had distressed him, but he had recognized that his loyalty was to his country rather than to the throne and he had taken the oath to the provisional government. He had readily co-operated with the soviet of sailors' deputies, but could not accept the rapid decline in discipline. When the sailors in a mass meeting on his flagship demanded the disarming of all officers, Kolchak refused and in a dramatic gesture drew his sword and threw it overboard. On his own insistence he was relieved of his command and he visited the U.S.A. and then England. Returning to Russia, he was shattered to learn in Vladivostok the news of the bolshevik revolution and the withdrawal of Russia from the war.

This breach of faith with the Allies affected him deeply and he at once offered his services to the British army in any capacity. The British authorities for unknown reasons sent him to Mesopotamia but recalled him when he reached Singapore, deciding that he would be of more use in the Far East. His first assignment there was to co-ordinate the numerous anti-communist forces in the region of the Chinese eastern railway. But he had no troops to uphold his authority; Ataman Semenov ignored him; the Japanese who supported Semenov gave him no help. He then decided to seek service in the volunteer army on the Don. He reached Omsk and there was persuaded to become minister of war in the new cabinet of ministers under the directory. While he was on a tour of the front, the officers, apparently, without his knowledge, planned their coup which took place the day after his return, when the directory was overthrown and he was unanimously invited by the council of ministers to become supreme ruler and commander-in-chief.

Trim and lean, with aquiline features, even his mouth shaped like the beak of an eagle, Kolchak had the appearance of a disciplined and dedicated soldier. To many among the Allied leaders who knew something of his service career and his high-principled conduct he seemed the perfect leader for a unified White government. But he was aloof and moody, nervous at times to the point of hysteria. He had no understanding of politics and no capacity for choosing the right men for responsible positions, and he was unable to make decisions. He saw corruption and mismanagement all around him but he lacked the ruthlessness and decision to crush it. In spite of his personal probity, his dedication to duty and his patriotism, he was to prove a tragic failure.[60]

Kolchak's rule opened with excesses of the kind that had made the Cheka feared and hated. A revolt in Omsk and the nearby town of Kulomzino on 21 December, organized by an underground communist group, was put down with savagery. Three hundred people were killed and a further 166 were shot after court-martial. A number of moderate left-wing politicians were released from the local prison by insurgents and promptly gave themselves up. But then a young lieutenant, named Bartashevsky, took some of these unfortunate politicians from the prison and had them shot on the banks of the Irtysh. Such brutality, for which Kolchak was not responsible personally, marked his regime with blood and antagonized many of his supporters.

In the first weeks of Kolchak's rule, rapid advances and impressive victories nevertheless suggested that he would soon enter Moscow and that the communist government would be in flight. At the end of December

1918 the Siberian army under General Gajda on the north of Kolchak's front took the town of Perm. This aroused new hopes of forming a junction with the small British units some four hundred miles to the north on the Dvina.[61] But the new optimism at the headquarters in Omsk was soon crushed by the advance of the Red Army which had crossed the Volga and by the end of 1918 had taken Ufa and Orenburg.

Early in 1919 Kolchak launched his offensive. His western army, some 40,000 strong, pushed back the Soviet 5th Army which was but a quarter of this strength, and on 13 March recaptured Ufa. In the following weeks his armies advanced so rapidly that they were threatening Kazan and Samara, while in the north the Siberian army had passed beyond Perm on the road to Vyatka.

Moscow now seemed well within his reach. But the weakness of his armies and his position in Siberia began to appear. Few of his troops were trained and they had no stomach for real fighting. They had advanced rapidly, because the Red Army troops facing them were weak and were threatened by serious peasant rebellions in the middle Volga region. Kolchak, too, found his regime was being increasingly undermined by the growing hostility of the Siberian peasants. They resented the arbitrary rule of the White officers who were not only corrupt and brutal, but inefficient. Kolchak and his ministers made no attempt to understand the peasants and their interests and imposed a crude militarization on the land, demanding taxes, recruits, and grain, and arousing hatred and hostility such as the committees of the poor and the grain requisitioning detachments had inflamed in Soviet Russia, where the peasants had at least been promised the land.

At the end of April, the Red counter-offensive began. Mikhail Frunze, a veteran communist, led a strong Red force which turned back Kolchak's western army. On 9 June Ufa was recaptured by the Red Army and the Whites retreated beyond the Ural Mountains. Already morale had broken among Kolchak's troops and many went over to the Red Army. In a pitched battle at the end of July near Chelyabinsk, the White forces suffered a serious defeat. On 14 November the Red troops took Omsk. Kolchak's armies were completely broken and in a growing flood his troops went over to the enemy.

During these months of the Red advance, Lenin was eager that the Red Army should press on to secure complete control over the Ural Mountain region. Trotsky and the Red commander-in-chief, I. I. Vatzetis were anxiously watching the progress of Denikin's army. Lenin's tactics prevailed and Vatzetis was replaced by S. S. Kamenev, formerly a tsarist colonel, who served the communist regime loyally.

Denikin had launched his offensive in May 1919. His army took Kharkov and Tsaritsyn and by the end of June the whole of the Don region was in their hands. On 3 July Denikin issued his 'Moscow Order' which declared the final objective of the campaign to be 'the seizure of the heart of Russia, Moscow'. This offensive involved a three-pronged attack: Wrangel, commanding the right-wing, was to advance up the Volga and join with Kolchak's army to take Moscow; Sidorin was to move northwards; Mai-Maevsky, commanding the left-wing, was to move north from Kharkov on Moscow.

The Soviet leaders were again on the defensive. During the summer of 1919 the Red Army in the south had suffered defeat after defeat and was becoming demoralized. Grigoriev, one of the Soviet commanders in the south, turned traitor and tried to set himself up as an independent ataman. Red troops defected or deserted in growing numbers. The peasants were anti-Soviet and unpredictable. The turmoil and anarchy which gripped the whole of the Ukraine, after the withdrawal of the Germans and Austrians, turned the steppes into a cauldron of warring partisans fighting savagely and suffering cruel reprisals.

Denikin's campaign reached its climax in October 1919 with the capture of Orel. Here he was only two hundred and fifty miles from Moscow. Tula, an important centre of the munitions industry, alone stood between him and the capital. But Denikin had failed to build up any reserves and he had no troops to guard his communications or defend his rear. This was important, for his positions were under attack by partisans and particularly by the Insurgent Army, led by the daring anarchist, Nestor Makhno.[62] Denikin himself, although a man of outstanding courage, ability, and integrity, was a soldier with no understanding of politics and although himself the son of a serf he failed to attract popular support. In making his rapid advance to Moscow he knew that he was taking a desperate risk and that he had to gain the capital in the autumn or early winter of 1919 or admit defeat.

At the time when Denikin was advancing on Orel, General Yudenich with his north-western army of some 18,500 troops launched an unexpected attack on Petrograd. It was a daring venture. The 7th Red Army guarding the approaches to the city was 25,000 strong. But Yudenich was seeking to support Denikin's advance on Moscow either by drawing off Soviet troops as reinforcements for Petrograd or by himself capturing Petrograd and so striking a severe blow at Red morale.

Yudenich began his surprise attack on 11 October and advanced rapidly. The Red Army fell back in disorder and panic began to spread among the troops. Yudenich's plan was to cut all the railway lines to the city as the first step before taking it by storm. He succeeded in cutting all lines except the Petrograd–Moscow line which remained in Red control.

The Soviet leaders were in a quandary. Denikin's threat to Moscow was the more serious danger and they therefore decided against rushing troops from the southern front to defend Petrograd. Lenin considered that the city must be abandoned. Trotsky would not accept this proposal. He rushed to Petrograd and personally took charge of its defence. In a fury of activity he worked to inspire the 7th Army so that Yudenich would be repulsed before his troops could enter the city. But, if the Whites gained entry, they were to be met by savage fighting in the streets and from every building, which would, he was confident, result in the virtual annihilation of the White army.

In the event, the Red 7th Army, driven back to the Pulkovo heights which formed the last line of defence of the city, stood firm. Here Trotsky rallied them and they repelled Yudenich's forces. By 23 October they had to withdraw from Tsarskoe Selo. This repulse was the decisive turning point in Yudenich's campaign. He had no reserves on which he could call and his force was too small to lay siege to the city. His army, drawing its main strength from the high proportion of former officers, fought stubbornly. As they retreated they continued to struggle, but by mid-November they had fallen back over the border and into Esthonia where the army was in due course disbanded.

The successful defence of Petrograd was Trotsky's achievement. The Red troops, taken by surprise, had been on the point of panic, when he himself had taken charge. He had organized, driven, and put new heart in the Red troops who had stood firm and then had pushed the Whites over the frontier. His great personal contribution was formally acknowledged by the award of the Order of the Red Banner, then the highest Soviet decoration. Throughout the civil war Trotsky's activity and leadership were of the greatest importance; he created the Red Army and more than any other Soviet leader brought victory to the Soviet regime.

Spring and summer 1919 had been a critical period for the Soviet regime. But in the autumn the tide had turned and after months of desperately fighting on the defensive, the Red Army had begun to advance, driving the Whites before them on all fronts. After the capture of Orsk on 14 November Kolchak's armies had disintegrated, thousands of his troops going over to the Reds. Kolchak himself, despairing of victory, nominated Denikin as his successor in January 1920. He then began to make his way eastwards to Vladivostok but was betrayed to the Soviet forces by the French General, Janin, and by the Czechs, and was shot.[63]

Denikin had reached Orel, but in doing so had over-extended his lines and overtaxed his forces. Moreover, the peasants and workers in his rear had become bitterly hostile, because of the savage excesses of his troops and the reactionary behaviour of his officers. On 20 October the Red Army drove him from Orel and four days later from Voronezh. Denikin hoped to re-form his armies as they fell back into the Don region. But morale had declined too far among them for any rallying to be possible. Moreover, Denikin himself, after this long retreat from what had been a position of strong advantage, had lost the confidence of his officers and men and of his Cossack allies. Towards the end of March with the help of British ships he evacuated some 35,000 troops to the Crimea, hoping again to rally his forces. But aware of the antagonism of increasing numbers of his officers, he nominated General Baron Peter Wrangel who had commanded on the Caucasian front to be commander of the White armies, and on 4 April he left Russia.[64]

The Whites made their last stand against the communist regime in the Crimea. They now had in Baron Peter Wrangel an outstanding leader who, if he had assumed command earlier, might have led the Whites to victory. A tall, dashing figure, wearing Cossack uniform, he was an aristocrat and devoutly Orthodox. He rallied the die-hard officers and conservatives, who saw in him a romantic embodiment of the tsarist tradition. But Wrangel was more far-seeing and progressive than Kolchak and Denikin, and had a far better appreciation of the military and political situation. He recognized in particular that the Whites must win peasant support even at the price of surrendering the land to them.[65]

The immediate task facing Wrangel was the restoration of discipline and the revival of the fighting spirit of his forces. The remnants of the volunteer army had been demoralized by the crushing defeats suffered in the long retreat from Orel. In the Crimea they were surrounded by refugees from Soviet Russia and there seemed no future for any of them. Moreover, the British government which had provided the bulk of their supplies now indicated that it, too, considered future struggle to be hopeless. The British undertook to negotiate with the Soviet government for the safety of all who had taken part on the side of the Whites, but they would do no more.

Wrangel himself at first felt that his only course of action was to ensure the safe evacuation of his troops and the refugees. He did not lose hope, however, and with driving energy he began to reorganize his army. He enforced discipline ruthlessly. Officers and soldiers found after drunken bouts in the streets of Simferopol were publicly hanged. He would tolerate none of the violence and unruliness which had earned for the White armies the hatred of the peasants and villagers throughout southern Russia. His severity and leadership soon revived the White army. In the summer of 1920 a communist acknowledged that Wrangel's army was 'qualitatively . . . the best fighting force of which the Russian and international counter-revolution ever disposed in armed struggle against the Soviet Republics'.[66]

Wrangel had strongly criticized Denikin for advancing headlong to Orel without securing his rear. He held that the Whites must consolidate themselves in each region as they captured it, and there produce such order and living conditions as would attract the people. For his first offensive he prepared carefully. The British government had bluntly warned him against renewing hostilities. The French were encouraging, but Wrangel knew that he could not count on them for supplies and support such as Denikin had had from the British. But a factor which helped him greatly was the outbreak of the Soviet–Polish war towards the end of April. The Soviet leaders deployed their best troops against the Poles and could not send reinforcements to the south.

On 6 June Wrangel launched his offensive. His army was far out-numbered by the Red forces holding the line north of Perekop, but he commanded seasoned troops who knew that they could expect no quarter from the communists. Wrangel's army surged forward, breaking through the Red lines. Within two weeks he had conquered the northern Tauride province. Here he stopped to consolidate his gains. He tried to introduce land reforms which would win the support of the peasants. But they re-jected the reforms and waged savage guerrilla warfare against the White troops. He tried to reach agreement with Makhno for joint operations with the insurgents against the communists, but Makhno simply hanged his envoys.

Wrangel decided now not to press his advance into the Ukraine where the peasantry were so hostile, but to turn to the Kuban and the Don where he could hope for Cossack support. The Soviet leaders recognizing, how-ever, that the Kuban was a region of anti-communism maintained an army of 30,000 troops there. They were nevertheless worried by Wrangel's advance and Trotsky himself hurried to Taganrog to direct operations.

Against such an overwhelming superiority of Red forces Wrangel's one hope of victory lay in speed of advance. But his generals proved hesitant and were forced to retreat. The next line of attack which Wrangel chose was north-westwards across the Dnieper and into the western Ukraine. Here he hoped to benefit from the Polish advance. But after crossing the river and seizing Nikopol his army suffered defeat at the hands of the Red forces and was thrown back over the Dnieper with heavy losses. At this time, too, the Soviet–Polish armistice freed the Red armies to reinforce the Southern Front.

In Moscow the Soviet leaders still did not underestimate the danger of Wrangel and his army which was, moreover, the last organized White force opposing them. Frunze who had been largely responsible for the defeat of Kolchak was given command of the Red Armies in the south. But it was an uneven struggle. Wrangel had some 35,000 men and no dependable source of supplies and munitions. He could not now retreat into the Crimea for the peninsula could not provide enough food for his troops. The Red forces were some 137,000 strong and could now be re-inforced from the north, and they had adequate arms and ammunition. Sensing the hopelessness of the struggle, the Whites began to lose heart. In the battle on the north Tauride front begun on 28 October Wrangel's army suffered disastrous defeat and was driven back into the Crimea.

On 7 November, the anniversary of the revolution, Red troops stormed the White lines holding the Perekop isthmus which were believed to be almost impregnable. But the Red troops elated by the prospect of victory fought bravely, ignoring heavy losses, and broke through these defences. Wrangel now ordered his men to fall back to the numerous Crimean ports for evacuation. In all, 145,693 people, a figure embracing not only the White troops but the families of many of them and a horde of refugees,

Nikolai Ivanovich Bukharin, 1926

Leo Borissovich Kamenev, 1919

Marshal Stalin and Winston Churchill, Livadia Palace, Yalta, 1945

were taken off by boats of every kind, including units of the French navy.

Wrangel had faced overwhelming odds. The Red Army was by this time a massive force of more than five million officers and men, disciplined, well led, and fighting with a furious revolutionary zeal. Wrangel had taken command of a small army, exhausted and broken by defeats and retreats. But he had transformed it into a brave and efficient force. He had then made a gallant attempt to destroy the communist Goliath. He was foredoomed to failure, as indeed all the White resistance, seen in retrospect, was doomed. With his withdrawal the organized struggle of the White forces against the communist regime came to an end.

Russia was near to exhaustion. Hunger, typhus and other epidemics, and severe economic crisis had followed war in ravaging the country. The Soviet government desperately needed peace. The anti-communist regimes along Russia's borders no longer had the support of the Allies who recognized that the Soviet government could not readily be overthrown and really wanted an end to the war. The result was that peace treaties had been signed by the Soviet Republic with Esthonia, Lithuania, Latvia, and Finland. With their traditional enemies, the Poles, however, the Russians made no headway in negotiating peace.

At the Paris peace conference, the Allies had not settled the eastern frontier of Poland. They had proposed the Curzon Line as the most suitable solution since it left on the east side a population the majority of whom were Russians, and a population to the west side with a majority of Poles. But this was not acceptable to the Poles. They dreamt of restoring to Poland the frontiers of the eighteenth century before the partitions whereby Catherine of Russia had annexed most of her territory. Poland, like Russia, had suffered in the war and now desperately needed peace, but this dream of national revival obsessed the Polish leaders.

In spite of urgent attempts by the Soviet leaders to begin peace talks and their apparent readiness to make territorial concessions, the Poles were evasive. Marshal Pilsudski, who had emerged as the military dictator of Poland, believed that Soviet Russia was weak and vulnerable, that a Polish invasion would ignite the Ukrainian nationalist movement, and that the downfall of the Soviet regime would result.

On 25 April 1920 the small Polish army launched a surprise attack into the Ukraine. Sweeping forward they captured Kiev on 6 May. The success of the campaign depended largely on the support of Petlura who had signed an agreement with Pilsudski. But Petlura was still unable to inspire a popular Ukrainian nationalist movement or to organize a strong army. He was not popular among his own people and his agreement with the Poles was not welcomed, for the Ukrainians while disliking the communists cherished an age-old hatred of the Poles.

The Poles were halted at Kiev. The famous Red cavalry army led by the dashing young Budyonny, formerly a sergeant in the tsarist cavalry, was mainly responsible for breaking the Polish advance. On 12 June the

G

Poles withdrew from Kiev and began their hasty retreat. The Red Army, commanded by Tukhachevsky, was now on the offensive and the troops were fired with visions of annihilating the Polish army and of supporting the Polish proletariat in creating a Soviet Polish Republic. This would, they believed, be but a short step from creating also a Soviet Germany and bringing world revolution nearer realization.

Before Warsaw, however, the Red Army was halted. Pilsudski advised now by General Weygand, Foch's chief of staff, who had come to Warsaw specially for this purpose, was determined to hold the city. He also planned a counter-offensive which would take the over-confident Red commanders by surprise. The Russian troops were weary from their head-long advance but still carried on by their crusading zeal. Pilsudski's counter-offensive was, however, immediately successful and the Red forces fell back as rapidly as they had only a few weeks earlier advanced.

The Soviet leaders were now desperate for an early peace. Their dreams of creating a Soviet Poland had dissolved in the hasty retreat of their troops and they now thought only of disposing of Wrangel and of coming to grips with the internal chaos of Russia. In their impatience for peace they conceded generous terms to the Poles in the preliminary treaty signed at Riga on 12 October. The Polish frontier was moved far to the east of the Curzon Line, and Poland gained a corridor to the Baltic Sea which deprived Russia of direct access to Lithuania and thence with Germany.

In the south the Soviet government had more success in establishing Russia's frontiers. In Transcaucasia the three anti-communist republics of Georgia, Armenia, and Azerbaidzhan were quickly occupied by Red forces. Each became a Soviet Socialist Republic, independent in name but in fact wholly subject to the R.S.F.S.R. The Soviet grasp on Transcaucasia was consolidated in March 1921 when a treaty was signed with Turkey, then under the rule of Mustafa Kemal's revolutionary government.

In Central Asia and the Far East the process of bringing the many regions under Soviet rule took longer. After the defeat of Kolchak the communists were able to extend their influence into this vast territory. They brought under their control the former protectorates of Khiva and Bokhara, establishing the former as the People's Republic of Khorezm. They took the old province of Turkestan. Siberia to the west of Lake Baikal had been made part of the R.S.F.S.R. after the fall of Kolchak. But the vast region to the east of Lake Baikal had remained mainly under the control of Ataman Semenov, supported by the Japanese. Gradually, however, the Red forces moved eastwards and in 1920 they had recovered sufficient territory to constitute the Far Eastern Republic, which for the time being retained nominal independence. The Soviet government accepted this situation because the Republic was a strong ally and because it served as a buffer between the R.S.F.S.R. and Japan, which was for Moscow the real enemy in the Far East.

The Japanese, in fact, withdrew to the east coast of Siberia, but showed determination to cling to this foothold on the mainland. Finally, the pressure of the United States and Britain, who strongly opposed Japanese expansion in Siberia, compelled them to withdraw. Troops of the Far Eastern Republic then gradually crushed or expelled the White forces which, with Japanese help, lingered in eastern Siberia, and on 25 October 1922 they entered Vladivostok. By this time the communists had secured a majority in the government of the Far Eastern Republic which voted in November in favour of its incorporation in the R.S.F.S.R.

The civil war which had been one of the most savage, inhuman, and destructive struggles in history, but a struggle epic in scale, had ended.

PART III

INTERREGNUM

CHAPTER TEN

NEP

THE cost in lives and human suffering of the civil war can never be known. Throughout the vast expanse of European Russia and Siberia the administration was chaotic and no records were kept. Men, women, and children vanished in their thousands, leaving no trace. But a census conducted in 1926 accounted for a population of 147 million and, calculated on the basis of normal population growth, this figure should have been 175 million. Twenty-eight million had disappeared. The refugees from the revolution and the civil war who made their way to western Europe and to China probably numbered a million. But in the course of three-and-a-half years of war against the Central Powers and then the civil war some 27 million Russians had perished. Many had died on the battlefields and in the countless guerrilla engagements, but many had died of typhus and other diseases and of malnutrition. No other country had endured such dreadful losses, but the ordeal was not yet at an end.

For Lenin and the Russian communist party the civil war had ended in victory, but only partial victory. The Red Army had swept the White forces from Russian soil, and the half-hearted attempts of the Allied powers to overthrow the Soviet regime had failed. But the communist certainty that world revolution would follow had proved a chimera. Lenin, Trotsky, and other communist leaders had during the darkest days of their struggle drawn strength from their conviction that world revolution was at hand. The indescribable cruelties and hardships endured by their peoples were to them in the inhuman arrogance of their messianic faith wholly justified by this coming revolutionary upheaval. Furthermore, they accepted as inevitable and desirable that capitalist societies everywhere would be violently overthrown and that class hatreds would be fomented, plunging all peoples into the abyss of misery which the Russians themselves were suffering. But to them violent revolution was a purification by fire and destruction which was necessary before the party could embark on its great task of creating a new society. It was like the fire of London which cleansed the city of the plague and destroyed the buildings which harboured it and so prepared the way for building a new city.

As late as July 1919, when the Soviet regime was facing one of its gravest crises, Lenin was proclaiming in Moscow: 'This is the last difficult summer, the last difficult July. If we hold out through it, and we certainly shall hold out, the victory of the world revolution is assured.'[1] In the previous March this faith had taken on a positive form when the third international, known as the Communist International or Comintern, had been established with Zinoviev at its head and had held its first congress in Moscow.[2] Nineteen communist parties and groups had full representation while delegates from sixteen other groups participated but had only consultative votes. The Comintern was, however, no more than a façade for apart from the Russian communist party, the groups were unrepresentative and insignificant in their own countries.[3] It was nevertheless a proclamation of communist missionary zeal and an earnest of determination to carry the ideology into the countries of the world. At the same time it was made clear during this first congress that workers of the world must rally in support of the regime in Russia, and further that Moscow was the sole source of inspiration and rulings, binding on all communists.[4]

The second Comintern congress held in Moscow from 21 July to 6 August 1920 was also jubilant over the prospects of world revolution. The Red Army was then advancing victoriously into Poland and this more than offset the disappointment over the collapse of the shortlived Soviet regimes in Hungary and Bavaria. This second congress, in seeking to create a single world communist party, laid down twenty-one conditions designed to bring all communist parties into conformity with the Russian party as a step towards subordinating them completely to Moscow.[5]

By November 1920, however, Lenin was no longer so sanguine about the imminence of world revolution. The severity of the world depression in particular had diminished the revolutionary zeal of the proletariat in the industrial countries. In the meantime he was concerned to maintain an equilibrium in which Soviet Russia could trade and coexist with the capitalist countries, growing strong in readiness for world revolution in the distant future. But now he turned his attention to urgent internal problems for, following upon victory over the White armies, the whole future of the communist party and the Soviet regime in Russia was suddenly in jeopardy.

The stark problem facing him was the economic survival of the nation. The decline in industrial and agricultural production was an inevitable outcome of the war. It had become more critical because anti-Soviet forces had during much of the civil war held over sixty per cent of Russia's railways and had denied access to the grain of the Ukraine, the cotton of Turkestan, and to the Donets Basin which was the source of sixty per cent of Russia's pig iron and seventy-five per cent of her iron ore. But the system known as war communism, operating through a new massive and grossly inefficient bureaucracy, had hastened the headlong plunge of the economy towards collapse. By according absolute priority to the Red Army the system had met its minimum needs, but in every other field it had led to disaster.

By November 1920 when the civil war had come to an end Russia was completely exhausted. Six years of total war under inhuman conditions

had reduced the people to a primitive existence in which they were freezing, starving, and disease-ridden. They had accepted their hardships just
as they had accepted communist rule while the civil war raged, but now
they could see no hope of change and they were rebellious. In many parts
of the country the peasants were already in open revolt. In the cities and
towns the people were in a desperate mood.

Among the communist leaders, however, the view had been gaining
ground that the system of war communism would be even more effective
in peacetime. It was a reflection of the utter failure of the communists,
accustomed to think in terms of the proletariat, classes, and the masses, to
understand the simple human factors in society.

Trotsky was the chief exponent of this view that war communism
could solve the economic crisis. Towards the end of 1919 he had begun to
withdraw from military affairs because he considered the civil war to be
virtually at an end. He was preparing to plunge into the problems of
economic reconstruction and, vabrant with confidence after his success as
commissar of war, he believed that he could restore the national economy.

On 16 December he submitted his theses on the economic transition
from war to peace. He obtained the approval of Lenin, and the central
committee adopted his proposals for 'the mobilization of the industrial
proletariat, liability to labour service, militarization of economic life, and
the use of military units for economic needs'.[6] He was tireless in proclaiming the need to apply to labour the same severe discipline which he
had enforced in the Red Army. He organized a deluge of propaganda,
even using theatres, cinemas, and gramophone records to explain to
workers and peasants the importance of labour discipline. He demanded
that armies, no longer needed in war, should serve in civil operations, such
as the repair of railway lines, wood-cutting, and harvesting. On his instigation the Red 3rd Army was renamed 'The First Revolutionary Army
of Labour' and assigned to works in the Urals.

This labour campaign soon roused a storm of protest. Troops resented
being kept far from their families and under military discipline as they
worked on civil projects. They began deserting in large numbers. Local
peasants, antagonized by the take-over of their districts by labour armies,
became obstructive. They burnt the timber and hay which the military
units had gathered. It was soon evident that the productivity of the labour
armies was negligible while the cost of maintaining them was enormous.

In the first months of 1921 the crisis in Moscow and Petrograd came
nearer to eruption. In January the starvation bread-ration was cut by one
third. In the following month a fuel crisis was officially announced. The
winter had been severe and snow-drifts had halted food and fuel trains
from the Ukraine, the Caucasus, and Siberia. The paper-making industry
and in Petrograd sixty-four of the largest factories, including the Putilov
works, had to close down for lack of fuel.

Anger mounted among the workers. Within the party itself rank-and-file members expressed their discontent more openly and cases were reported of members tearing up their party tickets in disgust. But more significant than this general dissatisfaction was the opposition within the party which had already hardened into two main groups. The democratic centralists, comprising former left communists, objected to domination by the central committee which, they claimed, was contrary to the principles of party democracy. The other group, known as the workers' opposition, comprised communists in the trade unions. They, too, resented the interference and control of the party centre. But they also opposed the leadership on the question of the role of the trade unions in the socialist state. The general view of the party leaders was that, since workers could have no grounds for opposing their own government, the sole function remaining to the trade unions must be to submit to party policy and to work for higher production. But this was far from acceptable to the trade unions and to many party members, whose opposition was at root a lack of confidence in, bordering on contempt for, the party leaders.

Trotsky's eruption into the field of economic reconstruction brought the tensions to explosion point. His demands for discipline and revolutionary zeal in industry were unwelcome to workers, already exhausted and embittered, and they antagonized the trade unions. The debate raged so violently that the central committee gave it urgent attention. But on the question whether the party should exercise more or less discipline and control, the central committee itself was divided. In preparation for the tenth party congress, which was to meet in March 1921, the matter was thrown open to public debate. Lenin, Trotsky, and the various groups each published their policies or 'platforms'. But the debate was disrupted by the explosion of popular discontent in open rebellion.

In the Ukraine the incredibly brave and elusive anarchist, Makhno, with his insurgent army, continued to defy the Red Army. In western Siberia rebellions by peasants during this winter were so serious that for a time the Trans-Siberian Railway was disrupted and this further aggravated the food crisis in Moscow and other cities. The most serious peasant risings were, however, in the Tambov province.

In the agrarian revolution of 1917 this province had been outstandingly turbulent and the Tambov peasantry had fought most savagely against the Soviet regime in 1920 and 1921. The leader of the Tambov rebels was a certain Antonov. He had been exiled for acts of violence committed during the 1905 revolution. He had returned to his native province after the tsar's abdication and proclaiming himself a socialist revolutionary had held the office of chief of police in the town of Kirsanov. Brave and daring like Makhno, he was not, however, fanatically devoted to the same anarchist principles and was rather a natural rebel against authority.

By the spring of 1921 Antonov had some 20,000 rebels under his command and the whole province, together with parts of the adjoining provinces of Pensa and Saratov, was aflame with savage guerrilla warfare.

The grain requisitions and the harsh punishments inflicted on those who resisted had brought the peasants to the point of elemental destructive fury, which had marked the great peasant revolts of Stenka Razin, Bulavin, and Pugachev against the tsarist regime.

Soviet authority ceased to exist in the vast area of Tambov province and neighbouring districts during the first months of 1921. Officials fled to larger towns and to other places of safety. But in April Tukhachevsky took command of the Red cavalry and special units drafted to the region, and the rebels were driven back. The abolition of requisitions, removing the main grievance of the peasants, facilitated his task. By the autumn of 1921 order had been restored and the Red units were left with only the task of tracking down and destroying the small bands of rebels who had hidden away in the forests and swamps.[7]

Inured to rebellions, strikes, and revolts, Lenin and the other Soviet leaders still did not attribute special importance to the unrest in these months. The new sullen attitude of the people was reflected in a rash of strikes in Petrograd late in February. Mensheviks made appeals for freely elected factory committees and socialist revolutionaries demanded the election of a constituent assembly. At the roots of these protests lay not only the desperate food shortage, but also strong and growing antagonism towards the party dictatorship. The government imposed a curfew on the city and declared martial law. Special patrols paraded the streets. It became dangerous to display open resentment. The people, lacking leaders and themselves worn out by deprivations, smothered their discontent. But neither this massive protest in the city of the revolution nor outbreaks in the countryside on the scale of the Tambov uprising brought the Soviet leaders to recognize that the people of the country were near to the end of their endurance and that they were bitterly hostile towards the regime. It took the mutiny of the naval garrison of Kronstadt to make them realize how explosive the mood of the people was.

Kronstadt, the island naval base in the Finnish Gulf guarding the approaches to Petrograd, had been a stronghold of bolshevism in 1917. Now, four years later, the garrison rebelled against the communist party, declaring it to be the enemy of the working classes. Numbering 15,000 sailors and soldiers recruited among the peasants, the garrison shared their rebellious mood. Accounts brought by new recruits from country districts of the grain requisitions, the activities of the Cheka, and the suppression of risings, had brought them closer to mutiny. The political commissars with their stern discipline and unending admonitions had added to the unrest in the fortress. The strikes and declaration of martial law in nearby Petrograd had finally brought them to the point of open mutiny.

On 1 March 1921 the sailors, soldiers, and workers on the island held a mass meeting. Speeches by Kalinin, president of the soviet executive committee, and by N. Kuzin, commissar of the Baltic Fleet, urging the garrison not to defy Soviet authority, were brushed aside. The sailors were especially hostile. Kronstadt rang with their shouts of 'Down with the Bolshevik tyranny!', 'For the Soviets—without the Communists!' and the rebels saw themselves in the role of liberators of Russia from the new dictatorship.

After many speeches the mass meeting unanimously passed a lengthy resolution setting out their demands to the government. The chief demands were for re-election of the soviets by secret ballot, freedom of speech and of the press for workers, peasants, anarchists, and left-wing parties, freedom of meetings of peasant associations and trade unions, abolition of political appointments and of requisitioning detachments, equalization of rations for all except workers in harmful occupations, and the right of peasants to possess their land provided they did not hire labour. These and the other less important demands involved outright rejection of the dictatorship of the communist party. They reflected the view held not only in Kronstadt but widely in the country that the communists had corrupted the ideals of the revolution.

On 2 March the garrison elected a revolutionary committee of fourteen members who set up their headquarters in the warship *Petropavlovsk*. Few of the members of the communist party on the island offered opposition to the mutiny and, indeed, most of them joined the rebels. The leading commissars and Soviet officials were arrested, but the revolutionary committee was careful to avoid executions and ill-treatment of prisoners. In fact, the mutiny might well have been resolved without bloodshed if the Soviet government had been more conciliatory. But Lenin, and Trotsky in particular, feared that readiness to negotiate would be interpreted as weakness. The Petrograd soviet meeting on the night of 4 March demanded absolute surrender by the garrison. Trotsky followed this with a threatening manifesto. Kronstadt refused to submit.

On the night of 7 March Soviet artillery from the northern and southern banks of the Neva began bombarding Kronstadt. The garrison was well armed and replied with its heavy guns. It was clear to the Soviet leaders that an attack must be made on the fortress while the bay of Finland and the Neva river were frozen, for once the ice began to thaw Kronstadt would be almost impregnable. The difficulty now was that advancing forces had to cross the expanse of ice where they would show up as easy targets to the batteries, machine-guns, and rifles of the 15,000 rebels. Trotsky considered that he could not count on the 7th Red Army stationed near Petrograd to fight against comrades in Kronstadt. He therefore chose special Cheka and communist units, again under the command of Tukhachevsky. But three attacks on the fortress were repulsed with heavy losses to the Soviet forces.

On 16 March, however, by camouflaging the troops in white sheets the Soviet units managed to cross the ice and reach the fortress. Fighting was furious and both sides suffered severe casualties. But by the morning of 18 March the Soviet forces had gained control. Most of the insurgent leaders escaped across the ice to Finland. The Cheka carried out ruthless mass executions of prisoners and hostages. The Kronstadt challenge to the communist regime had been crushed.

This rebellion nevertheless made a deep impression on Lenin. He could not ignore this warning of popular unrest. He recognized, too, that now at the end of the civil war the communist leadership was the object of popular hatred and contempt greater than had ever been directed against the tsars. For Lenin and the party it was a time of profound and disturbing readjustment. They had fervently believed that world revolution was at hand, that the proletariat of western Europe would rally to their aid and their leadership, and that the heroic drama of the civil war had heralded the transition to a socialist order. Suddenly they awakened to the fact that world revolution was still far off and that popular hostility, forcibly demonstrated in simultaneous rebellions by proletariat and peasants, threatened the very existence of their regime.

The urgent, overriding need was to deal with the economic chaos and by doing so to recover popular confidence and consolidate the rule of the party on a secure basis. Lenin knew, however, that his government could not tackle the vast economic problem without the support and co-operation of the peasants who formed the great majority of the population and whose products and demands dominated the economy. His first task was, therefore, to win over the hostile peasantry. This was the prime purpose of the series of decrees issued at this time which came to be known as the New Economic Policy.

From the start Lenin recognized that NEP would result in a mixed economy and the restoration of private enterprise. It would mean the reversal of so many of the principles which the bolsheviks had fostered and proclaimed. *Pravda* and other party organs had until a few weeks previously continued to condemn free trade and other forms of capitalism, while upholding the system of war communism. On 15 March 1921, however, the tenth party congress silently but unanimously adopted the new policy which was to restore the abhorrent capitalist practices.

Lenin's first great retreat had been in rejecting 'revolutionary war' and accepting the treaty of Brest-Litovsk. NEP was his second great retreat, made to win over the peasantry without whom the socialist revolution must fail. On each occasion, however, he was withdrawing before practical difficulties which he saw to be temporarily insuperable. His retreats were merely tactical and did not mean the relinquishment of basic communist policies.

Early in February 1921 during a discussion in the Politburo on agrarian policy Lenin had proposed the initial measure of NEP. This proposal, approved by the tenth Party Congress and enacted in the decree of 21 March 1921 of the all-Russian central executive committee (VTsIK), was to impose a tax in kind calculated as a percentage of the crop harvested in place of the requisitioning of surpluses. The tax was graduated so that the poor and middle peasants were less affected than the richer peasants. At the same time peasants who sowed greater areas or increased the productiveness of their lands were entitled to special rebates. The individual peasant was liable for payment of the tax due from him and collective responsibility was abolished. Moreover, a state fund was set up to supply consumer goods and agricultural equipment in exchange for surpluses voluntarily delivered in excess of the amount of tax. Such surpluses could also be traded on the open market.

The new policy was strictly commercial and aimed at increasing agricultural output by giving peasants the incentives of freely trading their surpluses. In this free market the efficient and prosperous peasants, known as kulaks, inevitably flourished, sometimes at the expense of the poorer peasants who were exploited. The bolsheviks had always held this exploitation to be the greatest evil of capitalism which must be met, not with legislation protecting the weak, but by annihilation of the kulak and the whole capitalist class. But now they had to accept the reintroduction of capitalism.

In agriculture NEP, launched hurriedly under pressure of peasant revolts and the Kronstadt mutiny, might well have yielded prompt results. But drought, affecting especially the lands in the Volga basin, brought a disastrous famine. Sovnarkom had on 28 March 1921 decreed the amounts of grain to be levied by tax in kind, but the drought cancelled these assessments. Relief measures were proclaimed in April, but the scale of the catastrophe was only fully realized in July when a non-party All-Russian Committee for Aid to the Hungry was appointed. Decrees provided for the evacuation of 100,000 people from the stricken lands to Siberia. The Hoover American Relief Administration gave invaluable aid and by the summer of 1921 was distributing food to some ten million Russians. But towards the end of 1921 more than twenty-two million people were facing starvation. Estimates of deaths from famine are unreliable, not only because records were not kept but also because famine is so often the indirect cause of death. But with this disaster coming after the world war, the civil war, the Red and the White terror, there seemed no limit to the sufferings which the Russian people were called upon to endure.

NEP was initially concerned with agriculture and internal trade but it spread naturally and inevitably to industry. Private trading dictated a return to the use of money as the basis of exchange and a revival of manufacturing for profit. Lenin had foreseen that the government could not in existing conditions revive industrial production and that private enterprise and management would have to be invoked. Under the new policy large-scale industry and transport remained nationalized and under state control but decentralized and grouped in trusts. But two decrees issued by Sovnarkom in May 1921 authorized small private industries in the countryside and provided for the leasing to private management of nationalized industries which the government could not operate. This policy was expanded until all industrial undertakings employing less than twenty people were denationalized and returned to their former owners or leased to private individuals or to co-operatives. To attract foreign capital and skill the government also invited foreign companies to lease certain nationalized large-scale industries, usually on twenty-five year concessions.

After recovery from the disastrous famine of 1921, NEP achieved impressive results in agriculture. In industry, however, the results were less impressive and even dangerous. The census of 1923 showed that 88·5 per cent of industrial enterprises, totalling 165,781, were under private management, while a further 3.1 per cent were run by the co-operatives. State-controlled enterprises amounted to 8·4 per cent of the total. To the communists who protested that reversion to capitalism would cancel all the gains of the revolution, Lenin replied that while the state retained control over the 'commanding heights' of large-scale industry and foreign trade this danger would not arise. Meanwhile the private *entrepreneurs*, the Nepmen, who emerged suddenly with the new policy, injected vitality and purpose into the stagnant economy. Small industries producing consumer goods began to flourish, but large-scale industries, producing capital goods which were needed in the long term to restore the economy but which met no immediate demands, were neglected. The output of small industries rose sharply, while heavy industry revived very slowly.[8] It was soon apparent that the 'commanding heights' could not control this violent upsurge of private enterprise.

The period of NEP was not only a time of economic revival but also of return to normal living. The savagery and destruction of the war and the civil war were past. With a natural resurgence of energy and purpose which NEP facilitated and the good harvest of 1922, coming after the famine of winter 1921–2, encouraged, the people set about rebuilding their lives.

The general desire for stability and normality was strikingly illustrated in the attitude to the family and to sexual morality. The extreme views which had been bandied about at the time of the revolution and some of which had been enacted concerning marriage, the care of children, free love, and abortion were no longer acceptable. They hankered now after the stability of conventional marriage and the satisfactions of family life.

A similar desire for the comforts of religious worship and for the restoration of the churches to their old places in the community was also noticeable especially in the country towns and villages. But this was not a strong movement. Moreover, the Orthodox church itself had been passing through internal crises which weakened it at a time when it might have rallied the faithful.

By 1917 a movement had gathered strength for restoration of the patriarchate which Peter the Great had abolished. A holy synod had decided by a small majority in favour of restoration and on 18 November 1917 Tikhon, metropolitan of Moscow, was elected patriarch. He at once came into conflict with the bolsheviks especially at the time of the famine of 1921–2 when the Soviet authorities decreed the seizure and sale overseas of ecclesiastical treasures for the relief of the hungry. Resistance to the execution of this decree led to arrests, casualties, and a number of executions of priests and others. This was also made the occasion and pretext for the launching of anti-religious campaigns and in 1922 *Bezbozhnik*, the anti-religious weekly, began publication.

The restoration of the patriarchate and Tikhon personally were, however, not acceptable to many Orthodox. A dissident group began in May 1922 publishing a new journal with the title *The Living Church*. The leaders of the group convened an assembly which set up 'the living church' and replaced the patriarch by a 'supreme church administration'.

The Orthodox were now divided between those who supported the patriarchate and those who belonged to the living church. The bitterness between them recalled the fury which had split the church at the time of the schism in the seventeenth century. For a time the living church was dominant. Tikhon had been in prison since his defiance of the Soviet government early in 1922. But the bolsheviks were anxious to be neutral and certainly did not intend to be committed to the living church, which was unpopular with the peasants and which attracted much unfavourable publicity abroad. In June 1923 Tikhon was freed on signing a declaration that he was 'henceforth not an enemy of the Soviet government' and that he would engage in no political activity. He was allowed to resume his patriarchal duties and many at once rallied to him. The living church began to wane. Meanwhile, both parties recognized the Soviet regime and on that condition the government was content for the time being to show tolerance.

The tenth party congress which met on 8 March 1921 while the Kronstadt revolt was at its height was to mark the beginning of a new era in the history of the party. The delegates who assembled in Moscow were then bewildered, angered, and intimidated by the general hostility towards communist rule and especially by the defiance of Kronstadt. They waited for guidance and leadership, and without Lenin they would have been lost.

In such a crisis Lenin demonstrated his practical commonsense and his unscrupulous talent for expediency. The tenth congress gave its approval to NEP. But Lenin saw that economic reform was not enough; he had to ensure the supremacy of the communist party. Here he showed his skill in manipulating delegates assembled in conference. First a series of resolutions were adopted following the moderate line set out in Lenin's 'Platform of the Twelve'. The resolutions condemned the extreme centralization in the party. They promised greater freedom from central interference and control at local soviet level and in the trade unions. They asserted that members must be able to take 'an active part in the life of the party' and, further, that 'the nature of workers' democracy excluded every form of appointment in place of election as a system'.[9]

The resolutions were designed to nullify opposition groups and had no other purpose. Soon they were to be ignored completely. Indeed, Lenin, who had no intention of allowing party democracy or of accepting dictation of rank-and-file members, had in hand resolutions cutting across these promises. Early in the congress he had remarked that it was time 'to put an end to opposition, to put the lid on it'.[10] Suddenly on the last day of the congress, he moved two new resolutions, one on 'Party Unity' and the other on 'The Syndicalist and Anarchist Deviation in our Party', which were both adopted.

The resolution on party unity referred to the existence of opposition groups as a source of danger and weakness. It forbade all forms of fractionalism and demanded the immediate dissolution of all groups with separate platforms, or their expulsion from the party. At the same time it purported to uphold the principles of party democracy. The second resolution rejected the claims of the trade union communists to direct industry. The trade unions were, in fact, to be merged into the state machine, functioning only as agents of government policy, especially charged with raising production.

The earlier resolutions had been no more than a smoke screen behind which Lenin worked to strengthen the power of the party and his own power as its leader. In spite of increasing restiveness and criticism among members, the dictatorship of the party bureaucracy and its immunity from control became stronger. Interference from the centre in local soviets and in trade unions became more direct and blatant. In May 1921, for instance, the communist 'fraction' of the metal workers' union, the oldest pro-bolshevik union, rejected the list of candidates nominated by the central committee to serve on the union's governing body. The central committee promptly overruled the union and appointed its own committee to run it.

A further late resolution adopted by the tenth party congress as part of the policy of strengthening the party was designed to make the election of members more selective and to subject the credentials of every existing member to close scrutiny, purging those who were unsatisfactory. This measure, too, was designed to eliminate opposition.

At the time of the tenth congress the party had some 730,000 members. The great influx had been after the revolution when as the party in power it had attracted many careerists. A registration of members was carried out and unworthy or unwanted persons were eliminated. During the civil war, when membership of the party might involve personal danger, mass recruitment was encouraged for it was felt that the wrong type was unlikely to join. After the end of the civil war the influx of careerists and, as revealed by the Kronstadt revolt and the strong opposition groups, of people inclined to independent views disturbed party leaders.

For the purge the central committee appointed a central checking commission of five which worked through local checking commissions. The purge was to be directed mainly against former members of other political parties and against officials with records of service under the tsarist regime. Warnings were issued against victimizing members who had belonged to the opposition groups, but the purge was widely taken to be directed to the elimination of actual and potential critics.

A fifth of the party, more than 136,000 members, was rejected in the course of this exercise.[11] But also, according to official figures, individual and group withdrawals from the party amounting to 14,100 members took place during 1921 and 1922. Many resigned because they disapproved of NEP and because of the party's denial of independent thought and criticism. Many felt no further need to support the party after the civil war and simply wanted to return to their own lives without interference.

Between March 1921 and December 1922 the number of members and candidates declined from 730,000 to 485,500. But the party emerged stronger than ever before. It had rid itself of its potential critics, its worst careerists, and its waverers and half-hearted supporters. By and large it comprised now a majority of young enthusiastic communists, ready to support their leaders without question and to work zealously for the party.

Lenin needed the party to be disciplined and obedient at this time when he was embarking on radical policies which alarmed many of the old bolsheviks. This applied particularly to his economic policy. As it got under way NEP seemed to be plunging the country into capitalism as it had existed in Russia in the first decade of the century. To ensure the success of NEP in the long term it was necessary that one or more of the leading industrial nations should embrace communism. But Lenin now recognized that this was not yet likely to happen. In the meantime, to further NEP it was important to revive normal trade relations with the capitalist West and to attract its financial support. But the West was deeply suspicious of the new revolutionary state which was committed to fomenting world revolution. England, France, and the U.S.A. were also insistent that the Soviet government should honour the repudiated debts of the tsarist government and pay compensation for foreign-owned industries nationalized by the bolsheviks.

The third congress of the Comintern, meeting in Moscow in June and July 1921, unanimously heeded Lenin's demand for a retreat from world revolution. In this way Lenin hoped to calm capitalist misgivings about trading with Soviet Russia. But while unanimous on the floor of the congress foreign delegates were dissatisfied with the subordination of the Comintern entirely to Russian interests. Many expressed strong opposition and the growing anger disturbed Lenin and his comrades. But the executive of the Comintern, centred in Moscow and completely under

Russian control, exercised its disciplinary powers, expelling the German group and warning others. Moreover, it brought before the congress a resolution on party structure which went even further than the twenty-points adopted in the second congress in subordinating foreign parties to Moscow. The fourth Comintern congress held in November 1922 accepted the principle that in its work priority must be given at all times to supporting Soviet Russia.

Meanwhile, under the stimulus of NEP Soviet exports and imports were rising and a number of minor trade agreements were signed. But Lenin's plans for trade pacts with the leading industrial powers failed. In Genoa in April the Soviet government sought to negotiate trade agreements with the Allied powers, which would result in *de jure* recognition of the Soviet regime and pave the way for capital aid to develop Soviet industry. But the negotiations broke down on Soviet refusal to repay loans.

While the meetings continued in Genoa, however, Soviet delegates were engaged in clandestine discussions with German representatives in nearby Rapallo. The resulting Russo-German treaty signed on 16 April 1922 was not only the first major diplomatic and commercial treaty to be concluded by the Soviet government, but was a significant achievement for both countries.[12] Germany, the defeated enemy, burdened by the treaty of Versailles, and Soviet Russia, the revolutionary outcast, were both to gain considerable economic, diplomatic, and military profit from it. The Allied powers, who had tried to prevent a Russo-German alliance, at once became more conciliatory. But while England and certain other countries recognized Soviet Russia in 1924, the U.S.A. and the majority of governments withheld recognition. Exclusion from the League of Nations and from other international organizations emphasized her continuing isolation.

While launching these measures to strengthen the party and also to develop the national economy, the Soviet leaders were working on the constitutional framework of their regime. On 26 December 1922 Stalin submitted to the tenth congress of soviets of the R.S.F.S.R. a resolution proposing a federal union with the three other Soviet republics—the Ukrainian S.S.R., the Belorussian S.S.R., and the Transcaucasian S.S.R.[13] The declaration and treaty of union were ratified four days later by the delegates of the republics assembled in Moscow as the first all-union congress of soviets of the Union of Socialist Soviet Republics (U.S.S.R.).[14]

The constitution of the U.S.S.R. was approved by the central executive committee on 6 July 1923 and ratified by the second all-union congress of soviets on 31 January 1924. It followed closely the fundamental laws, or constitution, of the R.S.F.S.R., adopted in July 1918,[15] in its definition of the civil rights and suffrage. The new provisions mainly concerned the division of powers within the union. The federal government had exclusive powers over foreign relations, trade, finance and the national economy, justice, education, and communications.[16] Residual powers vested in the governments of the union republics.

The all-union congress of soviets was the supreme power.[17] Comprising some 2,000 deputies, its main function was to elect the all-union central executive committee (CEC) of some 750 members.[18] The CEC in turn elected a presidium of twenty-seven members who, when the CEC was not in session, exercised its powers.[19] The CEC also appointed Sovnarkom, which, comprising the people's commissars, was a form of cabinet.[20] The chairman of Sovnarkom was the equivalent of a Western prime minister, while the chairman of the presidium of the CEC acted as head of state.

The constitution was an impressive legal document, but it was devoid of real meaning. All power, in fact, lay in the hands of the communist party to which the constitution made no single reference. The tentacles of the party machine reached out from Moscow to all parts of the country. The right of national self-determination and of secession which the constitution guaranteed,[21] and the plight of the national minorities which seemed assured of their independence by the creation of autonomous regions and republics, pointed to the real character of the regime. Communist policy on national minorities had been set out in November 1917 in the 'Declaration of the Rights of the Peoples of Russia'. This had promised the free exercise of the right of cultural development, full legal equality, and the right of self-determination. Lenin had insisted on self-determination for all national units. The problem was now to harmonize the national aspiration of each minority with the strongly centralized government and control over them which the Russians had always exercised.

In practice the right of self-determination was soon curtailed and then abolished. In December 1917 the independence of Finland was reluctantly recognized. But in the following January Stalin announced that independence of a national unit could only be granted upon the demand of the working class in the region and then self-determination had to be considered as part of the struggle for socialism.[22]

The constitution of the R.S.F.S.R. adopted in June 1918 had affirmed the rights of self-determination and secession, but two qualifications had been added the effect of which was to leave the decision to the party leaders in Moscow.[23]

Lenin was increasingly disturbed about the treatment of national minorities. He held the chauvinism of the Russian communists to be the main reason for the unsatisfactory handling of the problem. He became critical towards Stalin whom he had made people's commissar of nationality affairs in November 1917. Stalin had worked with ruthless efficiency in this office, especially in enforcing the control of Moscow over the parties in the territories recovered during the civil war.

This was, in fact, no more than a continuation of Lenin's own policy of a centralized party, wielding sole power from Moscow over Russian and non-Russian alike. But Lenin remained anxious about the national minorities. His anxiety was probably increased by the new realization that Stalin had built up his own group of supporters and that he at times quietly ignored Lenin's strictures. Matters came to a head over Georgia which had proclaimed its independence and had been recognized by the Allies. Georgia had become a social democratic stronghold, but one in which the mensheviks held the great majority of seats in the national assembly. On 7 May 1920 the government of the R.S.F.S.R. had signed a treaty with the menshevik government recognizing Georgia's independence, renouncing all Russian claims, and solemnly undertaking not to interfere in Georgian affairs. Soon afterwards the communists inside Georgia staged a rebellion and this was used as a pretext to send Red Army units into the republic.

Among the party leaders Lenin and others were uneasy about this perfidious breach of faith which Stalin and Ordzhonikidze, the two Georgians, supported and which they had probably engineered. Apparently, however, the misgivings of Lenin and the others were assuaged by assurances that the Allies had no intention of intervening on Georgia's behalf. But Lenin continued to urge on Ordzhonikidze, now virtually the ruler of Georgia, the need for moderation especially in handling the mensheviks. But by this time Lenin's counsels were no longer heeded.

CHAPTER ELEVEN

Lenin Dies

ON 12 December 1922 Lenin retired on doctors' orders to his private apartment in the Kremlin. Four days later he had a stroke which paralysed his right side. The cerebral sclerosis from which he was suffering and which may well have caused his father's premature death was spreading inexorably.

Confined to his apartment but in full possession of his faculties, he dictated notes and articles which Krupskaya, never more devoted than in these last months, delivered. He was now able to review the party and its policies, as he could not do when immersed in the furious activity of day-to-day crises and responsibilities. His review plunged him into an agony of anxiety. He saw ahead not a communist paradise but a pit of errors and sufferings. He recognized that many of his own mistakes lay at the root of the threatening troubles. He had directed the revolution, but had failed to lay secure foundations for the new communist state. He was disturbed by the treatment of the national minorities, but he was oppressed by the extreme centralization of power and by the monstrous bureaucratic machine which had so quickly come into existence.

On 25 December, only nine days after his second stroke, Lenin dictated what came to be known as his 'testament'. In it he expressed his fears about the instability of the party. The immediate danger was a split within the central committee between Trotsky and Stalin. He noted that 'Comrade Stalin, having become general secretary, has concentrated enormous power in his hands, and I am not sure that he always knows how to use that power with sufficient caution.'[1] His judgement on Trotsky was that he was 'distinguished not only by his exceptional abilities—personally he is, to be sure, the most able man in the present central committee —but also by his too far-reaching self-confidence and a disposition to be too much attracted by the purely administrative side of affairs'.[2] He then added the warning that 'These two qualities of the two most able leaders of the present central committee might, quite innocently, lead to a split; if our party does not take measures to prevent it, a split might arise unexpectedly.'[3] At this stage, however, he expressed no real preference between Stalin and Trotsky and, apart from proposing an increase in the size of the central committee, he seemed unable to suggest any action to prevent a schism.

A few days later Lenin dictated a memorandum criticizing the handling of the national minorities which closed with the comment: 'Evidently the whole scheme of "autonomization" was radically wrong and untimely ... I think that a fatal role was played here by Stalin's hastiness and administrative impulsiveness.'[4]

His growing hostility towards Stalin erupted again on 4 January 1923 when he dictated a postscript to his testament which read:

'Stalin is too rude and this fault, entirely supportable in relations among us communists, becomes insupportable in the office of general secretary. Therefore, I propose to the comrades to find a way to remove Stalin from that position and to appoint to it another man who in all respects differs from Stalin only in superiority, namely, more patient, more loyal, more polite, and more attentive to comrades, less capricious, etc. This circumstance may seem an insignificant trifle, but I think that, from the point of view of preventing a split and from the point of view of the relation between Stalin and Trotsky, which I discussed above, it is not a trifle, or it is such a trifle as may acquire a decisive significance.'[5]

The testament and postscript were not at this time circulated to the Politburo and were known only to Krupskaya and his secretaries. The party, having no inkling of Stalin's fall from favour, continued to regard him as one of Lenin's most able lieutenants. Among the papers, dictated by Lenin during January 1923, however, was an article, entitled 'Better Less But Better', which was to reveal his feelings publicly for the first time. The article was a savage attack on the people's commissariat of workers' and peasants' inspection, known as Rabkrin, and an indictment of 'bureaucracy not only in our Soviet institutions, but in our party institutions.'[6]

Stalin had been in charge of Rabkrin from its inception in 1920 until May 1922, and the article could only be interpreted as an attack on him. Every attempt was made by Stalin and his personal supporters to prevent its publication, but Lenin's authority was still not to be overruled and on 4 March it appeared in *Pravda*. Members of the party were staggered to realize that Stalin had forfeited the confidence and support of their leader.

Lenin prepared a second public attack, determined now, according to Krupskaya, 'to crush Stalin politically'. This attack was on Stalin's handling of the national minorities and in particular Georgia. He sent a telegram to the Georgian opposition leaders promising them his support at the twelfth party congress. Then realizing that he himself would not be well enough to attend he sent a memorandum to Trotsky, requesting him to 'undertake the defence of' his views because he could not depend on the 'impartiality' of Stalin or Dzerzhinsky. He begged Trotsky not to trust to any 'rotten compromise' that Stalin might propose.[7]

On the same day Lenin's antagonism reached a critical point. In a telephone conversation with Krupskaya Stalin spoke heatedly. He was evidently desperately afraid that the stricken leader was about to destroy his position in the party. But Krupskaya considered that on the telephone he had insulted her. Lenin was furious and at once wrote to Stalin, demanding that he retract his words and apologize or accept severance of relations between them.[8]

Lenin's health now began to decline again. On 9 March he had a third and far more severe stroke which paralysed his right side and partially his left, depriving him of the power of speech. Such a sudden and complete loss of the ability to write or to speak was a tragic fate for a man whose whole life had been taken up with communicating his ideas and directions. In his desperate thwarted efforts to express himself he became violent at times, trying to expel doctors, nurses, and secretaries from his room. The devoted Krupskaya attempted to teach him to write with his left hand, but without real success. In his enforced silence he seemed to retreat into himself. He had probably seen none of the party leaders since first retiring to his Kremlin apartment in December. After his third stroke, however, while prepared occasionally to receive peasant delegations, 'he decisively refused all meetings with impatient political leaders'.[9] In fact, he took no further part in party or public affairs.

At this time preparations were in hand for the twelfth annual congress of the Russian communist party. The congress was also to celebrate the twenty-fifth anniversary of the foundation of the party.[10] But the leaders and, indeed, members and non-members were dismayed by the absence of the leader. The bulletins on his health, issued after his third stroke, gave some hope that he might make a partial recovery, but members of the Politburo who could speak with the doctors knew that this was unlikely.

The Soviet leaders were, moreover, deeply disturbed by the growing discontent among rank-and-file members of the party. Complaints were mainly economic, but they gave rise to strong criticism of the Politburo, especially Zinoviev, Kamenev, and Stalin. From this widespread restiveness, two organized opposition groups had emerged, the Workers' Truth and the Workers' Group, and both were outspoken in attacking the concentration of power in the hands of the leaders.

The twelfth party congress, postponed until April in the vain hope that Lenin might be able to attend, was significant not for concrete results but for the preliminary skirmishes in the struggle for the leadership. Zinoviev and Kamenev in their speeches made eulogistic references to their absent leader which were to prove the beginning of the cult of Lenin. Their tributes were an indication of how deeply his presence was missed, but they were even more an invocation of his name and prestige to bolster their authority in the face of mounting criticism.

Stalin did not contribute to these fulsome tributes. He delivered straightforward reports to the congress on party organization and on the national minorities. He mentioned Lenin only to promote himself as a faithful follower. He repeated Lenin's strong criticisms of Rabkrin and of the bureaucracy endorsing them as just and correct, and himself moved the resolution to give effect for Lenin's proposals for reform. In his report on the national minorities he again supported all of Lenin's strictures and disarmed criticism of himself. By his earnest humility and devotion to both Lenin and the party he more or less disposed of the cloud that had hung over him since publication of Lenin's article 'Better Less But Better'. Not only did he extricate himself from a difficult position, but he emerged with an enhanced reputation for dignity and good sense.

In his report on industry Trotsky dealt with the economic crisis in which many of the opposition complaints were rooted. He explained that the purpose of NEP was to promote exchange of products between agriculture and industry, stimulating the output of both in such a way as to advance the country on the road to socialism. The consumer industries had achieved dramatic results, but medium and heavy industries were almost at a standstill. The immediate threat to NEP, however, was the rapid rise in prices of industrial products and the decline in agricultural prices. He illustrated the price movement with a diagram which gave it the name of the 'scissors crisis'.

Trotsky's brilliant exposition made most delegates understand for the first time the nature of the economic problem. But he was careful to refrain from proposing remedies, for this would have brought him into conflict with the other members of the Politburo.

Already the struggle for the leadership was taking shape. Trotsky and Zinoviev were the foremost contenders, and strong personal animosity existed between them. But Trotsky was isolated in the Politburo; all of its members, and especially Stalin, were antagonistic towards him. At this stage, however, all were determined to maintain party unity and to defeat the opposition. For this reason they had agreed on an armistice among themselves. Trotsky did not even oppose the troika or triumvirate which emerged during the twelfth congress and was entrusted with leadership of the party in Lenin's absence.

The triumvirate comprised Zinoviev, Kamenev, and Stalin. Zinoviev was the senior and saw himself as Lenin's successor. Born into a petty bourgeois Jewish family in Elizavetgrad (renamed Zinovievsk in 1924) he was, like Stalin, one of the less highly educated of the bolshevik leaders. He had in 1908 in Switzerland become Lenin's close disciple and adjutant. In April 1917 he had returned in the sealed train to Petrograd and by this time his position as Lenin's special henchman was acknowledged. One revolutionary who knew both Lenin and Zinoviev well noted that 'Whenever there was an unfair factional manoeuvre to be carried out, a revolutionary reputation to be undermined, Lenin would charge Zinoviev with the task.'[11] In March 1919 Lenin had appointed him president of the executive committee of the newly founded Communist International, a position of great prestige at this time when world revolution was impatiently awaited.

Zinoviev had a strong tenor voice and was an impressive orator. He could work long hours writing articles and drafting resolutions, and Lenin entrusted him with many tasks. But he was a man of straw, and no other bolshevik was so despised by his fellows as he was. The same revolutionary wrote of him that 'After Mussolini ... I consider Zinoviev the most despicable individual I have ever met.'[12] Beneath the bluster and the ready flow of words, he was a vain superficial man, lacking in real ability, in courage, and in principle. He was nevertheless generally accepted as the deputy leader in April 1923, when Lenin was absent and Trotsky held back from the leadership.

Lev Borisovich Kamenev, the second member, was also Jewish. The son of an engine driver who became a railway engineer, Kamenev had had a thorough education, finally studying law at Moscow University. He had the bearded face and handsome features of a sensitive Russian intellectual. By nature he was gentle and amiable and he was widely respected in the party. His failing as a bolshevik was his readiness to compromise and to avoid extremes. On matters of principle he could take a stand, even against Lenin, but in the long run he would toe the line for the sake of peace. Modest and lacking in ambition he did not contend for power or prominence.

Stalin, the third and most junior member of the triumvirate, was scarcely known outside the party ranks. To those who knew him he was an industrious mediocrity. Sukhanov wrote that Stalin 'during his modest activity in the executive committee produced—not on me alone—the impression of a grey blur, floating dimly across the scene and leaving no trace. There is really nothing more to be said about him'.[13] Trotsky, who considered him 'the outstanding mediocrity of our party', treated him with condescension and contempt.[14] Lenin had until the time of his illness tended to see in him no more than a faithful disciple and able organizer.

By April 1923, however, Stalin was already in a position of immense power. As people's commissar of nationalities, he had control over the 65 million non-Russians of the nation's 140 million population. As commissar of Rabkrin, which had virtually unlimited powers of inspection over the administration, he had control over the machinery of government. As a member of the Politburo during the civil war, he had in practice been responsible for the everyday management of the party. Moreover, he was from the beginning of 1919 a member of the organization bureau which posted and transferred party personnel as required. His appointment on 3 April 1922 to the office of general secretary of the central committee enhanced his authority further.

For two years quietly and in the background Stalin had been virtually the ruler of Russia. Lenin was the first to realize what great power he had gathered into his hands. The other members of the Politburo completely underestimated him. Moreover, they were so obsessed with the idea that a Bonaparte might emerge, as had happened after the French Revolution, and were so convinced that Trotsky was the threat, that they overlooked the Bonaparte in their midst.

Although not a member of the Politburo, Nikolai Ivanovich Bukharin was one of the best known and certainly the best loved among the leading bolsheviks. He was an active member of the central committee and editor of *Pravda*, but he was primarily a brilliant intellectual and theorist. He came into conflict with Lenin several times, demonstrating on each occasion his inflexibility and inadequacy as a practical politician. He was never a serious contender for the leadership. He was a man to be led, not a leader. He enjoyed the affection, but scarcely the respect of his comrades. Indeed, Trotsky wrote of him: 'This man's nature is such that he must always lean on somebody, be dependent on somebody, attach himself to somebody.'[15]

Fear of Trotsky had brought and kept the triumvirate together. He was, as Lenin had recognized, by far the most able member of the Politburo. No one had played a greater role in bringing about the October revolution or in creating the Red Army and winning victory against the Whites and other enemies of the regime in the civil war. His prestige and authority were such that he was acknowledged as Lenin's equal partner and, indeed, the names of Lenin and Trotsky were generally linked as the fathers of the revolution.

While he held the ultimate power, Lenin was not troubled by any sense of personal jealousy or rivalry. But others in the Politburo were intensely jealous and resentful towards Trotsky. He could be flamboyant and unbearably arrogant, reflecting the 'too far-reaching self-confidence', which Lenin had noted in his testament. Towards Zinoviev, Kamenev, and other lesser men, he was condescending and contemptuous. He treated Stalin as a minor functionary and his condescending attitude together with his western outlook intensified the cold implacable hatred that Stalin had secretly nursed towards him since their conflict during the civil war.

On Lenin's withdrawal after his second stroke, many in the party and among the people, and especially in the Red Army, were ready to accept Trotsky as their leader. Delegates to the twelfth congress were expecting him to assume the leadership. But he depended on Lenin's support and against the lesser men of the Politburo, who now banded together to prevent his succession, he seemed bewildered and indecisive. He was divided within himself between his respect for party discipline and unity and his contempt for its leaders as individuals. He refused to risk splitting the party in his own interest, but he was unable to deal with this new situation. His imperious will seemed paralysed, as he waited, desperately hoping that Lenin would recover.

On the surface, the twelfth congress had been harmonious but the following summer was a time of intense unease in the party. The opposition groups and the malcontents had no faith in the triumvirate and were disappointed that Trotsky had not come forward. Economic crisis and lack of leadership provoked further industrial unrest in July and August. The opposition gathered new support among rank-and-file members. Plans were even made for a mass demonstration on the lines of Gapon's march to petition the tsar on 'Bloody Sunday' (9 January 1905). But the GPU (State Political administration) uncovered the plot in time and arrested twenty-eight of the conspirators. Fourteen were later expelled from the party and fourteen were admonished. Such lenient treatment was not to continue for long.

Crisis overtook the party leadership in the autumn. Alarmed by the growing discontent the central committee had appointed special committees to investigate the 'scissors crisis', the grievances on wages, and the internal situation. Suddenly and unexpectedly on 8 October, Trotsky, his patience evidently exhausted, wrote a forthright letter to the central committee denouncing its economic policy and attacking its leadership. He criticized the procedures and the rigging of the twelfth congress and the practice of nominating rather than electing members to senior party posts. Clearly referring to Stalin, he attacked the growing 'secretarial psychology, the principal trait of which is that the secretary is capable of deciding everything'.[16] He roundly condemned 'secretarial bureaucratism' and demanded a return to 'party democracy—at any rate enough of it to prevent the party being threatened with ossification and degeneracy'.[17] Finally he warned that if no changes were made he would bring on 'a crisis of exceptional severity'.[18]

Trotsky's dramatic challenge was followed a week later by the declaration of the Platform of the Forty-Six.[19] This also denounced the party leadership for its incompetence in dealing with the economic crisis. The gravamen of its criticisms, however, was 'the ever increasing, and now scarcely concealed, division of the party between a secretarial hierarchy and "quiet folk", between professional party officials, recruited from above, and the general mass of the party . . .'[20] It went on to state that party members who were dissatisfied with or had doubts about decisions of the central committee or provincial committees were afraid to speak out even in private conversations. It denounced 'the regime of the dictatorship of a fraction within the party'.[21]

Anxious and unsettled by this angry opposition, especially now when Trotsky seemed about to place himself at the head of it, the central committee felt more acutely the lack of a leader. Zinoviev's inadequacy was exposed; the amiable Kamenev was incapable of leading; Stalin was wary and vulnerable to criticisms, especially for manipulation of the congress and the appointment of senior party officials.

On 25 October 1923 the central committee met with the central control commission and delegates of ten party organizations. Twelve of the members who had signed the Platform of the Forty-Six were invited to attend to give their views. But the sole published result of the three-day meeting was a resolution 'on the Internal Party Position' which included a condemnation of Trotsky's threatening letter as 'a profound political error'.[22] This part of the resolution would probably not have been included had Trotsky not been absent from the meeting through illness.

The party leadership had stood united against the opposition, but it had so far done nothing to remedy the complaints. On 7 November, however, Zinoviev in an article published in *Pravda* declared that it was 'indispensable to give practical application to workers' democracy within the party'.[23] Members, trade unionists, and even non-party men were invited to contribute to the debate to be published in the columns of *Pravda* on the predicament of the party. This debate continued during November filling pages of the paper but merely repeating the criticisms of the leadership in more restrained terms.

Throughout this period the triumvirate was obsessed with the danger that Trotsky might assume leadership of the opposition. As it existed, unorganized and without leaders, the opposition posed no serious threat but led by Trotsky it would split the party, and the triumvirate would then probably face defeat. At this point Trotsky for the first time in his strenuous career suffered a breakdown in health which lasted through the winter of 1923–24.[24] But to the members of the triumvirate Trotsky, although ill, remained a serious threat and they made overtures to him. The resulting resolution drafted by Zinoviev, Kamenev, and Trotsky, amounted to a compromise. It contained little more than a restatement of general principles and also a condemnation of the Workers' Truth and the Workers' Group and, by implication, of the Platform of the Forty-Six. Trotsky thus subscribed to the censure of all his possible allies. But he undoubtedly supported this resolution because he believed that it would preserve party unity, which was to him the paramount consideration.

This resolution, approved subsequently by the Politburo and the presidium of the central control commission did not, however, herald the long armistice that the triumvirate expected. On 11 December *Pravda* published a letter from Trotsky to a party meeting, apologizing for his absence and containing a statement explaining the resolution as he understood it. He evidently intended it simply as an explanation and not as an attack on the triumvirate or a denunciation of the resolution. At this time the opposition groups were, however, making special efforts to publicize their complaints in party meetings and Trotsky's letter appearing at this time was taken to be part of the opposition campaign.

On 15 December the triumvirate began its counter-offensive with an article in *Pravda* signed by Stalin, attacking Trotsky. Zinoviev next assailed him in a speech to a large meeting of party workers in Petrograd.[25] *Pravda* began publishing reports from meetings all over the country, most of them expressing confidence in the leadership and the heavy defeat of motions of support for Trotsky and the opposition groups. Arranging demonstrations of this kind was a technique which Stalin had already developed to a high degree.

Pravda continued to serve as a vehicle of the dispute. It printed two articles by Trotsky which were countered by a long article by Bukharin attempting to exploit Trotsky's past differences with Lenin. But this was the last time that the columns of *Pravda* were to be opened to party controversy. The paper now became exclusively the organ of the central committee or of the Politburo, publishing only official party statements.

Towards the end of December the party leaders began actively preparing for the thirteenth party conference to be held in mid-January 1924. The struggle against the opposition and the campaign denigrating Trotsky continued at all levels, and especially in the Red Army where his prestige remained high. But on 31 December a bulletin was published on Trotsky's health with the doctors' recommendation that he should retire to the Caucasus for two months' rest. As delegates to the conference assembled, Trotsky left Moscow. He was absent during this decisive stage in the struggle for the leadership.

The thirteenth party conference met in Moscow on 16 January 1924 and sat for three days. The selection of delegates for such conferences had been criticized by the opposition who held that the elections at provincial and district levels were rigged through the party secretaries, themselves appointed by the central committee. Moreover, opposition members had found themselves increasingly under pressure by the party machine. This pressure took the form of discrimination, such as being deprived of one's job or transferred to distant posts. Fear of discrimination was an important factor in the intimidation and the resulting dwindling of the opposition.

The triumvirate had planned its tactics with care. Stalin now coming into greater prominence spoke of the need to achieve party democracy, but the main part of his speech was a savage attack on Trotsky. After its session on international affairs the conference formally adopted resolutions on economic policy and on party affairs. By an overwhelming majority it approved the resolution on party affairs submitted by the central committee which held Trotsky responsible for the whole campaign against the leadership. The opposition, and Trotsky in particular, were guilty of 'not only an attempt to revise Bolshevism, not only a direct departure from Leninism, but a plainly declared petty bourgeois deviation'.[26] The resolution set out fifteen points for action which would strengthen party discipline and unity and eliminate opposition groups.

Party conferences were in general smaller in scale and their resolutions carried less authority than congresses and congress resolutions. The thirteenth party conference was exceptional. It put an end to the debates and criticisms which had come near to shattering party unity after Lenin's retirement, and it established the authority of the triumvirate. In doing so it killed all hope of free discussion and party democracy and set the course of further development firmly on the road which had at the beginning of the previous year caused Lenin so many misgivings. Also this conference advanced Stalin's position in the party hierarchy. He was no longer the junior member of the triumvirate but an equal, and by his careful manipu-

lation of committees, conferences, and congresses he had proved himself to
be indispensable. Quiet, wary, and nursing secretly his savage personal
antipathies, he bided his time.

Still unable to write or speak, Lenin took no part in these events. On 15
May 1923 he had been moved from the Kremlin to a rest home in Gorky.
Here during the next four months his condition improved. He was able to
walk unaided and his general health was better. A partial recovery seemed
possible.

On 21 October he insisted on being driven to Moscow. He managed
laboriously to climb the stairs to his old office in the Kremlin. For some
minutes he looked about the room, touching the familiar books on the
shelves, and probably recalling the tense hours of work, the meetings, and
the telephone calls which had filled his life there with excitement and
purpose. Now he was incapable of work and, as he knew, nearing the end
of his life. Having taken leave of his old headquarters he shuffled down
the stairs for the last time and was driven back to Gorky.

By the beginning of the winter his condition had deteriorated. His
strength was slowly ebbing. On 21 January 1924 he had a severe stroke
and within the hour he was dead. The newspapers were already in the
press, but special news-sheets were hurriedly printed and soon all Russia
knew that Lenin had died.[27]

Late on the evening of 21 January Zinoviev, Stalin, Bukharin,
Kamenev, Kalinin, and Tomsky drove in sleighs through the frosty moon-
lit night to Gorky. The body lay on a table around which flowers and fir
branches had been banked. Having paid their respects, the leaders hastened back to Moscow to attend a formal meeting of the central committee
and to prepare for the funeral. They returned to Gorky two days later to
escort the body to Moscow. There it lay in the Hall of Columns, known
now as the House of the Trade Unions, and the people queued for hours in
the freezing cold to file past and pay their respects just as they had done in
other years when the tsars had lain in state.

On 26 January the second all-union congress of soviets held a formal
session in homage to their dead leader. At this congress Stalin made a
powerful impact in the role of Lenin's devoted colleague and follower.
Kalinin, Krupskaya, and Zinoviev paid their tributes in restrained conventional style. But Stalin spoke differently. He had carefully cast his
speech in a form of commands and responses echoing the Orthodox liturgy
even to the point of using biblical wording.[28] To bolsheviks who had lived
in the West the emotional ritual of the speech probably sounded outland-
ish but the great majority of the members present were, like Stalin himself, rooted in the Russian soil and for them the speech, redolent of old
Russia, was moving and memorable. In fact, it was a remarkable performance which raised Stalin's prestige further in the party and contributed to
the general image of him as one of Lenin's most trusted comrades.[29]

The congress in this same session also approved certain proposals to

honour Lenin's memory. The first measure was to change the name of
Petrograd, the city of the revolution, to Leningrad.[30] The other decisions
were to embalm Lenin's body and to keep it in a special mausoleum to be
erected by the Kremlin wall near the graves of the bolshevik heroes
who had lost their lives in the October revolution.[31]

During the following weeks the Soviet press published articles and
reminiscences exalting Lenin. The cult, launched by lesser men to bolster
their authority, gathered amazing momentum. Russians were taught to
revere him for his great disinterested labours as father of the revolution.
They read of his love of children and of cats and of his hatred of all
suffering. He was the example, held up before each generation, of self-
discipline, industry, and self-sacrifice. He was, moreover, the embodiment
of the two most powerful attractions of Marxism, namely its positive
dogmas of action and of the power of men to create their own society, their
own paradise on earth. The legend presents Lenin as an inspiring example
and it is, perhaps, this legend that is his greatest legacy to Russia and to
the communist world.

The Lenin of history is less attractive. In spite of the descriptions of
Gorky and others of his humane qualities, he was a cold man, unconcerned
with normal human relationships.[32] He was the complete fanatic and a
demonstration of the devastating power of a fixed idea in a man with the
capacity to pursue it to the end. He had a powerful intellect, but constrained and harnessed it to the application of Marxism. He was selfless,
but he demanded and held complete power for he could not accept that
anyone but he himself was capable of leading the party. The morality of
his assumption that any action, no matter how cruel, evil, or ruthless, was
justified if it served the ideological end was terrifying. But, although his
actions were often sordid and devious and although he repels by his cold
fanaticism, his life possessed a certain grandeur, deriving from its dedication and its high moral purpose.

No political leader has had a greater impact on the twentieth century
than Lenin, but his achievements were limited. He was the father of the
October revolution, and without his leadership and drive it would probably not have taken place. He transplanted the wholly Western ideology of
Marxism in Russian soil, where it took root as Marxism–Leninism and
developed as a continuity of the Russian historical tradition. A reflection
of this was his creation of a disciplined party of dedicated bolsheviks
obedient to their leader, which carried on the Russian heritage of abso-
lutism and centralization, vesting power in one man and giving rise in the
future as in the past to terrible abuses. But he did not survive to build the
socialist society which he held as the ideal. The policies and methods
which he might have evolved in advancing on their road would have been
a true test of his greatness as a political leader. He died and left to other
men, schooled in his philosophy and methods and serving his high purpose,
to build on his bare foundations.

CHAPTER TWELVE

Stalin Emerges 1924–9

THE struggle for power entered upon a new savage stage after the death of Lenin but still it was waged under cover. No one was prepared yet to come into the open and to risk disrupting party unity. The strife was masked by polemics; major issues of the interpretation of Leninism, the true nature of NEP, the policy to be followed to achieve socialism were befogged by petty opportunistic arguments. Furious debates raged over hair-splitting analyses of dialectic, each participant seeking to prove himself more faithful to Lenin's teachings than the others. But the secret bitter struggle for power was the overriding factor of the period.

The party central committee met a few days after Lenin's funeral to endorse the resolutions of the thirteenth conference. One of these resolutions was to launch a membership drive among 'workers from the bench' and without any formal decision to purge the existing membership.

Stalin was undoubtedly behind these measures. His immediate purpose was to rout Trotsky and destroy the opposition groups. The terms for enrolling new members allowed wide discretion to local party officials. Likewise the purge, limited at first to Leningrad, Moscow, Odessa, and Penza, was said to be concerned only with 'non-proletarian elements'. The immense party machine, which Stalin was painstakingly erecting, was well able to enforce such measures to ensure that new members accepted the supreme authority of the party leaders and that opposition members were weeded out.

During the months February to May the 'Lenin enrolment', as it was called, produced remarkable results. The purge of 1921 and subsequent reviews had by the beginning of 1924 reduced the total membership from 650,000 to 350,000 with 120,000 candidate members. The new enrolment increased this figure by 240,000, and it began a policy of party expansion which was to continue in the years to come.

Lenin had always emphasized the importance of the quality rather than the size of the membership. But he had also been concerned about the smallness of its proletarian element. New measures were now always justified by reference to some statement by him. It was therefore claimed that the new enrolment, limited to 'workers from the bench', was in harmony with Leninism, because it increased the proletarian element in the party for the first time to more than half. But it had other effects which would have disturbed Lenin. The new proletarian predominance jeopardized the partnership of worker and peasant on which the regime was based. More serious was the danger of Great Russian chauvinism, aggravated by the fact that the new proletarian intake was almost entirely Great Russian. But this was part of an overall change in the character of the party which Lenin had not fully envisaged. The old revolutionaries had by 1923 dwindled to 10,000 and their number was diminishing rapidly. The need now was for a political party of managers and administrators able to run the affairs of this vast nation, and the new enrolment sought to meet this need.

Quietly and methodically by purges, by manipulating party appointments, and other methods, Stalin was extending his authority and entrenching himself at the centre of the party. But in May 1924 on the eve of the thirteenth party congress an unexpected incident threatened to cut short his career. Krupskaya sent Lenin's testament to the Politburo with the explanation that his expressed wish had been that it should be submitted to the next party congress after his death.[1] This communication agitated all the members of the Politburo. None of them, except possibly Trotsky, stood to gain from publication of the testament to the congress.

A plenary session of the central committee meeting on 22 May considered Krupskaya's report. The cult of Lenin had grown to the point that his every word was sacred and his recommendations were commands. But now the party leaders rallied to save themselves. Zinoviev and Kamenev urged their colleagues to retain Stalin's services in the Politburo and as general secretary and by implication to vote against Trotsky who, they thought, would press for publication of the testament. Trotsky, however, remained aloof and silent throughout the discussions. Finally, by thirty votes to ten overruling Krupskaya's objections, the meeting decided that the testament should not be read out to the whole congress but should be communicated in confidence only to the heads of delegations.[2] Thus Lenin's wishes were set aside and Stalin was spared.[3]

The thirteenth party congress opened on 23 May 1924. The dominant theme was the need to maintain party unity especially now when Lenin could no longer lead them. Krupskaya who had only the previous day seen Lenin's wishes suppressed made an impassioned plea for opposing factions to work together. Zinoviev, too, appealed for unity. He did not name Trotsky in his speech but clearly had him in mind when he called on the opposition 'to liquidate the controversy and come to the tribune of the congress and say, "I made a mistake and the party was right!" '[4] Loud applause followed this emotional appeal and neither he nor the others present realized that, in demanding not only submission to the party but also recantation, they were establishing a new principle and one which was to lead to their own humiliation.[5]

Trotsky made a dignified and honest speech but it did not help his case. He proclaimed his submission to the party, right or wrong, but refused to concede that he had been in error in his criticisms of the leadership. This fell short of the recantation that Zinoviev had enunciated. Stalin who had spoken with calm restraint in his report on the work of the party now attacked Trotsky for his opposition and his refusal to recant. The speech marked a further stage in the fall of Trotsky from a peak of prestige to a position of scorned isolation. In fact, the opposition had already been outmanoeuvred and defeated. The main resolution of the congress in extolling the central committee for its 'firmness and Bolshevik uncompromisingness . . . in defending the foundations of Leninism against petty bourgeois deviations' merely served to emphasize this defeat.[6]

Stalin and Zinoviev now worked to gain endorsement by the Communist International of the condemnation of Trotsky and the opposition. Many European communists had been appalled by the ferocious Russian attacks on Trotsky whom they revered more than Lenin.[7] But the collapse of the communist rising in Germany eased the task of Zinoviev as president of the Comintern in undermining Trotsky's position and removing his strongest supporters among the European parties. In the course of the thirteenth congress of the Russian party several European communist leaders had been invited to the platform and with one exception all had condemned Trotsky and the opposition.[8] The fifth congress of the Comintern, meeting in Moscow from 17 June to 8 July 1924 endorsed this excommunication. Ruth Fischer, a young demagogue who was the new leader of the German communists, set the tone with her vicious vilification of Trotsky. English, American, and French delegates echoed her speech. The congress called on Trotsky to come before it to justify himself. He refused, considering that further controversy would serve no purpose and might well bring about his expulsion from the party. His silence was taken as setting the final seal on his condemnation.

Within a few months Stalin and Zinoviev had, in fact, eliminated the opposition within the Comintern to the official Moscow line. They had taken a further major step towards recasting the international communist movement, degrading it to the status of a submissive offshoot of the Russian party. Trotsky and Lenin had founded the Comintern in the faith that it would become a truly world party into which the Russian party would ultimately be absorbed. But Stalin had no patience with and was, in fact, antagonistic towards this ideal.

For twelve months the triumvirate had been in power and had weathered storms of criticism. Zinoviev, Kamenev, and Stalin had seemed pathetically inadequate by comparison with Lenin and the opposition had voiced a general feeling of no confidence in them. They had survived because they had stood together, united mainly by fear of Trotsky's succession. But now, with Trotsky virtually defeated, their unity began to crumble. Stalin, whom Zinoviev and Kamenev had regarded as a reliable organizer but otherwise an inferior, had grown remarkably in power and status during the year. He even criticized them now for mistakes in doctrine. Direct conflict between the members of the triumvirate became in-

evitable. But Stalin held the greater power and was a master tactician. He
had quietly captured the confidence of the party, because he was modest
and moderate. He was also a silent man, who gave no hint of his thoughts,
but he was methodical and implacable as he prepared to dispose of his
rivals.

While Stalin kept his own interests constantly in mind, Trotsky seemed
intent on playing into the hands of his enemies. He was too proud and too
dedicated to forward his own personal cause. But he was also strangely
blind to the consequences of his actions. The cult of Lenin which to his
rational mind and Western outlook was abhorrent, as it would have been to
Lenin himself, had already become part of the mystique of Russian communism. Within the party and even outside it the cult had gathered an
authority which he did not understand. In June 1924 he published a
pamphlet which he intended as a salute to Lenin. But his references to the
great leader as an equal and a partner, while fully justified by past events,
now gave offence.

Trotsky, finding himself subjected to increasing attack, retired into
silence. Then suddenly he carried the conflict within the triumvirate to
explosion point. In September 1924 while resting in Kislovodsk in the
Caucasus, he was assembling his early speeches and articles for publication in the third volume of his collected works, then being published. As a
preface to this volume he wrote a long article with the title 'Lessons of
October'. It was a reasoned analysis of the progress of the revolution and
the part played in it by the present leaders. With characteristic outspoken
honesty he severely criticized several of them and described the sharp
conflicts that had taken place between Lenin and Zinoviev and Kamenev
on the eve of the October revolution. He even wrote of mistakes made by
Lenin. Stalin was not mentioned by name, partly because he had not been
prominent and partly because Trotsky scorned to attack him.

The volume was published in October and caused an immediate sensation. Few doubted that Trotsky was raking up the past to indict the
present leadership and many resented his attempts to cast doubts on the
infallibility of Lenin. Bukharin at once published an article in *Pravda*
entitled 'How not to write the history of October'. This was merely an
interim reply. Trotsky's article was too damaging and had to be countered
fully. The triumvirate gave this task to Kamenev who, as editor of the
official edition of Lenin's works, could write with special authority and
who had been most heavily attacked.

By digging up the past, however, Trotsky had played into the hands of
his enemies. From the time when he had escaped from Siberia in 1902,
and having made his way to London had joined Lenin there, until 1917
when he had become a member of the bolshevik party, Trotsky and Lenin
had constantly engaged in violent, often abusive, polemics. The differences between them were usually small and after 1917 they worked amic-
ably and closely together. But Stalin, Kamenev, Zinoviev, and other

enemies were now ready to exploit these early quarrels with Lenin in order to damn him in the eyes of the party.

Kamenev's reply, published in *Pravda* and *Izvestiya* on 26 November 1924 under the title 'Leninism or Trotskyism', ranged over the whole of Trotsky's early activities. It sought to prove, especially by quotations from Lenin often out of context, that Trotsky had always been opposed to bolshevism and Leninism. Stalin's attack was more brief, biting, and effective. A commission working on the history of the party had in 1921 come upon letters exchanged between Trotsky and Chkheidze in 1913 which the tsarist police had seized but had never published. Stalin quoted from these letters a statement by Trotsky that 'the whole foundation of Leninism at the present time is built on lying and falsification' and his further comment that Lenin was 'a professional exploiter of everything that is backward in the Russian workers' movement'.[9]

Stalin's speech sent a shock of horror and incredulity through the party. It seemed impossible that Trotsky could have written in such terms of the now revered and legendary leader. But Stalin's evidence was irrefutable and his charge that Trotsky had been all the time the bitter enemy of Lenin and Leninism was taken as proven.

A campaign was mounted against Trotsky. The press printed lengthy articles and reports of party meetings throughout the country condemning him. A fever of persecution gripped members who became oblivious of his outstanding services and his dedication to the revolutionary cause. At the same time all were amazed as the days passed that neither Trotsky nor those associated with him issued any denials or replies to these attacks. Such silence from one of the most forceful, brilliant, and outspoken orators and writers in the whole revolutionary movement seemed unbelievable and could only imply complete admission of guilt. On 13 December 1924 anticipating charges of suppressing a response *Pravda* published an editorial note that no communication had been received from Trotsky or his associates on the subject of Trotskyism. This seemed to be a final proof of guilt.[10]

The fury of the attacks had evidently stunned Trotsky. He had never expected that his 'Lessons of October' would loose such a hurricane of vituperation against him. For over a year now he had been the victim of a campaign of vilification mounting in virulence and intensity until it had now reached its climax. The persecution was not restricted to public attacks but undoubtedly took more subtle and sinister forms. Trotsky's private secretary, Glazman, for example, suffered so much from victimization that he committed suicide.

Under this strain Trotsky's health broke down. Doctors diagnosed fever and recommended rest in the Caucasus. But he now refused to leave his Kremlin apartment. Sick, solitary, and surrounded by hostility, he awaited the meeting of the central committee to be held on 20 January 1925. Five days before this date he wrote what is known as his letter of resignation to the committee. As in his declaration to the thirteenth party congress he expressed his loyalty and complete submission to the party but again refused to make any confession of error.

At the meeting of the central committee most of his enemies were eager for the kill. Proposals were made to expel him at least from the Politburo and the revolutionary military council. Zinoviev, Kamenev, and others wanted to expel him completely from the party. Stalin appeared as the moderate leader, devoid of vindictiveness and without personal interest in disciplining the opposition. He favoured relieving Trotsky of the office of president of the revolutionary military council, as Trotsky himself had proposed in his letter of resignation. He no doubt feared that Trotsky as head of the Red Army which he had created might be goaded into planning a military coup. But to Trotsky this would have been a betrayal of the revolution. Loyal to his principles he served the party, believing it to be the only true representative of the working class, and disregarded his personal interests. In fact, he was relieved of this office and continued as a member of the central committee itself and of the Politburo but only on sufferance.

With Trotsky out of the way the triumvirate quickly crumbled. Stalin controlled the central party machine, Zinoviev the Leningrad party organization. A few months earlier the triumvirate had appointed Uglanov to be secretary of the Moscow provincial party committee with the task of streamlining its work. Uglanov had transferred his support to Stalin. Kamenev found himself reduced to being no more than a figurehead in his own party organization, and being neither ambitious nor aggressive he apparently accepted relegation to a minor position.

Stalin and Zinoviev were the two remaining contenders for power. The struggle between them at once became enmeshed with the traditional rivalry of the two cities. Dormant for periods but never extinguished, the strong antagonism between them readily flared into active hostility. The Leningradtsi were in an arrogant mood. Theirs was the city of the revolution, the home of the proletariat and of true class consciousness; to them Moscow was still the old conservative capital with the peasant outlook.

During the summer of 1925 Zinoviev and Stalin both changed their ground, each conforming with the outlook of the city which provided his base. Formerly Stalin had taken the line that to the Marxist the peasantry must yield in importance to the proletariat. Zinoviev had stood by the peasantry. But now he gave priority to the interests of the proletariat while Stalin began to champion the peasantry.

The rivalry within the triumvirate and the Politburo centred at this time on the nature of NEP, the inner contradictions of which constantly troubled Marxists. Acute unrest among the peasants gave urgent practical point to the conflict. The great estates of the landlords had been divided into small farms. Individual farming on twenty-four or twenty-five million smallholdings had become the pattern. But the proportion of grain finding its way to the towns had fallen[11] with the result that food shortages constantly threatened. Meanwhile the peasants still had no confidence that their farms would be secure under the Soviet regime. They demanded greater concessions under NEP, particularly higher prices for their produce and better supplies of industrial goods; the more prosperous peasants called for abolition of restrictions on hiring labour, leasing land, and investing capital in agriculture. A peasant uprising in Georgia in the summer of 1924 was taken as a warning that similar uprisings could happen elsewhere in Russia. Stalin concluded that the party had lost contact with the peasants who must in future be handled more carefully.[12]

The Politburo was undecided on the policy to be followed. Bukharin and the right-wing bolsheviks favoured maximum concessions to the peasantry and the cultivation of harmonious co-operation between them and the proletariat. Bukharin argued that not only was the country dependent on them for food but also for the capital with which to finance industrialization. He went so far as to call on the kulaks to enrich themselves, holding that they had so much to contribute in grain and in capital and that they would in due course be readily absorbed into the socialist economy.[13]

Stalin leaned towards the right bolsheviks. He was anxious to encourage the poor and middle peasants, but was uneasy about the appeasement of the kulaks. Finally, however, he adopted Bukharin's policy. The fourteenth party conference meeting from 27 to 29 April granted numerous concessions to the peasants. The agricultural tax was cut by twenty-five per cent; restrictions on leasing land, hiring labour, and accumulating capital were virtually removed.

Zinoviev and Kamenev now seized on this policy to oppose Stalin and Bukharin. Expressing the strong misgivings of the left wing, they pointed to the danger that the prosperous farmers would become stronger and by withholding food from the towns would be able to undermine the soviets and make the restoration of capitalism possible. The correct policy for the party was to encourage large-scale farming which had been the most productive system under the tsarist regime, but now they would be collective farms. The movement from individual to collective farming should be achieved not by compulsion but gradually by persuasion and inducements, such as the supply of seed, fertilizer, and tractors. Once settled on the collective farms the peasants would see the advantages, especially in greater productivity. This policy would, however, call for greater emphasis on industrialization not only to meet the demands for industrial goods but also to provide for mechanization of agriculture and, more broadly, to create the balance needed in a socialist economy.

Zinoviev and Kamenev pressed their attacks on the right-wing further by arguing that according to the true interpretation NEP was not a positive step towards socialism but a temporary retreat into capitalism. Stalin and Bukharin at once condemned them as pessimists. Their stand was tantamount to saying that the revolution had come to a standstill and that the Soviet people, who had in the glorious October revolution shown the way to the proletariat of the world, lacked the creative capacity to advance farther. But rational argument on this and other points of dispute, such as the stabilization of capitalism, soon came to be of secondary importance. The debate became simplified as a struggle between the optimists who proclaimed their faith in the dynamic creative nature of the Soviet people and the pessimists who lacked this faith.

The embittered polemics moved towards a crisis. The two sides seemed fairly equal in strength. But Zinoviev and his supporters were in the dis-advantageous position of seeming to attack party unity, a concept of greatest emotional significance to members. Meanwhile neither side was prepared to engage the other publicly, and the meetings of the central committee in October 1925 passed off without explosion.

Like a spider at the centre of the great party web, Stalin waited patiently for his opponents to make a wrong step and deliver themselves into his grasp. The fourteenth party congress was approaching and both sides skirmished and prepared for it. The hostility between the Leningrad and Moscow party machines and between *Leningradskaya Pravda* and *Pravda* became acute. The Leningradtsi were so arrogant and provocative towards the central party organs that Zinoviev became alarmed and tried to restrain them. The mood of Leningrad was becoming like that of Kronstadt at the time of the 1921 revolt.

The congress opened on 18 December 1925. It began quietly, but ten-sion soon mounted. Bukharin attacked Zinoviev. Krupskaya answered with an earnest plea for party unity. The first opposition speaker, Lashevich, had difficulty in making himself heard above the organized noise and interruptions. He nevertheless spoke strongly against the 'cut-ting off' of Zinoviev and Kamenev from the party leadership. To this Mikoyan, already one of Stalin's chief lieutenants, replied that it was not a matter of 'cutting off' Zinoviev and Kamenev but of their submitting 'to the iron will of the majority of the central committee'.[14]

Kamenev dominated the fourth day. He delivered one of the most forceful speeches of his career. At first he was subjected to the usual interruptions, but he turned on his hecklers with the demand: 'If you have instructions to interrupt me, say so openly.' Many had known that the heckling was organized, but no one had openly challenged it before. The effect was to shame the delegates into silence.[15]

Kamenev expounded the opposition policy, and towards the end of his speech he electrified the congress by making a trenchant personal attack on Stalin. He brought into the open the rivalries which all had conspired to keep secret. He put an end to the myth of collective leadership and ex-posed for the first time publicly Stalin's growing role as dictator.

'We are against creating the theory of a leader,' he said, speaking for the opposition. 'We are against making a leader. We are against having the secretariat combine in practice both politics and organization and place itself above the political organ ... We think it harmful to the party to prolong a situation in which the secretariat combines politics and organization and, in fact, decides policy in advance.'[16]

A storm of heckling disrupted his speech but Kamenev was not to be silenced.

'I must say what I have to say to the end,' he shouted. 'Because I have more than once said it to Comrade Stalin personally, because I have more than once said it to a group of party delegates, I repeat it to the congress: I have reached the conviction that Comrade Stalin cannot perform the function of uniting the bolshevik general staff.'[17]

An uproar broke up the congress. Leningradtsi shouted their support of Kamenev, but it was noticeable that the counter-demonstrations in favour of the leadership, and particularly of Stalin, involved the great majority of delegates. When order was finally restored, the official spokesmen attacked the speech with fury. Kamenev had shown, they said, the true nature of the opposition as grounded not in principle but in personal jealousy and resentment of Stalin. Tomsky went so far as to proclaim that a system of individual leaders did not and could not exist. He closed with an appeal to Kamenev and Zinoviev to 'apply to yourselves the lesson which you taught Comrade Trotsky' and 'to bow your heads before the will of the party'.[18]

The debate continued. Other delegates from the opposition minority followed up Kamenev's attack, but the official majority stood firmly behind Stalin. On the fifth day of the congress Kamenev again attacked him, this time rather plaintively objecting to the fact that he usually got his way in the Politburo. 'Comrade Stalin is,' he said, 'evidently destined by nature or by fate to formulate propositions rather more successfully than any other members of the Politburo. Comrade Stalin is, I affirm, the leading member of the Politburo without, however, ever claiming priority; he takes the most active part in the settlement of questions; his proposals are carried more often than anyone's; and these proposals are carried unanimously.'[19]

The three rapporteurs of the congress—Zinoviev, Molotov, and Stalin —wound up the proceedings. Stalin, always displaying firmness in matters touching the party but otherwise moderate and impartial, denied any intention of 'cutting off' Zinoviev and Kamenev but demanded that they fall into line. The final resolution, probably drafted by Stalin and expressing the official policy, was carried by 559 votes to 65.

Stalin had won an overwhelming victory. But he was careful to avoid any appearance of vindictiveness. In the election of the central committee all the opposition leaders were returned. Later, when the central committee appointed the Politburo, all of the existing members—Zinoviev, Bukharin, Rykov, Stalin, Tomsky, and Trotsky—were returned, except Kamenev who was reduced to candidate membership, no doubt because of his personal attack on Stalin. The Politburo had, however, been increased from seven to nine members. Of the three new members, Molotov and, less reliably, Voroshilov and Kalinin were Stalin's men. Moreover, the opposition leaders fully understood that their membership of the Politburo was conditional on absolute support of the official line; no criticism or deviation would be tolerated.

Meanwhile, Stalin was following up his victory. *Leningradskaya Pravda* was given a new editor and the Leningrad press at once became the faithful mirror of official policy. Next Stalin took steps to remove Zinoviev and the other defeated opposition leaders who remained, nominally at least, in control of the Leningrad party machine. Early in January 1926 Molotov led a strong delegation to Leningrad to report to workers' groups on the congress. Members of the delegation appealed directly to the rank-and-file, ignoring the leaders. They addressed 63,000 workers, or eighty-two per cent of the party membership and secured more than 60,000 votes in favour of the official line. In short, the delegation brought about a massive swing of the majority of Leningrad members away from their leaders whom they had only a few weeks earlier empowered to oppose the central machine in Moscow. It suggested that the Leningradtsi were like sheep, ready to follow the latest leader, but this changeover was also a demonstration of the strength of the party and of the call of party unity, and also of Zinoviev's inadequacy. At the subsequent Leningrad party conference, Kirov was appointed first secretary of the Leningrad provincial party committee and other opposition members were replaced.

Stalin and the central machine were now in complete control of the single undivided party. Moreover, Stalin whom the other bolshevik leaders had scorned as incompetent in the field of doctrine was now the source of the new dogma of 'socialism in one country' which the fourteenth congress had endorsed. He had formulated this dogma almost casually and certainly without appreciating its coming significance. In autumn 1924, when searching for new pretexts to attack Trotsky, he had come upon the latter's theory of 'permanent revolution' enunciated in 1905. In denouncing this theory Stalin had stumbled upon 'socialism in one country'.

The controversy over the two theories was strongly influenced by the struggle for the leadership but its sources lay deeper, arising from the fundamental problem of applying Marxism to Russia. Originally Russian Marxists had acknowledged that because so backward economically Russia must first pass through a bourgeois revolution before a socialist revolution was possible. Lenin and Trotsky had argued that the proletariat in partnership with the peasantry would effect a bourgeois revolution and prepare conditions for the socialist revolution. Trotsky held, however, that having achieved the bourgeois revolution the proletariat would be bound to advance at once to the socialist revolution. He called this process 'permanent revolution', a term taken from Marx. Lenin had disagreed strongly with Trotsky on this point until April 1917 when he had changed his mind and, in effect, accepted Trotsky's doctrine.

The creation of a socialist economy was the next problem. Lenin and Trotsky agreed that it would be out of the question to build a socialist economy in Russia alone. They were counting on support from proletarian revolutions, expected at this time in the wealthy countries of the West. The bolsheviks as a whole had taken it for granted that their October revolution had been socialist in character. By 1924, however, after seeing revolutions fail in the West and particularly after the fiasco in Germany in 1923, Stalin alone had recognized that the theory on the building of socialism in Soviet Russia must be reviewed.

Stalin did not possess the educated or the analytical intelligence of Lenin or Trotsky, Kamenev or Bukharin, but he had a deep instinctive understanding of the mood, hopes, and needs of the party. As a Marxist–Leninist he was seeking to develop the doctrine logically in the new predicament; in effect, he was searching urgently for a policy which would controvert Trotsky and would meet the immediate needs of the country. He combed the works of Lenin and there found a few statements which suggested that Lenin had not ruled out the possibility of building 'socialism in one country'. Seizing on these rather thin references Stalin repeated them, creating the impression that Lenin had indeed believed in this possibility and, incidentally, that Trotsky had not believed in it. At the same time Stalin had taken care not to depart from the orthodox doctrine of internationalism. While arguing that Lenin had fully believed in socialism in one country, he had added that it was 'the beginning and the premiss of world revolution'.[20]

Stalin's theory was first discussed seriously by the Politburo in April 1925. Kamenev and Zinoviev agreed to its inclusion in the resolution to be submitted to the fourteenth party conference in December 1925, when it was accepted without attracting much interest. It seemed at first to be merely a matter of abstract doctrine. Then dramatically its real importance burst through as the inspiring policy that would carry Soviet Russia on from the glorious October revolution to socialism and communism. The emotional and national appeal of 'socialism in one country' was tremendous. National pride in the revolution expanded, embracing most Russians, with this declaration of independence of the West and of faith in the ability of this backward country to continue alone and unsupported in the vanguard. Russia, for long treated as lagging on the outskirts of civilization, would show herself to be advanced and the very centre of civilization in the world to come. Zinoviev and Trotsky who condemned the policy as 'national narrow-mindedness' and 'national messianism' were themselves denounced as men of little faith who did not believe in the great creative mission and power of the party and the Russian people.

Stalin as the exponent of this policy had shown himself to be the leader in the Leninist tradition. NEP had been Lenin's great contribution to the advance towards socialism. The recovery of the economy had by 1925 produced the situation in which 'socialism in one country' would take over from NEP and inspire the drive for industrialization and industrial social-ism. This was the constructive policy which Stalin alone offered the nation and it made his claim to lead irresistible.

In January 1926 after his sweeping victory at the fourteenth party con-gress Stalin wrote an article 'On Questions of Leninism'. He attacked the views expressed by the opposition at the congress on the NEP and the dictatorship of the party. But he also dealt with the two obstacles to the creation of socialism in one country. The first obstacle was the backward-ness of the Russian economy, but this was a challenge rather than an obstacle, and he damned the pessimists of the left for arguing that the obstacle was real and insuperable. In fact, the sole obstacle was that the capitalist powers in this period of stabilization of capitalism would attack the Soviet Union. Soviet Russia must, therefore, withdraw and in isolation pursue a policy of intensive industrialization. She would then, while pre-paring to repel any capitalist attack, surge irresistibly towards industrial socialism. This article, published in the party journal *Bolshevik* on 15 February 1926 and later with other articles in a volume with the title *Questions of Leninism*, provided the fundamental canon of the party in the years ahead.

The opposition leaders and their supporters, although defeated, were still at large. Their only hope of continuing the struggle against Stalin's dictatorship lay in working together. Even then they could not hope to make a real impact. Zinoviev no longer controlled the Leningrad party machine. He was still president of the executive committee of the Comin-tern, but Stalin was soon to remove him from this office. Trotsky could count on only a few supporters. But he remained the one man whom Stalin feared. He had consistently outmanoeuvred and defeated Trotsky in the councils of the party, reducing him to the position of a political outcast. But, like other members who knew Trotsky, he stood in awe of his great ability, his courage, and his high moral purpose.

During 1925 Trotsky had held himself aloof from public affairs. He had sat through the fourteenth congress without speaking. His one public statement had been a denial that he had assisted an American author, Max Eastman, whose book *Since Lenin Died*, published in New York, quoted long extracts from Lenin's testament and gave an account, subsequently shown to have been largely accurate, of the rivalries after Lenin's death. Trotsky and Krupskaya both dismissed the book as 'malicious inven-tion'.[21]

Early in spring 1926 Zinoviev and Kamenev approached Trotsky with proposals to act together. Trotsky at first showed no enthusiasm and he astonished Zinoviev and Kamenev by leaving at this time for Berlin where he had his tonsils removed. During the summer, however, the combined opposition was formed and at once became active. It had to advance its programme circumspectly. Marxism made no provision for an opposition and in a proletarian regime it could only be counter-revolutionary. The party apparatus under the control of Stalin was fully prepared for the opposition challenge. Moreover, during the past four years the bolsheviks had developed a horror of factions and of assaults on the unity of the party. Trotsky in presenting the opposition platform, therefore, used parallels from the time of the French revolution to stress the danger of the bureaucracy within the party. He held that antagonism between the proletariat and the bureaucracy was responsible for the failings of the regime. He urged the speeding up of industrialization, improvement of wages and conditions of workers, restraints on the growing strength of the kulaks and middle peasants, and greater support to the poor peasants. The opposition also criticized the leadership for its lack of revolutionary ardour, especially in failing to support the Comintern, and emphasized that since socialism was international the policy of socialism in one country was misconceived.

This programme was presented in part at the central committee meeting from 6 to 9 April 1926 and in full to the meeting from 10 to 23 July. Meanwhile Stalin was active in removing opposition supporters from positions of authority. Zinoviev ceased to be a member of the Politburo and his place was taken by Rudzutak. At the same time he was busily discrediting the policies of the opposition. He controlled the press and ensured that opposition policies were given extremely limited circulation and then in a distorted form.

Thwarted in their efforts to promote their ideas and their criticisms of the party machine, Trotsky, Zinoviev, and other opposition leaders grew desperate. They arranged demonstrations among party members in factories. This was a blatant violation of party discipline. Trotsky, Kamenev, and Zinoviev and three others fearing expulsion, at once published a statement admitting their guilt and pledging themselves to refrain from factional activity. But their action had played into Stalin's hands. The central committee, meeting from 23 to 26 October 1926, removed Zinoviev from the Comintern, Trotsky from the Politburo, and Kamenev ceased to be a candidate member. The opposition demand that their policy statement should be submitted to the fifteenth party conference to open on 26 October was refused. Their stand was further weakened by Krupskaya's changeover to the official side at this time.[22]

At the fifteenth party conference the opposition were in an impossible position. Their policy and criticisms were merely referred to in garbled form by Stalin as he condemned them. Opposition spokesmen could not make themselves heard above the uproar of jeers and demonstrations which burst forth automatically whenever they came forward to speak. The conference endorsed the official policy of 'socialism in one country' and howled disapproval of the pessimists, as all opposition members were now labelled, and they were damned with the invective which was now becoming standardized.

In 1927 the opposition attempts to press their case against Stalin and the party bureaucracy followed the same pattern but more feebly. They made full use of General Chiang Kai-shek's persecution of the Chinese communists in Shanghai in May 1927. On this point their case claimed wide sympathy within the party and embarrassed Stalin who had been criticized for continuing to support Chiang Kai-shek. But also in May 1927 an imagined threat of war served to unite the party and to offset such criticisms. In London the police raided the offices of the Soviet Trade Delegation and found evidence of subversive communist activities. The British government at once broke off diplomatic relations with the Soviet government. Many Russians believed that this was the prelude to war. The opposition at once pressed for the election of leaders commanding the confidence of the proletariat inside and outside the country. But this was not the time for change and Stalin made the more telling appeal for strong party unity in the face of common danger.

The campaign against the opposition steadily mounted in intensity. Thousands of meetings in party cells organized by the central secretariat passed resolutions condemning the opposition leaders. The OGPU, successor to the GPU, was harrying them. In effect they were already outlawed.

In anticipation of the fifteenth party congress which had already been delayed some months and was now to meet in December 1927, the opposition leaders prepared a third memorandum for circulation to delegates. Expecting that the central committee would refuse them permission to publish it, they had it printed clandestinely. It was an act of desperation. Within a few days the OGPU had found the printing press and arrested those involved. Trotsky and Zinoviev were at once expelled from the central committee. They now planned a last defiant gesture, well aware that it would result in their expulsion from the party. On 7 November 1927, the tenth anniversary of the October revolution, they organized demonstrations by their supporters in the streets of Moscow and Leningrad. Crowds of workers and others lethargically watched the processions. Then the police aided by organized mobs broke them up. This was the end of the left opposition. Trotsky and Zinoviev were expelled from the party. The fifteenth congress confirmed their expulsion and declared for the first time that support of the opposition was incompatible with party membership. Zinoviev, Kamenev, and others humbled themselves by renouncing their views as anti-Leninist and petitioning for readmission to the party. Trotsky did not sink so far and on 19 January 1928 he and some thirty others were expelled from Moscow. Trotsky was sent to Alma-Ata in Central Asia where he began his long exile.

During the five years following the death of Lenin no one could claim to be the sole undisputed leader of the party and the country. But Stalin was advancing inexorably towards this position and nothing is more striking than his complete victory over men like Trotsky and Kamenev who were in so many respects his superiors. The main reason for his success was his organizational genius and his mastery of the party machine. In this period he contributed most to the tremendous expansion and growth in the strength of the party. The dynamism and sense of mission which inspired even rank-and-file members were fundamental to this development. But from the centre of the party web he controlled and directed it.

When originally created in March 1922, the office of general secretary had been intended to co-ordinate the work of the numerous branches, committees, and offices of the party. But Stalin from the day of his appointment in the following April had made it the centre of power. By 1925 the secretariat had a staff of 767 officials and its authority reached out over the country. Its main department was Orgraspred formed in 1924 by the merger of the account and assignment and the organization and instruction sections. Its powers were wide. It made recommendations for appointments, promotions, and transfers not only to party offices but also to important positions in the commissariats, the trade unions, and industry. It kept dossiers on leading party workers and controlled their appointments. It advised on all matters of party organization. It maintained a team of instructors or inspectors who advised and inspected local committees and organs, taking care that dissidents were dealt with and that delegates chosen at every level were trustworthy supporters of the party and especially of Stalin.

The appointment and control of party secretaries throughout the country was the secretariat's chief function and the main source of its power. Secretaries at the various levels were in theory elected, but in practice they were carefully chosen and since no one could stand against them they were automatically elected. They were the key men, the 'apparatus' of the party which had itself developed into an immense organization. Its full-time officials numbered 15,325 in August 1922 and by 1925 this figure was about 20,000.[23]

Members had strong incentives to seek appointment in party organizations. Party officials received pay up to fifty per cent above that of government employees and, more important, they enjoyed special privileges. Zeal to serve the party in the great communist venture caused most officials to lead lives of fanatic dedication and austerity. But many succumbed to corruption or abused their powers.

The secretariat also had a secret section, maintaining close liaison between the party and the OGPU which could be called on to dispose of actual or potential opponents. Other departments of the secretariat dealt with the press, agitation and propaganda, village affairs, statistics, administration, party work among women, accounting, and the dissemination of appropriate information as distinct from propaganda. During the years 1924–7 Stalin made further changes and improvements in the secretariat, until it was functioning with ruthless efficiency as the nerve centre of the party.

The other committees of the central committee were the Politburo and the Orgburo. The responsibilities of the Orgburo were not clear, but included the making of the most senior appointments. Strictly it stood above the secretariat but in practice it was subordinate to it, for Stalin, dominating both organs, concentrated power in the secretariat.

The Politburo had by 1927 come under Stalin's control. Of its nine members Kuibyshev, Molotov, Rudzutak, and Voroshilov were his men. The other four members—Bukharin, Kalinin, Rykov, and Tomsky—had sided with Stalin in routing the left opposition, but he was soon to eliminate them. The eight candidate members who included Mikoyan, Kaganovich, Kirov, and Uglanov, were younger men who owed their advancement to their own ability and also to Stalin's favour.

The Politburo made most of the policy decisions but major matters under dispute, especially during the interregnum when the struggle for the leadership was involved, were transferred by Stalin to the central committee or to the joint plenum of the central committee and the central control commission, the latter's duties being the control of party and government and in particular the maintenance of party discipline. Debate in the central committee or the joint plenum being public, the discussion of problems there appeared to be more democratic, although the voting of the delegates carefully chosen through the apparatus of the secretariat was readily predictable. In fact, soon after Lenin's death the congresses and conferences of the party ceased to discuss and decide party policy. The opposition had voiced criticisms before them, but only as a minority whose views would be voted down by overwhelming majorities. After the defeat of the opposition the function of congresses and conferences came to be that of a public platform to which the leaders could make reports and which endorsed the policies put to them.

The party apparatus and, more specifically, the Politburo and the secretariat which Stalin dominated ruled the party and the country. But this vast, highly efficient party machine could only be secure in wielding power if it had control over the Red Army and the security organs. The army was a special problem. Towards the end of the civil war, a party congress (ninth congress in April 1920) had considered setting up a national militia in place of the regular army. Social democrats had always condemned standing armies but after the Kronstadt revolt, the peasant outbreaks, and the industrial unrest in 1920–1, the bolsheviks had recognized that an armed militia might be dangerous. Tukhachevsky, the most able of the communist military leaders, and others urged the need for a standing army. In 1924 a regular army of 562,000 men was instituted together with a system of universal military training for all socially reliable citizens, a phrase excluding priests, kulaks, and other elements from the old regime.

Trotsky had been people's commissar for war and head of the revolutionary military council until 1925, but had long before ceased to wield authority in military matters. Stalin nevertheless feared that he might influence the armed forces and this was a further incentive for him to assert direct party control over the army. The political directorate of the army had answered to the revolutionary military council, but in 1924 the directorate was brought under the central committee, which wielded its authority directly through political departments in army and naval units and these departments were independent of local party organizations.

A further reform affected the political commissars. The system of dual command had survived from the civil war when the chief duty of the commissar had been to ensure the loyalty of the ex-tsarist officers serving in the Red Army. The system was now causing resentment. Army commanders considered that their loyalty to the regime was beyond question and maintained that the commissars diminished their authority and the efficiency of their units. In 1925 army commanders were given sole command and the commissars were reduced to acting as their political assistants. In effect, this change was only nominal, for the commissars reported direct to their political authorities without reference to their commanders. Gradually, however, as the party leadership gained confidence in the political reliability of the army, single commands were established.

The increase in the number of party members in the army from 1924 to 1928 contributed greatly to this growing confidence. By 1927 members and Komsomol members accounted for 202,000 men or thirty-seven per cent of the army. Party members were, moreover, found mainly among the officers. This meant that often a commanding officer, responsible for military discipline, was also the party official entrusted with the indoctrination of his men. Party and military discipline were administered together and the dangers of dissident groups forming in the army were negligible. Leaving nothing to chance the OGPU maintained special units within the armed forces but independent of the military commands which vigilantly watched for unreliable elements.

The OGPU, the United State Political Administration, had been instituted on 15 November 1923 under the terms of the constitution of the U.S.S.R. It was the successor to the GPU which it followed in its powers and functions, except that it was independent of the NKVD, the People's Commissariat of Internal Affairs. Felix Dzerzhinsky was appointed chairman of OGPU and he served Stalin as zealously as he had served Lenin, when head of the CHEKA. The jurisdiction of OGPU was vaguely defined, but in practice it never lacked power to do whatever the party required of it.

The OGPU was responsible to Sovnarkom, the Council of People's Commissars. In fact, the OGPU answered to the party through the Politburo or the Orgburo, and Dzerzhinsky was a member or candidate member of both organs until his death in 1926. But the secretariat, which controlled appointments to the OGPU, was probably the channel by which Stalin maintained control over the security forces which were increasingly sinister and ubiquitous and at hand as an instrument of terror.

By 1927 the Komsomol, the Communist League of Youth, had a membership of two million. It had been set up in October 1918 independently of the party. At first it had claimed autonomous status and had only reluctantly accepted control by the party central committee. Among Komsomol members, aged between fourteen and twenty-three years, the spirit of independence and of revolution was strong. They did not tamely bow to directives from the central organs. Lenin made far less impact on them than Trotsky, and they tended to rally to him and later to Leningrad rather than to Moscow. But after the fourteenth party congress in December 1925 the Komsomol became a subordinate branch of the party, obedient to the directives of the central committee.

The position of the church and its relations with the Soviet regime were still unresolved. The patriarch, Tikhon, had been released from prison in June 1923 on signing a declaration, recognizing the Soviet government and undertaking not to engage in political activity. The patriarchal church had at once revived but the death of Tikhon in 1925 was followed by new troubles. The government arrested his appointed successors. When finally Metropolitan Sergii assumed the leadership he, too, was arrested, notwithstanding his instructions to all churchmen to observe strictly Tikhon's political neutrality.

The party's attitude was clear. It was committed to the creation of an atheistic society. Religious activity was considered to be counter-revolutionary and a ground for criminal prosecution. But the complete eradication of such an institution as the Orthodox church which had been an integral part of the life of the nation since its beginnings could not be effected simply by decree. Realizing this the party leaders showed uncertainty about the tactics to be adopted, for they could not completely ignore domestic or world opinion.

Meanwhile the church existed and its relations with the state had to be placed on some satisfactory basis. Tikhon's undertaking had served at the time, but it was recognized that the church could not stand aside from politics. By 1927 the Soviet leaders had made it clear that political neutrality was no longer acceptable and that they expected active co-operation in all fields.

The new basis for relations between the church and the state was provided by the proclamation made in July 1927 by Metropolitan Sergii. In it he promised the support and political co-operation of the church and its followers. 'We wish to be Orthodox and at the same time to claim the Soviet Union as our civil motherland, the joys and successes of which are our joys and successes, the misfortunes of which are our misfortunes ... Remaining Orthodox, we remember our duty to be citizens of the Union "not from fear but from conscience".' The émigré clergy, whose activities had exacerbated the difficulties of the church in Russia, were called on to give written guarantees of their loyalty to the Soviet government or face expulsion from the church. Finally the proclamation released the news that a permanent central church administration would be elected to manage the affairs of the church.[24]

On the basis of this renunciation of political and social leadership and of identification of the political interests of the church with those of the atheistic state, the church survived during the next sixteen years. But they were uneasy years. The Soviet government was hostile and continued to persecute the clergy and to discriminate against believers.

The most damaging assault on the church at this time, influenced by the collectivization campaign and the attempt to break down peasant opposition, was the decree of 8 April 1929 which brought angry protests from abroad. This decree made registration of all religious societies and groups of believers compulsory and limited their functions rigidly to the conduct of worship. Religious instruction, propaganda, and even recreational activities were expressly forbidden. Religious groups could gather and perform ceremonies of worship only in the buildings allocated to them by local authorities except for the administration of last rites and burials, and they had to meet all expenses, including the upkeep of buildings, by voluntary collections.[25] This was the beginning of a violent campaign against the church and religion.

During the NEP period the party had still not achieved control over industry and agriculture, but it was moving steadily towards the totalitarianism which was inherent in the system. At this time it was creating the machine to administer and enforce totalitarian rule. Also it was expanding party membership as the basis of its strength. For Stalin, too, the Lenin enrolment and the membership drives which followed brought into the party new members on whom he could rely for support. In the four years from 1924 to 1928 party membership grew from 472,000 to 1,304,471, including candidate members. Of the members of the party in 1927 one quarter were under twenty-five years old, over half were under thirty, and over eighty-five per cent were under forty. The ranks of the older bolsheviks were rapidly thinned by death, purges, and grief.[26] The party had the vitality of youth but suffered from its inexperience and above all from the low educational level of members. Fewer than one per cent had had higher education and less than eight per cent had even had secondary education; of the remainder the majority were barely literate and over two per cent were illiterate.

To remedy this deficiency an ambitious programme of educating party members was launched. By 1927–8 over 40,000 party schools with more than three-quarters of a million enrolments were functioning throughout the country. The schools gave special instruction not only to members but also to potential members. Soon the party schools were brought under the control of the secretariat, for Stalin saw that the system would train officials selected and well-indoctrinated to serve the party reliably.

In the midst of this intensive development of the party the struggle for the leadership was still not at an end. Stalin could not rest while any man capable of challenging or checking him remained in a position of authority. He had endorsed the policy of continuing NEP, thus gaining the support of the right-wing members headed by Bukharin, Rykov, and Tomsky, which had enabled him to rout Trotsky, Zinoviev, and Kamenev and the left groups. Now he turned on Bukharin, Rykov, and Tomsky and proceeded to eliminate them.

Again the almost perverse failure of his opponents to recognize his abilities and power helped Stalin in his task. Even after the fifteenth congress, Bukharin, Rykov, and Tomsky were convinced that the party's endorsement of their right-wing policy meant that they would soon take over the leadership from Stalin. Trotsky and others had warned against the swing to the right, but Bukharin saw in this swing victory for himself and other supporters of NEP. Moreover, he believed quite mistakenly that he could count on a majority of the new Politburo of nine full members and eight candidate members, elected on 19 December 1927 after the congress.[27] But he was soon to find that Stalin with the backing of the Politburo and using the immense powers of the secretariat was displacing his supporters from positions of authority in the party and the administration. For the present, however, Stalin carefully avoided open conflict. He had come out strongly in support of NEP in routing the left opposition groups, and he saw that he could not turn so soon against his allies and reject NEP which commanded wide support.

At some time shortly before or during the fifteenth congress, however, Stalin had reached a momentous decision. Grain supplies to the towns had been falling far short of requirements. Famine threatened. Late in December 1927 the central committee had ordered local party officials to make every effort to increase grain deliveries from the peasants. In January 1928 supplies were two million tons short of the minimum needed to feed the towns. The food crisis was so grave that the central committee threatened party officials with disciplinary action if deliveries did not improve, and in the following months many local officials were purged.

Against this background of recurrent food crises, Stalin had made his decision that NEP must be reversed, agriculture collectivized, and heavy industry developed rapidly; only in this way could socialism be achieved in Russia. Drastic changes in policy were involved, but for the time being he kept his decision to himself. Emergency measures to extract grain from the peasants gave rise to rumours that NEP would soon be abandoned. Categoric denials of any such intention were promptly issued. At a meeting of the central executive committee of the all-union congress of soviets Stalin introduced proposals which gave the first indication of the new line. But the suggestion of collectivization of agriculture met with such strong opposition that it had to be withdrawn.

By this time Stalin had become convinced that headlong collectivization and industrialization were essential to survival. The gradual development urged by the rightists was completely unrealistic. Already he was promoting the new call for a massive national effort of dedication and self-sacrifice to achieve socialism. Gosplan, the state planning commission, was working on an overall plan for industrial development, based on conservative estimates of agricultural expansion. But Kuibyshev, as head of the VSNKh, overwhelmed the Gosplan economists by demanding a 130 per cent expansion of industry in five years. To the charge that such a target was impossible, the reply was that 'Our task is not to study economics, but to change it. We are bound by no laws. There are no fortresses which bolsheviks cannot storm. The question of tempo is subject to decision by human beings.'[28]

The central committee meeting from 4 to 12 July 1928, debated the new policy and confirmed the existing line. It endorsed individual farming by small and medium-sized peasant families as the basis of agriculture for some years ahead and repealed the extraordinary measures against the kulaks, which it had approved in the previous year. Again NEP was affirmed as the only policy for the achievement of socialism. But this affirmation of NEP was deceptive. As revealed some years later the meetings of the central committee had been occasions of angry conflict. Stalin had forcefully argued the need to accelerate industrial growth by compelling the peasants to contribute the necessary capital. Bukharin, Rykov, and Tomsky had desperately opposed this change of policy, but now they were becoming uneasily aware of the dangers of challenging Stalin.

While the central committee was still in session, Bukharin had suddenly called on Kamenev. He was evidently highly excited and near to panic. He told Kamenev that Stalin 'will strangle us. He is an unprincipled intriguer who subordinates everything to his appetite for power. At any given moment he will change his theories in order to get rid of someone.'[29] Bukharin's immediate purpose was to reach some agreement with Kamenev and Zinoviev who had now been readmitted to the party. 'We consider Stalin's line fatal to the revolution,' Bukharin told Kamenev. 'This line is leading us to the abyss. Our disagreements with Stalin are far far more serious than those we have with you.' He called Stalin the 'Genghiz Khan of the General Secretariat' and warned Kamenev about keeping their conversation secret because the OGPU had them both under observation. But Kamenev was evidently far from convinced that Bukharin would win against Stalin for he stood aside, awaiting developments.[30]

Meanwhile Stalin himself avoided making the dispute with Bukharin public. He knew that strong opposition to his policy existed and he recognized the need to make a show of unity in the party leadership after the upheavals of the campaign against Trotsky. It was all the more necessary at this time when foreign delegates were gathering in Moscow for the sixth congress of the Comintern. Rumours of conflict were, in fact, denied in a special statement to the Comintern signed by Bukharin and the other members of the Politburo. At the same time a subtle campaign to denigrate Bukharin was conducted among the delegates.

The complete domination of the Comintern by the Russian party was demonstrated again at this congress. Using the occasion for preliminary skirmishes against the right wing, Stalin engineered a major change of policy. He had suffered severe criticism from Trotsky and others for supporting alliance with non-communist parties in China and Britain. He now abandoned this policy. The congress passed resolutions condemning rightwing reformists and especially so-called social democrats who, while claiming to seek unity with the communists, were really their most dangerous enemies. Bukharin and the other right-wing leaders tamely toed the party line.

The Comintern resolutions were a prelude to similar action in Russia. *Pravda* on 18 September 1928 expressed this clearly in stating that the struggle against the right-wing pro-kulak elements was equally necessary in Russia. At the end of September Bukharin himself, still nominally editor of *Pravda*, published an article with the title 'Notes of an Economist', which made the dispute public. His article was a well-argued statement of the right-wing policy towards industry and agriculture. But the time was past for arguments. Stalin had decided on his policy and was now intent on eliminating the right-wing. Bukharin, Rykov, and Tomsky made desperate attempts to undermine his power in the Politburo but in their loyalty to the principle of party unity they had weakened their position, and in any case they were no match for Stalin.

To the central committee in November 1928 Stalin enunciated certain of the principles basic to the new policy which were deep-rooted in his mind and which were to apply throughout the years of his reign. Socialism would be achieved, he explained, only by 'catching up with and overtaking' the capitalist countries in industrial and economic growth. Moreover, the rapid development of industry was essential to national defence, which was a first priority, since it was part of the communist dogma that the capitalist powers would attack and seek to destroy the young socialist nation. A further argument for rapid industrialization was the need to merchanize agriculture.

In December the central executive committee adopted a law removing the remaining guarantees of security of tenure to the peasant landholder. In the same month the eighth trade union congress approved the tremendous targets for industrialization submitted by Kuibyshev. The congress also adopted several resolutions which would facilitate the removal of Tomsky and other rightists from the senior trade union offices. Finally the congress elected five of Stalin's supporters to its praesidium, including Kaganovich, who was already established as one of the most trusted of Stalin's henchmen.

On 21 January 1929, the anniversary of Lenin's death, Bukharin
mounted a last desperate attack on the new policy. He made a speech,
which was published in *Pravda* and as a pamphlet, with the title of
'Lenin's Political Testament'. Supporting his arguments with lengthy
quotations he sought to show that Lenin would never have accepted
Stalin's policy. The article and its title must have reminded many members of Lenin's other testament, condemning Stalin.

Bukharin knew, however, that the end of the struggle was near at hand.
The OGPU had been keeping a watch on him for some time and his
approach to Kamenev was widely known. In February 1929 the control
commission summoned Bukharin, Rykov, and Tomsky before it on the
charge of plotting to form a faction with Kamenev. All three addressed a
protest to the Politburo against one-man rule in the party and against the
new policy of forcible collectivization and headlong industrialization and
on other scores. Stalin merely made use of their arguments to label them
as pro-kulak and enemies of the properly constituted authority of the
party. At the meeting of the central committee in April 1929 Stalin delivered a savage attack on Bukharin, and the central committee passed a
resolution condemning him as well as Tomsky and Rykov.

Still Stalin acted cautiously. The central committee's resolution was
circulated within the party but not made public. It served to warn his
opponents that they were on probation and that any slight act of opposition would mean expulsion from party organizations and from the party
itself. Bukharin and his colleagues recognized that they must lie low and,
remaining within the party, try to gain support in the Politburo and the
central committee. Stalin, still not wholly secure as leader, knew that it
needed only two members of the Politburo to vote against him for Bukharin to have a majority. Kalinin, for instance, sympathized with much of
the right-wing policy and Stalin therefore cultivated him. He could rest
secure only when he had eliminated his opponents beyond all hope of
rehabilitation.

The sixteenth party conference meeting from 23 to 29 April 1929
unanimously adopted the new policy, including the first five-year plan and
the collectivization of agriculture. Rykov himself proposed the resolution
for the adoption of the five-year plan. Bukharin and Tomsky obediently
went along with the other delegates. Indeed, the right-wing leaders were
again virtually estopped by their own conduct from attacking Stalin and
his policy. By the end of the year all three and their supporters had been
removed from the official party and other appointments which they had
held. They had also submitted to the humiliating procedure of public
confession and recantation. Like Trotsky, Zinoviev, and Kamenev they
had been completely vanquished and they played no further part in the
affairs of the party and the nation.

The celebration of Stalin's fiftieth birthday at the end of 1929 was a
tumultuous occasion. Statues and immense portraits of him appeared

everywhere. Party organizations throughout the vast country vied in prais-
ing him. Their tributes were extravagant and, for those who could remember, the celebrations contrasted with the modest toasting of Lenin on
his fiftieth birthday when he had warned members against the danger of
cults and ceremonies. But now the great propaganda machine of the party
was at work glorifying the leader. The slogan 'Stalin is the Lenin of today'
was the theme of the celebrations and already Stalin was overshadowing
the memory of Lenin. Stalin was the supreme and undisputed leader of
the party and the nation.

The new autocrat was, however, the heir of Ivan the Terrible and Peter
the Great rather than of Lenin. He wielded absolute power and was
aggressively nationalist in outlook and policy; his driving purpose was to
make Russia strong and equal, but independent of the Western powers
and, like Ivan, he was to develop a pathological suspicion of others. But
there the resemblance ended. Ivan had possessed a fiery majestic presence
and Peter had been a giant of a man, endowed with tremendous energies.
Both men had dominated their eras. Stalin was a small man with a withered arm, possessing great patience, cunning, and courage. He seemed to
have been thrown up by the convulsions of the times and often in danger
of being overwhelmed by them.

His rise to power had been undramatic and unexpected and yet, seen in
retrospect, inevitable. All of the bolshevik leaders, except Lenin in his last
years, had dismissed him as a mediocrity. This had, in fact, helped him in
his rise for no one had suspected or feared him until it was too late. Quiet,
moderate, and inscrutable, he had revealed nothing of the strength of his
ambition and his will to power. Even his closest colleagues had failed to
note his genius for manipulating men and committees and his mastery of
the party organization.

Stalin was not, however, merely a skilled manager of men who had risen
to power by his personal abilities and the weakness of his opponents. He
was a leader who embodied in himself the aspirations of the nation and
reflected their moods and needs. He was a national and not an international socialist like Lenin and the other old bolsheviks. A Georgian by
birth he had become a Great Russian with an intense feeling for his
adopted country. Alone among the bolshevik leaders he had never lived in
the West or learnt any Western language. He was Russian in outlook and
the new men whom he brought to positions of power—Kirov, Molotov,
Kaganovich, Kuibyshev, and Voroshilov—had the same cast of mind.
Moreover, he hated the intellectual and theoretical approach of Lenin and
other bolsheviks as much as their cosmopolitan outlook. This was the
source of much of his savage antagonism towards Trotsky who not only
aggravated his sense of inferiority but affronted his emotional attachment
to Russia.

Stalin was a dedicated communist, but he prided himself on being a
practical man, and he never allowed doctrine to obstruct Russian interests.

Within the communist framework he felt himself to be the heir of Ivan and Peter as a great Westernizer and a champion of the Russian nation. This was his strength as a leader and the main reason for the support and love which the great mass of the Russian people, while enduring so much, accorded to him during the twenty-four years of his reign.

PART IV

THE NEW REVOLUTION

CHAPTER THIRTEEN

Collectivization, Industrialization, and the Eradication of Opposition 1928–34

THE period of the first five-year plan was decisive in the history of Soviet Russia. Collectivization of agriculture and industrialization transformed the nation in these years and the Soviet political system took the form it was to hold into the 1950s. The magnitude and high pressure of these developments were so great that the Soviet leaders themselves recognized them as amounting to 'a profound revolution, a leap ... equivalent in its consequences to the revolution of October 1917'.[1] But the 1917 revolution had been destructive, a purging and clearing away of the old regime, while the new revolution was constructive, seeking to build afresh on a planned socialist basis, but this great leap forward was stained indelibly by the inhumanity with which it was enforced.

In its scale and character the new revolution recalled the reforms of Peter the Great. Stalin, like Peter, imposed innovation on Russia. In each era the mass of the people, patiently and with incredible endurance, struggled humbly and obediently to achieve the objectives set before them. Moreover, Stalin's purpose was the same as Peter's; both men were striving to drive Russia into a new age as a strong nation, able to defend itself and stand as an equal with the great powers of the West. But Peter had a broader outlook; he was determined that his people should in culture and their way of life participate as equals in Western civilization. Stalin, the son of a cobbler, his mind gripped in the straitjacket of communism, cared nothing for civilization and was concerned only with industrial and military might.

The need for collectivization of agriculture and for industrialization had long been agreed in the party. The critical debate concerned the tempo of change. Trotsky and the left wing had advocated rapid development in both fields. Bukharin and the right wing stood for gradual evolutionary change. They could quote in support of their policy Lenin's statement, made in 1919, that 'there is nothing more stupid than the idea of compulsion with reference to economic relations with average peasants'.[2]

Stalin had accepted this pro-peasant policy. He preferred gradual and moderate rather than drastic action, and at first he shrank from the dangers and the scale of conflict threatened by headlong collectivization. As late as the spring of 1929, while charging Bukharin and the right wing with promoting capitalism on the land, he was still endorsing their policy and arguing that 'individual poor and middle peasant farming plays and will continue to play a predominant part in supplying the country with food and raw materials'.[3]

Stalin was, however, temporizing. The threat of famine in the winter of 1928–9 was serious. The persistent shortfall in grain deliveries could only grow worse. The crisis facing the communist government was in fact a kind of nemesis. The bolsheviks had secured the passive support of the peasants during the civil war because they had allowed them to share out the large estates and to farm them as small individual holdings. But this had led to reduction in the grain surplus and now threatened famine which would plunge the country into chaos and destroy the regime. Collectivization was necessary not only to avert famine but also, since foreign aid and any real expansion of foreign trade were unlikely, to make the peasants yield the capital investment without which industry could not develop.

Stalin had no real sympathy or affection for the peasants. He did not share the compunction which Bukharin and others felt about compelling them to provide investment capital. Indeed, he resented the semi-independence which the peasants had enjoyed during the years of the NEP and the facts that they stood outside party control and by withholding their produce could hold the government to ransom. He was hostile towards the kulaks who were rapidly growing in wealth and could pose a threat. But he had continued to hesitate.

The magnitude of the problem could be gauged from the fact that the peasants numbered over a hundred million. The right-wing leaders were unable or unwilling to accept the responsibility for the suffering inevitable in driving them into collectives. But Stalin felt no restraints of humanity; he had courage and nerves of steel, and he was determined that Soviet Russia should grow powerful in the shortest possible time, regardless of the human cost. The sweep of events was again carrying the country towards the maelstrom of revolution and at some point he made the decision to plunge Russia into it.

In the year ended 1 June 1928 the number of kolkhozi[4] had increased from 14,830 to 33,258 and their membership from 194,200 to 416,700 peasant households. Gosplan had pronounced this as having been a period of rapid collectivization.[5] But this was a ripple compared with the tidal wave of the following year.

From confused beginnings the collectivization campaign began to gather impetus in 1929 and was soon to sweep across the country, leaving a trail of disaster like a new Mongol invasion. On 27 December 1929 Stalin proclaimed that '... We have recently passed from a policy of confining the exploiting tendencies of the kulaks to a policy of the liquidation of the kulaks as a class.'[6] This meant uprooting from their lands and homes and eliminating five to ten million people. At a conservative estimate more than five million kulaks were deported to Siberia and the arctic north, and of them at least a quarter perished. Many more were killed in their villages and in trying to defend their property.

On 5 January 1930 the central committee pronouncement, that realization of the objective of collectivizing the great majority of the peasants by the end of the plan period was entirely practicable, brought the campaign to a climax of fury. In October 1929 4·1 per cent of peasant households had been collectivized. Three months later this figure was 21 per cent. By 10 March 1930 more than half of all farmlands and more than half of the total peasant households had been collectivized. By 1 July 1934 this figure had become 71·4 per cent. It was a stupendous development, but wrought at terrible cost.

Stalin achieved this transformation by ruthless use of force and terror. Directives went out from Moscow to all local soviets to confiscate the property of kulaks, which was then to become part of the commonly owned and indivisible collectives. In practice this involved the land and livestock of all peasants, for those of the poor and middle groups who did not join collectives voluntarily were liable to be treated as kulaks.

Fearing that local soviets might not be able to stomach such militant action against friends and neighbours, he also sent 25,000 'workers with adequate political and organizational experience' from the towns and more followed to ensure enforcement of his policy. The pernicious committees of the poor, which had whipped up hatred, savagery, and destruction in the villages during the civil war, were revived to wage hostilities against the richer peasants. But the workers and party members were in most cases themselves peasants with village ties and as such not reliable, and the committees of the poor were less effective now when the land was divided into individual holdings. The OGPU thus became the chief instrument for the enforcement of collectivization.

The peasants in many provinces fought with blind destructive fury. The age-old craving of the Russian peasant had been to own his individual farm. He had for centuries endured serfdom and the commune and when serfdom was abolished in 1861 the commune had remained to constrict his freedom and independence. He had taken prompt advantage of Stolypin's reforms, allowing escape from the commune. War and the civil war had intervened, but the peasant had emerged with his own holding of land. Now the Soviet government was confiscating it along with his livestock and forcing him into a kolkhoz which was even more tyrannous than the commune had been. The peasant felt cheated and threatened by the very government which had promised him so much. He now fought savagely. The communists were his enemies and he did not hesitate to kill them on sight. Many villages were transformed into battlefields where the peasants with their wives and families stood against OGPU units, only to be shot down in the end.

Demonstrating most starkly the depth of the bitterness and hatred felt by the peasants was their slaughter of their livestock. To the peasant his horse, cow, his few sheep and goats were treasured possessions, a source of food and income especially in times of shortage. But faced with confiscation and transfer of these domestic animals to the kolkhozi, peasants slaughtered them. Of the 34 million horses in Russia in 1929, 18 million were killed. Some 45 per cent of cattle and 67 per cent of sheep and goats were slaughtered between 1929 and 1933. It happened not as part of an organized resistance, but as the instinctive defiance of hundreds of thousands of peasants.

By the end of the first five months of his campaign Stalin had become alarmed by the turmoil and violence convulsing the countryside. He could claim that his policy had achieved remarkable success in a brief time, but he recognized that the situation was growing dangerous. On 2 March 1930 he published his famous 'Dizziness from Success' article in *Pravda*,[7] calling for a halt to the forcible and planless herding of peasants and livestock into collectives. The time had come to consolidate gains, to put a brake on the ruthless drive, and to halt the excesses which he blamed on the extreme zeal of local officials. The article was followed by detailed instructions from the central committee 'On Distortions of the Party Line with reference to the Collectivization Movement', which prescribed greater care in the handling of peasants. Both the article and the instructions denounced as one of the most serious illegalities the treatment of thousands of poor and middle peasants as kulaks and ordered that this should be stopped. Other illegalities mentioned were the confiscation of the property of peasants under cover of collectivization and the arbitrary closing of churches on the ground, falsely alleged, of popular demand. Stalin had, in fact, unleased a new campaign of persecution against the church in 1928. Mass arrests of churchmen and the closing of churches took place all over the country. Believers, who were most numerous among the peasantry, were distressed by this campaign and for the party leaders it was convenient to blame it on local party officials.

Stalin's article and the subsequent directives emphasized, moreover, that joining a kolkhoz was voluntary, except for the kulaks, and that peasants should not be compelled. At once the peasants took these statements at their face value and exercised their right to withdraw. Within two months the proportion of households collectivized in the R.S.F.S.R. had fallen from 60 to 23·4 per cent.

After a few hectic months Stalin's agricultural policy thus faced collapse. The countryside was near to civil war. Within the party itself unrest over the collectivization campaign was widespread and gathering strength. At this point the opposition right-wing group, led by Bukharin and Rykov, might have promoted an alternative policy. They could claim that they had forecast the disasters that would follow adoption of the policy which Trotsky and the left-wing group had advocated and which Stalin was now enforcing so drastically. If Bukharin and Rykov had proclaimed their platform publicly, they would at once have rallied to their banner the over-

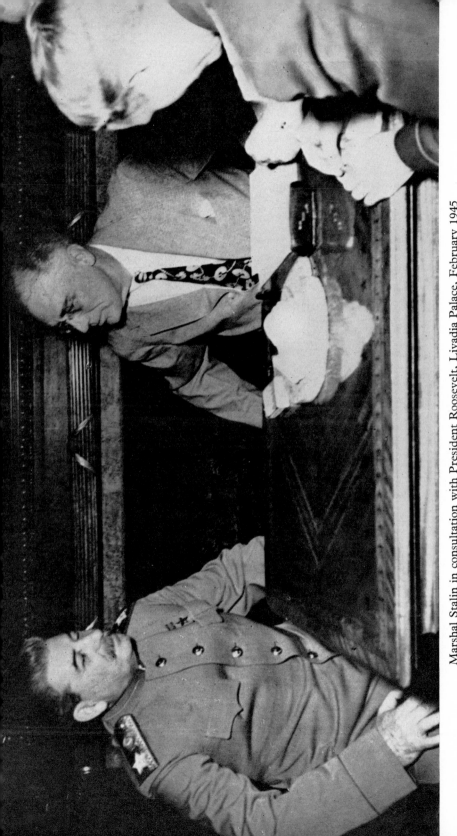

Marshal Stalin in consultation with President Roosevelt, Livadia Palace, February 1945

Marshal Georgii Constantinovich Zhukhov, 1945

whelming mass of the peasants and many members of the party as well as all anti-communists throughout the country. With such support they would have been in a position to assume power and Stalin would have been found to lead only a small minority in the party and the country. But Bukharin and the right-wing group made no attempt to stand as a legitimate opposition. In fact, they actively supported Stalin's policy, and Rykov and Tomsky travelled far afield to Tiflis and Sverdlovsk to defend the official line.

The extraordinary power of the mystique of the party had again asserted itself. Absolute devotion to the party bound Bukharin and his supporters, as it had bound Trotsky. Any suggestion that they might have led a Stenka Razin or Pugachev rising of the peasants against the Soviet government would have horrified old bolsheviks like Bukharin and Rykov. They were, in fact, doomed by their own loyalty to the party. What they strangely failed to realize was that their obedience was not to the will of the party expressed through the central committee and the Politburo, but to the will of one man, Stalin, who had quietly, almost surreptitiously, brought the party under his personal control.

The conflict and the final defeat of Bukharin, Rykov, and Tomsky within the Politburo had been kept from the public. But, having suffered this defeat, they were prevented by party loyalty from carrying the struggle further. At the sixteenth party congress held in June–July 1930 Stalin condemned them without, of course, giving any publicity to their policies and without making martyrs of them. Mild tributes were even paid to them for resisting temptations to rally the dissident peasants to their cause. Bukharin, Rykov, and Tomsky were re-elected to the central committee and Rykov was also re-elected to the Politburo. All honoured the unspoken agreement that the party must show a united front in this time of extreme crisis.

Meanwhile the movement away from the kolkhozi after Stalin's 'Dizziness from Success' halt was being reversed. At the sixteenth congress Stalin made it clear that the peasants must accept collectivization. By mid-1931 official statistics showed that 52·7 per cent of peasant households were collectivized. Six-and-a-half years after the beginning of the campaign 90·5 per cent of households were in collectives.[8]

An essential feature of the kolkhozi was to be the use of machine power and this became a pressing need after the slaughter of eighteen million horses which would have been used to work the land. For the mechanization of agriculture machine tractor stations, known as MTS, were set up to provide machines to work the collectives on the basis of a money payment or a share of the crop. Agronomists, veterinary specialists, and mechanics were attached to each station and courses of instruction were given to kolkhozniki. The MTS were not a complete innovation. In the period of the NEP the middle and more prosperous peasants had lent animals and equipment in return for the labour of the borrower or a share of his crop.

I

The MTS was a development of this practice on a planned basis. In 1929 only one MTS existed. Reporting to the sixteenth congress in the following year the people's commissar of agriculture, Y. A. Yakovlev, claimed that two hundred MTS had already been set up. By 1935 half of the tractor power needed in agriculture was being provided by tractors from the MTS. After 1932, moreover, all of the tractors in use were of Russian manufacture. But mishandling, neglect, ignorance, and sabotage hampered their full use on the land.

At the sixteenth congress Yakovlev had complained of the inequality in collectives, resulting from the different sizes of *usadba*, the allotments of land, which remained in the separate possession of the peasant households. But, unwilling to goad the peasants further, the central committee declared that the forced pooling of the *usadba* land was a mistake, committed by over-eager officials. The collectivized peasant must be allowed to cultivate his private holding. Moreover, the produce of the *usadba* made an important contribution in these years of food shortage. Indeed, private trade in food products which had been the essence of the NEP had been abolished in 1929, but in 1930 the markets had been reopened and had continued to play a vital role in the supply and distribution of food.

The five-year plan had forecast rich increases in production and improvements in the standard of living. But the extravagant forecasts proved false. By 1933 production had fallen below the levels of 1928. In the winter and spring of 1932–3 a terrible famine afflicted the whole country and especially European Russia, causing millions of deaths.[9] The famine was not a result of drought, but of peasant opposition to collectivization and forcible procurement of produce by the government at fixed low prices, and of the slaughter of livestock.

In the face of peasant recalcitrance the government resorted to reprisals. The OGPU acted with greater ruthlessness, carrying out mass deportations, enforcing the death penalty for many minor crimes, in particular for theft of grain, and generally whipping the peasants into obedience. Even while famine gripped the country and thousands were dying of starvation, the government continued to procure grain by force to maintain the level of exports; ruthlessness could go no further. The headlong drive for collectivization had succeeded in terms of the numbers of peasant households and hectares of land brought into the kolkhozi, but the cost had been untold human suffering, the loss of millions of lives, the enslavement of nearly one hundred million people and the destruction of their goodwill.

The drive for industrialization had also started on a moderate note. It had quickly gathered momentum and Stalin had become intoxicated by visions of Russia transformed into an industrial nation. Suddenly the drive had become a revolution with all the pressure of party and state behind it. The new impetus might well have caused a fatal dislocation of industry. The foundations for this industrialization campaign had, however, already been laid before the revolution by Sergei Witte's industrial policies. On these foundations the Soviet campaign relied initially. But no reference was made to this fact nor to the nucleus of experienced engineers and technicians, trained in this earlier period. They were to prove indispensable until Soviet replacements were available and then they were to be eliminated.

By 1927 industry had regained its pre-war level of production. Output had increased at the rate of twenty to thirty per cent annually, but as nearly all existing factories and plants had been restored to full operation, this rate was not expected to continue. Reporting to the fifteenth party congress in December 1927, Stalin had proposed that the rate of fifteen per cent annual increase in output should be accepted as satisfactory for the next few years. By mid-1929 the fever of industrialization had gripped him and he was demanding a fifty per cent rate of increase.

The campaign was mounted on military lines. The Politburo acted as the supreme headquarters and through the party machine and government administration maintained close centralized bureaucratic control over the economy. Incessant propaganda sought to drum into every worker a grandiose conception of his role as a partner in this great five-year exercise and demanded of him an ever-increasing output. Factories, departments, and workers' brigades in every branch of industry were ranged against each other in 'socialist competition'.

Among party members and young people, especially in the Komsomol, the campaign aroused tremendous enthusiasm. Faith in the party and in their role as the builders of a new country and a new communist world was an important element in the industrial achievements of this first plan. An American, John Scott, noted the speed and fervour with which workers erected new plant in the Urals and could not help being impressed by the pride they took in their work.[10]

The mass of the workers, however, did not share this spirit of enthusiasm. They were weary from long hours of labour and the unending pressure for higher production. Food shortages and the sharp decline in their living standards, aggravated by the flood of hungry peasants into the towns in search of work, added to the general disillusionment. As time passed the numerous claims, made by Stalin, that the plan would bring greater prosperity, merely intensified their bitterness. Absenteeism increased steadily as workers sought to escape the direction of labour and the harsh factory discipline. But this led to even more repressive measures. One day's absence brought instant dismissal and in December 1932 the internal passport system was introduced to allow a check to be kept on all citizens in towns, on building sites, and living in frontier areas.

Older workers in particular were antagonized by the change in their position in the factories. The mood of the revolution, which had carried into the NEP period, had developed in all a spirit of equality and of owning and belonging to their factories. Now under the pressure of industrialization they were subject to strict discipline such as they had not endured under capitalism. The revival of piece-work rates for time-rates, which Marx himself had condemned as a method of capitalist exploitation, recalled the old system which they had been told had gone forever. They found small consolation in being constantly reminded that the workers owned the factories, that Soviet Russia was the workers' state, and that they were no longer being exploited by a capitalist class. The grim realities of their daily lives made such political theory meaningless.

Industrial production nevertheless continued to rise. In the four-and-a-half years, which became the official period of the first plan, new blast furnaces increased the number of furnaces operating by a quarter and the output capacity by two-thirds. The new iron and steel centres of Magnitogorsk and Kuznetsk were founded and were in the course of the next decade to supersede the Dnieper and Donbas. Nearly half the machine tools in operation in 1932 had been installed during the plan period. In such branches of engineering as the manufacture of motor cars, tractors, and machine tools, the proportion of new equipment amounted to 80 per cent or more. A quarter of the total coal output came from pits opened within the period. Oil wells in production increased by 25 per cent and two-thirds of the plant for primary refining and nearly all cracking plant were installed in these years. The capacity of electric power stations was more than doubled.[11]

The plan had achieved its basic objective of building heavy industry on firm foundations.[12] Moreover, the production of large-scale industry had shown an increase of 118 per cent which, while falling short of the target of 133 per cent set for the final year of the plan, was a remarkable achievement. The main failures were in iron, steel, and coal output. Both pig-iron and steel had been scheduled to reach an output of 10 million tons by the end of the fifth year of the plan, but had failed badly in achieving only 6·2 million and 5·9 million tons respectively. Coal production was some 10 million tons short of the target of 75 million tons set for 1932–3. Special production campaigns were mounted in these industries.

Constructed under pressure and often by semi-trained personnel, many of the plants were defective. The main problem, however, was the shortage of trained workers who could master modern techniques and maintain normal operations. The great increase in the industrial labour force involved an intake of workers from the villages who were strange to machines and to factory life. Equally serious was the shortage of engineers and technical workers to take charge of plants and brigades of workers. To meet this urgent need in the first years of the plan, engineers and technicians were engaged from the U.S.A., Germany, Britain, and France.[13]

At the same time a massive campaign was launched to increase the number of technical schools at both university and secondary school levels, and to establish factory schools to give rudimentary training to workers. By 1933 some 200,000 students were studying in higher technical colleges, at universities, and secondary technical schools, known as *technicums*, were taking 900,000 students. Factory schools and special courses were able to train a million workers a year. The new training facilities, although imparting only superficial instruction, quickly began to ease the shortage of trained men and in the period of the second five-year plan they could start building on the foundations laid.

The plan coincided with the great economic depression which began in October 1929. The markets of the world closed, industries stagnated, and foreign exchange was frozen, while unemployment rose sharply in the capitalist countries. At first this was not without benefit to Soviet policies. Obsessed by economic collapse in their own countries, people in the West tended to put aside their misgivings about the Soviet regime and to look on Russia as an opening market. Soviet pursuit of trade and Western eagerness to participate forged new economic links. Russian exports increased sharply, reaching a total of 533 million dollars in 1930, while imports rose in value until 1931. But then both exports and imports declined sharply. As a percentage of world trade, Russia's share rose from 1·34 per cent in 1929 to 2·44 per cent in 1932, the peak year, after which it fell, showing that the Soviet economy was not immune from the influences of world economic trends.[14]

The level of Russian imports might have been maintained or even increased, but was held back by lack of capital, difficulty in raising loans, and discrimination against Soviet exports, chiefly on charges of 'dumping' goods at uncompetitive prices. As world prices fell, the Soviet government had to increase the volume of exports, especially grain, timber, and oil, to earn the foreign currency needed.

In 1931 'Torgsin' shops were opened in which Russians could purchase goods not normally available in exchange for precious metals, jewellery, and foreign currency. This was a useful source of gold and foreign exchange, while supplies lasted. Another method of procuring desperately needed imports was by direct barter; Canada, for instance, sent aluminium in exchange for Soviet oil. After 1933 the growing output of gold eased, but did not solve, the problem of payment for imports. The need to pay by immediate exports and through credits remained. Long-term loans were not available, partly because of world economic conditions and partly because of the widespread mistrust of the regime. But short-term commercial credits, of which Germany was the main source, caused Soviet foreign indebtedness to leap from 415 million rubles in October 1929 to 975 million rubles in June 1932.[15]

During this first plan period Stalin was a man possessed. He repeatedly hearkened back to the reign of Peter the Great, seeing himself first as a twentieth century Peter and only secondly as a socialist. He was imbued with the aspirations which, whether astir with vitality or merely dormant, had possessed Russia's rulers since Grand Prince Ivan IV in the fifteenth century. His appeal to nationalist as well as socialist sentiments had been inherent in his doctrine of 'socialism in one country'. But now he proclaimed publicly and as paramount the nationalist appeal.

In a speech delivered in February 1931 to the first all-union conference of workers in socialist industry, Stalin dwelt on the targets to be achieved. He then spoke with unconcealed fervour about Russia.

'The question is sometimes asked,' he said, 'whether it is not possible to reduce the tempo slightly, to hold back the movement. No, it is not possible, comrades! It is not possible to lower the tempo. On the contrary so far as strength and opportunities allow, it is necessary to increase the tempo. Our obligations to the workers and peasants of the U.S.S.R. demand this of us. Our obligations to the working class of the whole world demand this of us.

'To retard the tempo—this means to drop behind. And those who are backward are beaten. We do not want to be beaten! No, we do not want that! The history of old Russia was, among other things, that she was constantly beaten because of her backwardness. The Mongol khans beat her. The Turkish beys beat her. The Swedish feudal lords beat her. The Polish–Lithuanian nobles beat her. The Anglo-French capitalists beat her. The Japanese barons beat her. All beat her—for her backwardness. For military backwardness, cultural backwardness, governmental backwardness, industrial backwardness, agricultural backwardness. They beat her because it was profitable and went unpunished. Remember the words of the prerevolutionary poet: "Thou art poor. Thou art abundant, Thou art powerful, Thou art powerless, Mother Russia . . ."

'In the past we did not and could not have a fatherland. But now, when we have overthrown capitalism and power belongs to us, to the people—now we have a fatherland and we will defend its independence. Are you prepared for our socialist fatherland to be beaten and for her to lose her independence? If you do not want that, then you must in the shortest time liquidate her backwardness and develop the present bolshevik tempo in the construction of its socialist economy . . . We are fifty to a hundred years behind the advanced countries. We must make up this gap in ten years. Either we do this or they crush us!'[16]

This was the appeal to which the Russians responded. They would create in Russia a 'new America' and, in fact, the terms 'Americanization' and 'industrialization' were at this time used interchangeably. This was the metamorphosis of which the great Russian symbolist poet, Alexander Blok, had written in 1913 in his prophetic poem, 'New America'. Stalin, like many of his people, felt a sense of destiny as they pressed forward in pursuit of this goal. In his haste he was constantly overreaching himself and the progress of industrialization was bespattered with local failures and catastrophes that might have been avoided by greater prudence and foresight. But this surge of effort to achieve in a few years what for other nations had required decades was also part of the pattern of Russia's history and this fact, too, bred confidence and determination.

In these years of the first five-year plan the immense drama of collectivization and industrialization overshadowed important political developments which resulted in the elimination of opposition and the imposition of complete unanimity throughout Soviet Russia. Also in this period strict censorship of all information released to the public and the world became a feature of the regime. Such sparse news of political events as filtered into the Soviet press was enveloped and distorted by propaganda. But despite secrecy and censorship, distortion and propaganda, vital information seeped across the frontiers.

The sixteenth party congress (June–July 1930), known as 'the congress of the broad offensive along the whole front', was the first in the history of the party in which no opposition of any kind to official policy was expressed. Opposition groups had been defeated and silenced. At the congress Rykov and Tomsky contritely confessed that they had been in error and they bowed abjectly to the rule of the party. Party unity was stronger than ever before in spite of the unrest over the collectivization and industrialization campaigns. The sense of comradeship, of being members of the vanguard party, was further reinforced now by recognition of the need to stand together in the face of the critical challenges of the first plan period.

Stalin did not, however, rely on this strong party loyalty. Obsessed with holding power in his own hands, he went in dread of another leader emerging to challenge him. His greatest fear was that Trotsky might, like a phoenix, arise from the ruins of his political career and push him aside. He had always stood in awe of Trotsky's abilities and power of leadership. Early in 1929 he had had him expelled from Russia. But this had not calmed his fears and throughout the 1930s he maintained an intense and vicious propaganda campaign, depicting Trotsky as the most hateful enemy of the Soviet regime.

Stalin himself maintained an appearance of impassive calm during this desperate period. Only once, it is said, did his control break down. One evening at the house of Voroshilov, his wife, Nadia Allilyueva, voiced her distress over the famine and terror raging through the country. Stalin is said to have turned on her and to have abused her in the company which included several members of the Politburo. On the same evening she committed suicide.[17]

In the midst of national and personal crisis, however, Stalin continued tirelessly to note all signs of unrest and opposition. Two or three small groups are, in fact, known to have made attempts after the sixteenth congress to bring about changes in policy. The first comprised a number of fairly young members close to Stalin, who kept up a pretence of loyalty to him while trying to gain support for their opposition programme. Syrtsov, the leader of the group, was a candidate member of the Politburo and prime minister of the R.S.F.S.R. His purpose was to bridge the gulf between the left and right groups and his group was to be known, rather incongruously, as the 'Right-wing leftist block'. But its activities were soon uncovered by the OGPU. Syrtsov and his colleagues were removed from their offices, but apparently nothing further happened to them.

Late in the summer of 1932, when famine was beginning to spread through the Ukraine and in the North Caucasus and the people were gripped by a mood of savage desperation, another opposition group was uncovered. It was led by Ryutin, a former secretary of the Moscow party committee and a supporter of Bukharin. He drew up a two hundred-page indictment, known as 'the Ryutin platform', which denounced Stalin as the 'great *agent-provocateur*, the destroyer of the party' and as 'the grave-digger of the revolution and of Russia'.[18] Ryutin pledged himself to fight for the overthrow of Stalin. His policy was to slow down the pace of industrialization, to end collectivization and return to individual farming, and to restore party democracy. Copies of the Ryutin platform were sent to many prominent party members and to former oppositionists, including Zinoviev and Kamenev. Again the OGPU struck, arresting not only all who had taken part in preparing and distributing the platform, but also those who had received it.

In the Politburo Stalin called for the execution of Ryutin. It was a demand of tremendous significance. Opposition had been treated as a mistaken and even a dangerous activity. Recalcitrant members had been persecuted, expelled, imprisoned, and exiled, but never executed. Lenin had warned his supporters against applying the death penalty and following the fatal example of the French revolution which had devoured its own children, the Jacobins. But now Stalin was demanding that any form of opposition should be treated as a treasonable act against the state, punishable by death.

Within the Politburo, this proposal aroused strong antagonism and was rejected by a majority. Of the ten members of the Politburo, Molotov and Kaganovich would have supported Stalin; Kirov, Ordzhonikidze, Kossior, Rudzutak, and Kuibyshev probably voted against him. Voroshilov and Kalinin had wavered before and how they voted on this occasion is not known. But of those who almost certainly stood against Stalin on this occasion, all were soon to die by assassination or in mysterious circumstances. The fate of these prominent party leaders was a warning to all who dared to cross the general secretary.[19]

The conflict in the Politburo had concerned the application of the death penalty and the unleashing of terror within the party. No such conflict arose over the treatment of others and, indeed, the party had always openly recognized terror as a legitimate political weapon. For some time technicians, administrators, and members of the old intelligentsia, on which the regime had depended, but whom Stalin detested, had suffered persecution. Many had been condemned to death without trial; a chosen few were, however, tried under the arc-lamps of publicity and propaganda.

The first of these show trials peculiar to the Stalin era was staged in

1930. A number of economists and engineers were arrested in August of that year. All had held high office in Gosplan, VSNKh, the finance, trade, and agriculture commissariats, and similar offices. They were tried in three groups and two of the trials were public. The first group comprised industrial managers and engineers, charged with plotting in the interests of capitalists. The second group involved former mensheviks and included Groman, the chief economist of Gosplan, and Sukhanov, the historian of the revolution. The third group embraced economists mainly in the agricultural field.

The trials, elaborately staged and with all propaganda media deployed to distort and magnify, served several purposes. First, by showing the accused as self-confessed enemies of Soviet Russia, they aroused the patriotism of the people. Second, they provided an excuse and explanation for failures to reach the plan targets and for the drastic decline in living standards. The accused were denounced as 'wreckers' and 'saboteurs' and their confessions, although not credible to any detached observer, were seized on as the real reasons for economic failures. The trials also gave notice generally to the intelligentsia and especially technicians, engineers, and administrators among whom the collectivization and industrialization campaigns had aroused serious unrest, that the state was to be served without question and that its authority could not be challenged lightly. The propaganda machine laboured all these points with deafening monotony. In particular the 'bourgeois specialists' were denounced because they had deliberately sabotaged the plan or had by proposing conservative targets for production shown a contemptible lack of understanding and faith in the people.

In the 1930–31 trials all of the accused were duly condemned and sentenced to long terms of imprisonment. None is known to have survived. They made way for the new communist-trained intelligentsia who had been taught to eschew politics and to concentrate on new machines and techniques, on grandiose pioneering ventures and on management. They were men of narrow vision, devoid of interest in all but their own specializations. But they were energetic and fanatic in their devotion to the job in hand. Supported by the high enthusiasm of young party members they were to achieve remarkable results in striving after the goals set before them in the plans.

During these years, moreover, the party membership was thoroughly purged. Members who came under suspicion were interrogated, usually found guilty, and condemned in secret. From mid-1930 to the end of 1933 the party control commission passed judgement on 611 party members and candidates on charges of counter-revolutionary activity. During 1931, 1932, and the first half of 1933 regional organizations, together embracing 62 per cent of the total party membership, examined nearly 40,000 allegations of political deviation and as a result 15,442 members were expelled.[20]

Another group was uncovered a few months after Ryutin. Led by A. P. Smirnov who had been elected to the party central committee in 1912, the group included a number of old bolsheviks and trade unionists in Moscow, Leningrad, Rostov, and Ivanovo, whose aims were broadly the same as those set out in the Ryutin platform. All were found guilty, but probably on grounds of their ineffectiveness and age, they were treated leniently and forgotten.

The Ryutin group had been a minor affair, the work of amateurs who like the Decembrists in 1825 had no hope of success. But Ryutin was not forgotten. He had evidently made a deep impression on Stalin. The affair brought home to him more acutely the widespread opposition to him and his policies. In later years and especially during the notorious Moscow trials of 1936–8, the autumn of 1932 when Ryutin was exposed was taken as the starting point of anti-Soviet conspiracies and of the change of the right-wing opposition into a counter-revolutionary force. It marked the beginning of the intensification of security measures and of the massive purge which reached a climax in the Moscow trials. The Ryutin affair opened a new era of terror directed towards eradication of all opposition and the imposition of the silence of unanimity on Soviet Russia.

In planning to purge and subdue the party, however, Stalin faced certain difficulties. The Politburo, which controlled the party apparatus and the police in the last resort, had opposed him over the death penalty for Ryutin and the launching of a new terror. He needed therefore closer personal control over the security organs and to devise a means of by-passing the Politburo when necessary. For this purpose he advanced three men during 1933 and 1934, all of whom were his trusted agents. A. N. Poskrebyshev who had become head of his personal secretariat in 1931 spent his whole career as a key backroom official. His duties are not precisely known, but they undoubtedly involved close liaison with the OGPU. He served Stalin faithfully and was to disappear soon after the death of his master. Another of Stalin's trusted officers was A. I. Vyshinsky, an ex-menshevik and professor of law, who became deputy state procurator in 1933 and chief procurator in 1935, and was to play a sinister role in the political trials of 1936–8.

The most important of Stalin's new key men was N. I. Ezhov, who at the beginning of 1933 first emerged as a member of the new purge committee. Stalin's mistrust extended to the OGPU itself. Its tradition of fanatic service to the party as forged by Dzerzhinsky had bred a corps which might not, he suspected, be sufficiently amenable to his purposes. As a member of the purge commission and later of the Orgburo, Ezhov had full access to secret files on all party members including the officers and agents of the OGPU. This information and the experience of this work were to equip him well to serve as Stalin's special henchman and later as head of the security forces in place of Yagoda.

During these years Stalin was also looking beyond the party to threats of opposition among the national minorities. The treatment of the nationalities had troubled Lenin who had been displeased with Stalin's handling of the problem, especially in Georgia. A policy had, however, been agreed by the twelfth party congress in 1923. According to this policy Great Russian chauvinism and colonialism were the real dangers, for they undermined faith in the Russian proletariat on the part of the minorities who had been oppressed by the tsarist regime.

This policy, promoting respect for the nationalities, had produced striking results during the 1920s. National cultures revived and the prestige and popularity of the Soviet regime mounted. Inevitably, however, the policy aroused nationalist pride and local patriotisms. Moreover, treatment of the nationalities could not be kept apart from the peasant problem. The decision to enforce collectivization made revision of the policy towards the nationalities unavoidable.

Stalin had observed and enforced the official policy of denouncing Russian chauvinism, but he can hardly have believed in it. He had shown himself to be a Russian chauvinist at heart and unlikely to accept the principle of the equality of each nationality with the overwhelmingly dominant Great Russians.

Events in the Ukraine, the largest and most productive of the republics of the R.S.F.S.R. brought the problem to a head. Collectivization had met with savage opposition in the Ukraine which also suffered most severely from famine. Meeting in July 1932, the third all-Ukrainian party conference recognized that collectivization had been a substantial failure in their republic. In Moscow this setback was viewed with special concern and in January 1933 the central committee passed a resolution on strengthening Ukrainian party leadership. Postyshev was sent to overhaul the party organization and with him went a team of senior officials and several thousand selected party workers. Within a short time they had made drastic changes, especially in personnel, and had started a campaign against local nationalism.

Much of the strength of the opposition to collectivization and industrialization in the Ukraine had, in fact, come from fears that they would destroy national traditions. Nationalist sentiment, although never strong enough to unite the people in a bid for independence from Great Russian domination, remained active. The union for the liberation of the Ukraine, formed in 1929, and the Ukrainian national centre, led by the prominent Ukrainian historian, Hrushevsky, had wide support. Against them Postyshev and his men waged a merciless campaign. 'Bourgeois nationalist deviation' or 'nationalist deviationism' was the crime of thousands of Ukrainians. Systematically the republic and the Ukrainian party were purged of all who cherished even the mildest nationalist sentiments. At the same time similar purges were taking place in White Russia (Belorussia), in the Caucasus, and in Central Asia.[21]

Bourgeois and local nationalism had now become the great enemies.

Nothing more was heard of Great Russian chauvinism. The progressive nature of tsarist colonialism was suddenly revealed, taking its place as a logical development of the new nationalist interpretation of Russian history. The seventeenth party congress endorsed the new nationality policy with its slogan 'national in form, socialist in content'. It spelt the Russification of national cultures more ruthless and complete than had ever been enforced by the tsarist regime.

The seventeenth party congress, meeting from 26 January to 10 February 1934, was called 'The Congress of Victors'. The mood of the delegates was one of combined relief and exaltation. They were relieved because the party had endured through the grim struggle against the peasants, through famine, and through terror. They were exalted because in the period of the first plan Russia had been transformed. Collectivization of more than one hundred million peasants had been effected to the extent of over ninety per cent. The peasants seemed to have given up the struggle and to be patiently accepting the kolkhozi. A record harvest had been gathered in 1933 and this had helped greatly to relieve hardships and win acceptance of the new policies. Industrialization had failed to achieve the target set in the plan, but industry had made tremendous strides forward and, most important, the foundations of heavy industry had been laid for the second plan to build on. The sacrifices which it had involved were behind them and the price paid could be forgotten as the delegates looked to the future.

For Stalin the congress was a time for special gratification. His headlong drive for collectivization and industrialization had aroused deep unrest within the party, which had been reflected in opposition even within the Politburo. He had revived terror and instigated purges and show trials to eliminate actual and potential opponents. But the opposition challenge that he had anticipated had not materialized. He had routed the opposition leaders and at the congress had the satisfaction of hearing Bukharin, Rykov, Tomsky, Preobrazhensky, and others acknowledge their mistakes and praise his leadership in fulsome terms. Indeed, the Stalin cult which had been launched on his fiftieth birthday in December 1929 was carried to new heights at the congress with each speaker zealously adding to the laurels heaped on him as leader.

Another man receiving such acclaim might have felt secure. But Stalin never relaxed his vigilance and indeed he could detect many signs of incipient opposition and challenge around him. He could not have been pleased that the congress, on the recommendation of Ordzhonikidze, adopted a lower rate of growth for the second five-year plan than was proposed in the draft resolution submitted to the congress. Another setback was that in announcing the election of the new secretariat, comprising Stalin, Kaganovich, Kirov, and Zhdanov, Stalin's office was given not as 'general secretary' as it had been described since its foundation in

1922, but simply as 'secretary', a change which suggested that attempts would be made to reduce his powers.

The elections to party organs included several names that must have been unwelcome to him. Pyatakov, the witty and outspoken member, was elected to the central committee and among the candidate members were Bukharin, Rykov, and Tomsky, who evidently still enjoyed general respect in the party, despite their opposition to him. The plenum of the central committee, meeting straight after the congress, elected a new Politburo which included at least three members—Ordzhonikidze, Kirov, and Kossior—who could be expected to oppose Stalin's methods, and of the others he could still rely on the support only of Molotov and Kaganovich.

The growing ascendancy of Kirov probably disturbed Stalin most. S. M. Kirov had been his ally against Zinoviev whom he had succeeded as head of the Leningrad party organization. He had supported collectivization, but he may in 1933 have taken the line that the war against the peasants should be ended. Through this or some other stand, he apparently gained the reputation for being a moderate, and many saw in him the leader of moderate policies against Stalin's extremes. His rise had been rapid, far outstripping that of Ezhov, Stalin's special protégé at this time. He had become a member of the Politburo in July 1930 and of the purge commission when it was set up in April 1933. Young, handsome, and a Russian, he was extremely popular and at party meetings received applause second only to that accorded to Stalin. In fact, on his re-election at the seventeenth congress he was said to have received acclaim as great as that of Stalin.[22] Such incidents did not pass unnoticed by Stalin and evidently he was already preparing to strike.

By the end of the year Kirov was dead. Within the next five years 98 of the 139 members and candidates of the central committee, elected by the seventeenth congress, had been shot. Of the 1,966 delegates who attended this congress, 1,108 were arrested and did not survive. Only 59 delegates lived to attend another congress.[23]

CHAPTER FOURTEEN

Soviet Foreign Policy 1928–39

IN the first months of the revolution Lenin and his government had given no special thought to foreign policy. All policy, domestic and foreign, served the single purpose of consolidating and spreading the revolution. The capitalist powers were, they believed, about to follow in Russia's steps. World revolution was imminent. The U.S.S.R., which existed as the nucleus, would soon embrace all other countries.

The peace negotiations and resulting treaty of Brest-Litovsk with Germany had checked these unrealistic assumptions. The ending of the civil war, the withdrawal of interventionist forces from Russia, and the failure of attempts to bring about revolutions in Poland, the Baltic states, and Germany had made it clear that world revolution was still far off. Lenin began stressing that foreign policy must concentrate on strengthening the socialist revolution in Russia. Meanwhile the Soviet government needed a foreign policy to regularize its relations with other countries and to serve Russian national interests.

The policy which evolved was complex and often confused. It was based on certain assumptions, derived from Marxism–Leninism. Fundamental to this doctrine was the absolute denial of the possibility of permanent peace between 'the camp of capitalism' and 'the camp of socialism' into which the world was divided.[1] Further, the doctrine provided that the capitalist camp, fearing Soviet Russia as the leader of the revolutionary movement which must inevitably destroy it in the end, would make constant efforts, including the use of armed force, to isolate, weaken, and overthrow the Soviet regime. At the same time the capitalist camp contained within it the seeds of its own destruction. It was being steadily undermined by its own inherent contradictions, which had led to such conflicts as the first world war and would give rise to further disruption whenever capitalist powers joined in alliances, and especially when their purpose was to destroy the socialist regime.

Based on these assumptions Soviet foreign policy followed certain lines. The belief in the inevitability of conflict between socialist and capitalist camps was readily accepted by Russians. They had had a long history of invasions and plunder by their enemies, and in the 1920s, when isolated and weak after the revolution and the civil war, they were acutely troubled by a sense of being vulnerable, of living under the threat of capitalist attack. Thus a major element in Soviet foreign policy and one which was fervently supported by all Russians was determination to avert capitalist attacks by fomenting disagreements and rivalries within the capitalist camp, by seeking to intensify the contradictions inherent in the system, by preventing anti-Soviet coalitions, and by intensive peace and disarmament campaigns. This policy was defensive in character and a change from the aggressive policy of instigating revolution, which the old bolsheviks had urged, but the defensive policy was to prevail.

The Soviet government, in fact, pursued a dual policy which involved interplay and even conflict in application. The traditional pursuit of Russia's national interests and security by normal diplomatic methods was inescapable. But this basic purpose was now overlaid and buttressed by revolutionary doctrine. Marxism–Leninism required the fomenting of world revolution to be the primary objective of foreign policy. The communist international or Comintern had been set up in March 1919 expressly as the instrument of this policy. The Soviet government had at first been openly identified with the Comintern in its efforts to arouse class conflicts and bring about revolution in the capitalist world. But Russian national interests and the needs of revolution proved increasingly incompatible. Changes in emphasis and in priorities became more pronounced. World revolution seemed to decline to a mere shibboleth. But this was, like other apparent changes, deceptive, for among convinced communists it remained an integral part of Soviet policy as a long-term strategic aim.

In the 1920s the two primary considerations of Soviet policy, both rooted in national interest, were to secure Russia against attack along its immense frontiers and to put an end to Russia's isolation from the community of nations. Progress on both fronts was slow. Not only was Russia greatly weakened and the government in no position to negotiate, but the revolutionary aspect of Soviet policy inspired other nations with mistrust.

The first Soviet peace treaties were made in February–March 1921 with Persia, Afghanistan, and Turkey. They had been followed by trade agreements with Great Britain,[2] Norway, Austria, Italy, and Germany.[3] Such agreements gave only *de facto* recognition, but they were for the Soviet leaders an important step in the process of gaining acceptance among the nations of the world.

The four Baltic states had in 1920 recognized the Soviet government which for its part had acknowledged the independence of all states, except Rumania, along its western frontier. Rumania's annexation of Bessarabia was a barrier to any agreement with Soviet Russia and the two countries moved even farther apart when the Rumanian government made a military pact with Poland.

Centuries of bitter hostility separated the Poles and the Russians. The Soviet leaders fully shared the traditional Russian mistrust and hostility towards the Poles and were especially alarmed that they might build up a comprehensive alliance of all the border states under their leadership.

Holding a central position on the Soviet frontier and more populous and powerful than any of their northern and southern neighbours, the Poles were well placed to forge a strong, integrated system of alliances such as the Czechoslovaks had built up in the Danube Basin. But they proved wanting in statesmanship. The Polish Republic had emerged from the peace treaties obsessed with the idea of becoming a great power with its sovereignty extending over all the territories possessed by the old republic in 1772 before the first of the partitions of Poland. Absorbed by this ambition the Poles became aggressive and arrogant towards their neighbours, antagonizing them and finally forfeiting the position of leadership which they might have claimed. To its great relief the Soviet government was not faced with a strong alliance along its western frontier, but with the three distinct and weak sectors of the Baltic, the Polish frontier and Bessarabia.

In the spring of 1921 the launching of NEP had marked a major development in Soviet foreign policy. Lenin recognized that NEP depended on trade and finance from the capitalist powers. To allay their suspicions he had at the third congress of the Comintern in 1921 and the fourth congress in 1922 sounded a retreat from the policy of promoting world revolution. Contrary, however, to Lenin's sanguine hopes, this much publicized retreat was not enough to banish the mistrust of other countries, and the urgent needs of Soviet policy continued to be seriously hampered by this revolutionary mission.

Disappointed in its hopes at the world economic conference in Genoa in 1922 and conscious still of being an outcast, the Soviet government had achieved an outstanding coup when Chicherin in clandestine meetings with Rathenau, the German foreign minister, at nearby Rapallo, had agreed the terms of a pact of mutual friendship, which they signed on 16 April 1922. For the Soviet government it represented a major step towards re-entry into international affairs and it was to provide invaluable economic and technical assistance.

Great Britain and France remained for the Soviet leaders their most unrelenting enemies. France was bitterly hostile not least because her insistent demands for repayment of war debts were not met. The close links which France had with Poland tended to intensify her hostility towards Soviet Russia, while aggravating Soviet mistrust of France, who appeared to Moscow as the centre of anti-Soviet diplomacy.

Soviet relations with Great Britain were yet more complex and frustrating. The trade agreement made with Britain on 16 March 1921 had given satisfaction in Moscow, especially as other countries followed in making similar arrangements, but the agreement had not improved Anglo-Soviet relations. Chicherin was as staunchly anti-British as Lord Curzon, the foreign secretary, was anti-Soviet. Curzon objected to Soviet propaganda against Britain and her interests; Chicherin complained that the British were fomenting anti-Soviet sentiment in the Baltic states.[4] A number of incidents involving British nationals poisoned relations further. The arrest of English fishing vessels off the Kola Inlet in the spring of 1923 led the British government to send a cruiser north and in a stern note to threaten to break off trade relations unless compensation was paid. The note also demanded that anti-British and revolutionary propaganda should cease in Afghanistan, Persia, and India. Fearing hostilities and an end to trade with Britain, the Soviet government agreed to pay compensation, but in a note of 4 June gave a long and involved disclaimer of responsibility for anti-British propaganda.[5]

The election of Britain's first labour government, under Ramsay Mac-Donald, brought some improvement in relations. English socialists had a certain sympathy for the revolutionary regime, although confident that socialism would be introduced into England without the savagery and the excesses which had characterized the Russian revolution. The Labour government favoured recognition of the Soviet regime and the revival of diplomatic and trade relations. On 2 February 1924 Britain accorded *de jure* recognition to the Soviet government. Italy, Norway, Austria, Greece, Sweden, Denmark, France, and others promptly followed suit.

For Soviet Russia this was a major step from the isolated position of revolutionary outcast towards resumption of the diplomatic status which Russia had held before the revolution. The Soviet leaders recognized at this time, moreover, that the capitalist countries had entered upon a period of stabilization. They themselves were no longer under the immediate threat of internal and external enemies and, feeling more confident about the stability of their own regime, they began to think more of regularizing relations with other countries and less of revolution. An important factor in this change of emphasis was that Soviet expectations of imminent world revolution, diminished by early failures, had been virtually extinguished by the German fiasco in October 1923. This new stage in Soviet policy was at first called a 'breathing space' and in 1925 was defined as 'a long period of so-called peaceful coexistence between the U.S.S.R. and the capitalist countries'.[6]

In settling down to a long, but in their view not permanent, state of coexistence, the Soviet leaders were following in their foreign policy the same trend as in their domestic policy. Indeed, Zinoviev had claimed in May 1924, 'Never has our international policy been so closely bound up with our domestic policy.'[7] NEP had allowed a return to the immediate practical problems of the peasantry and the nation as a whole. The new foreign policy, based on coexistence, gave priority to Russian national interests over the pursuit of world revolution. Moreover, like NEP, it amounted to an acknowledgement of continuity with Russia's past. Soviet leaders had found that the tsarist heritage could not be discarded or ignored in foreign relations so readily as apparently it could be in the domestic field. The factors involved in protecting national security and in promoting national interests were largely the same. In their foreign policy they had begun taking up the traditional threads and building on the foundations laid by Ivan the Terrible and Peter the Great.

The internationalism of Trotsky, Lenin, and the old bolsheviks was being discarded. Soviet Russia, the citadel of socialism and of the revolutionary proletariat—just as Moscow, the Third Rome, had been the citadel of the Orthodox faith—was becoming the dominant theme. It gained further strength after the adoption of Stalin's doctrine of 'Socialism in one country'. Soviet leaders and ideologists still tirelessly maintained, and Comintern resolutions reiterated, that the development of Soviet economic and military strength was the greatest service that could be rendered to the international revolutionary movement, since Soviet Russia was the guardian of that movement until the proletariats of other countries were ready for revolution. Often communist propaganda, official policy statements, and the tirades loosed from Moscow upon the world masked a deep confusion in Russian minds over the real purpose of their foreign policies. Loyalty to the revolution inhibited admission that the fundamental objective of Marxism–Leninism was being put into storage, and that for all immediate purposes the security and interests of Soviet Russia were the dominant factors.

The improvement in Anglo-Soviet relations, brought by British *de jure* recognition was shortlived. The Comintern continued its anti-British campaigns in India, the Middle East, and Ireland. Notes of protest brought the regular response that the Soviet government had no responsibility for the Comintern's activities. In fact, the Comintern had become a serious embarrassment to the Soviet government and gradually all overt links with it were severed. By 1924 Moscow could assert that the Comintern was absolutely independent. But this claim had a hollow ring and served only to hold Soviet good faith in question.

Mistrust was unabated in Britain, but commercial and industrial interests were alert to the scope offered by NEP. For this reason the question of repayment of tsarist debts was shelved for later discussion and Christian Rakovsky, the first Soviet ambassador to London, was able to negotiate a new trade agreement, signed on 8 August 1924. But it was never ratified.[8]

The Zinoviev letter, released by the foreign office on 10 October 1924, struck all in Britain as a flagrant breach of the agreement and caused an uproar. The letter, signed by Zinoviev as president of the Comintern and by Kuusinen, the Finnish chairman and secretary of the Comintern, may have been a forgery. But its directions to the British communist party on spreading sedition and preparing for revolution were wholly in accordance with communist policy for achieving world revolution.[9] Publication of this letter had, moreover, followed another outcry when J. R. Campbell, editor of the communist paper *The Workers' Weekly*, printed an article appealing to British soldiers to refuse to fire on illegal strikers. He was charged under the Incitement to Mutiny Act, but the charge was withdrawn, and the Labour government was defeated on a vote of censure on its handling of this incident. Anti-communist feeling had a strong influence on the ensuing elections. A conservative government, led by Stanley Baldwin, was returned to power and on 21 November 1924 the Anglo-Soviet trade agreement was denounced.

Relations between the two countries remained unfriendly during the next four years. Communist propaganda in India and the Middle East was a constant annoyance to the British government. But the apparent attempts of Soviet agents to interfere directly or through the Comintern in British internal affairs were the main source of British hostility and served to keep alive the threat implied in the Zinoviev letter. Many believed that the Comintern had helped in promoting the general strike of May 1926. This belief received support from official protests made on 12 June against Russian trade union contributions to the strike fund and from publication of documents found in a police raid on the offices of the British communist party.[10] Demands for an economic boycott and for breaking off diplomatic relations with the Soviet Union gathered further strength. The climax came when on 12 May 1927 two hundred police raided the offices of Arcos Limited, an Anglo-Soviet trading organization, and took away three truck-loads of documents. many of which were said to prove that Arcos was a centre of communist espionage and propaganda.[11] On 27 May Chamberlain gave notice of the termination of the trade agreements and the breaking-off of diplomatic relations with the Soviet government.

The British action deepened Soviet convictions that the capitalist camp was engaged in sinister plans to attack Russia. But gradually during 1928 the need to resume normal relations was recognized. Trade between the two countries had dwindled seriously. Britain could not stand idle while German industry and even U.S.A. oil interests benefited. In October 1929 the new labour government resumed diplomatic relations.

In May of the following year a commercial agreement was signed. Trade began to improve, but it remained unbalanced. Britain was taking twenty-two per cent of Russia's exports in 1929, rising to thirty-two per cent in 1931, but, owing to exchange controls and to the fact that British industrialists had no government backing or guarantees, her exports to Russia were far less. Finally, on 17 October 1932 after the imperial conference in Ottawa, Britain denounced its trade agreement with Soviet Russia. This, and in March 1933 the dispute over the arrest of British nationals employed by Metropolitan-Vickers in Moscow, further depressed Anglo-Soviet relations.[12]

During these years Germany remained Russia's chief ally. The treaty of Rapallo (16 April 1922) formed the basis of Soviet foreign policy in Europe. Trade with Germany was of special importance to Soviet development in the NEP period and even more after the first five-year plan had been launched. Soviet leaders watched over German policy with a jealous anxiety, fearful that their ally might be drawn into reconciliation with the Western powers. The moderate parties in Germany were eager for good relations with the West but the left and especially the nationalist right, which nursed a bitter antagonism towards their former enemies in the field, wanted alliance with Soviet Russia. Nevertheless, after the abortive communist coup in Germany in October 1923 relations between the two countries cooled. An incident in the following year concerning the extraterritoriality of the Soviet trade delegation in Berlin led to angry exchanges. The Soviet government went so far as to break off economic relations, but they were soon restored.

The unresting suspicion of the Soviet leaders became acute when in October 1925 Germany participated in the Locarno pact. The pact could in their eyes only be a capitalist plot against the Soviet Union. Their anxieties were calmed, however, by a new trade agreement with Germany signed a few days later, containing a most-favoured nation clause and giving the Soviet Union special long-term credits to increase imports of machinery. But Moscow continued to view with deepest mistrust the possibility that Germany would be admitted to the League of Nations. The Soviet leaders regarded the League as an organization for collective action, probably in the form of economic sanctions, against the Soviet Union. But they opposed Germany's entry all the more anxiously, because it would accentuate Russia's isolation by marking her as the only major country in the eastern hemisphere outside the League, and because Germany, drawn into the capitalist camp, might be committed to collective action against her ally. They watched Stresemann, the German foreign minister, with special misgivings because he sought closer understanding with the Western powers. In fact, Stresemann, while wary of the bolsheviks, wanted good relations with both east and west. This was demonstrated by the treaty of Berlin which he signed with Chicherin on 26 April 1926, developing further their close political and economic ties and providing for regular consultation, as well as containing a neutrality clause. Reassured by this treaty, but without relinquishing its suspicions, the Soviet government accepted more calmly Germany's entry into the League of Nations in September 1926.

Trade continued to grow between Soviet Russia and Germany during these years. In 1928 Germany was taking 28·9 per cent of Russia's exports, particularly manganese ore, timber, oil, flax, and furs. From Germany, Russia obtained 28 per cent of her imports. This was of great importance to Germany at this time, since Russian purchases were mainly of machinery for which markets were lacking. In 1930 Russia took 8·1 per cent of Germany's machinery exports and this percentage had reached 30·5 per cent by 1932.[13] An important stimulus to this trade was the policy of the federal and state governments of giving guarantees to German industrialists and credits to the Russians. Moreover, in the years 1928–33 hundreds of German technicians and engineers were working and instructing in Russia. A further trade agreement in December 1928, the institution of a Russian committee specifically concerned with German trade, and a German Industry Week organized in Moscow in January 1929, all helped boost this trade.

By 1929 the Soviet government had gained recognition from the majority of foreign governments, with the exception of the U.S.A., and was already a force in international relations.[14] A notable achievement had been the Litvinov protocol, signed in Moscow on 9 February 1929 by Poland, Rumania, Latvia, Esthonia, and the Soviet Union. Some four months later Lithuania, Turkey, Persia, and Danzig also signed the protocol, leaving Finland alone of Russia's western neighbours standing apart from the system of non-aggression and neutrality.

The credit for penetrating the wall of mistrust and hostility, erected by these small countries between themselves and their mighty neighbour, belonged mainly to Maxim Litvinov, the deputy commissar for foreign affairs. He had taken increasing control over the affairs of Narkomindel after 1927 when Chicherin's health began to fail, but he succeeded him only in July 1930. The genial, comfortable, and respectable figure of Litvinov had become familiar in Geneva and other diplomatic centres. He had taken part with great effect in the world disarmament conference, expounding Soviet peace propaganda with forceful eloquence. But, although constantly attacking the capitalist governments, he himself retained the liking and respect of their representatives. It was perhaps felt by Western diplomats that, because he had an English wife and was so genial in personal relationships, he could not be an intransigent revolutionary. But Maxim Litvinov was a convinced bolshevik who had served the party faithfully even before becoming a member in 1903. He had been arrested abroad while trying to pass Russian bank notes which were the proceeds of the Tiflis 'expropriation'. In 1918 when in prison in England he had been exchanged for Bruce Lockhart, the British consul, then under arrest in Moscow.

The tendency among Western diplomats was also to credit Litvinov with the improvement in Russia's relations with the West in the 1930s, assuming that as Commissar for Foreign Affairs, he was the architect and director of Soviet Foreign policy. But aside from the fact that Litvinov, although he enjoyed Stalin's confidence, was not so highly regarded in Moscow as he was abroad, the direction of Soviet foreign policy was firmly in the hands of the party. The people's commissariat carried out the instructions of the central committee and, later, of the Politburo. Trotsky had during the short period when he was foreign commissar acted independently, but he was the exception. Chicherin who had succeeded him as head of Narkomindel was not even a member of the central committee and he, like Litvinov, acted within the strict limits of party directives.

The launching of the first five-year plan with its programme of headlong industrialization gave a new impetus to the conduct of foreign policy. In the process it brought marked changes in emphasis but it made no change in objectives; they remained, as under NEP, the pursuit of trade, foreign capital, normal diplomatic relations, and, above all, peace. Reporting in July 1930 to the sixteenth party congress, Stalin said: 'Our policy is a policy of peace and strengthening trade relations with all countries.'[15] Later in the same month Litvinov stated that 'the larger the scale of our constructive work, the more rapid its tempo, the greater our interest in the preservation of peace'.[16]

Propaganda for peace and disarmament had been a feature of Soviet foreign policy from the start. A lasting peace was, of course, impossible in the Soviet view until the capitalist causes of war had been eliminated. But disarmament would give some temporary guarantee of peace. It was also advantageous that the strong powers should be encouraged to disarm, while Soviet Russia built up her economic and military strength against the day when the inevitable conflict with the capitalist world broke out. In the 1920s and 1930s the peoples of the West with dark memories of the first world war earnestly desired peace, and pacifism was widespread. Soviet peace propaganda made a strong appeal and many were blind to its real purpose.

The first approach in 1924 to military reforms, which were to provide the basis of the Red Army, had brought home sharply to Stalin and the Politburo the military unpreparedness of the country. Frunze, who had succeeded Trotsky as people's commissar for war in January 1925, had spoken bluntly of Soviet weakness. Indeed, rearmament was an important, but unpublicized, purpose of the industrialization campaign. The first plan had established heavy industry and under the second plan the rebuilding of the defence industries got fully under way. But at no time was peace more crucially necessary than during this first plan when the whole nation was extended and concentrated on the gigantic tasks of collectivization and industrialization. War at this time would have meant the collapse of the economy and of the nation. The demand for peace, reiterated by all members of the Soviet government, was undoubtedly sincere. No longer did they mean by peace merely an absence of war; they now pursued a positive peace policy, calling for closer relations with the countries of the capitalist camp.

Trade was second only to peace among the objectives of Soviet foreign policy at the time of the first plan. Formerly trade had been regarded primarily as an instrument of foreign policy. Special concessions had been granted to Asian neighbours in an endeavour to destroy British trade and influence among them. Trade had been held out as an incentive to other countries to accord recognition to the Soviet regime. But such considerations now ceased to play an important part in policy. Industrialization depended on the import of machinery and the services of foreign technicians and, through trade agreements, loans, barter, and other means, the Soviet government strained to obtain them from the capitalist world.

Under the impetus of the plan, Litvinov sought to develop a closer, more tightly integrated pattern of treaties with Eastern Europe. The security of their western frontier was an obsession with all Russians. The threat in the early 1920s that Poland might head an anti-Soviet alliance along this frontier had not materialized. But the division of these border states into three weak sectors had not calmed Soviet anxieties, especially when actively threatened in the Far East.

In 1926 Poland had countered the Soviet approach for a non-aggression pact with the demand that such a pact must be part of a multilateral treaty embracing all the border states. The Soviet government then seeing a threat to their security in this demand had rejected it. When in November 1931, however, Litvinov again proposed a non-aggression pact to the Poles, he readily agreed to negotiate such a collective treaty. The Finns who had long and bitter memories of relations with Russia nevertheless signed on 21 January 1932 a non-aggression pact, guaranteeing the frontiers agreed in the treaty of Dorpat (14 October 1920) and establishing procedures for arbitration on disputes between the two countries. Four days later a pact was concluded between Soviet Russia and Poland containing similar conditions but excluding the specific guarantee of frontiers. The Poles believed that the terms of the pact protected them against any revisionist claims that might be made by Germany, and in particular that the pact secured them from any joint Soviet–German move against them. In February and May similar treaties were concluded first with Latvia and then with Esthonia, but these also excluded frontier guarantees.

In London to attend the world economic conference in June of the following year (1933), Litvinov proposed a multilateral treaty of non-aggression to be signed by all parties to the Litvinov protocol of 1929. This initiative bore fruit. On 3 July the Soviet Union, Latvia, Afghanistan, Esthonia, Persia, Poland, Rumania, and Turkey signed the treaty. Two days later Lithuania signed an identical treaty with the Soviet Union. Moreover, Yugoslavia, Czechoslovakia, Rumania, Turkey, and the Soviet Union all signed a separate pact which contained special provision for other countries to join.

Meanwhile, France had been involved in the Soviet network of treaties in Eastern Europe. France was moving away from the stubbornly anti-Soviet policy which she had pursued in the 1920s and was now growing uneasy about developments in Germany. The agreement between Poland and the Soviet Union had removed one of the major barriers to a Franco-Soviet understanding. Negotiations on a non-aggression pact and a trade agreement, already begun, were hurried forward and on 29 November 1932 the two countries signed a friendship pact and a trade agreement.

An added reason for Russian impatience in consolidating the security of the western frontier was the threatening situation that had developed in the Far East and the fear of being attacked simultaneously in the east and the west. But also the Soviet government was active in pursuing the Russian interests which had gathered strength in the Far East in the previous century, and between their eastern and western policies there was constant interplay.

In July 1919 the Soviet government had issued a formal manifesto, which it had reaffirmed in September 1920, renouncing all previous pacts infringing Chinese sovereignty, abandoning all claims to the Boxer indemnity, and affirming its readiness to treat with China on equal terms. But the Soviet treaty with Mongolia in November 1921 had antagonized Peking and not until May 1924 was a full treaty of accord signed by the Soviet and Chinese governments. By this time, however, Soviet and Comintern agents were active in south China, supporting the Chinese nationalist revolutionaries. Sun Yet-sen had founded the revolutionary party 'for the regeneration of China' and in particular to free it from the control and interference of foreign powers.[17] But, although relations between Soviet Russia and the Chinese revolutionaries of the Kuomintang were close, Sun Yat-sen did not accept communism. He knew and greatly admired Lenin, but he sought closer ties with the Soviet Union because she would be a useful ally against the great powers and a source of technical and military aid. He himself asked for political and military advisers, and the Soviet mission led by Adolf Joffe which went to China concluded an agreement whereby Soviet Russia would help the Kuomintang to unite China and free her from foreign domination, and undertook not to seek to impose communism on the country.

One member of the Soviet mission was Mikhail Borodin, whose real name was Gruzenberg, and he remained in China to serve as Sun Yat-sen's chief political adviser. In 1924 a military academy had been set up in Canton headed by General Chiang Kai-shek who had studied at the Moscow military academy. At the Canton academy he was assisted by a Red Army general, Vassily Blücher, known in China at this time as General Galen. Many other Soviet political and military advisers served the Kuomintang, and money and equipment flowed from Russia to enable Sun Yat-sen to carry through his revolution. By March 1927, the Kuomintang had mastered South China, including the Yangtse valley and the Chinese section of Shanghai.

The Soviet undertaking to support the nationalist Kuomintang rather than the Chinese communist party caused conflict in the Politburo. Trotsky wanted to back the Chinese communists and to make the revolution a communist revolution. Stalin, supported by Bukharin, persuaded the Politburo to back the nationalist movement since China was not ripe for communist revolution. Thus Soviet aid flowed to the Kuomintang with whom the Chinese communists on the directions of the Comintern cooperated.

On the death of Sun Yat-sen in March 1925, however, rifts appeared in the revolutionary movement. Chiang Kai-shek, who now became leader and received his main support from the bourgeois element in the Kuomintang, was uneasy about the alliance with Russian and Chinese communists who were pressing for a more radical agrarian policy. He favoured closer relations with the powers against which the nationalist revolutionary movement had originally been directed but which would, he believed, help China to modernize herself. In March 1926 he had several communist leaders arrested in Canton and they were executed on charges of conspiracy. In April 1927 he took vigorous action against the communists in Shanghai and elsewhere. Stalin nevertheless continued to support the Kuomintang. This was to prove a source of acute embarrassment to him and he did not escape sharp criticism within the party. In May 1927 Chiang Kai-shek took further drastic action against the Chinese communists. Meanwhile Chang Tso-Liu, the anti-nationalist dictator of Peking, sent police to search the Soviet embassy in Peking and seized papers proving subversive activities. The Soviet note of protest against this disregard of diplomatic immunity was rejected and on 14 December 1927 the Soviet government severed relations. The Soviet mission was withdrawn and consular representatives were expelled from all parts of China.

In Manchuria Soviet officials were at first unaffected. In May 1929, however, the consulate in Harbin was searched and soon afterwards Russian officials of the Chinese eastern railway were arrested. In the midst of this final collapse of Soviet Far Eastern policy the threat that this railway would be taken from Russian control caused most concern in Moscow. The Sino-Soviet treaty of 1924 had provided that the Russian-owned railway should be managed jointly by China and the Soviet Union until 1956 when China would take complete control. The Soviet government was not prepared to allow the Chinese to take it over in breach of this agreement. Soviet forces had been concentrated in the Far East under the command of General Blücher and despite attempts at intervention by signatories of the Kellogg–Briand pact they advanced into Manchuria. The Chinese government hastened to negotiate and in Khabarovsk agreed to the restoration of the Soviet consulates and to Russian control of the railways. But diplomatic relations were not re-established between Soviet Russia and China until 1932.

A graver and more effective threat to Soviet interests and security in the Far East arose in September 1931 when the Japanese invaded Manchuria. The emergence of Japan in the previous century had checked Russian expansion in the Far East. The treaty of Portsmouth in 1905 and the Russo-Japanese treaty of 1907 had brought a period of friendly relations. By the end of the first world war, however, the balance of power in the Far East had changed drastically. Russia had been greatly weakened; China was paralysed by the collapse of the old dynasty and by revolution; Germany had been eliminated; the Western powers were distracted by other problems. Japan occupied a particularly strong position and was ready to grasp at this opportunity to extend her possessions on the mainland.

The Japanese occupation of Manchuria, or Manchukuo as it was renamed, faced the Russians with a critical problem. Japan could not be intimidated by a show of force as China had been, and Russia had to avoid involvement in a major war at almost any cost. In the protests and negotiations which followed Japan's occupation of Manchuria the Soviet leaders acted with 'invincible restraint and impenetrable reserve'.[18] Such restraint was possible because the Japanese concentrated on creating a puppet regime in Manchuria. They had not threatened the Soviet north-east or Outer Mongolia, the buffer state where with the help of the Red Army the Mongols had created a people's republic under Moscow's influence. A Japanese advance from Manchuria would have compelled the Russians to take military action. But this did not arise and on 2 May 1933 Litvinov made the offer to sell the Chinese eastern railway to Japan for 650 million yen or 250 million gold rubles. After protracted negotiations the price of 170 to 175 million yen was agreed.[19] In the circumstances it was a realistic decision.

The Soviet government had thus been forced to recognize that the most immediate threat lay in the east, not in the west as had been assumed. The sale of the railway and acknowledgement of Japanese power in Manchuria had postponed the war which both Japanese and Russians believed to be inevitable between them, the former because Russia stood as an obstacle to Japanese expansion, the latter because communist ideology decreed it. Meanwhile Soviet troops were transferred to defend the Far Eastern frontiers and Outer Mongolia and hurried plans were made to develop heavy industry in support of this army. At the same time the Politburo observed a policy of strict neutrality towards Japan, refusing to collaborate with Great Britain and the U.S.A. in opposing Japan or even to take part in the Lytton commission, set up by the League, to investigate developments in Manchuria. But despite this careful neutrality, repeated Soviet attempts to negotiate a non-aggression pact with Japan were rejected.

The United States of America had steadfastly refused to recognize the Soviet regime. Reports of persecution of the church and of GPU terror had antagonized American opinion. But the deep emotional antipathy of Americans was rooted in resentment of communist doctrine and propaganda. The U.S.A. had during the 1920s enjoyed outstanding prosperity which seemed to them to offer positive proof of the success of capitalism and democracy. The claims of communism and its assaults on capitalist societies were brazen affronts which could not be tolerated. Any expression of sympathy for the plight of the Soviet Union or of understanding of communism was liable to be damned as 'un-American'. The U.S.A. was nevertheless scrupulous in respecting Soviet frontiers and only in 1922, then with reluctance, extended recognition to the Baltic states. U.S. pressure had been important in forcing the Japanese to withdraw from Siberia. Moreover, in the terrible famine of 1922–3, the Hoover relief mission, a great humanitarian undertaking, had saved hundreds and thousands of Russian lives.

Supremely confident in its economy and its strength the U.S.A. felt no need for relations with the Soviet Union and able to indulge its moral stand against communism. In any case the U.S.A. was losing nothing for trade between the two countries continued. A soviet trade organization, Amtorg, had been established in the U.S.A. and throughout the 1920s trade had flourished. Americans travelled freely to Russia despite the absence of diplomatic relations, and American engineers and specialists contributed notably to Soviet industrialization. American exports to Russia rose each year to a peak in 1930 when, amounting to a quarter of Russia's total imports, they exceeded those of all competitors.

By 1932, however, U.S. exports to and imports from Russia had dropped dramatically.[20] Germany displaced the U.S.A. in the Soviet market. At the same time American imports from Russia were reduced as a result of publicity against buying the 'products of slave labour' and against the 'Red trade threat' alleged to have arisen from Soviet 'dumping' of wheat, cotton, coal, manganese, and oil to embarrass the U.S. economy. Washington went so far as to place embargos on certain goods such as timber and cellulose.

In autumn 1929 the American cycle of prosperity suddenly came to an end with the crisis on Wall Street. The U.S. economy was severely affected and the virtual loss of the Soviet market came at a time when American industry could least afford it. Business interests began to press for recognition of the Soviet regime on the ground that it would help revive trade. In the last months of the Hoover administration the movement for establishing diplomatic relations was gathering strength.

Far more important, however, than the economic factors in bringing the U.S. to recognize the Soviet regime was the dramatic change in the balance of power in the Pacific. To counter the growing influence of Japan the practical steps which the U.S.A. could take were to refuse recognition to the Japanese puppet regime of Manchukuo, to strengthen the U.S. navy in the Pacific, and to extend recognition to the Soviet Union, also desperately concerned by the growing power of Japan.

The Roosevelt administration which assumed office in March 1933 was ready to act. Negotiations began and in November Litvinov visited Washington where the conditions of U.S. recognition were agreed. The Soviet press was jubilant over this diplomatic success and hailed the new Soviet–U.S.A. friendship. But relations were soon to be soured by disputes over Russian debts and propaganda, arising partly from confusion in the wording of the agreements signed in Washington, and partly, too, from the truculence of William C. Bullitt, the first U.S. ambassador to Moscow.[21]

The American government was determined to secure some repayment of the loan of $188 million, made to Kerensky's provisional government, and of further private claims, amounting to $400 million. Negotiations opened in Moscow early in 1934 and dragged through the year without progress. The Russians could make no concessions. U.S. claims concerned only seven per cent of Russia's war debt. Any accommodation reached on repayment would have brought immediate demands from Great Britain and France whose claims amounted respectively to seventy per cent and nineteen per cent. Exchanges over trade were more fruitful and on 13 July 1935 a trade agreement was signed.

The year 1933 was notable in world affairs. It was marked by the liquidation of Russian interests in Manchuria and by the new Soviet–U.S.A. accord, by the world economic conference and the world disarmament conference, both of which ended in failure. But the most ominous event of the year was the emergence of the national socialist party in Germany and the rebirth of German militarism. The nazi regime with its violently anti-communist programme and its blatantly aggressive intentions gave rise to a complete change in the orientation of Soviet policy. It had been based on alliance with Germany and antagonism towards Great Britain and France. But now it became a policy of collective security, anti-fascism, and united front alliances with not only socialist but also liberal and radical parties. The Comintern shelved its extreme revolutionary policies and fostered the popular fronts, and in 1936 left-wing popular front governments were formed in France and Spain.

The Soviet leaders were not at first greatly disturbed by German national socialism, complacently accepting it as a stage to be passed through on the road to proletarian revolution. Following the policy laid down by the sixth congress of the Comintern in 1928, that foreign socialist parties were the chief enemies, communists had even allied themselves with national socialists against social democrats. Moreover, nazi hostility was at first directed against the Western powers who had imposed the Versailles peace, and Hitler in a speech to the Reichstag on 23 March 1933 was not unfriendly in his references to Soviet Russia. In the nazi hierarchy the faction headed by Alfred Rosenberg was savagely anti-Russian, but others strongly favoured alignment with Russia.[22] Moreover, on 5 May 1933 the Soviet–German conciliation agreement of January 1931 extending the neutrality treaty of April 1926 was ratified. The comment of *Izvestiya* expressing Soviet policy was that 'in spite of their attitude towards Fascism, the people of the U.S.S.R. wish to live in peace with Germany and consider that the development of German–Soviet relations is in the interests of both countries'.[23]

Trade was the real bond. In 1932 Germany supplied 46·5 per cent of Russia's total imports, but by 1935 Great Britain had become Russia's chief market and Russian imports from the U.S.A. were growing. Germany made strenuous efforts to recover this trade. No less than four offers to extend credits in return for Soviet purchases were made without result in 1934. In 1935 when Germany's share of Russia's total imports had dropped to a mere nine per cent, an agreement was signed by which Russia obtained new credits of 200 million marks. In the next year a further credit agreement was signed and the German share of Russian imports rose to 22·8 per cent. But it was soon to drop again.

Nazi leaders had become increasingly aggressive and abusive towards Russia. Soviet leaders continued to express a desire for friendly relations with Germany. Stalin had not ruled out the possibility of alignment with nazi Germany against the capitalist powers of the West. To him and to communists generally there was nothing to choose between fascism and capitalism; the deciding factor was the security and benefit of Soviet Russia.[24] But Hitler himself rejected such an alignment. On 26 January 1934 he signed a ten-year non-aggression pact with Marshal Pilsudski. This immediately aroused Soviet suspicions that Germany and Poland had embarked on an anti-Soviet policy whereby Germany would support Polish annexations in the Ukraine, while Germany extended her grip on the Baltic. Hitler's rejection of a proposal made in the following April for a joint Russo-German guarantee of the inviolability of Finland and the Baltic states intensified Russian suspicions.

In the period of the first five-year plan trade had been the main factor, but in the years 1933–6 security and defence dominated Soviet policy. Litvinov pursued three distinct purposes. The first was to secure the eastern frontiers. This arose from Russian fears of being engaged simultaneously in the east and the west, and from recognition of the danger that Germany and Japan might join together against Russia. It had meant placating Japan by surrender of Russian interests in Manchuria, but it had also helped bring accord with the U.S.A. The second purpose was to continue the policy of preventing the formation of an anti-Soviet coalition of capitalist powers. A new urgency was now added to this purpose by nazi claims that Germany stood alone as a shield against the bolshevik menace. In the West the popular attitudes towards the nazi regime were pathetically muddled. Left-wing opinion went to extremes in condoning nazi barbarity as a justified reaction to the punitive terms of the Versailles treaty. Right-wing opinion was often gullible in its ready acceptance of nazi anti-Soviet propaganda.

Discussion of the so-called four-power pact of Great Britain, France, Germany, and Italy which would settle all current political and military problems in Western Europe aroused Soviet misgivings. In Moscow it was seen as an attempt by Great Britain to assume leadership in Europe and to prevent any alignment of Germany and Italy against France. The idea of the pact also antagonized Poland and the Little Entente, and France, determined to maintain her influence in Eastern Europe, secured significant changes in the draft text of the pact. But still Moscow viewed the proposal with hostility.

The policy of seeking friendly relations with other countries continued. In September 1933 a Soviet–Italian non-aggression pact was signed. Understanding with Turkey was strengthened by Soviet support of Turkish complaints under the straits convention at the league council. At the same time the Soviet government sought to deter Germany from war by revitalizing international organizations as a means of mobilizing armed force against German aggression, and by extending the Locarno pact to embrace countries to the east. Attempts to negotiate an Eastern security pact foundered on the opposition of Germany supported by Poland, but resulted in treaties with France and Czechoslovakia in 1935.

The policy of more active participation in international organizations was to lead in September 1934 to the entry of Soviet Russia into the League of Nations. Membership of the League with a permanent seat on its council represented a major development in Soviet policy. It pointed to a new confidence in the Soviet leaders who felt that Russia again belonged to the comity of nations and that membership of the League enhanced the international prestige of the Soviet Union. But, whereas the Soviet leaders saw the League as a potentially powerful anti-fascist organization, Western statesmen treated it as a useful forum where they could speak benevolently without committing themselves to action. The Soviet purpose of 'putting teeth into the Covenant' could make no headway when faith in the efficacy of the League was rapidly ebbing and suspicion of Soviet motives remained strong.

On 28 January 1935 Molotov made a full report to the seventh congress of soviets in Moscow on the foreign situation. He spoke of 'the expediency of collaborating with the League of Nations, although we (the Soviet government) are not prone to overestimate the importance of such organizations'.[25] He went on to condemn German racial theories and quoting with great effect from *Mein Kampf* spoke of Hitler's 'policy of territorial conquest' directed at Russia.[26] Molotov also referred to the growing military might of the Red Army and to the increased allocations in the Soviet budget for defence. His speech conveyed a calm confidence in the strength and ability of the Soviet forces to deal with any attack.[27] But already the Soviet leaders were desperately worried about the pace of German rearmament which, supported by German heavy industry, far outstripped the expansion of the Soviet armed forces which had only got under way in the previous year.

The Comintern was now deployed to play its part in organizing resistance to Hitler. Its seventh congress, which had been postponed since the previous year because of the international situation, met in Moscow in July–August 1935. The policy and directives of the Comintern at once underwent a major change in support of the new Soviet policy. The congress called for a united front; the social democrats and the bourgeois parties which had been so violently condemned in the past were now to be welcomed as brothers in the struggle against fascism. It was a striking example of the flexibility of communist policy.

The new Soviet role of anti-fascist champion and the new image of the Soviet Union as a peace-loving power which had discarded its revolutionary mission, were ably and tirelessly promoted by Litvinov who hated nazism. Stalin himself in his famous interview with the American editor, Roy Howard, on 5 March 1936 even maintained that 'to assert that we desire to bring about revolution in other countries by interfering with their way of life is to speak of something that does not exist and which we have never preached'.[28]

Many in the Western democracies who sympathized with the great socialist experiment of the Soviet Union readily allowed themselves to be deceived into believing that the Russian communist party had in fact abandoned the policy of world revolution, but considerable mistrust of Soviet intentions remained. This mistrust was indeed to prove justified. The Soviet agent, W. G. Krivitsky, revealed after his defection to the West that, while being interviewed by the Western press and promoting through every possible channel the policy of collective security against nazi Germany, Stalin was during the years 1934 to 1937 seeking in greatest secrecy to negotiate an agreement with Hitler and was rebuffed.[29]

The Spanish civil war (1936–9) raised serious problems for the Soviet government. Stalin was ideologically opposed to the fascist regime of Franco, but feared that a republican victory would aggravate anxieties in the West about communist revolutionary subversion. He therefore gave to the republicans support which was negligible compared with that given by Germany and Italy to Franco. At the same time the Soviet government denied categorically, despite irrefutable evidence to the contrary and despite membership of the 'non-intervention committee', that any Soviet aid was going to the republicans. In fact, the devious policies pursued by Stalin during the Spanish civil war intensified Western suspicions of Soviet good faith.

At this time of mounting antagonism between Moscow and Berlin and of the forging of the Berlin–Rome Axis (October 1936) Stalin was looking anxiously to the east. Rumours of a secret understanding between Germany and Japan were confirmed for Stalin by Krivitsky's coup in obtaining a copy of the correspondence between the two governments. This revealed a secret agreement to co-ordinate their policies in the east and west, and specifically their policies towards Russia and China.[30] The German–Japanese anti-Comintern pact of 25 November 1936 was a brief and comparatively innocuous defensive agreement, the real alliance being contained in the secret understanding. Incidents on the Manchurian border added to Moscow's fears and further troops were sent to the Far Eastern frontiers. A new security treaty was signed with the Mongolian Republic and in the following year a non-aggression pact was made with China. But such pacts could not allay the acute feeling in Moscow that Russia was a beleaguered nation threatened from the east and the west.

In March 1938 Hitler annexed Austria and the crisis over the Sudeten Germans in Czechoslovakia inevitably followed. Nazi threats of violence led to a series of anxious consultations between the British and French prime ministers and the dictators, and both Britain and France brought strong pressure to bear on Czechoslovakia to surrender the borderlands to Germany in the interests of peace. Contrasting with the readiness of Britain and France to capitulate ignominiously before Hitler's threats of aggression, the Soviet government at least proposed to stand firm.

The Soviet proposals were that Great Britain and France and the Soviet Union should present a strong and united front to Germany and at once prepare with the Czechoslovak high command a combined military plan. All three powers should invoke the League of Nations and prepare to enforce the provisions of the Charter in the event of German aggression. Moreover, Litvinov confirmed to the Czech government that Soviet Russia would stand by the terms of the mutual assistance pact of 1935 if France, too, would honour her obligations under this pact. But France was only too eager to back out of her treaty obligations and Britain showed no keenness to stand by France if she were involved in defending Czechoslovakia. The Soviet government was not consulted about, or included in, the Munich conference which, meeting on 28–30 September 1938, agreed to deliver Czechoslovakia into the hands of nazi Germany.

The Western powers had carefully refrained from taking up the Soviet proposals for collective action. Their mistrust of the Soviet Union had been mounting. At the time of the economic recession which hit the capitalist West in 1937, communist propaganda had become more strident and, in spite of the Soviet policy of developing collective security, had loudly predicted left-wing victory in Spain and the collapse of the capitalist powers. Another reason for Western antipathy and mistrust towards Soviet Russia was the series of show trials of prominent communists. Further, the savage purge of Red Army officers, which was still taking place in September 1938, made a deep impression abroad. In the opinion of many, Stalin's purge of the military hierarchy had 'destroyed the confidence of Western Europe in the strength of his army and the strength of his government'.[31] But, while influenced by strong doubts about the ability of Soviet Russia to give effective support against German aggression, the British and French refusal to treat her as an ally and to take up Soviet proposals for combined action was due mainly to mistrust of Soviet intentions. Certain influential politicians in the West went so far as to express the hope that Hitler would turn eastwards and, leaving the West in peace, would satisfy his ambitions at Russia's expense.

Stalin certainly interpreted the events of this period as showing that the Western powers had promised Hitler a free hand in the east in return for peace in the west. This was an important factor in the recasting of Soviet policy in 1939. Collective security was seen in Moscow as a failure; the Western powers were the enemies of the Soviet regime and were, in any case, too infirm of purpose and degenerate to make reliable allies. Russia's security demanded new measures, but the policy formulated in 1939 was to be the prelude to the second world war.

Lieutenant-General Vasily Ivanovich Chuikov (speaking), General N. Krylov, Lieutenant-General K. Gurov, and Major-General A. Rodomtsev in the dug-out headquarters of the Soviet 62nd Army, Stalingrad

Winston Churchill, President Truman, and Marshal Stalin at Potsdam, July 1945

CHAPTER FIFTEEN

Economic and Social Developments 1933-9

THE first five-year plan was in scale and achievement probably the greatest concentrated economic effort in human history. Results had fallen short of targets but the nation had succeeded decisively in the basic purpose of establishing heavy industry. This feat had, moreover, been accomplished in four-and-a-quarter years, for the plan had been declared fulfilled on 31 December 1932. Also, in concentrating into this brief period a development of such magnitude, which in other countries working on a smaller scale had taken a generation or more, the Russians had applied effectively the untested methods of economic planning. The cost had been high. The plan had been enforced ruthlessly and had involved incalculable human suffering and sacrifice. Stalin and his government had been prepared to pay this price and the Russian people had endured, as the British people had endured in the years 1820 to 1880. Now, only slightly abated, the tempo of development continued.

The second five-year plan for the years 1933 to 1937 had as its purpose 'the completion of technical reconstruction in the whole of the national economy'.[1] The goal was that four-fifths of all industrial output in Soviet Russia should be produced by 'new enterprises built or completely reconstructed during the First or the Second Five-year Plan periods'.[2]

Emphasis was laid on mastering techniques, consolidating the gains of the first plan, and increasing the productivity of labour. But the pressure was relaxed. Capital investment in the final year of the first plan had amounted to 24 per cent of the national income; in the last year of the second plan it was down to 19·5 per cent. The target for the annual increase of industrial output which had been 21 per cent during the first plan fell to 16 per cent under the second plan.[3]

The iron and steel industries after their failures under the first plan were set special targets. By 1937 the output of pig iron and steel was to be 16 and 17 million tons respectively, which represented an increase of over two-and-a-half times the 1932 figures. Even allowing for the fact that 107 new rolling mills, 164 open hearth furnaces, and 45 blast furnaces were to be brought into production during the second plan, the new targets demanded superhuman labours. The requirements for machine tools were likewise high, involving an approximate threefold increase in production.

New and vigorous steps were taken to exploit the vast and barely

K   271

tapped mineral resources of the country. Copper, zinc, tin, nickel, and bauxite were all urgently needed in the fast developing industries. Production of aluminium was already expanding, but only during the second plan was mining of nickel, tin, and magnesium begun.

The demand for consumer goods received greater attention. Textile, footwear, food-processing, and kindred industries were expanded and required to double or treble their output. In the towns accommodation and hospitals were to be increased by 33·3 per cent and 44 per cent respectively. But these targets were unrealistic. Improvements in popular welfare were secondary considerations while capital was so short. Heavy industry remained the first priority and claimed some three-quarters of the capital investment of the period.

Of special importance was the attention given to the shift in the geographic distribution of industry which had taken shape during the first plan period. A principal objective of the second plan was to ensure a more even allocation of industry throughout the country, to establish heavy industries where possible near sources of fuel and materials and to reduce the strain on the transport system. This movement resulted in the development of the second coal and steel industry in the Ural–Kuznetsk combine. Magnitogorsk, the centre of the new Ural industrial region, had started in 1931 as a collection of huts for the workers who were building the furnaces and rolling mills to process the local ores; eight years later it was a city of 146,000 inhabitants. Kuznetsk, known after 1932 as Stalinsk, in Siberia grew into a city in the same period. Karaganda in Kazakhstan was founded and became a city of 166,000 people within six years. This rapid growth of towns and cities was an indication of the tempo of industrial development in the 1930s.

The new distribution of industry was not wholly determined by economic factors. It had long been recognized that the concentration of industry in European Russia made it vulnerable to attack from the West, and this became an oppressive anxiety in Moscow after the rise of nazi Germany. Indeed, the industrial development of Central Asia was to prove of tremendous importance to Russia's survival in the second world war.

Another feature of the second plan was its attention to transport. Headlong industrialization had imposed excessive demands on the antiquated transport system. By 1934 inadequacy of transport had become a barrier to further expansion. Railway construction, heavy in its consumption of iron and steel, had had to yield priority to industrial development in the first plan. In the second plan, however, allocations of iron and steel to railway construction were trebled, and were applied primarily to strengthening existing lines. The Trans-Siberian and the network of railways connecting Leningrad with Donbas and Moscow with the Volga region were doubletracked.

More spectacular were the improvements made in the waterways. The great network of rivers played a major part in Russia's communications but river vessels and port facilities were dilapidated. A programme of rebuilding was started and canals were cut to speed river transport. The Baltic–White Sea canal, 141 miles in length, reduced the water route from Archangel to Leningrad from 2,840 to 674 miles and aided the economic development of Soviet Karelia. The Moscow–Volga canal, 80 miles long, linked the Moskva and Volga rivers, converting Moscow itself into a major river port.

Road construction had always been neglected and the existing roads were notoriously inadequate. A system of arterial highways was now laid down, linking Moscow with Leningrad, Minsk, Kharkov, the Crimea, the Caucasus, and the Urals, and connecting Leningrad direct with Kiev and Odessa. But road-building was slow and costly over the great distances in Russia, and especially in the new developing regions of Siberia and Central Asia. Airlines served many of these parts more efficiently and cheaply, and the second plan witnessed a remarkable expansion in air traffic. In 1933 regular internal air services covered 21,580 miles; by 1939 the distances covered were more than 100,000 miles, and the amount of freight carried by air was twenty times greater. Many districts which had depended for transport on horse and cart over rough tracks or in winter on sleighs suddenly leapt into the new age of air communications.

During the plans Russian workers were subjected by press and radio, by poster and cinema, and in lectures by party agitators to a ceaseless barrage of propaganda and exhortations to increase productivity. The effects of this strident campaign, supported by incentives and enforced by penalties, were probably considerable. But one method of encouragement which undoubtedly made a strong impact was the Stakhanovite movement. Alexei Stakhanov worked at the coal face of the Irmino mine in the Ukraine. By reorganizing methods of work he made it possible to keep the pneumatic drills in constant use. The output of his team increased so greatly as a result that they could earn nearly a month's normal wages for a day's work.

Government and party made Stakhanov a hero and launched the Stakhanovite mass movement to encourage workers to take initiative in improving the organization of labour and the application of techniques. Honours and financial rewards were lavished on all workers who contributed in this way to production. Russian industry benefited enormously from many improvements initiated by ordinary workers emulating Stakhanov.

During the second plan, collectivization was virtually completed. More than 90 per cent of all peasant households had been collectivized by 1936 and the figure reached 96·9 per cent in 1940. The savagery and bitterness which had marked the campaign in its early stages had subsided. Government policies now concentrated on consolidating and stabilizing the kolkhozi. But already the regime was deriving benefits from the new system. The harvests of 1933, 1934, and 1935 showed steady growth; 1936 was a drought year, but 1937 yielded a record harvest. Moreover, the system of 'forward contracts' for the procurement of grain ensured dependable supplies for the expanding industrial centres and for export. By 1935 food supplies to the towns were sufficient to allow the abolition of rationing. This procurement system, as revised by a decree of 19 January 1933, allocated the obligatory supply-quotas to be paid for at official rates which were so low as to be a form of tax in kind. In effect this was a repetition of the compulsory requisitions of war communism.

As a recompense for the obligatory deliveries, members of kolkhozi received certain privileges. Any surplus remaining after deliveries to the state could be sold on the open market, and the profit thus earned was distributed among members of the kolkhoz according to the number of days worked. In 1935 a new collective farm charter provided special rewards for individual farmers who by skill and labour raised productivity. The most important concession, however, was the right of every peasant household to a garden plot, adjoining the homestead, and to own a few head of cattle, sheep, and goats, and an unrestricted number of chickens and rabbits. All produce from the private holdings could be sold on the open market for the benefit of the household.

By the late 1930s the Soviet leaders could consider that collectivization had succeeded. The kolkhozi, numbering about 250,000, were more easily organized and controlled than the millions of individual holdings. Grain and other produce were more efficiently gathered for distribution to the towns. The MTS (machine tractor stations) had been developed until by 1938 they numbered 5,800, spread throughout the country, and employing a staff of nearly a million and a half. The MTS ploughed 71·5 per cent of the arable lands and threshed 95 per cent of the grain. Through these services and their educational work they were well placed to know of discontent, potential opposition, and slackness in the kolkhozi. By withholding their services, they could subdue any unruly, inefficient, or independent-minded kolkhoz. Prompt to take advantage of any organization to police the people, the party in January 1933 started organizing political departments in all MTS and drafted nearly 17,000 party members to serve in them. With such close control and with the concessions and inventives for improved productivity, the problems of Soviet agriculture seemed to have been solved.

The peasantry was, however, a great elemental force which could not be constrained and organized so simply into permanent submission. The peasants wanted to work their own soil and to live in freedom. They were not reconciled to the kolkhozi, which combined the repression of the old commune and of serfdom. The collective farm charter provided that the kolkhoz should be run by all its members over the age of sixteen who elected the chairman and board responsible for its management. In practice the chairman was nominated by the party and from Moscow came directives on the crops and acreages to be sown. The MTS while rendering services also supervised, inspected, and reported. The promised incentives were not always shared out according to work done. The peasant was nothing more than a labour unit, and his attitude towards the kolkhoz tended to be completely negative.

From centuries of experience the Russian peasant had become adept at evasion and he now exercised this skill with effect. He concentrated his attention on the garden plot, in which he had a personal interest. He worked perfunctorily on the kolkhoz lands, reporting late and breaking off early. An official investigation revealed that by 1939 over two-and-a-half million hectares of land had been diverted by peasants to their own use. Some peasants had gained possession of considerable holdings of land which they farmed lucratively. Government surveys of private plots followed and collective farm land was reclaimed. Severe penalties were imposed on peasants found guilty of diverting land or working less than a minimum number of hours a day or days a week. The demands on the peasants for work, obligatory deliveries, and expansion of acreages sown steadily increased. The result was that the grain crop in 1937 was 50 per cent greater than in 1928 and 33 per cent greater than in 1913, but the output in 1937 of animal products was probably smaller than in 1928 owing to the decline in the number of livestock.[4] Meanwhile the resentment of the peasantry against the regime and its collectives remained strong.

During the second plan period living standards nevertheless improved. Stalin had in 1928–9 made exaggerated promises that general prosperity would flow at once from the first plan. But the people had suffered severe food shortages and rationing and in the year 1932–3 famine. Food consumption over the whole population fell, according to some estimates by as much as 20 per cent between 1928 and 1932, but by 1934 it had been restored nearly to the 1928 level. Between 1934 and 1937 it rose by 9 per cent and in the towns by 20 per cent. But the consumption of foodstuffs apart from grain remained well below the standards of countries in the West. In the supply of such goods as textiles and clothing as well as in housing and other amenities, Russia lagged far behind the West. The most critical shortage was in housing, especially in the towns where the great influx of people had aggravated the shortage, and whole families had to be accommodated in one room.[5]

The task of the five-year plans was to ensure that Soviet Russia would 'overtake and surpass the most highly developed capitalist countries of Europe and the U.S.A.' in both *per capita* and absolute output. At the end of the second plan realization of this goal was still far off, despite tremendous progress in many fields. The third five-year plan was launched in 1938 with a programme of further development of transport, mineral deposits, and oil, especially in exploiting the new oil resources between the Volga and the Urals. Priority was still to be given to heavy industry, but consumer industries were to be greatly expanded. But the urgent needs of rearmament distorted these plans and the second world war was to inter-vene before the third plan could be completed.

In the period of these plans the whole nation was in a ferment of change, movement, and development. The population according to the 1939 census was 170 million, an increase of 23 million since the 1926 census. This was 5·5 per cent lower than the anticipated growth and due to famines in the early 1930s, especially in the Ukraine, Kazakhstan, and the Caucasus. But equally important were the movements of population and the changes in occupation. In thirteen years the urban population had doubled. The number of cities with more than 200,000 people increased from 12 to 39. The population of Leningrad rose from 1·69 to 3·19 million and that of Moscow from 2 to 4 million. Migration of some 20 million people from villages to the towns was the main factor in this growth and it was a demonstration of the effect of the revolution in agri-culture. The movement of the population eastwards was also reflected in this census. It showed that, while population growth had been about 11 per cent in European Russia, it had been about 31 per cent in Siberia and 38 per cent in Central Asia.

The late 1930s was also a time to review changes and seek for greater stability in social conditions. Just as in the period of NEP the people had shown a craving for normality after the chaos of the civil war, so now after the violent changes of the first five-year plan they sought a more stable way of life. In particular they demanded a revival of respect for the sanc-tity of marriage and family life. The early revolutionary ideas of free love, easy divorce and abortion, and ready acceptance of illegitimacy had proved unsatisfactory. The Soviet government recognized and gave effect to this general demand. The interests of the regime were served best by a stable, ordered, and obedient society, capable of discipline and cohesion in time of war which was the threat preying constantly on all minds in this period. Moreover, to meet the man-power needs of such a vast and rapidly developing country and also the demands of the armed forces, a high birth rate was essential. For this the stability of the family had to be encouraged and greater attention paid to such amenities as hospitals, crèches, nurseries, and housing.

The Soviet press opened a campaign against the high incidence of divorce and abortion and the decline in family life. A government decree followed on 27 June 1936 making divorce more difficult and costly to obtain and forbidding abortion except on grounds of health. The decree made extensive provision for the care of mothers through the building of more maternity homes, nurseries, and kindergartens, and also by raising the money allowances payable in respect of children, mothers with six or more children receiving a large bonus allowance. Through the press and other media the family, once dismissed as a decadent bourgeois institution, was now elevated as the fundamental social unit of society responsible for the welfare and training of its children. Moreover, children were now taught to respect and love their parents and to show them obedience.

In education, too, discipline was revived and a complete reform of the system was carried out in the 1930s. Soon after the revolution in 1917 Anatoly Lunacharsky, head of the state commission for education, had summarized the tasks ahead as the abolition of illiteracy as speedily as possible, the introduction of universal, compulsory, and free education, the setting-up of institutes to train 'people's teachers'. Subsequent decrees had provided for secular and co-educational schools, to be known as 'united labour schools'. Further innovations were the abolition of the old forms of discipline and of homework and examinations. Pupils were to take part in the running of their schools and teachers, known as 'school workers', were to break away from the old tsarist methods.

The liquidation of illiteracy was the first task. At the end of the previous century some 76 per cent of the people had been illiterate. By a decree of 26 December 1919 Sovnarkom had directed that the entire population between the ages of 8 and 50 should be obliged to learn to read and write Russian or their native language. While the country was torn by the civil war, implementation of this decree was difficult. By 1926, however, the percentage of illiterates had been reduced to 48·9 per cent. A joint decree of the party central committee and Sovnarkom on 26 January 1930 set up special local committees, attached to each regional and district executive committee, to concentrate on the abolition of illiteracy. These measures were evidently effective for by 1939 the percentage of illiterates had fallen to 18·8.

In general education, however, the innovations had been far from satisfactory. Teachers had no authority and were unable to enforce discipline. Schools were chaotic and pupils were unruly and ill-educated. A recasting of school syllabuses and a revival of discipline and examinations were decreed in August 1932. The brigade system of teaching was abandoned and teachers were required to revert to individual tuition. A further decree of 16 May 1934 abolished the united labour schools and set in their place the general educational schools, divided into three stages: the elementary or four-year school, the incomplete secondary or seven-year school, and the secondary or ten-year school. The programme was ambitious and its fulfilment was constantly hindered by shortages of trained teachers and of schools. In 1939 at the eighteenth party congress the aim in education was stated to be attainment of general attendance of the full ten-year school in towns and workers' settlements and of seven-year schools in the country. But war intervened before the new drive could get under way.

In higher education the innovations of opening universities and institutes to all citizens over sixteen and of providing 'workers' faculties' to prepare workers and peasants for higher education were soon abandoned. The need for specialists was acute and during the first plan gave rise to special decrees on the development of new cadres and on doubling the number of engineers and technicians in heavy industry. In 1936 higher education was reorganized and to be eligible students had to complete full ten-year school and to pass special competitive entrance examinations.

The egalitarian spirit which had been so marked in the early days of the revolution had diminished by the thirties. Titles, ranks, and academic degrees could serve as powerful incentives and they were now reintroduced. The word 'officer' had been banned in the armed forces. Senior personnel had been known only as 'commanders'. In September 1935 the traditional ranks from lieutenant to general were restored. Also the new title of Marshal of the Soviet Union was introduced, and Tukhachevsky, Budyonny, Yegorov, and Blücher were made marshals. As part of the policy of developing incentives special awards were created for outstanding work. The new titles included Hero of Socialist Labour, Distinguished People's Artist, and Distinguished Scientific Worker, and such titles were not only great honours, but carried special privileges.

A further development was the abolition of proletarian class privilege and the revival of fashions which had formerly been damned as bourgeois. In December 1935 the ban imposed soon after the revolution on the admission of people of undesirable social origin or their children to institutions of higher learning was lifted. Interest in clothing and fashions was allowed to revive. The austere tunic and cap which the early revolutionaries had proudly worn as their uniform was no longer obligatory. Russian women began to give attention to their appearance and limited production of cosmetics was permitted under the second plan.

The revival of so many of the practices of pre-revolutionary Russia which had been so hastily abolished did not, however, affect the campaign against the church. Metropolitan Sergii had evidently hoped that his proclamation made in July 1927 of the submission of the church to the state would buy the survival of Orthodoxy in Russia. The Soviet decree of 8 April 1929 and the campaign against the church, intensified by Stalin's determination to break peasant opposition, made the metropolitan realize that years of bitter struggle lay ahead. But as late as 1930 Sergii could still claim that some 30,000 churches remained open.[6]

The campaign against the church developed in ferocity during the late 1930s. The clergy were victimized. Attempts were made to paralyse the administration of the church by arresting the bishops, but the church managed to nullify this form of attack by maintaining a reserve of consecrated bishops ready at once to replace those arrested. Anti-religious propaganda became more strident, but was usually too crude to make a real impact. Moreover, attacks on the church, alleging that it was counter-revolutionary and an enemy of the state, carried small weight. Sergii's proclamation had been published in full in the Soviet press. All knew that the church was not opposing the state, but merely struggling to survive. For many Russians this persecution gave the church the added appeal of martyrdom.[7]

Gradually, however, the communist campaign, while fluctuating in intensity, was destroying the organization of the church. In 1935 Sergii had to disband the holy synod, a step which further crippled its administration and unity. He struggled against the increasing difficulties, but held tenaciously to the undertakings of neutrality and support in his proclamation of 1927. In his relations with *émigré* churchmen he was most careful to prevent the Russian church being involved in anti-Soviet agitation. He seemed to be fighting a losing battle, and yet he could derive some comfort from the number who remained faithful. In the period 1932–4 the campaign against the church had relaxed in some degree and by 1937 even the Soviet press was commenting on signs of a religious revival, especially among young people. In 1937 a census held throughout the Soviet Union included the question 'Are you a believer or not?' This census was declared invalid on the ground of incorrect procedures and falsifications, and its results were not released. But figures reported by anti-religious publicists, which may have been based on the census result, put the number of believers as high as 80 million in 1937.[8]

In compelling Sergii to abolish the synod Stalin was probably seeking to destroy the church administration in which he saw a potential organ of opposition. Further, he may have had in mind the danger that the new constitution to be adopted in 1936, in giving the clergy normal rights of citizenship including the right to vote, would enable the clergy to wield sinister influence in the general elections. Indeed, as the elections approached in 1937 the Soviet press made repeated charges that the clergy were subverting the elections.

During the great purge of 1936–8 the church suffered savage persecution, although it was probably no worse than that suffered by other important segments of Soviet society, including the communist party. But the toll on the church, already gravely weakened, was severe. Persecution was directed especially at the hierarchy. In 1930 Sergii had claimed the loyal support of 163 bishops, and fewer than 12 remained in 1939. Forty bishops were shot. Sergii himself seemed in danger of arrest. Some 10,000 churches were estimated to have been closed.[9] The church in 1939 was near to collapse.

On 1 February 1935 the plenum of the party central committee directed Molotov to propose changes in the 1924 constitution to the seventh all-union congress of soviets. The changes were to effect further democratization of the electoral system and to give recognition to the new class structure of the Soviet Union. The Congress unanimously approved Molotov's proposals and appointed a commission under the chairmanship of Stalin to draft a new constitution. On 1 June 1936 Stalin himself submitted a draft to a plenum of the central committee which approved it and it was presented to an extraordinary all-union congress of soviets for ratification.

On 12 June 1936 the draft was published and the people were invited to discuss it and to propose amendments. Andrei Vyshinsky, the procurator general of the Soviet Union, commented that 'the draft was read with delight and discussed in all the industrial and transport enterprises in sovkhozes and kolkhozes, and in government offices . . . The Soviet people greeted the appearance of the draft of the new U.S.S.R. constitution with enormous enthusiasm and approved it with one accord.'[10] In fact, many amendments were proposed but only a few minor, mainly verbal, changes were made in the draft as submitted by Stalin on 25 November 1936 to the extraordinary eighth all-union congress of soviets. The congress finally approved the constitution on 5 December 1936.

The nation-wide debate and then the unanimous approval of the congress of soviets were intended to establish beyond all question the legality of the regime and, consolidating political and economic developments, to provide the foundations of the new socialist society. The process of evolution from the dictatorship of the proletariat to socialism and then to communism was, the party maintained, advancing satisfactorily. Socialism had already been achieved, since both industrial and agricultural production had been socialized and the principle established 'From each according to his ability, to each according to his needs.'

At this stage when socialism existed and the exploiting class had been eliminated, the state should have withered away. The state existed solely to keep the exploiting and the exploited classes from violent struggle. In the Soviet Union now, according to Marx and Lenin, the state should have been unnecessary. The fact that the state and the dictatorship of the proletariat had not yet come to an end was, Stalin explained, due to 'capitalist encirclement'. It was clear, he maintained, that the dictatorship must continue while the Soviet Union was surrounded by capitalist powers intent on destroying their socialist society.

In his speech to the extraordinary congress Stalin explained that the constitution would bring the fundamental law of the state into conformity with the socialization of industry, the collectivization of agriculture, the liquidation of the kulaks, and the creation of the collective farm system. These developments had, he claimed, transformed the class structure of the Soviet Union. The population now comprised only the workers, the peasants, and the intelligentsia, living in harmony and serving the common interest. As distinct from bourgeois constitutions the draft of 'the new constitution of the U.S.S.R.', he said, 'proceeds from the fact that there are no longer any antagonistic classes in society; that society consists of two friendly classes of workers and peasants; that it is these classes, the labouring classes, that are in power . . .'[11] This meant that universal suffrage could be introduced and that the inequality between the voting power of workers and peasants could be abolished. Moreover, the electoral system could be revised since the communist party was sure of retaining power.

Speaking of the party's monopoly of power, Stalin said that the new constitution 'preserves unchanged the present leading position of the communist party of the U.S.S.R.' As guardian of the interests of workers and peasants the party provided 'democracy for the working people, i.e. democracy for all ... That is why I think that the constitution of the U.S.S.R. is the only thoroughly democratic constitution in the world.'[12]

The word 'democracy' was to come into frequent use in official speeches and statements in the Soviet Union. But it was not used in the same sense as in the West, where democracy meant government exercised by the people, freely exercising the right to choose and oppose. In the Soviet Union it meant the elimination of all actual and potential opposition and the compulsory support of the regime. 'The most thoroughly democratic constitution in the world' was a façade behind which the monopoly of power vested in the communist party within which it was held by one man, Stalin. In essence it was an autocracy such as the Russian people had known and accepted under the Romanovs.

The new constitution launched with fanfares of publicity was also intended to make an impact abroad. The Soviet leaders were increasingly conscious of public opinion in the Western democracies and anxious to gain good will. The constitution had been drafted and promoted with the needs of Soviet foreign policy in mind, for at this time the Soviet government was proclaiming collective security and seeking to forge with the Western democracies a strong common front against nazi Germany. In his speech to the congress Stalin said that 'Today, when the turbid wave of fascism is bespattering the socialist movement of the working class and besmirching the democratic strivings of the best people in the civilized world, the new constitution of the U.S.S.R. will be an indictment against fascism, declaring that socialism and democracy are invincible. The new constitution of the U.S.S.R. will give moral assistance and real support to all those who are today fighting fascist barbarism.'[13] Public opinion in the West was, in fact, greatly impressed by this constitution which seemed to guarantee human rights and to hold promise of democratic government as it was understood there. But within a few months terror was raging throughout Russia.

The constitution defined the U.S.S.R. as a federal state of eleven republics voluntarily united and each with the 'right freely to secede'.[14] The government of each union republic comprised a unicameral supreme soviet, directly elected. It appointed a presidium to carry on its legislative functions between sessions and a council of people's commissars as the responsible executive and administrative organ of the republic.

The highest authority in the Soviet Union was declared to be the supreme soviet, which consisted of two chambers, both elected for a four-year term. The soviet of the Union was directly elected on the basis of one deputy for every 300,000 persons. The soviet of nationalities was also directly elected, but on the basis of twenty-five deputies from each union republic, eleven deputies from each autonomous republic, five deputies from each autonomous region, and one deputy for each autonomous district.

The supreme soviet appointed the presidium which functioned as constitutional head of state. It consisted of a chairman, eleven vice-chairmen (one from each union republic), a secretary, and twenty-four members.[15] The soviet of people's commissars, appointed by the presidium and confirmed by the supreme soviet, functioned as the executive and administrative authority of the Soviet Union.[16] The three types of commissariat or ministry defined in the constitution were the all-union people's commissariats, responsible for functions within the exclusive jurisdiction of the federal government, the union-republic commissariats, with jurisdiction over functions shared by the federal and union-republic governments, and the republic commissariats, responsible for functions reserved to the union republics.

The federal government had exclusive power in such matters of national importance as foreign affairs, foreign trade, defence, finance, and planning. Certain functions, like agriculture, justice, health, were shared between federal and union-republic governments. A few minor functions were reserved to the union republics. The authority given to the central government was wide. The directives of the all-union soviet of people's commissars were binding on all inferior organs. In practice, the central government wielded supreme power and the constitution provided for a unitary rather than a federal system.

Two innovations made by the constitution were the new electoral system and the statement of fundamental rights and duties of the citizen. All elections were to be conducted 'on the basis of universal, direct, and equal suffrage by secret ballot' (Article 134). The right to vote belonged to 'all citizens of the U.S.S.R. who have reached the age of eighteen, irrespective of race or nationality, religion, educational and residential qualifications, social origin, property status or past activities...' (Article 135). This introduction of universal franchise and of the secret ballot seemed an impressive display of the confidence of the party that it had the full support of the people. In practice, however, the Soviet voter had a single list of candidates chosen by the party and he could vote for no others.

The extensive list of fundamental rights of citizens set out in Articles 118–128 was also impressive. But the rights were subject to the qualification that they must be exercised 'in conformity with the interests of the working class and in order to strengthen the socialist system' (Article 125). The sole judge of what conformed with these criteria was the party. In practice, moreover, these rights were frequently overridden or so circumscribed as to be worthless. Thus, freedom of conscience (Article 124), if exercised in the face of official hostility to all religion, carried disabilities and even the risk of persecution. Guarantees of the inviolability of the persons, homes, and correspondence of citizens were shown to be meaningless during the period of the great purge. The imposing judicial system and the office of procurator, carefully defined in chapter 9 of the constitution, also proved during the great purge to dispense justice not as it was understood in the West. Judges, for example, were said to be 'independent and subject only to the law' (Article 112) but, as interpreted by Soviet jurists, this meant that judges were subordinate to the Soviet regime which was the only source of law.[17]

The most noteworthy innovation in the constitution was its reference to the communist party which had not been mentioned in the constitution of 1924. Article 126 stated that 'the most active and most politically conscious citizens in the ranks of the working class and other sections of the working people unite in the Communist Party of the Soviet Union (bolsheviks) which is the vanguard of the working people in their struggle to strengthen and develop the socialist system and is the leading core of all organizations of the working people, both public and state'. This acknowledgement of the leading position of the party might have stated more explicitly that the party was the supreme power in the Soviet Union.

During the ten years from 1928 to 1938 the Russian nation had developed at an amazing pace, and the process was continuing. Russia had become an industrial power. The changes in the occupations of the people reflected this economic transformation. More than seventy-five per cent of the population had been engaged in agriculture in the NEP period and only ten per cent in industry: in 1939 agriculture claimed fifty-five per cent and industry twenty-five per cent of the population. Moreover, despite this reduction in the agricultural labour force, the total acreage under cultivation had increased by twenty-one per cent between 1928 and 1939. But agriculture lagged far behind all production targets and continued to be the most basic and intractable problem in the Soviet economy.

The industrialization drive had brought more dramatic results. Russian industry had lagged far behind that of Great Britain, France, Germany, and the U.S.A. By 1939 Russia had overtaken Great Britain and France and was closing on Germany in industrial production, and her goal was to surpass the U.S.A. But the low productivity of the Russian worker and other problems beset industrial growth.

From the chaos, devastation, and tragic sufferings of the past twenty-five years, Russia had nevertheless emerged as a dynamic nation. The people responded to the calls of their leader, although he had been guilty of mistakes, false promises, and savageries. The nation was on the move and gathering momentum.

Stalin and the party applied every possible means to drive the people to greater effort. Terror stalked the land. The secret police were ubiquitous and ruthless. All who dared to oppose or even to withhold support lived in fear of the long tentacles of the OGPU and the NKVD reaching out for them. They would then be torn from homes and villages to face execution or to expend their lives in the labour camps of the far north or of Siberia. But terror, while effective in destroying opposition and coercing laggards, was a negative instrument incapable of making a real contribution to a dynamic society. Incentives and honours rewarding greater effort and output, and the competition and emulation encouraged particularly by the Stakhanov movement were more important.

The appeal to Russian patriotism was a major factor in the surge of energy and enterprise which moved the nation. Stalin had in 1931 launched this appeal to the strong devotion to their homeland felt by all Russians when he had spoken of liquidating Russia's backwardness. But such patriotism offended against communist ideology which demanded service to the cause of the international proletariat. The anthem of the U.S.S.R. was the *Internationale* and its slogan 'Workers of the world, unite!' Nationalism, even Russian nationalism, was a bourgeois vice.

'Soviet patriotism' was the new conception evolved to meet the needs of both the ideology and of the nation, striving to advance and threatened by war. A decree issued on 16 May 1934 called for the preparation of new history textbooks from which the errors of Pokrovsky and the old bolshevik school of anti-nationalist historians would be eliminated. Stalin took a close interest in this project of reinterpreting Russian history. Certain of the rulers of the past were restored to places of honour. They included the great tsars, like Ivan the Terrible and Peter the Great, who had devoted their reigns to making Russia strong and with whom Stalin himself undoubtedly felt that he had close affinity. A. N. Tolstoy, the writer who enjoyed Stalin's favour although he had supported the Whites in the civil war, wrote an historical novel in which he portrayed Peter the Great as a great national hero. Outstanding films were made of the lives of Ivan and Peter and shown in all cinemas in the Soviet Union. But the greatest of all national heroes was now Lenin and it was a role which he himself would have abhorred. Idolatry of Stalin, described as Lenin's closest supporter, his indispensable right hand, and his true successor, was mounting. Portraits of Lenin, and increasingly of Stalin, were inescapable throughout the country. Trotsky and other alleged enemies of the Soviet people were blamed for all mistakes and failures. Stalin was portrayed as the culmination of Russian and Soviet history.

In the midst of this idolatry, of the strident propaganda, and the incessant exhortations to be better communists and to achieve greater production, the Russian people seemed like a cornfield swaying to winds, invoked by Stalin and the party. But the great winds were not commanded by Stalin or by the party; they swept through the country moving people and party alike. In the ferment of the times it seemed that individual Russians were afire with the feeling that they were conquerors and that Russia was at last, like Gogol's vision of the troika, 'overtaking the whole world'.

CHAPTER SIXTEEN

Terror and the Great Purge 1934-9

ON 1 December 1934 Sergei Kirov was shot in his office in Leningrad. A member of the Politburo, head of the Leningrad party organization, and evidently one of Stalin's closest comrades, he had risen rapidly in the party hierarchy and commanded wide popular support. His death shocked the whole nation.

The assassin was L. Nikolaev, a young communist in revolt against the policies of the party. It seemed a straightforward case of terrorism of the kind that the socialist revolutionaries had practised. But the circumstances were mysterious, suggesting that Nikolaev had had help from within the security forces and even from Stalin himself. Kirov had become so popular that Stalin may have seen in him a rival to be removed, or may have regarded his murder as a suitable pretext for the massive purge that he was secretly planning.[1] The facts will never be known fully, but it is certain that this assassination marked the beginning of four years of terror that paralysed the nation.

As the collectivization policy once launched had gathered a furious momentum, so the terror was to develop into a holocaust of savagery and suffering. For the first time the party itself felt the full impact of terror. But every organ of government and every segment of society were drawn into the vortex. Arrests ran into millions and of those executed or sentenced to forced labour, few were guilty of the charges laid against them. The dark and terrible period of the Stalin terror exceeded both the civil war and the collectivization campaign in horror.[2]

Stalin's motives in perpetrating this vicious purge and in allowing it to go to such inhuman extremes were complex. Lust for power, insanity, and malignity may have contributed to them, but to dismiss him as a monster or a dictator of 'incredible criminality' provides no adequate explanation. This is to be found in the nature of the man, of the Soviet regime, and of the international situation.

All bolsheviks saw themselves engaged in a massive and heroic endeavour to create a new society. The only matter in dispute between them was the path to be followed. Stalin believed fervently in this purpose and since the death of Lenin he had evolved and directed the policy designed to achieve it. He had disposed of Trotsky and displaced the other internationalists and, adopting a Russian nationalist approach, had made 'Socialism in one country' the basic principle. He had launched the great transformation through collectivization and industrialization, which would advance the nation towards socialism and at the same time equip it to stand against the hostile capitalist powers encircling it.

Stalin had identified himself with these policies as the only possible course of action. He was convinced, too, of his mission to lead the nation. Any other leadership and any other policies would mean disaster. All who opposed him or failed to support him were therefore enemies, and as such must be allies of the capitalists and potential destroyers of the new Soviet society. Such crudely simple reasoning was typical of the Soviet mind which converted every issue into a sharp conflict of opposites.

In Stalin this outlook was intensified by his own nature. Ambitious, vengeful, and convinced of his role as leader, he could not tolerate opposition. He had struggled patiently and relentlessly to secure power and was determined to concentrate it in his own hands. Nor could he forget the humiliations he had suffered at the hands of Trotsky, Lenin, and other old bolsheviks. He hated them for this reason and also because their internationalism and cosmopolitanism affronted his faith in Russia and her mission in the world. Both on personal grounds and in pursuit of the great communist vision, he was bound to see in the old guard real and potential enemies whom he had to eliminate.

Obsessed with the dangers of opposition and unnaturally suspicious, Stalin saw threats to himself and to the grand design all around him. Trotsky was the arch-enemy. His powerful intellect, impassioned activity, and the role he had played as leader jointly with Lenin made him the most dangerous rival. Stalin felt an implacable hatred and a fear of Trotsky which did not diminish even after he had exiled him from Russia in 1929. He had not dared to imprison or to execute him. But he brooded constantly on the damage that Trotsky might inflict, even from the small island of Prinkipo where by agreement with the Turkish government he was held.

Stalin's fears were not groundless. Trotsky had begun publishing from Prinkipo the *Byuleten Oppozitsii* (The Bulletin of the Opposition). Although modest in format, this bulletin was informed in its comment and bore the stamp of Trotsky's vigorous pen. Soviet officials travelling abroad brought back copies with them and it circulated among senior government and party officials, some of whom provided the up-to-date information for it. Trotsky's name gave it a real authority and it was influential, especially among those who had served under him.

During the momentous period of the first five-year plan, the *Byuleten* sought to weld the widespread discontent into a firm opposition movement and to displace Stalin. It published an economic survey of Soviet conditions at this time which closed with the comment: 'In view of the incapacity of the present leadership to get out of the economic and political deadlock, the conviction about the need to change the leadership of the party is growing.' Trotsky also reminded his readers of Lenin's will and his advice to the party to 'remove Stalin'.[3]

Among the old bolshevik leaders uneasiness about Stalin's direction of the country's affairs had mounted sharply during the first plan period. But whenever they had openly taken an opposition stand, Stalin had out-manoeuvred them and compelled them to recant. The fact was that none of them could offer an alternative policy. They disagreed with Stalin's methods but not his policies. Moreover, the opposition had been disrupted and confused by the repeated renunciations and surrender to Stalin of Zinoviev, Kamenev, Bukharin, Rykov, and other prominent members.

Stalin felt contempt for these men and probably did not regard them as dangerous. His agents were everywhere and he knew their movements and every word they spoke. On the other hand they were non-supporters and enemies. The assassination of Kirov may have disturbed him and made him feel insecure or he may have engineered Kirov's murder, intending to make this the pretext for a purge to eliminate the old guard. With their memories of serving under Lenin and Trotsky they would never prove dependable under his leadership. Whatever the course of events he clearly decided at this time on drastic action.

Stalin was keenly interested in history. He read widely, especially about Russian autocrats of the past. Peter the Great and Ivan the Terrible were two national leaders to whom he referred often and he had, incidentally, restored them to their rightful places in Soviet history books. Both had had to deal with problems similar to those facing him. At this stage, as he planned to destroy the old bolsheviks, he could not but have had in mind Ivan the Terrible's conflict with Prince Kurbsky and his purge of the boyars in the sixteenth century. Trotsky was his Kurbsky and the old bolsheviks were the conservative boyars, reluctant to accept his authority. Ivan had forged his special private police-army, the *oprichnina*, as he, Stalin, had carefully built up his security force within the OGPU and the NKVD.[4] Probably from this historical precedent his resolve to cleanse the party and the nation of these enemy-elements drew strength.

The international situation gave an added urgency to this decision. As a communist he was convinced that the capitalist powers were poised, wait-ing to attack Soviet Russia. Britain, France, Japan, and Germany were the most serious threats. He believed that he could make some deal with Hitler, and in the late 1930s he saw Japan as the immediate danger. This made the development of heavy industry a pressing priority; it also gave urgency to the need to clear away all discordant elements which might disrupt the unity of the nation and hamper his leadership in the coming struggle on which the survival of the regime depended.

At the beginning of 1934 Russia had seemed set for a period of com-parative calm after the fury of the five-year plans. The seventeenth party congress in January–February had demonstrated the strength and unity of the party. Stalin had been acclaimed. The former leaders of the opposition

—Bukharin, Rykov, Zinoviev, and Kamenev—had been permitted to address the congress and after confessing their errors had humbly paid tribute to his leadership. No discordant voice had disturbed the harmonious unity. Stalin himself had exclaimed that the congress had shown that 'there is nothing more to prove and, it seems, no one to fight'.[5] But, unresting, observant, and suspicious, he had undoubtedly noted the many incidents which suggested latent opposition to his rule.

During the year other events had also pointed towards a return to greater normality. The 1933 harvest had been above average and food supplies were improving. The persecution of engineers and others blamed for shortcomings in meeting production targets was halted in July on the orders of Vyshinsky, the deputy state procurator. In November, the central committee abolished bread rationing and endorsed a model statute, designed to improve conditions on collective farms.

More significant were the decrees in July dissolving the OGPU. It had long had a sinister reputation, especially among the peasants, and was dreaded even more than its predecessor, the Cheka, had been. The NKVD (Narodny Kommissariat Vnutrennikh Del—the people's commissariat for internal affairs), headed by Genrikh Yagoda, took its place.[6] It was given responsibility for all police and security functions and for the forced labour camps which were rapidly increasing in size and number. But its powers were stated to be subject to certain limitations in political cases. Also the procurator-general, a post soon to be held by Vyshinsky, had the power to supervise and veto its activities if they contravened the law. Such measures were taken to indicate new restraints on the security forces. But this consolidation of the police and security machinery of the Soviet regime, far from involving a reduction in its powers, was to forge the most savage instrument of repression in Russia's history.

The murder of Kirov opened a new inhuman chapter in which police powers were unlimited. A decree was at once issued, depriving those accused of terrorism of rights of defence, and a secret party directive required their speedy investigation and execution. Kirov's assassin, Nikolaev, and thirteen others, alleged to have been his accomplices, were charged with organizing a Leningrad centre to plot assassinations. They were tried in secret and shot. A hundred or more people arrested before Kirov's death on the charge of being counter-revolutionaries were found guilty of terrorism and shot. Twelve senior NKVD officers were arrested on charges of negligence. In the first months of 1935 several thousand Leningradtsi were arrested on suspicion of holding opposition sympathies and deported to Siberia.

Zinoviev, Kamenev, and their chief associates were imprisoned in Verkhne-Uralsk. Later in the summer they were tried in secret on the charge of plotting to murder Stalin. Two of the accused were shot and the others, including Zinoviev and Kamenev, were sentenced to imprisonment. This secret trial set a sinister precedent, for it was the first time that political opposition by members within the party had been tried and judged as a criminal act.[7]

The striking new development was, however, the concentration of terror on the party itself. Until 1934 the security police had preyed on the old intelligentsia, on former White Guards, kulaks, Nepmen, and opponents of the bolsheviks. The party had been to a large degree immune from the attentions of the OGPU. The few prominent members of the left and right opposition who had been arrested had been sentenced to administrative exile or, at worst, held in isolation. All had received fairly humane treatment and, compared with the unfortunates sent to forced labour camps, they were privileged. Such lenient treatment of party members was soon to cease.

Screening of the membership had become routine. In 1933 members and candidate members had numbered more than 3·5 million. By the beginning of 1934, purges had brought this figure down to 2·7 million, and in the course of that year it had fallen by a further 340,000. But then party records were said to be in serious disorder. In May 1935 the central committee directed that all party documents should be verified and a directive in December 1935 required the screening to be completed by the following February when local party organs were to issue new membership cards. In effect this prolonged the purge. By 1 January 1937 the number of members and candidates was below 2 million: in four years 1·5 million members and candidates had been eliminated from the party.

On 1 February 1935 the central committee plenum elected two new members to the Politburo. A. I. Mikoyan was already known as a staunch supporter of Stalin. The other new member was V. Ya. Chubar', probably a moderate, and soon to be removed. Of the two new candidate members, Zhdanov, who had succeeded Kirov in charge of the Leningrad party organization, was a Stalinist while the other, Eikhe, was like Chubar' a moderate and soon to be eliminated.

Two new appointments which were to prove more noteworthy were also made. One was the elevation of Ezhov to be in charge of the control commission in place of Kaganovich, who was given the task of supervising and reforming the people's commissariat for transport. A newcomer at this stage was Nikita Khrushchev, who in March 1935 was made first secretary of the Moscow party organization. His rise since his arrival in Moscow from the Ukraine in the autumn of 1929 had been remarkable. Starting as an apprentice fitter in the Donbas, he had been slow to interest himself in politics. He had not joined the party until 1918 although he had had ample opportunity. Lazar Kaganovich, the Jewish leather worker, who had played a major role as a bolshevik leader in the Donbas and who was only a year older, had joined the party in 1911. But gradually, by his energy and ruthless drive, Khrushchev had won recognition.

Kaganovich, a staunch Stalinist, had in supervising the construction of the gigantic hydroelectric project of the Dnieproges, the symbol of the new Soviet Russia, and in other undertakings, demonstrated a genius for organization. He needed men like Khrushchev, whom he had watched at work in the Ukraine. In the 1930s when Kaganovich was in charge of the modernizing of Moscow, including the building of the Metro, so that the city would outshine Leningrad and be a capital worthy of a great industrial nation, Khrushchev had worked under him. In 1933 he had become deputy to Kaganovich in charge of the Moscow party organization and in the following year had been elected a member of the central committee. Now he had become head of the Moscow party organization, a position of major importance.

Khrushchev had proved himself as a leading member of the new Stalinist *élite*. He learnt quickly and approached every task with an urgent practical need to produce results. Moreover, accepting completely the need for discipline and obedience in the party, he supported Stalin wholeheartedly, never questioning his policies, and furiously condemning all who might be identified with opposition. Applying his mind and energies wholly to the practical tasks entrusted to him, he had no time to think about policies. He saw communism as the only way to remove obstacles to unlimited progress, which for him meant the development of Soviet Russia into a rich and powerful nation, and only under Stalin's leadership was this possible. His blind faith was to falter during the war, but in the 1930s, dedicated to the heroic task of building a new nation, he did not pause to question the purges, the public trials, or any line taken by Stalin.

Two other men, both strong Stalinists, gained prominence at this time. One was G. M. Malenkov, who became assistant director of the cadres department of the party secretariat and was to work closely with Ezhov in purging the party. The other was L. P. Beria, an NKVD officer then serving as first secretary of the party in Transcaucasia. He won recognition by publishing a revised version of the history of the party in Transcaucasia in which special tribute was paid to the work of Stalin.

In May the society of old bolsheviks and, a few weeks later, the society of former political prisoners and exiles, two strongholds of old-guard revolutionaries, were disbanded. The significance of these changes only became apparent in the following year.

None of these measures, however, not even the purge of the party membership, amounted to the severe reprisals generally expected after the murder of Kirov. The continued improvement in the supply of food and other goods, the steady expansion of industry, and the constant exhortations to greater labours took the thoughts of the people away from purges and security measures. In February 1935, just two months after the murder of Kirov, the seventh congress of soviets had approved a decree on the need for a new constitution and had elected a drafting commission. Stalin was chairman and its members included Bukharin, Radek, Sokolnikov, and Vyshinsky. Bukharin and Radek were mainly responsible for the draft of what was to be called 'the Stalin constitution'. It occurred to few that Stalin might be planning to destroy old colleagues who were now working side by side with him on a matter of this importance. In the press and at meetings the principles of the new constitution, to be proclaimed 'the most democratic in the world', were under discussion. The promises of universal suffrage and of guarantees of the rights of the citizen made the dread arm of the OGPU and the NKVD seem remote. But Stalin was biding his time and cautiously waiting before he struck.

Towards the end of July 1936, only a few weeks after publication of the draft of the new constitution, a top secret directive went out to all party organizations. Bearing the title 'On the Terrorist Activity of the Trotsky-ite–Zinovievite Counter-revolutionary Block', it called for a special vigilance in seeking out and denouncing enemies of the regime and ordered a fresh review of the party membership.

Throughout these months the great purge was slowly but positively getting under way. Arrests, secret and usually in the dead of night, were growing more frequent. The security police were reaching out more widely and striking more often, but their activity was still apparently under cover.

The purge broke suddenly upon the nation in August with the public Trial of the Sixteen. Zinoviev, Kamenev, and fourteen others were arraigned on the charges of organizing a secret terrorist centre under the direction of Trotsky in exile, of planning the assassination of Kirov, and of plotting attempts on the lives of Stalin, Voroshilov, Kaganovich, and Zhdanov. All sixteen were found guilty, sentenced to death, and promptly shot.

The trial, conducted in a full blaze of publicity, caused a sensation. The accused, especially Zinoviev and Kamenev, were old bolsheviks who were household names but all, with one exception, had pleaded guilty to the fantastic charges laid against them. Their evidence had, moreover, impli-cated others and Vyshinsky, as prosecutor, made known that he had ordered investigations of Rykov, Bukharin, and Tomsky. A few days later, Tomsky, the gallant old bolshevik trade unionist, committed suicide, presumably to avoid investigation and the shame of having to confess publicly to such charges as Zinoviev and Kamenev had admitted.

Tomsky's suicide and Stalin's evident intention of destroying the old bolshevik guard and all potential opposition may at this stage have rallied some belated support for them. The terror seemed to falter briefly. On 10 September 1936 the investigation of Bukharin and Rykov was declared at an end, as no basis for any charge against them had been uncovered. Ordzhonikidze, the people's commissar for heavy industry, apparently spoke in defence of his deputy, Pyatakov. But opposition merely hardened Stalin's determination to eliminate such opponents. Suddenly on 18 February 1937 Ordzhonikidze died, it was said, of heart failure.[8]

At the time of the Trial of the Sixteen in August 1936 Stalin was with Zhdanov at the holiday resort of Sochi on the shores of the Black Sea. He may well have been disturbed by the announcement that no charges would be made against Bukharin and Rykov. On 25 September he and Zhdanov sent to Kaganovich, Molotov, and other members of the Politburo in Moscow a telegram which read: 'We deem it absolutely necessary and urgent that Comrade Ezhov be nominated to the post of People's Commissar for Internal Affairs. Yagoda has definitely proved himself to be incapable of unmasking the Trotskyite–Zinovievite block. The OGPU is four years behind in this matter . . .'[9]

On the following day Ezhov was appointed head of the NKVD. Yagoda was made people's commissar for posts and telegraph. Sweeping changes were at once effected in the security service. The older officers many of whom had first served in the Cheka under Dzerzhinsky were replaced. Stalin mistrusted them, probably suspecting that they might have sympathy with the old bolsheviks, and that they might not be amenable to his purposes in other ways. Of the six most senior security officers under Yagoda, only one survived and he belonged to the new generation.

The appointment of Ezhov marked the beginning of what Russians called the Ezhovshchina, the period of savage terror which lasted until late in 1938. NKVD officers arrested, interrogated, and arbitrarily imprisoned, sent to labour camps, or shot thousands of citizens. The flimsiest pretext could lead to arrest and severe sentence. Russians who had visited another country or had friends or families abroad were promptly taken in for questioning. The arrest of the head of a department, a trade union branch, an industrial combine, or a party organization automatically involved every member of his staff and of their families and friends. The net would then spread wider and wider until all were drawn into it. Some of the unfortunates would be released after examination, but the great majority suffered detention in some form or execution.

A purge hysteria began to grip the nation. The people, fearing arrest and unbalanced by the uncertainty of their daily lives as well as by the relentless propaganda and exhortations to show vigilance, denounced neighbours, colleagues, and even members of their own families. Queues formed outside NKVD headquarters and people waited patiently to file their denunciations. Human dignity and integrity were forgotten. Terror demeaned the whole nation.[10]

Towards the end of January 1937 the second great show trial was staged. This, the Trial of the Seventeen, was directed against the so-called anti-Soviet Trotskyite centre, said to have been led by Pyatakov, Sokolnikov, Radek, Serebryakov, and Muralov. The charges were more widely drawn than for the first public trial. The accused were alleged to have conspired with the active help of the German and Japanese governments to overthrow the Soviet government by force; they had also organized espionage, subversion, and sabotage on behalf of foreign governments and had planned to restore capitalism in Russia. Again, demonstrating Stalin's obsessive hatred, Trotsky was denounced as the sinister figure in the background, who had inspired and organized this monstrous conspiracy to destroy the Soviet regime.

The charges, straining the credence of any impartial observer and certainly fabricated, were nevertheless found proven. Indeed, according to an eyewitness account, 'all defendants seemed eager to heap accusation upon accusation upon themselves—*mea culpa maxima*. They required little cross-examination by the prosecutor. In the case of one defendant the prosecutor even had to admonish him to get down to the case and not embroider his testimony with additional crimes . . .'[11] Of the accused, thirteen were sentenced to death and promptly shot. Four, including Radek and Sokolnikov, were sentenced to ten years' imprisonment.

Leading party members were increasingly perturbed about the purge and especially the charges of treachery and sabotage laid against old bolsheviks who had proved themselves in so many crises. But few had the temerity or courage to voice their misgivings. Stalin and the NKVD seemed to have hypnotized them by fear. At the plenum of the central committee in February–March 1937, however, several members evidently questioned this mass persecution. Pavel Postyshev, the secretary of the Ukrainian party organization, expressed his anxieties boldly. 'I personally,' he said, 'do not believe that in 1934 an honest party member who had trod the long road of unrelenting fight against enemies for the party and for socialism would now be in the camp of the enemies. I do not believe it . . .'[12] But protest of this kind was tantamount to a confession of guilt as an accessory. In the following months Postyshev and more than ninety other members who were present at this plenum were arrested and shot.

Early in 1937 storm clouds began to gather over the Red Army. The evidence of Pyatakov and Radek in the Trial of the Seventeen had implicated senior commanders. Marshal Tukhachevsky, the commander-in-chief, who was not on good terms with Stalin was seen to be under suspicion in the spring. In May the system of political commissars was reintroduced. Dual command, whereby the military commander had at his side a political commissar who endorsed his orders, had always been strongly resented by the army and had gradually given place after 1925 to the single command system. The commissar had become the deputy of the military commander and had authority only in political matters. The revival of political commissars as joint commanders was ominous.

The Red Army, in fact, had a clear record of supporting Stalin and his regime. Even during collectivization the army, although recruited almost wholly from the peasant class which suffered so terribly from this campaign, had apparently not wavered in its allegiance. In earlier purges of the party the army had been found to harbour fewer unworthy elements than the party in general. In 1929, when 11·7 per cent of the membership had been purged, the percentage of the army members purged was only 3·5 per cent. Again in 1933 the army had lost only 4·3 per cent, whereas

17 per cent of the civilian membership had been purged. Moreover, party membership in the Red Army was increasing rapidly. By the end of 1934 all senior commanders and 93 per cent of divisional commanders were party members. But neither its record of allegiance nor the fact of party control saved the army from terror and purge. Stalin, keeping in mind always the decisive part that army revolts had played in the history of Russia and other countries, was determined that the Red Army should never be able to challenge his leadership.[13]

On 11 June 1937 *Pravda* published the statement that Marshal Tukhachevsky and seven other prominent Red Army generals were to be tried in secret. All were found guilty of 'espionage and treason to the Fatherland' and shot. According to press reports they had engaged in espionage on behalf of Germany and Japan and had conspired to surrender Soviet territory in the Ukraine and the Far East to those two countries in return for military support to overthrow the regime.[14]

The Red Army now suffered the full ferocity of the purge. Officers and soldiers were arrested in hundreds and many were executed. The higher commands were especially afflicted. According to reliable estimates, 35,000 men or approximately half of the officers of the Red Army were purged. This figure included three of the marshals, the two survivors being Voroshilov and Budyonny, old supporters of Stalin, 13 of the 15 army commanders, 220 of the 406 brigade commanders, 75 of the 80 members of the supreme military council, including all commanders of military districts, and all 11 vice-commissars of war.[15]

This purge, disrupting organization and destroying morale, came at the time of a massive build-up of the Soviet armed forces. Early in the 1920s Frunze, the commissar of war, and others had warned that the Red Army, despite its great resources of man-power, would be unable to stand against Western armies, unless fully equipped with modern techniques and machines of war. This required rapid development of the heavy industries able to produce such equipment. The Soviet leaders, and especially Stalin, were aware of this need for industrial support to the army and gave it all priority.

The first five-year plan provided the foundations for heavy industry and under the second plan defence industries were developed some two-and-a-half times as fast as the rest of industry. Budget allocations for the army and navy increased from 1,430 million rubles in 1933 to 23,200 million rubles in 1938 and to 56,800 million rubles in 1940. Equipment in both services was modernized, special attention being given to tanks, artillery, and planes.

At the same time the size of the regular army was expanding rapidly. In 1934 it was increased from 562,000 to 940,000, and in the following year to 1,300,000. In 1939 the territorial system was abolished and all national military units were dissolved, and the army was placed on a cadre basis. In the same year a decree made service in the armed forces compulsory for all citizens and the period of service was increased.

By the mid-1930s the Red Army had become more efficient and better disciplined than at any time in the past. Tukhachevsky with his outstanding abilities for strategy and organization, his energy, and his talent for leadership had gathered around him a staff of able officers and was making progress with his modernization of the army and its doctrines. But some of his advanced ideas, such as the massing of tanks for attack, were dismissed as heresy. His outlook disturbed conservative and inefficient men like Voroshilov and Budyonny. His prestige and popularity in the Red Army aroused jealousy, and Stalin in particular had watched him with misgiving.

At this time, when the Red Army was growing strong and confident, Stalin struck and virtually decapitated it by removing its leading commanders and so many of its officers. The general staff was thrown into disorder. The mechanization policy was dislocated and the allocation of guns, tanks, aircraft, and other equipment was no longer co-ordinated. A mood of bewilderment and uncertainty took the place of the confidence and the professional pride of officers and men. The young officers, although trained in modern methods and devoted to the party and its leader, were unsure of themselves. They needed time to gain experience and build confidence, and time was short. The Spanish civil war, which was still raging at this time, offered the opportunity of giving some of these new officers training and experience under fire, but only a small number benefited.

The purge applied not only to the military but also the political officers of the Red Army. Jan Gamarnik, head of the political directorate and responsible for administering the party organization within the forces, had committed suicide to avoid arrest. In his place L. Mekhlis, a loyal Stalinist, was appointed. He promptly removed most of the political officers and promoted men of the new generation to their places. They were key appointments now when the dual command system had been restored. They had the special duty of ensuring that the army was under the party's close control. But the efficiency and morale of the Red Army and Navy were shattered, and it was to require the shock of war and defeat to revive them as a fighting force.

In December 1937 the first general election to the supreme soviet under the new constitution took place. It was claimed that 96·8 per cent of the electorate had voted. Of them 89·844 million, or 98·6 per cent, had voted for the communist block. Only 632,000 which was less than one per cent had voted against the official candidates, all of whom were returned.[16] The press proclaimed the result as a massive vote of confidence in Stalin and the Soviet government. Soviet propaganda extolled the new democratic constitution and the elections held under it. But in the midst of the terror and the purge hysteria which gripped the nation, the claims rang false.

The third of the great show trials, the Trial of the Twenty-one, took place in March 1938. The chief accused were Bukharin, Rykov, and Krestinsky, all of whom had been members of the Politburo, Yagoda, the former head of the NKVD who had launched this terror, Rakovsky, who had been chairman of the Ukrainian Sovnarkom and Soviet ambassador to England and France. The charges against them included the usual crimes of espionage, terrorism, and sabotage, all inspired and organized by Trotsky from abroad. Bukharin and Rykov were alleged to have been the leaders of the anti-Soviet block of rightists and Trotskyites which had carried on espionage on behalf of foreign governments. The accused had conspired with Germany and Japan to surrender Soviet territory in return for rewards and military help. They had plotted the murder of Stalin and other members of the Politburo, and had perpetrated numerous acts of sabotage with the purpose of destroying the regime. Yagoda faced the additional charges of having murdered his predecessor in command of the NKVD, Menzhinsky, and of plotting the murder of his successor, Ezhov; he was also charged with being an accessory to Kirov's assassination and with the murder of Kuibyshev and Gorky. Bukharin faced the additional charges of conspiring with the left socialist revolutionaries in 1918 to murder Lenin, Stalin, and Sverdlov.

All of the accused duly confessed their guilt in court except for Bukharin who, while pleading guilty to the general charges, refused to confess that he had planned to kill Lenin in 1918. Krestinsky caused a stir when he retracted the confession he had already made under interrogation. After a further twenty-four hours in the hands of the NKVD, however, he returned to court and confessed. One of the witnesses, Boris Kamkov, a socialist revolutionary terrorist, held up proceedings when he consistently refused to give the evidence demanded by the prosecution. His testimony was required to prove that Bukharin had plotted to kill Lenin in 1918. The charges were nevertheless taken as proved. Three of the accused were sentenced to imprisonment. The other eighteen were sentenced to death and shot.

The three public trials of this period, accompanied by shrill propaganda and denunciations in the press, on the radio, and at countless meetings throughout the country, which were addressed by carefully briefed agitators, caused bewilderment among the Russians. The old bolsheviks who had been virtually eliminated had worked with Lenin in promoting the revolution and then in creating the regime. Now they were told that these same men had all along been capitalist agents and wreckers. But living in fear of the terror and the ubiquitous agents of the NKVD, Russians were silent and even among themselves they hesitated to talk of such matters.

Opinion abroad was also bewildered. Speculation and condemnation of

Soviet methods were rife. But the confessions of such men as Zinoviev, Kamenev, Radek, Bukharin, and Tomsky made commentators hesitate to dismiss the trials as stage-managed to enable Stalin to rid himself of all whom he considered rivals. Such men as Sir Bernard Pares, who had devoted himself to the study of Russia and to interpreting Russia to the West, considered that the charges of sabotage had been 'proved up to the hilt' and that all the evidence was convincing.[17] Likewise Joseph E. Davies, the U.S. ambassador in Moscow from 1936 to 1938, reluctantly concluded that the case against the accused had been proven. He found, too, that the general opinion in foreign embassies in Moscow was that the trials had clearly established the existence of a conspiracy to overthrow the government.[18] But these conclusions of eyewitnesses were mistaken. The revelations to the twentieth and twenty-second party congresses, made after the death of Stalin, indicated that the charges were fabricated. The confessions of the accused were extracted by methods of mental and physical torture, by blackmail, and by treachery.[19] Moreover, those who appeared at the public trials and who confessed were few in number, while those tried in secret or merely interrogated without trial and who did not confess numbered thousands.

The purge reached out from Leningrad and Moscow into the regional organizations of the party and the government. No sector of the population was immune. The union republics suffered, but none more severely than the Ukraine. Stalin was particularly mistrustful of the Ukrainians. He could not forget that they had allied themselves with the Germans in 1917 and that Ukrainian nationalism made them liable to deviate from Moscow's policies. In 1933 when collectivization had reduced Ukrainian agriculture to chaos he had sent Postyshev to Kiev to purge the party. Postyshev had evidently carried out his instructions, but in 1937 he himself had been purged. Meanwhile Stalin's suspicion of Ukrainian loyalty had been aggravated by Hitler's openly expressed plans to annex the Ukraine and by the danger that Ukrainian separatism might again lead to an alliance with Germany.

In January 1938 the Soviet press announced that the central committee of the Ukrainian communist party had elected N. Khrushchev as acting first secretary. By this time the former party leaders in the Ukraine— S. V. Kossior, P. P. Postyshev, V. Ya. Chubar', and G. I. Petrovsky—had already perished and most of the senior party and government officials had been purged. Khrushchev's task was to rebuild the party organization and government and to revive the shattered economy. His appointment was a mark of Stalin's confidence in him as a dependable supporter and as an administrator.

The Ukraine, as the major grain-growing region, was crucial to the Soviet economy. The expansion of the industrial labour force made increased grain supplies even more important. Agriculture had not yet recovered from the collectivization campaign in the Ukraine and both party organization and membership there were at a low ebb. Khrushchev with his aggressive energy and urgent practical approach set to work on both fronts. He had had no real experience of agriculture, but he learnt readily by visiting farms and examining difficulties at first hand. His methods were simple, but his application of commonsense and relentless drive evidently brought results. Two good harvests relieved anxiety about grain deliveries, and he was quick to declare that the problem had been solved. He himself was already emerging as a national leader. In 1938 he was promoted to be a candidate member of the Politburo and in the next year he became a full member.

Meanwhile the purge continued unabated. Hundreds and thousands of people were arrested daily and a great many of them were sentenced to forced labour. GULAG, the main administration of corrective labour camps, which was a department of the NKVD, was responsible for the vast web of labour camps which spread over Russia, but which were most concentrated in Siberia and the extreme north. The flood of political prisoners who poured into these camps during the Ezhovshchina were put to heavy labour such as cutting timber, mining coal, and building roads. For every kind of work a production target was fixed and prisoners who met their target received food sufficient for survival (500 to 600 grams of bread a day and hot meal of some kind). Prisoners who failed to reach their target received only 300 grams of bread a day, a diet below starvation level. Many of the political prisoners, and especially the older ones, were unaccustomed to hard physical labour and perished. The conditions of political prisoners were all the more intolerable because, as enemies of the people, they were treated as the lowest form of prison life. Criminal prisoners were evidently allowed and even encouraged to persecute them.

The number of prisoners crowded into these camps can only be estimated. The two most reliable estimates available give the total number 'living in detention under the NKVD' during the Ezhovshchina as between seven and fourteen million or between seven and twelve million.[20] Deaths from hard labour, under-nourishment, and the harsh conditions, especially in winter, were appallingly high. But already forced labour camps had become part of the Soviet regime, accepted as a system whereby political and criminal prisoners could be isolated, and at the same time made to serve the state in developing the remote and inhospitable regions of the country.[21]

By the beginning of 1938, however, the mounting fury of the Ezhovshchina had begun to disturb Stalin. The original purpose of eliminating the old bolsheviks and their supporters had been achieved. But under Ezhov's direction the purge had spread until, like a malignant plague, it was out of control. Stalin with the instinct for pulling back from disaster which he had displayed nearly eight years earlier with his 'Dizziness from Success' speech, evidently decided to call a halt before the purge destroyed the regime.

The first sign of what was to be called 'the Great Change' was a resolution by the central committee plenum in January 1938 with the title 'Concerning the Mistakes of Party Organizations in Excluding Communists from the Party, Concerning Formal-Bureaucratic Attitudes towards the Appeals of Excluded Members of the VKP(b) and Concerning Measures to Eliminate these Deficiencies'.[22] The new enemy of the party was declared to be the communist-careerist. He had taken advantage of the purge to denounce his superiors and to secure his own promotion. He was guilty of spreading suspicion and of weakening the party. The resolution laid down a ten-point plan to halt the mass expulsions and to rehabilitate those who had been wrongly expelled. At once a purge of communist-careerists was launched and a press campaign reported on the release and rehabilitation of victimized party members.

The real halt to the great purge came, however, in July 1938 when Lavrenti Beria was appointed Ezhov's deputy. In effect, he took control of the NKVD, although it was not until December 1938 that Ezhov was removed and made commissar for inland water transport. Soon afterwards he disappeared. Now came the arrest, trial, and execution of NKVD officials on charges of extracting confessions from innocent people. This endorsed the belief of many loyal communists, that fascists had insinuated themselves into the NKVD and the government, and had been responsible for the countless cruelties and injustices of the Ezhovshchina. Their loyalty to the party undiminished, they now welcomed the purge of the NKVD. This explanation was officially endorsed and encouraged, for it conveniently removed the responsiblity from the shoulders of Stalin and the Politburo.[23]

The NKVD itself was now purged as ruthlessly as every other Soviet organization had been. It was common for prisoners to find themselves joined in their cells by the examining magistrates who had interrogated them.[24] So drastic was this purge that, as in the party, nearly all senior officers of the NKVD were removed and the new young men had to be promoted quickly to fill the chief posts. But the great change was felt more widely in the easing of conditions in prisons and labour camps and the fact that the more savage methods of interrogation were applied less often. The most heartening sign to the oppressed populace, however, was the release of prisoners, many to be reinstated in their old positions and even promoted. The tension was suddenly lifted in some degree from the lives of Russians in prison and outside.

Stalin himself emerged from this period in an unassailable position. He had instigated the purge and, although it had gone much further than he had envisaged, he had waited until it had reached a danger point before calling a halt. But he had retained the support of his people. Evidently he had not been identified in the popular mind with this monstrous repression. The Russians had blamed the boyars for the excesses of Ivan the Terrible, and in later centuries the tsar's officials, rarely the tsar himself.

Now they blamed the NKVD, and Stalin enjoyed the same immunity from popular censure. Moreover, his role as leader of the nation was being constantly magnified by the propaganda organs of party and state. He was seen rarely in public, but portraits of him were inescapable, and he was taking on the image in the popular imagination of a demi-god, omniscient and omnipresent. He lived in the Kremlin in Moscow where the ancient tsars had lived; already he was being accepted with something of the same faith and allegiance that had been shown them.

The main factor, consolidating and strengthening Stalin's position, was, however, the advance to power of the new Soviet *élite*. The old generation of revolutionaries and intelligentsia had been almost completely destroyed. The new men were young, tough, and devoted to him. They were of humble origin and not highly educated, but eager and quick to learn. An English economist, who spent a year from mid-1936 working and studying at the Economic Research Institute of Gosplan in Moscow and lived in the students' hostel of the All-Union Planning Academy, observed that the academy was a kind of party school for training party members of unimpeachable loyalty for senior posts. 'Notwithstanding all their variety of personal character, these people were very alike, so far as I knew them, in their rather simple-minded and ruthless practicality. Marxist theory and Soviet policy as expounded by Stalin suited them exactly. I could not and cannot imagine a leader better suited to them. In the opinion of one of them there were about 50,000 party members of their general status and these were the "masters of the country". The purge which throughout this period was mounting to its climax worried them not at all in any way apparent to me either for their own safety or for pity.'[25] This new generation of carefully selected and trained party members was to be the main support to Stalin's power and to provide the executors of his will in building the new Soviet Russia.

The transformation of the managerial class in party and state was a positive result of the purge. But the terror also fostered a malaise in the form of unwillingness and fear of taking initiative or responsibility. Obeying the instinct of self-preservation officials followed instructions to the letter, reluctant to do more for fear of exposing themselves to criticism or worse. In the vast Soviet bureaucracy this negative attitude caused interminable delays and inefficiency. But the impact of this attitude was most disastrous in the Red army and navy. The young officers, hurriedly promoted to replace those who had been purged, were untried and unsure. Morale had fallen throughout the armed forces and the general feeling of insecurity and caution stifled confidence and initiative. The demoralization of the Red Army and the dire effects of the purge were to cause major losses and to bring the whole nation close to disastrous defeat in the coming months.

On the whole, however, Soviet Russia had probably emerged stronger from this period of terror and purge. The nation was united and equipped with a potentially more dynamic and efficient management at all levels. But the result had been achieved by ruthless methods entailing needless sufferings, as had happened in the collectivization campaign. But now, before the people with their extraordinary resilience could recover and return to normal living, they had to endure a far greater ordeal.

PART V

THE GREAT PATRIOTIC
WAR

CHAPTER SEVENTEEN

Preludes to War 1939–41

THE Soviet policy of collective security collapsed on the signing of the Munich agreement of 29 September 1938. Stalin and the Politburo had endorsed this policy with misgivings; Maxim Litvinov, the commissar for foreign affairs, had worked sincerely to realize it, believing that it offered the only hope of deterring Hitler from war. But the weakness of Britain and France and their mistrust of Soviet Russia had made any real collective agreement impossible.

To the Russians, Neville Chamberlain, the British prime minister, was the arch-villain of the period and the object of their contempt and detestation. In their view he had made a shameful surrender to Hitler, which, far from securing 'peace in our time', had merely brought war nearer. But they also saw in him a sinister enemy of the Soviet Union.[1] He made no secret of his hatred of communism and the Soviet regime, but so did Churchill and others, whom they respected; his villainy was that he sought to isolate the Soviet Union and encourage Germany to march eastwards in the belief that war could be kept in the east and that Britain and the rest of the world could enjoy peace, while fascism and communism destroyed each other.[2]

The winter of 1938–9 was a time of anxiety in Moscow. Russia needed peace. The people had harsh memories of the horrors of war, and the thought of another war, especially after the hardships of their lives since the revolution, was not bearable. Stalin and the party leaders were also determined to avert war, because they knew that Russian defence industries and the Red Army itself were in no condition to withstand a strong attack. Russia would again be 'beaten for her backwardness'. Defeat would destroy the Soviet regime and all hope of creating the new society to which the party was dedicated.

The problem was where to turn for allies. The U.S.A. avoided commitment. Britain and France were not dependable, and Munich had shown them to be so morally bankrupt that their support would be of small value. Meanwhile Germany, Japan, and Italy behaved with increasing arrogance. The war in Spain was going badly for the republicans. The Poles, fanatically anti-Russian, had sent Colonel Beck, their foreign minister, to Berlin, evidently to make some deal with Hitler. To the Russians each day seemed to bring more ominous events.

Desperately anxious to gain time to prepare against the inevitable war with Germany, Stalin now kept the door open even to an understanding with Hitler. In his speech to the eighteenth party congress on 10 March, he defined the principles of Soviet foreign policy and stressed that 'We stand for peace and the strengthening of trade relations with all countries ... We stand for peaceful, close, and good-neighbourly relations with all the neighbouring countries, having common frontiers with the U.S.S.R.' [3] It was a hint that his government was ready to consider discussions and the Germans took note.

On 15 March nazi troops invaded Czechoslovakia. Hitler announced that he had taken Bohemia and Moravia under German protection. Slovakia was detached and became a puppet state. In Moscow this violation of Czechoslovakia had been expected; it was indeed, they considered, an inevitable result of Chamberlain's appeasement. The news of nazi troops in Prague nevertheless startled all Russians. Litvinov at once sent a note of protest to Berlin that this latest German action 'enlarged the elements contributing to the state of alarm already created in Europe and dealt a fresh blow to the feeling of security of the nations'.[4]

Public opinion in the West was outraged by the rape of Czechoslovakia. In Britain, Chamberlain, who in his statement to the House of Commons on 15 March had merely expressed disapproval, was evidently shaken by the outcry, and stirred to action. In Moscow the British ambassador called on Litvinov to enquire what the Soviet Union would do if Hitler attacked Rumania.[5] Litvinov responded on the same evening with the proposal that representatives of Britain, France, the U.S.S.R, Poland, and Rumania should meet without delay to discuss measures to avert such a danger.[6] This marked the beginning of the abortive tripartite discussions between Soviet Russia, Britain, and France which were to aggravate Soviet mistrust of Britain even further.

The British government rejected the proposed meeting and suggested on 21 March that the Soviet Union, Britain, France, and Poland should issue a declaration that in the event of any new act of aggression the four powers would consult on action to be taken. Litvinov, although incensed by the rejection of the practical Russian proposal, agreed to sign the declaration, provided that Poland was also a signatory. But Colonel Beck, as anti-Russian as Chamberlain himself, did not favour such a declaration. He proposed a Polish–British agreement of mutual assistance which might later be broadened to include other powers. Chamberlain now took a headlong plunge. On 31 March he announced the Polish–British pact, which on 13 April was extended to include Rumania and Greece. In effect, Britain was undertaking to defend countries, two of which lay directly between the Soviet Union and Germany and were inaccessible to her. If Germany attacked Poland or Rumania, Britain could do nothing without the support of the Soviet Union. Chamberlain and Halifax nevertheless continued obstinately to avoid a direct agreement with the

Soviet government. Churchill, Eden, and others were quick to point out that British foreign policy had seldom been so ineptly handled.

Under pressure from parliament and public opinion, the British government then proposed that Soviet Russia should give similar unilateral guarantees to Poland and Rumania. Moscow was not prepared, however, to adopt this proposal, especially as the two countries concerned would probably reject such an offer. On the basis of a French move for a joint Soviet–French declaration of mutual assistance to each other and to Poland and Rumania, Moscow on 17 April put forward a plan for an Anglo-Franco–Soviet pact of mutual assistance. It would include a military convention and provide guarantees of the independence of all states along the Soviet border from the Baltic to the Black Sea.[7]

The Soviet three-power pact was a positive proposal which might well have deterred Hitler or have delayed his plans considerably. Chamberlain rejected it on the grounds that it would offend Poland, that it would incense Germany, and that it would commit Britain and France to the defence of Finland and the Baltic states. Negotiations dragged on, but in Moscow it was recognized that Russia stood alone and must act to preserve her own interests.

On 3 May Litvinov was replaced by Molotov as people's commissar for foreign affairs. The change caused a stir in the West, giving rise to speculations about a new direction in Soviet foreign policy. Litvinov had carried out the directives of the Politburo, of which he was not a member, and he did not originate policy. But he was known as an ardent Westerner and an advocate of collective security. The Germans disliked him and, as a Jew, he was an object of nazi abuse. His replacement signified Russian recognition of failure of the policies pursued, while he was foreign commissar and, in fact, it forecast change.

The new commissar for foreign affairs, Vyacheslav Mikhailovich Molotov, whose real name was Scriabin, was already chairman of Sovnarkom (the council of people's commissars), an office akin to prime minister. He had joined the party in 1906 and, specializing in party organization, had held many responsible posts. Since the early 1920s he had been one of Stalin's most trusted supporters. He stood second only to Stalin in authority and prestige, but was evidently content to play a secondary role. Sturdy, practical, and dignified he impressed his own people as a strong, dependable statesman of the kind the country needed. In fact, although he had neither experience nor knowledge of foreign affairs, he was tougher and probably more suited to the office of foreign minister than Litvinov at this juncture. Abroad he was hardly known at the time of his appointment. He was quick to make an impact by his granite-like presence and his relentless pursuit of Russian interests.

Soviet foreign policy did not, however, change suddenly. Molotov's report on 31 May 1939 to the Supreme Soviet on the international situation was, like Stalin's speech of 10 March, critical and mistrustful of

Britain and France, but it was primarily an attack on Germany and Italy.[8] The Soviet government was still anxious to conclude a mutual assistance pact with both capitalist powers. In London, Chamberlain and Halifax found themselves under greater pressure to negotiate with Russia. Towards the end of May the British and French ambassadors in Moscow delivered new proposals for a tripartite pact. The terms submitted made action under the pact subject to cumbersome League of Nations procedures; they sought to avoid a convention on military aid and they excluded the Baltic states. It was a further demonstration of confused thinking and of the reluctance of the British and French governments to come to an agreement with the Soviet regime. Showing patience and restraint the Soviet government replied on 2 June 1939 with a new draft which, while maintaining the purely defensive nature of the proposed agreement, was specific about the countries to be guaranteed against aggression and the commitments of the three parties.[9]

On 8 June 1939 Halifax informed Maisky, the Soviet ambassador in London, that the British government hoped to speed the negotiations by sending a representative to Moscow. But, whereas Chamberlain and Halifax had gone to Berlin to negotiate, they sent only a foreign office official, William Strang, to Moscow. It seemed to be a deliberate affront and, as Churchill noted, it 'gave actual offence'.[10] A courteous but pressing invitation to Halifax to go to Moscow was waved aside.[11] Meanwhile Hitler was increasingly belligerent towards Poland. Tardily recognizing the mounting seriousness of the situation, the British and French governments began to seek more urgently to reach some agreement with the Soviet Union. Late in July the British government agreed to send a military mission to Moscow. The Russians expressed eagerness to receive such a mission as soon as possible and hoped that Lord Gort, the chief of the imperial general staff, would lead it. But Chamberlain appointed an elderly retired admiral, Sir Reginald Plunkett Ernle-Erle-Drax, who travelled by passenger steamer and arrived in Moscow on 12 August without instructions and without authority to sign any military convention.

The mission was abortive. The main obstacle was Soviet insistence that a military convention must include provision for Soviet troops to pass through Poland in the event of war with Germany. The British and French governments rejected this provision. The Poles, carried away by their centuries-old hatred of the Russians, declared that they need not and would not accept Soviet military aid.[12] Neither Britain nor France were prepared to bring pressure to bear on the Poles. Indeed Chamberlain and others were inclined to rate Polish military strength above that of Soviet Russia and were anxious not to offend Warsaw by pressing the Soviet condition. The Poles were soon to pay a tragic price for their failure to understand the situation and for their suicidal obstinacy.

Hitler and his ministers had been following these developments closely.

Hitler was ready to attack, but wanted assurance that Soviet Russia would not take a stand with Britain and France in defence of Poland. The first German approaches to Moscow, suggesting a review of Soviet–German relations, were evidently made on 30 May 1939, while the Anglo-French–Soviet negotiations were still under way. The Russians returned a non-committal reply. In August they rejected a proposal, made by Ribbentrop, for a secret protocol, dividing the countries from the Baltic to the Black Sea into Soviet and German spheres of interest. But a German note, delivered in Moscow on 15 August, received a more sympathetic response. The Soviet government welcomed the German desire for a serious improvement in relations and suggested a trade and credit agreement to be followed by a non-aggression pact or a reaffirmation of the neutrality pact of 1926, and the conclusion of a special protocol defining spheres of interest.[13] A Soviet draft for the non-aggression pact was ready on 19 August and on the same day a trade and credit agreement was concluded.[14]

Hitler, worried about the presence of the Anglo-French military mission in Moscow and impatient to order his troops, poised on the Polish frontier, to march, increased his pressure on Moscow. On 20 August he sent an urgent telegram to Stalin, asking him to receive Ribbentrop on 22 or at latest on 23 August. Stalin agreed. He had by 17 August, the date of the Soviet note, begun actively considering the possibility of a pact with Germany, but it was possibly only on 19 or 20 August that he made his final decision. By then the Anglo-French military negotiations had reached deadlock and the Poles had reaffirmed their refusal of all access to Polish territory to Russian troops. Another factor, which influenced Stalin, was the fighting which was still continuing with Japan and the probability that a pact with Germany would lead to the signing of a similar pact with Germany's ally, Japan.

On 22 August the Soviet–German negotiations for a non-aggression pact were announced. On the following day Molotov and Ribbentrop signed the pact and a secret protocol in Moscow.[15]

The Russian people were bewildered by this change in policy. They were accustomed to think of their country as leading the anti-fascist struggle, and the Soviet press had consistently told them that this was part of the Soviet mission in the world. Now by an abrupt reversal of policy they found themselves on friendly terms with the nazis. No one would have dared, especially with the purge so fresh in their memories, to criticize the new development. In any case all accepted that Stalin and Molotov knew what they were doing and the general reaction was that it was a shrewd move to keep Russia out of war.[16]

On 31 August 1939 Molotov reported to the Supreme Soviet. He spoke now with strong anti-British and anti-French bias. Soviet attempts to reach agreement with Britain and France had failed for reasons which he explained. He went on to justify the new Soviet–German pact as designed to put an end to the enmity between the two countries. He stressed that the pact formed part of the policy of peaceful coexistence, formulated by Lenin and endorsed by Stalin, and that the Soviet Union was pursuing its own independent policy without obligation to involve itself on either side. He made no mention of the secret protocol which defined spheres of interest, providing that 'In the event of a territorial and political transformation' in the Baltic states, the northern frontier of Lithuania would represent the dividing line between their respective spheres; on such a transformation taking place in Poland, their spheres of interest would be bound approximately by the line of the rivers Narev, Vistula, and San. The question of the maintenance of an independent Poland was noted as something for future consideration between them.[17]

On the day after Molotov's address to the Supreme Soviet, Hitler invaded Poland. On 3 September the Anglo-French ultimatum, demanding the withdrawal of German troops from Poland, expired and both countries were then at war with Germany. On 10 September the Soviet government decreed partial mobilization. Meanwhile negotiations had started with Japan to end the heavy fighting which had been raging since May along the frontier between the Mongolian People's Republic and Manchukuo. Molotov and Togo, the Japanese ambassador, agreed to end hostilities and to set up a commission to establish the frontier.

Stalin had watched the German advance into Poland uneasily. It was a ruthless demonstration of the highly mechanized efficiency of the German army. It confirmed his belief that the Red Army was still neither equipped nor trained to meet such an attack. Russia needed time and meanwhile everything must be done to strengthen her western frontiers.

On 17 September the Red Army began its occupation of eastern Poland. The basic purpose was defensive, but Russian action was also inspired by the animus, rooted in centuries of bitter antagonism between Russian and Pole. All sense of charity and sympathy were missing from Molotov's speech of 17 September. He spoke with contempt of the 'internal insolvency and obvious impotence of the Polish state', which had become 'a fertile field for any accidental and unexpected contingency that may create a menace to the Soviet Union'. For this reason and to protect 'its blood-brothers the Ukrainians and White Russians inhabiting Poland', the Red Army had crossed the Polish frontier.[18]

The Polish army and air force had already been crushed by the German advance, and the Red Army advance was almost unopposed. The NKVD went in with the army and was soon deporting 'hostile or unreliable' Poles, Ukrainians, and White Russians to the east in thousands. Some 14,500 Polish troops, including 8,000 officers, surrendered to the Red Army. They were disarmed and interned in three prisoner-of-war camps in Katyn Wood near Smolensk. Nothing more was heard of them until the spring of 1943 when extensive mass graves were unearthed at Katyn.[19]

On 28 September Ribbentrop paid his second visit to Moscow and at once agreed with Molotov the tentative division of Poland. A secret protocol also made Lithuania part of the Soviet sphere of interest. Next, the Soviet government imposed treaties of mutual assistance on Esthonia (29 September), on Latvia (5 October), and Lithuania (10 October). The Baltic states over which Peter the Great had fought to secure Russia's access to the Baltic Sea, were still essential to the defence of Leningrad. He had waged war in Finland, too, for the same purpose. The Soviet need for a protective shield to the important naval base of Kronstadt, which Peter had established, was also crucial in the face of the German threat.

In 1938 the Soviet government had made approaches to the Finnish government to lease certain territory along the northern shore of the gulf. The Finns, jealous of their independence and suspicious of the Russians, had refused. On 14 October 1939 the Soviet government made urgent representations in a note to the Finnish government. Stalin now requested in exchange for other territory certain islands in the Gulf of Finland, a thirty-year lease of the Hango peninsula, and frontier adjustments in the Petsamo area and on the Karelian Isthmus.[20] Again the Finns rejected the Soviet proposals. A further exchange took place but it was clear that the Finns would not yield.

On 31 October 1939 Molotov reported to an extraordinary session of the Supreme Soviet on the international situation. His speech demonstrated a gross insensitivity to world opinion and was of a kind to antagonize countries which might otherwise have been sympathetic to Soviet policy. Referring to Poland which had been so ruthlessly crushed, he said scornfully that 'one swift blow ... first by the German army and then by the Red Army, and nothing was left of this ugly offspring of the Versailles treaty...' He spoke in the same contemptuous tone of the ineffective British and French guarantees to Poland. Soviet Russia was, he stressed, neutral in the war between Germany and Britain and France, but he went on to explain how the whole conception of 'aggression' had changed: Germany now stood for peace; Britain and France wanted to continue the war, and were therefore now the real aggressors. Such sophistry did not impress opinion in the West or even in Russia. Then his references to Soviet gains from Poland of some 13 million people and 196 square kilometres at the price of only 757 casualties and 1,860 wounded sounded inept when, as was generally known, the Polish army had been crushed by the Germans and the Poles were in no condition to resist the Russian invasion.

Reporting on negotiations with Finland, Molotov explained that the problems of Soviet security were all the more acute because Leningrad, a city of 3½ million, was only 32 kilometres from the Finnish border and within range of artillery fire. He then outlined the Soviet proposals, designed to ensure the defences of Leningrad and Kronstadt. It was clear that he had in mind defence against German attack.[21]

Negotiations with the Finns continued, but made no progress. On 13

November Stalin broke them off. His patience was exhausted. He was desperately anxious to secure his frontiers against German attack. Since the Finns would not concede the territory requested, he decided to use force.

On 30 November 1939 a massive Soviet attack was launched on Finland by land, sea, and air on the pretext that Finnish artillery had fired on Soviet frontier villages. Voroshilov was in command of Russian operations. His main force was the 7th Army Group which was to break through the Mannerheim Line, a strongly fortified zone, some twenty miles deep, running diagonally across the Karelian Isthmus. This was the basis of the Finnish defence system and here the bulk of the Finnish artillery and infantry was concentrated. The Red 7th Army Group, after breaking through the Mannerheim Line, was to move on to Helsinki and then to the Hango Peninsula. From north of Lake Ladoga the Red 8th Army Group was to cross the Finnish frontier and then moving southwards attack the Mannerheim Line defences from the west. The Red 9th Army Group in positions farther north and along the frontier was to cut off all communication with Sweden. Within the Arctic Circle the 14th Army Group was to take the ice-free port of Petsamo and the surrounding region. Voroshilov was confident that the campaign would take not more than two weeks.

The small Finnish conscript army with reservists was some 300,000 strong. The Soviet forces initially numbered about 600,000 and more than a million additional troops were to be brought into action. But the morale of the Finns was high and they were united in their grim determination to defend their country. Moreover, although small in number, they were highly trained and skilled in the mobile and aggressive guerrilla warfare, known as *motti* fighting.

On 30 November the Red Army Groups began their ponderous advance and at once suffered appalling losses. Their artillery made small impression on the Finnish defences and the armour of the Soviet tanks was too thin to withstand Finnish gunfire. To the north the 8th, 9th, and 14th Army Groups became strung out as they advanced. Units were cut off and the Finns destroyed them one by one. By the end of the year a stalemate had been reached on the Karelian Front and fighting had stopped in all sectors.

For the Russians this failure against a nation of only 3 million people was a bitter humiliation. Despite the paucity of news in the Soviet press, many suspected that the Red Army, which they had always been told was invincible, was not doing well. People in Leningrad or who had contact with Leningradtsi knew that hospitals were overcrowded and that the flood of wounded was growing. Stalin was alarmed, especially because by comparison with the ruthless efficiency of the German war machine in western Poland, the Red Army had proved lumbering and inefficient. He was now determined to bring the war to an end as quickly as possible and before other countries rallied to the defence of the Finns with equipment and troops.

World opinion had been appalled by the attack on Finland. On 14 December the general indignation found expression in the expulsion of the Soviet Union from the League of Nations. In Britain, the U.S.A., and in France people followed closely this unequal contest in which the small Finnish nation fought so bravely and effectively against the great bully. In England and France volunteers came forward to fight with the Finns. Efforts were made to help by sending war materials, but Germany and neutral Norway and Sweden stood in the way and only very small quantities of equipment reached the Finns. So strong was public opinion and so misguided were the governments of Britain and France, that serious consideration was given to declaring war on Soviet Russia. Chamberlain even considered that there would be strategic advantage in fighting Hitler and Stalin simultaneously and 'killing two birds with one stone'.[22]

In the first weeks of 1940 Red troops massed for decisive action against Finland. Some one-and-a-half million men were concentrated in or immediately behind the narrow Karelian Isthmus. Heavy field guns and tanks were assembled. Throughout January, Red artillery and the Red air force bombarded the Mannerheim fortifications. On 11 February General Timoshenko, now in command of the southern front in place of Voroshilov, who, however, remained commissar for defence, ordered the advance. Thirteen infantry divisions, covered by aerial and artillery bombardment, moved forward. Casualties were terribly high, but more and more Red troops were poured in to maintain the relentless pressure. On 15 February the Mannerheim Line was breached and on the following day the sheer mass of troops forced the Finns to give up the western half of the line. Timoshenko threw in fresh divisions. The Finns were being overwhelmed by numbers and constant bombardment. They hoped for an early thaw which in the marshes, lakes, and streams of this wooded region would have bogged down the Red forces, but spring came late.

On 3 March Vyborg was taken. The Finns opened negotiations on 8 March and on 12 March in Moscow they signed the peace treaty. The Russians gained the bases needed for their defences and certain other territories which they had not included in their original demands. But they did not attempt to occupy Helsinki and were careful not to overreach themselves in Finland. The price of these gains was, however, 48,745 killed or missing and 158,863 wounded, according to official Soviet figures, and the actual losses were probably far higher.[23]

The Soviet–Finnish war had been costly and unnecessary.[24] The Germans secretly and Britain and France openly took delight in this humiliation of Soviet armed might. They noted that only with difficulty and at terrible cost had the Red Army managed to conquer an army one-fiftieth its size and were convinced that the purge had undermined morale and reduced efficiency until it was no more than a massive, primitive force.

But the lessons of Finland which had exposed the Red Army to its first real test since the civil war, were not lost on Stalin and the High Command. They were realists, and they enforced reforms with a new urgency. Zhukov was to call 1940 the 'year of the great transformation' of the Red Army. In producing this result the Soviet–Finnish war was to prove an important preparation which helped save Russia from conquest by Germany.

The Finnish war had indeed revealed major faults in the Red Army. The purge had seriously damaged morale, especially among officers. Inexperienced and under the supervision of the political commissars and of the sinister special section of the NKVD, they were afraid to take initiative of the kind that fighting against the Finns demanded. Timoshenko, who became commander-in-chief and commissar for defence in place of Voroshilov, and Shaposhnikov, the chief of staff[25] and other commanders evidently opposed the system of dual command, for in August 1940 the single command was restored and a campaign to raise the status and authority of officers was developed. Moreover, they instituted intensive courses to train staff officers and carried out sweeping revisions of the military manuals. Lack of experienced officers had been felt acutely during the war, and over 4,000 officers, selected from those dismissed in the great purge, were recalled. Among them were Rokossovsky, Rotmistrov, and Tolbukhin, all to become marshals of the Soviet Union, and others for whose services Soviet Russia was to be grateful.

In April the Supreme Soviet approved the budget for 1940, voting an enormous increase in defence expenditure. In the Finnish campaign the Soviet troops had been ill-equipped, unsuitably clothed for mobility in the severe cold, and untrained in use of skis. Red tanks were too thinly armoured to resist Finnish shells. Eighteen months later the Red Army was well equipped for winter warfare and their ski-troops were highly organized and trained. Also armour was developed and the new T-34 was being mass produced to replace the tanks used against the Finns.

Special attention was paid to discipline, which had been a weakness in the Finnish war. No trace of the old idea of equality of officers and men remained. Unquestioning obedience was now exacted. Ranks were restored to NCOs in December 1939 and on 8 May general officers were again granted ranks of major-general, lieutenant-general, colonel-general, and army general, in addition to the highest rank of marshal of the Soviet Union.[26] The professional pride of the Red Army had been hurt and with a tremendous effort the damage done by the purge, by political interference and by complacency was now being repaired.

The Russians had nevertheless derived some feeling of greater security from their territorial gains in Poland and Finland, but in the spring and early summer of 1940 this was destroyed by Hitler's lightning advances. In April, nazi troops occupied Norway and Denmark; in May they invaded the Low Countries and forced the evacuation of the British army at Dunkirk. But most shattering to the Russians was the collapse of France and the German occupation of Paris on 14 June. Although informed that French, like British morale, was low, they had not expected a collapse so prompt and so abysmal. They had heard much about the Maginot Line, and Stalin and the Soviet commanders expected it to be as near impregnable as the Mannerheim Line had been. For the French and especially their army the Russians developed a sudden deep contempt.[27]

Towards Britain after the Dunkirk evacuation Russian feelings were mixed. Mistrust was deep, but it eased slightly when Chamberlain resigned and Churchill became prime minister. The Soviet press was now more factual in its reports on the war in the West and on 5 June it printed Churchill's post-Dunkirk speech. His ringing declaration—'We shall never surrender'—stirred Russian admiration, which grew with the reports of the Battle of Britain and in the subsequent months. Russians were conscious that Britain was alone facing Germany and Italy, who had declared war on 10 June, and their great fear was that Britain might make peace with Germany, freeing Hitler to turn eastwards.[28]

Stalin and Molotov continued, however, to show meticulous care in observing the terms of the pact with Germany. Towards Britain, they maintained a stiff neutrality. Molotov rejected British proposals for a trade agreement and refused to receive Sir Stafford Cripps in Moscow as a special or extraordinary plenipotentiary, but they accepted his appointment as British ambassador.[29]

Meanwhile Stalin showed his alarm over the collapse of France by hurriedly occupying the Baltic states and compelling Rumania to cede both Bessarabia and Bukhovina. Also in June the presidium of the Supreme Soviet decreed new labour laws, imposing an eight-hour working day and a six-day week on all workers with severe penalties for absenteeism. Workers could not move without official sanction and were liable to be drafted. The severity of this *ukaz* awakened Russians further to the gravity of the situation and to the need to increase output.

On 1 August, Molotov reported to the seventh session of the Supreme Soviet and, while reaffirming Soviet neutrality and the importance of the Soviet–German pact, he was less savage in his attacks on British imperialism than in the past. Significantly he stressed now that 'the end of the war is not yet in sight. It is more probable that we are now approaching a new stage in which the war between Germany and Italy on the one side and Britain assisted by the United States on the other will become more intense.' He also reported on Soviet gains of territory which with the resulting increase in Soviet population of twenty-three million people 'greatly augmented the strength of the Soviet Union'.[30] But Stalin recognized that the new population, even though combed by the NKVD, would not be dependable in time of crisis. Meanwhile Soviet efforts to strengthen relations with other countries had only limited success. Yugoslavia alone was to sign a treaty of friendship. Finland, Rumania, and Hungary were already under German influence, Bulgaria vacillated between Germany and Russia and then joined the former.

A brief item appeared in the Soviet press on 24 August, which did not pass unnoticed even in this anxious period. It reported the murder of Trotsky in Mexico City on 21 August. Stalin, who never forgot or forgave an enemy and whose hatred of Trotsky had not dimmed, had finally claimed his victim.[31]

News of the blitz on London and other British cities, which began on 7 September, although reported briefly in the Soviet newspapers, was followed closely by Russians. Sympathy for the British in their time of trial was mingled with pleasure that the Germans were at last suffering setbacks. Underlying these reactions was interest in the bombing of a great city like London, an interest sharpened by foreboding that this might also be the fate of Russian cities.[32]

Relations between the Soviet Union and Germany remained formally correct, but became increasingly strained during 1940. The Russians had occupied the Baltic states and had annexed Bessarabia and Bukhovina without notifying the Germans in advance. Hitler had strong misgivings about the Russians being so near to the Rumanian oilfields which were essential to German war operations and he would not tolerate the Russians in the Balkans. Stalin was alarmed by the growing German threat, especially in the Balkans. A further source of anxiety in Moscow was that German troops had been reliably reported to have been seen in Finland and that German armaments were being sent there in quantity. Then on 27 September a ten-year pact between Germany, Italy, and Japan, but excluding Soviet Russia, was signed in Berlin. Molotov immediately demanded information and was not mollified by the reply that the pact did not affect relations between Germany and the Soviet Union, as it was directed solely against the United States.

In October, Ribbentrop wrote to Stalin, proposing that in view of the impending collapse of Britain, Molotov should visit Berlin to discuss 'a long-term delimitation of mutual interests'.[33] Molotov arrived in Berlin on 12 November and at once found that Hitler and Ribbentrop were concerned only with discussion on how the British Empire should be shared out between the Axis powers. They suggested that Russia should expand southwards into India and the region of the Persian Gulf. But Molotov showed no interest. He was not to be deflected from Russia's immediate interests. He was not in the least awed by Hitler and infuriated him by asking questions and demanding specific answers concerning German plans in Finland, Rumania, Bulgaria, and Turkey. The meetings were inconclusive.[34]

In the first months of 1941 Soviet–German relations continued to be formally correct. On 10 January Molotov and Schulenberg, the German ambassador, signed a pact settling the frontier between the two countries from the Igorka River through Poland to the Baltic Sea. On the following day they signed a further agreement on repatriation and property claims in the Baltic states and on trade. But relations between them were becoming more tense and now they broke into open disagreement. On 1 March 1941 Bulgaria joined the Axis and German troops moved into the country. Molotov at once sent a note to the German ambassador complaining that the German government had violated the security interests of the Soviet Union. Two days later Vyshinsky, now deputy commissar for foreign affairs, informed Bulgaria that the Soviet government disapproved of the decision to admit German troops, on the grounds that it would lead to an extension of the sphere of war.[35] Next Hitler demanded that Yugoslavia should join the Axis and the Belgrade government agreed. But on 27 March a successful revolt against the country becoming a German puppet state resulted in the formation of a new government, which looked to Moscow for support. On 5 April Stalin and Molotov signed a pact of friendship and non-aggression with the new Yugoslav regime. A few hours later the German army invaded the country and Belgrade was mercilessly bombed. The Soviet government had concluded a non-aggression, not a mutual assistance pact, and was in any case in no position to help. But the Yugoslavs, resisting bravely, inadvertently helped the Russians, for the fighting in Yugoslavia caused Hitler to postpone his invasion of Russia from 15 May until 22 June.

Stalin and Molotov derived some comfort from a Soviet–Japanese non-aggression pact, signed in Moscow on 13 April. The Japanese were planning to strike at Singapore, while Britain was engaged against the Axis powers. They were anxious, nevertheless, to ensure Russia's neutrality. Stalin was quick to seize on this guarantee that he would not be involved in war simultaneously in the west and east.

Tension in Moscow was mounting. On May Day the traditional military parade in the Red Square was marked by the appearance of new equipment, especially motorized units and the new T-34 tanks. Such displays were intended to maintain popular morale and to warn any potential enemy. Stalin and the high command knew, however, that the Red Army was still far from ready to face the *Wehrmacht*. On 5 May Stalin addressed an assembly of hundreds of young officers, newly graduated from the military academies. He spoke frankly of shortages of equipment and inadequate training of troops. The Soviet government would, he said, use every means to delay the German attack until the autumn, for this would in effect postpone it until 1942 and by then the Red Army would be better prepared. In fact, he stressed that the war would 'almost inevitably' be fought in 1942.[36]

The flight of Hitler's deputy, Rudolf Hess, to Scotland on 10–11 May gave rise to anxious speculation about the possibility of Britain and Germany making terms which could only be at the expense of Russia. Suspicion of the West and particularly Britain, while sometimes dormant, was usually active and never extinguished.

Stalin now concentrated on appeasing Hitler so that he would hold off his invasion. Although neutral he ostentatiously closed down Soviet embassies and consulates in German-occupied countries, such as Belgium, Greece, and Yugoslavia. He issued through TASS denials of reports of disagreements between the Soviet Union and Germany.[37] He rushed deliveries of valuable raw materials to Germany under the terms of the trade agreement of 11 January. Of particular importance were deliveries of 2 million tons of petroleum products, 140,000 tons of manganese, and 26,000 tons of chromium. But the German government made no response to these gestures of goodwill. Finally on 13 July, exactly eight weeks before the German invasion, TASS issued a statement which assured Russians and the world that rumours of discord between the Soviet Union and Germany were without foundation, that German troop movements had, 'it must be assumed', no bearing on Soviet–German relations, and that '...rumours that the U.S.S.R. is preparing for war with Germany are lies and provocations'.[38] The *communiqué* was evidently a final desperate attempt to appease Hitler and a reflection of what Stalin himself wanted to believe. But Hitler had already decided to attack and gestures of this kind made no impression on him.

At dawn on 22 June Schulenberg, the German ambassador, went to the Kremlin and read out to Molotov the text of the document he had just received by telegram from Berlin. Molotov listened silently to the crude allegations which Ribbentrop had included in the statement. Usually so unemotional and stolid, Molotov listened to the end and then quietly but with all the bitterness which the Russian people were to feel he said: 'This is war. Do you believe that we deserved that?'[39]

CHAPTER EIGHTEEN

The War: The Time of Disaster
June 1941–November 1942

AT 4 a.m. on 22 June 1941 the German invasion of Soviet Russia began along a front some 1,500 miles in length. The sixteen months that followed were to be for the Germans a period of tremendous gains; for the Russians they were months of humiliating defeats and of appalling tragedies and devastation, the fruits of monstrous miscalculation and mismanagement.

For the invasion the Germans had concentrated between 3 and 5 million officers and men, 32,000 guns, 9,000 tanks, and 5,000 aircraft. This force advanced in three main groups. Army Group North moved from the region of Koenigsberg through the Baltic states towards Leningrad. Army Group Centre advanced from the frontiers of Belorussia, north of the Pripet Marshes, in the direction of Moscow. Army Group South, supported by Rumanian divisions, surged into the Ukraine from positions along a line from Lublin down almost to the mouth of the Danube. In the far north from Petsamo to the Gulf of Finland, four German divisions supported the Finnish army in advancing east into Soviet Karelia and south towards Leningrad.

The immediate objectives of Hitler and the High Command were to take Leningrad, to destroy the Red Army west of the Dnieper in the northern theatre, and to occupy the Ukraine. In the first stage the German armies were to advance to the line of Leningrad–Orsha–Dnieper and then consider further operations. But so swift was their progress that they had no time to pause. By the end of July, Leningrad seemed about to fall; Smolensk had been taken and the way was open to attack Moscow; in the south Zhitomir had fallen and Kiev was soon to follow. Soviet Russia seemed about to collapse as ignominiously as France in June of the previous year.

The unreadiness of the Red Army and the Russian failure to take obvious precautions were among the most extraordinary and costly mistakes of the war. Stalin was primarily responsible. He had refused in the face of the strongest evidence and of repeated warnings to accept that the German invasion was at hand. He knew that the Soviet armed forces were not strong enough in 1941 to withstand the onslaught of the *Wehrmacht*. He calculated that the Red Army would be ready in 1942 and he gambled on

319

NORTHERN
FRONT

L. Onega

Olonetz

Vyborg   L. Ladoga

Helsingfors

Hango   Gulf of Finland   Leningrad   Tikhvin

Stockholm

Tallinn

Lake
Chudskoe   Novgorod

Pskov   Starayay
Russa

Kalini

NORTH
WESTERN
FRONT   Riga   Volokolamsk

BALTIC
SEA   R. Dvina   Vitebsk   Vyazma

Kovno   Smolensk   M

Danzig   Königsberg   Vilna   Orsha   Kaluga

ARMY GROUP
NORTH   Grodno   Minsk   T

Belostok   Bryansk   Orel

WESTERN FRONT   Starodub

Warsaw   Brest   Gomel   Ku

Vistula   Litovsk

ARMY GROUP   Pinsk   Mozyr

CENTRE   Sumy   Bielgo

Lublin   Lutsk

Cracow   Rovno   Kiev   Kha

Lvov   Zhitomir   Khar

ARMY GROUP   SOUTH   Kremenchug

SOUTH   WESTERN   Vinnitsa

FRONT

Kirovograd
Dniepropetrovsk

Krivoi Rog   Dnieper   Zap

SOUTHERN   Nikolaev   Melitop

FRONT

Odessa   Kherson

R. Danube   Simferopol   Feodo

Sevastopol

BLACK   SEA

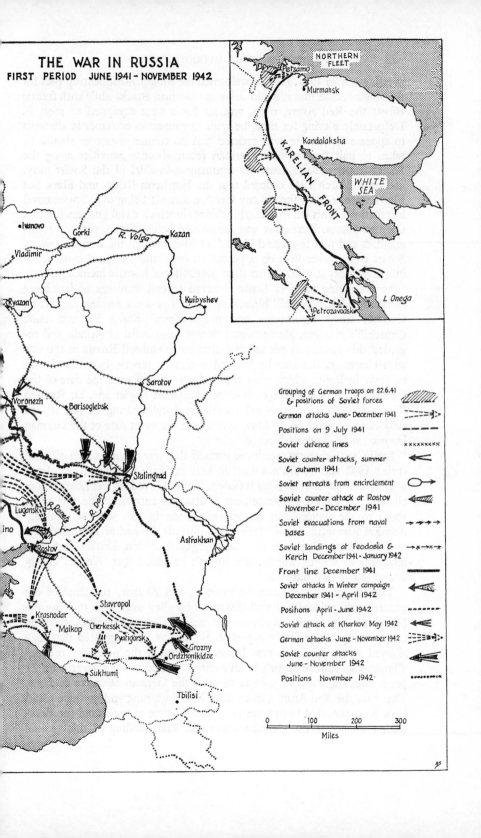

THE WAR IN RUSSIA
FIRST PERIOD   JUNE 1941 – NOVEMBER 1942

NORTHERN FLEET

Petsamo

Murmansk

Kandalaksha

WHITE SEA

KARELIAN FRONT

L. Onega

Petrozavodsk

Ivanovo

Gorki

R. Volga

Kazan

Vladimir

Ryazan

Kuibyshev

Saratov

Voronezh

Borisoglebsk

Stalingrad

Lugansk

R. Donets

R. Don

ino

Rostov

Astrakhan

Stavropol

Krasnodar

Maikop

Cherkessk

Pyatigorsk

Grozny

Ordzhonikidze

Sukhumi

Tbilisi

Grouping of German troops on 22.6.41 & positions of Soviet forces	
German attacks June–December 1941	
Positions on 9 July 1941	
Soviet defence lines	
Soviet counter attacks, summer & autumn 1941	
Soviet retreats from encirclement	
Soviet counter attack at Rostov November–December 1941	
Soviet evacuations from naval bases	
Soviet landings at Feodosia & Kerch December 1941–January 1942	
Front line December 1941	
Soviet attacks in Winter campaign December 1941–April 1942	
Positions April–June 1942	
Soviet attack at Kharkov May 1942	
German attacks June–November 1942	
Soviet counter attacks June–November 1942	
Positions November 1942	

0   100   200   300

Miles

averting war in 1941. He had welcomed the Molotov–Ribbentrop pact for the single reason that it might delay the German attack, while with frantic efforts the Red Army, navy, and air force were equipped to meet it. Desperately playing for time, he went to dangerous extremes in attempts to appease Hitler. He even ordered that no counter-measures should be taken to halt the intensive German reconnaissance activities along the Soviet frontier. Kuznetsov, the commander-in-chief of the Soviet navy, had on 3 March 1941 ordered that the Northern, Baltic, and Black Sea Fleets were to open fire on any German aircraft flying over Soviet naval installations. This led to several incidents in which naval gunners fired on German planes. Kuznetsov was summoned before Stalin, severely reprimanded, and told to rescind his order.[1] Moreover, in the frontier regions Soviet troops were kept on a peacetime basis and stationed some miles inland in order to avert the smallest possibility of frontier incidents.

In the spring of 1941 Stalin received several warnings of imminent German attack. Churchill himself sent him a personal message, reporting German troop movements and preparations.[2] Stalin brushed aside Churchill's message. He remained deeply mistrustful of Britain and regarded this gesture as yet another attempt to embroil Russia in the war with Germany. But also he ignored numerous reports from the Soviet embassy in Berlin which were conclusive and even gave the date of the German invasion.[3] Intelligence reports from the Soviet spy, Dr Richard Sorge, in Japan, over several months and culminating in the report, radioed to Moscow on 15 May, which gave the exact date of the German invasion were similarly ignored.[4]

Stalin had evidently convinced himself that war could be held off until spring 1942 and he did not want to hear evidence to the contrary. Even after Hitler had launched his invasion, Stalin delayed several hours before allowing an official announcement of Russia's entry into the war to be made to the nation. But he was not alone in this wishful thinking. Admiral Kuznetsov has recorded that towards the end of 1940 Zhdanov told him that Germany was fully engaged against Britain and 'was incapable of waging war on two fronts'; he added that 'We can calmly attend to our own business'.[5]

Timoshenko, the commander-in-chief, and Zhukov, the chief of the general staff, evidently shared this view, for they were slow to bring the Soviet forces to combat readiness and even to alert commanders when the German attack was firmly expected. Kuznetsov has suggested that they allowed eleven hours to pass before they issued the necessary orders.[6] Timoshenko sent telegrams to all military commands at midnight on 21 June, directing them to prepare to meet the German offensive at dawn. This gave the Red Army a mere three hours' warning and no force could have been expected to prepare in so short a time to withstand the devastating impact of the German onslaught. The wording of this general order also suggested that even in these last critical hours Stalin and the High Command were still hoping to avert the attack.[7]

Stalin, Zhdanov, and the High Command were in some degree the victims of their own propaganda. This had induced in the nation an outlook of self-deception and false optimism, ill-equipping them to face such an enemy as nazi Germany. The essence of this propaganda was the might of the Red Army and the principle that any attack on the Soviet Union would end with the complete rout of the enemy on his own territory. Thus the *Draft Field Regulations of 1939* stated that:

> 'The Soviet Union will meet any enemy attack by a smashing blow with all the might of its armed forces.
>
> 'If any enemy inflicts war upon us, our Workers' and Peasants' Red army will be the most fiercely-attacking army the world has ever known.
>
> 'The military activity of the Red army will aim at the complete destruction of the enemy and the achievement of a decisive victory at a small cost in blood.'[8]

Soviet strategy laid all emphasis on offensive warfare. Defence played a subsidiary role and little attention was given to retreat or to the possibility of large forces having to break out of encirclement. The traditional Russian strategy of retreating into the depth of the country and then striking at the enemy, as Peter the Great had done at Poltava, was not considered, but was to be forced on the Red Army in this war and then at terrible cost.

The Red Army was the pride of the nation and Russians were encouraged to believe that it was invincible. When it suffered devastating defeats at the hands of the Germans, the nation was shocked and bewildered. But the Red Army had been seriously weakened by the purge, especially of officers, and, while much had been done, it was still inadequately trained and equipped for modern *blitzkrieg* warfare. The official Soviet view was that at the time of the German invasion Soviet industry 'was able ... to supply all necessary equipment for the army to create reserves to replace losses and to provide new formations with equipment once the war had begun. All this, together with vast raw material resources, meant that economically the Soviet Union was prepared to repel fascist aggression.'[9] But, while budget allocations for defence had been increased and the planned capacity and output of the armament industries stepped up, the results were disappointing. New models of aircraft and tanks were slow to reach production and then were produced in small quantities. Of the old type tanks in service seventy-three per cent were in need of repairs.[10] The production of guns, mortars, and automatic rifles was grossly inadequate. Another serious shortage was in trucks and lorries; horses and farm tractors had to be used frequently to draw guns.[11] But in artillery, which had been a Russian speciality since

Peter the Great had created the first modern Russian army, the Russians claimed superiority. The rocket mortars, known as *katyusha* mortars, were being produced in quantity at the beginning of the war and were to have a devastating effect. Nevertheless, shortages and obsolescence of equipment in service were to cost hundreds of thousands of Russian lives and to bring the nation close to defeat.

According to Russian sources the Germans had a numerical superiority of four or even five to one, and at the time of the invasion German officers and soldiers were certainly better trained and more experienced.[12] Many Soviet troops were raw conscripts. Tank crews had often had as little as one-and-a-half or two hours' experience in tanks before going to the front. Pilots in the Red air force with fifteen hours' and some with only four hours' flying experience were posted to operational squadrons.[13]

The official Soviet history of the war, examining the state of the Red forces and Soviet defences in June 1941, concluded that sound plans had been made by the general staff, but that they had been carried out 'too slowly and too late'. The further judgement was that the commissariat for defence and the general staff would not have acted so incompetently 'if there had not been the unjustified repression of the leading commanding and political cadres of the army in the 1937–8 purge'.[14]

At 7.15 on the morning of 22 June the Soviet High Command sent out its first operational order. It avoided the word 'war' and referred to 'unprecedented aggression'. It instructed troops to resist the invader, but specified that 'unless given special authorization, troops will not cross the frontier'.[15] By the time this order was received at the fronts, the Red armies were already in full retreat. Many Soviet defence posts received neither the midnight alert nor this first operational order. German Army Group Centre intercepted frantic Russian signals, requesting instructions. One signal read: 'We are being fired on. What shall we do?' The reply from the local army command was 'You must be insane. And why is your signal not in code?'[16]

The Germans had achieved complete tactical surprise along the whole front. They took full advantage of the resulting chaos. They caught Soviet troops in their camps and barracks, and even in their beds. They found field fortifications uncompleted or unmanned, and easily took and destroyed them. The Red air force, its aircraft caught on the ground, lost some 2,000 planes in two days. The *Luftwaffe* had complete mastery of the air and its planes bombed and machine-gunned Soviet troops incessantly, preventing belated and desperate attempts to organize resistance. The only temporary halts to the German advance were caused by the groups of Red Army men who resisted with suicidal bravery. But among the Russians, attacked by German planes and overrun by this relentless destructive advance, many were seized by panic and tried to flee. During these first days of the war hundreds of thousands of Russians were killed; the total number will never be known.

In Moscow and throughout the country the people waited anxiously for news and guidance. Molotov broadcast an official pronouncement, explaining the position, stressing the peaceful policies pursued by the Soviet government and denouncing the perfidy of Hitler and the nazis. He spoke of the great patriotic war of 1812 when Russians had united to destroy the invader and expressed faith in the Russian people's ability to smash the German invader. On the evening of 22 June Churchill's broadcast with its forthright honesty and its assertion that Britain would never make terms with Hitler, but would support Russia and all who opposed the nazis, gave the Russians some encouragement. But above all else they were awaiting evidence that they had a leader. In national crises in the past Russia had rallied to the tsar in the faith that he would lead the nation to safety, and they desperately needed such a leader now.

For twelve days Stalin waited. He may have been stunned by the suddenness of the German attack which he had persuaded himself would not happen yet; he may also have been appalled by the ordeal which now faced the nation. But when on 3 July he broadcast to the nation, he spoke as the leader they had been awaiting. Russians everywhere and especially in the armed forces felt, as they listened, an 'enormous enthusiasm and patriotic uplift...' General I. I. Fedyuninsky who was to play a distinguished role on several fronts, wrote that 'We suddenly seemed to feel much stronger.' [17]

With a profound instinct and feeling for the mood and needs of the people, Stalin spoke to them sincerely and forthrightly of their predicament. His opening words—'Comrades, citizens, brothers, and sisters, fighters of our army and navy! I am speaking to you, my friends!'—were so different from his usual words of address and at once united him with them. He explained the position and dwelt on the unexpectedness and perfidy of the German onslaught. He rallied them by stating bluntly that they were now engaged in a life-and-death struggle against a cruel enemy and that there could be 'no room in our ranks for whimperers and cowards, for panic-mongers and deserters; our people should be fearless in their struggle and should selflessly fight our patriotic war of liberation against the fascist invaders...'.[18] He ordered retreating troops and civilians to leave the earth scorched and spoke of the newly formed state defence committee in which all power and authority of the state were vested. His speech was not eloquent but entirely apt, and it rooted him in the hearts and minds of the Russian people as the great national leader who would bring them through the tremendous ordeal now facing them.

The Russians needed such inspiration and leadership at this stage, for from all fronts came news of disaster. The state defence committee had divided the Soviet forces into three major groups or 'directions', each with its own command. Voroshilov, supported by Zhdanov as the senior party member of the region, commanded the north-western direction. Timoshenko, supported by Bulganin, commanded the western direction.

Budyonny, supported by Khrushchev, commanded the south-western direction. But none of them was able to halt the German advance.

The German Central Army Group, moving from the region of Brest-Litovsk, drove north of the Pripet Marshes along the Smolensk–Moscow line. In a rapid pincer movement the Germans closed on Minsk, which fell on 28 June. Eleven Soviet divisions were trapped. The German command claimed 300,000 prisoners, 3,000 tanks, and 1,800 guns captured.

Red troops resisted strongly at some points. At Borisov, they fought desperately to stem the German advance so that reserves could be brought up and defences organized in depth on the road to Smolensk and to Moscow. But the *Luftwaffe*, holding complete mastery of the air, bombed and machine-gunned the Russians constantly. The death rate was appalling as the Germans rapidly advanced with Guderian, the tank general, leading his panzer divisions in the van.[19]

On 16 July in another pincer movement the Germans closed on Smolensk. Here they met with stubborn opposition and the struggle continued into August. The Russians were now fighting in defence of Moscow. Their morale was higher and they were operating as a front rather than in small unco-ordinated pockets. The Germans were feeling the strain of their headlong advance, and their tanks and equipment had begun to need maintenance and renewal. In the Smolensk fighting, the Russian artillery was used for the first time with full effect, and the *katyusha* rocket mortars proved their worth. At this time, too, Hitler had rejected Guderian's plan for a massive attack on Moscow, spearheaded by his panzer divisions. Guderian was convinced that by keeping up the momentum of the advance, Moscow could be taken. Hitler had decided that the Ukraine and the Crimea should be the immediate objectives. He detached forces to strengthen Army Group South. His decision probably saved Moscow.[20]

In the north the German advance was equally rapid. The plan there was to drive north-east through Pskov and to take Leningrad. The Finns were to advance on the city from the north. By mid-August the Germans had nearly achieved their objective. Pskov fell on 12 July. Another German force took Riga, occupied Latvia and pushed swiftly into Esthonia. Red troops struggled desperately to hold Tallinn, the Esthonian capital and a major Soviet naval base. On 26 August, however, they were driven out and the surviving troops and equipment were evacuated by sea under heavy German air force and torpedo-boat attacks to Leningrad. Yet another German force moved north along the eastern side of Lake Chudskoe (Peipus) to the Baltic coast. Other German detachments were moving eastwards to cut the city off from that side and to join with the Finns who were advancing to Petrozavodsk.

Leningrad was in danger. The city had no fortifications of any kind in the south and south-west. All attention had been concentrated on protecting it from the north and the war against Finland in the winter of

1939–40 had been fought for this purpose. Hurriedly civilians were mobilized to dig trenches and to prepare what defences they could. Battalions of workers, students, and even schoolchildren were formed. By 10 July the Germans had reached the Luga river and Russian defence works were far from complete. But Leningradtsi fought spiritedly in defence of their city for which they had strong pride and affection. They slowed down the German advance, but could not hold it. Inexorably the Germans crossed the Luga and closed on the city. Voroshilov thought all was lost and gave way to panic. Only in September when Zhukov was hurriedly appointed to take over his command were the defences of Leningrad properly organized and the city prepared for its long and heroic resistance.[21]

In the south the German advance was at first held at Lvov and at other points, but only briefly, and then it gathered momentum. One force took Zhitomir and directly threatened Kiev. Another German force, moving farther south, took Dniepropetrovsk and, in spite of the order of the Soviet Supreme Command that the Dnieper Line must be held, crossed the Dnieper. The three important cities of Kherson, Nikolayev, and Krivoi Rog were also captured.

Meanwhile from the north the Germans were striking in the direction of Konotop. Kiev was being isolated at the top of a narrowing salient and in danger of encirclement. Without reserves with which to oppose the two German advances, Budyonny and Khrushchev decided to withdraw to the east. On 11 September they informed Stalin of this intention, but he at once ordered them to stand fast at Kiev and to resist the German advance from the north. He also appointed Timoshenko to take over Budyonny's command. On 13 September Timoshenko arrived in Kiev. Three days later the Germans closed the gap. Four Russian armies were encircled. They had already suffered heavy losses and in the struggle to break out of the encirclement many thousands more were killed or taken prisoner. It was the most crushing defeat that the Red Army had yet suffered.[22]

The state defence committee had been vested with supreme power in mobilizing all resources of the country and it had at once set about organizing the economy and the industry of the nation as well as its armed forces to wage war to the end. On 16 July it revived the military commissars. One reason for this measure was probably fear of conflict between the army and the party, especially as Rokossovsky, Tolbukhin, and others who had suffered in the great purge might be anti-party at heart. But another and a more important reason for reviving the military commissars was that in the first weeks of the war many units had shown panic and had fled before the enemy. The commissars had the special task of strengthening morale and arousing the fighting spirit of the troops. But neither reason had real validity at this time of national crisis. The strong force of patriotism and the need to defend their country and their homes against a cruel and arrogant enemy far outweighed any thoughts of party.

The same factors and, under the stress of war, the emergence of real leadership in the armed forces forged a morale which drew strength from hardships and was to carry the Red Army to Berlin. Military commissars and the system of dual command were abolished in the autumn of 1942.

The NKVD maintained 'rear security units' armed with automatic weapons to halt any panic flights by troops. The NKVD had been responsible for the frontier guards who had borne the first impact of the invasion and NKVD units were to fight alongside the Red Army in several desperate engagements. The NKVD also took charge of Russian prisoners who escaped from the Germans and detachments which had broken through an encirclement. Such officers and men were treated as suspects, disarmed and interrogated, and then often posted to particularly dangerous parts of the front where they could prove themselves afresh or die. As time passed, the Red Army with the strong confidence of fighting and maintaining its own discipline became the more intolerant of NKVD interference. Security police continued to be present, but they interfered less and their activities tended to be concentrated more in the rear of the army.

Stalin himself evidently accepted this development and the army's impatience of political interference. He had undoubtedly recognized that the great purge had seriously damaged the Red Army and had imperilled the regime. He had learnt a lesson and was now quick to replace the political generals and old civil war leaders, like Voroshilov and Budyonny, with professional soldiers. Timoshenko, Shaposhnikov, and Zhukov proved their worth in these testing months, but others failed and passed into obscurity.

The summer and autumn of 1941 were, in fact, a proving time for Soviet commanders. The desperate struggle in retreat from the ruthless efficiency of the German war machine showed up the commanders who were incompetent and lacking in leadership. But these terrible set-backs and defeats also brought forward a number of extremely able commanders who were to save the Red Army and the nation from collapse and were then to lead Russia to victory.[23]

On 20 July Stalin became commissar for defence with Timoshenko as assistant commissar, and on 7 August he was proclaimed commander-in-chief of the Russian forces. The Stavka, the general headquarters of the Soviet High Command, which had been set up on 23 June, a week before the state defence committee, became on 10 July the Stavka of the Supreme Command. Initially it comprised Stalin, Molotov, Voroshilov, Budyonny, Shaposhnikov, and the chief of staff, Zhukov, but soon it was to be expanded to include the senior commanders of all arms of the fighting forces. Its function was to advise the state defence committee and it produced most of the major operational plans. The existing general staffs of the Red Army, navy and air force worked to the Stavka and translated its directions into action. Another separate command, set up in August, was the chief of the rear areas, with responsibility for ensuring the best use of transport and supplies throughout the country.

Stalin had in his speech of 3 July also referred to the *opolchenie* and the partisan units which were already being formed. The *opolcheniya* were levies of citizens and, going back through Russia's history, levies of nobles and gentry with their serfs in time of national crisis. *Opolcheniya* had been formed to expel the Poles from Muscovy at the beginning of the seventeenth century, in 1812 to expel the French, and at other times. The *opolchenie* expressed the resistance of the people when the nation stood in danger. In Moscow, Leningrad, Kiev, and other cities the workers and other citizens now formed *opolcheniya* in support of the Red Army, but in Leningrad the volunteers were more numerous and zealous than in Moscow and even more than in Kiev, where morale and support for the Soviet system were lower. But barely trained and inadequately equipped these units could not stand for long against the highly mechanized German forces.

The Society for Furthering Defence, Aviation, and Chemical Warfare, known as Osoaviakhim, also came under pressure in this time of crisis. This society had been founded in 1927 for the military training of civilians. Its activities had expanded rapidly until it had developed some 3,500 driving and maintenance centres and numerous air training centres. The air force relied on it to train a reserve of pilots and aircrews. The state defence committee made the organization responsible for training all male citizens between the ages of 16 and 60 and women between 18 and 50 in civil defence groups and especially in anti-aircraft and anti-gas defences. Stalin also ordered the formation of partisan units in all occupied territories where they would harry the enemy, setting fire to forests, destroying telephone and telegraph installations, blowing up bridges and mining roads.

On 2 October 1941 Hitler issued an Order of the Day to the German troops facing Moscow: 'Today is the beginning of the last great decisive battle of this year.' The German offensive had, in fact, already begun with Guderian on the southern flank of Army Group Centre, leading his panzer divisions towards Tula. On 2 October he took Orel, but then he was held up by Russian tanks.

Meanwhile from the region south of Smolensk a strong German force and another from the region of Vyazma moved on Moscow. Soviet troops were concentrated opposite these regions in anticipation of the two-pronged onslaught. The German command had planned to encircle these Red troops, while their panzer and mechanized divisions swept round against Moscow. But the four Red Armies fought desperately for over a week, holding the German infantry and tank divisions, although at fearful cost. The Russians were thus able to extricate many of their troops from the encirclement and to dig them into fortified positions on a line running from Kalinin in the north through Kaluga to Tula. But on 12 October the

Germans took Kaluga and, still more dangerous, they captured Kalinin two days later. Fierce fighting raged south of Kalinin in the Volokolamsk sector, only fifty miles north-west of Moscow, and the Russians were slowly being forced back on the capital.

The fall of Moscow now seemed inevitable. Already on 12–13 October the state defence committee had ordered the evacuation of many commissariats and government offices and the whole diplomatic corps, as well as armament industries and scientific and cultural organizations. All were sent without delay to Kuibyshev and farther to the east beyond the Volga river. By the end of the month some two million people had been removed from the city.

Air raids on Moscow had begun in July and had continued through August. Anti-aircraft guns, arranged densely in three circles around the city, put up a formidable barrage. Ten or fifteen planes out of 200 managed to get through in the first raid. The few incendiaries and high explosive bombs dropped on this and subsequent raids caused little damage. In fact, the Germans, confident that they would soon take Moscow, did not press their air raids. But within the city the people, lacking adequate first aid facilities, short of food and without heating as winter came upon them, waited grimly for heavy raids. The fact that the Germans were inexorably closing on the city gave rise to feelings of desperation.

News of hasty evacuations, the stringent air raid precautions, and press reports of continuing disasters and the falling back of Red troops on the western front suddenly reduced Moscow to a state of panic. Red troops continued to fight stubbornly and they were managing to stem the German onslaught. But within the city fear of German occupation turned into a panic which gripped thousands from the humble citizen to the high party and government officials. People stampeded at the railway station to catch any train to the east. Officials fled in cars without the permits needed to leave their places of work and residence. The majority of the population was suddenly completely demoralized. The minority remained, grimly determined to fight to the end.

This *bolshoi drap* or great panic reached a climax on 16 October. On the following day, Shcherbakov, secretary of the central committee, broadcast that Stalin himself was in Moscow and that the position of the capital was critical, but he sternly denounced rumours that the surrender of the city was imminent. On 19 October a state of siege was proclaimed. The commandant of the city and his NKVD forces were empowered to set up tribunals for the summary trial and execution of spies, diversionists, and those who gave way to panic. The fact of Stalin's presence in the city and the stern measures taken in the state of siege helped to restore order. But also the German advance had begun to slow down.[24]

Casualties had been extremely heavy on both sides in this battle for Moscow. The Germans were amazed by the number of trained reserves brought forward in new formations during the fighting. The resilience of the Red Army took them by surprise. Moreover, they found that they could no longer easily rout the Russian forces as in the first weeks of the war. They were meeting with more savage and stubborn resistance. Reports of the brutality of the Germans in their treatment of prisoners and in occupied territory were beginning to be known among Russian troops and added a new ruthlessness to their fighting. The Germans themselves were also suffering from exhaustion and finding difficulty in keeping their armies supplied. The roads were not yet frozen over, but muddy, and motorized units were constantly bogged down so that supplies and munitions were slow in reaching their fronts. They needed vehicles with tracks rather than wheels. Meanwhile Guderian's panzer divisions had to be supplied by special airlifts. But the main factor in bringing the German advance on Moscow to a halt was the hardening resistance of the Russians themselves.

On 6 November during the lull in the German offensive, the twenty-fourth anniversary of the revolution was celebrated. It took place underground this year in the marbled Mayakovsky station of the Moscow Metro. Hundreds of delegates managed to attend as well as representatives of party organizations and of the armed forces.

Stalin spoke. The Russians had, he said, lost 350,000 killed, 378,000 missing, and 1,020,000 wounded; the Germans had lost $4\frac{1}{2}$ million in dead, wounded, and prisoners. Russian casualties had certainly been greater and German casualties smaller. But even allowing for distortions, the figures were awe-inspiring and impressed with the tremendous scale and cruel destruction of this struggle.

Without passing over the grim losses and devastation suffered by Russia or the savage struggle lying ahead, Stalin expressed supreme confidence in ultimate victory. The Germans had counted on the Soviet regime collapsing and on Britain and the U.S.A. joining them against Russia, or at least standing aside, while they concentrated on the war against Russia. They had been wrong on both counts. But Stalin then turned to the absence of British and American forces on the European mainland which was undoubtedly helping the Germans. This was to be the beginning of the Soviet propaganda for a second front which was to mount in intensity both as a reflection of desperation, as the Red Army was forced to retreat, and as an excuse for the failure to hold the German advance. It was to poison relations with Britain for a time and to a lesser extent with the U.S.A.

The other disability to which Stalin referred was the German superiority in tanks and aircraft. The Russians had been fighting with obsolete tanks and planes. The new Soviet T-34 tanks and the Mig fighters were better than the German equivalents, but owing to the massive evacuation of industry to the east, production was still grossly inadequate. More tanks, aircraft, and other equipment had to be produced without delay if the country was to survive.

German arrogance, the strident and humiliating *Ubermensch* propaganda, and the savage and often bestial treatment of Slav peoples taken prisoner and in occupied territories, had incensed all Russians. Stalin referred to the nazi claims of racial superiority with angry scorn. He proclaimed the greatness of Russia in words which aroused the patriotism of every civilian and every soldier.

'And it is these people without honour or conscience, these people with the morality of animals, who have the effrontery to call for the extermination of the great Russian nation—the nation of Plekhanov and Lenin, of Belinsky and Chernyshevsky, of Pushkin and Tolstoy, of Gorki and Chekhov, of Glinka and Chaikovsky, of Sechenov and Pavlov, of Repin and Sigrikov, of Suvorov and Kutuzov! The German invaders want a war of extermination against the peoples of the Soviet Union. Very well then! If they want a war of extermination, they shall have it! Our task now . . . will be to destroy every German, to the very last man who has come to occupy our country. No mercy for the German invaders! Death to the German invaders!'[25]

On the following morning Stalin reviewed the now traditional parade on the Red Square. But the troops whom he addressed were on their way to the front. The distant rumble of guns was the background to his speech, lending his words a dramatic immediacy. Again he appealed to the patriotism of the people; they were fighting now not for socialism or the proletariat of the world but for Russia and home. The enemy was at the gates of Moscow, the matrix of ancient Muscovy and the centre of Russia.

'The war which you are fighting [he said] is a war of liberation, a just war! May you be inspired in this war by the heroic examples of our great ancestors—Alexander Nevsky, Dmitri Donskoi, Kuzma Minin, Dmitri Pozharsky, Alexander Suvorov, Mikhail Kutuzov! May the victorious banner of the great Lenin be over you! Death to the German invaders! Long live our glorious country, its freedom, its independence! Under the banner of Lenin—forward to victory!'[26]

Reports of the two speeches circulated rapidly among the troops. Soviet aircraft dropped copies in occupied territory. Every Russian read them avidly. Stalin's two speeches, in fact, brought a dramatic and extraordinary rise in morale and in the fighting spirit of Red troops. Moscow stood as firmly as a rock and Moscow was the heart of Russia. All accounts of this period by Russians and by foreign observers confirm both the upsurge of national feeling and the veneration of Stalin as the national leader. He himself had from the days of the revolution and even earlier thought of himself as a Great Russian and had championed the nationalist policy against the internationalism of Lenin, Trotsky, and other old bolsheviks. Far from appealing to the pride and love of Russians for their country as an expedient to ensure survival of the regime, he spoke from the depth of his own being: to him, as to all Russians, Moscow was *Matushka Moskva* and the Soviet Union was Holy Russia.[27]

The British and American declarations of support for Soviet Russia, to which Stalin had made warm reference in his speech of 6 November, were followed up quickly with offers of help. A British military mission flew to Moscow. Stalin and Molotov discussed with Stafford Cripps, the British ambassador, the terms of an Anglo-Soviet declaration. When Stalin finally wrote to Churchill in response to the broadcast speech of 22 June, he proposed the prompt opening of a second front. To Churchill this was unrealistic and he proposed basing fighter squadrons near Murmansk and naval operations in the Arctic. A few days later Churchill again wrote to Stalin, informing him of the 200 aircraft and other supplies soon to be shipped to Russia. But Stalin's reaction was and continued to be to demand more. His attitude was that Russia was now fighting the war and Britain, her only ally at this stage, must help. Underlying his dealings with Churchill, too, was suspicion of Britain and the mistrust that never really diminished that Britain would save her men and arms and leave it to Russia to fight.[28]

The question on the minds of both Churchill and Roosevelt at this time was how long Russia could stave off defeat. British military opinion was that Russia would be crushed. General Mason Macfarlane, head of the British military mission in Russia, considered, however, that Russia would survive. The U.S. military attaché in Moscow expected an early collapse. Against the background of conflicting views, Roosevelt sent Harry Hopkins as his personal representative to confer with Stalin on U.S. aid. The real purpose of the visit was to enable him to form his own impressions and to report directly to the president. Harry Hopkins arrived in Moscow on 30 July and his reports on his four-day visit were to be of real significance in the development of both U.S. and British relations with Russia.

In the course of their meetings Hopkins was strongly impressed by Stalin as a man and a national leader.[29] Stalin's realistic survey of the military situation and of the kind of aid which he required confirmed Hopkins in the view that Russia would not fail. 'Give us anti-aircraft guns and aluminium and we can fight for three or four years,' Stalin said, and Hopkins saw in this and other requests the determination of a man planning a long war.[30]

On the basis of the Hopkins' report, Churchill and Roosevelt proposed a meeting in Moscow to consider 'apportionment of our joint resources'. Lord Beaverbrook, appointed by Churchill, and Averell Harriman, appointed by Roosevelt, began their meetings in Moscow towards the end of September when the battle of Moscow was mounting to a grim crisis. The conference discusions were cordial, and Russian demands for military equipment, machinery, and raw materials were almost totally agreed. Beaverbrook played a dominant part in this conference and, as an ardent supporter of unlimited aid to Russia, he was warmly received by Stalin and Molotov. The Russians were reassured and gratified by the prospect of massive help from the U.S.A. and from Britain.[31]

Britain and Russia had co-operated in August in the joint occupation of Iran. The Shah was pro-German and the allied fear was that Hitler would seek to use Iran as a base from which to attack Russia. The occupation was important also because it ensured the supply route from the Persian Gulf to the Caspian Sea. But Anglo-Soviet relations did not remain cordial. Churchill was, for instance, unwilling to declare war on Finland or on Hungary and Rumania all of whom were now at war with Russia. The agreement between Russia and the Polish government in exile, signed by Maisky and Sikorski in London on 30 July, was also to give rise to difficulties. Meanwhile, as a direct result of the Beaverbrook–Harriman discussions, Churchill informed Stalin on 6 October of two convoys, carrying much needed planes and tanks, to arrive in Archangel on 12 and 29 October respectively, and on 6 November a U.S. loan to the U.S.S.R. of $1,000 million free of interest to finance lease–lend supplies was announced.

The first German offensive against Moscow had come to a halt before the end of October. Frantic preparations had begun at once for a second offensive. In the ten days before this new offensive was launched the Russians feverishly strengthened their positions and massed reserves behind the city. Also Zhukov was on 24 October given command of the northern front, including Moscow. Timoshenko commanded the southern front. Voroshilov and Budyonny were made responsible for organizing reserves in the rear.

The fact that the city had not fallen in the first offensive and the tremendous influence of Stalin's speeches on the anniversary of the revolution had raised morale. All recognized that a bitter struggle lay ahead, but there was general confidence that Moscow would be held. Moreover, the evacuation had reduced the population of the city and its industries by more than half, as though clearing it for action.

The German onslaught was directed first to the north-west of Moscow in the Kalinin–Volokolamsk sector of the front. Here the Germans had superiority in tanks and guns. They broke through to Klin to the north and to Istra, only fifteen miles to the west of Moscow. Russian resistance was fierce and marked by countless heroic incidents. The twenty-eight men of Panfilov's anti-tank unit, who destroyed eighteen German tanks on the Volokolamsk road and who died to a man, the last survivor holding grenades and throwing himself under a tank to blow it up, were the stuff of legends and were typical of Russian resistance.

Fighting was equally desperate to the south-west of Moscow. Here the immediate German objective was the old industrial city of Tula which stood in a narrow salient and was in danger of being encircled. Guderian and his panzer group had on 22 November failed in an attempt to seize

Georgi Maximilianovich Malenkov

Marshal Rodion Jakovlevich Malinovsky, 1957

Tula. He persevered now in trying to encircle the city. On 3 December he succeeded, but the Russians rallied and cleared the road to Moscow. Guderian continued to attack but, stoutly defended, Tula survived.

By the end of November, the German offensive had begun to weaken. The troops were oppressed by the cold and, unlike the Russians, they were ill-equipped for winter warfare, having only summer uniforms, greatcoats and blankets.[32] Hundreds of Germans became incapacitated from frostbite. Morale began to fail. The new Russian T-34 tank, now appearing in greater numbers, were proof against the German 37 mm. tank-guns. German losses were extremely heavy, amounting to 55,000 dead, over 100,000 wounded or frostbitten, 777 tanks, 297 guns and mortars, and other equipment.[33] Feelings of despair showed among the Germans for the first time during the Russian campaign.[34]

The Russians, too, had suffered fearful casualties, but with the resilience that so often astonished the Germans they were already preparing a winter counter-offensive. On the Moscow front from Kalinin in the north to Yelets in the south, the Soviet Supreme Command launched its attack on 5–6 December. Progress was at first rapid. German troops gave way to panic in some sectors. Kalinin, Klin, Istra, and Yelets, and then Kaluga and Volokolamsk were liberated. But the winter was severe and both sides were suffering from the cold. The Red troops were handicapped by lack of motor transport and had difficulty in maintaining supplies to their front lines. By mid-January the Germans had nevertheless been pushed back from Moscow in some places a distance of 200 miles. But this was on the northern flank. On the line of Rzhev, Gzhatsk, and Vyazma the Germans stood firm. Hitler had overruled his generals and ordered that this line, extending to Orel and Briansk, should be held. He intended that Vyazma in particular should serve as the centre for a new offensive against Moscow in the spring.

The Soviet Supreme Command had been overambitious in this winter counter-offensive and the Red Army showed that it still lacked the experience of organizing and conducting a large-scale offensive operation.[35] The plan to encircle and destroy the strong German forces between Moscow and Smolensk was unrealistic. Troops were diverted in an attempt to retake Briansk and Orel, when they should have been concentrated against Vyazma. Reserves and supplies of equipment were inadequate for such major objectives and reserves that were available were not deployed effectively. But underlying these disabilities was the fact that the nation was not yet producing armaments on the scale required, and shortages of basic materials had 'reacted badly on the performance of the troops and on the tempo of the offensive, and often prevented their taking advantage of opportunities to destroy strong groups of the enemy'.[36] By the end of March 1942 when the thaw began the Russian advance had come to a halt and a wave of disappointment had

M

spread among the Red troops. Too much had been expected of this winter counter-offensive. The real gains were nevertheless considerable.

The Battle of Moscow had been a titanic struggle. More than 2 million men, 2,500 tanks, 1,800 planes, and 25,000 guns had been involved. Casualties had been terrible. But for the Russians the battle had ended in victory. They had suffered the concentrated impact of German *blitzkrieg* strategy, but had proved able to counter-attack and to push the enemy back at several points. They had begun destroying the myth of German invincibility, which had been growing dangerously among them. Moreover, they had relieved Moscow, which was not only a city of great strategic importance, but the capital and its fall would have had a disastrous effect on the morale of the whole nation.

The armament shortage, which had so gravely hampered Russian resistance and had nearly proved fatal in October 1941, was due not only to German occupation of important industrial regions and sources of power and raw materials, but also to the evacuation eastward of Soviet industry. Within a few days of the beginning of the German offensive the Soviet government had decided that all basic industries must be removed from European Russia to the east. The vulnerability of Soviet industry had long been on the minds of Soviet leaders and under the five-year plans industry had been developing in the east, particularly in the region of the Urals. But now the evacuation of industry had become urgent and vital.

On 4 July the state defence committee directed Gosplan to prepare for the co-ordination of industries already in the east with those to be transplanted there. The move had already begun with the evacuation of the armoured plate mill from Mariupol to Magnitogorsk. The transfer of twenty-six armaments plants from Leningrad, Moscow, and Tula was followed by the move of the Zaporozhie steel mills, an undertaking which required 8,000 railway trucks. The work of dismantling, loading, and transporting went on day and night, and air attacks were not allowed to hinder the work. This effort demanded superhuman labour as was exemplified in the evacuation of the vast tube-rolling mill at Dniepropetrovsk. Its removal started on 9 August and the last trainloads of dismantled plant reached Pervouralsk on 6 September: by 24 December the plant was again in production.

From the end of June until the end of October, 283 large and 136 smaller industrial enterprises were transferred from the Ukraine to the east. Ninety-two industrial works, producing war materials, were evacuated from Leningrad, but then the German blockade halted further transfers. Belorussia was subjected to air bombing and German forces quickly swept over it, but some 100 minor industrial units were got away in time. The removal of industries from Moscow did not start until October, but by the end of November 498 industrial units had been moved to the east. With the factories and plants hundreds of thousands of workers were also transferred to set them up on new sites and to restore production.

The evacuation of 1,523 industrial units, many of them enormous and including 1,360 major armament plants, was a tremendous undertaking and in human terms a magnificent achievement. But many enterprises could not be moved in time and were seized by the Germans or destroyed before withdrawal in accordance with Stalin's scorched-earth policy. In the long term the establishment of these industries in the east enabled Russia to produce the tanks, guns, and other equipment needed to defeat the enemy. In June 1941–2, however, the inevitable drop in production brought the nation near to calamity, especially in the autumn of 1941 and spring of 1942. But by incredible efforts, many transplanted industries were brought into production by the end of 1941. Industrial output began to rise towards the end of the summer of 1942 and then increased rapidly.[37]

The winter offensive which had relieved Moscow had also brought some small relief to Leningrad. Far more than Moscow, Leningrad had endured a tragic ordeal during the autumn and winter of 1941 and 1942, and the people had behaved with greater fortitude. Indeed, their endurance was epic in quality, but at the sacrifice of nearly a million dead, many from starvation. In the history of the war in Russia, in which Russian dead were to amount to the appalling total of 20 to 25 million, the siege of the 3 million people of Leningrad remains as one of its most moving and courageous chapters.

By mid-July the Germans had established a bridgehead on the right bank of the Luga river and poured through the breach in the Luga defence line, some 125 miles from Leningrad. The people came forward in thousands to build defences. By the end of July nearly a million civilians from all walks of life and including schoolchildren were working day and night to build defences for the city. In all they managed to dig 340 miles of anti-tank ditches, 15,875 miles of open trenches, and to erect 400 miles of barbed-wire defences, 190 miles of forest obstacles, mainly of felled trees, and 5,000 wooden or concrete firing points, as well as complex defences within the city.[38]

On 8 August the Germans, now regrouped, launched their offensive. They outflanked the Luga line to the west and east, and advanced in two prongs, one south-east of the city towards Lake Ladoga and the other south-west towards the Gulf of Finland. On 21 August they took Chudovo and on 30 August they took Mga, thus cutting Leningrad's railway communications. Against fierce resistance they reached the south bank of Lake Ladoga and the left bank of the Neva, taking Schlusselburg. To the south-west they broke through to the Gulf of Finland, but the Russians managed to hold a bridgehead at Oranienbaum, opposite Kronstadt. Leningrad was now cut off from the rest of Russia, its only line of communication being the dangerous route across Lake Ladoga.

Voroshilov, Zhdanov, and Popkov, chairman of the Leningrad soviet, were alarmed. On 21 August they proclaimed an appeal to the people to resist to the end, fortified by 'the strictest revolutionary discipline'.[39] But the Leningradtsi stood in no need of such exhortations. Among them, moreover, were many who were angry that the authorities, in particular Voroshilov, Zhdanov, and Popkov, had been so shortsighted, tardy, and incompetent in preparing the city to defend itself. Some were critical of the Red Army for failing to hold the German advance, but lacking equipment and without reserves the troops had fought and continued to fight bravely. Here and at many other points in 1941–2 the mismanagement and unpreparedness were the fault of Stalin, the High Command, and senior officials: their crass bungling was redeemed by the soldiers, workers, and other ordinary citizens, but at an appalling price.

Early in September the Germans began bombarding the city with heavy guns and by air. Fire-watching was quickly reorganized and incendiary bombs were promptly dealt with. But the delayed-action bombs and landmines caused heavy casualties among the civilian volunteers in the early stages. Meanwhile extensive defences had been prepared within the city. 'Factories, bridges, and public buildings were mined and would have blown up at signal; stone and iron wreckage would have crashed down on the heads of enemy soldiers and halted their tanks. The civilian population, not to mention the soldiers and sailors were prepared to fight in the streets. The idea of house-to-house fighting did not simply mean self-sacrifice: its object was to destroy the enemy.'[40]

The Germans, admitting their inability to take Leningrad by storm, now waited to starve the city into surrender. Hitler had ordered that its capitulation should not be accepted, especially as it would present danger of epidemics and would be mined, but it must be 'wiped off the face of the earth'. But Leningrad had no thought of capitulating. Zhukov had replaced the panic-stricken Voroshilov and had reorganized its defences.[41] The front which had been chaotic was stabilized. The Leningradtsi could not be sure, however, that the Germans had abandoned the idea of storming the city. They continued their frantic preparations for resisting the enemy street by street. Every military and naval battery that could be mustered was set up as part of the defences. The guns of the Baltic Fleet were concentrated in its defence, including those of the cruiser *Aurora* which had started the storm of the Winter Palace in 1917.

Leningrad with its population of nearly three million people was under siege. The authorities had not given serious attention to evacuating people to the east until it was too late. In June and early July children had been sent away because of air raids, but they had been sent to places which were directly on the route of the German advance. Hurriedly they were brought back and some of them were moved to the east in time. Workers and their families, some 40,000 in all, went to reassemble and tend industrial plant evacuated to the east. But thousands of old people, invalids, and children, who merely consumed food, had been allowed to remain.[42]

Food reserves were minimal. Popkov sent a telegram to the state defence committee in Moscow on 6 September, just two days before the German blockade closed on the city, stating that little food remained and requesting immediate supplies by rail. As with evacuation of old people and children, all had been left too late. Meanwhile on the basis of the rationing, introduced on 18 July, grain and flour stocks were sufficient for thirty-five days, meat for thirty-three days, fats for forty-five days and sugar for sixty days. But food stocks were further reduced by damage in air raids, and inadequate organization made distribution critically uneven. On 2 September the rations were reduced to twenty-two ounces of bread a day for workers, fourteen ounces for office workers, and eleven ounces for children and dependents. Ten days later the rations were further reduced: they were then below starvation level and winter was approaching.[43]

By the end of September coal and oil supplies were exhausted. Electricity could be used only at staff headquarters at Smolny and certain other key points. Young people formed wood-cutting teams and went to the forests to the north of the city. Here, although suffering from hunger and cold, they built a narrow-gauge line to the nearest railway line, ensuring a supply of timber.

Three times between 1 October and 20 November food rations were further reduced. Deaths from starvation began to mount. 'Death overtook people anywhere. As he walked along the street, a man might fall and not get up. People would go to bed at home and not rise again. Often death would come suddenly as men worked at their machines.' [44] Burial was a problem. The dead were usually dragged on sleds without coffins to the cemetery. Often relatives or close friends, lacking the strength to haul the sled, had to abandon it, leaving to the authorities the rest of the task. At the cemetery people did not have the strength to hack graves in the hard frozen earth. Special squads were given extra rations to bury the dead. In December, 52,881 people died of starvation and still more reached the threshold of death. In January and February the deathrate reached a peak when in sixty days 199,187 people died.[45]

'To fill their empty stomachs and deaden the pains of a hunger which can be compared with nothing else, the inhabitants resorted to all sorts of ways to procure food. They trapped crows and hunted down the surviving dogs and cats. They took anything that could be used as food from their medicine chests: castor oil, vaseline, glycerin. Soup and jelly were prepared from carpenter's glue. But by no means all the people of the vast city had these supplementary sources of nourishment available to them.' [46]

Leningrad's sole lifeline lay across Lake Ladoga. A harbour was built at Osinovets. Tugs and barges at Novaya Ladoga loaded food and munitions brought by rail via Tikhvin from the east and crossed the lake. Autumn gales made the voyage hazardous at any time, but now German aircraft from airfields only twenty-five miles away kept up constant patrols and mercilessly bombed and machine-gunned the little convoys. But with extraordinary courage and fortitude the men of the Ladoga flotilla and the crews of the barges brought important supplies to the city during the autumn of 1941. In quantity the food, amounting to 25,228 tons, represented only twenty days' rations, but every day counted.[47]

By mid-November, however, the lake was no longer navigable. Attempts were made to bring supplies by air, but German planes bombed airfields and attacked Russian air convoys. The survival of the city was further imperilled when on 9 November the Germans took Tikhvin. This was the important railway junction for the transport of supplies to be taken across the lake by the ice road. An alternative route lay from Zaborie to the east of Tikhvin by a road, built through forest along paths frozen solid. This road was completed by early December, but the route was impracticable. All hope depended on the freezing of the surface of the lake to the uniform thickness of two metres. Many lorries were lost because they ventured on the ice too soon. The other important factor was to recapture Tikhvin. On 9 December, fighting with desperate courage, Red troops retook Tikhvin and also Voibokalo. This meant that supplies could eventually be brought by rail from Vologda and Moscow to Voibokalo and thence by lorry over the shorter ice route to Leningrad. Meanwhile, since the Germans had destroyed all railway bridges between Tikhvin and Volkhov, supplies had to be carried long distances by bad roads and in the bitter cold of winter. By the beginning of January 1942, however, the railway was in use and supplies became better. But much rebuilding and reorganization of the railways were needed, often under heavy air attack by German planes, and only in February 1942 did conditions in Leningrad improve notably.

In the spring, anticipating epidemics with the thaw, the city authorities ordered a general inspection and clean-up of the city. The task was given to Komsomol units. It was then that thousands of bodies were discovered under the snow in trenches, ditches, and shelters, lying where they had fallen weeks and even months earlier. They were some of the casualties of the horrifying winter siege of Leningrad. Of those who survived, many were too weak to recover and they lingered only briefly.[48]

On 22 January 1942 the state defence committee decreed the evacuation of 500,000 people from the city. They were taken by the ice road and, after May, by ship across the lake. The evacuation of these pale, exhausted survivors continued until by the end of the year nearly a million people had been moved. Food was no longer a problem, for the city held only some 650,000 people by November 1942, but the Germans, although driven back from their close siege positions, still maintained the blockade. Red Army attempts to break it failed in 1942 and during that year of defeat and disaster for the Russians in the south, Leningrad remained on guard against another German offensive.

The Russians had by the end of 1941 stabilized their fronts at Leningrad and Moscow and had even in places pushed the Germans back. In the south, however, the German offensive continued eastwards and southwards, and the Red Army suffered several of its most disastrous and humiliating defeats. After the capture of Kiev in September 1941 the Germans found the way to the east open before them and in the course of the next two months they conquered the whole of Eastern Ukraine and most of the Crimean Peninsula. Odessa, holding down one German and eighteen Rumanian divisions, offered some small relief in the general gloom. Cut off from the rest of Russia, this important naval base resisted attack, despite heavy bombing, and was captured, fighting strongly to the end, only in mid-October.

The Germans had occupied the Crimea in the autumn, except for the strong garrison at Sevastopol. To relieve this garrison and then to liberate the Crimea, the Soviet Supreme Command planned a combined operation from the Caucasus with the immediate objective of recovering the Kerch Peninsula. It was an ambitious operation, but mismanagement by the Soviet commanders as well as lack of co-ordination and shortage of equipment were to bring it to disaster.

On 29 December the Russian force, supported by the Black Sea fleet, landed on the eastern side of the Crimea. The weather was stormy, but some 40,000 troops were put ashore. They retook Kerch and Feodosia and occupied the Kerch Peninsula. Instead of preparing strong defences and organizing effective offensives at once, however, Kozlov, commander of the Kerch Army Group, Mekhlis, his commissar, and other senior officers 'wasted time on lengthy and fruitless sessions of the War Council'.[49]

On 8 May 1942 Manstein launched a strong attack on the Russian positions. German aircraft had already bombed them severely and the Russians could only retreat to their prepared defences at the Turkish Wall. The Germans promptly dislodged them. They fell back to Kerch and began a chaotic evacuation of the peninsula in the course of which they abandoned nearly all their equipment.

The state defence committee at once took disciplinary action against the commanders of this bungled operation. Lieutenant-General Kozlov and many other officers were demoted. Mekhlis was made an example. He was extremely unpopular among senior officers of the Red Army in part for his sinister role in the army purge of 1937–8 and in part for his ardent advocacy of the revival of military commissars and the dual command system. At the time of the Kerch disaster he was vice-commissar of defence and a head of the political administration of the Red Army. He was now dismissed from both posts and reduced to the rank of corps commissar.

The disaster of the Kerch operation was followed in the same month (May 1942) by the rout of three Soviet armies at Kharkov. The plan of the Russian offensive to liberate Kharkov was for one force to strike north and the other south, and then to encircle the city. But the Germans, too, had planned an offensive in the Kharkov region, and they were holding strong forces in reserve. The Russian attack came first on 12 May. The Germans repelled the attack and then struck at the Soviet 9th Army, forcing it to withdraw to the Donets river, thus exposing the flank of the Soviet troops advancing on Kharkov. The Germans encircled many of the Red units, who suffered heavy casualties, amounting according to German claims to 200,000 killed or taken captive. Again, according to the official Soviet history, the Supreme Command had underrated German strength and had insisted on launching the offensive against the advice of senior officers, like Khrushchev, who were on the spot and saw the dangers.[50]

Kerch and Kharkov had been disastrous routs for the Russians. The fall of Sevastopol, although a defeat and felt throughout the country as a national tragedy, was so redeemed by the courage of its defenders as to become a moral victory. The Germans had occupied the Crimea in the autumn of 1941 and on 30 October had begun their siege of the naval base. Manstein launched his first attack on this stronghold from 30 October until 21 November. Sevastopol was, however, defended by three semi-circular defence lines and by sailors and marines of the Black Sea Fleet who were renowned for toughness and courage. The first German attack made small impression. But the Germans and Rumanians were vastly superior in man-power, guns, and tanks, and the *Luftwaffe* had mastery of the air. Manstein's second attack, lasting from 17 to 31 December, was more successful. The Russians were forced back to a line some five miles to the north of the stronghold.

The Russian landing on the Kerch Peninsula had halted the German–Rumanian assault and German troops were transferred to Kerch from positions before Sevastopol. News of the recapture of Kerch by the Russians raised the spirits of the beleaguered troops and civilians who became confident that the liberation of the whole Crimean Peninsula was at hand. Their disappointment was bitter when they learnt of the ejection of the Russians from Kerch. All knew that this meant the doom of Sevastopol and all in the stronghold prepared to resist to the end.

The German 11th Army and the Rumanian divisions commanded by Manstein, had been tied down for months at Sevastopol and they were needed in the drive eastwards. For the third attack, therefore, Manstein brought all his forces to bear. He opened the attack on 2 June with aerial bombardment, lasting for six days without respite. Damage and casualties in Sevastopol were heavy. On 7 June the German and Rumanian troops advanced and savage fighting raged for more than three weeks before they were able to occupy the city. Of the 106,000 Russian troops in Sevastopol, few got away. The Germans claimed 90,000 prisoners; the Russians admitted that 26,000 wounded were taken into German captivity. But on both sides the number of killed was appallingly high.[51]

Towards the end of June, the Germans launched a major offensive eastwards. Their objectives were to break through the Kursk–Voronezh sector, taking Voronezh from which they could advance to Tambov and Saratov, threatening Moscow from the east. They could also advance on Stalingrad and from there move southwards into the Caucasus, taking the valuable oil wells. It was a grandiose scheme which had to be modified and, for the Germans, it was to lead to disaster.

On 28 June the Germans began their attack in the Kursk–Voronezh sector. They broke through the Russian defences at Kursk and made for Voronezh. The Soviet Supreme Command was keenly aware of the dangers that would result from the fall of Voronezh. The immediate concern was that the Germans would advance from Voronezh to Saratov and stop the supplies of oil transported up the Volga river. They would be able to cut Moscow's communications with the east from which all food supplies came. They would also threaten Moscow with encirclement. But the Red Army fought stubbornly on the newly formed Voronezh front and halted the German advance. Without pressing their attack further, the Germans turned south, moving down the right bank of the Don in the direction of Stalingrad.

Farther to the south the other German advance continued. Voroshilovgrad (Lugansk) fell on 19 July. By the end of the month the occupation of the Donbas was completed with the capture of Novocherkassk and Rostov. The Donbas, which was the source of more than sixty per cent of Soviet coal, was the heart of the southern industrial region, the whole of which was now under German occupation. The region embraced the engineering and chemical industries, based on the coal of Donbas and the iron ore of Krivoi Rog and Kerch. Many industries had been evacuated to the east, but the loss of such vital coal and mineral sources raised crucial problems. Frantic efforts were made to sink new mines and to increase coal output in the Urals, the Kuzbas, and the Karanganda regions. But time was needed before the coal and minerals could be produced in quantity in the east. Meanwhile, desperate shortages of aluminium, copper, tin, nickel, and ferro-alloys and coal were holding back the output of armaments.

News of the loss of Rostov sent a wave of despair through the country. Far from having exhausted their capacity for offensive operations, as Soviet propaganda had alleged after the Battle of Moscow, the Germans continued to advance in an irresistible wave, and they were now clearly heading for the Kuban and the Caucasus. The fall of Rostov also shocked the nation, because it emerged that officers had lost their nerve when attacked and that Red Army troops had fled in panic. Strong disciplinary measures were at once taken against all who without orders had abandoned the city. Many were shot for desertion or flight in the face of the enemy, and generals and other officers were demoted.

The disgrace of Rostov brought on a crisis in the morale of the nation and was followed by a campaign of exhortations to the Red Army. The two themes in the Russian press, reflecting the feelings of all Russians at this time, were a deep love and reverence for Holy Russia, touched with self-pity, and a black hatred of the Germans. Liberation of occupied territories in the winter counter-offensives had uncovered innumerable savageries, committed by the Germans. Some incidents became legends. Zoya Kosmodemianskaya, an eighteen-year-old girl and a member of the Komsomol from Moscow, set fire to a barn in German-occupied territory near Moscow in November 1941. She was caught and tortured, and her body was found hanging from a gallows by the liberating troops. Pictures of the gallows appeared in all Soviet newspapers and her fate, like that of many others, fired the imagination of the people. Not only German brutalities but German arrogance and contempt for Holy Russia and all things Russian intensified the love of homeland and hatred of Germans among the Russians.

After the fall of Rostov, strong criticism of the Red Army also began to appear in the press and to be heard among the people. Red Army men were made to feel that the nation was profoundly disappointed in them. A new call for iron discipline and death to the coward and the panic-monger was sounded. Army orders strengthened army discipline to the point that any officer or soldier who disobeyed an order or showed cowardice was to be summarily shot. In exercising this power political commissars were evidently over-zealous, for on 9 August *Red Star*, the army newspaper, had to declare in strong terms that there was a clear distinction between the real coward and panic-monger and the man who had temporarily lost his nerve.[52]

The status of officers was raised not only by appeals to the personal honour of every officer, but by special measures designed to increase their authority and prestige. The Orders of Alexander Nevsky, of Suvorov, and of Kutuzov, all great Russian military leaders of the past, were instituted as decorations for officers only. Another major change was forecast in the same issue of *Red Star* which had warned commissars against shooting troops indiscriminately on grounds of disobedience or cowardice. This was the injunction that commissars must limit their activities to political work. Friction had clearly developed between officers and commissars over the application of the new iron discipline, and *Red Star* made it clear that enforcement of discipline was the responsibility of officers. On 9 October the Supreme Soviet abolished the system of dual command.[53]

The nation was in peril and at such a time Stalin was concerned with the morale and professional competence of the Red Army and not with the primacy of the party. He recognized too that the people were united in fighting for Russia. He himself had sounded the call, rallying them to the cause of Holy Russia, and from the start of the war he had been cautiously enlisting the support of the Orthodox Church. This support was important because religious faith remained strong in the country, and especially among soldiers of the Red Army of peasant origin. Also, as even Stalin may have appreciated, religious faith could be a source of fortitude and strength in the midst of the tragedies of war. Another factor was that the Germans encouraged the church and in propaganda broadcasts made much of the revival of religion in German-occupied territories. Furthermore, Stalin was keenly aware that the suppression of the church and anti-religious propaganda in Russia had antagonized public opinion in the United States and American aid was desperately needed, especially in 1942 when the evacuated industries still lagged in production.

The Orthodox Patriarch, Sergii, had issued a statement on 22 June 1941, declaring the support of the church for the regime and calling on all Christians to fight the German enemy. Soon afterwards *Bezbozhnik*, the atheistic propaganda magazine, closed down. But the Soviet authorities were cautious in their handling of the church. One bishop, Sergii the Younger, who had been sent to the Baltic states after their annexation by the Soviet Union, had defected to the Germans. It was significant, too, that in October 1941 when Moscow was threatened, the Soviet government, recognizing his great propaganda value in the hands of the Germans, had ordered the evacuation of the Patriarch to Ulyanovsk in the east. But from the autumn of 1941 co-operation between church and state began to grow and in 1943 it was to become notably cordial as part of Stalin's policy of uniting the Russian people.

The crisis in national feeling after the fall of Rostov and the new measures strengthening discipline and exhorting officers and men to fight to the death in the defence of their country tempered morale further in the armed forces. Stalin's order—'Soviet soldiers! Not a step back!'—which was read out to all troops on 30 July, had not halted the Russian retreat from the German advance into the Caucasus and eastwards towards Stalingrad. But it marked the beginning of a new grim resolution which was soon to be proved in the fires of Stalingrad.

Throughout August the Russians were driven southwards. The rich agricultural region of the Kuban was in enemy hands by 20 August and, with the great grain-producing lands of the Ukraine already under German occupation, the food shortage became acute. Von Kleist's Army Group A was now moving into the Caucasus. In their advance to the south-west the Germans took Krasnodar and the important oil centre of Maikop. To the south-east they pressed ahead rapidly towards the two main centres of the Soviet oil industry, Grozny and Baku.

Inside the Don bend to the north the German advance was slower as Russian resistance mounted in the second half of July. The Soviet command needed time to build up reserves and prepare defences at Stalingrad. But these defences were far from complete by the end of

August when the Germans reached the outskirts of the city. In fact, by 14 August the whole of the territory within the Don bend was in German hands, except for certain Russian bridgeheads in the north, and the Germans were advancing on Stalingrad not only from the south but also from the north-west and the north. For two weeks fierce fighting raged in the territory between the Don and the Volga.

Hitler had ordered that Stalingrad should be taken on 25 August. Two days earlier 600 German planes bombed the city, causing extensive damage and some 40,000 casualties among civilians. On this same day the Germans managed to reach the Volga bank north of the city and to avoid encirclement the Russian units, located south of this break-through, fell back to the city. Early in September the Germans broke through to the Volga to the south of the city.[54] Thousands of civilians escaped across the Volga, but both the army and the civil authorities were firm in their resolve to fight to the end to save Stalingrad. Already before the battle there was a general feeling among Russians that it would prove a turning point in the war. Faith in Stalin's leadership was also reflected in the belief that the city bearing his name could not fall into German hands.

During the German advance the Soviet 62nd Army to the east and the 64th Army to the south-east of Stalingrad had resisted bravely. The German plan to encircle and destroy both armies failed and they had fallen back, the 62nd Army inside and the 64th Army to the south of the city, where they endured the full weight of the enemy attack during the coming months.

Stalingrad was a vast city, stretching for some miles along the Volga bank. Mamai Hill, the highest point in the city, divided the industrial north from the administrative and residential districts of the south. By 13 September when the first major German onslaught on the city began, the bridgehead held by the 62nd Army commanded by Chuikov was on average five miles in depth. But in the north the Russians still held the Orlovka salient. Again the Germans had complete air superiority and their planes were making as many as 3,000 sorties a day. In tanks, too, they had superiority and they were well supplied with ammunition, unlike Chuikov who was to run desperately short. The Russian guns and aircraft as well as the main supply centre were based on the opposite bank where the Volga was about a mile wide. The concentration of Soviet artillery and *katyusha* mortars on the left bank of the river was to play a vital part in the defence of the city. The Russian gunners maintained constant fire, damaging German equipment and inflicting heavy casualties.

On the eve of the first German offensive at Stalingrad morale among the Russian troops was low. Many showed anxiety to escape the hell of incessant bombardment. Chuikov describes his meeting with the former commander of the 62nd Army who had already despaired of holding the city. But many, like Chuikov himself, were ready for a long cruel struggle. Chuikov had on the eve of the first German offensive declared to

Khrushchev and Yeremenko that he and the 62nd Army would 'either hold the city or die there'. Russian morale was raised, too, by the order of the war council of the Stalingrad front that 'the enemy must be smashed at Stalingrad'.[55]

The Germans, confident that the city was almost in their hands, launched their offensive on 13 September. Their objective was to take Mamai Hill, where Chuikov had his command post, and then break through to the Volga. Continuous bombing and shelling forced Chuikov to move to a strongly protected dug-out near the central station. The Germans advanced into the central part of the city. They were already jubilant with success and, forgetting to take precautions, they lost hundreds of men. But more troops took their place and the fighting reached within 800 yards of the Russian command post. Chuikov then ordered his reserve of nine tanks to halt the German drive.

On the night of 14–15 September the plight of the Russians was critical. But General Rodimtsev's 13th division of 10,000 was sent in from across the Volga. They recaptured Mamai Hill and in the savage fighting of the next two weeks they won fame for saving the city. But the cost was heavy. Rodimtsev's division was so reduced in strength that it could play only a small part in the remainder of the battle. On 21–22 September the Germans fought their way to the central pier on the Volga. This divided Chuikov's army and necessitated establishing other points at which ships of the Volga river flotilla, after making their hazardous voyage, could land reserves and supplies. Other troops landed were Batyuk's division, comprising mainly Siberians, who were tough and skilful fighters, and Gorishnyi's division; both were to win fame in this battle.

Making full use of their superiority in tanks and planes and having taken most of central Stalingrad, the Germans began a mass attack on the industrial part of the city in the north. The fury of the onslaught, supported by incessant dive-bombing, made even Chuikov wonder if his army could survive another day. He sent an urgent appeal to the war council for reserves. Two infantry regiments were sent across the Volga that night. Chuikov deployed them to reinforce the troops defending the Red October Plant. On 28 September the Germans continued their attack. Losses were appalling on both sides in this savage fighting, but grimly the Russians held on. They had acquired a mastery of camouflage and of barricade fighting, and were at their best in attacking at night. The Germans with their superiority in tanks and aircraft attacked by day. Chuikov, noting that their pilots were not accurate in bombing, devised close combat tactics whereby the distance from the enemy was kept at a hand-grenade's throw, and thus gained for his lines some immunity from air attack. On the following day the Germans ejected the Russians from the Orlovka salient north of the city.

In October the fighting was mainly concentrated in the industrial north of the city and for the Russians the situation was often desperate. At the beginning of the month Major-General Guriev's 39th Guards Division and the division of Colonel Gurtiev reached Stalingrad and were plunged into the fighting. Indeed every Red Army man who fought in Stalingrad was to win fame and to earn the gratitude of the Russian people.

On 14 October the Germans opened the offensive which they were confident would bring the final collapse of Stalingrad. Chuikov considered that, if they had planned their attack effectively, they might have succeeded within a couple of hours, so decimated were the Russian divisions. The Germans moved forward more than a mile. They took the Tractor Plant and drove through a wedge which again divided the Russian army. On the following day they pressed their attack strongly, supported by heavy aerial bombardment of the Russian bridgeheads. Reinforcements of General Ludnikov's division were brought across the Volga to take the places of the killed. Chuikov had to move his command post again, this time to a cave in the Volga cliffs about 1,000 yards from Mamai Hill. The Germans maintained the pressure of their attacks until 23 October. By then their strength and the strength of the Russians was nearing exhaustion. Chuikov had brought into the front every man he could find, including cooks, storekeepers, tailors, and others. All had fought bravely and the city had not fallen. But the struggle continued.

On 11 November the Germans mounted their last major assault. They concentrated their forces in a desperate attempt to push their way across the Russian bridgehead to the Volga. At one point they reached the river, but nowhere else did they succeed. The Russian defences remained strong and the troops brought in as reinforcements, especially the sailors of the Pacific Fleet, fought indomitably. Gradually the German offensive declined.

Only a few days later—on 19 and 20 November—the great Russian counter-offensive from the north and the south of Stalingrad was launched. It was to develop to plan, encircling the German 9th Army and marking the turning point of the war in Russia.

Chuikov and his men in the narrow bridgehead inside Stalingrad had been informed of the counter-offensive on the previous evening. When they heard the distant rumble of gunfire before dawn on 19 November, they knew what it portended.[56] Russian morale had never been higher than during the last weeks of the struggle to hold the city and now they were relieved and jubilant. But the Germans continued to fight.

The Volga was now covered with ice floes and no longer navigable. In any case the opening of the counter-offensive meant that no further reinforcements would be available for the 62nd Army. Supplies of food and ammunition were limited to what could be brought by small reconnaissance aircraft. When in mid-December the Volga froze over, troops began to bring supplies by sledge.

During December the Russians fought to close the Barricades salient, held by the Germans in the north and to reunite their forces. This was achieved on 23 December. The next task was to recapture the Red October Plant. The Germans had prepared defences of such strength in the plant that the building had to be destroyed by close-range artillery fire. Sniping and street-to-street fighting continued throughout December. The Germans struggled desperately, buoyed by the confidence that Manstein's army would advance from the south to relieve them. Chuikov observed that few prisoners were taken 'since the Hitlerites would not think of surrender'.[57] Not until after the failure of Manstein's attempt to break through did morale among the German troops begin to decline noticeably.

The epic struggle of Stalingrad had almost closed and the city had neither surrendered nor had it been taken.

CHAPTER NINETEEN

The War: The Russian Recovery
November 1942–December 1943

THE announcement on 22 November of the counter-offensive at Stalingrad aroused the Russian people to a fever of excitement as well as giving them a deep sense of relief. At last the Red Army had halted the German advance. The liberation of the occupied territories and the final defeat of nazi Germany could now begin. In this new mood of high optimism, few Russians realized that a long struggle lay ahead.

Three Red Army groups took part in the counter-offensive. On 19 November Rokossovsky, commanding the Don Army Group, and Vatutin, commanding the south-west Army Group, attacked from the north-west of the city. On the following day Yeremenko, commanding the Stalingrad Army Group, attacked from positions to the south. All three army groups advanced rapidly. They took Kalach and cut the two railway lines, used to supply the Germans in Stalingrad. Vatutin crushed the Rumanian 3rd Army, taking 30,000 prisoners, and routed several German units. On the fifth day of their offensive they completed the encirclement of the Germans in Stalingrad.

The planning of this major operation, carried out chiefly by Stalin, Zhukov, and Vassilevsky, who had consulted with the three group commanders, had begun in August. All had been prepared in great secrecy. Troops and masses of equipment had been assembled, mainly at night, within the Don bend north of the city, where they had been dispersed and camouflaged. Difficulties of transporting men and equipment across the Volga for the Stalingrad Army Group had been even greater. But, although flying frequent sorties and bombing the railway lines north of the Don and east of the Volga, the Germans never realized the magnitude of the preparations for the offensive.

In their planning, moreover, Stalin, Zhukov, and Vassilevsky tried to ensure that the Red Army had superiority in men and equipment. In the event the three Russian groups together had 1,050,000 men, some 900 tanks, 13,000 guns, and 1,100 planes. The Germans had a similar number of troops, only 700 tanks and 10,000 guns, but 1,200 planes. In the sectors where the main Russian attack fell, however, they had a three to one superiority in troops, and four to one in guns and mortars.[1]

Once Rokossovsky, Vatutin, and Yeremenko had closed their lines,

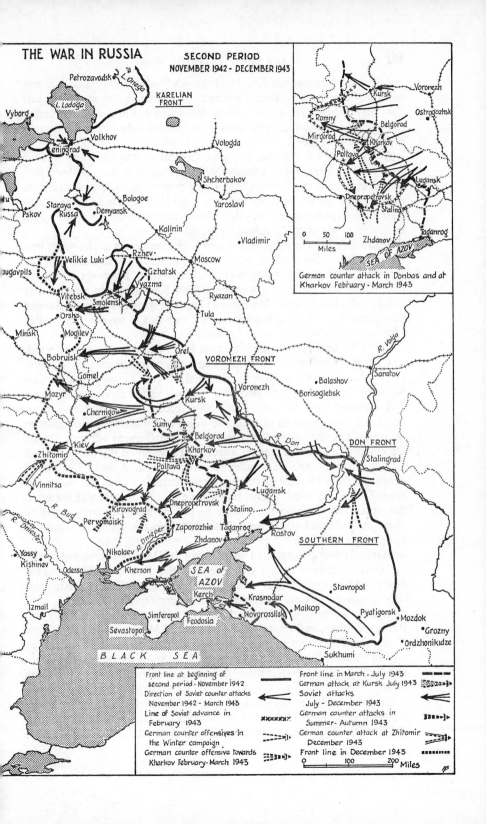

THE WAR IN RUSSIA — SECOND PERIOD NOVEMBER 1942 – DECEMBER 1943

German counter attack in Donbas and at Kharkov February – March 1943

Front line at beginning of second period - November 1942
Direction of Soviet counter attacks November 1942 - March 1943
Line of Soviet advance in February 1943
German counter offensives in the Winter campaign
German counter offensive towards Kharkov February - March 1943

Front line in March - July 1943
German attack at Kursk July 1943
Soviet attacks July - December 1943
German counter attacks in Summer - Autumn 1943
German counter attack at Zhitomir December 1943
Front line in December 1943
0   100   200 Miles

trapping the German 6th Army and the 4th Panzer Army, their fear was that the Germans would make a concerted effort to break out. The Russian lines lacked strength and depth. But when at the end of November the Germans attempted a break-out it was not the concentrated operation expected, and it failed.

At this time the Russian Supreme Command was working on 'Plan Saturn'. This was a broad offensive with the objective, first, of destroying or taking captive the German forces now trapped in Stalingrad and then of occupying the whole of the territory within the Don bend, so that with Rostov again in Russian hands the German armies in the Caucasus would be unable to withdraw by this main route.

Meanwhile the Germans had reorganized their forces in the south into the new Army Group Don under the command of Field-Marshal von Manstein. Part of this group was concentrated at Tormosin inside the Don bend. The other part was centred on Kotelnikovsky, some ninety miles south of Stalingrad. Manstein's objectives were to break the Russian encirclement and release Paulus's forces, and also to oppose the Russian advance across the Don and to the west.

On 12 December Manstein's force in Kotelnikovsky struck northwards and, notwithstanding strong Russian opposition, fought its way to within twenty-five miles of Stalingrad. Alarmed by this advance, the Russian Supreme Command postponed Plan Saturn, and ordered Malinovsky's 2nd Guards Army to hold Manstein's force at the Myshkova river. Malinovsky's troops had to cross the Volga and make forced marches in blizzards, but they arrived in time to halt the German advance. On 24 December the Russians counter-attacked. They hurled the Germans back to Kotelnikovsky and sixty miles farther to the south-west. But during the period from 19 to 23 December when Manstein's force was only some twenty-five miles away, Paulus might have broken out. He did not grasp this opportunity apparently because he had no authority from Hitler to abandon Stalingrad and, indeed, Hitler was to order Paulus to stand fast in the city to the end.

Manstein now concentrated on guarding the Rostov–Taman gap so that the German armies in the Caucasus and the Kuban could withdraw. Malinovsky was planning to drive through to Rostov. To the north Vatutin's South-west Army Group was advancing rapidly westwards. Supported by Soviet air sorties, this force crushed the Italian 8th Army and Rumanian units, and forced the withdrawal of Manstein's left flank from Tormosin. The Germans were retreating hurriedly from the Caucasus by way of Rostov. Threatened now by Vatutin from the north and Malinovsky from the north-east they fought more stubbornly to keep this route open.

Trapped in Stalingrad since 23 November the German forces under Paulus had no hope of escape after Manstein's failure to break through the Russian ring. Food supplies were running short. The cold was severe and the Germans suffered severely from lack of winter clothing. Paulus had been promised a daily airlift of at least 500 tons of food and ammunition. But fighter protection for the German transport planes was no longer possible from the positions to which the Germans had had to retreat. Soviet fighters were attacking the transport planes with increasing success and effectively reduced the supplies reaching the beleaguered German armies.[2]

On 8 January, while troops from the Don front stood ready to attack, Rokossovsky called on Paulus to surrender. The terms offered included a guarantee of safety to all German officers and troops and repatriation at the end of the war. Paulus on Hitler's orders rejected the Soviet offer. On the morning of 10 January the Russians opened a barrage from 7,000 guns and mortars on the German positions. But when they advanced they still met with strong opposition. On 17 January Rokossovsky again called on Paulus to surrender and to avoid unnecessary bloodshed. Again Paulus refused. The Russian onslaught continued. German casualties were terrible, but although demoralization was spreading, resistance continued to the end. On 26 January Russian troops, advancing from north and west, joined at Mamai Hill with Chuikov's 62nd Army, which throughout these weeks after the encirclement had continued its grim struggle. Finally Paulus surrendered.

In the first two-and-a-half weeks after the encirclement 140,000 Germans had perished. A further 100,000 had died between 10 January and 2 February. Prisoners taken numbered only 91,000. Thousands of Germans had fought on because discipline remained high, but mainly because they feared the Russian troops, and the revenge they might exact for the atrocities committed by the Germans. According to eye-witnesses, however, Germans taken prisoner were treated reasonably.[3]

In the savage cold of January–February 1943, Stalingrad and the surrounding country where battle had raged had become a grotesque white desert, strewn with corpses frozen solid in strange attitudes, helmets filled with snow, lorries, tanks, and other equipment lying in twisted ruin. All bore witness to the ferocity and havoc of the fighting which, as though by some miracle, men had survived and from which the Russians had wrested victory.

The German defeat at Stalingrad had put an end to Hitler's grandiose plans for the conquest of the Caucasus and ultimately of the Middle East. He had, in fact, overreached himself. His original plan of launching a concentrated onslaught on Stalingrad and, after taking the city, then moving south might well have succeeded. But the ease with which Rostov had been captured had persuaded him that the Russians lacked the will, training, and equipment to resist effectively. He had therefore divided his forces in an attempt to take Stalingrad and the Caucasus simultaneously, and his armies had suffered defeat.

The speed and success of the southward advance of the Germans in the summer and autumn of 1942 had, nevertheless, caused Stalin and the Supreme Command great anxiety. The Russians had been routed from the vast area of the Kuban and from the north Caucasus, but as the Germans plunged farther southward Russian resistance had stiffened. The Russians had made extensive defence preparations and had brought in reserves under great difficulties. On the Transcaucasian front, running from the Terek river to the north-east of Mozdok and Novorossiisk, they halted the Germans.

One question constantly on the minds of Stalin and the Supreme Command as the Germans were plunging southwards concerned the loyalty of the Cossacks and the Moslem peoples. Since the early days of the war, when the Western Ukraine and the Baltic states had been lost, the fighting had taken place on east Ukrainian and Great Russian territory, where the people, even if not enthusiastically pro-Soviet, were loyal to Russia. Stalin was alert to the dangers of disaffection. For this reason he had in August 1941 deported the Volga Germans, who had originally been encouraged to settle in Russia by Catherine the Great, to Kazakhstan and to northern Siberia.[4]

The Cossacks had, since the beginning of the Muscovite state, been an unpredictable people, usually supporting the tsar but always ready to rebel against his authority. The Cossacks, like the Moslem peoples of the Caucasus and of Central Asia and the Tatars of the Crimea had suffered under the Soviet regime, especially during the collectivization campaign, and had ample grounds for being anti-Soviet. The Germans, aware of this latent disaffection, clumsily tried to take advantage of it. The Cossacks were exempted from *Untermensch* status and were encouraged to enlist in the German army. By late 1943 some 20,000 Cossacks, or men claiming to be Cossacks, were fighting in German-sponsored units.[5] This was, however, a small percentage of the Cossack population of the Kuban, Terek, and the Don, most of whom resisted the Germans staunchly.

Among the Moslem peoples of the Caucasus, towards whom the Germans behaved almost benignly, the Karachai and Balkars, the Ingushi and the Chechens, and to the north the Kalmyks, all displayed pro-German sympathies in some degree. But the hurried withdrawal of the Germans from the Caucasus after the Russian victory at Stalingrad had allowed too short a time for anti-Soviet feeling to be organized. But these peoples were at the end of 1943 and in the spring of 1944 to suffer cruelly and excessively as punishment for their latent disloyalty.[6]

The Red Armies had begun to move westwards even before Stalingrad had fallen. Impatient to liberate all Russian territory, the Supreme Command had drawn up a plan for an advance on a broad front which would carry the Red forces to the Dnieper by spring 1943. This proved over-ambitious. In January 1943 Soviet forces of the southern front, as the Stalingrad front was soon to be known, commanded now by Malinovsky, advanced in the direction of Rostov. General Petrov, commanding the

Black Sea forces, was to advance to Krasnodar and join up with Malinovsky's group. This operation was intended to close the Rostov gap and also the route to the Taman Peninsula. But the Russians, slowed down by German resistance, by supply difficulties, and by shortages of equipment, were unable to prevent most of the German forces reaching the Taman Peninsula or escaping through the Rostov gap. Not until 12 February 1943 was Krasnodar recaptured and two days later Rostov and Voroshilovgrad were again in Russian hands.

Farther to the north, however, the Russian winter offensive was more successful. On the Voronezh front, General Golikov's forces regained Voronezh itself and eagerly pushed westward. At Kastornoye they destroyed the Hungarian 2nd Army, claiming more than 100,000 Hungarians killed or taken prisoner. Sweeping across the Kursk province Golikov's troops began liberating the north-eastern Ukraine and the northern part of the Donbas. On 16 February they fought their way into Kharkov and continued their advance until they were within twenty miles of the Dnieper.

Early in March 1943, moreover, the Germans withdrew from the Vyazma salient, only 100 miles from Moscow, which they had fought so obstinately and at such great cost to hold in the winter campaign of 1941–2. The ending of this threat to Moscow was a source of general relief in the capital. On the Leningrad front and the Volkhov front, too, the Red forces drove a gap in the German blockade lines seven miles in width and including the town of Schlusselburg. A railway was at once built, giving Leningrad communications with the rest of Russia to the east. But this corridor was frequently shelled by the Germans and indeed the city was to be exposed to shelling until the end of 1944, but Leningrad was no longer in the grip of the blockade.

In his order of the day on 23 February, the twenty-fourth anniversary of the Red Army, Stalin warned against underestimating the German forces. 'The enemy has suffered defeat, but still has not been conquered.' He ordered the Red Army to redouble its efforts.[7] The nation was exulting over the victory at Stalingrad and the liberation of vast areas in the Red Army's westward advance. The dangers of over-confidence were real. Stalin's warning proved timely. A few days after his Red Army Day speech the Germans counter-attacked. The Russians, lacking supplies and their lines of communication over-extended in their headlong westward offensive, had to withdraw from Kharkov and the northern Donbas. Among the Russians the general dismay was salutary and they recognized that the war was far from won.

At the end of March a pause came in the fighting along the German–Soviet front, which lasted until early July 1943. It was a period of furious preparation for the summer campaign which was to prove a crucial trial of strength. Hitler was determined to recover the German losses of the winter of 1942–3. The defeat at Stalingrad had been a major set-back to

German arms and to his own prestige. The new German Tiger and Panther tanks were now in production and, supported by the new Ferdinand self-propelling guns, they would, he was confident, ensure a resounding German victory. He had decided already that this decisive action should take place in the Kursk salient. From there his armies would strike north to capture Moscow and east to take Stalingrad, thus expunging the disgrace to German arms.

The Soviet Supreme Command also recognized the importance of the Kursk salient. They were urgently concentrating troops and equipment and preparing ground defences for this battle. More than 500,000 railway wagon loads of equipment, brought from the east to the Kursk salient, was an indication of the scale of the Soviet preparations. But the Russians were now drawing confidence not only from the quantities of armaments coming into service, but also from their quality. Much of this new Russian equipment was superior to the German equivalents. The time when Red troops lacked automatic weapons and when Soviet planes and tanks were outnumbered and outclassed had gone.

Soviet industry had, in fact, achieved extraordinary results since the gigantic evacuation in the autumn and winter of 1941–2. The evacuation had indeed dislocated production during 1942. This factor and the German occupation of the southern industrial region, centred on the Donbas, had contributed greatly to the Russian failure to stem the German advance in 1942. But throughout this year the evacuated industries, the expansion of existing plants, and the opening of new mines and industries had all added to the mounting tempo of production. As early as the autumn of 1942 the growing output of armaments had begun to be felt in the Red forces. In 1943 deliveries were already at such a level as to allow the staggering concentration in the Kursk salient and also the arming of Red forces on other fronts with the most up-to-date tanks and weapons.

This achievement was the result of the labours, heroic in scale and character, of thousands of men and women. Labour was conscripted and allocated where needed. Conditions, especially in winter and in the new industries or the plants transferred to the east, were terribly hard. Special rations were given in many of these industries to enable workers to keep up with the demands for higher output. The stamina of these men and women was extraordinary. Russian women, in fact, worked in mines, in industry, and agriculture, often in place of men, and their readiness, endurance and devotion were among the most remarkable aspects of the Russian war effort.

Coal, electric power, and metals were the most acute shortages. New coal mines were frantically sunk and old mines were expanded in the Urals, Kuzbas, and Kazakhstan, and thousands of miners, mainly women, were trained in the work at the same time. By 1943 all three coal regions were increasing their output month by month. At Chelyabinsk a great power station was built in six months in 1942 instead of the two or three years normally required. It supplied electric power to the numerous armament works in the region. The Kuznetsky combine, responsible for producing a third of all the iron and steel produced in the country, rapidly increased its output. To the five enormous blast furnaces of the Magnitogorsk, a sixth blast furnace, the largest in Europe, was added in 1943, and it was built in six months.[8]

The results of the increases in output from existing and new plants in the form of equipment for the armed forces was dramatic. In 1943 the total production of heavy and medium tanks was 16,000, of light tanks 3,500, and of self-propelling guns 4,000. This output was eight-and-a-half times greater than in 1940 and almost four times greater than in 1941. Moreover, the Soviet tanks included the improved T-34, considered by many to have been the best medium tank in the war, and the heavy IS tank, which the Soviet experts proclaimed as 'the best heavy tank in the world'.[9]

The Red Army had suffered particularly from German superiority in automatic weapons and in aircraft. Special priority was given to the production of both items. In 1943 the output of sub-machine-guns was treble that of the previous year and of machine-guns two-and-a-half times greater. Total aircraft production in 1943 was 35,000 planes, an increase of 37 per cent over 1942.[10]

Supplementing Soviet production were the equipment and other supplies provided by Britain and increasingly by the United States. The aircraft and tanks sent in 1942 and 1943 found little favour with the Russians.[11] But other British and American supplies were extremely valuable and contributed notably to the effectiveness of the Red forces. American trucks, lorries, and jeeps, of which 210,000 were received from June 1941 to April 1944, were particularly valuable in giving the Red Army greater mobility. Food and clothing, mainly from the U.S.A., also contributed to welfare and fighting efficiency. Large shipments of much needed metals, such as copper, aluminium, nickel, zinc, and steel, and of raw materials and high-octane fuel, as well as of machinery of various kinds, were also important factors in the Russian war effort.

The Soviet attitude to these supplies was that they were the least that the allies could contribute in the absence of a second front, while Russians were dying in thousands in the war against the common enemy. Indeed, Soviet reluctance to acknowledge this aid or to express any appreciation was to exacerbate relations for a time with Britain and the U.S.A.[12]

As summer approached in 1943, German and Russian preparations in the Kursk salient mounted in intensity. Hitler was convinced that 'Operation Citadel', involving simultaneous German onslaughts from Orel in the north and Belgorod in the south of the salient, would trap the Red Armies. Liquidation of the salient would greatly shorten the front which he was determined to maintain from the Gulf of Finland to the Sea of Azov. German prestige and initiative would be restored and his grandiose plans for conquest of Soviet Russia west of the Ural Mountains would resurge.

Among the German commanders at the Kursk salient, however, there were misgivings about attacking the Russians where they were so strongly entrenched and reinforced. The Germans needed a marked superiority in the latest tanks to succeed. The new Panther and Tiger tanks and Ferdinand mobile guns were rushed to the front. Hitler postponed the attack once to allow a greater build-up of German armed might, until on the eve of battle some 3,000 German tanks and 2,000 aircraft had been massed.

In the early hours of the morning of 5 July, after exchanges of gunfire, the Germans launched their attack, striking south from Orel and north from Belgorod, intent on encircling the four Soviet armies concentrated within the salient. The Panther and Tiger tanks met with a storm of shellfire from massed artillery and anti-tank guns. The Germans desperately pressed their attacks, and their losses of troops and equipment were appalling.

On the northern front of the salient on 5–6 July the Germans gained some ten kilometres at the cost of 25,000 men killed or wounded, some 200 tanks and mobile guns, and 200 aircraft destroyed.[13] By 9 July the Germans had moved little farther forward on this front and only some thirty miles on a narrow front in the south. On 13 July when the two German forces, which were to join in annihilating the four Soviet armies in the salient, were still more than 100 miles apart, Hitler reluctantly ordered the operation to be discontinued.

While inflicting heavy losses on the enemy in this battle for the Kursk salient and holding strong reserves in readiness, the Soviet Supreme Command on 12 July launched a devastating counter-offensive on the Orel salient, still in German hands. Soon afterwards another counter-offensive was launched to recapture the Belgorod–Kharkov bulge. On 5 August the Red Army liberated both Orel and Belgorod and on 23 August Kharkov was retaken. The German summer offensive, from which Hitler had hoped to extract a decisive victory, had been completely broken, and the Russians had seized the initiative.

On both sides losses had been appalling in this clash of tanks and artillery on a scale and with an intensity never before known in warfare. In fifty days of constant fighting German killed and wounded and missing amounted to more than half a million officers and troops. They included, moreover, the most experienced commanders, NCOs, and men, who had in the past given Hitler's armies a strong advantage.[14] Loss of equipment was also heavy. Between 2,000 and 3,000 tanks, many of them the newest types, had been destroyed and vast quantities of other equipment. Russian losses were similarly heavy, but the Red forces could replenish from its vast reserves of manpower, and Soviet industry, now fully geared to the needs of war, could provide ready replacements of equipment of all kinds. The Red Army drew strength also from the knowledge, confirmed in battle, that all their equipment was as effective or more effective than any of the equipment opposed to them. Moreover, buoyant from victory, the Russians were now experienced, well equipped, and with a developed appreciation of the mobility and initiative demanded by modern warfare.

In the Battle of Moscow in the winter of 1941 the Russians had stemmed the enemy advance without halting it. In the battle of Stalingrad they had inflicted a major defeat on the Germans. Partially at Moscow and completely at Stalingrad they had destroyed the myth of German invincibility. They had at Stalingrad also halted the German advance. But in the Battle of the Kursk salient they had crushed the German summer campaign, and they had destroyed the German capacity for mounting another major offensive in the war. From this time the Germans could only retreat, compelled to follow a defensive strategy.

The Russian plan to advance on a broad front, liberating all territory under German occupation up to the Dnieper river by the spring had proved impossible. All operations had been held back, while forces had concentrated for the decisive battle of the Kursk salient. Then, as soon as the outcome was clear, the Russians renewed their westward drive and now with a new confidence and a furious energy. The Germans resisted stubbornly at all important positions, but it was now the Russians who seemed invincible. In the south the whole of the Donbas was liberated by early September and in the following month the Taman Peninsula, Zaporozhie, Melitopol, and Dniepropetrovsk were retaken. The Crimea was already partly cut off from the mainland and hopes were high that the Red Army would plunge southwards and free the whole peninsula, but this was only achieved in the spring of the following year.

In October the Red Army began forcing the Dnieper, crossing it at certain points. On 6 November Kiev was liberated and, pressing ahead impatiently, Red forces recaptured Zhitomir two days later. In the north the Russian advance was less spectacular. But on 25 September Smolensk was recaptured, thus relieving Moscow completely of the threat of attack.

By the end of 1943 the Red Army had recovered nearly two-thirds of the vast territories conquered by the Germans in their great eastward advance of 1941–2. But most of Belorussia, the Western Ukraine, and the Baltic region were still in German hands. Leningrad, too, although no longer completely blockaded, was still being shelled by German guns. As the year came to an end, the Supreme Command was urgently planning to drive the Germans from Soviet territory. Russians everywhere, and especially in the Red forces, felt the desperate need to cleanse their land of the German invader.

The experience of the Red Army in liberating territories occupied by the Germans had intensified this sense of urgency. The savage inhumanity of German treatment of prisoners-of-war and the people in occupied territories had been fearful. Reports of German cruelties had been published since early in the war, but the liberation of vast territories had revealed the terrible scale of German barbarity. The Russian nation, although inured to purges, to mass coercion, and to forced labour, was deeply shocked and embittered.

On the basis of captured German documents, the American historian, Alexander Dallin, has calculated that the Germans took 5,160,000 Russian prisoners between June 1941 and May 1944. Of these 818,000 were released with worker or military status. The survivors who were finally liberated numbered 1,053,000. Thus more than three-and-a-quarter million men had died, exterminated in massacres, by starvation, and by exposure. The number of Russian civilians, including women and children, done to death by similar methods probably far exceeded this figure: the full toll will never be known.[15]

Russian prisoners were deliberately starved to death. This treatment of thousands of men was justified on the ground that German troops must feed off the land and all possible food surpluses had been sent to Germany where rationing was severe. But this extermination policy was also justified as part of the *Untermensch* theory, which condemned Russians as sub-human, and on the ground that the 'Jewish–Bolshevist system' must be destroyed. Any prisoner suspected of being Jewish or a bolshevik in fact or in sympathy, or of considering or being capable of escaping was shot at once. Others, penned in the open without shelter of any kind and without food, died in their thousands, especially in the cold of autumn and winter in 1941 and 1942.

Kharkov, the first large city to be liberated, provided a revelation of German barbarity. The population of Kharkov, normally about 900,000, had been swollen to some 1,300,000 by the influx of people, fleeing before the invader. As the Germans approached, however, thousands fled farther to the east. The Germans found some 700,000 people when they took the city; only half this number survived their occupation. Of the others, 120,000, mainly young people, were sent to Germany as slave labour. Between 70,000 and 80,000 died of hunger or exposure. The Germans executed about 30,000, a figure which included 16,000 Jews. The others had fled into the country, some to fight with the partisans, and others simply to hide.[16]

Orel, a city which had endured two years of German occupation, contained on liberation only 30,000 of its 114,000 population. The Germans had murdered some 12,000 people and had sent more than 20,000 as slave labour to Germany. But many thousands had escaped to the neighbouring forests to fight with the partisans. Alexander Werth, who was one of the first of the war correspondents to visit the newly liberated territory, has described the exhumation of bodies from a trench, containing 5,000 or more victims. About half were Russian prisoners-of-war who had died from disease or starvation. But half were men and women who had been shot at the back of the skull. Regularly on certain days of the week the Gestapo execution squad had come for its victims.[17]

Every Russian city, town, or village, occupied by the Germans, suffered the same cruel fate. The Jewish populations were always shot or killed in gas chambers and their bodies burnt. At Babyi Yar, near Kiev, some 100,000 Jews were massacred. Ukrainians and the Moslem peoples received better treatment, because they were thought to be actual or potential enemies of the Soviet regime. The fiendishness of the nazis was, in fact, concentrated against the Russians. But towards the end of 1942 they modified their treatment of the Russians, offering prisoners-of-war the alternatives of starvation or of joining the Russian Army of Liberation, usually known as the Vlasov army. Most prisoners, including senior officers, refused to serve under Vlasov and they died either by shooting or starvation, but a few in Dachau and other concentration camps managed to survive.

Andrei Andreivich Vlasov, born in a peasant family in the Nizhni Novgorod province, had fought with the Red forces in the civil war. He had not suffered in the great purge of 1937–8 and, promoted to the rank of lieutenant-general after his effective command of troops on part of the front in the Battle of Moscow, he was one of the rising young Soviet generals. During the summer of 1942 on the Volkhov front, however, he was captured. To those Germans who advocated organizing a Russian anti-Soviet movement, Vlasov was the kind of man needed. Tall, lean, and deliberate he was a powerful personality with a natural ability to command men, although apparently neither brilliant nor even above-average in intelligence.[18]

Vlasov agreed readily to collaborate with the Germans and issued to all Russian officers and 'comrades of the Soviet intelligentsia' an appeal to join him in striving 'with all strength and means to overthrow the universally hated Soviet regime'.[19] The plan was to create this army of liberation by bringing thousands of Soviet nationals under the unified command of a native ex-Soviet general. But the plan was never realized. The army remained a 'phantom', as Hitler called it, for he categorically rejected the idea of a Russian army under such a command, fighting side by side with the German forces.[20] The units that were recruited were scattered and largely commanded by German officers. Vlasov himself was never to exercise command over it. The army of liberation was therefore primarily a propaganda weapon, which the Germans hoped would unsettle and undermine the loyalty of Red troops and Soviet citizens. In this they grossly misjudged the mood of the Russian people. Hatred of the Germans for the suffering and devastation they had inflicted had been brought to white heat by the revelations of German arrogance and fiendish inhumanity in occupied territories. Any Russian who collaborated with the enemy was a traitor beyond redemption. Far from undermining loyalty to the Soviet regime, Vlasov and his supporters were the objects of Russian contempt.[21]

Ex-Soviet citizens serving in the German army in 1943 and 1944 nevertheless numbered over half a million. Many of them were Ukrainians, Belorussians, Cossacks, and from the Caucasus. Known as *Hilfswillige*, they were at first accepted reluctantly by the Germans who, fearing armed mutiny, used them only in very small units and even as individual recruits, all marks of national identity being carefully suppressed.[22]

In the circumstances the number of Soviet prisoners who collaborated is surprisingly low and the fact of collaboration cannot be taken to indicate anti-Soviet or anti-Stalin animus. The Soviet prisoner-of-war often had the choice between starving to death or enlisting as a *Hilfswillige*. If he took, as most did, the courageous decision to starve rather than serve the Germans, he could in 1943 and 1944 cherish the slender hope that he might be liberated by the Red Army. The German SS usually shot all surviving prisoners before retreating, but, if the prisoner escaped this fate, he would still have to face interrogation by the NKVD.

All Red Army men who had been taken prisoner and the civilians in liberated territories were treated as suspects, who might have been trained by the Germans to act as spies, saboteurs, or diversionists. Every Red Army soldier had to explain himself and why he had allowed himself to be taken prisoner instead of fighting to the death. Civilians had to account for their activities while under German occupation. Alexander Werth, who visited Kharkov in February 1943, soon after the liberation of the city, wrote: 'Nor was the return of the Russians an occasion for unanimous rejoicing in Kharkov. I saw two large letter-boxes, marked UNKVD —the Ukrainian Security Police—into which people were invited to drop denunciations and other relevant information ... And at the former Gestapo prison, now burnt out, I could see civilian prisoners being escorted into the basement for questioning by the NKVD. Scared relatives were hanging about the prison, some with parcels of food.'[23]

War and the barbarities of the German occupation had bred a new callousness among the Russians, but the mentality of the police state, especially in the handling of liberated prisoners and civilians, added cruelly and unnecessarily to the sufferings of the Russian people at this time.

The treatment of liberated prisoners-of-war is not mentioned in Soviet writing of the war, but the partisan or guerrilla movement has had wide publicity. The partisans, brave men and women who often endured terrible hardships and who perished in large numbers, have become romanticized as folk heroes. From its complexity and because so many partisans were killed, full information about the movement will always be lacking. Without doubt, however, the partisans became an extremely effective force which made a real contribution to Russian operations against the enemy.

In his first great broadcast of the war Stalin had ordered the creation of partisan groups and 'the eruption of partisan war everywhere to blow up bridges, roads, to damage telegraph and telephone communications, to set fire to forests, stores, supply trains', and to make conditions insupportable to the enemy.[24] Two weeks later the central committee had issued instructions on 'the Organization of the Struggle in the Enemy Rear'. The press called for spontaneous resistance by every Russian in occupied territory, reviving traditions of popular uprisings against the French invaders in the previous century. But, as the highly mechanized German armies surged across the Russian plain in 1941, unarmed bands of peasants could do little to halt their advance. Undoubtedly groups of Red Army officers and men who had escaped and other brave individuals engaged in sabotage. But in the chaos in Belorussia, the western Ukraine, and in western Russia in the first months of the war they had little effect.

During 1942, however, the organizing of the partisans and the supply of equipment and ammunition to them began to transform the movement. In May 1942 the Supreme Command set up in Moscow a Central Staff of the Partisan Movement and later similar planning centres were instituted for partisans in Belorussia and the Ukraine. This was a recognition of the great potential value of the broad mass movement which was growing rapidly, stimulated by the arrogance and brutality of the German invaders, and by the deportation of thousands of young Russians to Germany as slave labour. The forests, covering a large part of Belorussia and in the northern Ukraine as well as in the regions of Briansk, Orel, and Leningrad, were especially suited to partisan activity. In the Briansk region, according to Soviet claims, 30,000 Hungarian troops were engaged solely in fighting partisans. In the terrible winter of 1941–2 some 10,000 partisans were operating in the rear of the Germans before Moscow, Kalinin, and Tula. Partisans were credited with killing 18,000 of the enemy in the Battle of Moscow. In the autumn and winter of 1942 the partisans, already well organized and supplied, inflicted considerable damage on the Germans at Stalingrad. They constantly disrupted the long supply lines of the enemy and added greatly to Manstein's difficulties in trying to force a corridor through the Russian lines to allow the German 6th Army to escape.[25]

By the end of 1943, 220,000 partisans were fully armed and active in the Ukraine and as many as 360,000 armed partisans were harrassing the enemy in Belorussia. In three years the Germans lost 500,000 killed, including forty-seven generals, in Belorussia alone as a result of partisan activity. Soviet claims for the partisans in the Ukraine were that in the same period 460,000 Germans were killed and 5,000 railway engines and 50,000 wagons were wrecked or damaged, and other sabotage carried out. Partisans were active on this scale throughout other Russian territories under enemy occupation.

The Germans suffered not only from severe damage to military organization and supplies, but also from the constant tension of being on guard against the lurking partisan danger, especially at night. They reacted savagely. Any village suspected of helping the partisans or of harbouring pro-partisan sympathies was eliminated. The villagers, comprising usually women and children, were deported and all buildings were burnt to the ground, but more often the whole population was shot. In the Kaluga province alone 20,000 villagers were shot and the same story was repeated in every occupied province. Indeed, in the measures of revenge and repression, taken as a result of partisan activity, there seems to have been no limit to the atrocities of which the Germans were capable.

The partisan movement and the boldness of partisan activities grew steadily. More than half a million partisans, well armed, supplied, and organized, were fighting behind German lines in 1943. They were a reflection of the popular hatred and of the uprising of the Russians against an enemy who had stirred the whole nation to a fury of hatred.

CHAPTER TWENTY

Russia and the Allies
May 1942–November 1943

THE Russians had reacted with prompt gratitude to the British and American declarations of support, made so soon after the German invasion. The Soviet leaders had approached relations with their new allies with a real cordiality. The common purpose of defeating Germany and destroying nazism brought Soviet Russia, Britain, and the United States together in a way that held promise of future understanding. But in 1942, as the Red Armies reeled back from the German *blitzkrieg* and the need for help became more and more desperate, Russian suspicion of the good faith of Britain and America began to take root.

The two problems of a second front and of Poland were the early sources of misunderstanding. In September 1941, when the grim battle for Moscow was imminent, Beaverbrook and Harriman had been warmly received in the capital. Both had shown understanding of Russia's predicament. Beaverbrook in particular proposed the fullest support for Russia, including the opening of a second front in Western Europe in 1942. Stalin had stressed the need for a second front in a letter in July to Churchill. But neither this initiative nor Beaverbrook's advocacy, on his return from Moscow, of a dramatic invasion of the continent in support of the Russians, impressed Churchill. The fact that Roosevelt and General Marshall were ready to consider this major operation, although the United States was not yet able to provide trained men or basic equipment, especially landing craft, for the purpose, placed Churchill in a difficult position.

In Moscow the Soviet leaders continued to press for a second front. In their desperation they were impervious to all argument designed to show why it was impossible in 1942. They assumed, and bitterly resented, that their allies were holding back. Churchill seemed to appreciate their tragic predicament, but remained convinced that a second front was impossible so soon.[1]

In April 1942 Stalin wrote to Churchill that Molotov would come to London to discuss two draft agreements on which opinions diverged. The two drafts arose from Soviet proposals, made to Anthony Eden, the British foreign secretary, on his visit to Moscow in December 1941, that Britain should recognize Soviet frontiers in the West as at the time of the

365

German invasion. This meant recognizing Soviet occupation of the Baltic states, of the new frontiers with Finland and Rumania, and with Poland. Eden had refused to commit himself on these proposals, but had agreed to convey them to the British and U.S. governments and to include them in the matters for negotiation for a formal Anglo-Soviet treaty. Churchill was disposed to accept Soviet occupation of the Baltic states and the frontier with Finland. The U.S. government expressed strong opposition on the ground that the Soviet proposals involved direct violation of the Atlantic charter.

Molotov arrived in London on 20 May and began discussions on the following day. He specifically requested British recognition of Soviet occupation of eastern Poland. But this was rejected as incompatible with the Anglo-Polish agreement of August 1939. Eden also rejected Molotov's suggestion of a secret agreement, recognizing Soviet claims on Rumania. The talks, although friendly, were reaching deadlock. On 23 May, however, Eden proposed that, in place of a territorial agreement, they should negotiate an Anglo-Soviet treaty of alliance for twenty years. Molotov obtained approval from Stalin and on 26 May the treaty was signed.

Molotov's other and indeed his main purpose was to press for a second front. On 22 May he had a long meeting with Churchill who explained at some length the British view of future operations on the continent.[2] 'Molotov is a statesman,' he later wrote to Roosevelt, 'and has a freedom of action very different from what you and I saw with Litvinov.'[3] But Molotov was also extremely tenacious in pursuing Soviet interests and, when towards the end of May he left London for Washington, he was evidently intent on securing American commitment to a second front in 1942.

In Washington Molotov, in fact, found a far greater readiness to consider this operation without raising insuperable obstacles. Indeed, according to the official Soviet *History*, Roosevelt twice assured him that a second front would be opened in 1942.[4] When Molotov returned to London on his way back to Moscow, he brought with him a draft statement for public release, after British approval, which contained the sentence: 'In the course of the conversations full understanding was reached with regard to the urgent tasks of creating a second front in Europe in 1942.'[5] Churchill now found himself in a difficult predicament and felt obliged to accept this statement, justifying it on the ground that it would mislead the Germans and cause them to hold more troops in readiness in the West. At the same time, to ensure that the Russians were not misled, he handed Molotov an *aide-mémoire*. It stated that, although preparations were in hand for a landing on the continent in August or September 1942, 'It is impossible to say in advance whether the situation will be such as to make this operation feasible when the time comes. We can therefore give no promise in the matter, but provided that it appears sound and sensible we

Nikita Sergeyevich Khrushchev, 1964

Alexei Nikolayevich Kosygin, 1966

shall not hesitate to put our plans into effect.'[6] In the coming months Churchill was usually to hedge every British undertaking with such caveats about feasibility; not unreasonably the Russians interpreted this practice as indicating not caution but reluctance to help.

On his return to Moscow Molotov was hailed as the bearer of firm undertakings from Britain and the U.S.A. to launch a major invasion of Europe in 1942. The Soviet press published the *communiqué* and the texts of the Anglo-Soviet and the Soviet–American agreements. The Supreme Soviet met in special session in the Kremlin on 18 June to ratify the Anglo-Soviet treaty, but the leading topic of the proceedings and of the press was the second front.

In the previous month the Red forces had suffered disastrous defeats at Kerch and then at Kharkov. Sevastopol, although fighting heroically, was doomed. German forces were massing to crash their way through Kursk to Voronezh and then to the Volga. To the Russian people beset by such catastrophes a second front in the West seemed their only hope of drawing off German divisions and sparing them the deaths of yet more thousands of their menfolk and the further devastation of their country. When it did not come, faith in their allies was deeply shaken.

Within a few weeks of Molotov's return to Moscow, Anglo-Soviet relations began to decline. The immediate reason was British difficulty in maintaining the north Russian convoys, carrying British and American war materials to Murmansk and Archangel. The convoys had begun in August 1941, but by the following March the accumulated supplies in Allied ports far exceeded available transport. Both Russians and Americans were pressing the British to provide escorts and to run more convoys. Churchill acquiesced but with great reluctance. British naval resources were fully extended, as neither of the allies appreciated. Moreover, the Germans had stationed U-boats and planes in northern Norway and by March 1942 the warships *Tirpitz*, *Sheer*, and *Hipper* were waiting at Trondheim. The April convoy, PQ13, had lost five of its nineteen merchantmen in attacks by German aircraft and destroyers, and the cruiser *Trinidad* had been sunk. On 18 May, PQ16, a convoy of thirty-five ships, got through with a loss of eight ships. But convoy PQ17 which sailed from Iceland on 27 June, bound for Archangel, lost twenty-three ships in what Churchill called 'one of the most melancholy naval episodes in the whole war'.[7]

On 17 July Churchill wrote to Stalin, explaining the British decision to suspend the convoys for a time. Stalin's reply was curt. He made it clear that failure to maintain the convoys for fear of losses and postponement of the second front until 1943 were acts of bad faith and near-treachery at this time when Russia was so desperately hard-pressed.[8] Churchill wrote again on 30 July informing Stalin that a large convoy would sail for Archangel in the first week of September and offering to meet him. Stalin responded at once with an invitation for him to visit Russia.

N

Churchill arrived in Moscow on 12 August. He had undertaken this mission with misgivings. He had always hated the 'wicked regime' of the bolsheviks. He made the journey now from a sense of duty to explain Allied military plans and their reasons for postponing the second front until next year. But he was also eager to meet Stalin, 'the great revolutionary chief and profound Russian statesman with whom for the next three years I was to be in intimate, rigorous but always exciting and at times even genial association'.[9] From the outset he was clearly impressed by Stalin who bluntly expressed his disappointment and his disagreement with Allied military reasoning. But Stalin was quick to recognize the significance of 'Operation Torch', the plan for the British–American campaign in North Africa. Indeed, Churchill noted 'the Russian dictator's swift and complete mastery of a problem hitherto novel to him. Very few people could have comprehended in so few minutes the reasons which we had all so long been wrestling with for months. He saw it all in a flash.' [10] After further meetings with Stalin and Molotov, Churchill departed at dawn on 16 August, feeling 'definitely encouraged by my visit to Moscow'.[11] But, despite the understanding which Churchill thought he had forged with Stalin, Anglo-Russian relations were to decline further as the great trial at Stalingrad approached.

The Russians regarded Britain and to a lesser extent the U.S.A. with sullen suspicion. Churchill's visit, which had received little publicity, was of interest only in so far as it furthered the opening of the second front. The *communiqué*, released at the end of the visit, contained the usual references to the common purpose of Soviet Russia and Britain, but the absence of positive statements on the second front confirmed the general misgiving that it was to be delayed. The visit of Wendell Wilkie, as the personal representative of the American president, aroused more interest and enthusiasm. Wilkie suggested irresponsibly that the U.S.A. was ready to launch the second front in 1942, but that British military leaders and Churchill himself were raising obstacles. Soon after his departure Soviet propaganda organs began to mount a vicious anti-British campaign.

Early in October in replies to questions submitted by the Associated Press correspondent in Moscow, Stalin stressed the urgent importance of a major operation in Western Europe to relieve the pressure on the Russian front. He commented that 'help from the Allies to the Soviet Union had so far been of little effect' and that effective aid demanded simply 'the full and timely fulfilment by the allies of their obligations'.[12]

The next step was that Molotov released a note to the effect that the nazi leaders in allied hands should be tried as criminals without delay. This was a reference to Rudolf Hess, Hitler's deputy, who had flown to Scotland in May of the previous year on a private peace mission and was still held in custody. *Pravda* even alleged that Britain was 'a sanctuary for gangsters' and that Hess was enjoying diplomatic privileges as an accredited envoy.[13]

The Soviet purpose in stirring up anti-British feeling was evidently to create some diversion and to make Britain a scapegoat at a time when the news from the Stalingrad front was depressing. But this propaganda also reflected the real bitterness felt by Russians at this time. Sharp British reactions caused the Soviet authorities to drop the references to Hess, but Russian antagonism towards Britain remained. During October, too, Stalin's letters to Churchill were marked by surliness.

In his report on 6 November 1942, the twenty-fifth anniversary of the revolution, in which he reviewed the military situation, Stalin stated that the absence of a second front was the chief reason why the Germans had been able to hold the initiative and gain major successes in Russia during 1942. Referring to the position in the first world war when there had been a second front, Stalin sought to demonstrate that current Russian losses and sufferings were primarily due to Allied failure to invade Europe. The arguments were specious, but the Russians, bewildered still by the spectacular advance of the Germans, the ineffectiveness of the Red Army, and the failure of Stalin and their other leaders, readily accepted them.

Stalin went on to express his confidence that sooner or later the Allies would launch a second front. He then dwelt at length on the value of the Anglo-Soviet–American coalition which would be victorious against the Axis powers. His speech closed on a note of strong confidence. Preparations were well advanced for the great counter-offensive at Stalingrad later in November. Probably also he knew that the allied landing in North Africa, about which Churchill had told him, had begun and that the Germans were in retreat in the western desert. The auguries were good. In his Order of the Day he conveyed his new confidence to the Russian people in a phrase—'Soon there will be a holiday in our street!'—which made them feel that the worst was behind them.[14]

News of the North African landing, released two days later, cheered the Russians. They did not accept this operation as a second front, but it showed that the Allies were in earnest. Stalin in replies to further questions from the Associated Press correspondent, praised the 'masterly destruction of the Italo-German forces in the western desert'. He paid tribute to the 'first-class organizers who had accomplished this difficult military operation'. As in his comments to Churchill, he showed full appreciation of the importance of the North African landing in grasping the initiative, undermining German authority in the Axis and demoralizing Hitler's allies, and shaking France from her 'condition of inertia'.[15]

After the battle of Stalingrad the Soviet attitude towards the Allies became more cordial. Russians shed their anxieties about survival and were confident, at times over-confident, about ultimate victory. While still demanding a second front, they acknowledged the importance of the North African victories and of the bombing of Germany. The Allies could no longer be accused of inactivity. Moreover, in 1943 Allied shipments of aircraft, vehicles, food, and raw materials mounted considerably. In particular, American vehicles and food were valued in the Red Army.

At this time the one discordant factor in relations between Soviet Russia and the Western powers was the Polish problem which, rooted in more than 300 years of Russo-Polish animosity, seemed insoluble. Under the agreement signed on 30 July 1941 by Maisky and General Sikorski, diplomatic relations had been established with the Polish government in London. The Poles undertook to mobilize an army in Russia, commanded by a Pole, to be approved by the Soviet government and under the orders of the Soviet Supreme Command. The Soviet government also promised to grant amnesty to all Poles held prisoner on Soviet territory. Two problems overcast this agreement from the beginning. The first was Soviet refusal to give any undertaking to restore Poland to her frontiers as they were before the German and Russian invasions of September 1939. The second concerned the Poles and in particular the war prisoners, including twelve to fifteen thousand officers and NCOs, deported to Russia in 1939. The Polish government pressed for information about these officers. By the end of 1941 some 400 had been located in a camp near Vologda, but the others were missing. Failure to find these men aggravated Polish mistrust.

Formation of the Polish army in Russia which was to fight alongside the Red Army progressed. By December 1941 General Anders had 73,415 Poles under his command. But it is doubtful whether these Poles, all with recent and bitter memories of being prisoners in Russian hands, had any real intention of fighting on the Russian front. According to Soviet sources, the Poles during the critical months of 1941 when their help would have been valuable, consistently found excuses for not being sent to the front. In fact the existence on Russian soil of this army, led by Anders and other violently anti-Soviet officers, had become a source of resentment and even anxiety to the Russians. Any breakdown of the Soviet regime, and until Stalingrad this possibility could not be excluded, might lead to Anders' army running amok or emulating the exploits of the Czech Brigade in the civil war. When Churchill proposed that the Poles with their dependents should be allowed to leave Russia by way of Iran and fight on the Western front, Stalin readily agreed. The Russians were indeed glad to be rid of them, although their departure on the eve of the great conflict at Stalingrad gave the impression of desertion in the face of the German enemy.[16]

To Stalin, looking ahead to the peace settlement at the end of the war, Poland was perhaps the most intractable problem of all. He was a realist and did not pretend that the age-old hostility between Russian and Pole would suddenly disappear. At the same time he was determined that Russia should not have on her frontiers after the war a hostile Poland, under the control of such anti-Russian elements as Anders and most of the members of the Polish government in London.

Early in 1943 the basic features of Russia's policy towards Poland began to emerge. The Polish frontier in the east was to follow the Curzon Line and in compensation the Poles were to expand westwards at the expense of Germany. The territories in eastern Poland, annexed by Russia in September 1939, were inhabited by Ukrainians and Belorussians and, according to Soviet claims, they rightly belonged within the Soviet Union. In spring 1943 the Soviet press began a campaign against the Polish government in London, asserting that it was not representative of the Polish people. Next the formation of the Union of Polish Patriots was announced. Its president was Wanda Wassilewska, a Polish writer who had become a Soviet citizen in 1939 and later a deputy in the Supreme Soviet. She was married to Alexander Korneichuk, a Ukrainian playwright who had been appointed vice-commissar for foreign affairs with responsibility for Slav countries. Apart from her the members of this Union of Polish Patriots, who included a few officers who had refused to leave Russia with Anders' army and a number of young Poles, were unknown. This bold attempt to organize a pro-Soviet government which would take over from the well-known and apparently entrenched Polish government in London which had Allied support, seemed at this time unlikely to succeed.

In April 1943 the Germans announced that they had found at Katyn near Smolensk mass graves containing the bodies of several thousand Polish officers. These were the officers concerning whom the Polish government had been plaguing the Soviet government for information, and it was now widely alleged that the Russians had massacred them in spring 1940. The Soviet government at once issued a frantic denial of these allegations. The Polish government stated that it did not accept the German charges, but proposed that the International Red Cross should carry out an impartial investigation of the graves. The Soviet government indignantly rejected this suggestion. Despite Russian denials, however, many assumed that the 12,500 officers and NCOs on whom no information could be obtained had, in fact, been killed and buried by the NKVD at Katyn.

On 27 April 1943 the Soviet government suspended diplomatic relations with the London Poles on the ground of their attitude to the Katyn allegations. The Soviet press intensified its campaign, castigating them as imperialists and German agents. At the same time Wanda Wassilewska, as president of the Union of Polish Patriots, published an important article in *Izvestiya* in which she called upon every Pole to recognize that Soviet Russia was his natural ally and that 'such an alliance is a matter of life and death to his country, especially now when Europe's and Poland's fate is being settled on this [the Russian] front'. She went on to state that a new Polish army would soon be formed in Russia to fight with the Red Army. It would owe allegiance not to the London government but to the Soviet Union until the new Polish government had been formed. The

Tadeusz Kosciuszko Division was announced on 9 May and was built up rapidly. The strength of the division was soon in the region of 15,000 officers and men, mainly from the parts of eastern Poland annexed by the Russians. These Poles evidently recognized that they must forget the past, even the recent past of Katyn, and come to terms with Soviet Russia, if Poland was to survive. Germany was the real enemy and by October 1943 the Kosciuszko division was fighting alongside Red troops.

In the spring and early summer of 1943 Soviet relations with the Western Allies at the official level became notably cordial. In part this was due to anxiety that the break with the London Poles should not disturb relations with the West. In the main, however, this cordiality flowed from Soviet concern to reach real understanding with Britain and the United States in negotiating a three-power peace at the end of the war. But among the Russian people during the first six months of 1943 and especially in June, as they awaited the crucial campaign in the Kursk salient, there were ominous suspicions. The second front had not yet materialized. The Russians, severely rationed and working intolerably long hours, felt strongly that their allies had not yet proved their worth or their good faith. The Allied victory in North Africa, on which Stalin had sent warm congratulations to Roosevelt and Churchill,[17] and which the Soviet press had reported, was welcomed by the Russians, but as prelude to the second front. Stalin in his Order of the Day on 1 May referred in enthusiastic terms to the victorious Allies in North Africa and to the bombing of Germany as 'heralding the formation of a second front in Europe'.[18] Indeed the message issued by the Sovinformbureau on 22 June 1943, the second anniversary of the German invasion, stated that 'without a second front victory over Germany is impossible'.[19]

Among Russians, moreover, rumours were current that the Germans had made approaches to the Allies for a separate peace, and they feared that the Allies might accept. The fact that among the Allies rumours were rife that a separate Molotov–Ribbentrop agreement was possible was an indication of the constantly gnawing mistrust at the roots of the alliance. Stalin in his Order of the Day denounced German talk of peace and the rumours in the Western press that any of the Allies might come to terms with Germany, 'as though it is not clear that only the complete destruction of the Hitlerite armies and the unconditional surrender of Hitlerite Germany can bring Europe to peace.'[20]

At this time Stalin made a significant gesture of goodwill towards the Allies in dissolving the Comintern. This association of communist parties, established in 1919 by Lenin with the purpose of fomenting world revolution, had always represented for the Western powers the direct threat of militant communism. The resolution of the presidium of the executive committee of the Comintern, dissolving it, was hailed in Britain and America as clearing the way for real understanding and close co-operation with Soviet Russia.

For Stalin, the opponent of internationalism and the author of *Socialism in one Country*, the decision to disband the Comintern was a logical step.[21] Before and even more after the German invasion, it had been an embarrassment. In reply to a question put to him by an English press correspondent, concerning the impact of this dissolution on international relations, Stalin was explicit. He explained that it would put an end to the lies, spread by the nazis, that Moscow intended to interfere in the affairs of other states and 'to bolshevize them', and that the communist parties of various countries acted not in the interests of their peoples but on orders from outside. It would facilitate the work of patriots of the freedom-loving countries, irrespective of political and religious beliefs, in the struggle against fascism. The dissolution of the Comintern was, in fact, 'correct and timely'. His explanation concentrated on the immediate task of destroying the nazi menace, but it also contained reference to the 'organization in the future of the co-operation of peoples on the basis of equality'.[22]

Stalin had declined invitations from Roosevelt and Churchill to meet with them early in 1943. He wrote that he could not be away from Moscow and suggested that they discuss problems by correspondence. He added an expression of his confidence that both leaders would honour their promises to open the second front in the spring of 1943. In fact, despite the cordiality of official Soviet references to the Allies during these early months of 1943, Stalin's correspondence with Churchill and Roosevelt had become unfriendly and even offensive. He was critical of the delay in Anglo-American operations in North Africa and unenthusiastic about the proposed landing in Sicily, which 'cannot replace the second front in France'. He recalled that the second front had been admitted as a possibility in 1942 and as a firm expectation not later than the spring of 1943, and he stressed the need to embark on this operation not later than the early summer.[23] When on 30 March Churchill informed him that the March convoy to north Russia must be postponed because of the concentration of a powerful German battlefleet at Narvik, Stalin replied angrily that this meant 'a catastrophic diminution of supplies or arms and military raw materials' for the Russian forces at a critical time.[24]

In May 1943, as the build-up for the offensive on the Kursk salient was reaching a climax, all Russians waited in a fever of anxiety for the outcome of this crucial battle. At this time Roosevelt and Churchill informed Stalin that the Anglo-American invasion of Western Europe would be postponed until the spring of 1944. Stalin exploded in anger, charging the Allies with bad faith and in his letter of 24 May to Churchill he stated bluntly that 'the preservation of our confidence in the allies is being subjected to a severe stress'.[25]

The great Russian victory at the Kursk salient made the second front no longer a matter of life and death. But the damage had been done in entrenching in Russian minds the conviction that, while Russians died in hundreds of thousands, the Allies were concerned with strategy and saving the lives of their own troops. No Russian could believe that two such mighty industrial powers as the United States and Britain were incapable of mounting an invasion of Europe late in 1942 or certainly in 1943.[26]

For all his ready understanding of the strategy of war and of the difficulties of sea-borne invasion, Stalin was mistrustful of Churchill and Roosevelt, and no man was more tenacious in harbouring mistrust. At the same time he was earnestly seeking close relations and co-operation with them, and believed that peace after the war would depend on the three powers remaining united.

Relations declined further between Russia and Britain in the autumn of 1943. The North Russian convoys had been suspended since March. Molotov sent for the British ambassador at the end of September and asked that they should be resumed. Churchill, after applying strong pressure on the Admiralty, informed Stalin of his plans to send four convoys, the first to sail on 12 November and the others at twenty-eight-day intervals. Molotov's request had been peremptorily worded. Churchill's reply of 1 October was formal and hedged with conditions and explanations, intended to guard against Soviet charges of bad faith, if any change in plans became necessary. Further, Churchill formally demanded relaxation of the Soviet restrictions applied to British naval personnel, serving in north Russia.[27] This letter offended Stalin who responded so sharply and negatively that Churchill, in fact, refused to accept the reply and returned it personally to the Soviet ambassador. Eden who was at this time on his way to Moscow to attend the foreign ministers' conference there, managed in talks to restore understanding.[28]

Stalin had already in August agreed that a meeting of the three heads of government was 'absolutely desirable'.[29] At the same time he declined to leave Moscow. He gave approval for an exploratory meeting of foreign ministers and proposed that it should take place in Moscow in October. In these meetings, which lasted twelve days and ranged widely, Soviet concern was primarily that Operation Overlord, as the Allied invasion of Western Europe had been named, should take place in spring 1944 and no later. The Americans eagerly endorsed this understanding, while the British were more cautious because of commitments in the Mediterranean. Eden, in the course of a long meeting, nevertheless found Stalin 'in excellent humour and at no point in the evening was there any recrimination about the past or any disposition to ignore real difficulties that face us'.[30]

Although their meetings were intended to be exploratory, the foreign ministers reached firm agreement on setting up a European advisory committee in London to deal with problems arising in Germany and on the continent after the collapse of the Hitler regime, and a special commission for Italy. They signed a four-power declaration, the fourth power being China, on unconditional surrender of their enemies. They also agreed a statement which was an important step towards a United Nations organization. This gave special satisfaction to the U.S. secretary of state, Cordell Hull, who feared that Russia might become isolationist after the war. It also reassured the Russians who entertertained similar fears of a revival of American isolationism. In fact, as both Eden and Cordell Hull reported to their respective heads of government, the conference had given real evidence that Soviet Russia was eager for permanent friendship and co-operation with Britain and the United States.[31]

Only after lengthy correspondence and discussion was Teheran agreed as the venue for the meeting of Stalin, Churchill, and Roosevelt. Other venues, such as Cairo and Basra, had been suggested. Stalin was not, however, prepared to move farther from his own frontiers than Teheran. His reason was that as commander-in-chief of the Soviet forces he could not leave Moscow, but that for this important summit meeting he would go as far as Teheran which had direct communications with Moscow. The major factor in his insistence that the Allies must come to Moscow or, as a special concession, to the Soviet frontier was, however, concern for Russian prestige. The Russians were carrying the real burden. The Allies were operating on a small scale, while Russia was suffering the full horror and destruction of war and was now repelling the enemy. It was for the Allies to come to Moscow. This feeling of national pride and the acute sensitivity of Russians in matters of their prestige were to burgeon further, and they were not free of arrogance as in 1944 they won greater triumphs. But pride and arrogance were superficial and passing: at root their attitude was that, as in the thirteenth century Russia had shielded Western Europe from the Mongol Hordes of Chingiz Khan, so now in the twentieth century Russia was defending the West against the German hordes; the West owed Russia a debt of gratitude and respect that should be paid.

The conference in Teheran opened on 28 November 1943 and the discussions of the three heads of state were extremely amicable. Future action against the Germans was the basic theme. The British and Americans had agreed on Operation Overlord, to take place in May or at the very latest by the beginning of July 1944. The Anglo-American armies in Italy would continue their northward advance to Rome and farther. Other projects discussed were a landing in the south of France and action on a smaller scale in the Eastern Mediterranean. Stalin, speaking bluntly but genially, stressed the primacy of Overlord. Lengthy discussions ranged over other theatres of action, but he returned persistently to the importance of the cross-channel invasion. Churchill, hedging unnecessarily on firm undertakings to launch the invasion in May and on occasions behaving petulantly, was undoubtedly the main cause of Stalin's persistence on this point.[32]

On 30 November Churchill, in fact, had a long private meeting with

Stalin in which he reassured him of Britain's earnest intention to pursue the cross-channel invasion with all vigour. Stalin replied frankly that the Red Army was war-weary and was counting on a successful Allied invasion of northern France. For this reason he was anxious to establish that the operation would be undertaken on time as promised.[33] He also undertook to launch a large-scale attack on the Russian front to coincide with the Allied invasion. Later in the day he was gratified by the formal assurance to Roosevelt and Churchill that Operation Overlord would take place in May.

In their formal and informal sessions the three war leaders discussed the future of Poland and Germany and Churchill made a plea for lenient treatment of Finland with which Stalin expressed agreement. But in his insistent references to Poland and his plea for Finland, both countries on Russia's borders and of direct importance to Russian security, while distant from Britain, Churchill undoubtedly angered Stalin, who nevertheless remained calm. In their military conclusions, set out in a document which all three initialled, they agreed on supporting Yugoslav partisans and on seeking to persuade Turkey to come into the war with a Soviet guarantee of support if Bulgaria declared war on her. But the basic fact of the conference was agreement on the invasion of northern France in May of the following year.

The Teheran meeting brought together the three men who, in Churchill's grandiloquent words, 'controlled a large preponderance of the naval and three-quarters of all the air forces of the world, and could direct armies of nearly twenty millions of men, engaged in the most terrible of wars that had yet occurred in human history.'[34] Of these three men Stalin clearly emerged as the dominant figure. He was incisive in his comments, clear about his objectives, patient and inexorable in pursuing them and, strangely, he seemed to emerge as the most attractive personality. A small man, not striking in appearance, he possessed a powerful feline charm. Roosevelt fell under his spell. Churchill often appeared unnerved in his presence.[35]

Stalin had made a similar impact on all who had attended the meeting of foreign ministers in Moscow in the previous month. General Deane, head of the U.S. military mission, noted that one could not fail to recognize 'qualities of greatness in the man' and this was the impression of all who met him.[36]

CHAPTER TWENTY-ONE

Victory in Germany
14 January 1944–9 May 1945

AFTER, but only after, the victory at Stalingrad did Stalin assert his role as military leader. Praise of his name had been muted, almost silent, during 1941 and 1942. After Stalingrad the Soviet press and every organ of propaganda in Soviet Russia burst into full chorus, acclaiming 'the military genius of Stalin'. For the remainder of the war this praise mounted in a crescendo of extravagance.

Driven by an insatiable need for both adulation and power, Stalin jealously guarded his position as dictator. He had been keenly aware that the overwhelming advances of the German armies in the first eighteen months of the war had exposed his leadership to destructive criticism. He claimed, although it was untrue, that the Germans had succeeded in 1941, because they had perfidiously taken the Red Army by surprise. But the disasters of 1942 could not be attributed still to surprise attack. The excuses then given were the failure of the Allies to open a second front and, after the disgrace of Rostov, the failure of the Red Army itself. Russians, who recognized that Stalin and the party were largely to blame for these catastrophes, were silent. Indeed, despite Stalin's disastrous miscalculations, the Russian people instinctively held to their faith in him. He was their man of steel and their leader who had in his speeches of 3 July and 7 November given them strength. He had remained in Moscow in the grim days of October 1941 and with Zhukov had saved the city. After Stalingrad they were ready to hail him as the great architect of victory.[1]

Moreover, after the decisive battle of the Kursk salient, Stalin gave rein to his Russian patriotism. The press extolled Great Russian nationalism in terms that were almost jingoist. Tsarist ideas were revived. Nine Suvorov schools, set up at this time to train an officer *élite*, were modelled directly on the tsarist cadet schools. The curriculum required a high standard of general education and included training in good manners and dancing. Officers graduating from these schools were to be not only dedicated professional soldiers, but gentlemen, such as were, they believed, produced by West Point and Sandhurst.

The campaign to raise the status of officers, begun after the fall of Rostov in July 1942, had continued. Epaulettes which had been the hated

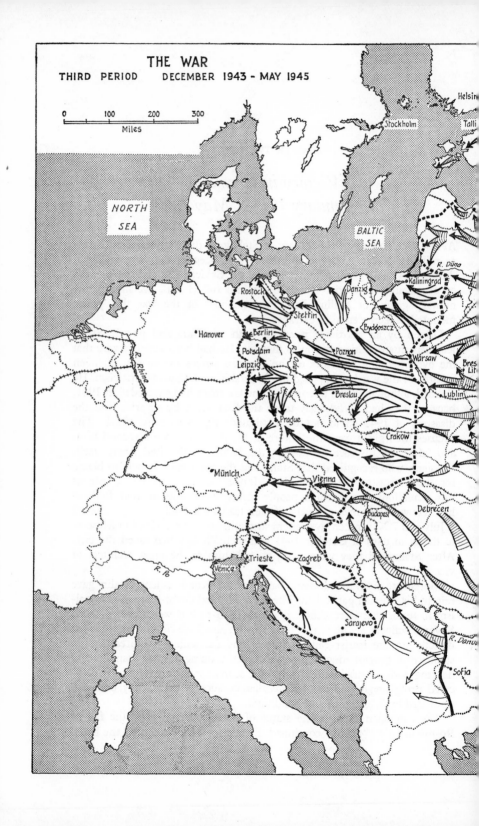

THE WAR
THIRD PERIOD   DECEMBER 1943 - MAY 1945

0   100   200   300
Miles

NORTH
SEA

BALTIC
SEA

Helsir

Stockholm

Talli

R. Düna

Kaliningrad

Rostock

Danzig

Stettin

Bydgoszcz

Hanover

Berlin

Poznan

Warsaw

Bres
Li

Potsdam

R. Oder

Leipzig

Breslau

Lublin

R. Rhine

Prague

Crakow

Münich

Vienna

Debrecen

Budapest

Trieste

Zagreb

Venice

R. Po

Sarajevo

R. Danu

Sofia

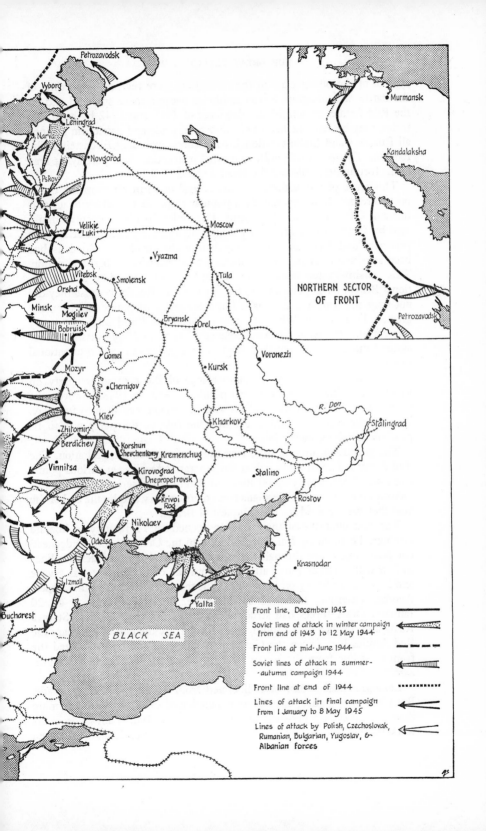

NORTHERN SECTOR OF FRONT

Petrozavodsk
Vyborg
Leningrad
Narva
Novgorod
Pskov
Velikie Luki
Moscow
Vyazma
Vitebsk
Smolensk
Tula
Orsha
Minsk
Mogilev
Bobruisk
Bryansk
Orel
Mozyr
Gomel
Kursk
Voronezh
Chernigov
R. Dnieper
Kiev
Kharkov
R. Don
Stalingrad
Zhitomir
Berdichev
Korshun Shevchenkovsky Kremenchug
Vinnitsa
Kirovograd
Dnepropetrovsk
Stalino
Krivoi Rog
Rostov
Nikolaev
Odessa
Izmail
Yalta
Krasnodar
Bucharest
BLACK SEA

Murmansk
Kandalaksha
Petrozavodsk

Front line, December 1943

Soviet lines of attack in winter campaign
from end of 1943 to 12 May 1944

Front line at mid-June 1944

Soviet lines of attack in summer-
-autumn campaign 1944

Front line at end of 1944

Lines of attack in final campaign
from 1 January to 8 May 1945

Lines of attack by Polish, Czechoslovak,
Rumanian, Bulgarian, Yugoslav, &
Albanian forces

symbol of the officer class in the revolution, were revived at the time of the battle of Stalingrad. Soviet uniforms became more splendid and, as the Red Armies expunged the disgraces of 1941 and 1942 by great victories, they became the heroes of the nation. Pride and patriotism gripped all Russians and Stalin's nationalist measures, including Eisenstein's film *Ivan the Terrible*, made on his personal instructions and portraying Ivan as his forerunner, reflected the general mood.

This wave of nationalism and the revival of so much from the tsarist past were not, however, merely a popular response to victory or an outburst of Great Russian chauvinism. The nation had been deeply humiliated by German *Untermensch* propaganda and the treatment of Russian prisoners and civilians. Since long before the revolution Russians had been sensitive to criticism that theirs was a primitive or barbaric nation. This sensitivity remained acute. Stalin in 1943 refused to allow additional British naval personnel to be sent to north Russia, because they did not treat the Russians as equals. But German racist policy had been the greatest insult of all. When the tide of war turned and ultimate victory was certain, Russians felt a resurgence of faith in Holy Russia and reassured themselves by recalling the past and giving expression to national pride.

Stalin did not overlook the importance of the communist party on which the regime and his personal position rested. In 1943, however, the people were jubilantly nationalistic and this mood was allowed full play. In the following year and afterwards the role of the party was to be proclaimed with growing force.

The year 1944, indeed, gave Russians every reason for exultation. The Red Army launched no less than ten separate offensives at various points along the front, nearly 2,000 miles in length. In a series of remarkable victories they drove the Germans from their country and by the end of the year they were poised for the conquest of Berlin.

The first offensive of the year was opened on 14 January to liberate Leningrad completely from blockade. From the Oranienbaum bridgehead one Red force broke through the strongly fortified German defence lines to join with another force, attacking from the east. Fighting was savage and losses were heavy on both sides. But the Germans were hurled back. Another offensive, launched at this time, liberated Novgorod on 20 January. Other forces had struck westwards from the region of Staraya Russa and, farther to the south, from Kholm. By the end of February the Red Armies had driven the Germans to the west and had stabilized the front on a line from the Narva river in the north, running to the southeast.

Leningrad had at last been liberated from its thirty-month blockade. But it was now a ghost city. Of its population of some three million, more than a million had perished during its tragic ordeal. Thousands of its workers, the vanguard of the Russian revolutionary proletariat, had been evacuated to serve industries newly established in the east. Thousands more Leningradtsi had been evacuated in 1943 when the blockade had been breached. Only 600,000 were present to welcome their liberators. The retreating Germans had left behind them a trail of destruction, including the beautiful and historic buildings of Tsarskoe Selo, renamed Pushkin after the revolution, which Catherine I had built for Peter the Great in 1714–15 and which subsequent monarchs had embellished. But most tragic was the death or dispersal of the real Leningradtsi who had given the city its lively individuality as the most Western outpost of Russian thought and culture.[2]

The second offensive took place in the Ukraine in extreme weather conditions in February–March. Red Army advances on four distinct fronts cleared the Germans from the southern and eastern parts of the Ukraine. By the end of 1943 the Russians had liberated Kiev and, forcing the Dnieper at many points, had established themselves west of the river. Hitler was determined to hold the western bank of the Dnieper and to eject the Red Army from their new bridgeheads. He ordered his troops to stand fast in the Korshun–Shevchenkovsky salient, some fifty miles south of Kiev. The German plan was to attack to the north and south of the salient. But in forming this plan Hitler and his High Command had no appreciation of the strength of the 1st Ukrainian Front, commanded by General Vatutin, to the north of the salient, or of the 2nd Ukrainian Front, commanded by General Konev, to the south. The two Russian commanders were co-ordinating their offensives to encircle the Germans in a repetition of the Stalingrad victory.

On 24 January the Red Armies began their offensives, the first Ukrainian Front moving south-east from the vicinity of Belaya Tserkov, the second Ukrainian front moving westwards from above Kirovograd. On 3 February they joined at the small town of Zvenigorodka, thus completing the encirclement of the German divisions within the salient. Inexorably the Red forces closed. On 9 February they took Gorodishche and five days later Korshun itself. The Germans made an attempt to break out and another German force tried to force a passage through the Russian lines to relieve their beleaguered comrades. Both attempts failed. On 17–18 February the Russians finally liquidated the enemy divisions within the salient. It was a period of concentrated slaughter and German losses were severe. Their attempt to hold this salient had cost them 55,000 dead and 18,000 prisoners as well as 500 tanks and other equipment.

The German 8th Army, although severely mauled in its attempt to break through the Russian encirclement of the Korshun salient, now sought to dig into positions on a line running from east of Vinnitsa down almost to Kirovograd. The thaw had already begun and in the deep Ukrainian mud military operations were taken to be impossible. The Germans believed that they had time to prepare strong defences. But on 5 March General Konev launched his mud-offensive. The difficulties were enormous. Russian supplies had to be brought in by air-lifts, but the T-34 tank stood up to the conditions and Konev's offensive gathered momentum. The Germans, taken completely by surprise by this operation which they had thought impossible, abandoned their equipment and fell back in disorder. Konev's forces moved rapidly to the Bug river and on to northern Rumania which they invaded towards the end of March.

To the north the 1st Ukrainian Front was now commanded by Zhukov, for Vatutin had been killed on 1 March by a band of Ukrainian nationalists. This front advanced more slowly. Drawing nearer to German territory, the Russians were meeting stronger opposition. But they continued to press forward along a wide front and by mid-June Zhukov was poised to strike at Lvov.

The 3rd Ukrainian Front, lying farther to the south and commanded by General Malinovsky, opened the third major offensive of the year on 9 March. Advancing rapidly from north-west of Krivoi Rog, the troops of this front swept westwards to the Bug river. On 28 March they captured Nikolaev and on 10 April liberated Odessa.

The 4th Ukrainian Front, commanded by General Tolbukhin, began the task of liberating the Crimea on 11 April. Hitler with foolish obstinacy sought to hold the peninsula even after the Russians had recovered the Ukrainian territories in the north. The Russians invaded the Crimea first from the Sivash, the salty inlet to the north. At the same time Red units attacked German defences in the Perekop Isthmus. A special Black Sea army, commanded by Yeremenko, had landed and captured Kerch, Feodosia, and Yalta, and had pursued the German and Rumanian troops to the walls of Sevastopol. Tolbukhin waited for two weeks while massing guns, tanks, and other equipment, but his assault on the citadel, when launched, was devastating, and on 12 May Sevastopol was liberated. In 1941–2 the Russians had held out for 250 days against vastly superior German forces: in 1944 the Red Army, now with marked superiority, took only thirty-five days to achieve the same goal. German losses were, moreover, 100,000 officers and men killed or taken prisoner.[3]

Late in May a pause came in the fighting which lasted until mid-June. The front was now stabilized on a line which, except for the great Belorussian bulge, ran from Narva south through northern Rumania to the Black Sea. Germany's satellites were acutely uneasy. At the time of the invasion of northern Rumania by the Red Army, Molotov made the official announcement that the Soviet government had no territorial claims on Rumania and had no intention of changing the existing social order. Stalin in his Order of the Day on 1 May paid warm tribute to the Allies, whose invasion of northern France would, he knew, happen very soon. He laid stress on the fact that 'the liberation of Europe and the smashing of Germany on her own soil can be done only on the basis of joint efforts from the Soviet Union, Great Britain, and the United States as they strike from the east and the west.'[4] Referring to the satellites he stated that they must see now that Germany had lost the war. 'But,' he added ominously, 'their governments cannot be relied upon to break with Germany and the sooner the people take over and make peace the better.' [5]

Preparations were mounting for the Soviet summer offensive which would clearly strike strongly at the Belorussian bulge, the only Soviet territory still in German occupation. The Russians were expected to drive the Germans westwards and to enter Poland. This made the Polish problem more acute. Stalin had in April made cordial gestures to the Roman Catholic Church, intended to impress Roman Catholics in the United States and also to appease the Polish Catholic clergy, most of whom were anti-Russian. A major development, late in May, was the statement, issued by the Union of Polish Patriots, that the People's Council of Poland had been set up in Warsaw on 1 January 1944 by the democratic parties and groups struggling against the Germans. This national council had, the statement continued, received the enthusiastic support of the Polish people. The council had now sent delegates to Moscow for discussions with the Union of Polish Patriots, to inspect the Polish army, and to establish relations with the Allied governments, including the Soviet government. Stalin and Molotov, it was also announced, received the delegates with great cordiality. The Polish government in London promptly denounced the national council as a group of nonentities under Moscow's orders and without popular support. This council was, however, already beginning to act as a provisional government, and it was to provide the basis of the Lublin committee which was soon to serve as the government of Poland.

The opening of the long-awaited second front on 6 June was warmly welcomed by the Russians. The general goodwill towards the Allies was expressed by Stalin in a statement in *Pravda*. He referred to the operation of forcing the Channel along a wide front and the mass landings in northern France as 'unquestionably a brilliant success for our Allies. One must admit that the history of war does not know of an undertaking comparable to it for breadth of conception, grandeur of scale, and mastery of execution.' [6] This was the opening of a period when the Soviet press referred to the Allies with great warmth and even published a full statement of the arms and materials which they had sent to the Soviet Union since June 1941.

The fourth offensive of the year was launched along the Karelian Isthmus against the Finns on 9 June. Within two days Red troops had broken through the Finnish lines. By 19 June they had broached the Mannerheim Line and had taken the important town of Vyborg. To the north of Lake Onega the Red Army made another thrust. By the end of July the Finns had been driven back behind their own frontier.

The major Russian summer offensive, the fifth offensive of the year, was, however, directed at the Belorussian bulge. For this massive operation the Russians had made thorough preparations. Their armies were grouped in four fronts—the 1st Baltic Front, commanded by General Bagramian and the 3rd Belorussian Front, commanded by General Cherniakhovsky, both under the general command of Marshal Vassilevsky, and then the 1st Belorussian Front, commanded by General Rokossovsky and the 2nd Belorussian Front, commanded by General Zakharov, both under the general command of Marshal Zhukov. In these four fronts were concentrated 166 divisions, 9 brigades, and reserves, 31,000 guns and mortars, 5,200 tanks, and self-propelled guns, and more than 6,000 aircraft. They now enjoyed a tremendous superiority over the enemy in men and especially in weapons. Their ratio to the Germans in men was 2:1; in guns and mortars 2·9:1; in tanks and mobile guns 4·3:1; in aircraft 4·5:1. Ninety to a hundred trains arrived daily bringing supplies to the four Russian fronts. Trucks nearly 12,000 in number were ready and capable of delivering 25,000 tons of fuel, rations, and ammunition to the front lines on every journey.

The organization behind this massing of men and arms and the preparations for maintaining supplies during the fighting were impressive. They demonstrated how swiftly the Russians had mastered the basic problems of mounting operations on such a scale, which had hindered them in the past.[7]

Hitler had ordered his armies to hold the line of Vitebsk–Orsha–Mogilev–Bobruisk which was the most easterly part of the Belorussian bulge. The German command was, in fact, expecting the Red Armies to attack not directly against the Belorussian part of the front, but to the south of the Pripet Marshes. The Russian forces had been concentrated in great secrecy and the Germans had been misled by Russian reconnaissance operations, mounted on a large scale for this purpose. When on 23 June the Russians launched their offensive, they took the Germans by surprise.[8]

In the first five days of the offensive the Russians broke through the enemy lines at six places on this 450-mile front. They routed the Germans at Mogilev and Orsha, and encircled and destroyed strong German forces at Vitebsk to the north and Bobruisk to the south of the front. Hitler's orders to his troops to stand firm at the Berezina river were to no purpose. The Russian offensive had developed a furious momentum which swept the enemy back. On 1 July Borisov was liberated and then in a swift movement forces of the 3rd and 1st Belorussian Fronts encircled and destroyed the German 4th Army. On 3 July Minsk, the capital of Belorussia, was liberated.

The headlong Russian advance continued on a broadening front. In the south the troops of Rokossovsky's 1st Belorussian Front, advancing into Poland, took Lublin on 23 July and five days later captured Brest-Litovsk. To the north Cherniakhovsky's 3rd Belorussian Front captured Vilno on 13 July and pressed westwards towards east Prussia. All along this front now, however, the Russians, weary from their rapid advance, were meeting with increasingly desperate and stubborn resistance, and their progress was far slower.

Meanwhile on other fronts the Red forces were driving the Germans before them. In the sixth offensive of the year, Konev's 1st Ukrainian Front on 13 July struck south of the Pripet Marshes and, advancing swiftly, invested Lvov which they took after fierce fighting on 27 July. By the end of the month Konev had reached the Vistula river. In the north Maslenikov, commanding the 3rd Baltic Front, took Pskov and advanced into Esthonia in July. Another advance carried the Red Army into Latvia. For a time the German Army Group Nord was cut off from Lithuania and East Prussia, but then managed to break through to the south-west of the Gulf of Riga.

German losses of men and equipment were heavy in Belorussia and on the other fronts. Indeed the position was the reverse of two years ago when the Germans, seemingly invincible, had swept across the Russian plain, inflicting terrible destruction and casualties. Now the Germans were suffering. In the encirclement to the east of Minsk alone they had lost 100,000 men, most of whom had surrendered. Overall losses in the Belorussian campaign were in the region of 350,000 men. Army Group Mitte had been destroyed and Field-Marshal Model was appointed in place of the defeated Field-Marshal Busch, with the task of rushing all troops he could muster to the disintegrating eastern front.[9]

On 17 July Moscow witnessed a parade, lasting three hours, as 57,600 German prisoners, taken in the Belorussian campaign, marched through the city. They included several generals and hundreds of officers. The Russians watched them in silence and probably without the intense hatred felt by the Red troops at the front who had seen so much evidence of German savagery.[10] Everywhere the Germans had left a trail of death and destruction. The Germans had, it was estimated, murdered more than a million people during their occupation of Belorussia. This included the Jewish population and partisans and their families. Anticipating their withdrawal they had devised special equipment to destroy crops. The only areas saved from being turned into desert were those under partisan control.

The climax of German inhumanity towards people who fell into their hands was the vast murder-camp of Maidanek, two miles from Lublin. Here with great thoroughness the Germans had built gas chambers, incinerators, and disposal units, with the normal capacity of killing and cremating 2,000 people a day. In groups of 200 and 250, the victims, Jewish, Russian, and Polish men, women, and children were stripped of all clothing and possessions and packed into gas chambers. The corpses were loaded into lorries and taken next to the incinerators. Beside them stood great mounds of human ash which German guards used to fertilize their vegetable gardens.

It is estimated that the Germans put one-and-a-half million people to death in Maidanek.[11] All Red troops in the vicinity of Lublin were ordered to visit this camp so that they would understand the nature of their enemy and allow no feelings of pity or generosity to hinder them in the further task, now that they had driven the Germans from Russia, of destroying the nazi regime.

At this stage further tragedy was to beset the Poles in the premature and abortive Warsaw Rising of August–September 1944. This was to lead to bitter recriminations being levelled at the Russians and to bring discords between Russia and the Allies.

On the liberation of Lublin by Rokossovsky's 1st Belorussian Front on 23 July, the formation of the Polish Committee of National Liberation, soon to be known as the Lublin committee, was announced in a manifesto. The committee claimed to have been appointed by representatives of the peasant party and other democratic elements in Poland and to be recognized by Poles abroad, including the Union of Polish Patriots and the Polish army in Soviet Russia. It denounced the London Poles and declared its acceptance of the 1921 constitution until a constituent assembly had been elected and had enacted a new constitution. The manifesto made a strong appeal for Slav solidarity and asserted that Poland's frontiers with Russia should be settled by agreement on an ethnical basis.[12]

Two days after publication of this manifesto the Soviet government released a statement that the Red Army and the Polish army were now both engaged together in liberating Poland. It stressed that the Soviet Union had no intention of annexing Polish territory or making changes in the Polish social order. The Red Army was on Polish soil, solely for the purpose of helping the Poles to drive the Germans from their country. On 26 July the Soviet government signed an agreement with the Polish Committee of National Liberation concerning relations with the Soviet Supreme Command and co-operation between the Red Army and the administration set up by the committee, especially in organizing Polish forces to drive out the Germans. The agreement also provided that the committee would take over completely the administration of all Polish territory as soon as it had been liberated.[13]

Towards the end of July in the sixth offensive of the year Rokossovsky's 1st Belorussian Front had begun advancing through Poland towards the Vistula. But after forty days of unbroken campaigning the Red forces were fatigued and their offensive was losing momentum. Supply lines were over-extended and the Red air force had temporarily lost its superiority over the enemy. Moreover, the Germans were now throwing in strong reserves which further slowed the Russian advance.

In Warsaw the capture of Lublin by Rokossovsky's forces on 23 July and the Russian advance to the outskirts of Praga, the suburb on the bank of the broad Vistula opposite to Warsaw, made liberation seem at hand. Already on 24 July the commander of the *Armija Krajowa* in Warsaw,

General Bor-Komarowski, who was anti-Russian and a supporter of the London government, had made the decision to order the uprising before the Red Army reached the city. His purpose was to free Warsaw by Polish action and to win support for the London regime. This seemed all the more timely because Mikolajczyk, the head of the London government, was at that time in Moscow for talks with the Lublin committee.

Polish forces in Warsaw numbered about 40,000 and had supplies for seven to ten days' fighting. They were, however, ill-equipped to stand against the strong mechanized German divisions. Bor-Komarowski and the AK had deliberately avoided contact with Rokossovsky and any attempt to co-ordinate their uprising with the operations of his troops. Rokossovsky would undoubtedly have warned them that their action was premature. On the other hand Moscow radio on 29 July broadcast an appeal to the people of Warsaw to rise. This was the usual appeal made to occupied territories which the Red Army was approaching. In Warsaw, however, it was naturally taken to mean that the Red Army was on the point of launching its assault. In the event the Poles fought bravely in what became a popular uprising, but they had no chance. The Germans with inhuman ruthlessness proceeded to destroy the city and all who were in it.

Meanwhile the inactivity of the Red forces on the Vistula aroused the suspicions of Churchill, Roosevelt, and others in the West that Stalin was deliberately leaving the city to its fate. The London Poles were active in fomenting these suspicions. On 4 August Churchill sent a cable to Stalin, reporting that British planes were dropping some supplies to the Poles and seeking assurance that Russian aid was at hand. Stalin's reply was unco-operative.[14] On 14 August Churchill requested Eden to send a message to Stalin through Molotov, asking him to send all help possible to the Poles in Warsaw. Two days later, however, Vyshinsky asked the U.S. ambassador to call and read out to him the statement:

'The Soviet Government cannot, of course, object to British or American aircraft dropping arms in the region of Warsaw, since this is an American and British affair. But they decidedly object to American or British aircraft, after dropping arms in the region of Warsaw, landing on Soviet territory, since the Soviet Government do not wish to associate themselves either directly or indirectly with the adventure in Warsaw.'[15]

On 16 August, also, Churchill received a message from Stalin, stating that he had given orders for arms to be dropped to the Polish insurgents. But he condemned the uprising as 'a reckless and terrible adventure' from which the Soviet Supreme Command must dissociate itself.[16] Churchill consulted urgently with Roosevelt and on 20 August they sent a joint appeal to Stalin to help Warsaw. Again Stalin responded unhelpfully. He was not prepared to be moved by Churchill's quixotic intercession on behalf of Poles, led by elements as hostile to Soviet Russia as the Germans themselves; he was also strangely insensitive or indifferent to world opinion. On 10 September, after the fighting in Warsaw had continued for six weeks, Russian support came in the form of artillery fire on the eastern suburbs of the city and of Soviet planes dropping supplies, 'but few of the parachutes opened and many of the containers were smashed and useless'.[17] Finally on 2 October, Bor-Komarowski surrendered to the Germans. More than 300,000 Poles had perished in the uprising and the city had been almost completely destroyed.[18]

The Russians now struck against the remaining German satellites. The Rumanians in particular were anxious to make peace. They had suffered heavy casualties in the war and had been antagonized by German arrogance. The defeat of Germany was in sight and they wanted to make peace with the Allies as soon as possible.

On 20 August the 2nd Ukrainian Front, commanded by General Malinovsky, and the 3rd Ukrainian Front, commanded by General Tolbukhin, launched their offensive from the Moldavian and Bessarabian fronts and advanced rapidly into Rumania. This offensive, the seventh of the year, was an outstanding success. The German Army Group Sud-Ukraine comprised two German and two Rumanian armies, and they were overwhelmed by the Russians. The German 6th Army of sixteen divisions was encircled south-west of Kishenev and almost completely destroyed. Likewise the Rumanian 3rd Army in positions near the Black Sea was trapped. The Red Armies swept southwards and on to Bucharest.

Rumanian troops now offered little resistance and even in some places turned their guns on their German allies. In Rumania the opposition had been growing to the two Antonescus who were responsible for the pro-Axis policy. On 23 August King Michael had ordered their arrest and had appointed General Sanatescu to lead the country. The Soviet government on 25 August broadcast a statement, confirming its earlier declaration that it did not propose to make changes in the Rumanian social order and undertaking not to destroy the Rumanian army but to give it all help if it would fight against the Germans and Hungarians.[19] The King and Sanatescu accepted Soviet armistice terms and Rumanian troops began actively fighting against the Germans at Bucharest, in the Carpathians, and in Transylvania. On 31 August the Rumanians, supported by Malinovsky's troops, liberated Bucharest.

A new coalition government was now formed in Rumania which included representatives of the four main political parties, including Patrasceanu, the communist, now minister of justice. This government, a few days after its formation, sent a delegation to Moscow where it concluded a formal armistice with the Soviet, British, and United States governments.

Bulgaria raised different problems. The Soviet Union, unlike Britain and the United States, was not at war with Bulgaria. Indeed, because of pro-Russian feelings there, and the weakness of the regime, Stalin had shown great restraint towards the Bulgarians, even when the Germans established a military and naval base there. But the provocations had become worse as the Red Army swept into Rumania, especially when the Bulgarians allowed German ships to escape from their ports.

On 5 September the Soviet government declared war on Bulgaria and on 8 September troops of Tolbukhin's 3rd Ukrainian Front invaded the country. They were warmly welcomed by the Bulgarians. A new government promptly declared war on Germany and on 28 October in Moscow it signed an armistice with the Soviet Union and the Allies.

Meanwhile the Finns, too, had come to terms. The Russian offensive along the Karelian Isthmus early in June had pushed the Finns back to their frontier. The Red Army had, however, made no attempt to advance into Finland, for it was Soviet policy to treat the whole of Scandinavia as a neutral block with which the Soviet Union would maintain cordial relations. Early in August the pro-German President Ryti resigned. The Finnish parliament at once passed a new law conferring full presidential powers on Field-Marshal Mannerheim. Hitler sent Field-Marshal Keitel to Helsinki to ensure that the Finns did not intend negotiating a separate peace with Soviet Russia. But Mannerheim informed them that the Finnish government no longer regarded the Ryti–Ribbentrop agreement as being in force.

On 25 August the Finnish minister in Stockholm made a formal request to Madam Kollontai, the Soviet ambassador, that a Finnish armistice delegation might be received in Moscow. The Soviet government agreed, subject to the Finns proclaiming their breach with Germany and disarming all German troops in Finland. After exchanges over these conditions, a cease-fire to apply on 4 September along the 1940 Finnish frontier was agreed.

The terms of the armistice, signed in Moscow on 19 September, included the severe provision for the payment of 300 million dollars in reparations over six years, later extended to eight years. The Soviet government took a lease on Porkkala Udd, near Helsinki, as a military base and renounced claims on Hango. In its place the Russians took the Petsamo area in the north which was important for its nickel mines and because, like nearby Murmansk, it was an ice-free port on the Arctic Ocean.

The German troops in Lapland were not disarmed by the Finns, but ejected by the Red Army in an offensive in October. The Russian forces under Marshal Meretskov broke through the German defences and captured the Petsamo area. Then, crossing the Norwegian frontier, they took Kirkenes which had served as an important airbase from which German planes had attacked the north Russian convoys.

Early in October Red forces under Tolbukhin's command, advancing westward through Rumania, had joined with the Yugoslav irregulars of Tito's committee of national liberation. Russian and Yugoslav troops had entered Belgrade together on 20 October, warmly welcomed by the people. One of the purposes of the Red Army's advance into Yugoslavia was to be able to launch an offensive on the Germans and Hungarians, concentrated in the region of Budapest, from the south. On 20 October troops of Malinovsky's 2nd Ukrainian Front captured the important town of Debrecen in eastern Hungary. But their rapid advance became slower and the resistance of both Germans and Hungarians was more stubborn, as they moved eastwards in November and approached Budapest.

Hungary lay directly across the route of the Russian advance from Rumania and Yugoslavia into southern Germany. Hitler, although threatened more immediately from the east, was determined to halt the Russian advance in Hungary and had strongly reinforced the German armies at Budapest. The Germans had in October arrested Admiral Horthy, the head of the Hungarian government, fearing that he might, like the Rumanian king, dismiss the fascist government as the Red Army approached. The fascist leader, Szalasi, had taken over the government of the country and with him Hitler had agreed to make a stand at Budapest. In Russian-occupied Hungary a Hungarian provisional national assembly and then a provisional government had been formed towards the end of December. But the Hungarian people generally were not ready, as the Rumanians, Bulgarians, and Yugoslavs had been, to welcome the Russian liberators.

As the Red Armies swept westwards, Churchill became increasingly disturbed about the spread of Soviet influence in Eastern Europe. He accepted that Rumania and Bulgaria were already under Soviet domination. He was concerned for the future of Poland, Greece, and Yugoslavia, with all of whom Britain had special relations. Moreover, he was worried that the United States 'were very slow in realizing the upsurge of communist influence which slid on before, as well as followed, the onward march of the mighty armies directed from the Kremlin'.[20]

After consulting Roosevelt, Churchill wrote to Stalin offering to go to Moscow in October for preliminary discussion of the many problems to be agreed by the three Allied leaders. Stalin responded with a warm invitation. He had on 30 September reiterated his inability to leave Moscow, even for a meeting with both Roosevelt and Churchill at The Hague or elsewhere in the West. He evidently still considered it appropriate that the others should come to him.

Churchill, accompanied by Eden, arrived in Moscow on 9 October and received a tremendous welcome. Stalin had never been more charming and cordial as a host, and Churchill responded warmly. The Russians generally seemed far more friendly than at the time of his visit two years earlier, no doubt because their fortunes in the war had changed so dramatically. Churchill was particularly impressed by the thunderous ovation which Stalin and he received when they appeared in their box in the Bolshoi Theatre at a gala performance. At his press conference on the eve of his departure on 18 October, Churchill won Russian approval by his warm tributes to Russian achievements and to Stalin, and by his evident desire for understanding between the three powers in ensuring peace after the surrender of nazi Germany.

Real progress was, however, slight in the talks which Churchill and Eden had with Stalin and Molotov. At their first meeting it had been agreed that Mikolajczyk and two of his ministers should be invited to Moscow for discussions with representatives of the Lublin committee on the future government of Poland. But their meetings were fruitless, for they could not agree on the division of seats in a future government. On the Balkans Churchill believed that he had achieved a broad understanding with Stalin.[21] They reached general agreement on the partitioning of Germany, the treatment of war criminals and other matters.[22] Churchill had not raised the points in dispute with the Soviet government concerning the United Nations organization which was under active consideration by the three powers. On the request of Roosevelt he left this subject for discussion at the meeting of the three leaders which, Roosevelt had suggested, and Stalin and Churchill had agreed, would take place at a Black Sea port in the near future.

In December, General de Gaulle visited Moscow. Obsessed with the mission of asserting the greatness of France at a time when, especially in the eyes of the Russians who had fought heroically, French greatness was far to seek, his visit was not a success. De Gaulle was striving at this stage to establish a role for France, free of dependence on Britain and the United States, by signing a Franco-Soviet pact. Stalin kept Churchill informed about the French proposals, and agreed to Churchill's preference for a tripartite pact which included Britain. This was unacceptable to de Gaulle. The Russians offered then to agree a Franco-Soviet pact in return for French recognition of the Lublin committee, and finally signed the pact without insisting on this condition. But de Gaulle left Moscow, incensed by Russian contempt, hardly hidden, for the French war record.

As 1944 closed, the Red Armies were preparing intensively for the final attack on Germany. Their front lines ran from the borders of east Prussia through Poland, Czechoslovakia, Hungary, and Yugoslavia. They had made spectacular advances through the year and the morale of the Red troops was magnificent as they saw victory over a cruel and hated enemy within their grasp. They took keen pride in the fact that they had developed an efficient and seasoned army which was now superior to the German *Wehrmacht*. Through the centuries the Russians had looked on the Germans as the paragons of discipline and efficiency, and now they had proved themselves able to rise to higher standards. Moreover German man-power reserves were rapidly diminishing; German industry was unable to make good the losses of armaments, suffered in the war. On the other hand the Red Army, although only slightly larger in the numbers of its troops, was now magnificently equipped with the finest armaments and in ample quantities.[23]

On the Western Front in December the Anglo-American forces found themselves seriously threatened by Rundstedt's offensive in the Ardennes sector. German pressure was maintained and Eisenhower, the supreme Allied commander, was acutely anxious to know whether the Russians could undertake any operation to relieve the pressure on the Allies in the West. He had, in fact, sent his deputy, Air Marshal Tedder, to Moscow for the purpose, but Tedder had been grounded by bad weather.

On 6 January 1945 Churchill sent a message to Stalin asking whether in their predicament they could 'count on a major Russian offensive on the Vistula front or elsewhere during January'. Stalin responded immediately. The Russians were, he stated, preparing an offensive, but the weather was unfavourable. 'Nevertheless, taking into account the position of our Allies on the Western front, GHQ of the Supreme Command has decided to accelerate the completion of our preparations and, regardless of the weather, to commence large-scale offensive operations against the Germans along the whole of the Central Front not later than the second half of January.' [24] He was to improve on this generous undertaking, for on 12 January the great Russian offensive was launched, although the weather made air support impossible.

Russian preparations for this massive offensive had been completed early in January. The 1st Belorussian Front commanded by Marshal Zhukov, and the 1st Ukrainian Front, commanded by Marshal Konev, together had 2,200,000 troops with 32,143 guns and mortars, 6,460 tanks and self-propelling guns, supported by 4,772 aircraft. The Red forces had vast superiority over the enemy divisions opposing them.[25] North of Warsaw the 2nd Belorussian Front, commanded by General Rokossovsky, was to launch its offensive in the direction of Danzig at the same time. Farther to the north the 3rd Belorussian Front, commanded by General Cherniakhovsky, was to advance into East Prussia. The 4th Ukrainian Front, commanded by General Petrov, was to plunge westwards through Czechoslovakia. Such was the formidable array of armies poised to advance on Germany.

The main offensive was by the 1st Ukrainian and the 1st Belorussian Fronts, co-ordinating their advances. The former was to strike from the bridgehead west of Sandomir in the direction of Radomsko. The latter was to advance from the two main bridgeheads south of Warsaw and a smaller bridgehead north of the city, which they were to take and then advance in the direction of Poznan. The Germans had built strong defence lines between Warsaw and the Oder river. They recognized that the Russians would advance on Berlin by this direct approach. They were not, however, expecting this advance so early. Thirty German divisions were held in Courland and the Russians would, it was assumed, attack this force first; in fact, the Soviet Supreme Command decided to deal with these divisions at leisure after the main offensive had been completed. The Germans had also expected the main Russian attack to fall in the region of Budapest. Thus, while their defences on the Warsaw–Berlin line were well prepared and manned, they had not brought in reserves and concentrated forces in this sector as expected.

Konev's 1st Ukrainian Front advanced after a heavy artillery barrage on 12 January. His troops pressed forward rapidly. On 18 January they took Piotrkow and on the following day Cracow, which the Germans evacuated so hurriedly that they had no time to destroy it. Four days later Konev's troops were plunging into Upper Silesia and had begun fighting along the Oder river north of Steinau, where they established a bridgehead on the west bank.

The advance of Zhukov's 1st Belorussian Front was even more spectacular. He launched his offensive on 14 January and three days later Warsaw was liberated. By 29 January his forces had encircled Poznan and had reached the outskirts of Frankfurt.

Rokossovsky's 2nd Belorussian Front had at the same time swept across northern Poland. By the end of January he had established a front, running from east of Elbing, through Marienburg down to Bromberg (Bydgoshch) which had been taken by Zhukov on 23 January. Farther north Cherniakhovsky's 3rd Belorussian Front had swept through East Prussia and by the end of the month was poised to strike at Koenigsberg.

Throughout February and March the Russians pressed their offensive along the whole front. They now gave special attention to operations in eastern Pomerania, Upper and Lower Silesia and East Prussia to destroy the enemy on the flanks of the main line of advance on Berlin. At the same time they were broadening their bridgeheads on the left bank of the Oder in the vicinity of Küstrin and Frankfurt. They were meeting constantly with desperate, at times suicidal, resistance from the Germans, now fighting on their own soil and defending their capital.

On 10 February Rokossovsky's 2nd Belorussian Front began a new advance northwards on Danzig. The bitter cold added to the savagery of the fighting. Russian losses were heavy, but they pressed ahead relentlessly. Early in March, Danzig was cut off by land and on 28 March Gdynia fell to the Russians. But in Danzig fierce fighting continued for several days before the Russians took it. Rokossovsky now began to move westwards along the Baltic coast towards Stettin.

The 3rd Belorussian Front, now commanded by Marshal Vassilevsky, after the death of Cherniakhovsky from wounds received in battle, was completing the conquest of East Prussia. Koenigsberg still resisted, but on 9 April this stronghold fell. Many Red Army divisions were now brought south to the Oder bridgeheads in readiness for the final offensive on Berlin. Konev's 1st Ukrainian Front advanced through Upper and Lower Silesia to the Neisse, and here, too, the Red forces established their positions and prepared intensively for the Berlin offensive.

In the south the 2nd and 3rd Ukrainian Fronts, commanded respectively by Malinovsky and Tolbukhin, had faced strong resistance from both Germans and Hungarians. Hitler had reinforced his armies in Hungary and Szalasi, the Hungarian fascist leader, who had displaced the Horthy government, commanded spirited fighting troops. Together the Germans and Hungarian forces barred the way to Austria.

On 13 February the Russians took Budapest after long and bitter fighting. The Debrecen government in Russian-occupied Hungary had already in the previous month signed an armistice with the Soviet government. The enemy had, it seemed, been conquered in Hungary and the Red Army could continue its advance into Austria and southern Germany. But on 6–15 March German and Hungarian forces made a bold counterattack from north and south of Lake Balaton. They advanced deep into Russian-held territory before Tolbukhin was able to bring in reserves and crush them. The Russians then swept northwards into Austria and on 13 April Tolbukhin and Malinovsky took Vienna.

On every front the Germans were now resisting with a desperate ferocity. The swift approach of the Russians inspired terror among them. Nazi propaganda had instilled the fear that they would act with the savagery of barbarians. Not even in the heat of battle, however, did the Red troops perpetrate such cruelties or behave as the Germans had behaved in Russia. Indeed, most Germans realized that their own troops and their nazi regime, especially the SS troops, had treated Russia and her people with gross inhumanity and they feared a savage revenge. Civilians gave way to panic on the approach of the Russians and many committed suicide. The roads to Berlin were blocked by refugees seeking safety there. The weather was icy with up to thirty degrees of frost at night. Thousands died of exposure and frostbite, and those who reached the city found it devastated by air raids, carried out by as many as 1,000 bombers, flying in nightly from the West. The Germans were meeting their nemesis.

Early in February, Stalin, Roosevelt, and Churchill met in conference at Yalta on the Black Sea coast. At this time the Russians were making spectacular advances on all fronts and had reached the Oder river. In the West the British and American armies were recovering from the Battle of the Bulge and had yet to cross the Rhine, while in Italy their advance had come to a halt. It was a factor that might have been expected to influence the Russian approach to this momentous meeting, when matters affecting the peace of the world were under consideration. There was, however, nothing in the discussions, as reported by Churchill and Stettinius, to suggest that the military situation influenced Stalin's attitude to his allies or persuaded him to take a strong line. Indeed, the three war leaders talked frankly in their discussions and achieved in their meetings a wide measure of agreement and understanding, except on Poland. In later years the Yalta conference was to be condemned by many in the West as a capitulation to Soviet Russia in which Stalin had cleverly outwitted the ailing president. In fact, this conference demonstrated the extent to which the Russians at this time were prepared to compromise and to work in good faith with their allies.

At the first plenary session on 5 February, the future of Germany was discussed. All agreed that Germany should be dismembered after her unconditional surrender. On Roosevelt's suggestion the foreign ministers were instructed to produce a plan within a month for the division and control of Germany. Stalin and Molotov did not press their earlier objections to French participation and on Churchill's insistence it was agreed that France would have an occupation zone in Germany and be represented on the control commission. A special commission, to meet in secret in Moscow, was to examine the complex problem of German reparations.

The second session considered the proposed world organization for peace. At Dumbarton Oaks discussion on the question of voting rights in the Security Council had resulted in deadlock. Roosevelt had put forward a compromise proposal which was now discussed. His proposal was that each member of the council should have one vote. Conflicts would be divided into the category of those calling for economic, political, or military sanctions, and the category of those which could be settled by peaceful means. Sanctions could only be applied if the permanent members of the council were unanimous and, if one of those members was itself a party to the dispute, it could nevertheless take part in the discussions and vote. Herein lay the right of veto which was to become an important element in the council's functioning.

Stalin took a close interest in this compromise proposal and sought with blunt honesty to clarify the position. 'The greatest danger,' he said, 'is conflict among ourselves, because if we remain united the German menace is not very important. Therefore we must now think how to secure our unity in the future and how to guarantee that the three great powers (and possibly China and France) will maintain a united front.' [26] He then referred to the Russo-Finnish war and the fact that the British and French had managed to expel Russia from the League of Nations. He was anxious for guarantees against repetition of such a situation, which would break up the unity of the great powers. When the conference resumed on the following day, Stalin announced that the Soviet government was satisfied with the new voting procedure and with the provision that the three powers must be unanimous. [27]

On the subject of the nations to be included as founder members of the world organization, the Soviet demand at Dumbarton Oaks had been for sixteen membership votes, one for each republic of the Union. Britain and the United States had been disturbed by this demand. But Molotov now announced that the Soviet government would be content if three, or at any rate two, of the Soviet republics, namely the Ukraine, Belorussia, and Lithuania, became original members. It was further agreed that the first conference of the world organization should meet at San Francisco on 25 April.[28] The states which had declared war on Germany by 1 March or which had already signed the United Nations declaration would be invited. On all of these major issues Stalin agreed readily and showed himself ready to compromise. Churchill wrote in a report to London on 8 February that 'In spite of our gloomy warnings and forebodings, Yalta has turned out very well so far.'[29]

Poland who, so Roosevelt remarked, 'has been a source of trouble for over five hundred years', again proved an intractable problem.[30] This had been for Roosevelt and Churchill the most urgent reason for the conference and according to Churchill it 'was the first of the great causes which led to the breakdown of the Grand Alliance'.[31]

Stalin expressed his policy on Poland clearly. Throughout history Poland had been a corridor through which Russia's enemies had advanced to attack her; Germany had used this corridor twice in the last thirty years. Russia wanted a strong and powerful Poland who could herself guard this corridor. But in wanting a strong, free, and independent Poland, Stalin did not add expressly that he would not tolerate the old regime, now represented by the London government which comprised men who were sworn enemies of Russia. The London Poles had, in fact, displaced Mikolajczyk, the one Polish leader in whom all three heads of state had confidence, because he favoured agreement with the Lublin government. It was obvious that such a government would be only too ready to keep the corridor open and would pose a permanent threat to Russia.

Already in the previous December, Stalin had informed Roosevelt that the Soviet government proposed recognizing the Lublin committee as the provisional government of Poland. Roosevelt had objected that only a small part of Poland west of the Curzon Line had so far been liberated, and that the views of the Polish people on the Lublin committee could not yet be known. But on the recognition of the Lublin government Stalin stood firm.

A fundamental difference divided the Soviet and Western approaches to this problem. Stalin was concerned for Russian security and, after the ordeals of two major wars, he considered this paramount. Churchill and Roosevelt were upholding democratic principles and, even more, they were concerned to prevent the spread of communism.

In seven of the eight plenary sessions of the conference Poland was discussed. The Curzon Line, drawn in 1918 on ethnographical grounds by Curzon, Clemenceau, and a United States representative, was agreed as the eastern frontier of Poland which would be compensated at Germany's expense. The western frontier would run down the Oder river but both Roosevelt and Churchill opposed extending it so far west as the Western Neisse river. The final delimitation of this frontier was to await the peace conference.

On the composition of the Polish government, argument continued. Finally it was agreed, as set out in the joint declaration, that the Lublin committee provisional government should be 'reorganized on a broader democratic basis, with the inclusion of democratic leaders from Poland itself and from Poles abroad', further that Molotov and the U.S. and British ambassadors in Moscow should consult with all Polish leaders with a view to reorganization of the government along these lines, and that the 'Polish provisional Government of National Unity shall be pledged on the holding of free and unfettered elections as soon as possible on the basis of universal suffrage and secret ballot.'[32]

The formal agenda of the conference contained no reference to the Far East. The Americans at this stage feared that the war against Japan might continue for a further two years and they were anxious for the Russians to help hasten its end. Roosevelt and Harriman raised this question informally with Stalin on 8 February. Stalin agreed to enter the war against Japan two or three months after the surrender of Germany on terms which included preservation of the *status quo* in Outer Mongolia and restoration of Russia's position, as it had been before the Russo-Japanese war of 1904–5. This meant specifically the restoration to Russia of southern Sakhalin and the adjacent islands, internationalization of Darien with safeguards for the predominant Soviet interests in the port, and revival of Russia's lease of Port Arthur as a naval base. It included also joint operation by a Soviet–Chinese company of the Chinese eastern railway and South Manchurian railway with recognition of the pre-eminent Soviet interests, but with Chinese sovereignty in Manchuria guaranteed. Stalin also asked for the Kurile Islands. On these conditions and subject to the concurrence of Chiang Kai-shek, which Roosevelt undertook to obtain, agreement was reached.[33]

In the course of the informal dinners at the Teheran meeting and now at Yalta, the three heads of state achieved a greater understanding of one another and of their respective problems. Stalin evidently set great store by this kind of relationship. He went out of his way to express his faith in their alliance, 'that it should not lose its character of intimacy, of its free expression of views. In the history of diplomacy I know of no such close alliance of three Great Powers as this, when allies had the opportunity of so frankly expressing their views.' But he was worried about its endurance after the war. The alliance of the great powers and the United Nations were for him the principles on which hope for peace in the future must be based.[34]

When the three men parted on 11 February, they probably realized that they would not all three meet again. Roosevelt was frail and failing. In him Stalin and the Russian people as a whole felt that they had a friend and in him they saw a statesman. For Churchill, too, they felt respect and even affection, for despite his bouts of being difficult and his occasional petulance, he had courage and had been an indefatigable war leader. But when, five months later, the three heads of state met at Potsdam, two new men were present.

In early April 1945 along the Russian front, Red troops waited impatiently for the final onslaught on Berlin. All felt a desperate need to reach the capital before the Allies. After all that Russia had suffered at the hands of the Germans, they had to conquer the German capital by force of arms. For the enemy to surrender there to American and British forces would have been an unbearable anti-climax, depriving them of their bitterly-won right to destroy their savage and arrogant enemy in his last stronghold.[35]

Before dawn on 16 April Zhukov's 1st Belorussian and Konev's 1st Ukrainian Front began their offensive, in which more than three-and-a-half million troops were involved on both sides. Artillery and aircraft had pounded the German defences and then, while it was still dark, Zhukov had ordered his forces to advance along the whole front. The Red tanks were guided by massed searchlights which incidentally blinded the German gunners.[36] Relentlessly the Russians pushed forward, making full use of their great superiority in men, tanks, and guns. Soviet planes more than 4,000 in number flew as many as 15,000 sorties on the first day of the offensive, bombing and machine-gunning enemy defences. The German forces, over half a million strong, defending Berlin put up savage resistance. But they could not hold the Russian advance.

While Zhukov's forces were advancing on a broad front from bridgeheads on the Oder river, Konev's troops struck out from positions to the south on the Neisse river and swept north-westwards. Against this offensive, too, German troops fought with fanatical bravery. Casualties were heavy on both sides. But from the east and south-east the Russians surged forward. The outcome of the battle was already certain; the Russians were concerned to end it in the shortest possible time.

By 23 April troops of both fronts had broken into Berlin and the savage fighting continued inside the city. On the following day detachments from the two commands, moving from the north and from the south made their junction in the south-eastern part of the city. On 25 April further detachments joined at Ketsin, north-west of Potsdam. Red forces had now completely encircled the capital. Also on 25 April troops of the 1st Ukrainian Front and of the American army met at Torgau on the Elbe.

Within Berlin, however, the bitter fighting continued. The Germans had thrown in their last reserves and they fought bravely. Russian planes maintained constant bombing of the German positions. On the night of 26 April alone 563 sorties dropped 569 tons of bombs on these small targets.[37] The climax of the battle was the storming of the Reichstag on 30 April in which the Russians had to fight the Germans room by room through the building. Only on 2 May did the Reichstag garrison capitulate, having lost 2,500 officers and men killed or wounded; 2,604 Germans were taken prisoner.[38] Resistance in Berlin now ceased. On 8 May in Berlin Field-

Marshal Keitel, representing the German High Command, surrendered to Marshal Zhukov.

Czechoslovakia had not yet been completely liberated. Red forces had been fighting there since the beginning of the year. Only on 9 May was Prague finally taken. That day was proclaimed from Moscow as Victory Day, and the whole Russian nation celebrated joyfully.

o

PART VI

THE COLD WAR

CHAPTER TWENTY-TWO

Potsdam and the End of the Alliance
1945–52

SOVIET RUSSIA had emerged triumphant from the most tragic and terrible war in her history. No longer weak and an outcast, her standing among the nations of the world had been transformed, and she now commanded respect as one of the two great world powers. Twice before in her history—after Peter the Great's victory over Charles XII of Sweden in 1709 and again after the defeat of Napoleon in 1812—Russia had achieved a similar predominance. But she had in each period allowed her strength to dissipate. Now with a seasoned and victorious army of some twelve million men, superbly equipped, and a people strongly behind their leader, Russia seemed more powerful and secure than ever before in her history, and Stalin was determined that there would be no relapse.

The Russian people were jubilant and united in a deep sense of national pride that they had endured this terrible ordeal and had come through with honour. In his speech of 24 May 1945 at an impressive reception in the Kremlin for Soviet military leaders Stalin had paid tribute to the Russians, 'the most remarkable of all the nations of the Soviet Union'.[1] With his sure instinct for popular feeling, he was expressing the general sense of achievement. The great victory parade in the Red Square on 24 June was the nation's tribute to the Red Army. Marshal Zhukov took the salute and Marshal Rokossovsky commanded the parade. But Stalin himself, standing on the Lenin mausoleum at the foot of which hundreds of captured German banners were cast down, dominated the scene, and no Russian would have disputed this arrangement.

The general elation was tempered, however, by the tragedies they had suffered and were still suffering. Countless women waited for news of their menfolk and, as days passed, realized that they were widows. Thousands of children had become orphans. Casualties at the fronts and in German-occupied territory had been on such a horrifying scale that few who survived were without bereavements.[2] Moreover, the mass of the people were still severely rationed for food, clothing, and housing, and they continued to work long hours under hard conditions. Many had died as a result of overwork and undernourishment. The industrial force included a large element of adolescents and by 1945 women comprised fifty-one per cent of all workers in industry, while agriculture depended almost entirely on female labour.[3] The people were now confidently expecting that life would become easier, that food and other goods would be more plentiful, and that somehow they would be rewarded for their endurance in the war. But their expectations were to wait long for realization.

Soviet Russia, for all her standing as one of the two most powerful nations in the world, was near to economic ruin. Material losses had been disastrous in magnitude, amounting to about one quarter of all Soviet property. Nearly 2,000 towns and 70,000 villages had been destroyed and 25 million people rendered homeless, as well as 31,000 factories, employing more than 4 million people, 84,000 schools, and 40,000 miles of railway lines laid in ruins. A tremendous labour of reconstruction faced the nation.

The immediate problems were to revive agricultural output and to rebuild industry, while reconverting it to the pressing civil needs of the massive reconstruction programme. Already in summer 1943 directives had been issued for the return of livestock and machinery and the grant of loans for seed in liberated territories. It was claimed that within two years after liberation more than 26,000 collective farms and 1,000 motor tractor stations had been re-established in the Ukraine alone.[4] But by the end of the war only a small fraction of the productive capacity of the devastated regions had been restored. Agricultural machinery and fertilizers were first priorities for post-war production. The reduction in livestock was critical. Compared with 1940, when the level of livestock was already desperately low as a result of the collectivization campaign, the number of cattle was 87 per cent, of cows 82 per cent, of sheep and goats 76 per cent, of pigs 38 per cent, and of horses 51 per cent of the 1940 figures. In the liberated territories the figures were still lower.[5]

Soviet industry had produced phenomenal results in its output of aircraft, tanks, guns, and other war materials. In the first half of 1945 this output had amounted to nearly 21,000 planes, 9,100 tanks, 6,300 self-propelling guns, 62,000 guns of all types and calibres, 873,000 rifles, pistols, and machine guns, 82·1 million shells, bombs, and mines, and 3·3 milliard cartridges.[6] But this record masked the fact that Soviet industry as a whole had suffered disastrously in the war.[7] All the great industrial regions that the Germans had occupied had been reduced to ruins. Reconstruction had begun in 1944. The important Donbas mines and the Kharkov Tractor Plant were in production by the summer of 1945. In Krivoi Rog and Zaporozhie, Odessa and Rostov, Leningrad and Stalingrad, work had started on reviving and rebuilding. But the enormous task of reconstruction got under way properly only on the adoption of the fourth five-year plan in March 1946.

Already in 1943 the Soviet leaders were thinking about the problem of financing post-war reconstruction. One method was to depend on Russia's own severely diminished resources. This meant maintaining the nation in the same austere conditions, deprived of consumer goods and restricted in food and housing, as by their own labours the people rebuilt industry and agriculture. Another source of finance, to which Stalin attached importance, was massive reparations from Germany and her satellites. He had already exacted from the Finns an undertaking to pay 300 million dollars in reparations over a period of six years. But when at Yalta he had raised the subject Churchill in particular had raised objections.[8]

Substantial long-term credits from the United States would assist greatly in the financing of Soviet reconstruction and this form of help was much in the minds of the Soviet leaders. It would relieve the people of the need to continue living so austerely and working under the same pressure as during the industrialization campaign and the war. Strict communists viewed with misgiving such dependence on a capitalist power, seeing it as a betrayal of Marxism–Leninism. Others saw in acceptance of such help the danger that Russia's security would be jeopardized.

Stalin himself evidently considered that the value of a sizeable loan from the United States would outweigh the objections. He was concerned less with the principles of Marxism–Leninism than with the recovery and security of Russia. In conversation with Stettinius on 5 February Molotov 'expressed the hope that the Soviet Union would receive long-term credits from the United States'.[9] In the previous weeks Molotov had discussed the matter with the U.S. ambassador, Harriman, and on being told that it would require an act of congress, he had asked that it should be submitted to congress before the end of the war. But no U.S. loan or credits of any kind materialized.[10] Indeed, promptly after 8 May, celebrated in the West as Victory-in-Europe Day, lease-lend supplies were curtly halted, although the Soviet Union was pledged to enter the war against Japan.[11]

During these first months of 1945 several angry exchanges took place between Stalin, Roosevelt, and Churchill. They served as dramatic evidence of the unsleeping mistrust of the Russians and of their readiness to challenge their Allies at times with insulting frankness. Stalin in particular was often intemperate in his language. In February, General Karl Wolff, commander of the SS in Italy, made contact with the American intelligence service in Switzerland. He was told that negotiations could not be considered, but two 'exploratory meetings' with him took place. The Soviet government was informed and at once charged the Allies with denying facilities for a Soviet representative to be present. Stalin believed that Britain and the U.S.A. were negotiating a separate surrender in southern Europe, and apparently from his own intelligence sources he had received reports that this was happening. He charged Roosevelt and Churchill with breach of faith and falsehood. Both replied so forthrightly that Stalin was clearly shaken that his charges had caused such deep offence. He ended his letter of 7 April to Churchill with the comment:

> 'My messages are personal and strictly confidential. This makes it possible to speak one's mind clearly and frankly. This is the advantage of confidential communications. If, however, you are going to regard

every frank statement of mine as offensive, it will make this kind of communication very difficult. I can assure you that I had and have no intention of offending anyone.'[12]

Other disputes arose and the Russians, as soon as their suspicions were allayed, dismissed them as being no more than disturbances on the surface of the alliance. When in April, Himmler, the nazi leader, offered through Bernadotte, the head of the Swedish Red Cross, to surrender the German forces in Norway and Denmark to British, American, or Swedish troops, the offer reached London first through the British ambassador in Stockholm. Churchill at once informed Stalin by cable and stated that his proposed reply to Himmler was that nothing less than unconditional surrender simultaneously to the three major powers would be acceptable. Stalin at once cabled his agreement, adding the words: 'Knowing you, I had no doubt that you would act in this way.' Churchill was touched and replied: 'I am extremely pleased to know that you had no doubt how I would act and always will act, towards your glorious country and yourself.' [13] But the trust and goodwill between the two leaders was to be shortlived and they were soon to be sundered by the cold war towards which both contributed.

Poland remained the intractable problem. In January 1945 the *Armija Krajowa* had been dissolved on orders from the Polish government in London and converted into an underground organization. General Okulicki, who had replaced Bor-Komarowski after the Warsaw rising, was head of this Polish underground, which was active against the Russians in Poland. Anti-Russian feeling among the Poles was intensified by propaganda from the London government and by the church. The Soviet government asserted that over a hundred Red Army officers and men in Poland, as well as numerous Polish communists, had been assassinated by this underground. Indeed, Alexander Werth on arriving in Poland with a large group of Western correspondents, witnessed a special anti-Russian demonstration provided for their benefit, and in proof of the fact that the underground was active, two unfortunate Russian soldiers were shot outside the hotel where the correspondents were staying.[14] In March, Okulicki and fifteen others among the leaders of this underground were arrested and taken to Moscow. A general outcry was raised in the West, but in June they were tried in public and found guilty, but given lenient sentences.

The death of Roosevelt saddened the Russians. They had greater faith in him than in any other Western leader, certainly greater than in Churchill. But Roosevelt's death also disturbed them deeply for they feared the worst from his successor, Truman. As yet he was unknown to them, but the fact that in 1942 he had seriously proposed in the senate that America should alternate aid to Hitler and Stalin in such fashion as to ensure that Russia emerged as an exhausted victor, was far from encouraging.[15] His first act, directly affecting Russia, had been the cutting-off of lease-lend, which, particularly in the manner in which it had been done, had given offence. It did not augur well for future relations. But when Truman sent a personal representative to Moscow with assurances that he intended to pursue Roosevelt's policy of co-operating with the Soviet Union, Stalin and Molotov welcomed him, all the more because the envoy was Harry Hopkins whom they trusted.

The main purpose of Hopkins' mission which lasted from 26 May to 6 June, was to discuss the Polish question. Roosevelt and Churchill had considered that Stalin was not honouring the Yalta agreement. Hopkins managed to persuade Stalin to invite Mikolajczyk and two London Poles as well as certain important non-Lublin Poles in Poland to Moscow for discussions. As a result a new Polish provisional government was set up and on 5 July both the United States and Britain accorded it recognition. Neither of the Western powers was satisfied with the compromise government, but recognized that Stalin had come far to meet their objections and that they must accept it.

Hopkins also interceded with Stalin for the Polish underground leaders, then awaiting trial in Moscow. He pointed out that their release would make a good impression in the West. But, resisting Churchill's pressure, he refused to allow this mediation to interfere with the more important matter of bringing together the Lublin and other Poles for discussion. Grudgingly Churchill expressed himself satisfied with what Hopkins had achieved on the Polish issue, pending the meeting of the three heads of state, now arranged to take place in Berlin on 15 July.[16]

While Hopkins was in Moscow, the San Francisco conference had reached deadlock on an issue which threatened the whole conception of the United Nations with failure. Departing from the agreement reached at Yalta, Molotov had instructed Gromyko to insist now that a dispute could not even be discussed by the Security Council without the unanimous vote of the five permanent members, unless the dispute was one that could be settled by peaceful means.

Stettinius stated on 2 June that the United States could not join a world organization in which the power of veto was so extensive. He then cabled instructions to Harriman and Hopkins in Moscow to raise the matter directly with Stalin. At their meeting Molotov attempted to defend his instructions to Gromyko, but Stalin told him not to be ridiculous and at once accepted the American position.[17]

Stalin was deeply concerned for Russia's security in the West. Already he was looking ahead to the time when Germany would rise from her present ruins and, thirsting for revenge, strike in a third attempt to conquer Russia. He recognized that American troops would not remain indefinitely in Europe. Roosevelt had said at Yalta that they would withdraw within two years, and many contingents were already moving to the Far East. This would leave only the British to support Russia in preventing renewed German aggression in the coming decades. But Britain had been gravely weakened by the war and it remained to be seen how quickly she would recover. Also Stalin with sharp memories of Chamberlain and Munich, and with exaggerated suspicions that the Cliveden and other anti-Russian circles were influential, still held some mistrust of Britain.

His policy of alliance with the United States and Britain and participation in the United Nations also involved other uncertainties. Many factors, fundamental to American policy, made him unsure whether close alliance with the U.S.A. was possible. The American open-door expansionist policy, entrenched by the fear that the American system would suffer disastrous depression if expansion overseas did not continue, was one such factor. Another was the assumption, held by many Americans as an article of faith, that the United States was the symbol and agent of positive good in the world while the Soviet regime was evil. This assumption, giving rise to an outburst of national fervour and backed by the knowledge that America was strong while the Soviet Union was devastated and weak, might well destroy the alliance and even lead to an American attack. Such frightening possibilities intensified Stalin's feeling that Russia was dangerously vulnerable.

Long before the end of the war, he had begun pursuing the basic precaution of ensuring Soviet domination in Eastern Europe as a barrier against aggression from the West. The communist parties and pro-Soviet elements in Czechoslovakia, Rumania, Bulgaria, and Yugoslavia were being organized. At this stage it was expedient that they should co-operate with other political parties and in Rumania the Soviet authorities even cultivated the goodwill of the king. Poland was the weak link in this defence barrier. The Poles who clung tenaciously to their Russophobia could be won over or dealt with in other ways, but this required time. Meanwhile Stalin was disturbed by the increasing pressure from his allies on behalf of the Poles, which threatened what he considered to be Russia's basic defence needs, and made him suspect that the Western powers were seeking to isolate Russia by a *cordon sanitaire*.

Churchill was already perturbed by the growth of Soviet influence in Eastern Europe and the Balkans, by the Soviet attitude to Poland and reluctance to give the Allies access to Austria and other territories, occupied by the Red Army. He expressed his anxiety to Truman, seeking to brief him on the dangers of Russian and communist expansion. He wrote that an 'iron curtain' had been drawn down upon Russian-occupied Europe, and he envisaged the advance of the Russians 'to the waters of the North Sea and the Atlantic'.[18] His attitude, increasingly shared by the Americans, and Stalin's mistrust, allied with determination to preserve the security of Russia, were to make the continuance of the Grand Alliance impossible.

At Teheran and Yalta the three heads of state had been men mature in experience, outstanding in ability, and secure in office. United by common purpose they had met to discuss immediate and future problems and they had achieved the beginnings of genuine understanding. At the Potsdam conference which began on 17 July, two new heads of state attended, supported by newly appointed foreign ministers; all were politicians of limited experience in international affairs and of moderate ability. The task of the three heads of state was now far more difficult because the defeat of Germany had removed their immediate common purpose. For none of them was the purpose of ensuring world stability a cause strong enough to override immediate gains, national pride and prestige, and mutual suspicions. Moreover, a new factor—the successful explosion of an atom bomb in the Mexican desert—now bedevilled the alliance.

Churchill was given this momentous news on 17 July, the first day of the Potsdam conference. His immediate reaction was that the strength of the Western powers had been enormously enhanced while that of Soviet Russia had been correspondingly reduced. Also Russian participation in the war in the Far East would no longer be needed or desirable. This, too, was Truman's reaction. The Americans had been anxious for Russian help to bring the struggle against Japan to an early end. They had been pleased and relieved at Yalta when Stalin had committed himself to entering the war within three months of the defeat of Germany, and they had readily accepted his terms. An item in Harry Hopkins' mission to Moscow on behalf of Truman in May 1945 had been to confirm that Russia would participate in the war. Now with the atom bomb in his armoury, Truman felt that American arms alone should reap the glory of reducing Japan to unconditional surrender. Indeed, he was now anxious that Japan should surrender before Russia declared war, for then the Russian conditions could be evaded, although, according to the record of the agreement, 'they were to be fulfilled without question following the defeat of Japan'.[19]

Truman consulted with Churchill on how best to tell Stalin of this new weapon. Stalin had been, so Churchill wrote, 'a magnificent ally in the war against Hitler and we both felt that he must be informed of the New Fact which now dominated the scene, but not of any particulars'.[20] The president would mention it informally to Stalin after one of their meetings. A week later Truman told Stalin, and Churchill observed that Stalin seemed delighted and clearly had no conception of the significance of the new development.[21]

While Stalin could not have appreciated from Truman's informal statement the importance of the new weapon, he was quick to recognize the change in the attitude of the two Allies towards Russia. One American general wrote that 'We were in a position to be tough and indifferent',[22] and this feeling inspired the behaviour of the Western powers. Truman was truculent. Bevin, the new British foreign minister, was 'aggressive'.[23]

This change in the attitude of the Americans and British at Potsdam gave dramatic confirmation of Stalin's worst fears and suspicions. Moreover, it offended him deeply as an act of ingratitude and rejection. Russia had suffered cruelly in casualties and destruction to save herself and the world from nazism. To Stalin and to all Russians, while they paid tribute to Britain's stand and to America's aid, it was clear that, if Russia had not destroyed German armed might, Hitler would have conquered Britain and have carried the war into North America.[24] They had deserved the respect and consideration of the Allies, not their arrogance and condescension. But the American and British heads of state and their foreign ministers, antagonized by what they considered Stalin's unreasonable demands and emboldened by possession of their new weapon, were evidently not concerned to understand Russia's predicament or outlook.

The Potsdam conference in its thirteen plenary sessions ranged widely. Many matters were held over for consideration by the peace conference or by the council of foreign ministers, set up primarily to prepare the peace treaties with Germany, Finland, Hungary, Rumania, Bulgaria, and Italy. The Americans and the British were already highly critical of Russian policy in the liberated countries, especially Rumania and Bulgaria. The Russians countered with criticism of British activities in Greece. Strong words were exchanged as well as accusations of violations of the agreements reached at Yalta. But it was on Germany and Poland that the chasm, separating Russian from the United States and Britain, widened most notably.

Discussions on Poland now concerned the frontiers, for all three powers had recognized the Polish provisional government. The Curzon Line had been accepted as the eastern frontier. It was a matter of compensating the Poles for the territory lost to Russia by extending the western frontier at the expense of Germany. Stalin's proposal was that the Polish frontier should run west of Swinemünde to the Oder river, leaving Stettin on the Polish side, then along the Oder and the western Neisse to Czechoslovakia. Churchill strenuously maintained that the Polish frontier should not extend beyond the eastern Neisse. To push it to the western Neisse 'would rupture the economic unity of Germany and throw too heavy a burden on the powers occupying the Western Zones, especially as to food and fuel'.[25] Moreover, it was inequitable, since the Poles would have to transfer only two or three million people from east of the Curzon Line, whereas the Polish frontier proposed by the Russians would involve the transfer of seven or eight million.

Stalin was not, however, concerned with inequities in his dealings with Germany, but about his defence barrier and maintaining it as far to the west as was practicable. Churchill was removed from the subsequent discussions at Potsdam which resulted in Truman and Attlee accepting the Oder–Neisse line provisionally as the western frontier of Poland.[26]

In a declaration signed several weeks before the Potsdam conference, the United States, Britain, the Soviet Union, and France had agreed to divide Germany into separate zones, administered by each country, with Berlin as a fifth zone similarly partitioned. No central German government was set up, but an Allied Control Council, comprising the military commanders of the four powers, had jurisdiction in matters concerning Germany as a whole. Implicit in these arrangements was that Germany would not be dismembered. The drastic Morgenthau plan for partitioning and transforming Germany into an agricultural country, which Roosevelt and Churchill had initialled in September 1944, had subsequently been discarded. Soviet policy was to maintain Germany undivided and under the strict control of the four powers.

At Yalta, Roosevelt and Churchill had accepted in principle the Russian demand for reparations. They were anxious, however, to avoid a repetition of the calamitous experience of reparations after the first world war. The Russian proposal to exact twenty million dollars in reparations from Germany, half to go to the Soviet Union, had given rise to disputes, but this figure had been agreed as a basis for discussion. Maisky had been appointed chairman of a special Allied commission to examine the subject. But the commission after numerous meetings was unable to reach agreement.

At Potsdam, Stalin and Molotov pressed constantly for agreement on a figure for reparations. The Americans and the British refused to be committed. They had been incensed by reports that the Red Army was removing property and equipment which could not be classified as booty of war. They had expected that no property other than war booty would be removed without a strict accounting so that its value could be charged against the reparations allocations to be agreed. This and other practical difficulties finally led the Americans to abandon the Allied intention of treating Germany's economic question as a whole. Byrnes proposed that each country should satisfy its reparations claims out of its own zone. Some forty per cent of the value of German 'industrial equipment deemed unnecessary for a peace economy' was in the Soviet zone. Byrnes proposed that ten per cent of such industrial equipment in the Western zones should be given to Russia. Further, the Soviet government could exchange food or coal for additional equipment that they wanted in the American and British zones.[27]

Stalin and Molotov argued strongly against this arrangement. They accepted it in the end as part of a deal in which they were conceded the right to collect German assets throughout Eastern Europe and in which the Western powers recognized the Oder–Neisse frontier 'provisionally'.[28] But this imposed compromise led inevitably to Russia extending her economic and political control more tightly over her zone and the whole of Eastern Europe. At the same time, the Soviet proposal for joint administration of the Ruhr having been rejected, the Western allies excluded the Russians from their occupation zones. The policy of maintaining Germany as a unity under strict allied control was destroyed. Germany was divided between East and West.

During these weeks the Soviet forces in the Far East were being built up in readiness for Soviet entry into the war against Japan. Some forty Red Army divisions had been held in the Far East throughout the war. Stalin could never be sure that Japan would not attack in spite of the Soviet–Japanese pact. He had maintained correct diplomatic relations with the Japanese government, even in 1943 and 1944 when Soviet forces in the West and American forces in the Pacific were beginning to move towards victory. Always he had kept in mind the fact that the Japanese Kwantung Army of approximately one million officers and men stood ready in Manchuria to march.

On 5 April 1945 the Soviet government denounced its pact with Japan. The grounds were that Japan had assisted Germany in many ways during the war and that Japan was carrying on hostilities against the United States and Britain who were the allies of the Soviet Union. Already in previous months the Japanese, no doubt fearing Russian participation on the side of the United States and Britain, had begun seeking the intercession of Russia in ending the war, while avoiding unconditional surrender. The Soviet ambassador in Tokyo was approached several times and Japanese endeavours to persuade the Soviet government to mediate culminated in a proposal that the emperor would send Prince Konoye to Moscow on 12 July for discussions. No answer was made to this proposal.

The Americans were now eager to forestall Russia's entry into the war. The Yalta agreement had contained provision that Stalin's proposals concerning Outer Mongolia and the ports and railways would require the concurrence of Generalissimo Chiang Kai-shek and that the American president would take measures on the advice of Stalin to obtain this concurrence.[29] The Soviet–Chinese talks, lasting two weeks before the Potsdam conference and then from 7 to 14 August, were apparently drawn out by Chiang Kai-shek on American instructions. The Potsdam ultimatum to Japan on 26 July, demanding immediate unconditional surrender was evidently also intended to bring the war in the Far East to an end before the Soviet forces were ready. The Russians complained that they had not been consulted about this ultimatum and when they asked that publication should be held for three days they learnt that the text had already been released.[30]

The Japanese rejected this ultimatum, according to official U.S. and Soviet sources. But the Japanese were by this time facing defeat. They had made many attempts to negotiate an armistice. It seems probable that they were anxious to accept the ultimatum, subject only to the preservation of the position of the emperor. On 2 August the Japanese ambassador called to see Molotov about the ultimatum, but the Soviet government, eager to declare war before Japan could make peace, was unresponsive to his requests for clarification. Six days later the ambassador called again on Molotov, this time to receive the Soviet declaration of war.

On 6 August, two days before the Soviet declaration, the atom bomb was dropped on Hiroshima.[31] This awesome event disturbed the Russians deeply. The Soviet press reported the news only briefly, but everyone realized that here was a devastating new development which could threaten them. Stalin is reported to have summoned five of the foremost Soviet scientists to the Kremlin on the following day and to have ordered them to develop a Soviet atom bomb in the shortest time possible and regardless of cost.[32] The Russians felt that, although they had destroyed Germany, their greatest enemy, they were now desperately vulnerable from another quarter.

The Soviet declaration of war, announced on the same day as the report in the Soviet press of the Hiroshima bombing, merely deepened the general depression among the Russians. No one wanted another war and the feeling towards Japan was of sympathy rather than hostility. But, aware that troops had been moving for some time to the Far East, they were resigned and concerned only that the war should be brief.

Under the general command of Marshal Vassilevsky the Baikal Front and the 1st and 2nd Far Eastern Fronts had marked superiority over the Kwantung Army, especially in tanks, guns, and aircraft. The Russians were highly trained and seasoned troops who advanced swiftly into Manchuria. The Japanese fought bravely, but their counter-attacks failed completely to hold the Russian advance.

The Soviet command was intent on seizing the areas, which Stalin had specified at Yalta, before the Americans could occupy them. The declaration of surrender by the Japanese emperor on 14 August was dismissed by the Soviet chiefs of staff as only a general statement. On 17 August Marshal Vassilevsky sent his own ultimatum to the commander of the Kwantung Army to surrender by noon on 20 August. Japanese units continued to fight for some days, but officially the Japanese army surrendered on that day.

During these few days Soviet air-borne troops had seized the ports of Dairen and Port Arthur. The Soviet Pacific fleet in a series of combined operations ensured the occupation of southern Sakhalin and the Kurile Islands. Of these acquisitions the recovery of Port Arthur gave Stalin special satisfaction. In his broadcast to the nation on 2 September, the day on which the formal capitulation of Japan was signed on board the U.S. warship, *Missouri,* he recalled the Russian defeat in the war against Japan in 1904–5. Then, he claimed, the Japanese had unexpectedly struck at the Russian fleet at Port Arthur as they had later struck at Pearl Harbour. He spoke with pride of the fact that Russia had exacted her revenge at Port Arthur and had now secured her access to the Pacific by occupying southern Sakhalin and the Kuriles. No Russian patriot could have shown greater pride in these achievements.

In the following months relations between Soviet Russia and the Western powers declined sharply. The division into two camps became more marked as Stalin believed that the menace of American domination was pressing inexorably on Russia. The foreign ministers met in London,

Moscow, and Paris to draft the peace treaties and settle problems of post-war relations, and their bitter wrangling threatened to be interminable. Byrnes and Bevin constantly criticized the regimes in Bulgaria, Rumania, Hungary, and Yugoslavia for being totalitarian. Molotov insisted that Russia was entitled to the security of having friendly governments in the neighbouring countries of Eastern Europe. He argued that the Western powers had no right to impose their conception of democracy on other countries. But the Western powers without being explicit claimed this right, confident that the free elections on which they insisted would result in each case in an anti-communist government. Moreover, they were prompt to rebuff any attempt to extend Soviet influence beyond Eastern and Central Europe. When Molotov proposed that the former Italian territory of Tripolitania should be placed under Russian trusteeship, Bevin was incensed by what he considered a threat to the British Commonwealth, and both he and Byrnes rejected the proposal.

The conflict that developed over Iran and its outcome provided what Stalin considered a sinister demonstration of the American threat to Russia. British and Soviet forces had in an agreed operation occupied Iran early in the war, because they feared that the pro-German Shah might make Iran available for a German invasion of Russia from the south. American forces had later shared in the occupation which ensured that Iran was open for the transport of war supplies to Russia. Towards the end of the war the withdrawal of the occupation forces by a certain date was agreed. But the Soviet units remained after this date and were accused of seeking to establish a regime in northern Iran, friendly to Russia. The Soviet reply was that they needed to hold their troops in Iran to bring pressure on the legal Iranian government to grant oil exploitation rights which the Soviet Union desperately needed to compensate their shortage of oil, caused by German damage to Soviet oilfields.

American and British pressure on Russia to honour her agreement mounted and threatened a major clash. Finally Stalin yielded and withdrew his troops. But America at once stepped in with dollar aid and with advisers, including military advisers. Iran quickly came under American domination which was as complete as Russian domination over Rumania and Bulgaria. The difference was that Iran, remote from the United States, was on Russia's borders, and the Americans were free to establish military installations there as and when they wished. The Western powers had thus secured an important strategic and economic position from which, the Russians believed, they could attack them. The Western powers also compelled Russia to desist in her attempts to share in the control of the Dardanelles and access to the Black Sea.

Churchill's militant speech on 5 March 1946 at Fulton in the United States, known as his 'Iron Curtain Speech', in effect proclaimed the division of the powers into the communist and the Western blocks. He advocated a strong political and military 'fraternal association' of the

United States and Britain and the Commonwealth, which by maintaining the balance of power against the Soviet block would guarantee peace. The Charter of the United Nations had had as one of its basic purposes the prevention of nations forming blocks and holding power and the peace of the world in balance between them. Churchill had prefaced his speech with the usual assurances that he sought to preserve peace and to reach closer understanding with the Soviet Union, but to Stalin and his government it seemed clear that he had issued a warning and a threat to Russia which made closer understanding impossible. The speech was, Stalin declared on 13 March 1946, 'a dangerous act, calculated to sow seeds of dissent and hinder collaboration among the allied nations. It has harmed the cause of peace and security. Mr Churchill has now adopted the position of a warmonger.' [33]

Stalin recognized, moreover, that, although no longer prime minister, Churchill's speech represented the views of both American and British governments. Truman, the U.S. president, had shared the platform with him at Fulton. In Britain the labour party expressed disagreement, but the labour government was following the policy which he advocated.

A few dissenting voices were raised. In the U.S.A. Henry Wallace, the secretary of commerce, declared that 'We should be prepared to judge [Russia's] requirements against the background of what we ourselves and the British have insisted upon as essential to our respective security. We should be prepared, even at the expense of risking epithets of appeasement, to agree to reasonable Russian guarantees of security.' [34] But neither Truman nor Attlee nor their foreign ministers were prepared to concede that any Russian claims were reasonable, so long as the Soviet government refused to retreat from Eastern Europe.

Progress was slow at the peace conference which began its meetings in Paris on 29 July 1946. The Soviet government was now relying on obstructive tactics to avoid being continually out-voted by the Anglo-American block. The conference nevertheless reached agreement on many subjects, including the terms of the peace treaties with Germany's former allies. The council of foreign ministers met in New York in November 1946 to settle final details. Treaties with Italy, Hungary, Finland, Rumania, and Bulgaria were finally signed in February 1947.

In March the council of foreign ministers met in Moscow to work on the problems of the German peace treaty. But no agreement could be reached on the main issues. The Russians still demanded reparations of ten billion dollars to be paid by Germany in capital, current production, and labour. The Western powers still refused to accept this figure firmly and held that reparations should be paid from capital only. The Russian demand, that the industrial region of the Ruhr, located in the British zone, should be placed under four-power control, was firmly opposed by the United States and Britain. Russia maintained that the German lands, placed under Polish control, an arrangement accepted reluctantly and provisionally by the Potsdam conference, must now be considered to be permanently part of Poland.

The evident determination of Stalin and Molotov to extend Soviet control over Germany and to exact reparations beyond the terms agreed exasperated the Western leaders. They interpreted it as blatant aggrandizement and evidence of communist militancy. Stalin was, however, concerned primarily to secure Russia against future aggression and by means of reparations to gain such economic aid as he could for reconstruction. His fear and suspicion were that the Western powers would allow Germany to recover her industrial and military strength and would then use her as an ally against Russia. The decision of the United States and Britain to merge their zones intensified Stalin's fears. At every stage he opposed American and British policy in Germany and refused to countenance German unity, unless he had some guarantee that the German government would be at least friendly to Russia.

To check the further extension of Soviet power and influence and to bring pressure on the Soviet government to co-operate on Western terms, Truman on 12 March 1947 proclaimed his doctrine of the containment of Russia. This would be effected by granting military and economic support to countries which, while outside the Soviet sphere of influence, were considered to be menaced. The policy was buttressed by the theory propounded mainly by G. F. Kennan, an influential state department officer who had served in the U.S. embassy in Moscow, that strong pressure from outside would bring the collapse of the Soviet regime. He argued that communism was an alien and evil creed, contrary to Russian traditions and history, and that the Soviet leaders could maintain the regime only by use of force.[35]

Meanwhile America was disturbed by the slow economic recovery of Europe and especially Britain from the war. Haunted by the spectre of a revival of the great economic depression, America sought to exorcize it by underwriting the rapid economic recovery of Western Europe and thus solving American problems by an expansion of its overseas markets and investments. This policy which was a concomitant of the Truman doctrine was launched in general terms in the summer of 1947 by Secretary of State George Marshall. He had not specified in his speech that this American aid would be open to the Soviet Union, but at a press conference he stated that he saw no reason why the plan should not include Russia. But it may be doubted whether the U.S. congress would have sanctioned the extension of what came to be known as the Marshall plan to Soviet Russia, except on terms completely unacceptable to Moscow.

Acting on the assumption that the Marshall plan was open to Russia, the British foreign minister, Bevin, invited Molotov to Paris to discuss it in the hope that it would bridge the gulf between the two blocks. The Soviet attitude to the Marshall proposals was very cautious. Disappointed in their earlier hopes of American aid and deeply disturbed by the threat of American domination, Stalin and Molotov suspected a trap. They were quick to reach the conclusion that the Marshall plan was as much part of the American policy of open-door expansion as the Truman doctrine of containing and destroying communism and that it spelt danger for Russia.[36]

Molotov left Paris abruptly after a few days. He had made it clear that the Soviet Union would not participate. Moreover, he made haste to bring pressure on Hungary, Poland, and Czechoslovakia, who had accepted the plan, to withdraw. This had the result of deepening the division between the communist and the Western worlds. Stalin was now convinced that the West was an organized block, led and supported by the great power of the United States, and devoted to the destruction of the communist world. Soviet policy was now to develop Eastern Europe as an integrated block, economically and politically independent of the West. The Western powers interpreted this to mean that Moscow was planning a general offensive which would even include military action. The rift was complete. The 'cold war', a period of bitter recrimination, unbridled suspicions, and mutual animosity, had begun.

During the next three years Stalin consolidated the Soviet block, extending it where possible, and at times going dangerously close to provoking the Western powers to a major conflict. He hastened the process of transforming countries in the Soviet sphere into people's democracies, regarded as a transitional stage between capitalism and socialism, by eliminating all non-communist elements. This strengthened Soviet control over Rumania, Bulgaria, Hungary, Czechoslovakia, Poland, and Albania.

The one country to resist Soviet pressure and to assert its independence was Yugoslavia. The Yugoslav communists, led by Tito, had gained power without Moscow's help and they saw no reason for accepting Soviet dictation. Stalin, infuriated by this defiance of Moscow, the citadel of communism, vented his anger in accusations of heresy, revisionism, and betrayal of the revolutionary cause. Tito was, however, unmoved even when Stalin had the Yugoslav communist party expelled from the Cominform (Communist Information Bureau), the modified Communist International, revived in September 1947, and moved the headquarters of the Cominform from Belgrade to Bucharest.

This political integration of Eastern Europe with Soviet Russia was accompanied by economic integration. On 25 January 1949 Comecon (Council for Economic Mutual Assistance) was set up, embracing the Soviet Union, Czechoslovakia, Bulgaria, Hungary, Poland, and Rumania.

In response to the formation of the Federal Republic of Germany on 8 May 1949 by the German population of the American, British and French zones, the Russians set up the German Democratic Republic in their zone. But, while disturbed by the degree of independence accorded to the West Germans, the Soviet government was alarmed by the North

Atlantic Pact, signed on 4 April 1949 by the United States, Britain, Canada, France, Belgium, the Netherlands, Luxembourg, Norway, Denmark, Iceland, Italy, and Portugal. The pact provided for a military alliance in which all signatories would receive prompt aid if attacked in Europe or North America. It established the permanent North Atlantic Treaty Organization to maintain a defence force, comprising troops provided by the member states. The pact was part of a general programme for bringing the countries of Western Europe into closer economic and military partnership. But also, as the Russians feared, this movement embraced Western Germany and soon, on American insistence, it was to include German rearmament.

To Moscow this Western alliance, although said to be defensive, was readily adaptable for offensive action against Russia. The inclusion of Western Germany as an equal and German rearmament were horrifying developments. Stalin watched this rapid evolution of Western policy anxiously and intensified the process of building up the strength of the Soviet Union and of the whole communist block. In an attempt to secure Berlin completely under Soviet control he began in June 1948 to bar all deliveries of goods by land and water from Western Germany to the American, British, and French sectors of the city. The Western powers countered by sending supplies by air. Stalin was faced with raising the barriers to land and water communication from the West or risking war by using force to stop the airlift. He was not prepared to provoke a major war and at the end of September 1949 the Western powers were able to use the normal land and sea routes.

Conflicts between the two blocks had already come to dominate the work of the United Nations. Soviet representatives had exercised the right of veto forty times by the end of 1949, while the United States and Britain had not used it once. Soviet Russia was pursuing an obstructionist policy as the whole world could see. But since the anti-Soviet vote was always in the majority in both the General Assembly and the Security Council, the Western powers could and did ensure the rejection of Soviet proposals in the Security Council without having to resort to the veto.

The disputes between the Soviet Union and the Western powers over the international control of atomic energy revealed the extent of the chasm separating them, and the complete absence of trust made this chasm unbridgeable. In November 1945 the American, British, and Canadian governments declared their readiness to share with members of the United Nations detailed information on the industrial use of atomic energy, provided that effective safeguards could be agreed against its destructive use. Early in 1946 the United Nations appointed an Atomic Energy Commission. In June 1946 the American Baruch plan was presented to the commission. This plan proposed setting up an atomic authority with control over the production of fissionable materials. When the system of control was operating effectively and all the states had formally renounced the atom bomb, the United States would cease making them and would dispose of its existing stocks. Full information on production of atomic energy would then be vested in the authority and its decisions would be by majority vote without any right of veto.

The Baruch plan was hailed in the West as a practical and, since at this time the United States alone held the secret of the atomic bomb, a generous proposal. Stalin considered, however, that the plan would put the Soviet Union at a serious disadvantage. During the transitional period, while effective control of atomic energy production was being established, the United States alone would be free to use the atomic bomb in the event of war against Russia. Moreover, the transitional period might be prolonged. He also rejected the proposal that foreign inspectors would be free to investigate all installations. Mistrusting the United States and Britain and believing that they were hostile to Russia and the Soviet regime, he was not prepared to admit such inspectors who would surely include among them Western spies. Also the atomic authority when set up would almost certainly have an anti-Soviet majority, and he could not put Russia at its mercy.

Soviet counter-proposals accepted the need for strict international control over the mining and production of atomic materials and conceded other major points, but demanded destruction of existing bombs before the control was established. The proposals merited consideration, but the Western powers rejected them. In September 1948 Vyshinsky moved in the General Assembly that the permanent members of the Security Council, as a first step in disarmament, should reduce all armed forces by one third within one year and should accept an absolute prohibition of atomic weapons. An international agency working within the framework of the Security Council would enforce and supervise these measures. In November, further Soviet resolutions called for the absolute prohibition of atomic weapons and an efficient international control over production and use of atomic energy.

Rejection of the Soviet proposals and the adjournment on 25 July 1949 of the Atomic Energy Commission *sine die* convinced Stalin that the Americans and British were not acting in good faith, while they in turn held doubts about the good faith of the Soviet leaders in making them. Stalin considered, however, that the Western powers were concerned to maintain their own advantage and to dominate the production of atomic materials in the world through the atomic authority. He continued to fear also that they might be tempted to take advantage of their sole possession of the bomb to strike at Russia. Without doubt Stalin and all Russians felt relief when in September 1949 their scientists exploded an atom bomb.

Soviet Russia and the United States also came into conflict in the Far East. Both countries had supported Chaing Kai-shek's nationalist government in China. Stalin had regarded the Chinese communist party as being of small consequence, and where Russia's interests or security were involved he did not hesitate to disavow the local communists. At Yalta he had agreed to conclude a treaty of alliance with the nationalist government and to assist it in liberating China from the Japanese yoke. In the post-war period, however, both the Soviet and the American governments began to realize that Chiang Kai-shek's regime had become corrupt and ineffective, and that the Chinese communists, vigorously led by Mao Tse-tung, alone offered hope of reform and stability. The Communist People's Liberation Army swept the nationalists from the country. Chiang Kai-shek fled with the remnants of his army and regime to Formosa (Taiwan). On 1 October 1949 the Central People's Government of the Chinese People's Republic was proclaimed. A new nation of some 500 million had become part of the Soviet block and as its leader Soviet Russia's prestige was greatly enhanced.

This dramatic change in China faced the United States with a dilemma. It was clearly futile to attempt to restore Chiang Kai-shek. But as the champion of the anti-communist crusade, the U.S. government could not accord recognition to Mao Tse-tung's regime. Formosa was therefore taken under American protection and the nationalists continued to receive U.S. support. Indeed, on American insistence nationalist China retained its permanent seat on the Security Council, while the effective government of China, because of American opposition, went unrepresented in the United Nations.

In June 1950 the Korean People's Democratic Republic, encouraged by the victory of the Chinese communists and undoubtedly with the approval and possibly with the support of Moscow, invaded the Republic of Korea in the south. The resulting war was to bring the world close to a major conflict.

Informally at Yalta or subsequently the Americans and Russians had agreed that after the defeat of Japan Soviet troops would occupy northern and American troops would occupy southern Korea until a Korean government had been elected. In November 1946 elections held in North Korea resulted in the United Democratic National Front, led by Kim Il-sen, a Korean communist, forming a government. In October 1948 the Soviet government accorded recognition to this regime. The United Nations commission in Korea reported unfavourably on the regime, but could take no action.

In the south the American military government was intent on establishing a national assembly of ninety members, half elected and half nominated. A United Nations commission, sent to Korea to supervise the creation of a free state, by deciding to allow elections in the south gave recognition to the division of the country in two parts. Two governments were thus in existence. The withdrawal of the occupation forces was announced; the U.S. forces were to be withdrawn by July 1949, the Soviet forces by Christmas of 1948.

Hostility had already begun to mount between north and south. Each government claimed to be the *de jure* government of the whole country. On 25 June 1950 war broke out between them. The Security Council met immediately. It passed a resolution declaring that North Korea had committed an act of aggression and calling for the withdrawal of their forces from South Korea. When the North Koreans did not respond to this summons to cease hostilities and withdraw to the north of the 38th parallel, the Security Council agreed that military and other assistance, under a unified American command, should be given to the South Korean Republic. The absence of the Soviet representative from the Security Council meetings had made it possible for these resolutions to be passed.

The Korean crisis brought Soviet Russia and the United States into angry conflict at the United Nations. The Soviet government supported the North Koreans. It accused the United States of perpetrating aggressive armed intervention in the internal affairs of Korea and attacked the Security Council's resolutions as being gross violations of the United Nations charter. In the West the general belief was that Moscow had instigated the invasion of South Korea. The action of communist China in sending troops to fight with the North Koreans against the U.N. forces convinced the Western powers that they were facing a new threat. Truman declared that the attack on Korea had made it plain that communism had gone over from subversion to the conquest of independent nations by armed force. He expressed fears of a communist invasion of Formosa and ordered the American 7th Fleet to the defence of the area. The conflict was threatening to explode into a major war. When on 23 June 1951 the Soviet representative at the United Nations proposed a conference to discuss possible armistice terms, the Western powers at once agreed. The negotiations were protracted and only in 1953 was an armistice agreed.

Meanwhile the United States had decided to take independent action to conclude a peace treaty with Japan. In October 1950 an American memorandum, setting out proposed peace terms, was handed to the Soviet representative at the United Nations and circulated to other interested countries. Soviet objections centred on three main points. The first was the proposal that Japanese sovereignty with the right to rearm and to be free of occupying forces would be recognized. Not only Russia, but Britain and others were disturbed by this provision. The United States had, however, put aside memories of Pearl Harbour. Communist Russia and China were now the enemies. The new policy was to take Japan under her protection and to establish her as a powerful bastion against communism in the Far East. For this reason the peace terms contained provision also that foreign powers should have the right with Japanese agreement to station troops on Japanese territory.

The Soviet government objected strenuously to these terms, while noting that provision was made for the formal cession of the Kurile Islands and southern Sakhalin, as Roosevelt had agreed with Stalin at

Yalta. Moscow insisted, too, that China had the right to be consulted, particularly since the Chinese more than any other nation had suffered from Japanese aggression and would strongly oppose the rearming of Japan. But the United States was adamant in her refusal to recognize the Chinese People's Republic. Communist China was a threat to American security in the Far East and could therefore be neither recognized nor consulted. On 8 September 1951 in San Francisco the peace treaty with Japan was signed by most members of the United Nations, but the Soviet Union, Poland, and Czechoslovakia refused to sign it.

Nothing weighed so heavily on Stalin and his government, however, as the Anglo-American policies designed to revive Western Germany as an economic and military power. In particular Stalin was anxious to prevent the integration of a German army as part of NATO and the West European defence organizations. In March 1952 he proposed that the four allied powers should meet without delay to discuss a German peace treaty. In the exchange of notes that followed, he conceded many points. Germany would have the right to have armed forces for her own defence, but not to form an alliance directed against any power which had taken part in the war against her. He accepted the principle of free elections throughout all Germany, conducted under the auspices not of the United Nations but of the occupying powers, as provided by the charter. But the exchange ended in deadlock, mainly because the Western powers were not to be deflected from their intention of integrating an armed West Germany into the Western block.

Thus within a few years of the end of the war the Grand Alliance of Soviet Russia, the United States, and Britain had been sundered. Stalin had thought of post-war security for Russia and for the world in terms of co-operation between the three powers directly and through the United Nations. He had hoped for Western support in the reconstruction of Russia. He needed peace and stability for this task and then for developing Russia so that she would overtake the capitalist world. He believed in communism as a system superior to capitalism and that communist Russia would rise above the capitalist West in peaceful competition. He had no thoughts of war. Russia had suffered too much from wars and another war, especially now when nuclear weapons would be used, would probably destroy the Soviet regime and retard Russia's development a hundred years or more.[37]

To this end the policy he now pursued was based on conclusions or assumptions which seemed clear to him and to others in his government. From the time of the Potsdam conference the policy of the United States and Britain evidently had been concerned to keep Soviet Russia weak and to impose American domination. This was demonstrated by their denial of what he considered the just demands for reparations and their refusal to recognize Russia's security interests in Eastern Europe. American aid clearly spelt domination or at least pressure to modify or abandon communism. American proposals for nuclear controls were, he considered, designed to maintain American ascendancy. As anti-communism in the West generated greater moral fervour and became a crusade, he began actively to fear American aggression. This fear was aggravated by the many influential voices in the West which were raised in support of once-for-all military action against communist Russia. To Stalin and to the Russian people the capitalist West had become an aggressive enemy and, while obstructing Western policies by every means possible, their tasks must be to make Russia strong and fully able to compete and defend herself against them.

CHAPTER TWENTY-THREE

The Great Reconstruction

VAST problems of readjustment and reconstruction faced Russia at the end of the war. The dislocation of national life and the devastation had been stupendous in scale. Many experts considered that a decade or more would be needed to restore the country to the conditions of early 1941. The people were desperately weary. The war had taken heavy toll not only in killed and wounded, but also in labour which had reduced many to exhaustion. But the easier life, expected as the reward for wartime sacrifices and for victory, did not come. The new economic plan made the staggering demand that reconstruction should be completed and that production should be lifted above pre-war levels within five years. So long as the nation remained weak and vulnerable, they must continue to work under the same pressure. With extraordinary resilience and courage the Russians turned to their new task.

The first problem was to resettle people who had been scattered widely and to utilize them productively. This was urgent because the man-power shortage was acute. More than eight million men had been demobilized from the armed forces within a few months of the end of the war. Some four-and-a-half million people returned from German slave labour and other camps. Eight million or more people had been evacuated beyond the Urals. Many endured severe hardships in returning to their homes. They suffered from food shortages and the desperate lack of housing forced them to live in dug-outs, ruins, and generally in primitive crowded conditions. All who were able, however, were at once involved in the great labour of reconstruction.

The priorities and tempo of post-war development were laid down in the fourth five-year plan which the Supreme Soviet had adopted on 18 March 1946. Significantly Stalin had within a few days of the dropping of the bomb on Hiroshima given orders to Gosplan to prepare this development programme. The plan made heavy industry the main priority. Building materials, steel, and machinery were in urgent demand as reconstruction and re-equipment got under way. Also, as relations with the Western powers deteriorated, Stalin was determined to provide the foundations upon which a strong armaments industry could be permanently based.

The plan called for an overall increase in industries' output by 1950 of 48 per cent above pre-war levels. This would require the restoration of more than 3,000 medium and large industrial plants and the construction of a further 2,700 plants. The new construction included 45 blast furnaces, 165 open hearth furnaces, 90 electric furnaces, 104 rolling mills, and 63 coke batteries, restored or newly erected. Further, 250 new collieries and iron ore mines with a total combined output of 35 million tons were to be opened. Estimated on the basis of an increase of 50 per cent in the capital equipment provided for each worker, the labour productivity was expected to rise by 36 per cent over the pre-war years.[1]

The targets to be achieved in only five years and after the strains of war seemed impossibly high. But they were part of Stalin's vision of the day when Soviet output would exceed that of Western Europe and the United States. This long-term goal, requiring 'perhaps three new five-year plans, if not more', as he explained at the beginning of 1946, would mean trebling the pre-war output of steel to 60 million and of coal to 500 million tons annually. The target for steel was double the U.S. output in 1938, but below the U.S. wartime peak of 81 million tons in 1944. The coal target was more than double the British pre-war output, but below the U.S. wartime peak. The target figure for oil of 60 million tons was not quite double the pre-war output and only a third of U.S. production in 1940.[2] Stalin was presenting only approximate production figures, but they were a reflection of bold vision and an indication to the people of the magnitude of the tasks before them.

While heavy industry continued to claim priority the plan provided for some expansion of industries producing consumer goods. It stated that the output of foodstuffs and consumer goods generally should on the basis of a 17 per cent annual increase reach and surpass the pre-war levels by 1950.[3] In fact the proposed increases were far below those planned for heavy industry. In the case of cotton and woollen textiles they were actually lower than the target figures set in the first and second plans before the war. Russians recognized and accepted that for some years ahead they must continue to live austerely.

The planned increases in agricultural production were fairly modest. Grain output was to rise by 1950 only 7 per cent above the 1940 level. But crops, such as cotton and flax, required in industry, were set higher targets. For animal production, which had been drastically reduced during the war, the increases were 39 per cent for cattle, 75 per cent for sheep and goats, and 200 per cent for pigs. But these increases were over the animal population in 1945, one of the lowest levels ever reached. In fact, while the number of collective farms was planned to rise above pre-war levels, the restocking of the farms would, it was realized, take far longer than five years.

The plan gave special attention to the revival of the old industrial centres of western and south-western Russia, which had in most cases been razed to the ground. Not only were these centres to be rebuilt and brought into production but by the end of the plan period their total output was to be 15 per cent above the pre-war level. This did not mean, however, that the eastward movement of industry, begun in the 1930s, was to be reversed. On the contrary this trend was maintained and strengthened by a higher planned growth in the output of the eastern industrial centres, which were playing an increasingly dominant role in the national economy.[4]

The transport system needed urgently to be developed to serve in the restoration and expansion of industry. The war had imposed a heavy strain on transport, especially in the Urals and Siberia where armaments industries had poured out tanks, guns, and other equipment, and from which the main food supplies had been sent westwards. But under the new plan the total freight to be carried by rail, water, and road would rise, according to estimates, by as much as a third above the pre-war level. The plan therefore made extensive provision for extending and improving the transport system.[5]

The achievements under the plan were remarkable. By 1948 wartime devastation had been made good in industry and overall industrial output had already exceeded the production levels of 1940. By 1952 the output was two-and-a-half times greater than pre-war. But in agriculture the recovery was disastrously slow.

While tackling these formidable tasks, the nation was rapidly returning to a peacetime basis. The state committee of defence was dissolved on 4 September 1945 and the appropriate organs of the party and state resumed their responsibilities. Martial law was ended in all parts of the country except those territories which had been acquired after 1939. On 10 February 1946 the general election of deputies to the Supreme Soviet were held. The last elections had taken place in 1937 and deputies had retained their seats beyond the usual term. But this was of no great importance. The elections in which the people could vote for only the one party candidate, involved no choice of government or policy, and simply provided an opportunity for a mass declaration of support for the leader of the party. Dutifully Russians cast their votes in a poll claimed to represent ninety-nine per cent of the electors.

The Supreme Soviet met in March to elect its presidium and the council of people's commissars. It approved the adoption of the Western title 'ministers' in place of 'people's commissars'. It confirmed with acclamation Stalin's position as chairman of the council of ministers or prime minister, and indeed it made few changes. Kalinin, now old and failing but popular, resigned from the chairmanship of the presidium of the Supreme Soviet and his place as titular head of state was filled by Nikolai Shvernik.

Power resided, however, not in the Supreme Soviet but in the party, and specifically in the hands of Stalin himself. He remained prime minister and was also in effect the first secretary of the party. His personal prestige among his people had never stood higher than in these post-war years and his authority was beyond challenge. He felt no need for the support of the all-union party congress which was legally the source of authority in the party and, according to the party rules, had to meet every three years. No congress had met since 1939 and not until October 1952 was another convened. The plenum of the central committee met seldom and even the Politburo seems to have been largely disregarded. Stalin reigned as autocrat, wielding absolute power over state and party.

Among the men in authority below him, however, personal rivalries were leading to manoeuvring for position and prominence. Stalin himself undoubtedly observed and even fostered these rivalries which in no way challenged his position and which prevented any one of his senior colleagues gathering too much power into his hands. Malenkov had held a powerful position since the time of the great purges. He was close to Stalin and had been from 1941 until 1945 a member of the state committee of defence. Early in 1945, however, Zhdanov had returned to Moscow from Leningrad and, ambitious, tough, and dogmatic, he was evidently ready to challenge Malenkov. Supported by Voznesensky, he attacked Malenkov's work as chairman of the Committee on Rehabilitation of Liberated Areas, and particularly his handling of the dismantling of German industry. His attack was so effective that Malenkov was forced to retire for a time into the background. But suddenly in July 1948 he returned to the party secretariat and his career was clearly on the mend. Moreover, a few weeks later, on 31 August 1948, Zhdanov suddenly died, apparently from natural causes.

Again in control of the party organization, Malenkov introduced important changes affecting the role of the party in industry, reviving the system set up in 1934 by Kaganovich, but changed by Zhdanov in 1939. The main factor was the introduction of greater centralization of party control over industry in this period of rapid reconstruction and expansion. The party secretariat was reorganized so that closer attention could be given to all branches of industry, while decentralizing the party's control over the distribution of personnel.[6]

Feeling the strength of his position, especially after the death of Zhdanov, Malenkov next attacked the handling of party policy in the Ukraine, which had been for some years the domain of Khrushchev. The dispute really centred on the perennial problems of agriculture which at the end of the war was in a desperate state. The pressing need was thought to be the restoration of party control over the collective farms, where it had always been weak. The peasants had, however, continued to resent the collective system. Many had hoped that at the end of the war the system would be abolished and they had begun expanding their private holdings by taking the land of the collectives. On 19 March 1946 the council of ministers and the central committee directed in a joint resolution that all land and equipment, alienated by the peasants, should be restored to the collectives. Within a year, some fourteen million acres of land, grabbed by the peasants, had been recovered.[7] Other serious problems were the corruption of local party and government officials and failure to observe the rules governing collectives.

Under the chairmanship of Andreev, a Council on Collective Farms was made responsible for restoring some order on the land, and this meant to Stalin and Malenkov the strengthening of party control. The great obstacle had always been the very small number of communists on the collectives, and the council now launched a campaign to increase their number. At the same time it sent selected communists to rural districts so that primary party organizations could be formed as widely as possible. Some progress resulted. A third of all collective farms had party organizations by early 1948, but support for the party on the land remained, as it had always been, half-hearted, and agriculture continued to show few signs of reviving.

The communist party and its ideology had never been able to win the confidence and support of the Russian peasant. Stubbornly resisting party directives, he gave as little as he could in time, labour, and interest to the collective farm and devoted himself to his private holding. There he had the incentive of working his own piece of land and of being able to sell its produce in the free market. The government increased taxation on the income gained by peasants from their private holdings and required farmers with cows, sheep, and poultry to deliver part of their produce to the state at the fixed low prices given for all such compulsory quotas. Stalin even considered that the private holdings should be abolished. But such measures made no difference to agricultural output. Poverty was widespread and many peasants lived near to starvation level. Malenkov and others made bold claims, while Stalin was alive, that agriculture was recovering rapidly. But figures, released after his death, showed that production was still desperately low.[8]

Khrushchev had taken a special interest in agriculture in the Ukraine. Since 1938 he had been first secretary of the Ukrainian party. He had retreated with the Red Army to Stalingrad, serving as a high-ranking political officer, and had returned with the army taking part in the liberation. From 1944 to 1947 he held office both as first secretary of the party and chairman of the council of ministers of the Ukraine.

In 1946 when the Ukraine suffered a fearful drought and the harvest failed, the central committee in Moscow, probably on Malenkov's instigation, strongly criticized the appointment and administration of party personnel in the Ukraine. This was a direct attack on Khrushchev. In March 1947 Kaganovich was sent to the Ukraine where he took over the office of first secretary, leaving Khrushchev as chairman of the council of ministers. Details of this crisis are not known, but Khrushchev survived the attack. When Kaganovich returned to Moscow later in 1947, he again became secretary of the Ukrainian party.

Towards the end of 1949, Khrushchev was summoned to Moscow to serve in the central committee secretariat and also as secretary of the Moscow regional party organization. Stalin's purpose in bringing to Moscow this dynamic and assertive leader, who was also one of the party experts on agriculture, may well have been to counter-balance Malenkov who was becoming too deeply entrenched as the heir apparent.

Khrushchev at once became involved in agricultural reform. He launched an important new policy, directed at amalgamating collective farms into larger units. By the end of 1950 the number of collective farms had been reduced from 252,000 to 121,400 and by the end of 1952 to 94,800.[9] He maintained that this reform would make the farms more manageable and efficient, especially in facilitating mechanization. Moreover, the reorganization would enable the party to exercise greater control. But the party was still unable to wield a strong influence in agriculture and Khrushchev's changes had no real effect on agricultural production. The Russian peasant still lacked incentives and he was even less attracted by the new vast collectives than he had been by the smaller farms.

Khrushchev also advanced radical proposals for settling the peasants of these new collectives in towns, known as agro-towns or, more modestly, as 'collective farm settlements', where they would enjoy amenities such as peasant villages had never known. This concern for the welfare of the people and appreciation that it could aid production were among the novel aspects of Khrushchev's approach to practical problems, but they also exposed him to criticism by his colleagues.

Malenkov and Beria were his main opponents in the Politburo. At the nineteenth party congress Malenkov strongly attacked his concern for the welfare of the consumer and his neglect of the major production problems in agriculture. His stand against Khrushchev on this basic policy certainly had the support of Stalin who was concerned not with consumer welfare but with the basic problem of production and the need to ensure that agricultural output surged ahead on a level with industrial output. Khrushchev suffered a rebuff, but he retained his position and indeed by his vigorous personality and flow of positive ideas he had made an impact in Moscow.

Stalin was present at the nineteenth party congress, which met in Moscow on 5 October 1952, but took no part in the proceedings, except to deliver a brief closing address. He was now husbanding his strength, but he showed no signs of decline. His standing and supreme authority were acknowledged by every speaker in most fulsome terms and the whole congress rose to give him the tumultuous standing ovation which had now become traditional. He was still the autocrat, completely in command of the party and the nation. But, while never mentioned, the succession was undoubtedly exercising many minds.

Malenkov was the senior secretary after Stalin and regarded by many as the obvious successor. He received the greatest acclamation of the congress after Stalin and he presented the main report of the central committee. Beria was, however, a strong contender. His position as head of the security organization and of the ministry of the interior with control over the internal security troops gave him real power. He also had considerable responsibilities in managing the national economy and in developing atomic energy. Khrushchev held no comparable position of influence. But he had acquired control in party organizational affairs, enabling him to appoint his own supporters to key positions in the party and this was soon to prove an important source of power. One other possible contender who had the seniority and the status to succeed Stalin was Molotov, but he had never shown interest in advancing his personal position.

At the congress Khrushchev presented a report on proposed changes in party organization, which were duly approved. The most important change was to transform the Politburo into a presidium of the party central committee and to abolish the Orgburo, concentrating its work in the hands of the party secretariat. The new presidium at the apex of the party organization was a large committee of twenty-five members and eleven alternates. No explanation was given for this major change. At the time it was taken to have the purpose of rejuvenating the topmost authority by introducing younger members. Khrushchev subsequently declared that Stalin was preparing to dispose of the old Politburo members, such as Molotov and Mikoyan, and to bring in younger men.[10]

The congress also approved the changing of the party's name to the Communist Party of the Soviet Union. The addition of 'bolsheviks' in parentheses at the end was abolished. Presumably Stalin felt that the word 'bolsheviks', meaning majority-ites, was no longer relevant or desirable when the party ruled supreme and unopposed, and he had no qualms about breaking with tradition. Another change was the rearranging of the duties of party members so that the first duty was now to maintain party unity. The new rules also demanded that members should be more fearless in self-criticism and should give special attention to the need for party discipline.

This revision of the duties of members was in keeping with the ideological drive, launched soon after the end of the war. During the war the emphasis had been on nationalism and the patriotic duty of every Russian to fight for his country. The Western powers had for a time ceased to be capitalist enemies and had become democratic allies. But now with the great tasks of reconstruction before them and the deepening dangers of the cold war, the people needed, so Stalin and the party hierarchy considered, to be strengthened ideologically. The tenets of Marxism–Leninism were emphasized afresh and the basic differences between the Soviet Union and the capitalist world were restated.

Zhdanov as a secretary of the central committee had had special responsibility for ideological affairs. He took a leading part in launching this new campaign. A bigoted communist he was well suited to the task.

He imposed the conception of socialist realism as the goal of all forms of art. He mounted attacks on Western influence in the arts of 'formalism' and in scholarship as 'objectivism'. He harried Soviet writers, artists, and musicians, condemning them to produce their work in private or to remain unproductive, apart from paying the obligatory occasional lip-service to party ideology.

The country was so united and the party so strongly entrenched at the end of the war that the need for an ideological campaign was questionable. The anxiety of party leaders that the army might become a challenge had led to the revival of dual command. But this had clearly hampered the fighting efficiency of the army and on 9 October 1942 the single command system had been restored. But the military commander still had a political deputy at his side. The two branches remained separate and political officers, although deputies, could report independently to their political superiors. Relations between commanders, concerned with the discipline and efficiency of their troops, and political deputies, responsible for political indoctrination, readily became discordant. But the interests of the party were safeguarded not only by political officers, answering to the chief political administration, but also by the special security units, posted at vital points throughout the services.

At the same time the party had strengthened its mass base in the armed forces. Standards of admission to membership were relaxed and the intake of officers and men had increased rapidly during the war. By October 1952, 86·4 per cent of all Soviet officers were members of the party or the Komsomol. In 1942 alone 1·34 million new members had been admitted. By 1 January 1945 the overall size of the party had reached the record level of 5,760,369 and by September 1947 the figure was 6,300,000. At the time of the nineteenth party congress the total membership was 6,882,145.[11] But applications were by this time being subjected to careful scrutiny and many wartime members who had proved to be inadequate in political knowledge or inefficient or untrustworthy were weeded out.

The wartime recruitment ensured also that the party was a party of youth. The average age of party members was considerably reduced by the intake from the armed forces. By 1946, 63·6 per cent of the membership was under thirty-five years old. Another noteworthy feature was the improvement in the educational qualifications of members. By 1947, 6·32 per cent had received higher education and 20·54 per cent had received higher education, both striking improvements on pre-war figures.[12] The intake of women members had also risen from 14·9 per cent in 1941 to 19·2 per cent in October 1952, a recognition of the fact that women had played an outstanding role in the war.[13]

The party had made strong efforts to broaden its social base by recruiting members among the leading workers and collective farmers. Success had, however, been very limited, especially in rural areas where party representation remained significantly lower than in urban areas. More-

P

over, the real strength of the membership continued to come from the administrative, managerial, and technical intelligentsia. This was part of the general trend towards social differentiations which the war had accelerated.

The policy of raising the status of officers and the cult of the uniform had continued after the war. The practice of wearing uniforms, with marks of rank, spread to certain ministries, to the coal and iron ore industries, and to the transport system. Differences in income, supported by status distinctions, led to different standards of living. The factory director, the senior government servant, and the numerous party officials enjoyed living standards and privileges far above those of the worker, the clerk, and the ordinary members.

For those who had achieved senior and influential positions and who had money as a result, it was possible to give their children advantages and a better start in life. In 1940 fees had been introduced for secondary and higher education and the policy had continued. An extensive scholarship system ensured that the gifted children of humble parents would receive a full education. But the average child of parents who held a senior position and had money could attain higher education which would not be open to the average child of poor parents. Within this growing upper class as among senior officers of the armed forces a loyalty and fellowship naturally developed. The idea of a classless society, which had always been unrealistic, was now rapidly being eroded, as the Soviet regime found that it needed an élite not only in the armed services but in every sphere of responsibility.

The average age of the party membership had fallen, but the average age of the top leadership had risen appreciably, for men, least of all old men, do not readily surrender power. Of the voting delegates at the eighteenth congress in 1939, 49·5 per cent were under thirty-five; at the nineteenth congress only 5·9 per cent were under this age. Delegates over the age of fifty had amounted to only 3 per cent in 1939, but in 1952 they comprised 15·3 per cent.[14]

Stalin himself was undoubtedly aware of this ageing of the leadership. He had no thought of himself abdicating or retiring. But by his abolition of the Politburo and creation of the greatly enlarged presidium of the party he had undoubtedly intended to bring younger men into the top leadership. At the lower levels of the hierarchy, however, the problem remained untouched and, while he continued in absolute command, the party and government remained fairly rigid in character.

Stalin himself was nearly 73 at the time of the nineteenth congress. He had become, according to Khrushchev, 'even more capricious, irritable and brutal; in particular his suspicion grew. His persecution mania reached unbelievable dimensions.'[15] This had been demonstrated by the Leningrad affair which had followed on the death of Zhdanov. Disturbed by the promotion of Voznesensky, whom Stalin had made first deputy of the council of ministers, and of A. A. Kuznetsov, elected secretary of the central committee, Beria had aroused Stalin's suspicions against them. Both Voznesensky and Kuznetsov were purged, together with Rodionov, the chairman of the council of ministers of the R.S.F.S.R., Popkov, the first secretary of the party in Leningrad, and others. The party central committee subsequently carried out an examination of the whole affair and proved it to have been fabricated. The innocent who had suffered were rehabilitated, but posthumously in several cases.[16]

The campaign, lasting from 1946 to 1950, against Western influences which reasserted the party's domination of all artistic and intellectual life in the country, also developed into a purge. Denunciations, especially of Jews as 'rootless cosmopolitans', culminated in 1952 in the execution of a number of outstanding Jewish writers. Not least in its anti-Jewish character, the whole campaign was destructive and it reduced the intellectual life of the nation to sterility.

The 'doctors' plot' which also had an anti-Jewish element, was mounting to a climax when Stalin died. This plot, subsequently denounced by Khrushchev as a fabrication, arose from allegations that a terrorist group of nine prominent doctors, of whom seven were Jews, had been uncovered. A woman doctor, named Timashuk, wrote to Stalin that the doctors were deliberately prescribing the wrong treatment with the purpose of cutting short the lives of certain eminent people. Timashuk was herself an agent of the state security and presumably wrote the letter on someone's instructions. Stalin, his unresting suspicion having developed into a mania in these last years, acted on the letter and took a personal interest in the investigation of the alleged plot.[17] Soon confessions had been obtained, proving that the doctors had in fact killed Zhdanov and Shcherbakov, and that they were planning to undermine the health of the country's leading military personnel. The doctors were said to be American spies who had contact with U.S. intelligence organs through Jewish charities.

Preparations for the public trial of the doctors mounted until it was clear that the trial would be on the scale of the great purge of the 1930s. Within the Kremlin tension spread. The trials were clearly intended as the prelude to another terror. Voroshilov, Molotov, and Mikoyan were under suspicion, according to Khrushchev, and if three such stalwart colleagues of Stalin could be purged, there would clearly be no limits to the victims.[18] The nation was spared this horror by the death of Stalin.

CHAPTER TWENTY-FOUR

Stalin Dies

THE end was sudden. According to Khrushchev's account, Stalin had invited his close colleagues to his dacha for dinner one Saturday. All had enjoyed a pleasant evening, for Stalin was in good humour. On the following Sunday Khrushchev was surprised when Stalin did not ring him as usual to discuss business, and more surprised when he did not return to the Kremlin on the Monday morning. But on that evening the head of the bodyguard rang to say that Stalin was ill. He had suffered a stroke and was unconscious. Khrushchev, Malenkov, Bulganin, and Beria hastened to the dacha and stayed there for the next three days. He remained unconscious. He revived briefly and, although paralysed and unable to speak, he tried to joke with them. Shortly afterwards he suffered another stroke and on 5 March he died. Khrushchev said that he wept, adding 'After all we were his pupils and owed him everything.' [1]

The news of Stalin's death stunned the nation. Many Russians wept as Khrushchev had wept. Even those who felt the threat of a new terror lifted from them, and the artists and intellectuals who had suffered savage repression, especially since the war, were shaken. He had been their man of steel. He had held the reins of government firmly in his hands and had wielded power with a sense of purpose and direction. His death meant for the great majority of Russians that the nation had been cast adrift.

Stalin, an autocrat in the Russian historical tradition, had ruled as the tsars had ruled. Like them he had commanded the obedience and the devotion of the overwhelming majority of his people. Anthony Jenkinson, an Englishman who visited the court of Ivan the Terrible, wrote of him that 'He is not only beloved of his nobles and commoners, but also had in great dread and fear throughout all his dominions, so that I think no prince in Christendom is more feared of his own than he is, nor better beloved.' [2] Jenkinson's words could be applied to Stalin. During the terror and the collectivization campaign, when so many suffered from his ruthlessness, the Russians as a whole did not vilify or even blame him. They tended to accept their inflictions as part of the pattern and spirit of their history and they held to their faith in him.

Stalin's position as national leader derived its legal justification from the communist party and from Marxism–Leninism just as the authority of the tsars had been buttressed by the Orthodox church. But the strength of his hold on the loyalty of the people was rooted in nationalism. A

Georgian, not a Russian, he spoke the language with a distinct accent to the end of his days. But with the fervour of a migrant or a religious convert to another creed, he had adopted Great Russia as the nation to which he belonged. He had believed in Russia and her people and in their mission in the world. Indeed, he had embraced the messianic idea which since the sixteenth century had been deeply embedded in the Russian outlook. Resurging with new vigour after the revolution, this sense of mission had the same goal of reinvigorating civilization and specifically of purging the West of its self-seeking individualism and materialism, but now communism was the means of this goal.

Like Lenin, Stalin believed that he alone was capable of leading Russia along her destined road and that any means, no matter how ruthless, were entirely justified in maintaining himself in sole power to pursue this goal. To the end of his life, according to Khrushchev, in his speech of 25 February 1956, he was convinced that the crimes which he committed were justified by this great purpose.[3] But, while his purges and his ruthless driving campaigns caused widespread sufferings among his people, he did not rule by fear. A despot may keep a nation obedient and quiescent for a time by coercion and terror. Such negative instruments cannot, however, release and direct the dynamism which transformed Russia from a primitive illiterate nation into a highly industrialized, technologically advanced and literate nation within the twenty-five years of his reign.

The small quiet man whom Sukhanov had dismissed as a 'grey blur' and whom Trotsky had called 'the outstanding mediocrity of our party' had become one of the most remarkable men in history.[4] He could indeed claim to stand with Peter the Great, for he thought and acted on a grand scale and his achievements were similar. He had possessed an inexorable will which he imposed on the whole nation of 200 million people. Marshal Zhukov stated, after his death, that 'with his tough demands he achieved the impossible' and this was part of his greatness.[5] But this iron will had not been merely a blind instrument. He had possessed an extraordinary mastery and understanding not only of politics and economics, but also in the technical fields of industry and military affairs. In his meetings with Western leaders and their experts he had always demonstrated a swift and complete command of the subject of discussion. He had brushed aside non-essentials and cut through confusion and rhetoric to reach to the roots of any situation. Several times he had disconcerted Churchill by laying the problem bare and with a blunt realism exposing the real dangers.[6]

Allied with these great abilities were a nerve of steel, patience, and courage. Only twice in his long career, so far as is known, had he lost this self-mastery. The first time was in his outburst on the telephone to Krupskaya when he knew that Lenin was intending to denounce him to the party. The second time was in June 1941 when the Germans invaded Russia.[7] Throughout the months of the German advance across Russia to

Moscow and to Stalingrad he alone had borne the full responsibility for Russia's survival. He had recognized and later admitted that he had made serious mistakes,[8] but in these months of trial he had shown tremendous fortitude as he rallied the nation in defence of Moscow and then for the great counter-attack at Stalingrad. Long before the war had ended he was thinking actively of Russia's recovery and in 1946 he had launched the great reconstruction which restored the nation as an industrial power within a brief period.

As a statesman and ruler Stalin's greatness is undeniable. But the means which he used were often extreme and inhuman in their ruthlessness. In many minds the means have overcast the achievements, bringing such judgements as that he suffered from paranoia,[9] that he was 'a man of incredible criminality',[10] and 'one of the two or three worst men who ever lived'.[11] It will be for historians, in decades to come, free from the pressures of ideology and cold war, to evaluate the man and his reign dispassionately.

PART VII

THE THERMONUCLEAR
POWER

CHAPTER TWENTY-FIVE

The Succession to Stalin
1953–8

THE sudden removal of Stalin's absolute control over party and government faced the nation with a crisis of leadership. The Soviet regime had evolved no machinery for transferring power. Inherent in Lenin's doctrine of a small disciplined group of revolutionaries, forming the vanguard of the proletariat, was the principle of dictatorship. Stalin had gathered power into his hands after Lenin's death and had annihilated his opponents. He had held that in a totalitarian state all opposition was dangerous. But he had appointed no successor and had made no provision for selecting one so that the same ruthless struggle for power again threatened.

At the same time the need for change and relaxation from the harsh demands of the government had become acute among Russians. Stalin's will had remained a terrible driving force which none could resist. But with age his keen intelligence and instinct had become blunted and he seemed unaware that the great effort of post-war reconstruction had been followed by a creeping stagnation in industry and that agriculture remained backward and unproductive. He had become increasingly doctrinaire and unconcerned that his demands on the people, especially after all that they had endured, were excessive. The general longing for some relaxation in conditions of living and for relief from terror and police persecution was growing. It made itself felt as soon as Stalin's control was removed, and it affected all fields of the national life, even tempering the struggle for power.

The immediate reaction of the senior party leaders to Stalin's death was to draw together, maintaining party unity before the nation and the world. Evidently Malenkov, Bulganin, Beria, and Khrushchev had planned during Stalin's last hours to assume the leadership. On 7 March the decision of a joint meeting of the party central committee, the council of ministers, and the presidium of the Supreme Soviet was announced, which effected wide changes in senior personnel and organizations. Chief among them was the reduction in the size of the party presidium from twenty-five to ten members and from eleven to four alternates.

The full members and the posts to which they were assigned were in order of rank: 1. G. M. Malenkov (chairman of the council of ministers);

2. L. P. Beria (minister of internal affairs and first deputy chairman of the council of ministers); 3. V. M. Molotov (minister of foreign affairs and first deputy chairman of the council of ministers); 4. K. E. Voroshilov (chairman of the presidium of the Supreme Soviet); 5. N. S. Khrushchev (secretary of the party central committee); 6. N. A. Bulganin (minister of defence and first deputy chairman of the council of ministers); 7. L. M. Kaganovich (first deputy chairman of the council of ministers); 8. A. T. Mikoyan (minister of internal and external trade and deputy chairman of the council of ministers); 10. M. G. Pervukhin (minister of electric power stations and the electrical industry).[1]

Malenkov had long stood out as Stalin's most likely successor. Now as prime minister and as senior secretary of the party central committee he seemed to have achieved this position. Among the eight senior members of the presidium, however, a concerted move against him had already started. Under their pressure he asked to be released from his duties in the secretariat, a request which the central committee granted at its meeting on 14 March. The same meeting made Khrushchev first party secretary. In relinquishing his position in the secretariat Malenkov made a mistake, for as Stalin had shown, and as Khrushchev was to prove again, control of the party apparatus was the real source of power.

In this early period of the collective leadership three men stood out in the struggle for the succession. Malenkov was still in a strong position as head of the government. Beria, commanding the police and security forces, was also well placed to bid for supreme power. Khrushchev, extending his control over the party organization, remained in the background in these early months, but was to emerge as strongest of the three. Molotov, Kaganovich, and Voroshilov were the Stalinists. Molotov in particular was respected for his staunchly held views, but he had no organization behind him to support a claim to the leadership. He was, moreover, not in touch with the new mood for change, which Malenkov was seeking to meet. Bulganin, the minister of defence, might have developed a position of strength but he apparently had no real support from the armed forces, and was not seen as a serious contender for power.

The presidium was to divide on many issues, but it was unanimous on the need to eliminate terror and to curb the security organs. On 27 March 1953 an amnesty decree liberated thousands of prisoners and marked the beginning of a thorough review of the forced labour camps and a considerable improvement in prison conditions.[2] On 3 April Beria's ministery of internal affairs announced that the 'doctors' plot' had been a fabrication and that all responsible for it would be punished. But already Beria was evidently disturbed by the extent of the reforms and restraints which his presidium colleagues planned to impose on the police and security forces, which had under Stalin developed into a private army, beyond the control of party and government. Since this police army provided the base from which he hoped to seize power, Beria struck early.

The steps which he took to secure control of the presidium are not known. But they failed completely. His colleagues, recognizing the threat that the powerful police army presented and fearing a renewed terror, directed against them by Beria, were ready. As a precaution they had even called on the high command for support, and Red Army detachments had moved into Moscow in readiness for any attempt by Beria to seize power.

On 10 July 1953 *Pravda* reported that Beria had been removed from all posts in party and government and had been expelled from the party as an enemy of the people. It stated that 'Beria's evil scheming to seize power began with trying to set the Ministry of Internal Affairs above the party and the government and to employ the agencies of the MVD, both in the centre and locally, against the party and its leadership, against the government of the U.S.S.R. . . .'[3] Further charges against Beria were that he had damaged the collective farm system, hindered the country's food supply, and had been guilty of 'illegality and high-handedness'. He was even held to have been 'an agent of international imperialism', who had planned to eliminate the party and restore capitalism.[4] On 24 December 1953 the Soviet press announced that, after a secret trial, Beria and six associates had been executed by a firing squad.

In the following months several of the security police chiefs who had been involved in the Leningrad affair and the doctors' plot were executed. In Georgia a number of security police leaders and M. D. Bagirov, an alternate member of the presidium, and three of his associates, all of whom had been close to Beria, were shot.[5] But Beria was now the chief scapegoat for the crimes of Stalin's reign. 'The question arises,' Khrushchev declared to the twentieth party congress, 'why Beria who had liquidated tens of thousands of party and Soviet workers, was not unmasked during Stalin's life. He was not unmasked earlier because he had utilized very skilfully Stalin's weaknesses; feeding him with suspicions, he assisted Stalin in everything and acted with his support.'[6]

At the same time the police and security organs were reorganized and their powers curbed. The party enforced its control at every level. The MGB (Ministry of State Security) which had been absorbed into the MVD (Ministry of Internal Affairs) was re-established as a separate organ with the title KGB (Committee of State Security). A secret *ukaz* in September 1953, only published three years later, abolished the MVD special board which had exercised the independent power to sentence any brought before it. In April 1956 another *ukaz* repealed the 'Kirov decrees' which had provided the legal basis for mass executions by the security police at the time of the great purge. Moreover, certain functions, carried out by the MVD in the past, such as the economic projects which were administered by GULAG (The Chief Administration of Corrective Labour Camps), an MVD subsidiary, were now transferred to the appropriate ministries. These and other measures introduced after Stalin's death were part of the general policy of reducing and even eliminating terror and police persecution from the lives of the people and of ensuring that the party retained active control over the security organs, which were nevertheless retained as part of the machinery of the Soviet state.

During 1953 Malenkov remained prominent. He reported on behalf of the presidium to the central committee plenum which condemned Beria and his associates. He made the chief speech to the Supreme Soviet in August 1953. He appeared to be entrenching his position as head of the government, but he was, in fact, rapidly losing ground. In his Supreme Soviet speech he had forecast a number of policy changes which were to divide the presidium and range the majority against him. In domestic policy he had proclaimed a new consumer goods programme which would correct the excessive concentration on heavy industry, and he had announced increases in the prices paid to collective farmers for their obligatory deliveries of produce. In foreign policy he declared a more conciliatory line towards the West. On all of these new directions in internal and external policy conflicts arose and they were to be intensified by the underlying struggle for power.

During the first six months after Stalin's death Khrushchev had remained in the background. But he was making full use of his control over the party apparatus and in the autumn of 1953 he began appointing his own supporters to important party positions in Moscow, Leningrad, and farther afield. On 13 September 1953 the central committee confirmed his position and bestowed on him the formal title of first secretary. Also in September his report on agriculture began a series of far-reaching reforms. In this first report he spoke bluntly of the backward condition of agriculture, but in his proposals he did not depart greatly from the new direction, already announced by Malenkov. He emphasized incentives and increases in capital investment, both designed to raise production. He stressed in particular the need to train agricultural specialists and mechanics and to redistribute personnel from offices to productive work on the collective farms. He estimated that by spring 1954 100,000 agricultural specialists would have been transferred from offices to machine tractor stations, so that each collective would have the advice and guidance of at least one specialist. Fifty thousand party members would also be drafted from cities to rural party offices and to the MTS to strengthen party control and stimulate production.

The 1953 grain harvest had been poor, falling far short of the needs of the growing urban population. The new proposals had been concerned primarily with dairy produce, meat, and vegetables, but now the emphasis moved to grain. Khrushchev came forward with grandiose plans to deal with the grain shortage effectively and quickly. On 23 February 1954 he reported his proposals to the central committee where their boldness and vast scale aroused enthusiasm. In the presidium, however, his colleagues, especially Molotov, Malenkov, and Kaganovich, were disturbed by the gamble involved, but Khrushchev himself was always a gambler and, presumably, his critics advanced no alternative plans capable of dealing with the grain crisis.

Khrushchev's chief proposal was to cultivate vast areas of virgin land in Siberia, Kazakhstan, the Volga, the northern Caucasus, and the eastern regions. In the first stage in 1954–5 thirty-two million acres of land would be ploughed and sown. This area would be expanded until by 1960 the virgin land under cultivation would exceed 101 million acres. To settle the new regions some 150,000 workers and technicians, mainly young people, would be mobilized and scales of financial rewards were prepared to encourage them to stay and others to migrate to the new lands. The main appeal, made through the party and Komsomol, was, however, to the sense of service, pioneering, and adventure of students and others of the younger generation.

The great gamble in this tremendous project was the climate. The virgin lands were in regions where winters were long and severe, and droughts were frequent. But Khrushchev with his driving enthusiasm considered the massive investment of human energy and capital justified. In 1954 adequate rainfall resulted in a good harvest, but in the following year droughts reduced the harvest sharply. In 1956, however, a record harvest was garnered and, despite droughts in the following years, the grain yielded gradually improved, except in Kazakhstan where dust storms added to the difficulties. But Khrushchev could claim some success for his policy, although the future of the virgin lands was beset by massive problems, especially the need for large-scale measures to conserve the soil.

Khrushchev's other proposal was to grow more productive crops. He was eager to expand the acreage of maize as an animal feed. In cattle and pigs Soviet farming was desperately poor, and he was determined that in animal husbandry the Soviet Union should overtake the United States. In January 1955 he announced a programme for greatly expanding the maize acreage as part of plans to raise the output of meat, milk, and butter. In fact, the increase in pigs from 30·9 million on 1 January 1955 to 58·6 million on 1 January 1961 was undoubtedly aided by the new feed. In general, however, the maize crop was disappointing.

Khrushchev and Malenkov came into more direct conflict over industrial policy, which became a struggle between priorities of heavy and light industry. Malenkov had called for a greatly increased output of consumer goods to be achieved at the expense of heavy industry and armaments. Indeed, his policy involved considerable reductions in military expenditure. The budget allocation for defence was cut from 110 billion rubles in 1953 to 100·3 billion in 1954. In his eagerness to secure prompt results from the consumer industries he was prepared to draw on raw material stockpiles which the High Command considered essential to defence planning. Malenkov justified this switch of priorities from heavy to light industry by his policy of reducing tension in international affairs and seeking understanding with the West. But this was not acceptable to the High Command nor to Molotov and other members of the presidium. Indeed, in April 1954, under pressure from the presidium, he had had to modify certain of his pronouncements on foreign affairs.

Malenkov had by this time ranged the presidium, the party, and the High Command against him, and his fall had become inevitable. Khrushchev delivered the final attack against him in a speech to the central committee towards the end of January 1955. He asserted the priority of heavy industry and armaments and, without naming Malenkov, clearly referred to him in condemning 'incorrect reasoning, alien to Marxism–Leninism ... a belching of the rightist deviation, a belching of views hostile to Leninism' on the part of those who claimed that light industry should overtake other branches of industry. This denunciation marked the end of Malenkov's bid for power. A few days later, on 8 February, he resigned as chairman of the council of ministers. He had failed as Stalin's successor because he had lost control of the party and had tried to base himself on the government apparatus. But the major factor in his failure was that he lacked strength of leadership. 'He wrote a fine speech for others,' Khrushchev remarked later with some contempt, adding, 'When he took command he was no good at all.' [8]

Bulganin took Malenkov's place as chairman of the council of ministers. Marshal Zhukov moved to the ministry of defence, vacated by Bulganin. Both changes were instigated by Khrushchev who himself remained first secretary. He had evidently assured the High Command that in return for support against Malenkov, he would protect their interests, and the promotion of the popular Marshal Zhukov was part of this undertaking. Next he brought about the demotion of Molotov and Kaganovich. Both had strongly opposed the policies of Malenkov, which had made them Khrushchev's allies, but they now also opposed his policies. In particular Molotov disagreed with Khrushchev's determination to effect a reconciliation with Tito of Yugoslavia whom Stalin had ostracized from the communist block. The central committee, now containing many of Khrushchev's supporters, rejected Molotov's defence of the Stalinist policy and, although he remained minister of foreign affairs for the time being, his authority declined sharply. The position of Kaganovich, too, was diminished. But, like Molotov and Malenkov, he remained a member of the presidium.

At this juncture a dramatic event shook the whole communist movement. This event was Khrushchev's denunciation of Stalin at the twentieth party congress in February 1956. His speech staggered the Russian people and deeply disturbed the communist parties abroad. It was an unexpected and, from the Soviet point of view, even an irresponsible action, designed primarily to further the political fortunes of Khrushchev. Stalin who had been the colossus, bestriding the communist world, was now the object of denigration by his underlings as they struggled to succeed him.

The evil excesses of Stalin's dictatorship were already being corrected before the twentieth congress, and it was clearly the intention of all members of the presidium, including Molotov, that this process should continue. Starting immediately after his death the Kremlin doctors had been officially exonerated and an amnesty, followed by two further amnesties, had released hundreds of thousands of prisoners and led to the closing down of many forced labour camps. The arrest of Beria had been followed by an extensive revision of police powers and personnel. Gradually, too, the national worship of Stalin was being stopped. His body had been placed beside that of Lenin in the mausoleum on the Red Square, but the ubiquitous portraits of him had been removed and the incessant expressions of homage to him, his work, and his writings were no longer heard. Indeed, on 21 December 1953 *Pravda* failed even to mention his birthday.

The emphasis now in the press and all party meetings was on collective leadership and the return to party control through regular meetings of its legally constituted organs which Stalin had increasingly ignored. The new leaders were especially concerned to demonstrate that, although they had been close to Stalin, they had not perpetrated the terror and the purges, and that they were now eliminating them from the national life. One change made with this purpose was to open the Kremlin so that it could become an historical museum, rather than remain the sinister fortress which Stalin, like the early Muscovite tsars, had made it.

Far-reaching de-Stalinization had thus been carried out, but discreetly and without any need for denunciations of the leader who, despite terrible excesses and mistakes, had held the nation united and had led it through crises and war to its position as one of the two great powers in the world.

At the twentieth party congress, meeting in Moscow in February 1956, Mikoyan opened the attack on Stalin and the cult of personality. But Khrushchev's detailed denunciation, delivered in closed session at the end of the congress, caused the sensation. He recalled Lenin's fears that Stalin would not 'always be able to use this power [as Secretary General of the party] with the required care'.[9] Then, after brief tribute to Stalin's leadership against Trotskyites, rightists, and bourgeois nationalists, he charged him with 'glaring violations of revolutionary legality', resulting in the deaths of thousands of honest communists. He had weakened the Red Army by executing Tukhachevsky and other able officers. He had failed to make the necessary defence preparations against the German invasion, although he had had ample warning. Khrushchev alleged that he had interfered in the conduct of the war with dire results. He had erroneously broken off relations with Yugoslavia. In his last years, suffering from persecution mania, he had perpetrated the Leningrad affair and the doctors' plot and was at the time of his death preparing another terror. These and other failures had resulted when the cult of personality had developed after the seventeenth congress in 1934 and the collective leadership of the party had been abandoned.

In his indictment Khrushchev was careful, however, to avoid attacking Stalin's basic policies. Indeed, his speech was as much a defence of these policies with many of which he himself had been closely associated, as it was an indictment of Stalin's personal misdeeds. He went to extremes in criticizing Stalin as military leader and in trying to demonstrate that he, Khrushchev, had boldly stood up to him. His purpose was, in fact, to persuade the party and the nation generally that a fresh start was being made. The government would rule now not by terror and compulsion, but by calling on the initiative of the people and encouraging their co-operation.

The speech was a bold gamble in Khrushchev's bid for power, but it had unexpected repercussions which were to bring him close to disaster. Within Russia the full text of the speech was not released. Its main points were filtered through party organizations with great care and the denunciation of Stalin was minimized. He had been revered so deeply by the Russian people that he was part of the fabric of their lives and beliefs. The mere fact that he had been criticized in the party congress caused a deep and lasting shock at all levels of Soviet society.

Among communists abroad, reactions to the speech were more open. Foreign communists had been excluded from the secret session of the congress which Khrushchev had addressed. A copy of the text, bearing all signs of authenticity, had, however, come into the possession of the U.S. State Department which released it to the world on 4 June 1956. This caused considerable debate, and statements by foreign communist leaders or parties, while approving generally this demonstration of Soviet self-criticism, showed less than the spontaneous and unanimous support which Moscow expected and usually received from communist parties abroad. Togliatti, the Italian communist leader, even questioned whether Soviet society might not be revealing 'certain forms of degeneration'.[10]

Khrushchev had launched this de-Stalinization campaign for internal consumption and in the teeth of strongest opposition from Molotov, Malenkov, Kaganovich, and Voroshilov. He had not expected that the full text of his speech would be published abroad. The Russian party, the leader of world communism, had thus exposed its weakness and invited criticism from communists and capitalists in a way that Stalin himself would never have permitted. On 30 June 1956 the central committee adopted a resolution, published in *Pravda* two days later, which contained a ponderous clarification of the proceedings of the twentieth congress.[11] But this did not close the matter, as the Soviet leaders hoped. More serious repercussions followed later in the year, especially in Poland and in Hungary. Khrushchev's speech was, in fact, to prove the first step in the disintegration of the communist solidarity which Stalin had created and maintained.

At the twentieth congress Khrushchev nevertheless strengthened his hold on the party. Five new alternate members, all of them his protégés, were appointed to the presidium: L. I. Brezhnev, first secretary of the Kazakhstan party; Marshal Zhukov; E. A. Furtseva, first secretary of the Moscow city organization; D. T. Shepilov, editor of *Pravda*; N. A. Mukhitdinov, first secretary of the Uzbek party. The central committee, elected by the congress, contained 53 new members in the total membership of 133, and 76 new candidate members in the total of 122 candidates. The newcomers were in most if not all cases Khrushchev's choice. In June 1956 Shepilov became minister of foreign affairs, displacing Molotov, and Kaganovich, too, was demoted.

By the autumn, however, Khrushchev was in difficulties. Unrest had broken out in Poznan in July. It had long simmered beneath the surface in Poland, where resentment of Russian domination was strong. The de-Stalinization speech at the twentieth congress had ignited a fuse which exploded popular discontent. To pacify it, Moscow changed some of the Polish leaders who were too closely identified with Russian control. Among the Poles brought forward at this time was Wladislaw Gomulka, whom Stalin had imprisoned as a nationalist and who had only recently been released from prison. He was regarded with some suspicion by the Russian leaders. In mid-October the Polish communist party decided, however, to make Gomulka first secretary and also proposed to remove Rokossovsky, the extremely able Russian marshal, from the Polish ministry of defence which he had headed since 1949. The Polish decisions alarmed Moscow. Khrushchev and Mikoyan, significantly accompanied by Molotov and Kaganovich, who had opposed the rehabilitation of Gomulka, left hurriedly for Warsaw to intervene. Their meetings with the Polish party leaders were stormy. Khrushchev was truculent and threatened to use force, if they did not heed Moscow's wishes. He was disturbed to learn that the Poles were prepared to resist even though they knew that they must be crushed by the might of the Red Army. Gomulka clearly had support throughout the country. He made it clear that he had no intention of trying to take Poland out of the Soviet block, but he asserted Poland's right to run her own affairs without the close Russian supervision which she had suffered since the war. Khrushchev felt compelled to yield to the Polish demands.

In Hungary the Russians faced a far more desperate challenge. They had recognized the dangers of an Hungarian revolt. Mikoyan had gone to Budapest earlier in the summer to dismiss Rakosi, the staunchly Stalinist leader. But Moscow was uneasy about the Hungarian choice of Imre Nagy, just released from prison, to head their regime, for he was known as an even more ardent nationalist than Gomulka in Poland. On 23 October, revolution broke out in Hungary. The strong popular demand for independence and the savage antagonism towards Russians, which Hungarians had demonstrated during the war, could be restrained no longer. At the beginning of November, Imre Nagy declared that Hungary would leave the Warsaw Pact, the communist equivalent of the North Atlantic Treaty Organization, and so withdraw from the Soviet block. Khrushchev and his colleagues in the presidium discussed urgently the steps that they should take and finally decided on military force. The Hungarians fought with desperate courage against the Red Army, suffering heavy casualties, but they had no chance of success. Within a few weeks the revolution had been crushed. Imre Nagy had been shot and new leaders, supported by Red Army units, had been installed, but a deep bitterness remained. Moreover, Tito, the Yugoslav leader, was outspoken in his support for the Hungarians in their struggle to free themselves from Russian domination. This also reflected badly on Khrushchev, for he had insisted, against the opposition of Molotov and others, on trying to effect a reconciliation with Tito and on bringing Yugoslavia back into the communist block.

At the plenum of the central committee in December 1956 Khrushchev, who had dominated earlier meetings, did not speak. The plenum considered industrial planning and in particular approved extension of the powers of the state economic commission. Pervukhin was made its chairman with overriding powers in directing the economy. Members of the presidium, who saw in these changes the strengthening of the government organization and a setback to Khrushchev who based himself on the party, at once supported them. At its session on 12 February 1957 the Supreme Soviet endorsed this reorganization in economic planning.

This was a major reverse for Khrushchev, but he was not yet defeated. His energies erupted and his initiative sharpened in such a predicament so that when his opponents thought him beaten he suddenly counter-attacked. He had been actively rallying supporters and working out his own economic policy since the central committee plenum which he had sat through in silence. On 13 February, the day after the Supreme Soviet session, he addressed a meeting of the central committee, specially convened to hear his proposals. He outlined bold reforms which involved abolishing a number of central ministries and creating new regional economic councils (sovnarkhozy) to take over direction of industry on a regional basis. At the centre Gosplan was to serve as the supreme planning authority, while the state economic commission was to be so reduced in its powers as to survive only in name.

This plan for a massive decentralization of the economy and control through numerous local authorities, the sovnarkhozy, instead of the powerful but remote ministries in Moscow was thrown open for public discussion. Early in May the presidium of the Supreme Soviet appointed I. I. Kuzmin, one of Khrushchev's colleagues in the party secretariat, to serve as the new powerful chairman of Gosplan and as first vice-chairman of the council of ministers. On 10 May 1957 the Supreme Soviet itself endorsed Khrushchev's plan for decentralizing the administration of industry.

The plan and the manoeuvres to ensure its adoption were part of Khrushchev's struggle for power. But also they were intended to restore the predominant authority of the party over industry as in every other field of the national life. He was the chief force behind the new drive, started in 1954, to increase and diversify the party membership. By January 1959 the total had increased by some fourteen per cent to 8,239,131 members, and by October 1961, when the twenty-second congress was held, this total, including candidate members, had reached 9,716,005. At the same time the marked trend towards recruiting white-collar workers was checked. By July 1961 members in forestry and agriculture accounted for 23·3 per cent, which was far higher than in previous years.[12]

Khrushchev believed passionately in the party's role and that in industry it was being usurped by the large and inefficient central ministries. For this reason he gave the name of anti-party group to his adversaries. Malenkov had now joined with Molotov and Kaganovich in the struggle to defeat Khrushchev. With their supporters they were a formidable group, and they awaited their opportunity to bring him down. In the meetings of the central committee and the Supreme Soviet which had approved Khrushchev's proposals for the decentralization of industrial administration, seven members of the presidium—Molotov, Malenkov, Kaganovich, Bulganin, Voroshilov, Pervukhin, and Saburov—had remained ominously silent. They formed a majority in the presidium. In June they faced him with their united opposition and called on him to resign as first secretary. The presidium met almost continuously from 18 to 21 June, while debate raged over this challenge. Khrushchev fought stubbornly and refused to resign. He maintained that only the central committee, which had appointed him, could call for his resignation, and he demanded an immediate meeting of the central committee to resolve the conflict. But the presidium majority refused to convene a special meeting for this purpose.

News of the crisis in the presidium spread rapidly among members of the central committee. Khrushchev had been active since his appointment as first secretary in securing the election of his own supporters and now he used every means to inform them of the need for a special meeting. The alternate members of the presidium stood by him and of them Zhukov in particular was active. While the presidium was in session a group of central committee members sent a letter, demanding that a meeting be convened. Next a band of Khrushchev's supporters made their way into the Kremlin, determined to confront the presidium, then in continuous session, with their demand. Special guards had been posted to prevent access, but the presence of Zhukov, the minister of defence, in this group made such measures ineffective. Finally Khrushchev and Mikoyan, Voroshilov, and Bulganin were deputed to receive the delegation. By this time the presidium majority had recognized that they could no longer refuse to convene a special meeting.

Meanwhile members of the central committee were arriving in Moscow from all parts of the country, many of them by military aircraft, provided on the orders of Zhukov himself. In all 309 members were present for this meeting of the central committee which began on 22 June. No fewer than 215 members came forward to speak for Khrushchev. The presidium majority found themselves outmanoeuvred and isolated. Voroshilov and others among them wavered and then went over to support Khrushchev. Molotov sturdily maintained his opposition. The final resolution of the central committee, condemning the anti-party group for opposing the party on important issues affecting industry, agriculture, and foreign policy, was said to have been passed unanimously, except only for Molotov, who abstained from voting.

This resolution, published in *Pravda* on 4 July, concentrated the blame on Molotov, Malenkov, Kaganovich, and Shepilov.[13] All were expelled from the presidium, the central committee, and their other appointments. The fact that Bulganin, Voroshilov, Pervukhin, and Saburov had been members of the anti-party group only emerged later and for the time being they retained their offices.

Khrushchev had emerged triumphant from this strong challenge. He at once consolidated his position by enlarging the presidium to fifteen and the new members appointed were his supporters. Marshal Zhukov advanced from alternate to full membership. The other new members were Brezhnev, Shvernik, Furtseva, Aristov, Belyaev, Ignatov, Kozlov, and Kuusinen. But several of them were to have only a brief presidium career. Zhukov was in the following October dismissed, not only from the presidium, but also from the central committee and the Supreme Soviet. He had given Khrushchev strong support against Malenkov and against the anti-party group, but then he had evidently sought to subordinate party to army interests, and in particular had given military training priority far above political instruction in the armed forces. Under Stalin's rule the party had always been sensitive to the possibility of challenge by the Red Army which enjoyed tremendous prestige among the people and never more than in these post-war years. Khrushchev showed himself equally anxious to forestall such challenge and to secure the party permanently from such a danger.

The central committee passed a resolution, confirming Zhukov's dismissal on the ground that he had underestimated and curtailed the leadership of the party in the army and navy.[14] Zhukov's outstanding leadership during the war had gained him the love and respect of his troops and of the people. The fact that he could be dismissed so peremptorily was an indication of the strength of the party and of its grip on the nation.

After the defeat of the anti-party group, the appointment of the new presidium, and the expulsion of Zhukov, Khrushchev's position was supreme. The twenty-first congress, meeting in January 1959, rang with praises of his 'Leninist firmness', his 'tireless energy', and his dedication to the party. It seemed that the cult of another personality was about to develop. But Khrushchev possessed the honesty and humility to recognize that he could never achieve the stature of Stalin and that, even had he wished, he could not have built up such a cult to bolster his authority. He had to rely, for reasons of necessity and probably also preference, on consultation and persuasion rather than the domination of his will and by terror. At the twenty-first congress certain of his closest supporters made savage attacks on members of the anti-party group, evidently intended to destroy finally all confidence in Molotov, Malenkov, Kaganovich, and others. They were not expelled from the party, nor were they executed, but were allowed to pass into the obscurity of retirement.[15] This was a real proof that Stalin's ruthless methods belonged to the past.

Although in fact the supreme leader in Soviet Russia, Khrushchev continued to hold only the office of first secretary for some months after his defeat of the anti-party group. On 27 March 1958, however, he became also chairman of the council of ministers, and so was head of both party and state. He was now truly Stalin's successor.

CHAPTER TWENTY-SIX

Soviet Foreign Relations
1953–64

To Stalin Russia was 'a besieged fortress encircled by capitalism'.[1] Briefly during the period of the Grand Alliance he may have thought that the military conflict could be avoided and that the three powers could maintain the stability of the world. Another war was unthinkable to him and to his people. His concern was the defence and security of Russia rather than militant communism. But after the Potsdam conference and the explosion of the atom bomb, he had become convinced that the capitalist powers were planning to attack, while Russia was devastated and at their mercy. Obsessed with the danger that Russia would yet again be beaten for her backwardness, he had driven his people to greater efforts. Development of heavy industry had priority. Nuclear research and armaments evidently had even higher priority; for in August 1949 Russia had exploded her first atom bomb, and in August 1953, within six months of his death, the hydrogen bomb was part of the Soviet armoury.

No nation can, however, endure indefinitely the driving pressure which Stalin had imposed. After his death a mood of relaxation crept over the nation, and it was notable in the conduct of foreign policy. Malenkov, as chairman of the council of ministers, first announced a more conciliatory line in a speech in March 1954. He recognized that war involving the hydrogen bomb would result in 'the destruction of world civilization'.[2] Khrushchev, Molotov, Kaganovich, Voroshilov, and Bulganin, who were already working to bring about his downfall, all made speeches in the following weeks condemning this new line. Khrushchev in a bombastic outburst in June claimed that Russia was ahead of the West in developing the hydrogen bomb. He asserted further that a nuclear war would destroy capitalism, not world civilization.[3] But in the preceding April, bowing to the majority view of the presidium, Malenkov had already modified his original statement, and had declared that war 'would inevitably lead to the collapse of the capitalist socialist system,' rather than of world civilization.[4]

Behind these exchanges in the struggle for power, the new Soviet policy of reducing international tension continued. As a result of a hint made by the Soviet delegate to the United Nations, which the other powers grasped eagerly, that the Soviet government was prepared to discuss a cease-fire in Korea, the Korean armistice was signed on 27 July 1953. In August, Moscow announced that Germany would not be required to pay further reparations after 1 January 1954, and in January of the following year the Soviet government declared the state of war with Germany to be ended. In the Far East tension eased when the Soviet Union agreed to transfer all rights in Manchuria to the Chinese People's Republic. Then early in 1955 the Soviet offer to revive discussions on an Austrian peace treaty resulted on 15 May in the signing of the treaty by the Soviet Union, the United States, Great Britain, and France. A few months later the Soviet government also concluded a treaty with Japan, bringing to an end the state of war which had existed for ten years.

The list of Soviet concessions was considerable. They marked a break from Stalin's policy of standing firm and conceding nothing. At the same time the new leaders were unyielding on what they considered to be basic Russian interests. Thus domination of Eastern Europe, as part of Russia's defence against attack from the West, was strongly maintained. Control over Poland was relaxed slightly in 1956. Gomulka was reluctantly recognized, but only on the clear understanding that Poland would remain part of the Soviet block. In Hungary, when Nagy announced policies which meant taking the country out of the Soviet block and probably joining with the Western powers, the Red Army crushed the revolt with severity, causing much bloodshed. On Germany, too, the new Soviet leaders were to prove as inflexible as Stalin had been.

Soviet attempts to reduce international tension had only limited success. This was due partly to the fact that on major matters in dispute they were immovable. It was partly due also to the advent of John Foster Dulles as secretary of state of the new U.S. administration, which took office in January 1953. Dulles opposed communism with a righteous fanaticism. A ruthless, intransigent, and devious corporation lawyer he concentrated his undoubted abilities and energy on the immediate problem, ready to use any means, but always proclaiming his moral ends, to win his case. As the dominant spokesman of the Western block, he was a formidable figure. Within his first year of office he proclaimed the policy of liberating the countries under Soviet domination and the threat of 'massive retaliation', both of which sounded in Moscow like near-declarations of war. The 'liberation' policy came to be the same as Truman's policy of containment and 'massive retaliation' was the atomic deterrent in more aggressive guise. Indeed the Soviet leaders might have looked on him as a useful ally, since he was so active in arousing resentments and mistrust within the Western alliance. But in his championship of the European defence community with West German participation, his organizing of security pacts, such as CENTO and SEATO, and his exercises in 'brinkmanship', he alarmed Moscow.

Western nuclear superiority had ended with Russia's successful explosion of a hydrogen bomb in August 1953. This event gave impetus to the general move towards a summit meeting to seek solution of matters disturbing East–West relations. The foreign ministers met in Berlin in January 1954, but their discussions were unproductive. Dulles was said to have been masterful in his handling of Molotov,[5] but he, like the other Western ministers, failed to reach any closer understanding with him on Germany. They pressed the usual Western proposal for free German elections, which would result in dissolution of the German Democratic Republic. Molotov countered with the suggestion that the East and West German regimes should come together in the first instance to form an all-German government, that all occupying troops should be withdrawn, and that Germany should solemnly undertake not to join military pacts against any of its former allies. He made it clear that free elections which might result in the resurgence of a Germany, hostile to Russia, would never be acceptable. Eden and others were prepared to consider a neutralized Germany. Dulles, at first adamant that the all-German government must be aligned with the West, moved to the position that such a government should be free to choose its own alignments, confident that a united Germany would join with the West. For the Russians, whose country had suffered terrible devastation and some fifty million casualties in two German invasions, and who now actively feared the revival of Germany, supported by Western arms, the Western proposals were merely a demonstration of hostility towards Russia. But the Berlin conference at least served the purpose of clarifying the issues on Germany.

In April 1954 the Geneva conference began its meetings which continued until July, seeking agreement on peace in Korea and Indo-China. Chou En-lai represented the Chinese communists. On Korea no progress towards a peace treaty was made and the existing armistice agreement was confirmed. The problems of Indo-China dominated the conference. Ho Chi-minh the Vietnamese communist leader, who had been trained in Moscow, was advancing southwards against the French. Communist China had increased supplies to him after the armistice in Korea had relieved her of commitments to the North Koreans. After the fall of the French garrison at Dienbienphu on 7 May, it seemed only a matter of time before the whole of Indo-China was under communist domination.

The French had already appealed for American help. Dulles had decided that this communist thrust to the south must be halted, but that the U.S.A. could participate only in some collective effort. Eden was unwilling, however, to commit Britain to military action at a time when the conference was seeking a settlement in Geneva, especially as military action in Indo-China would have aroused Indian opposition. Furthermore, he did not trust Dulles and suspected that the Americans would leave the British to carry the military burden after the collapse of the French. Dulles withdrew from the conference, but the threat of American intervention and the able negotiations of the British and French representatives with the Chinese and Russians resulted in an armistice being agreed on 20 July 1954. Vietnam was partitioned along the 17th parallel and elections were to be held throughout the country within two years.

In September 1954 the South-East Asian Treaty Organization was established by the U.S.A., Britain, France, Thailand, Pakistan, and New Zealand. In this same month a conference of nine Western powers opened in London and resulted in an agreement to end the occupation of Western Germany and to make Germany and Italy members of the Brussels treaty with Germany contributing twelve divisions and a tactical airforce. The U.S.A. and Britain confirmed that they would maintain their forces on the continent. Moreover, West Germany was to be admitted to NATO. The West German government undertook not to manufacture atomic weapons, long-range missiles, or strategic bombers. Furthermore the defensive nature of the Atlantic and Brussels treaties was stressed, and the Germans pledged themselves never to resort to force to achieve reunification or to modify existing frontiers. At this time Dulles was also organizing a Middle East alliance, embracing the countries along the southern borders of Russia. The Baghdad pact, which was concluded in April 1955, embraced Turkey, Iran, and Britain, joined soon afterwards by Pakistan and Persia. This pact was proclaimed as a bulwark against Soviet aggression, but to the Russians, conscious of their vulnerability in the south, the pact was further proof of the aggressive intentions of the Western powers.

In 1955 Bulganin had replaced Malenkov, but neither he nor Khrushchev, who was the dominant force in the collective leadership, was yet secure in his authority. The presidium was nevertheless united in its attitude towards the new organization of West European defence, including Germany, and the menace of NATO and the Baghdad pact. The cuts in the military budget, made by Malenkov, were promptly restored. In the spring of 1955 the first Russian IRBM (intermediate-range ballistic missile) was successfully fired. On 14 May the Eastern Security Treaty (Warsaw pact), providing a military organization within the Soviet block, was signed in Warsaw by the Soviet Union, Rumania, Poland, the German Democratic Republic, Hungary, Czechoslovakia, Bulgaria, and Albania.

The summit conference which met in Geneva in July 1955 was expected in the West to produce important results.[6] Western opinion had been encouraged in its optimism by the sudden and unexpected Soviet agreement to the Austrian peace treaty, signed in Vienna on 15 May 1955. The visit of Bulganin and Khrushchev to Belgrade in May–June to restore relations between Soviet Russia and Yugoslavia also made a favourable impression in the West. But the summit conference failed to achieve most of what was hoped of it. The agenda comprised reunification of Germany, linked with European security, disarmament, and development of contacts between East and West. The crucial item was Germany. The Russians were now urging that the West should recognize East Germany and, predictably, they rejected all proposals to reunify Germany by free elections. At the same time they made great play of proposals for disarmament. Dulles was worried that West German opinion might be influenced by the Austrian peace treaty and the talk on disarmament and seek reunification within the Soviet block. But this did not happen and the ruthless suppression of the Hungarian revolt in the following year put an end to any latent hopes in Germany that this might provide a solution.

The summit conference nevertheless introduced a new, more cordial atmosphere, called by many the 'spirit of Geneva', into international relations. The agreement on cultural exchanges, the only specific result, seemed part of this new spirit. For the Russians it had been a partial success.

Two broad purposes of Soviet foreign policy were, first, to reduce international tension and the hostility towards the U.S.S.R. and, second, to disrupt the Western block and especially to destroy NATO. From Geneva the Russians, while achieving no progress in disrupting the Western block, could draw satisfaction from the general reduction of international tension.

The meeting of foreign ministers in the autumn showed that on the fundamental issue and in their attempts to dismantle NATO, the Russians were even more obdurate. They demanded the 'liquidation of all foreign bases', which meant the withdrawal of American and British troops from the continent. They pressed for a European security system in place of NATO. They made great play of their disarmament proposals, knowing them to be unacceptable to the West. They offered the alternatives of reunification of Germany with the abolition of the security system which the West considered essential or the maintenance of that system and the indefinite postponement of unity for Germany. Russia's obsession with her security against the resurgence of a powerful Germany and a third invasion dominated the meetings.

Many of the Soviet proposals also had the propaganda purpose of appealing to the uncommitted countries, like India, and the newly independent nations of Asia and Africa. In December 1955 Bulganin and Khrushchev had visited India. Moscow directly and indirectly through satellites in Eastern Europe was already in touch with Egypt. Khrushchev promised full support for all colonial peoples, struggling for freedom. Here was a vast new world to be won for communism. But the Russians, like the Americans, were to find that, while their aid was welcomed, these countries were reluctant to be absorbed into one or the other block and to sacrifice their newly won independence.

In 1956 Soviet foreign policy developed in a way which aroused new hopes of an understanding in the West. The twentieth party congress was of importance not only for Khrushchev's speech, launching the de-Stalinization campaign, but also for his restatement of the fundamentals of Soviet foreign policy. Malenkov had soon after the death of Stalin proclaimed a new line, which acknowledged the dangers of the thermonuclear age. He had amended his statement under pressure of the majority of the presidium. But at the twentieth congress Khrushchev developed the new direction further and proclaimed the policy of peaceful coexistence. He confirmed that conflict between the socialist and imperialist camps and the victory of communism were inevitable. But he now maintained that 'war is not a fatalistic inevitability. Today there are mighty social and political forces possessing formidable means to prevent the imperialists from unleashing war ... For this it is necessary for all anti-war forces to be vigilant and mobilized; they must act as a united front and not relax their efforts in the struggle for peace.' [7] The choice was between war and peaceful coexistence and, war being no longer inevitable, Soviet policy was one of peaceful coexistence. Further, he conceded the possibility of a society moving from capitalism to socialism without violent revolution, which was a major departure from Marxist–Leninist doctrine. But the immediate practical objective continued to be to overtake the West in economic and military strength. There was also the need to attract the support of the vast uncommitted world by proving the superiority of the communist system.

The full significance of peaceful coexistence was lost in the heated exchange of accusations, threats, and counter-charges between East and West over Soviet armed intervention in Hungary and the abortive Anglo-French invasion of Egypt in November 1956. The first months of the following year were taken up mainly by efforts to repair the damage caused within the two blocks. In Russia Khrushchev's struggle for power had ended in June with his rout of the anti-party group. The need to consolidate the Soviet block, which had been deeply shaken by the Hungarian crisis, gave rise to a conference of East European leaders in Moscow at which the Soviet leaders offered economic concessions and sought in other ways to recover the goodwill of their allies. In the West the healing of the deep rift which separated the U.S.A. and Britain occupied the attention of Eisenhower, the U.S. president, and Macmillan, the new British prime minister. At a meeting in Bermuda, they agreed that American IRBMs should be maintained in Britain, an agreement which marked the restoration of some degree of Anglo-American understanding. But the confidence of the U.S.A. and of the West in their security, based on the assumption of overwhelming American nuclear superiority, was soon to be shattered.

In August 1957 the Russians successfully tested their first inter-continental ballistic missile (ICBM). They had overtaken and clearly beaten the Americans in the missile race. They had the capacity, possessed by no other nation, of striking across seas and continents with the thermonuclear missiles. A few weeks later on 4 October they launched *Sputnik*, the first earth satellite, which virtually proved their claim to have achieved the

ICBM. *Sputnik* was a more spectacular success, for people of many nations saw and heard the satellite as it orbited in space.

This was a time of triumph for the Russians. Starting behind the West with its vaunted technological skills and resources, they had achieved clear superiority. Khrushchev and the Soviet press were prompt to claim that this was the pattern which communist society would follow in asserting its superiority over capitalist societies. But this was premature. The U.S.A. successfully tested her first ICBM less than three months later. Moreover, the American decision in May 1957 to equip NATO with missiles was adopted by the NATO council in December, when it was also decided that IRBMs should be set up in Turkey, Greece, and Italy. *Sputnik* was to be the beginning of a momentous rivalry between the U.S.A. and the U.S.S.R. for superiority in strategic capabilities and in space exploration.

Shortly after the successful launching of *Sputnik*, a conference of world communist leaders met in Moscow. The conference embodied its decisions in a forthright declaration, which reaffirmed the tasks of the party and the goals of world communism. It presaged a grand offensive to bring the third world of the uncommitted nations into the communist camp and to lead the anti-colonial and nationalist movements in their struggle against the imperialist West. Soviet ICBMs and the *Sputnik* had become powerful propaganda weapons.

Mao Tse-tung, the Chinese communist leader, attended the Moscow conference in person, and the conference became an occasion to demonstrate Sino-Soviet solidarity. But beneath this display of accord disagreement had long existed, in part rooted in the history of Sino-Russian relations and in part in their independent roads to revolution. Mao had established his regime with little help from Russia. Indeed, he did not forget that Stalin had subordinated the interests of the Chinese communists to Russian national interests. Moreover, while accepting the seniority of the Soviet leaders and their party, Mao regarded himself and his party as their equals. In particular, he was always prepared to pronounce authoritatively on Marxist–Leninist doctrine. But he had been prepared to accept Stalin as a strong and purposeful leader of the communist movement in the world, and to refrain from open criticism.

Conflicts between Moscow and Peking had sharpened after Stalin's death, particularly over the new conciliatory element in Soviet policy. In the interests of communist unity, however, the Chinese communists had expressed their views with careful restraint. The twentieth congress of the Russian party and Khrushchev's attack on Stalin had so angered them, however, that they became more open in their criticisms. They were even now reluctant to destroy communist unity and Mao Tse-tung's purpose in going to Moscow had been to resolve their differences. But the latent conflicts were aggravated by personal incompatibilities, for Mao appears to have formed a poor opinion of Khrushchev as an opportunist and an unworthy successor to Lenin and Stalin.

The profound difference which existed between them inevitably led to a widening gap in the communist movement. Mao Tse-tung was strictly orthodox in believing that military conflict with the capitalist world was inevitable. He now rejoiced because the Russians, leaders of the communist world, possessed the hydrogen bomb and had superiority in intercontinental missiles. He had in a speech to the Moscow conference declared that a nuclear war, while destroying capitalism, would not destroy communism, and he did not fear the terrible destruction that nuclear weapons might inflict on China. His fanaticism was untouched by any feelings of humanity. By contrast Khrushchev and others in the presidium appreciated what nuclear war would mean, and bitter memories of the sufferings and casualties in the war against Germany reinforced their determination to avoid such a war. Thermonuclear weapons and ICBMs were needed to enable them to negotiate from strength with the West and to ensure Russian security. They were not for use in destroying capitalist societies in the interests of the revolutionary struggle. Mao sought to bring pressure on the Russians to make use of their nuclear power, but Khrushchev resisted all pressure. He was convinced that communism would triumph over capitalism, but it would, he believed, do so by its essential superiority as a system, and not through the holocausts of thermonuclear aggression in which Russia and her block would suffer as much as the Western block.

Seizing the initiative after the Russian triumph in launching *Sputnik*, Khrushchev mounted a diplomatic offensive. He was the more eager to achieve results by this means in order to prove to the Chinese that negotiations rather than nuclear weapons were the better way to deal with the West. The facts that Western Europe was moving towards union, that the Western powers were actively seeking to collaborate in the use of nuclear arms in NATO, and that the U.S.A. had succeeded in firing an ICBM in August 1957 added further urgency to the Soviet diplomatic campaign.

Khrushchev had in March 1958 become chairman of the council of ministers and had achieved full power. His objective now was another summit conference. His chief aims were to negotiate an agreement as a result of which NATO would be dismantled, or at least shorn of its nuclear weapons, and to reach a satisfactory decision on Germany. The concern of all Russians over the rearmament of West Germany was obsessive. Even after the addition of thermonuclear weapons to the Soviet armoury, this anxiety about West Germany as a potential threat to Russian security remained.

In summer 1958 the movement towards a summit conference was overtaken by two crises. A nationalist revolt in Iraq, leading to British and American military precautions in Jordan and the Lebanon, involved strong exchanges with Moscow. The Russians were, however, unable to halt the British and American preparations, but then Iraq withdrew from the Baghdad pact and the crisis dissolved. The other crisis was in the Far East where the Chinese communists threatened to invade the off-shore islands of Quemoy and Matsu, but were deterred by threats of American military action.

Khrushchev now seized the initiative afresh. In November 1958 he demanded that the Potsdam powers should abandon the occupation of Berlin which would then become a free city within the German Democratic Republic. He allowed the Western powers six months in which to concede these demands, and at the end of this period the Soviet Union would, if necessary, carry out these terms unilaterally with the G.D.R. This was an ultimatum which could only lead to war unless the Western powers capitulated. In the event the West did not yield and Khrushchev did not attempt to carry out this threat.

The Berlin crisis, which nevertheless continued into 1961, resulted from the Russians' determination to drive the allies from the city so that they could consolidate their hold on East Germany. For the present they accepted that German reunification on their terms could not be achieved and that the rearmament of West Germany as part of the Western block could not be prevented. But with Berlin under their control as part of East Germany, they could concentrate more on propaganda and economic penetration of the uncommitted countries in their drive towards communist victory.

During 1959 Khrushchev maintained his pressure for a summit conference. He visited the U.S.A. in August–September and had affable conversations with President Eisenhower. Finally in December the Western powers agreed to a summit conference. Khrushchev hoped that by persuasion mixed with intimidation he would be able to pursue the policy of peaceful coexistence on Russian terms. But the conference, held in Paris in May 1960, proved abortive. The Russians broke off the discussions when a Soviet missile brought down an American U-2 reconnaissance plane, flying over Sverdlovsk. The Berlin crisis remained unresolved. But Khrushchev continued to hold the initiative. At the same time he was now facing the mounting crisis in the world communist movement which was to explode later in the year in the great schism between the Russian and Chinese parties.

In November 1960 the communist parties of the world again met in Moscow. Their final declaration, like that of the conference three years earlier, expressed bold confidence in the coming victory of communism. The conference appeared to proceed in an atmosphere of full accord. Only in the course of the following year did information and rumour, reaching the West, indicate that the conference had witnessed the opening of a real schism. It had marked the end of Russia's unquestioned domination of the world communist movement. The Chinese communists had asserted their independence and began increasingly to challenge Moscow's leadership.

The difference between Russian and Chinese parties, which had emerged after the twentieth party congress in 1956, now affected doctrine, strategy, and tactics. Attempts at the 1957 conference to resolve these differences in the interests of communist unity had failed, for they affected the fundamentals of communism. Relations between the two parties deteriorated rapidly. The Chinese loudly denounced Yugoslav revisionism. They criticized the Russians for being half-hearted in their support when the Chinese were threatening to invade Quemoy. They strongly resented Russian refusal to share with them nuclear secrets and weapons. The final breakdown had been marked by Moscow's recall in August 1960 of all the Soviet technical advisers, who had been guiding the development of Chinese industry.

Behind the antagonism, intensified by these and other events, lay the basic disagreements on communist doctrine and strategy and the new Chinese rivalry for the leadership. Already in the underdeveloped countries Peking was challenging Moscow's leadership. Moreover, the Chinese were appealing for Afro-Asian support, claiming that Russia, a European power with an imperialist past, could not speak for the peoples of Asia and Africa. In the underdeveloped countries wars of national liberation were, the Chinese maintained, the true revolutionary road to socialism, but the Russians favoured communist political and economic subversion, since wars of national liberation might well escalate into nuclear wars. Russian recognition of the horror and dangers of nuclear war and their policy of peaceful coexistence were anathema to the Chinese. They continued to assert that nuclear war would destroy the imperialist, but not the socialist block, and they damned peaceful coexistence as pernicious revisionism. The communist world was split and, it seemed, irrevocably.

Although deeply involved in the Sino-Soviet conflict and in rivalling the Chinese in supporting 'the war of national liberation' which was building up in Vietnam, Khrushchev's main concern was Berlin. In 1961 he provoked a new crisis over the city. Again he was hoping to be able to impose his terms by intimidation. Kennedy, the U.S. president, had taken office in January 1961. He had at once been involved in a crisis over Cuba, resulting from an ill-conceived attempt by anti-communist Cubans, aided by the U.S. central intelligence agency, to invade the island. But the landing in the Bay of Pigs had been promptly crushed by Castro's forces. The Americans found themselves in a humiliating position, but Kennedy refused to take military action against Cuba, recognizing that it would antagonize world opinion. Soon after seizing power in 1959 Castro had turned to Russia for aid and support in his struggle to make Cuba a socialist state. Khrushchev had readily responded and in 1961–2 Soviet aid to Cuba had increased steadily until it gave rise to a dangerous crisis.

In 1961, however, Khrushchev was seeking a settlement with the West on Berlin. He was confident of success. Russian prestige and strength had been further boosted in April 1961 by the spectacular achievement of putting the first manned space satellite into orbit, and Yuri Gagarin, the first man in space, was acclaimed by the world. This technological success would surely impress on the West the extent of Russia's power and make the Americans more amenable to negotiations on his terms.

President Kennedy made his first official visit to Europe in May–June and early in June he and Khrushchev met in Vienna. Taking advantage of the occasion, Khrushchev personally handed to Kennedy an *aide-mémoire* which was, in fact, couched in the language of an ultimatum. It renewed the Soviet demand of November 1958 for the allied military evacuation of West Berlin which would become a free city with all access under the control of the German Democratic Republic. It repeated the threat that, if the Western powers did not concede these demands the Soviet Union would sign a peace treaty with the G.D.R. unilaterally. Khrushchev returned to Moscow in a truculent mood and was evidently convinced that the U.S.A. and her Western allies would not fight to maintain the *status quo* in Berlin.

Khrushchev had, however, misjudged the determination of Kennedy and the support that he had in the West in resisting such threats. Towards the end of July, Kennedy announced increases in the American armed forces and, making it clear that Moscow, not Berlin, was the source of world tension and the threat to peace, he declared unequivocally that the U.S.A. would not surrender or submit to Soviet terms, but would fight. Meanwhile the crisis hanging over Berlin was disrupting East Germany from which refugees were pouring in a growing flood, rising to 10,000 a week in July. Finally on 13 August the G.D.R. government built a wall dividing East and West Berlin. By thus halting the mass exodus which threatened to undermine the East German regime, the tension in Berlin, but not the bitterness aroused by the wall, was slightly relieved. When shortly afterwards, the U.S. government declared that negotiations over Berlin would be renewed at the end of the meeting of the U.N. General Assembly in September, Khrushchev welcomed the chance to retreat with dignity from the terms of his ultimatum.

The crisis over Cuba in the following year which threatened the world with a thermonuclear war was probably the result not of deliberate provocation but of Khrushchev's complete misjudgement of the American outlook and temper. The Russians had not forgotten that soon after the end of the war Stalin had under strong American and British pressure withdrawn his occupation forces from Iran, whereupon the Americans had moved in with aid and military advisers. More recently, Dulles had organized in the Baghdad pact (April 1955) the Middle Eastern countries, bordering on the Soviet Union, and then, in December 1957, the NATO council had approved the American proposal to mount IRBMs in Turkey, Greece, and Italy, where they would threaten the Russian cities and in-

dustrial centres. This had been a demonstration of Western, and specifically American, power and superiority, which the Russians had resented,
but had been forced to accept. When Castro defied the U.S.A. and turned
to Soviet Russia with whom Cuba signed a security pact at the beginning
of 1962, Khrushchev seized the opportunity to set up Soviet missile em-
placements near to American shores. Russia's ability to do this was a
token of her new power and parity with the U.S.A. It was, moreover, an
act of confrontation which would, Khrushchev hoped, make the U.S.A.
more amenable and ready to negotiate on Berlin and NATO. He probably
had no thought that the U.S.A. would be prepared to wage a full-scale
war to compel the removal of Russian missiles from Cuba.

In July the Cuban minister of defence and in August the finance
minister visited Moscow for discussions. The terms of the Soviet–Cuban
security treaty were negotiated, providing for the mounting of Soviet
missiles in Cuba. Even before TASS announced this treaty on 2 September, equipment for the missile sites was arriving from Russia and
being assembled by Russian technicians. But only on 16 October, as a
result of photographs taken by a U-2 reconnaissance flight, did Washington have positive evidence of the advanced construction of intermediate
and medium-range ballistic missile sites in Cuba.

The American reaction was prompt and dramatic. This was a direct
threat of a kind that the U.S.A. had never known. The immense power of
her nuclear armoury was brought to full readiness. In Washington the
possible courses of action, including invasion of Cuba, were discussed and
planned. On 22 October President Kennedy addressed the nation and the
world by television and radio in a measured and firm speech in which he
declared American readiness to go to war, if necessary, to eliminate this
threat. He explained the initial preparations which he had ordered. They
included imposing a quarantine on shipments of all offensive military
equipment to Cuba. All ships bound for Cuba were liable to search and, if
carrying such equipment, to be turned back. Kennedy declared that a
missile launched from Cuba on any nation in the Western hemisphere
would be regarded as an attack by the Soviet Union on the U.S.A. who
would retaliate directly and fully. Further, he announced that he had
requested an emergency meeting of the Security Council to take action
against the Soviet threat. Finally, he called on Khrushchev to 'halt and
eliminate this clandestine, reckless, and provocative threat to world
peace ...', adding that Khrushchev had 'an opportunity now to move the
world back from the abyss of destruction'.[8]

Four days later an exchange of notes began between Washington and
Moscow. It concluded on 28 October with Khrushchev undertaking to
withdraw all Soviet missiles, subject to Kennedy undertaking not to invade Cuba.[9] Taken aback by the scale of the crisis and terrible dangers of
nuclear war which suddenly threatened Russia and the world, Khrushchev
had readily yielded to the American demands. He did not want war and

Q

certainly not over the island of Cuba, so small and remote from Russia.[10] But this crisis also marked an important stage in the deep, almost secret rivalry between the Soviet Russia and the U.S.A. for superiority in missiles and nuclear striking power, which had underlain the cold war since the Potsdam conference. At times the Russians had achieved a clear ascendancy, as in 1957 when they had successfully tested the first ICBM and had launched *Sputnik*, but they had held the advantage only briefly. By the time of the Cuban crisis, Khrushchev must have recognized that the U.S.A. possessed the greater power. But the rivalry continued.

The Cuban crisis had nevertheless shocked the Russian and American leaders with the realization that they had brought the world close to Armageddon. They at once began seeking some form of truce in the interest of their own survival. A period of reduced tension ensued, which resulted in August 1963 in the signing by the U.S.A., the Soviet Union, and Great Britain of a nuclear test-ban treaty, and the installation of direct teleprinter communication, the 'hot line', between Moscow and Washington to ensure that by prompt exchanges they would avoid ever again approaching so near to disaster. But as though by some tacit fatalistic agreement the arms race continued.

Within their respective blocks, however, both Russians and Americans found that the Cuban crisis had aggravated disagreement. In the West growing uneasiness, that decisions on the use of nuclear weapons, involving all members, should vest solely in American hands, led to the Nassau agreement in December 1962 in which the U.S.A. and Britain agreed on sharing control of the Western nuclear arms. Next came the American project of a multilateral force, in which allies would have some control over one NATO nuclear weapon. But the French, moved by nationalism and visions of a united Western Europe, serving under French leadership as a third force, rejected this proposal.

At the heart of Europe's problems lay the reunification of Germany. For Khrushchev and his government, West German government was 'bellicose, militarist, revenge-seeking'.[11] But Moscow's terms for accepting the reunification of Germany were not acceptable. Germany remained divided.

Within the Soviet block the divisions became sharper. The Chinese communists were increasingly vehement in condemning peaceful co-existence as a betrayal of Marxism–Leninism. Both Moscow and Peking endorsed 'wars of national liberation', but they differed over the Russian insistence on the struggle for peace and peaceful coexistence. Indeed the Chinese were prompt to accuse the Russians of 'capitulationism' because they agreed to withdraw their missiles from Cuba rather than plunge the world into a nuclear holocaust. The successful firing of a Chinese atomic bomb in Sinkiang province in October 1964 was an event boding ill for the future.

The assassination of President Kennedy on 22 November 1963

appalled the Russians who had come to respect him as a sincere and responsible leader. But this tragedy also alarmed them. They feared that it would somehow be attributed to communist action and indeed the first reactions of Lyndon Johnson and the presidential guards was that a communist plot had brought about the president's death. Moscow was prompt to deny all complicity and to express sincere regrets. But the danger was again apparent that nuclear war might suddenly erupt from the deep mistrust and rivalry of the two great powers.

Meanwhile the U.S.A. continued its policy of containment under new titles, such as 'Flexible Response', in answer to the Soviet policy of competition in peaceful coexistence. The intensive post-war rivalry for the support of the new uncommitted nations in Asia and Africa, while continuing, declined in importance. The third world of the under-developed countries made it clear that they wanted the aid but not the tutelage of either block. Indeed the failure of communism to make any real appeal among most of them had clearly emerged by the mid-sixties.

Caution marked the policies of the U.S.A. and the Soviet Union, as each realized that survival was at stake, and the deposition of Khrushchev from power in October 1964 removed an element of unpredictability and opportunism from the conduct of Soviet policy which had faced the world with three major crises, and which had disturbed the Russians most of all.

CHAPTER TWENTY-SEVEN

Khrushchev 1958–64

SOVIET RUSSIA was now competing as an equal with the United States for superiority in nuclear weapons and in the exploration of outer space. But Khrushchev recognized, especially after his visits to Western Europe and North America, that in standards of living the Russian people lagged far behind. He believed sincerely that communism offered the one perfect social and economic system and that it was superior to the unplanned methods of capitalism. But he accepted that communism must demonstrate its superiority by affording the Russians a way of life that was clearly better. Only by this means, and not through revolutionary wars as preached by the Chinese, could communism attract world support and achieve ultimate victory over capitalism.

Khrushchev, a typical Russian peasant in his short stocky build, was a man of dynamic energy and outstanding ability. He was a hustler who got things done. A practical man he demanded immediate tangible results. He had proved his abilities in the Ukraine, in the modernization of Moscow and during the war, when he was carrying out tasks given to him by Stalin, but he needed such supervision. Wielding power alone he was to show lack of stability. He was too readily carried away by grandiose visions and by his own enthusiasm. His mistakes were on a grand scale. He demonstrated these qualities and failings during his six years in supreme power when he was striving to introduce new efficiency into Soviet industry and agriculture and to lead his people closer to the communist millennium.

The immediate task was to overtake and surpass the West in every field, and at this time all Russians were filled with optimism. The years from 1955 to 1958 had been a time of rapid growth in industrial output and, after the record harvests of 1958, even in agriculture. The success of Russian missile tests and then of *Sputnik* which had made such a deep and dramatic impression on world opinion had intoxicated them with a sense of pride and confidence in their power to attain greater heights.

The long-term programme, adopted by the twenty-second party congress in October 1961, reflected this mood.[1] It revealed the magnitude of the developments to be achieved in the course of the next two decades. By 1970 Soviet production per head of population was to rise above that of the U.S.A. By 1980 industrial output would have increased by not less than 500 per cent and the national income of the Soviet Union would have grown by 400 per cent, while the real per capita income would have risen by over 250 per cent. Agricultural output would increase by 150 per cent in the first decade and by 250 per cent by the end of the second decade. Amenities forecast for workers and farmers in this period included ample housing and consumer goods, a 35–36-hour working week, free gas, heating, public transport, factory and school meals, and a considerable expansion of welfare services.[2]

The party programme was explicit about the hard work needed to achieve these goals. It stressed that communism 'does not release the members of society from work. It will by no means be a society of anarchy, idleness, and inactivity...'[3] Indeed, to gain these results, the programme laid down that it would be necessary 'to raise productivity of labour in industry by more than 100 per cent within ten years and by 300 to 350 per cent within twenty years'.[4] The goals were challenging, but the nation accepted that they were within reach.

This was, however, the longer-term programme. The immediate priorities were laid down by the sixth five-year plan (1956–60) and then the seven-year plan (1958–65).[5] They were similar to previous plans, but radical changes were introduced into the organization and methods used to implement them.

Under Stalin in the post-war years all control had been over-centralized. The vast ministries in Moscow with their massive bureaucracy had directed every detail of production and had shackled industry and agriculture. This factor, dulling initiative, together with the lack of incentives, and the weariness after the exhausting labours of the war and the post-war reconstruction, had led to growing stagnation. Promptly after the death of Stalin the pressure on the people had been relaxed and more attention had been given to incentives and consumer goods. The period of rising productivity had resulted. Khrushchev, eager to accelerate this development, had launched his grandiose virgin-lands policy and the beginnings of other reforms. After 1958 when he had secured full power in his own hands, he embarked on even bolder plans in his impatience to revitalize industry and agriculture.

The plan for decentralizing industry which the Supreme Soviet had approved on 10 May 1957 had eliminated more than 140 all-union, union republic, and republic ministries. In their place it had set up 105 regional economic councils (sovnarkhozy) which exercised on a regional basis the authority which the ministries had wielded centrally. The reform sought to revive local initiative and to raise efficiency. Overall co-ordination of industrial policy vested in Gosplan, the central planning office.

The chief danger in the new system was that local interests would predominate. Khrushchev himself had recognized this threat of 'tendencies towards autarchy' and had alerted the party to fight against them.[6] The capacity of the Soviet regime to carry out large-scale reorganization within a brief period was again demonstrated. In April 1958 it was announced that industrial enterprises, responsible for almost three-quarters of the industrial output of the nation, had already been transferred to the sovnarkhozy. But at once difficulties began to multiply. The most serious was localism. Despite warnings and admonitions by party officials many sovnarkhozy gave absolute priority to local needs. Regional managers illegally diverted central funds to local developments. Moscow immediately applied stricter supervision. Local officials were denounced and punished. The process of centralization was halted and then gradually reversed. In 1960, new controls were instituted by establishing sovnarkhozy for each of the three largest republics—the R.S.F.S.R., the Ukraine and Kazakhstan.

In May of the following year the whole country was divided into seventeen economic regions, each with a council responsible for co-ordinating its economic development. In November 1962 the central committee decreed further centralization. The sixty-seven sovnarkhozy of the R.S.F.S.R. were merged until only twenty-two to twenty-four remained. Similar reductions in the number of councils were made in other Soviet republics. The councils were also restricted in their authority. New construction, design, and technology were made the responsibility of the Soviet State Industrial Committee for Construction and the state industrial committees. Among other organizational changes, the new All-Union Economic Council was set up to ensure that the annual plan targets were reached.

Khrushchev had tried to streamline organization and to bring a new efficiency into Soviet industry. But he had to retreat before the upsurge of parochialism. The Russians had been held too long in the straitjacket of Moscow's control. They had seized on the first relaxation of this control to devote capital and attention to their own regions, the interests of which had always been subjugated to the national priorities. This was the conflict between national and provincial or state interests which existed in the U.S.A., Australia, and other large federations, but whereas they had struck some balance, the Soviet Union lurched from excessive centralization to sudden decentralization, damaging the economy in the process. Until they worked out a gradual and satisfactory devolution of authority from Moscow, they had little hope of achieving a balance.

In agriculture, too, Khrushchev launched massive changes. Reporting to the central committee on 17 January 1961 he declared his objective. 'You know, comrades, that I am an optimist. I believe that we can overtake the United States of America in these five years in per capita output of farm products. The whole question is how to organize the work.'[7] But again he showed excessive concern with organization rather than with reviving initiative and providing incentives for workers on the collective farms.

The 1958 harvest had been followed by three poor harvests in succession. Animal husbandry continued to produce disappointing results.

Khrushchev sought the answer to greater productivity in correcting the over-centralization in agricultural planning and control. Wider responsibility was given to managers of collective and state farms. In particular they would have the power to decide the acreage to be sown with each crop, when it should be sown and when harvested.

A more drastic change was Khrushchev's decision to abolish the machine tractor stations. They had played an outstanding part not only in mechanizing agriculture but also in ensuring the presence and control of the party throughout the vast rural areas. The party attached special importance to this function, for resentment against the Soviet regime lingered among peasants. By 1958, however, party members were far more numerous among collective farmers, mainly as a result of the membership drive, mounted by Khrushchev in rural areas after Stalin's death. The party was now felt able to do without the MTS. The important fact was that the collective farms were, as a result of mergers, large enough to maintain their own machinery and by eliminating the division of responsibility between MTS and collective farms, greater efficiency could be introduced into agriculture.

Khrushchev's reform, approved by the Supreme Soviet on 31 March 1958, caused an upheaval. The machinery of the MTS, which was to be sold to the collectives, amounted to 512,000 tractors and 221,000 harvesters as well as other equipment. Many collective farms had difficulty in financing these purchases. By 1 July 1959, however, ninety-four per cent of the collective farms had, it was claimed, bought their equipment for cash or on credit.[8] Another problem was the transfer of MTS personnel, who in 1957 had numbered more than two million, to the collective farms. The MTS staffs had been a rural upper class, receiving higher salaries than the collective farmers. It was specified that they had to receive the same salaries on transfer and such differentials naturally aroused discontent on the collective farms. A nucleus of MTS staff remained to carry out the duties of the repair and technical service stations (RTS) which took over the MTS functions of repairing machinery, and providing new equipment, spare parts, fuel, fertilizers, and other supplies as well as hiring out to collective farms heavy equipment for roadbuilding and similar special projects. The RTS proved unsatisfactory and on 21 February 1961, the All-Union Farm Machinery Association was set up in their place with a network of district and inter-district machinery associations. But the new system at once proved cumbersome and inefficient.

The ministry of agriculture, which had held overall responsibility for planning and administration, suffered drastic reorganization under a decree announced on 21 February 1961. Its powers were reduced mainly to running agricultural research institutions. But this change left the nation without any central government organ with responsibility for planning and supervising production. In March 1962 yet another major reorganization took place with the creation of a new all-Union committee on agriculture and similar committees at republic level, charged with planning and co-ordinating production, the fulfilment of quotas, and the general requirements of agriculture. But Khrushchev was soon complaining in strong terms about shortfalls in deliveries of machinery, fertilizers, and other necessities.[9]

The improvements in the prices paid for produce, compulsorily delivered to the state, provided more effective incentives for higher production. Under Stalin the complex price-system had meant extremely low payments for the fixed quota deliveries, but higher prices for above-quota deliveries. The payments to the collective farmers were so low, however, as to be a disincentive. In autumn 1953 the prices for compulsory quotas and for above-quota deliveries of most products were greatly increased. Grain deliveries were treated separately; compulsory quota prices were held, but prices for above-quota deliveries were raised tenfold. Gradually, however, the large difference in prices for above-quota and quota deliveries was reduced, until the differential was about three to one. The average income of collective farms nevertheless rose considerably. In 1958 and again in 1961 further changes were introduced to spread payments more equitably and to step up the income actually received by farm workers. Measures had to be taken also to halt the widespread corruption and abuses of the procurement system. Khrushchev spoke at length in his report to the central committee in January 1961 on the evasions, false reporting, and general corruption on the collective farms. A major purge of party, government, and farm officials followed.[10]

At lower levels, too, Khrushchev harried and reorganized agriculture in his furious drive to improve output. The merging of collective farms to make larger units, a movement which he had initiated in 1950, had continued. The number of collective farms at the end of 1960 had been reduced to 44,000 each with an average of 6,800 acres under cultivation, and containing some 400 households. At the same time he was expanding the state farms where they offered greater productivity. Between 1953 and 1959 the collective farm share of lands growing grain had fallen from 89·5 per cent to 66·8 per cent, while that of the state farms had risen from 8·7 per cent to 32 per cent.[11] But this policy resulted in many farms becoming too big and posing new problems of management and administration.

All these and other changes in agriculture, although dealing with real problems, failed to solve the crucial problem of incentives. The benefit of the increased prices paid to collective farms for their produce filtered down to farm workers by means of a complex system of workday credits after prior deductions by the collective for taxes, seed, emergency reserves, and other payments. The workers on poor or average and even on flourishing collective farms received very small rewards in money and kind for their labours. They had to rely on their household plots and domestic animals to supplement their incomes, and these plots were their first concern.

The household plots, in fact, made an important contribution to the national food supplies. In 1959 the private sector of Soviet agriculture, consisting mainly of private plots, produced nearly half of the total meat and milk output, over 80 per cent of the eggs, 60 per cent of the potatoes, and 46 per cent of the green vegetables consumed in the Soviet Union.[12] In 1963, 23·8 per cent of all field crops and 45·6 per cent of livestock products were produced on private plots occupying only about 3·1 per cent of the total arable land.[13]

The party and government frowned on these household plots, which distracted farm-workers from giving their best to the collective farms and encouraged the 'petty bourgeois propensities' which Khrushchev constantly denounced.[14] The striking difference between the output of the vast collective farms and the output of the minute household plots gave dramatic proof of the indifference of the peasants towards the collectives and of their capacity to cultivate the land intensively. But the government had been unable to eliminate the private sector because of its food production. Khrushchev made strenuous efforts to curtail the private plots in the hope that peasants and others would then give more time and attention to the collective farms. Heavier taxation on livestock, cuts in allocations of fodder, restrictions on keeping animals on private plots, and pressure on farm-workers to sell their cows and other stock to the collectives were some of the methods applied. The result was, however, that between 1959 and 1962 the output of these plots fell only slightly, while working time expended on this smaller output increased by 5 per cent.[15] Khrushchev could go no further, for he was not prepared to abolish the private sector completely.

Agriculture consistently lagged behind industry in the drive for greater productivity and continued to act as a brake on the economy. Inefficiency, bureaucracy, over-centralized control, and other factors hampered development. At root, however, the reason for the near-stagnation was the failure of the communist party to understand and come to terms with the Russian peasant. Only at the time of the NEP had the peasants really accepted the regime. They had not forgotten the collectivization campaign which had cheated them of their land. The collective farms seemed to many of them to embody all the worst features of serfdom and the village commune, and they hated the new army of party bureaucrats even more than their fathers had hated the landlords. They were hounded by exhortations to greater productivity and subjected to harsh punishments for failures to work as prescribed by the party leaders. Their resistance was passive, but whenever opportunity offered, they displayed deep peasant cunning in evading regulations and in enriching their household plots, the one concession the regime allowed them. When supervision slackened, they expanded their plots by taking land from the collective farms. The party was, in fact, engaged in a running battle with the peasantry and, while agriculture continued to stagnate and the nation depended to such a great extent on food production of the private sector, the party was clearly the losing side.

As the older peasant generations with their bitter memories and their deep resentment of the Soviet regime passed from the scene, however, the new generations began to show greater readiness to co-operate. They were better educated and able to grasp opportunities for advancement. They have been said to show less interest in household plots and even to be prepared to abandon them if the incentives on the collective farm were adequate. The long struggle of the regime to gain the support of the people on the land may be drawing towards an end.

During the years since Khrushchev had become autocrat, the nation had suffered increasingly from frustration and disappointment. The hopes, surging from the period 1955 to 1958 and symbolized by *Sputnik* orbiting the earth, had not been realized. Khrushchev had blustered across the scene like a high wind, breaking up the surface but leaving the deep-rooted problems untouched. Under his leadership the nation had drifted in a state of change and turmoil.

In international relations he had instigated three major crises which, even though only partially reported by the Soviet press, had disturbed the Russian people. Moreover, the communist world, which had been a strongly united block under Stalin, except only for Yugoslavia, had fallen apart and was now in disarray. The Russians had no sympathies for Mao Tse-tung and the Chinese communists. They recognized in particular that nuclear war would mean the devastation of the world, and the Chinese demand that Russia's nuclear weapons should be used to further the revolutionary cause probably struck them as irresponsible. While they probably did not blame him for the schism with China, they may well have blamed him for speeding the process whereby Russia was losing the leadership of the communist movement.

Judging by criticisms subsequently levelled at him, however, Khrushchev's failures in domestic policy were the real reasons for his downfall. In agriculture he had wrongly applied administrative rather than economic remedies. His campaigns and policies had been positively harmful, especially his drive to enlarge collective and state farms, which was condemned as *gigantomania*. His discrimination against the private sector, the household plots of peasants, workers, and employees, was condemned.[16] In industry he had abolished central ministries and then had set up new ones. He had decentralized and then recentralized. He had interfered in management and had granted wider powers to managers. Finally he had attempted to reorganize the party itself, so that at every level one half was concerned with supervision of industry and the other of agriculture.

By autumn 1964 Khrushchev's colleagues in the presidium, all of whom, except Mikoyan, owed their advance to him, had decided that a return to greater stability was essential. They may well have reflected popular feeling in reaching this decision. The means that they used and the pressure that they brought to bear on him are not known, but this time they were effective.

On 16 October 1964 the Soviet press announced that the central committee, meeting two days earlier, had granted Khrushchev's request to be released from office 'in view of his advanced age and the deterioration in the state of his health'.[17] On the following day *Pravda*, while not mentioning his name, indicted him for 'hair-brained schemes, half-baked conclusions and hasty decisions and actions, divorced from reality; bragging and bluster; attraction to rule by fiat; unwillingness to take into account what science and practical experience have already discovered'.[18]

Suddenly Khrushchev's name vanished from the newspapers; his picture was nowhere to be seen; his collected speeches no longer crowded the bookshops and library shelves. He was not executed, the fate that would have befallen him under a Stalinist regime, but retired to live out his days in comfort. But such retirement into complete oblivion must be galling to a man who had always been so active.

Khrushchev's ebullience, eccentricity, and basic humanity had gained him some goodwill in the West. He had appeared as an approachable man with whom negotiations might be possible. Despite the Berlin and Cuba crises the tendency in the West was to give him the credit for the general lowering of tension between the two blocks after Stalin's death. It may be doubted, however, whether he had endeared himself to his own people. Their reaction to his downfall was apparently complete passivity, indicating indifference or tacit approval.

Khrushchev had assumed the leadership at the end of an era, but for all his energy, commitment, and imagination he had failed to forge policies that would carry Russia purposefully into the new era. He had launched numerous large-scale reforms, some of which might have proved to be on the right lines, but when they did not produce prompt results he had reversed them or made further radical changes. The result of his hectic activity was that the growth rate in industry and agriculture was declining and the nation was drifting. His record as supreme ruler was one of failure.

CHAPTER TWENTY-EIGHT

Brezhnev and Kosygin
1964–7

AFTER deposing Khrushchev, the presidium at once declared that collective leadership had been re-established. The same declaration was made after the death of Stalin. On each occasion it probably represented a real intention that power should vest in a group rather than in one man. But the succession to Lenin and then to Stalin had been resolved each time within some four years by the emergence of a new autocrat.

Many were now expecting this pattern to be repeated. The Russian people have throughout their history accepted and preferred the rule of one man, and under the Soviet regime the structure of party and government favoured it. Moreover, the two men who succeeded Khrushchev seemed so lacking in qualities of leadership that the tendency has been to regard them merely as caretakers. But Russia had been in a state of transition since the death of Stalin and, while individual bids for the supreme power will happen, it is possible that the historical pattern of autocracy may be broken.

Leonid Brezhnev succeeded to the office of first secretary and leader of the party. Alexei Kosygin became chairman of the council of ministers and head of the government. Both were extremely able and experienced men. They lacked Khrushchev's dynamic energy and personality, but possessed the stability and discipline needed after the disorder of his rule. Brezhnev's career had been almost entirely within the party apparatus and he owed his rise in the party hierarchy mainly to Khrushchev himself. Kosygin's experience, although broader, had been gained primarily in industry, administration, and economic planning. But, following after Stalin and Khrushchev, both men seemed to be eclipsed even as they took up their formidable responsibilities.

Brezhnev and Kosygin were not, however, the undisputed rulers of the Soviet Union. They were evidently the chief members of a team which included Nikolai Podgorny and probably also Alexander Shelepin, Mikhail Suslov, and Dmitri Polyansky. Podgorny began his rise in senior administrative posts in the Ukraine and then served in Moscow. But he owed to Khrushchev his promotion to the post of first secretary of the Ukrainian party. He became a candidate member of the presidium in May 1958 and a full member two years later. Since June 1963, when

Khrushchev brought him to Moscow as a member of the party secretariat, he has gained increasing prominence. Mikhail Suslov joined the secretariat of the central committee in 1947 after extensive experience as a party official in the provinces. He only became a full member of the presidium in July 1955, but has apparently specialized in ideological work.

Podgorny and Suslov are both in their sixties like Brezhnev and Kosygin, but Shelepin and Polyansky, the two other probable members of the governing group, are in their forties. Alexander Shelepin was chosen by Stalin himself to maintain control of the Komsomol and in 1952 after twelve years' service he was appointed first secretary. In 1958 he was made head of the KGB (committee of state security) and next became a secretary of the party central committee. In autumn 1962 he took charge of the important Party-State Control Committee and was also appointed a vice-premier and a party secretary, thus holding high office simultaneously in party and state. A Russian from Voronezh, he has had vast experience at the centre of power and, having satisfied Stalin, his ability and ruthless devotion to the party are beyond doubt.

Dmitri Polyansky is reputedly the most dynamic and efficient of the governing group. He served for some years in the Crimean party organization. In March 1958 he was appointed chairman of the council of ministers of the R.S.F.S.R. and an alternate member of the presidium. He owed his promotion to Khrushchev, whom he supported strongly against the anti-party group in June 1957. He was an active member of the central committee and now of the presidium, but his career has lacked party experience of the depth that Shelepin has had.

In the collective leadership, headed by Brezhnev and Kosygin, and including some or all of these men, Kosygin has appeared as the outstanding leader. Although so reserved and with a face so heavily lined and set in expression as to be almost inscrutable, he has made an impact on those who have had dealings with him. Russians have seen him as an exceedingly able and dedicated man, who can be trusted to serve Russian interests. But, whilst most of his career has been in industry and he first achieved real prominence as chairman of Gosplan, he has had long experience of the party machine.

At the age of 15 he served with the Red forces in the civil war, and joined the party in 1927. He received technical training in the Leningrad Technical Institute and was for a time an engineer in the Siberian textile industry. Returning to Leningrad in 1937 he directed a small factory and worked also in a district party office. Suddenly in 1938 he was mayor of Leningrad and in the following year a member of the party central committee. By 1940 he was a full member of Politburo. He survived subsequent purges and was evidently regarded by Stalin as a sound technocrat and economist. But his career was not spectacular. Malenkov and Khrushchev were evidently reluctant to use his services. He was omitted from the Politburo in 1953 and became only a candidate member of the presidium in 1957, although he had opposed the anti-party group. In May 1960 he regained his full membership. Standing aside from factions, independent in judgement, and unmoved by strong ambitions, he has served as required. With his wide experience of industry, administration, and economic planning he was the man most qualified to lead the government at this juncture.

The aftermath of Khrushchev's rule was confusion and disorder in the economy, in the communist block, and in Soviet foreign relations. But the problems which faced the Soviet leaders were not wholly of Khrushchev's making. They arose inevitably in the new era, following Stalin's death. The most pressing problems arose from the state of the Soviet economy. The fact was that the national economy was slowing down and the Russian leaders were alarmed. One estimate was that the rate of growth, which in the late 1950s had been as high as 12 to 15 per cent annually, had fallen to 2·5 per cent and was thus lower than that of the leading countries in the West. Official Soviet estimates put the growth rate at 8, 7, 6, 5 per cent respectively for each of the four years 1960–4. While slightly less gloomy, these figures still showed a steady decline in a period when the seven-year plan required that the economy should leap ahead.[1]

The failure in agriculture was a major factor in this decline. Brezhnev declared at the plenum of the party central committee in March 1965 that agricultural output had during the previous five years grown by only 1·9 per cent, compared with 7·6 per cent in the preceding five-year period. The seven-year plan (1959–65) had set the target at a 70 per cent increase in output. By 1964, however, the growth had been no more than 10 per cent. A factor which forcefully impressed on Soviet leaders the need to deal urgently with this crisis was the failure of the harvest in 1963–4. This had involved the nation in importing more than ten million tons of grain at the enormous cost of $1,000 million.[2]

The policies of Khrushchev were held largely responsible for this slowing down of agricultural growth. The merging of collective and state farms which had resulted in vast unmanageable units was halted. The trend towards separating industry and agriculture, as though they were independent of each other, marked by his division of the party in 1962 into industrial and agricultural committees, was reversed. The campaign against the private sector was stopped. The government declared that private plots would not be reduced, and the many restrictions imposed on them were abolished. The rights of collective farmers to a specified size of plot and the livestock which he was entitled to keep were redefined. Individual farmers, workers, and employees were to be allowed credits, repayable on easy terms within five years, to enable them to buy livestock. In these and other measures the government acknowledged the importance of the private sector. At the same time it was recognized that only when the collective and state farms were providing farm workers with adequate rewards and food supplies would the private plots and the private sector as a whole begin to wither away.[3]

The near-stagnation of agriculture was also a result of the low priority accorded to it over the years. Industrial development has always been the first concern of the regime, and agriculture has suffered from serious discrimination in the allocation of investment capital, the provision of equipment, fertilizers, and other necessities to growth.

The new Soviet leaders have come to grips with these problems. The total investment in agriculture in the 1966–70 five-year plan will be raised to 71 milliard rubles, which is about the same as the total investment over the previous nineteen years.[4] Supplies of machinery will be increased. By 1970 tractors will be produced at the rate of 625,000 a year, and agriculture will then have 1,780,000 tractors in service. Trucks, which have always been in short supply, will be manufactured in far greater numbers; in the plan period 1,100,000 trucks will be supplied to agriculture, compared with 394,000 in the previous five years. Fertilizers, too, are to be produced in greatly increased quantities, amounting by 1970 to fifty-five million tons of mineral fertilizers a year, which is double the amount planned for 1965.

Reforms in the state procurement system and the prices paid for produce, and adjustments in the taxation levies on collective farms, will help rationalize long-term planning. The new financial provisions will, in fact, give the collective farms greater independence and should stimulate production. They will no longer labour under the handicaps of low-priority and neglect. Farmers will attain a higher standard of living, comparable with that of industrial workers, and new incentives will result in greater productivity.

The effects of this new approach to agriculture will only be clear towards the end of the plan period. According to the report of the central statistical board on the 1966 results, the gross output of agriculture has exceeded the output of 1965 by approximately 10 per cent. The grain harvest amounted to 170·8 million tons, as compared with 130·3 million tons in 1965. Increases in livestock and products of animal husbandry were also reported.[5] At long last a turning point appears to have been reached in Russian agriculture.

The decline in industrial growth, while less severe than in agriculture, has still been serious. According to Soviet figures the average annual rate of industrial growth has fallen from 21 per cent in the period 1948–51 to 8·5 per cent in 1963, and to an estimated 7·8 per cent in 1964.[6] Kosygin, reporting to the Supreme Soviet on 9 December 1964 soon after the dismissal of Khrushchev, referred to many of the causes of these declining figures. Steel, electricity, and rail transport had reached their plan targets, while coal and gas had failed and fuel shortages had handicapped many factories. Excessive administrative interference and over-centralization had hampered industry and agriculture. His comments pointed to the overall need to streamline industry and to raise productivity by encouraging initiative and offering greater incentives.

A new approach, associated with Professor Yevsei Liberman of the University of Kharkov, came under discussion as early as 1962. Liberman maintained that the two chief sources of inefficiency were, first, the payment of bonuses for reaching or over-fulfilling the plan target with the result that management sought, often by most devious methods, to have the targets set as low as possible; the second source was that managers received a multiplicity of instructions from the central ministries which tied their hands down to the last detail.

Liberman proposed a plan of great simplicity, designed to give managers full scope for initiative and at the same time to make it in their interest to use all plant efficiently in order to attain maximum rather than minimum targets. His proposal was that management and workers in each enterprise should receive incentive bonuses, based wholly on the rate of profit earned on the total capital investment in the enterprise. The bonuses would be so calculated that the greater the profit planned and achieved, the greater the bonus would be. Furthermore, managers would receive only minimal instructions from the centre, and the challenge to attain and exceed their plan targets would be for them to meet, with the incentive of substantial rewards for success.

Liberman's plan with its similarity to the basic principle of capitalist industry aroused opposition among Marxists. It clearly offended against socialist ideals. But the Soviet leaders were practical men who recognized that, while Soviet industry lagged in efficiency and productivity, communism would remain only an ideal. They recalled that Lenin's NEP had been criticized on similar grounds. They rejected all suggestion that the plan would revive private enterprise, and justified it as a means of increasing productivity.

Khrushchev had shown interest in this policy, but had been unsure. Kosygin with his greater knowledge and experience of industry and economic planning, has evidently been strongly attracted by the ideas of Liberman, who has been called his protégé. But Kosygin is also a politician, who must heed the objections expressed within the party. He has, however, introduced Liberman's system. As from 1 April 1965, when 400 consumer-goods factories were brought under this system, it has spread rapidly and apparently with good results. More than 673 enterprises, employing some two million workers, had changed over by the end of 1966, and about half of Soviet industry, involving nine million workers, would be functioning on this basis at the end of 1967.[7]

Industrial output for the first year of the new plan has, according to the Soviet Central Statistical Board, over-fulfilled the target figure of 6·7 per cent by a growth of 8·6 per cent. Of special interest in the figures released is the rise of 9 per cent in industries producing cultural and household goods. During the year, moreover, 1,850,000 flats and in rural districts

370,000 houses were completed, and eleven million people moved into new or improved accommodation.[8] Such results point to the drive to meet the popular demands for housing and consumer goods. Indeed, the sense of purposeful direction and the policies adopted suggest that in industry as in agriculture a new era in the development of the Soviet economy is beginning. For this reason the Soviet leaders are even more anxious for peace.

The twenty-third party congress, convened late in March 1966, was the first to be held since Khrushchev was deposed. The main task of the congress was to approve the five-year plan for 1966–70. The proceedings were evidently calm and business-like, demonstrating the approach of the new leaders and contrasting with the flamboyance of Khrushchev. No attempt was made, however, to arraign him by name, although by implication his leadership was severely criticized. The Congress, in considering the state of the party, heard strong calls for greater stability in the tenure of party appointments and for closer attention to the suitability of applicants for membership, an indirect criticism of Khrushchev's large-scale recruitments. The congress revived the name 'Politburo', which had been changed to 'presidium' by the sixteenth congress in 1952. The title 'general secretary' also replaced 'first secretary', a change justified by reference to Lenin, but not to Stalin.

In the political report, delivered by Brezhnev in a speech of over four hours, no new lines of policy were declared or forecast on Vietnam, Germany and Europe, relations with Mao Tse-tung and the Chinese communists, and disarmament. But they were the problems of foreign policy most on the minds of the Soviet leaders who were clearly anxious to continue the *détente* with the West.

After the failure of Khrushchev's attempts to evict the Western powers from Berlin and to force an agreement on Germany, the Soviet government evidently decided to postpone for the time being its search for a satisfactory solution of the German problem. This did not mean, however, that Russian fears of the resurgence of Germany had passed. On the contrary throughout 1966 and into 1967, when the crisis of Vietnam and the Sino-Soviet dispute were demanding attention, the Soviet press continued to devote much of its space to the German problem. On 29 March 1966, reporting on behalf of the central committee, Brezhnev declared that:

Western Germany increasingly becomes the centre of the danger of war; revanchist passions there have reached boiling point . . . The politicians on the banks of the Rhine are dreaming that, after they have succeeded in getting hold of atom bombs, they will overthrow the frontier posts and will realize their most cherished dream of changing the map of Europe and taking revenge for their defeat in the Second World War . . . They are dreaming in Bonn of involving the U.S.A. more deeply and also other NATO allies in their revanchist plans . . .[9]

This remains the underlying Russian fear and one of the most important factors in Soviet foreign policy. Indeed, it has dominated their military strategy so that, instead of giving priority to bombers and ICBMs able to strike at North America, they have maintained airfleets and IRBMs, directed at Western Europe from which, they have evidently decided, attacks are more likely.

The danger that the war in Vietnam may escalate further has nevertheless been pressing. The Vietcong communists, directed from Hanoi and supported by both the Russians and the Chinese, are stubbornly fighting a 'war of national liberation' to conquer South Vietnam. The U.S.A., maintaining the policy of the containment of communism, has intervened in increasing strength. By the end of 1965 some 200,000 U.S. troops were involved. By March 1967 this figure had more than doubled and the U.S. congress approved the allocation of $4,500 million for military expenditure in Vietnam. The serious escalation of the war and the evident intention of the U.S. government to continue fighting until the Vietcong are defeated or come to reasonable terms, ensuring the independence of South Vietnam, place the Soviet leaders in a dilemma.

The threat of being engaged on two separate fronts has throughout history worried Russians. But the problem now is more complex. Soviet Russia and the United States are the outstanding great powers. But communist China with her population of 700 million is potentially the strongest power of all, especially as, despite her backward economy, she will in due course possess nuclear weapons. One fear oppressing the Russians is that by some means Peking and Washington may reach an understanding, leaving Russia alone to face them.

Russia is therefore anxious to come to terms with the West and especially with the U.S.A., by far its most powerful member. Moreover, this move towards reunion with the West has, since the beginning of the Muscovite state late in the fifteenth century, formed part of the pattern of Russia's history. The reason why it has not been accomplished has been, in the view of many Russians, that the Western powers have always taken advantage of her backwardness to invade and plunder, but for many in the West the potential might of Russia has always loomed as a threat. To the Russians in the twentieth century it has been axiomatic that such reunion would be possible if Russia was strong, but Russian strength, combined with militant communism, has continued to frighten the West and has given rise to the cold war. The spread of communism to China has complicated the position further and the Vietnam war has added to this complexity.

The prestige and authority of the Soviet party, already damaged by the de-Stalinization campaign and subsequent events, would be further diminished if the Americans were to inflict an outright defeat on the Vietcong. This would also probably lead to a permanent U.S. garrison, based in south-east Asia. But equally unwelcome to Moscow would be an

American withdrawal. This would leave Vietnam to become a Chinese base from which to foment communists' revolutionary activities over vast areas of southern Asia, from which the Chinese would exclude the Russians.

Since the twentieth congress of the Soviet party in February 1956, relations between Russia and China have deteriorated sharply. The two countries are now engaged in ferocious exchanges. Apart from mutual charges of betrayal of Marxism–Leninism, there have been accusations of bad faith over Vietnam. The Chinese have alleged that the Soviet government is secretly acting in collusion with the Americans to bring about a compromise peace. The Russians have accused the Chinese of holding up supplies of Soviet arms to North Vietnam in an attempt to demonstrate Soviet treachery towards 'the war of national liberation'.

The Soviet view is that China is 'a seriously sick country' in the grip of a pernicious personality cult. The Chinese celebration of the anniversary of Sun Yat-sen in November 1966 gave force to this line. The celebrations virtually overlooked Sun Yat-sen, concentrating on Mao Tse-tung and his designated successor, Lin Piao. Mao himself was proclaimed to be far above Marx, Engels, Lenin, and Stalin. Indeed as the Chinese communists became increasingly chauvinistic, their standing among communists was further damaged by the destructive 'cultural revolution', in which the undisciplined gangs of young Red Guards had a free hand to destroy whatever they found in their way. Their unruly activities led to fighting in many provinces, threatening the country with civil war, and serious cracks appeared in the monolithic unity of the party under Mao.

The Soviet leaders, in the interests of Russian security rather than world communist unity, have sought to rally all communist parties behind Moscow and to apply pressure for the replacement of the Chinese leaders by others who would co-operate. A *communiqué*, issued on 13 December 1966 after a meeting of the plenum of the Soviet central committee, set out the three main principles of Soviet policy towards China: first, the Chinese communist party was basically sound and the Soviet party would always strive for good relations with it; second, Mao Tse-tung and his associates could no longer be accepted as communists, for their policies and behaviour were anti-Marxist, and they must now be strenuously opposed; third, another world conference of communist parties, like the conferences held in Moscow in 1957 and 1960, should be held after careful preparation.

Soviet efforts to rally communist parties in a conference which would condemn the Chinese party and re-establish the unity of the international communist movement have met with limited success. Of the total of eighty-one parties represented at the 1960 conference in Moscow, only sixty-five could by the end of 1966 be counted on to support the Soviet party. Moreover, seven of the major ruling communist parties—China, Albania, North Korea, North Vietnam, Rumania, Yugoslavia, and probably Cuba—were definitely opposed to the conference. The parties of Japan, Italy, and Norway were also opposed to it, and the French communist party was hesitant.

In this and other developments, such as the refusal of the general council of the communist World Federation of Trade Unions to expel the Chinese delegation, the Soviet leaders have had dramatic and conclusive evidence that the monolithic unity and unquestioned Russian leadership of the world communist movement belong to the past. 'Polycentrism' is the term now used to describe the freedom of all parties to interpret Marxism and to act in the light of their own interests. Only Yugoslavia dared to assert this right under Stalin, but now Rumania and others have seized their independence.

For Stalin the unity of the world communist movement had been of value in contributing to Russia's security. International communism into which Soviet Russia would merge, as envisaged by Lenin and Trotsky, had never interested him. He had dissolved the Comintern in 1943 and his successors had abandoned the Cominform in 1956, because both organizations had been hindrances to Russian policy.

The support of fraternal communist parties, even though no longer welded into a strong union, is not, however, something to be sacrificed. The Soviet leaders are making every effort to hold this support, but this involves the pursuit of conflicting policies. As champion of communism the Russians continue, although less vehemently, to condemn the policies of the imperialists and especially the U.S. intervention in Vietnam. At the same time they have pursued a more conciliatory policy towards the West, hoping for some agreement which will ensure greater security. But the Vietnam crisis, which provides a test for Soviet dedication to the communist cause, has also involved the U.S. government in a costly war from which it seeks escape. In return for Russian support in negotiating a settlement in Vietnam, the U.S.A. is evidently prepared to set aside matters of dispute in Europe, and specifically to cease pressing for solutions unacceptable to the Soviet leaders on West Germany and German unity, and to accept some form of reconciliation with Russia.

The dilemma facing the Soviet leaders is thus acute. But their immediate and long-term concern is Russian security, and Chinese hostility makes it a matter of urgency. Their hope is that reconciliation with the West and security can be encompassed within the policy of peaceful coexistence. Competition between the socialist and the democratic-capitalist systems is inevitable. But the militant crusading spirit of the Russian revolutionaries and of the American capitalists has diminished. At the same time the development of nuclear weapons and missiles has faced them with the choice between war and destruction or peaceful competition. Appreciation of these factors and of the dangers of the Vietnam war has moved Russians and Americans to seek some basic accommodation which will secure their own survival and world stability. But the mistrust between them is slow to dissipate.

The Russo-American arms-rivalry is the most acute demonstration of this mistrust. In the mid-1950s the U.S. B-52 Stratofortress had been followed by the Soviet Tupolev-20, an intercontinental bomber of similar capability. In August 1957 the Russians had shaken the Americans by the successful test-firing of an ICBM and then by the launching of their space satellite. The arms race was intensified with the U.S.A. taking the lead. But at this time it was recognized that the approach of the two powers was different. U.S. reconnaissance revealed that the foremost Soviet concern was strategic defence rather than strategic attack to which the U.S.A. gave priority. Estimates also showed that during the 1950s the Soviet Union had spent three times more on anti-aircraft defences than the U.S.A. The Soviet High Command also maintained air and naval patrols to keep seaborne enemies at a distance from Russian shores. Such defences were of small value in an age of intercontinental bombers and missiles, but they demonstrated how active were the fears of the Russians that the Americans with their great armoury of offensive weapons were planning to attack.[10]

In 1962 the U.S. *Minuteman* came into service. Its capability of annihilating all Soviet ICBMs on their launching sites, the positions of which were known by reconnaissance from artificial satellites, naturally alarmed the Russians. By the mid-1960s, however, they had equivalent missiles in service. The race continued and, although the U.S.A. held larger stocks of the newest weapons, the two powers were approaching stalemate. But next it emerged that the Soviet government was developing at tremendous cost an anti-ballistic missile defence system, deployed initially around Moscow. This evidently threatened a further intensification of the missile rivalry, which would be so costly and menacing that the U.S. president took the initiative in proposing negotiations to halt further competition. On 2 March 1967 Kosygin responded with an acceptance of this invitation to discuss halting the missile race. From such discussions agreement may result to extend the 1963 test-ban treaty to cover underground nuclear tests, and the general acceptance of a non-proliferation treaty may find wider acceptance among non-nuclear powers.[11] But progress, if any, will be slow.

Russia now finds herself passing over the threshold into a new era. For more than a decade after the death of Stalin, the nation faltered, as though unsure of the new course to be followed. Many Russians argued that the hard discipline of Stalin's rule must be maintained so long as the West, and specifically the United States, actively threatened. All Russians have been agreed that the nation must never again be caught unprepared as she was in the first and at the beginning of the second world war. For reasons of defence and because she is a modern industrial and technologically advanced nation, the development of missiles and space exploration must continue, but preferably on terms concerted with the United States or under international treaties such as the Outer Space Treaty, agreed at the United Nations in December 1966.

Concentration on heavy industry, defence, and technology is, however, no longer enough. It was accepted in the iron age of Stalin as essential to national survival, but the struggle for survival has been won. In the thermonuclear age Russia is advanced and for all practical purposes level with the United States. Her security is seen to rest on maintaining this position.

The new task is to develop the economy and to evolve a more liberal system so that the Russian people may enjoy the richer life for which they have struggled and sacrificed. The general demand among them for a better way of life has made itself felt increasingly in the 1960s. The policies launched since Khrushchev was deposed may well revitalize the economy. The mounting demand for a more liberal regime raises greater problems. Soviet leaders have reacted with caution. For them it is not simply a matter of reluctance of the party hierarchy to accept diminution of their power, but of maintaining Russia strong and united. Since the formation of the Muscovite state, the nation has depended on an authority wielding power at the centre. In a country so vast liberalizing reform will involve decentralization in some degree and that may lead to weakness of a kind that in the face of American, Chinese, or German threats of domination by infiltration or force could be fatal. Resolution of this problem will be a gradual hesitant process, demanding patience.

The past fifty years have been for Russia a time of trial and suffering on a scale that few other nations have endured, but they have been years of dramatic achievement. The coming years may well prove less dramatic, but they will scarcely be less important. The attainment by the Russian people of a more liberal and rewarding way of life, possibly involving some modification of communist ideals, is bound up with the reunion of Russia with the Western community of nations. Nothing is more vital in importance not only for Russia herself but also for Western civilization and for the peace and stability of the world.

NOTES AND BIBLIOGRAPHY

Notes to Prelude

1. W. H. Chamberlin, *The Russian Revolution 1917–21* (London, 1935), I, p. 91.
2. Bernard Pares, *The Fall of the Russian Monarchy* (London, 1939), pp. 467–8.
3. V. V. Shulgin, *Dni* (Belgrade, 1925), p. 270.

NOTES TO CHAPTER 1

1. Ian Grey, *Peter the Great* (London, 1962), pp. 403–6.
2. Grey, *Ivan the Terrible* (London, 1964), pp. 178–81; *Ivan III and the Unification of Russia* (London, 1964), pp. 44–69.
3. H. Seton-Watson, *The Decline of Imperial Russia 1855–1914* (London, 1952), pp. 14–18.
4. Isaac Deutscher, *Stalin: A Political Biography* (London, 1949), p. 49. *Katorga*, the Russian name for imprisonment in a penal settlement or fortress, derives from distant times when prisoners were chained to galleys, and it continued to strike a note of dreaded severity.
5. Grey, *Peter the Great*, pp. 135–7 and *passim*.
6. W. E. Mosse, *Alexander II and the Modernization of Russia* (London, 1958). A short but excellent study of Alexander and his reforms.
7. *ibid.*, p. 180.
8. *ibid.*, p. 173.

NOTES TO CHAPTER 2

1. Grey, *Ivan the Terrible*, p. 59.
2. For an interesting and graphic account, apparently based on fact, of similar treatment of the radical, independent individual, but on a much larger scale, in the Soviet Union, see the novel by Valery Tarsis, *Ward 7*, translated by Katya Brown (London, 1965).
3. A. I. Herzen, *My Past and Thoughts*. Translated from the Russian (London, 1967).
4. One day in 1878, General Trepov, governor of St Petersburg, was visiting the prison where accused populists were being held for a mass trial. One young prisoner angered him and he ordered him to be flogged. The flogging was so savage that the young man went mad and some years later died as a result. The cruelty and injustice of this flogging incensed revolutionaries and several planned revenge. Vera Zasulich went with a crowd of petitioners who visited the governor to beg relief or remedy from their grievances. When her turn came she did not speak, and drawing a revolver, fired point blank, but wounded him only slightly.
Vera Zasulich had been a revolutionary since the age of seventeen. During the years 1869 to 1871 she was in prison and then in exile in Kharkov. It was soon after returning from exile that she made her attempt on the life of Trepov.
Her trial and acquittal sent a current of excitement throughout Europe. She became a heroine not only to the people of Russia but also in other parts of Europe. After her acquittal, she was hidden by friends. She escaped over the frontier and found asylum in Switzerland and took part in

the main revolutionary movement, but strangely enough she became a staunch opponent of terrorist methods. She returned to Russia in 1879–80 and then lived abroad until 1905, when she returned again to Russia, this time as the enemy of Lenin and she was to oppose the bolshevik revolution of 1917.

Franco Venturi, *Roots of Revolution* (London, 1960) pp. 596–8; Avrahm Yarmolinsky, *Road to Revolution: A Century of Russian Radicalism* (London, 1957), pp. 219–21.

5. Leonard Schapiro, *The Communist Party of the Soviet Union* (London, 1960), p. 16.

6. The best biographies of Lenin available are David Shub, *Lenin* (New York, 1955), and Bertram Wolfe, *Three who made a Revolution* (New York, 1948); but see also Louis Fischer, *The Life of Lenin* (London, 1965), which contains a mass of material.

7. A. Kerensky, *The Crucifixion of Liberty* (London, 1934), p. 13, for a school report on Lenin. Kerensky's father had been headmaster of Lenin's school.

8. Karl Radek, *Portraits and Pamphlets* (Moscow, 1933), I, p. 27.

9. Maxim Gorky, *Days with Lenin* (London, 1932), p. 5.

10. Bruce Lockhart, *Memoirs of a British Agent* (London, 1932), pp. 237–8. Angelica Balabanov, the Ukrainian revolutionary, first met Lenin in 1906 and wrote:

'To be honest I must admit that I cannot remember just when and where I first met Lenin, though I believe it was at a meeting in Bern. I already knew who he was and the position he represented, but he made no personal physical impression upon me at the time. Lenin had no exterior characteristics that would lead one to single him out among the revolutionary figures of his day—in fact, of all the Russian revolutionary leaders he seemed externally the most colourless. Nor did his speeches at the time impress me, either by their manner or by their content.'

Angelica Balabanov, *My Life as a Rebel* (London, 1938), p. 84.

11. Lenin, *Letters of*, translated and edited by Elizabeth Hill and Doris Mudie (London, 1937).

12. Krupskaya, *Memories of Lenin* (London, 1930), I, p. 72; see also Louis Fischer, *op. cit.*, p. 37.

13. Recent biographers have sought to discover women in Lenin's life apart from his mother, Maria Alexandrovna, and his wife, Krupskaya. Mr Louis Fischer asserts that he truly loved only Inessa Armand, a strikingly beautiful young revolutionary of French origin.

See Louis Fischer, *op. cit.*; Robert Payne, *The Life and Death of Lenin* (London, 1964); Stefan Possony, *Lenin, the Compulsive Revolutionary* (London, 1964).

14. Schapiro, *op. cit.*, p. 24.

15. *Novy Mir*, June 1963, p. 175.

16. Lenin, *Letters of*, p. 57.

17. Lenin himself was conscious of the loyalty of the workers to the tsar and the regime, and in his pamphlets and articles, written in 1895 and 1896 from prison and exile, he was most careful not to affront them. See Leonard Schapiro, *op. cit.*, p. 27.

18. Shub, *op. cit.*, p. 35.

19. Schapiro, *op. cit.*, p. 49.

20. *ibid.*, p. 52.

21. Shub, *op. cit.*, p. 40.

22. *loc. cit.*

NOTES TO CHAPTER 3

1. The Uniate Church was a sect of the Orthodox Church, founded under Polish auspices in 1596 and primarily the work of the Jesuits. Its members were Orthodox believers who retained most of the Orthodox rites and liturgy, but acknowledged the supremacy of the Pope. The Uniate Church was anathema to all true Orthodox believers and was persecuted and proscribed by several Russian sovereigns. It was officially reunited with the Russian Orthodox Church in 1874.

2. Pares, *op. cit.*, p. 33.

3. Rodion Malinovsky, a young metal worker and an active trade unionist, arrived from Kiev in 1911 and joined the bolshevik party school, established near Paris by Lenin and Krupskaya. Lenin regarded him as representative of the new pattern of the professional proletarian revolutionary, and advanced him rapidly. In 1912 Lenin chose him as one of the six bolshevik deputies to serve in the fourth Duma. He visited Lenin frequently in Cracow and elsewhere, usually staying at Lenin's house. He enjoyed Lenin's complete confidence.

On 8 May 1914 Malinovsky resigned his seat in the Duma and went into hiding in Germany. He took this step to avoid public exposure as a secret agent of the police. It became clear, however, that he had been sent to join Lenin and the bolsheviks by the tsarist police and that he had reported faithfully to them on the people and activities of the party. Once elevated to the bolshevik hierarchy he was, of course, privy to the innermost secrets of the party, which he carefully reported.

Several members of the party had warned Lenin that Malinovsky was a police spy, but he refused to believe them. After the revolution, however, the secret Okhrana files fell into Soviet hands and those showed conclusively that Malinovsky had all the time been an extremely well-paid agent of the police.

Later, when head of the Soviet government, Lenin once remarked to Gorky, 'But I never saw through that scoundrel, Malinovsky. That was a very mysterious affair.' Maxim Gorky, *op. cit.*, p. 58; Louis Fischer, *op. cit.*, pp. 81–2.

4. For a fuller account of his astonishing career see B. I. Nikolaevsky, *Aseff: The Russian Judas* (London, 1934).

5. Schapiro, *op. cit.*, p. 64; cf. Gapon, *The Story of my Life* (London, 1905), p. 170.

6. Fischer, *op. cit.*, pp. 82–3.

7. Twelve years later a simple soldier, serving as one of the guards of the ex-tsar, remarked how the popular idea of Nicholas as a terrible tyrant had vanished from his mind on personal contact with him. 'His eyes were good and kind . . . The impression he made on me was of a man who was kind, simple, frank and ready to talk.' Bernard Pares, *op. cit.*, p. 495.

This was a true impression of Nicholas, part of whose personal tragedy was that he made no contact with, or impact on, his people. He was a little man, lost in the immensity of his realm and unknown by his people. By contrast his father, Alexander III, who possessed nothing of the goodness of his son, was a big man and a strong, confident autocrat, who made an impact on his subjects and was better loved by them.

8. The Russian equivalent for 'trade union' is *professionalny soyuz* or *profsoyuz* and is derived directly from these first unions of the professions. Trade unions are still known as *profsoyuzi* in the Soviet Union.

9. Pares, *op. cit.*, p. 80.

10. *loc. cit.*
11. Bernard Pares, *History of Russia* (London, 1947), pp. 488–9.

NOTES TO CHAPTER 4

1. The name Kadet was formed from the initials of the party name—Ka De. For further detail concerning the formation and policy of the Kadet Party see P. N. Milyukov, *Vospominaniya (1859–1917)* (New York, 1956), and George Fischer, *Russian Liberalism* (Harvard, 1958).
2. Schapiro, *op. cit.*, pp. 73–4.
3. Deutscher, *op. cit.*, p. 78.
4. Schapiro, *op. cit.*, p. 80.
5. Stalin in the foreword to his *Sochineniya* (Moscow, 1946–8), (Vols. i–viii) referred to his Stockholm controversy with Lenin and confessed that, through narrow-mindedness and lack of theoretical insight, he and other *praktiki*, as those favouring this treatment of the land question were called, had failed to understand that Lenin was already then looking forward to the Russian revolution as it would be when it passed from its 'bourgeois democratic' to its socialist phase. Stalin confessed that he himself had thought that the two phases would be separated by a long period of capitalist development; he could not, he admitted, then conceive of a socialist revolution taking place before the working class had grown to form the majority of the nation. Deutscher, *op. cit.*, pp. 83–4.
6. Pares, *The Fall of the Russian Monarchy*, p. 93.
7. *ibid.*, p. 111.
8. *ibid.*, p. 97.
9. *loc. cit.*
10. Wolfe, *op. cit.*, pp. 358–70.
11. V. I. Kokovtsov, *Iz moevo proshlovo* (Paris, 1933), I, pp. 232–3; Pares, *op. cit.*, pp. 97–8.
12. Azef at first indignantly denied that he had been a police agent, but the evidence was damning. A party 'court of honour' found him guilty in January 1909. He escaped abroad and his name survives, not as that of a Russian Judas, but as an example of the corruption to which police repression gives rise.
See for further detail concerning Azef's extraordinary career B. Nikolaevsky, *op. cit.*
13. Seton-Watson, *op. cit.*, p. 259.
14. Pares, *op. cit.*, p. 124.
15. *ibid.* A detailed account of the plot and assassination of Stolypin, which differs in some respects from Pares' account, has recently been published in the Soviet Union. See *Voprosy Istorii* 1966, No. 1, pp. 134–44; No. 2, pp. 123–40.
16. *ibid.*, pp. 124–5.
17. Iliodor, *Svyatoi Chort* (Moscow, 1917), pp. 5–6; Felix Yusupov, *Rasputin* (London, 1927), pp. 51–2; Kokovtsov, *op. cit.*, II, pp. 35–9.
18. Haemophilia was introduced into the Romanov family by Nicholas II's wife, the Empress Alix, who was a carrier through her grandmother, Queen Victoria.
Dr Victor A. McKusick, Professor of Medicine, Johns Hopkins University, considered that the mutation in the x-chromosome occurred in Edward, Duke of Kent, father of Queen Victoria, who became the first to transmit the mutation. Victoria's third child, Alice, married Louis IV, Grand Duke of Hesse. Of her seven children, three—two daughters and a son—received the mutant gene. The son died early from haemophilic haemorrhage. The elder

daughter bore three sons of whom two were haemophilic. Alix, the younger daughter, had four daughters and the tsarevich who was a haemophilic.

See Victor A. McKusick, *Human Genetics* (New Jersey, 1964), pp. 39–40.

19. Pares, *op. cit.*, p. 115.

20. Kerensky, *op. cit.*, p. 169.

NOTES TO CHAPTER 5

1. Kerensky, *op. cit.*, p. 169.

2. Anna Vyrubova, *Memories of the Russian Court* (London, 1923), p. 104.

3. M. V. Rodzyanko, *The Reign of Rasputin* (London, 1927), p. 111.

4. See note 3 to Chapter 3, on Rodion Malinovsky.

5. F. A. Golder, *Documents of Russian History, 1914–17* (New York, 1927), pp. 29–37.

6. Lenin, *Sochineniya* 4th ed., Vol. 21 (Moscow, 1948), pp. 1–4, 17. Lenin subsequently embodied his theses on the War, entitled *Zadachi Revolyutsionnoi Sotsial-Demokratii v Evropeiskoi Voine* in a manifesto of the central committee of the R.S.D.N.P. (The Russian Social-Democrat Workers' Party) under the title *Voina i rossiiskaya Sotsial-demokratiya. ibid.*, pp. 11–18.

7. Kerensky, *op. cit.*, pp. 222–3; Bernard Pares, *The Fall*, p. 333.

8. S. Kohn and Meyendorf, *The Cost of the War to Russia* (New Haven, 1932), p. 14; N. N. Golovin, *The Russian Army in the World War* (New Haven, 1931), p. 202.

9. General Sir A. Knox, *With the Russian Army, 1914–17* (London, 1921).

10. Pares, *op. cit.*, p. 190.

11. *ibid.*, p. 199.

12. Samsonov, believing that he had betrayed the tsar's trust by allowing himself to be surrounded and defeated in this way, apparently went into the woods and shot himself. Pares, *op. cit.*, pp. 200–1.

13. The Germans called this the Battle of Tannenberg, recalling and expunging the dishonour of the defeat of the German knights by Poles, Lithuanians, and Russians at Tannenberg in the year 1410.

14. *ibid.* p. 205.

15. *ibid.*, p. 210.

16. *loc. cit.*

17. Knox, *op. cit.*, p. 249.

18. Witte was so active in proclaiming his view, that Russia should seek economic alliance with Germany and France against England and that Russia should withdraw from the war, that the British ambassador, Buchanan, protested to the tsar and issued a public denunciation of his policy.

Sir George Buchanan, *My Mission to Russia* (London, 1923).

19. Pares, *op. cit.*, p. 207.

20. *ibid.*, p. 228.

21. *ibid.*, p. 201.

22. *ibid.*, p. 207.

23. *ibid.*, p. 251. See also *Imperatritsa Aleksandra Fedorovna, Pismak Imperatoru Nikolaya II* (Berlin, 1922), 1, pp. 117–19, 133–41, and *passim*.

24. Pares, *op. cit.*, p. 250.

25. Kohn and Meyendorf, *loc. cit.*

26. Golovin, *op. cit.*, p. 97.

27. Pares, *op. cit.*, p. 374.

28. Nicholas sent his cousin, Grand Duke Georgi, to the front to award decorations among officers and men. On his return he reported frankly on the anger at the front over the incompetence of Sturmer's government. But he was deeply impressed by the front line divisions whose fighting spirit was

splendid. Reflecting the general feeling among the troops, he concluded his report of 27 January with the words, 'I believe that the hour of victory may be much nearer.'

Pares, *op. cit.*, pp. 374–5.

29. *ibid.*, pp. 391–2.

30. Attempts had been made to kill him earlier, but he only became really concerned for his safety after the denunciation in the Duma on 2 December. He brooded on his death and wrote a prophecy which, if true, was strangely accurate. In it he foretold that he would die before 1 January (Old Style) and that, if killed by peasants, the tsar would have nothing to fear, for his dynasty would endure, but if murdered by one of the tsar's relations, then not one of the imperial children would remain alive for more than two years.

ibid., pp. 398–9.

31. Although consistently opposed to the war, Rasputin was apparently not in German pay; no evidence has been found to support this charge against him.

loc. cit.

32. The secrecy which had been an essential part of the plans had been forgotten in the panic of this horrifying evening. But Yusupov had been right in anticipating that no real attempt would be made to charge or punish the assassins. All knew who they were, but the murder was condoned by the whole city. Grand Duke Dmitri was posted to the army in Persia. Yusupov was sent to his country estate. The other conspirators did not face criminal proceedings. Yusupov. *op. cit.*, pp. 148–82; Vyrubova, *op. cit.*, pp. 178–86.

33. Vyrubova, *op. cit.*, p. 186.

34. Rodzyanko, *op. cit.*, pp. 246–7.

35. Buchanan had cabled the foreign office in London for permission to speak openly to the emperor on behalf of the British government or personally and not as ambassador. In due course he was authorized to give a personal warning.

In the audience which took place at Tsarskoe Selo on 12 January 1917, Buchanan said: 'Your Majesty, if I may be permitted to say so, has but one safe course open to you—namely, to break down the barrier that separates you from your people and to regain their confidence.'

Drawing himself up and looking hard at him, the emperor asked: 'Do you mean that I am to regain the confidence of my people or that they are to regain my confidence?'

'Both, sir,' Buchanan replied, 'for without such mutual confidence, Russia will never win this war . . .'

Buchanan also referred to the fact that the empress was discredited and accused of working in German interests, and that Protopopov was bringing Russia 'to the verge of ruin. So long as he remains Minister of the Interior there cannot be that collaboration between the Government and the Duma which is an essential condition of victory.'

Buchanan, *op. cit.*, II, pp. 42–9.

36. Rodzyanko, *op. cit.*, pp. 252–4.

NOTES TO CHAPTER 6

1. The best description of the confusion and excitement in Petrograd at this time is by Sukhanov, *The Russian Revolution 1917*, edited, abridged, and translated by Joel Carmichael (London, 1956), pp. 1–5. But also see Kerensky, *op. cit.*, pp. 232–40.

2. Chamberlin, *op. cit.*, I, p. 76.

3. *ibid.*, p. 78.

4. *loc. cit.*

5. Petrograd was said to have borne the brunt of the fighting in the March revolution, and the revolt there was on the whole so easy and even good-natured that it is something of a surprise to learn that losses of life were estimated by the statistical department of the Petrograd city council at 1,315 killed, wounded, and injured, of whom 53 were officers, 602 were soldiers, 73 police, and 587 other citizens. Figures quoted by Chamberlin, *op. cit.*, I, p. 85.

6. Sukhanov, *op. cit.*, pp. 72–3.

7. For text of Order No. I, see Chamberlin, *op. cit.*, I, pp. 429–30.

8. Golder, *op. cit.*, pp. 308–10.

9. Pares, *op. cit.*, p. 469; Chamberlin, *op. cit.*, 1, p. 93.

10. Golder, *op. cit.*, pp. 298–9; Pares, *op. cit.*, pp. 469–70; cf. Chamberlin, *op. cit.*, I, pp. 94–5.

11. Subsequently Lloyd George, the British prime minister, disturbed by left-wing agitations in England against the ex-tsar, sent instructions to Buchanan to withdraw the offer of asylum or, in the phrase used, to inform the provisional government that the offer of asylum was no longer 'insisted on'.

Buchanan, distressed by this perfidious treatment of a man who had been a sincere ally and was now dethroned and rejected by his own people, had tears in his eyes as he delivered this verbal message to Tereshchenko, the new foreign minister.

M. R. Kerensky, *The Murder of the Romanovs* (London, 1935), pp. 116–18; Meriel Buchanan, *The Dissolution of an Empire* (London, 1932), pp. 196–9; Pares, *op. cit.*, pp. 475, 479; Chamberlin, *op. cit.*, II, p. 96; Kerensky, *op. cit.*, pp. 296, 316.

12. Golder, *op. cit.*, pp. 301–2.

13. Chamberlin, *op. cit.*, I, p. 112.

14. Quoted by Chamberlin, *op. cit.*, I, p. 116.

NOTES TO CHAPTER 7

1. Sukhanov, *op. cit.*, p. 270.

2. The famous 'sealed' carriage which transported Lenin from Berne was, of course, not sealed. The party of thirty-one, which included Lenin, Krupskaya, Inessa Armand, Zinoviev, Sokolnikov, and Karel Radek, occupied a special carriage with their own cook. The conditions under which they travelled, stipulated in writing by Lenin and accepted by the Germans, were that the party would be exempt from inspection of documents and luggage, and would in effect enjoy diplomatic privileges, except that they had the right only to transit and could not alight at any point before their destination. The German High Command was indeed as anxious to transport Lenin to Russia as Lenin was to return, for both parties had the same urgent purpose, namely to put an end to Russian participation in the war.

A detailed account of the negotiations which resulted in this journey is given in Louis Fischer, *op. cit.*, pp. 107–13. See also Michael Futtrel, *Northern Underground: Episodes of Russian Revolutionary Transport and Communications through Scandinavia and Finland 1863–1917* (London, 1963), pp. 154–7.

3. Agitation and slogans, 'Down with Lenin', 'Back to Germany', began to appear almost at once. Sukhanov wrote that 'On April 14th–16th (Old Style) all the papers carried a resolution of the immemorially revolutionary sailors of the Baltic Fleet crew who had been at the station as guard of honour: 'Having learnt that Comrade Lenin came back to us in Russia with the consent of His Majesty the German Emperor and King of Prussia [*sic*],' the

sailors wrote, 'we express our profound regret at our participation in his triumphal welcome to Petersburg. If we had known by what paths he had returned to us, then instead of the enthusiastic cries of "Hurrah", exclamations of indignation would have resounded: "Away with you, back to the country you have passed through to us".' Sukhanov, *op. cit.*, pp. 297–8.

4. *ibid.*, pp. 272–3.
5. *ibid.*, p. 276.
6. Schapiro, *op. cit.*, p. 162.
7. Golder, *op. cit.*, pp. 320–36.
8. Chamberlin, *op. cit.*, I, p. 151.
9. Sukhanov, *op. cit.*, p. 362.
10. *ibid.*, p. 368.
11. *ibid.*, p. 451.
12. *ibid.*, pp. 424–73.
13. The truth of the charges that Lenin and his colleagues were German agents has been furiously debated. Lenin, Zinoviev, and Kamenev vehemently denied it. The evidence released by the ministry of justice on 18 July depended on the testimony of two dubious witnesses. The first was Ermolenko, a former police agent, who had been captured by the Germans at the front and sent back to Russia to engage in sabotage. He reported that the Germans had told him that Lenin was one of their agents. The second witness was a merchant, Z. Burstein, who testified that in Stockholm a German espionage organization headed by Parvus (Helphand) passed money to the bolsheviks.

Parvus was a former social democrat who had been a member of the Petrograd soviet in 1905 and was closely associated with Lenin and Trotsky. During the war he became a highly successful financier. He was never really trusted by the German or the Russian social democrats; the latter in particular held it against him that he supported German war policy, but they made use of his services. Parvus was said to have contact with Lenin through Haniechi and Kozlovsky, a member of the party close to Lenin. Two letters from Lenin in April 1917 refer to money transactions with both men. Documents in the German foreign ministry show that from 1915 onwards the Germans were eager to subsidize revolutionaries in Russia and also that large sums were paid to Parvus. The German motive in paying these subsidies was the same as the bolshevik motive, namely to take Russia out of the war. Certainly at this time and in subsequent weeks the bolsheviks were spending lavishly on propaganda and on arming the Red Guard and they had no other known source of finance.

Any charge that, because Lenin was receiving money from the German government, he was obedient to their orders would seem untenable. Lenin was dedicated to the cause of revolution and, as he demonstrated repeatedly, he was ready to use any tactics to further this purpose. Acceptance of German money, which was treason in the eyes of most Russians at this time, was to him wholly justified. Moral laws had no relevance. As in 1904–5 he had tried to take advantage of schemes financed by the Japanese government to bring about the defeat of Russia in the Russo-Japanese war, so now he would not have hesitated to accept German aid to bring about a Russian defeat and withdrawal from the war. If charged with disloyalty to his native land, he would have replied that patriotism was bourgeois sentimentality and that his loyalty was to the toiling masses. Chamberlin, *op. cit.*, I, pp. 176–83; Schapiro, *op. cit.*, pp. 175–7; see also 'Lenin and Japanese Money' by Vadim Medish in *The Russian Review*, April 1965 (Vol. 24, No. 2). A fascinating study of Parvus appeared in 1965: (Z. A. B. Zeman and W. B. Scharlan),

The Merchant of Revolution: The Life of Alexander Israel Helphand (Parvus) 1867–1924 (London, 1965). See also M. Futtrel, *op. cit.*, p. 161 and *passim*.

14. Sukhanov, *op. cit.*, p. 290.

15. *ibid.*, p. 471.

16. The government made every effort to find Lenin, but he eluded them. He hid in a loft, belonging to a bolshevik labourer near Sestroretsk, some twenty miles from Petrograd. He moved then to a hut in a hayfield and was smuggled from there to Helsinki and thence to Vyborg in Finland. He remained in Vyborg, until the eve of the November revolution. Chamberlin, *op. cit.*, I, p. 183.

17. *ibid.*, I, p. 186.

18. *ibid.*, p. 199.

19. *ibid.*, p. 198.

20. Sukhanov, *op. cit.*, p. 536.

21. *loc. cit.*

22. Schapiro, *op. cit.*, p. 171.

23. *ibid.*, p. 167.

24. *ibid.*, p. 169; Chamberlin, *op. cit.*, I, p. 292.

25. The central committee at this meeting also appointed a Political Bureau or Politburo, intended to direct party affairs until the uprising. Its members were Lenin, Trotsky, Sokolnikov, Budnov, Zinoviev, and Kamenev. The inclusion of the two latter suggests that they were certainly not in disgrace for their strong and continued opposition to Lenin. The Politburo apparently failed to function, probably because Lenin himself, feeling that it did not support him completely, ignored it.

26. John Reed, *Ten Days that Shook the World* (New York, 1922), p. 337.

27. Sukhanov, *op. cit.*, p. 640.

28. Bruce Lockhart, *op. cit.*, p. 278.

NOTES TO CHAPTER 8

1. 'The State and Revolution', *Sochineniya Lenina*, 4th ed., Vol. 25, p. 457.

2. James Bunyan and H. H. Fisher, *The Bolshevik Revolution 1917–18 Documents and materials* (Stanford, 1934), p. 133.

3. Sukhanov, *op. cit.*, p. 628.

4. Bunyan and Fisher, *op. cit.*, pp. 125–8.

5. *ibid.*, pp. 128–32.

6. Lenin, *Sochineniya*, 4th ed., Vol. 26, p. 446.
This land decree of 8 November is usually hailed by Soviet and Western historians as 'a brilliant piece of political insight' and 'a masterpiece of political dexterity' (Chamberlin, *op. cit.*, I, p. 326). Such praise for a deliberate deception, misleading millions of peasants, may deserve such praise, but in this deception, which subsequently gave way to forced collectivization, were the roots of much of the suspicion which the Soviet peasants have continued to feel towards the central government, which has consistently failed to solve the agrarian problem.

7. Bunyan and Fisher, *op. cit.*, pp. 211–15.

8. Lenin at once wrote a manifesto damning them as 'those of little faith, all waverers and doubters who let themselves be frightened by the bourgeoisie' (Chamberlin, *op. cit.*, I, p. 352) and they were known thereafter as the 'waverers'.
This was an example of Lenin's talent for labelling and discrediting his opponents. They did not really merit the epithet of 'waverers', for like many in the socialist movement they believed in socialist unity and resigned on grounds of principle.

R

9. Bunyan and Fisher, *op. cit.*, pp. 282–3.
10. *ibid.*, pp. 298–9.
11. Lenin, *Sochineniya*, 4th ed., Vol. 35, pp. 137–8.
12. *ibid.*, pp. 304–16.
13. *ibid.*, p. 323.
14. *ibid.*, pp. 601–4.

At the close of 1917, the general state indebtedness was sixty billion rubles of which about one quarter was distributed as follows:

	million rubles		million rubles
England	7,500	U.S.A.	500
France	5,500	Japan	200
Germany	1,250	Switzerland	200
Holland	750	Italy	100

Bunyan and Fisher, *op. cit.*, pp. 601–4.
15. *ibid.*, pp. 285–98, 574–8.
16. *ibid.*, pp. 295–8. See also E. J. Scott, *The Cheka* (St Antony's Papers No. 1, London, 1956), for an interesting account.
17. Until 1 January 1700, Russia had calculated the years from the beginning of the world. Peter the Great introduced the Julian calendar which was eleven days behind the Gregorian calendar in the eighteenth century and thirteen days behind in the twentieth century. Peter was influenced by the fact that England used the Julian calendar at this time. Gregory XIII's calendar, introduced in 1582, was suspect to Protestant and Orthodox alike as a papist invention; it was not adopted in England until 1752, and it was the Gregorian calendar the Soviet government now introduced.
18. In the first weeks of their rule the bolsheviks treated the Orthodox church with tolerance, but this changed in January 1918. Church properties were requisitioned; state support for religious institutions and offices was withdrawn; chaplains were discharged from the armed services; church printing presses were seized. The church replied with protests, appeals, anathemas, and excommunications. The decree of 5 February, separating church and state, reaffirmed the right of freedom of conscience, but party supporters were encouraged to repudiate religion in all forms and to struggle actively against religion. Bunyan and Fisher, *op. cit.*, pp. 590–1.
19. *ibid.*, p. 361.
20. *ibid.*, p. 385.
21. *ibid.*, pp. 389–91.
22. *ibid.*, pp. 125–8.
23. J. W. Wheeler-Bennett, *Brest-Litovsk: The Forgotten Peace. March 1918* (London, 1938), pp. 126–7.
24. *ibid.*, p. 162.
25. *ibid.*, p. 192.
26. Bunyan and Fisher, *op. cit.*, p. 506.
27. Trotsky also repeated in this speech the ludicrous story that the Allies were in secret agreement with the Germans on the peace terms to be imposed on Russia.

Referring to Hoffmann's map, which he had brought with him from Brest-Litovsk, he said:

'The Allied Governments are responsible for these [terms]. London gave its tacit approval to Kuhlmann's terms. I declare this most emphatically. England is ready to compromise with Germany at the expense of Russia. The peace terms which Germany offers us are also the peace terms of America, France, and England . . .' (Bunyan and Fisher, *op. cit.*, p. 506).

Within a few days Trotsky was making contact with Allied representatives in Petrograd to enquire what aid they could offer the Soviet Government against a further German advance.
Wheeler-Bennett, *op. cit.*, pp. 251–2.
28. *ibid.*, p. 225.
29. *ibid.*, pp. 226–7.
30. Lenin, Trotsky, Stalin, Sverdlov, Sokolnikov, Zinoviev, and Smilga voted for the motion; Bukharin, Joffe, Lomov, Krestinsky, Dzerzhinsky, and Uritsky voted against it.
Bunyan and Fisher, *op. cit.*, pp. 512–13.
31. *ibid.*, pp. 517–19; Wheeler-Bennett, *op. cit.*, pp. 255–7.
32. Wheeler-Bennett, *op. cit.*, p. 257.
33. Jane Degras (ed.), *Soviet Documents on Foreign Policy*, I (London, 1951), pp. 50–5 for text of the treaty.
34. *ibid.*, pp. 49–50.

NOTES TO CHAPTER 9

1. Bunyan and Fisher, *op. cit.*, pp. 553–60.
2. Wheeler-Bennett, *op. cit.*, p. 277.
3. Bunyan and Fisher, *op. cit.*, pp. 528–9.
4. Lenin was, up to the moment when he mounted the platform to address the congress, ready to abandon his policy of ratification if he could secure firm guarantees of help from the Allies' governments against Germany and Japan. In February he had sent Kamenev to London and Paris to persuade the Western Allies to give such help, but Kamenev's mission had been a complete failure. Meanwhile Bruce Lockhart was urging the British government to help and Sadoul was imploring the French government to promise support, but their efforts were unavailing.
The U.S. ambassador, Francis, promised action, especially in preventing Japanese invasion of Siberia and the seizure of Vladivostok, but this, too, inspired no confidence and in the end brought no results. Lenin therefore mounted the platform and demanded ratification of the treaty.
Wheeler-Bennett, *op. cit.*, pp. 283–304; Bruce Lockhart, *op. cit.*, pp. 221–32.
5. Bunyan and Fisher, *op. cit.*, pp. 544–7.
6. *ibid.*, p. 530.
7. Nicholas Berdyaev maintained that, when the old consecrated Russian empire fell, the new one which was formed was also consecrated, an inverted theocracy. Marxism, itself so un-Russian in origin and character, assumed a Russian style approaching Slavophilism. Even the old Slavophiles' dream of transferring the capital from St Petersburg to Moscow, to the Kremlin, was realized by the Red communists, and Russian communism proclaimed anew the old idea of the Slavophiles and Dostoevsky—*ex Oriente lux.*
The messianic idea of Moscow the Third Rome was not achieved and a final cleavage in the idea took place between the apocalyptic and the revolutionary forms. Instead of the Third Rome in Russia the third International was achieved, and many of the features of the Third Rome passed to the third International, which was not international but a Russian national idea, and it represented a transformation of Russian messianism.
Nicholas Berdyaev, *The Origin of Russian Communism* (London, 1937), pp. 170–3. See also N. Zernov, *Moscow The Third Rome* (London, 1938), pp. 95–112.
8. Stalin, *Sochineniya*, Vol. IV (Moscow, 1946–8), pp. 6–14.
9. Bunyan and Fisher, *op. cit.*, pp. 419–20.

10. *ibid.*, pp. 426–7.

11. The Czechoslovak national council in Paris had made an agreement with the French government on 16 December 1917, placing the Czechoslovak legion under the French Supreme Command with the understanding that it would be transported to France to fight on the Western Front.

12. The bolshevik leaders maintained from the first that the Allied government had prepared and instigated the Czechoslovak revolt. Lenin himself stated: 'It has long been established that Anglo-French Imperialism took a direct and immediate part in the Czechoslovak Revolt.' Trotsky believed that French officers had actually directed the revolt.

Another of Lenin's allegations was that the Czechoslovaks who had then been fighting for over a month had been bought by Franco-British imperialists for fifteen million rubles and induced to rebel. But up to this time the Czechs had depended on Russian and Ukrainian credits. It is indeed clear that, far from being bought by the Allies, the Czechoslovaks received less support from them than from the Soviets. The Allies were in fact caught by surprise by the Czech revolt and they were slow to exploit it.

The Soviet allegations are effectively examined by J. F. N. Bradley in an article, 'The Allies and the Czech Revolt against the Bolsheviks in 1918' in the *Slavonic and East European Review*, XLIII, 101, June 1965.

13. David Footman, *The Civil War in Russia* (London, 1961), pp. 13–17.

14. Bunyan and Fisher, *op. cit.*, p. 569.

15. *ibid.*, pp. 572–4.

16. Quoted by Isaac Deutscher, *The Prophet Armed: Trotsky 1879–1921* (London, 1954), p. 408.

17. Bunyan and Fisher, *op. cit.*, pp. 569–71.

18. Footman, *op. cit.*, p. 139.

19. On 8 July 1919 the office of Extraordinary Plenipotentiary of the Council of Defence for the Supply of the Red Army was also established to deal with this serious problem.

From its earliest days the Soviet government has delighted in appointing such commissions and giving them long resounding titles.

20. James Bunyan, *Intervention, Civil War and Communism in Russia* (Baltimore, 1936), p. 428.

21. *ibid.*, p. 468.

22. *ibid.*, pp. 466–7.

23. *ibid.*, p. 469.

24. *ibid.*, pp. 476–9.

25. *ibid.*, pp. 472–3.

26. Chamberlin, *op. cit.*, II, p. 44.

27. This account of the fifth congress and of the attempted socialist revolutionary coup is based on the eye-witness account of Bruce Lockhart, *op. cit.*, pp. 292–302.

28. Bruce Lockhart, *op. cit.*, pp. 181–2. See also Savinkov's account of his career in *Memoirs of a Terrorist* (London, 1936).

29. Chamberlin, *op. cit.*, II, pp. 57–8.

30. *ibid.*, p. 59.

31. The bolshevik intention was to stage a trial of the tsar before a revolutionary tribunal, as Charles I and Louis XIV had been tried. Trotsky had cast himself in the role of chief prosecutor.

Trotsky stood firmly for evacuating the imperial family when Ekaterinburg was threatened, but the Politburo would not risk the possibility of their being rescued.

Deutscher, *The Prophet Armed*, p. 418.

32. It seems hardly possible that Anastasia could have escaped with her

life from this cellar. Yurovsky and his guards were thorough. They killed even the children's spaniel, and each body bore several wounds. But this period and Russian history in general abound in improbable and impossible events.

On 28 February 1967 the Court of Appeal in Hamburg rejected the claim of sixty-six-year-old Frau Anna Anderson to be recognized as Grand Duchess Anastasia, last surviving daughter of Nicholas II. Litigation, which has continued since 1933, will continue if the intention to appeal to the German Federal Supreme Court in Karlsruhe is implemented.

N. A. Sokolov, *Ubiistvo Tsarskoi Semi* (Berlin, 1925); P. M. Bykov, *The Last Days of the Tsardom* (London, 1937); Paul Bulygin, *The Murder of the Romanovs* (London, 1935); Pierre Gilliard, *Thirteen Years at the Russian Court: Last Years of Nicholas II*, translated from the French (London, 1921).

33. W. H. Chamberlin, whose history of the Russian revolution is still the leading study of the period, allows his republican bias to carry him away to the point that he is incapable of writing of the tsar with charity. His account of the end of Nicholas and his family, suggesting that their deaths were a kind of retribution for Jewish *pogroms* and for every massacre that occurred under the tsarist regime, is regrettable.

Chamberlin, *op. cit.*, II, pp. 84–95.

34. Bunyan, *op. cit.*, p. 502.

35. *ibid.*, pp. 507–24.

36. Maxim Gorky visited Lenin while he was convalescing and wrote subsequently:

'I came to him when he had hardly regained the use of his hand and could scarcely move his neck which had been shot through. When I expressed my indignation, he replied, as though dismissing something of which he was tired: "A brawl. Nothing to be done. Everyone acts according to his lights!"

'We met on very friendly terms, but of course there was evident pity in dear Ilyitch's sharp and penetrating glance, for I was one who had gone astray. After several minutes he said heatedly: "He who is not with us is against us. People independent of the march of events—that is a fantasy. Even if we grant that such people did exist once, at present they do not and cannot exist. They are no good to anyone. All, down to the last, are thrown into the whirl of an actuality which is more complicated than ever before. You say that I simplify life too much? That this simplification threatens culture with ruin, eh?" Then the ironic, characteristic "H'm, H'm . . ." His keen glance sharpened and he continued in a lower tone: ". . . You think the Constituent Assembly could have coped with that anarchy? You who make such a fuss about the anarchy of the country should be able to understand our tasks better than others. We have got to put before the Russian masses something they can grasp. The Soviets and Communism are simple." '

Gorky, *op. cit.*, pp. 39–40.

37. Fanya, sometimes Fanny or Dora, Kaplan was of the same breed as Maria Spiridovna. When a young girl under the tsarist regime she had been exiled to Siberia as an anarchist. Later she had become a right socialist revolutionary and a supporter of the constituent assembly.

After shooting Lenin she tried to escape but was captured and taken to the Lubyanka, the dreaded headquarters of the Cheka. Here she was seen by R. H. Bruce Lockhart, the British agent, who had also been arrested. He wrote:

'She was dressed in black. Her hair was black and her eyes, set in a fixed stare, had great black rings under them. Her face was colourless. Her

features, strongly Jewish, were unattractive . . . Her composure was un-
natural. She went to the window and, leaning her chin upon her hand,
looked out the window and into the daylight. And there she remained,
motionless, speechless, apparently resigned to her fate, until presently the
sentries came and took her away.' (Bruce Lockhart, *op. cit.*, p. 320.)

Fanya Kaplan was shot by the commandant of the Kremlin, Malkov, on
instructions of the Cheka on 3 September. Malkov's subsequent career was
obscure and he was pensioned off in 1936. His death was reported in the
Soviet press on 23 November 1965.

Angelica Balbanov, a Russian socialist and friend of Lenin, returned to
Russia from Stockholm and at once visited him in the rest house. She wrote:

'Only when the time came for me to leave did we refer to what had
happened to him and indirectly to the Terror that followed. When we
spoke of Dora Kaplan, the young woman who had shot him and who had
been executed, Krupskaya [Lenin's wife] became very upset. I could see
that she was deeply affected at the thought of revolutionaries condemned
to death by a revolutionary power. Later, when we were alone, she wept
bitterly when she spoke of this. Lenin himself did not care to enlarge upon
the episode.'

Balabanov, *op. cit.*, p. 209.
38. Bunyan, *op. cit.*, p. 240.
39. *ibid.*, p. 227.
40. *Memoirs of Ivanov-Razumnik*, translated by P. S. Squire (London,
1965), p. 29.
41. Chamberlin, *op. cit.*, II, p. 79.
42. Ivanov-Razumnik, a member of the revolutionary intelligentsia, was
not a member of any party, but had been closely associated with the left
socialist revolutionaries. He was arrested by the Cheka in February 1919, and
the detached irony and restraint of his account of his arrest, interrogation,
and imprisonment make the Terror more understandable in individual, as
distinct from mass, terms.
Memoirs of Ivanov-Razumnik, pp. 15–56.
43. Bunyan, *op. cit.*, p. 232.
44. Chamberlin, *op. cit.*, II, pp. 74–6.
45. Bunyan, *op. cit.*, pp. 283–4.
46. The main gold reserve of the former imperial government had been
evacuated from Petrograd to Samara to prevent it falling into the hands of
the Germans. The bolsheviks had moved it in barges to Kazan, when the
Czechoslovak legion threatened Samara, and on the capture of Kazan this
vast treasure of 650 million rubles in value came into the hands of the White
Russians. When the Red Army threatened, it was evacuated to Chelyabinsk,
thence to Omsk, and farther eastwards.
Bunyan, *op. cit.*, p. 292.
47. *ibid.*, pp. 283–4.
48. *ibid.*, pp. 333–4.
49. *ibid.*, pp. 340–66.
50. Mikhail Nikolayevich Tukhachevsky was to become one of the first
marshals of the Soviet Union and the leading military figure in the Soviet
Union until purged by Stalin in 1937.
Born into an impoverished noble family with estates in the Smolensk and
Ryazan provinces, Tukhachevsky developed broad intellectual and cultural
interests. Music was his great passion and he made violins as a hobby. He
attended an officers' training school, was commissioned in 1914 and posted

to the famous Semyonovsky Guards Regiment. He fought bravely in the first world war and, taken prisoner early in 1915, was held in the fortress of Ingolstadt where a French prisoner at the time was Captain Charles de Gaulle. He escaped in 1917 and returned to Russia on the eve of the October revolution. He joined the Soviet side and soon afterwards became a member of the communist party. A. I. Todorsky, *Marshal Tukhachevsky* (Moscow, 1965).

51. Bunyan, *op. cit.*, p. 301.

52. *ibid.*, p. 303.

53. Deutscher, *Stalin*, p. 203.

54. *ibid.*, p. 204.

55. Stalin, Voroshilov, and Budyonny claimed credit for this victory at Tsaritsyn. Trotsky's version, which was accepted by most Soviet generals until the purges in the 1930s, was that the victory belonged to the command of the southern front. Lenin apparently accepted Trotsky's version, for it was after the lifting of the siege of Tsaritsyn that Lenin yielded to Trotsky's demand for the recall of Stalin and gave him a free hand in dealing with Voroshilov whom he at once transferred to the Ukraine.

Trotsky's estimates of Voroshilov and Budyonny were not wide of the truth. Both men were dashing and successful leaders of partisan and cavalry units, but possessed neither the talent, experience, nor training to command an army. Both failed disastrously as commanders in the early months of the second world war and were promptly relieved of their commands.

Deutscher, *Stalin*, pp. 204–5; L. Trotsky, *Stalin*, 2nd ed. (New York, 1946), pp. 288–305.

56. On 4 October the party central executive committee on Lenin's instigation adopted a resolution 'that Soviet Russia will offer all its forces and resources to aid the German revolutionary government. The all-Russian central executive committee has no doubt that the French, English, American, and Japanese proletariat will be in the same camp as Soviet Russia and revolutionary Germany.' Bunyan, *op. cit.*, pp. 151–2.

57. Sir Charles Maynard, the British general commanding, has in his account of 'The Murmansk Venture' explained the purpose of the intervention as directed entirely against the Germans.

C. Maynard, *The Murmansk Venture* (London, 1928), pp. 1–9.

58. Britain, fearing a Turco-German advance through the Caucasus into Afghanistan and India, had hurriedly improvised plans to bar the way. In January 1918 a small force, commanded by Major-General Dunsterville, and known as Dunsterforce, set out from Baghdad for the Caspian with the purpose of securing the road and investigating the conditions in Baku.

The second British mission, commanded by Major-General W. Malleson, left Quetta in June 1918 and reached Meshed in mid-July. Its purpose was to keep a watch on developments in Transcaucasia and to stop enemy agents finding their way to Afghanistan and Baluchistan, and to prepare against a Turkish advance.

Both military missions were defensive in character and of very minor importance. Soviet propaganda has, however, inflated them into the first stages of a long-term Anglo-American capitalist plot to take possession of Transcaucasia and Transcaspia.

Major-General L. C. Dunsterville in *Adventures of Dunsterforce* (London, 1921) has given a lively account of his mission and of the short occupation of Baku in August 1918.

An authoritative and fascinating account of the Malleson Mission is given by Colonel C. H. Ellis, who was a member of the mission, in *The Transcaspian Episode* (London, 1963). He also gives the most acceptable account of the shooting of the twenty-six bolshevik commissars in Ashkhabad in September 1918, which Soviet propaganda has magnified as a British atrocity.

59. Degras, *op. cit.*, I, pp. 137-9.

60. Elena Varneck and H. H. Fisher, *The Testimony of Kolchak and other Siberian Materials* (Stanford, 1935); Peter Fleming, *The Fate of Admiral Kolchak* (London, 1963).

61. The British units in North Russia had no information on Kolchak's plans, but they knew of the vague talk that the White forces from Siberia should join with them in an offensive on Moscow.

Lord Ironside, then Chief of Staff to the commander-in-chief of the Allied Forces in North Russia with headquarters in Archangel, wrote in his diary of the many rumours, following the victory of the Siberian army in Perm: 'To have received a destitute Czech corps of 70,000 men [*sic*] in our northern region in the depths of winter would have constituted a formidable problem.'

Ironside (Lord), *Archangel* (London, 1953), p. 89; Maynard, *op. cit.*

62. Nestor Makhno, born into a poor peasant family in the southern Ukraine, became an anarchist at the time of the 1905 Revolution. In 1907 at the age of eighteen he was sentenced to life imprisonment for helping to murder a police officer and he was in prison in Moscow until March 1917. During the civil war he led a wild insurgent army of peasants, who fought with ferocity against Austrians and White forces and, after a period of alliance with the Red Army in 1919-20, against the bolsheviks. A man of tremendous energy, courage, cunning, and capable of great cruelty, he was the hero of the peasants. In 1921 he was finally defeated by the Red Army. He escaped into Rumania and thence into Poland, and eventually to Paris where he died, ill and destitute, in 1935.

Footman, *op. cit.*, pp. 245-302.

63. Footman, *op. cit.*, pp. 236-42; Fleming, *op. cit.*, pp. 193-217.

64. A. I. Denikin, although of humble birth, achieved high rank. He was an able general, but he lacked any understanding or sympathy for the peasants, whom he antagonized by restoring the estates to the landlords in regions under his control. After his final defeat by the Red Army he escaped into Turkey, thence to Belgium, France, and finally to the United States where he died.

For his account of his life see *The Russian Turmoil* (London, 1922); *The White Army* (London, 1924), *Put' Russkovo Offitsera* (New York, 1953).

65. P. N. Wrangel finally escaped to Belgium where he died in 1928. *Always with Honour* (New York, 1958) contains his own account of his career.

66. Chamberlin, *op. cit.*, II, p. 320.

NOTES TO CHAPTER 10

1. *Izvestiya*, 13 July 1919. Quoted by Chamberlin, *op. cit.*, II, p. 348.

2. Jane Degras, (ed.) *The Communist International 1919-43 Documents* I (London, 1956), p. 17.

The first International, comprising the socialist and anarchist groups, had been formed in 1864 and had dissolved in 1876. The second International, comprising socialist and labour parties, had been founded in 1889 and had lapsed into inactivity. The international socialist conference, held in Berne in February 1919, had sought to recreate the second International. The Moscow congress denounced and repudiated the Berne congress.

3. One participant wrote subsequently that most of the delegates 'had been handpicked by the Russian central committee from so-called Com-

munist parties in these smaller nations which had formerly comprised the Russian Empire . . . or they were war-prisoners or foreign radicals who happened to be in Russia at the time.' *ibid.*, p. 6.

4. The manifesto of the second world congress of the Communist International declared, *inter alia*, that:

'The struggle for Soviet Russia has merged with the struggle against world imperialism. The question of Soviet Russia has become the touchstone by which all the organizations of the working class are tested . . . The Communist International has proclaimed the cause of Soviet Russia as its own. The world proletariat will not sheathe its sword until Soviet Russia is one member in the World Federation of Soviet Republics . . .'

ibid., p. 177.

5. For the text of the twenty-one conditions, see *ibid.*, pp. 166–72.

6. Chamberlin, *op. cit.*, II, p. 293.

7. Antonov escaped capture for some months. But Cheka officials knew that they could count on him returning to his homelands. On 24 June 1922 they found him and his brother hiding in a house in a village in the Borisoglebsk district of the province. They surrounded the house, set it on fire, and shot the Antonovs as they tried to escape. *ibid.*, p. 439.

8. The output of small, rural and artisan industry was in 1920 just over a quarter of the output of 1912, but by 1921 it had risen to 35 per cent and 1922 to 54 per cent of the 1912 output.

On the other hand large-scale industry had in 1920 fallen to 15 per cent of the 1912 level and had in 1921 reached only 17 per cent and 1922 to 20 per cent of 1912 production. Carr, *op. cit.*, p. 310.

9. *KPSS v rezolyutsiyakh*, Vol. I (Moscow, 1953), pp. 517–27 and 534–49.

10. Schapiro, *op. cit.*, p. 211.

11. By the beginning of 1922, 136,386 members had been purged: 11 per cent were said to have been guilty of 'refusing to carry out party directives' and they undoubtedly included many actual and potential members of the opposition; 34 per cent were expelled for 'passivity'; 25 per cent were guilty of drunkenness, careerism, and bourgeois modes of life; 9 per cent were guilty of extortion, bribe-taking, etc.; nearly 5 per cent of those expelled were former members of other parties.

Schapiro, *op. cit.*, p. 232.

12. *Dokumenti Vneshnei Politiki C.C.C.R.*, V. (Moscow, 1961), pp. 233–4 for the text of the treaty.

13. A. A. Lipatov and others (editors), *Istoriya Sovetskoi Konstitutsii v Dokumentakh* (Moscow, 1957), pp. 390–1.

14. *ibid.*, pp. 392–8.

15. *ibid.*, pp. 142–57.

16. *ibid.*, pp. 460–1.

17. *ibid.*, p. 462.

18. *ibid.*, p. 463.

19. *ibid.*, p. 465.

20. *ibid.*, p. 467.

21. Chapter 2, Clause 4 reads: 'The right of free secession from the Union is guaranteed to each of the Union Republics.' *ibid.*, p. 462.

22. Stalin, *Sochineniya* (Moscow, 1946), Vol. IV, pp. 30–7.

23. The first qualification proposed a federal union of states, organized on the Soviet model, 'as one of the transitional forms on the path to complete unity.' The second qualification declared that on the issue of secession the decision as to who was to be regarded as the bearer of the will of the nation

must be taken 'according to the stage of historical development of that nation'.
KPSS v. rezolyutsiyakh, 7th ed. (Moscow, 1953), I, p. 417.

NOTES TO CHAPTER 11

1. E. H. Carr, *The Interregnum 1923–24* (London, 1954), pp. 258–9.
2. *loc. cit.*
3. *loc. cit.*
4. *ibid.*, p. 262.
5. *ibid.*, p. 263.
6. *ibid.*, p. 264.
7. *ibid.*, pp. 265–6; Deutscher, *The Prophet Unarmed. Trotsky 1921–29* (London, 1959), p. 90.
8. *ibid.*, p. 342; according to Isaac Deutscher, *loc. cit.*, Lenin only 'threatened' to 'break off all personal relations', but Trotsky refers to the 'severance of all personal and comradely relations with Stalin'.
L. Trotsky, *Moya Zhizn* (Berlin, 1930), I, p. 375.
In the text of Lenin's letter, read out by Khrushchev to the 20th party congress in the secret session on 25 February 1956, the sentence is as follows:
' I ask you, therefore, that you weigh carefully whether you are agreeable to retracting your words and apologizing or whether you prefer the severance of relations between us.'
The Anti-Stalin Campaign and International Communism, edited by the Russian Institute, Columbia University (New York, 1956).
9. *loc. cit.*
10. The Russian communist party had been founded at the congress meeting in Minsk on 13 March 1898.
11. Balabanov, *op. cit.*, p. 244.
12. *ibid.*, pp. 243–4.
13. Sukhanov, *op. cit.*, p. 230.
14. L. Trotsky, *Chto i kak proizoshlo* (Paris, 1929), p. 25.
15. L. Trotsky, *Moya Zhizn* (Berlin, 1930), I, p. 311.
16. Carr, *op. cit.*, p. 296.
17. *loc. cit.*
18. *loc. cit.*
19. *ibid.*, pp. 367–73 for the text of this Platform; Deutscher, *op. cit.*, pp. 113–15. Whether or to what extent Trotsky was the direct sponsor of the Platform of the 46 is uncertain.
20. *loc. cit.*
21. *loc. cit.*
22. *ibid.*, p. 301.
23. *loc. cit.*
24. During the anxious weeks before Lenin's severe stroke in March 1923, Trotsky was confined to bed with an attack of lumbago. But late in October 1923 he went duck-shooting and caught a chill which gave rise to what he called 'a dogged, mysterious infection the nature of which still remains a mystery to my physicians'. The intermittent fever continued into January 1924 when he set out for the Caucasus to recuperate. One cannot but suspect that anxiety over Lenin's health and his own future in the party contributed to his ill-health.
Trotsky, *op. cit.*, II, pp. 220, 234, 238; Trotsky, *Stalin* (New York, 1946), p. 381.
25. In this speech Zinoviev evidently coined the word 'Trotskyism' which was to become part of the Soviet vocabulary of abuse and condemnation.

Carr, *op. cit.*, p. 317.

26. *ibid.*, p. 339.

27. The announcement of Lenin's death was followed by a flurry of rumours that he had asked for poison, that he believed that he had been poisoned, and that he revealed before his death that he was dying of poison. Trotsky suggested that Stalin may have poisoned Lenin. Stalin certainly had ample motive and opportunity, but it seems likely on the known evidence that Lenin died of natural causes.

Trotsky, *op. cit.*, pp. 372–8, 380–1.

28. Stalin, *Sochineniya* (Moscow, 1947), Vol. VI, pp. 46–51; see also Carr, *op. cit.*, pp. 347–8.

29. The absence of Trotsky was conspicuous. He had left Moscow a few days earlier and had received the news of Lenin's death in Tiflis in a code message from Stalin on the evening of 21 January. On the following day he telegraphed Moscow to ask when the funeral would take place. Stalin replied that it would be on Saturday, 26 January. This would not have allowed time for him to reach Moscow, for the journey from Tiflis took four days. In fact, the funeral was on 27 January and Trotsky might just have arrived in time. Trotsky alleged that Stalin misinformed him deliberately so that he could not participate.

Trotsky, *Moya Zhizn*, II, pp. 249–51; Deutscher, *op. cit.*, p. 133.

30. Lenin was not closely associated with the city that bears his name and lived there for only a few short periods. The city indeed remains peculiarly the city of Peter who created it as a gateway to Western Europe. He stamped it permanently with his ideas and personality and, to this author, it is still St Petersburg or Petrograd.

Grey, *Peter the Great* (New York, 1960), pp. 220–8, 436–9.

31. Krupskaya was strongly opposed to this apotheosizing of Lenin and in this she undoubtedly reflected his own strong feelings. In a letter of thanks for the innumerable expressions of sympathy which she received on the death of Lenin, Krupskaya wrote:

'I have a great request to you: do not allow your mourning for Ilich to take the form of external reverence for his person. Do not raise memorials to him, palaces named after him, solemn festivals in commemoration of him, etc.: to all this he attached so little importance in his life, all this was so burdensome to him. Remember how much poverty and neglect there still is in our country. If you wish to honour the name of Vladimir Ilich, build crêches, kindergartens, houses, schools, libraries, medical centres, hospitals, homes for the disabled, etc., and, most of all, let us put his precepts into practice.'

The letter was printed in *Pravda* on 30 January 1924, but the forms of external reverence for the person of Lenin were already multiplying and developing into a mighty cult.

Carr, *op. cit.* p. 349.

32. Lenin could be kind, encouraging, and thoughtful towards colleagues, but his occasional acts of kindness were usually calculated. Writing to one colleague concerning the electrification of the R.S.F.S.R., he expressed his delight, especially as 'I swore madly at you (almost to an outrageous degree)' over an earlier incident. 'Write another [book] after a thorough rest ... Greetings and congratulations on your magnificent success.'

Lenin, *Letters* of, p. 473.

NOTES TO CHAPTER 12

1. Lenin had proposed in the testament that his views should be considered by the next, i.e. the eleventh congress. It was accepted, however, that Krupskaya knew his true wishes. Nevertheless, disliking Stalin as a man and fully sharing Lenin's misgivings that he was dangerous in high office, Krupskaya was undoubtedly anxious to bring Stalin down. She was to demonstrate this again in the coming months.

2. L. Trotsky, *The Suppressed Testament of Lenin*, with two explanatory articles (New York, 1935), pp. 11–14, 17.

3. According to Stalin, he offered his resignation to the central committee immediately after the congress. But the central committee, including Trotsky, insisted that he should retain his offices. If this is true, it offers yet another example of Trotsky's strange conduct. Most members of the central committee, including in particular Trotsky, Zinoviev, and Kamenev, were soon to regret their support of Stalin.
Stalin, *Sochineniya* (Moscow, 1949), Vol. X, pp. 175–6.

4. Carr, *op. cit.*, p. 362.

5. Certain delegates present were taken aback by Zinoviev's demand for recantation. Krupskaya without taking Trotsky's part, made a dignified protest against Zinoviev's 'psychologically impossible demand'. This did not, however, hold the congress from condemning Trotsky for his refusal to recant.
Deutscher, *The Prophet Unarmed*, pp. 138–40.

6. Carr, *op. cit.*, p. 265.

7. Towards the end of 1923 the central committees of the French and Polish parties had protested strongly against these attacks on Trotsky. Moscow had ignored their protests.
Deutscher, *op. cit.*, pp. 140–1.

8. The exception was the French delegate Boris Souvarine, editor of *L'Humanité*, who spoke up for Trotsky and reported that the central committee of the French communist party had decided by 22 votes to 2 to protest against these attacks on Trotsky.
Deutscher, *op. cit.*, p. 146.

9. E. H. Carr, *Socialism in one Country 1924–26*, Vol. II (London, 1959), p. 17.

10. Trotsky in fact prepared a 54-page memorandum with the title *The Purpose of this Explanation* which was intended for eventual publication, but it remained among his papers and was found after his death.
Carr, *op. cit.*, pp. 28–9.

11. Although the production of grain had risen and in 1926–7 was above the production for 1913, the proportion finding its way to the market had fallen. The bulk of the grain had before the war come from the large estates of landowners and kulaks, but now it came from the middle and poor peasants, who were eating more and leaving less for the market.
Schapiro, *op. cit.*, p. 339.

12. Deutscher, *Stalin*, p. 301.

13. The three categories of poor, middle, and prosperous peasants were never precisely defined. Judging by the size and distribution of farms, those between 15 and 27 acres comprised about half and farms greater than 27 acres comprised some two-fifths of all the land. The remaining one-tenth comprised holdings less than 15 acres.
The middle peasants, forming 66·8 per cent of the village population, were the backbone of the farming system and were moderately well off. The

poor peasants, comprising 21·1 per cent, had farms too small and poor to maintain a family.

The prosperous peasants or kulaks—the word means literally 'a fist'—were a vague category, said to comprise 3·9 per cent. Under the tsarist regime they had been certain of the richest members of the commune who through money-lending and mortgages had held the poorer members in their grip. Under the Soviet regime up to 1928 they were the prosperous peasants, owning the larger farms with animals and equipment, who, while working the land themselves, hired labour and leased further land. They were, in short, the most efficient, hardworking, and well off of the farmers.

Schapiro, *op. cit.*, pp. 336–7.

14. Carr, *op. cit.*, p. 136.
15. *ibid.*, p. 137.
16. *ibid.*, p. 138.
17. *ibid.*, p. 138.
18. *ibid.*, p. 139.
19. *ibid.*, p. 140.
20. *ibid.*, p. 42.
21. Eastman had obtained the text of the testament from a reliable source, either Trotsky himself or Krupskaya, for it had not been published in the Soviet Union and was known only among senior party members.

The denial of the truth of this account by both Trotsky and Krupskaya, both of whom knew it to be true, is more difficult to understand. Trotsky's explanation three years later was that he had been forced to make the denial by the Politburo and by the opposition who wanted an end to the conflict. Krupskaya who since Lenin's death had been constantly persecuted by Stalin probably acted under the same pressure. In the case of Trotsky, however, one suspects that it would have required more than pressure to make him issue a deliberate mis-statement; it is more probable that he considered that he was serving the interests of the party by avoiding a major split.

Deutscher, *op. cit.*, pp. 201–2; Carr, *op. cit.*, pp. 64–5.

22. Krupskaya later explained that she had defected from the opposition side because it had carried its criticisms too far and was endangering the party and the regime.

Before her defection, however, she took care to arrange for Lenin's testament to be transmitted to foreign communists, and both testament and its postscript were published in the *New York Times* on 19 October 1926, a week before the fifteenth conference opened.

Schapiro, *op. cit.*, p. 302.

23. Merle Fainsod, *How Russia is Ruled* (Harvard, 1963), p. 181; Schapiro, *op. cit.*, p. 317.

24. Sergii's proclamation was condemned by many churchmen as a cowardly capitulation and even an act of apostasy. He had, it was suggested, been suborned during his months in prison in 1926–7. Others defended his proclamation as an act of great statesmanship which preserved the episcopacy and enabled the church to survive.

William C. Fletcher, *A Study in Survival: The Church in Russia 1927–1943* (London, 1965), pp. 28–37.

25. Fletcher, *op. cit.*, pp. 46–7.

The text of the decree is given in *International Conciliation* (Documents: Carnegie Endowment for International Peace), 1930, pp. 303–17.

26. The high suicide rate among party members sheds an interesting sidelight on the times. Of all members who died in the first quarter of 1925, 14·1 per cent were suicides, and of candidate members 11·9 per cent were suicides.

Many of these had probably suffered beyond endurance during the war and the civil war and were reduced to taking their lives. But many suffered from sheer disillusionment over the failure of the revolution which, they had believed, was the harbinger of a new age.

Schapiro, *op. cit.*, p. 310 note.

27. Stalin had the votes of Molotov, Kuibyshev, Rudzutak, and Voroshilov which with his own vote gave him a majority. For some reason Bukharin thought he could secure the vote of Voroshilov, who had been Stalin's close associate since the time of the civil war when they had stood together against Trotsky. Kalinin was the other uncertain vote, but when the time came he voted with Stalin. Of the eight candidate members all except Uglanov were Stalin's men.

Schapiro, *op. cit.*, pp. 362, 670; Deutscher, *Stalin*, p. 312.

28. Schapiro, *op. cit.*, p. 364, quoting S. C. Strumilin in *Planovoe Khoziaistvo*, No. 7, 1927, p. 11.

29. B. Souvarine, *Stalin* (London ed.), p. 485.

30. Kamenev made a record of this conversation which later came into the hands of supporters of Trotsky. They had the record printed clandestinely and circulated in Moscow. This was to prove a weapon in Stalin's hands in the elimination of Bukharin.

Schapiro, *op. cit.*, pp. 364–6.

NOTES TO CHAPTER 13

1. *History of the C.P.S.U.* (Moscow, 1946), p. 291.

2. Naum Jasny, *The Socialized Agriculture of the U.S.S.R.* (Stanford, 1949), p. 30.

3. Deutscher, *op. cit*, p. 319; Stalin, *Voprosy Leninizma* (Moscow, 1939), p. 242.

4. Kolkhoz is an abbreviation for the Russian name for collective farm, which is a special kind of co-operative. A kolkhoz usually embraces several villages, and the inhabitants, pooling their land and labour, are rewarded according to results. The kolkhoz makes heavy deliveries of produce at prices fixed by the state, and these deliveries take the place of taxes. In fact, kolkhozi are under the direction of the party and the government, who appoint the kolkhoz chairmen.

For a thorough examination of the kolkhoz system, see Jasny, *op. cit.*, chapters XIII–XVI.

5. Gosplan, the Russian abbreviation for the State Planning Commission, was set up in 1921 to plan and co-ordinate the economic activities of the state. Groman and others who had drafted the first five-year plan, setting conservative targets for production to avoid disrupting the economy, were strongly criticized by the party leadership and replaced. Jasny, *op. cit.*, pp. 304–5.

6. Stalin, *Sochineniya*, Vol. 12 (Moscow, 1949), p. 169.

7. *ibid.*, pp. 191–9.

8. The few individual peasants who remained outside the kolkhozi and who were not declared to be kulaks were left alone after the initial drive for collectivization. But they were victimized and their lives became exceedingly difficult. They had to pay higher taxes and deliver more of their produce to the state, and they suffered in other ways.

Jasny, *op. cit.*, pp. 308–9, 312–13.

9. *ibid.*, p. 323.

10. John Scott, *Behind the Urals* (London, 1942), pp. 58–9, 76, and *passim*.

11. Maurice Dobb, *Soviet Economic Development since 1917* (London, 1948), pp. 255–60.

12. Remarkable as this achievement was, it was gained mainly by drawing on the experience and advanced technologies of the industrialized countries of the West, and especially the United States.

An interesting feature of the informal relations existing between the U.S.A. and the U.S.S.R.—the American government had not yet accorded diplomatic recognition to the Soviet Union—was the arrangement whereby American companies gave of their experience, patents, and engineers to help in Soviet economic reconstruction.

Naum Jasny, *Soviet Industrialization 1928–52* (Chicago, 1961), pp. 97–9; see also Wladimir Naleszkiewicz, 'Technical Assistance of American Enterprises to the Growth of the Soviet Union 1929–32' in *The Russian Review*, January 1966.

13. The total number of American industrial and agricultural experts, engineers, and mechanics employed in Soviet territory from 1928 to 1933 was probably about 2,000.

Hundreds of Soviet students and engineers studied in the U.S.A. in the 1930s and returned to their country to act as instructors and leaders of industry. Naleszkiewicz, *op. cit.*; W. H. Chamberlin in *The Soviet Planned Economic Order* (Boston, 1931), p. 82.

Estimates of the number of foreign specialists engaged in Russia during the first five-year plan vary. On 25 February 1930, Molotov stated that 850 foreign experts and 550 foreign skilled workers were employed in Soviet factories. He added, 'Most of these came from Germany. The recruiting of new workers from Germany and also from America will be increased in the future.' In March 1931 a director of the Supreme Council of National Economy stated that 'about 5,000 foreign specialists and workmen were then employed in Soviet industry'.

Max Beloff, *The Foreign Policy of Soviet Russia 1929–1941*, Vol. I (London, 1947), p. 31 note.

14. Beloff, *op. cit.*, p. 32.

15. League of Nations, *World Economic Survey 1932–33*, p. 72 note; Beloff, *op. cit.*, p. 30.

16. Stalin, *Sochineniya*, Vol. 13 (Moscow, 1951), pp. 38–9. This speech reversed the bolshevik anti-nationalist interpretation of Russian history by which tsarist Russia had been depicted as the oppressor of weaker nations. The anti-nationalist conception was expressed most fully by the historian, M. N. Pokrovsky, but in 1934–6 he was officially disowned and stated to have been in error. The historian, B. D. Grekov, representing the national bolshevik interpretation of Russian history, succeeded him. This nationalist conception was to reach a climax in the second world war.

C. E. Black (ed.), *Rewriting Russian History* (New York, 1956). See also Chapter 21.

17. Another report holds that Stalin murdered his wife. See Boris I. Nikolaevsky, *Power and the Soviet Elite*, edited by Janet D. Zagoria, London, 1966, p. 73.

A. Barmine, *One who Survived* (New York, 1945), p. 264; V. Serge, *Portrait de Stalin* (Paris, 1940), pp. 94–5.

18. W. G. Krivitsky, *I was Stalin's Agent* (London, 1939), pp. 203, 296–7; Schapiro, *op. cit.*, p. 392 note.

Krivitsky was a trusted officer in Soviet military intelligence who defected after the terror had begun. His account is exciting, especially his final escape to the U.S.A. He closes with an account of his evasion of 'Stalin's long arm of vengeance' in New York. But he died in Washington in 1941 in circumstances which suggest that Stalin's agents struck again and this time with effect. Much of the information in his account has been confirmed by subsequent official statements.

19. The Politburo in 1932 comprised Stalin, Kaganovich, Voroshilov, Kalinin, Kirov, Kossior, Kuibyshev, Molotov, Ordzhonikidze, and Rudzutak. The group which opposed Stalin on this issue probably included Kirov, Kossior, Rudzutak, Ordzhonikidze, and Kuibyshev.

Kirov was to be assassinated, possibly on Stalin's orders. Kossior was shot. Kuibyshev was said to have died from a heart attack, but the circumstances surrounding his death have aroused suspicion of murder.

Krivitsky, *op. cit.*, pp. 205–8; Schapiro, *op. cit.*, p. 393.

20. T. Szamuely, 'The Elimination of Opposition between the 16th and 17th Congresses of the C.P.S.U.' in *Soviet Studies*, January 1966, Vol. XVII, No. 3. An excellent paper to which I acknowledge my indebtedness.

21. The eastward movement of industry began in the first plan period and was a feature of the two subsequent plans. For political reasons people, tainted with local nationalism, may have been transferred from the Ukraine to the new industrial centres to the east. There is evidence of Ukrainians moving to other parts of Russia and of Great Russians moving into the Ukraine to work in the expanding industries there.

Beloff, *op. cit.*, p. 37 and note; W. E. D. Allen, *The Ukraine* (Cambridge, 1940), pp. 324–30, 362–70.

22. Schapiro, *op. cit.*, p. 398.

23. Khrushchev in his secret speech to the twentieth party congress on 25 February 1956. See *The Anti-Stalin Campaign and International Communism* edited by the Russian Institute, Columbia University (New York, 1956), pp. 22–3.

NOTES TO CHAPTER 14

1. The Soviet constitution of 6 July 1923 in its introductory Declaration described the position as follows:

'Since the time of the formation of the Soviet republics the states of the world have been divided into two camps: the camp of capitalism and the camp of socialism.

There—in the camp of capitalism—national enmity and inequality, colonial slavery and chauvinism, national oppression and pogroms, imperialist brutalities and war.

Here—in the camp of socialism—mutual confidence and peace, national freedom and equality, peaceful coexistence and the brotherly collaboration of peoples.'

D. A. Gaiduk and others, *History of the Soviet Constitution 1917–1957* Collected documents (Moscow, 1957), p. 226; Beloff, *op. cit.*, I, p. 2.

2. The treaties and subsequent trade agreements were made by the R.S.F.S.R. The U.S.S.R., when established in December 1922, took over the treaties as part of its overriding responsibility for foreign affairs.

3. The first Russo-German agreement was concluded on 19 April 1920 and dealt with the repatriation of prisoners of war and civilians. This agreement was on 6 May 1921 extended to embrace trade between the two countries.

4. Of the numerous Soviet notes, the reply of 27 September to Lord Curzon's note alleging violations of the Anglo-Soviet Treaty is typical.

Degras, (ed.) *Soviet Documents on Foreign Policy*, I, pp. 257–62.

5. *ibid.*, pp. 396–403.

6. During this peaceful coexistence, however, so the party confidently asserted, the contradictions between the two camps would not weaken, but would grow.
KPSS v rez. Vol. II, p. 74; Schapiro, *op. cit.*, p. 353.

7. E. H. Carr, *Socialism in one Country*, Vol. III, Pt. I (London, 1964), p. 9.

8. This agreement replaced the agreement signed on 16 March 1921. Article 16, which was to be much quoted in the subsequent exchanges, contained a firm undertaking by each party to refrain from hostile propaganda or subversive action against the other.
For text of this and the other main articles, see Degras, *op. cit.*, pp. 453–7.

9. The Zinoviev letter remains a mystery. Its authenticity is unproven. Rakovsky on behalf of his government dismissed it as 'a gross forgery and an audacious attempt to prevent the development of friendly relations between the two countries' (*ibid.*, pp. 471–2).
The original was never produced, but the official explanation was that it had been obtained through secret service sources. If this was so, it would be expected that it would have been exclusively in official hands, but copies reached the *Daily Mail* newspaper and conservative party headquarters at the same time, if not earlier, than the copy reached the foreign office. The release of the letter by the foreign office was complicated by certain anomalies in procedure. Moreover, the text of the letter was inaccurate in some of its details and strangely uncharacteristic in some of its wording. There are, in fact, good grounds for regarding it as a forgery, produced by a group of White Russian émigrés in Berlin.
On 18 December 1966 the London *Sunday Times* published the disclosures of a Madame Prina Bellegarde, the widow of one of a group of White Russians, then in Berlin, who in response to the request of 'a person of authority in London' concocted the letter. In subsequent correspondence in the British press, this account was questioned, but it seems acceptable, in spite of certain mysteries still unresolved, surrounding the letter.
A fuller account of the incident is to be found in Arnold Toynbee, *Survey of International Affairs 1924* (London, 1928), pp. 247–50, which in Appendix VI, pp. 493–5, gives the English text of the letter.

10. Degras, *op. cit.*, II, pp. 118–19.

11. *ibid.*, pp. 202–8.

12. Arnold Toynbee, *Survey of International Affairs 1934* (London, 1935), pp. 368–70.

13. Beloff, *op. cit.*, p. 33.

14. The chief countries which withheld *de jure* recognition were Spain, Portugal, Holland, Belgium, Switzerland, the Little Entente, Bulgaria, and Hungary. In Asia, China had broken off relations when the Kuomintang purged itself of its communist wing. Of the countries of North and South America, Mexico and Uruguay alone had accorded recognition.
ibid., pp. 5–6.

15. *Political Report to the 16th Party Congress* (London, 1930), p. 32; Beloff, *op. cit.*, p. 28.

16. Beloff, *op. cit.*, pp. 27–8.

17. Victor A. Yakhontoff, *Russia and the Soviet Union in the Far East* (London, 1932), pp. 144–5.

18. Beloff, *op. cit.*, p. 78.

19. *ibid.*, p. 173.

20. U.S. exports to Russia in 1924 amounted to $42·1 million and imports from Russia were $8·2 million; in 1930 these figures were respectively $114·4 million and $24·4 million.

In 1932 U.S. exports dropped to $12·5 million and imports from Russia to $9·1 million.
U.S. official statistics, quoted by Beloff, *op. cit.*, pp. 119–20.
21. Of U.S.A.–Soviet relations after 1933, Sumner Welles, the former American under-secretary of state, wrote:

'Unfortunately the supervision of Soviet-American relations in Washington and Moscow was largely entrusted by this [the U.S.A.] government to men who proved incapable and unsympathetic to the task of bettering the ties between the two countries . . .'

Sumner Welles, *The Time for Decision* (New, York 1944), p. 246.
22. Beloff, *op. cit.*, pp. 95–6 note.
23. *ibid.*, p. 97.
24. Bukharin and others, mainly old bolsheviks, did not share the ruthless logic of Stalin's outlook. They would have preferred alliance with the more civilized imperialists and capitalists rather than with the barbarous and belligerent nazis. At the seventeenth party congress in January 1934 Bukharin made a fierce attack on Hitler. If a policy of alliance with Germany had been proposed at this time, it would probably have met with resistance within the party.
Schapiro, *op. cit.*, p. 481.
25. Degras, *op. cit.*, III, p. 106.
26. *ibid*, pp. 111–12.
27. *ibid.*, pp. 114–15.
28. *ibid.*, p. 166.
29. Krivitsky, *op. cit.*, pp. 37–40. Documents from the German foreign ministry which fell into Allied hands after the second world war have confirmed Krivitsky's report.
Schapiro, *op. cit.*, p. 485 and note.
30. Krivitsky, *op. cit.*, pp. 30–7.
31. J. E. Davies, *Mission to Moscow* (London, 1942), pp. 116, 129–38.

NOTES TO CHAPTER 15

1. Maurice Dobb, *Soviet Economic Development since 1917* (London, 1948), pp. 269–70; *The Second Five-year Plan* (Gosplan), (Moscow, 1936), p. 93.
2. *Narodno-Khozyaistvenny Plan na 1935 god*, 2nd ed. (Moscow, 1935), p. 10.
3. The draft of the second plan was only firmly adopted after a trial during the first year of the period. Results during this year were the most disappointing of the whole of the 1930s, and the targets in the final form of the second plan were reduced below those in the preliminary draft, thus reversing what happened in the first plan, the final targets in which had been considerably increased above those in the preliminary drafts.
Dobb, *op. cit.*, p. 270.
4. *ibid.*, p. 288.
5. The figures given are the estimates made by Colin Clark and set out in his *Critique of Russian Statistics*, pp. 24–5, 54–69. For comment and criticism of these estimates as being too conservative, see Dobb, *op. cit.*, pp. 286–8.
6. Fletcher, *op. cit.*, p. 45.
7. The part played by Metropolitan Sergii was at times difficult to understand. His proclamation had been severely criticized by some Orthodox clergy. But his action in giving interviews to the Soviet and foreign press in

February 1930 in which he flatly stated that 'Persecution of religion never has and does not exist in the U.S.S.R. . . . .' defies understanding. Evidently he undertook to give the interviews at the behest of the Soviet government, then most anxious to secure goodwill and trade abroad and to counter rumoured threats of a Christian crusade against communism. The questions and answers were vetted in advance by the Soviet government, and Sergii's answers were patently false. An émigré Metropolitan commented that 'the interviews caused a scandal not only among us abroad, but also in Soviet Russia. The people were indignant: what . . . the church lies?!'
Fletcher, *op. cit.*, pp. 48–55.
8. Fletcher, *op. cit.*, pp. 74–6, which also quotes even higher estimates.
9. *ibid.*, p. 80.
10. Quoted by Merle Fainsod, *op. cit.*, p. 371; Andrei Vyshinsky, *The Law of the Soviet State* (New York, 1948), p. 122.
11. Stalin, *Voprosy Leninizma*, 11th ed. (Moscow, 1939), p. 516.
12. *ibid.*, p. 524.
13. Fainsod, *op. cit.*, p. 372; Stalin, *op. cit.*, p. 571.
14. The eleven union republics were the R.S.F.S.R., the Ukrainian, White Russian, Georgian, Armenian, Azerbaidzhanian, Kazakh, Kirghiz, Uzbek, Turkmenian, and Tadzhik republics.
   The Transcaucasian S.R.S.R. was dissolved in 1936 and the constituent countries of Georgia, Armenia, and Azerbaidzhan were raised to union republic status. At the same time the Kazakh and Kirghiz autonomous republics were promoted to union republics.
15. The presidium was subsequently reorganized to comprise a chairman, fifteen vice-chairmen, a secretary, and sixteen members.
16. This soviet was in 1946 renamed the council of ministers.
Merle Fainsod comments:

'This reversion to tsarist and bourgeois terminology was variously hailed as a manifestation of the pull of traditionalism, as a symbol of the Soviet search for respectability, and as another Machiavellian manoeuvre to quiet the fears of the West. Whatever the underlying pattern of motivation, the old wine continued to ferment in the new bottles.'

(*op. cit.*, p. 380.)
17. *ibid.*, p. 375.

NOTES TO CHAPTER 16

1. On 25 February 1956 in the secret session of the twentieth party congress, Khrushchev commented on the strange circumstances of Kirov's death. A month and a half earlier Nikolaev had been arrested for suspicious conduct, but he had been released after questioning, although he was carrying a revolver at the time. One of the security officers, assigned to guard Kirov, was killed in a motor accident on his way to headquarters to give evidence, and the fact that he died while three other passengers in the car were unharmed, suggested that he had been disposed of before he could give evidence. Khrushchev said further that 'After the murder of Kirov, top functionaries of the Leningrad NKVD were given very light sentences, but in 1937 they were shot. We can assume that they were shot in order to cover the traces of the organizers of Kirov's killing.'
The Anti-Stalin Campaign, p. 26.
   Khrushchev's comments confirm much of the account of the mystery, given by Boris I. Nikolaevsky, which is the fullest available. Boris I.

Nikolaevsky, *Power and the Soviet Elite* (London, 1966), pp. 69–102. See also Krivitsky, *op. cit.*, pp. 205–8.

2. The poet, Anna Akhmatova, whose son was arrested in 1937 and only released after Stalin's death, has expressed something of the personal tragedy of the terror in her poems and especially in *Requiem* (Munich, 1964).

3. Deutscher, *Stalin* (London, 1961: O.U.P. paperback edition), pp. 349–50.

4. Grey, *Ivan the Terrible*, pp. 151–83.

5. Fainsod, *op. cit.*, p. 195.

6. Maxim Litvinov wrote in his journal of his first meeting with Yagoda in 1926, that he was 'a strange mysterious fellow, one of those adventurers thrown up in large numbers during the revolutionary period'.

Maxim Litvinov, *Notes for a Journal* (London, 1955), p. 23.

7. Stalin presumably obtained the support of the Politburo for this basic change in party practice. The more moderate members of the Politburo either approved or felt compelled to acquiesce. Dr Leonard Schapiro suggests that Kuibyshev in the Politburo and Maxim Gorky outside it may have tried to restrain Stalin. Yagoda was later charged with poisoning both men and he may have done so on Stalin's orders or may have been forced to confess to these crimes to divert suspicion from those who were guilty. The sudden and mysterious death of Kuibyshev, announced on 26 January 1935, and the attacks on Gorky's work, hitherto held to be beyond criticism, may lend some support to this hypothesis.

Schapiro, *op. cit.*, pp. 402–3; Fainsod, *op. cit.*, p. 434.

8. Khrushchev in his speech on 25 February 1956 to the secret session of the twentieth party congress, declared that Ordzhonikidze had been a victim of the persecution of Stalin and Beria and that he had been 'forced to shoot himself'.

The Anti-Stalin Campaign, p. 69; Schapiro, *op. cit.*, p. 409.

9. *The Anti-Stalin Campaign*, p. 26.

10. Krivitsky, *op. cit.*, p. 272.

11. Davies, *op. cit.*, pp. 36–7.

12. *The Anti-Stalin Campaign*, p. 29.

13. No evidence of an army plot to displace Stalin or to destroy the regime has ever come to light. The Nuremberg trials for German war crimes revealed no contacts between the Germans and Tukhachevsky or the other Soviet commanders. Indeed, as Dr Schapiro has pointed out, the right time for such a conspiracy to remove Stalin would have been 1929 or 1930; by 1937 it was already too late.

Schapiro, *op. cit.*, pp. 424–5; Krivitsky, *op. cit.*, pp. 233–66; but see Deutscher, *Stalin*, p. 379, who suggests that the generals did indeed plan a coup.

14. A full examination of the Tukhachevsky affair is contained in John Erickson, *The Soviet High Command 1918–1941* (London, 1962), pp. 461–6, 481–8, 737.

Khrushchev in his speech to the twenty-second party congress said:

'Such outstanding military commanders as Tukhachevsky, Yakir, Uborevich, Kork, Yegorov, Eideman, and others fell victim to the mass repressions. . . . A rather curious report once cropped up in the foreign press to the effect that Hitler, in preparing the attack on our country, planted through his intelligence service a faked document, indicating that Comrades Yakir and Tukhachevsky and others were agents of the German General Staff. This "document" allegedly secret, fell into the hands of President Benes of Czechoslovakia who, apparently guided by good intentions, forwarded it to Stalin. Yakir, Tukhachevsky, and others were

arrested and then killed. Many splendid commanders and political officials of the Red Army were executed.'
Fainsod, *op. cit.*, p. 436 note.
Sir Winston Churchill confirmed that Benes told him of passing on such a document. W. S. Churchill, *The Second World War*, Vol. I (London, 1948), p. 225.
See also Krivitsky, *op. cit.*, for his account of the framing and liquidation of the Red Army leaders.
Tukhachevsky has been completely rehabilitated as a hero of the civil war and as an outstanding military leader in the tradition of Suvorov and Kutuzov. See Todorsky, *op. cit.*, N. I. Koritsky and others (editors), *Marshal Tukhachevsky: Vospominaniya Druzei i Soratnikov* (Moscow, 1965).

15. Raymond L. Garthoff, *How Russia makes War: Soviet Military Doctrine* (London, 1954), pp. 220–1.
16. *Istoriya VKP (b) Kratky kurs* (Moscow, 1946), p. 336.
17. Schapiro, *op. cit.*, p. 428.
18. Davies, *op. cit.*, pp. 37–8.
19. W. G. Krivitsky's account of the extorting of confessions is convincing. He lists the four main methods which were used to persuade the old bolsheviks that it was their duty to make a false confession. First in importance was physical and mental torture; the second was evidence, often distorted, from the accumulated secret reports, gathered by agents on each individual over the years and kept in Stalin's secret cabinet; the third was conventional frame-ups by means of *agents-provocateurs*; the fourth and by no means least important factor was direct deals negotiated between Stalin and certain of his pivotal prisoners and involving promises that family, friends, and colleagues would be spared if by confessions the accused would help in uncovering the general conspiracy. A further factor was that the accused were often prepared to sacrifice 'honour as well as life to defend the hated regime of Stalin, because it contained the last faint gleam of hope for that better world to which they had consecrated themselves in early youth'.
Krivitsky, *op. cit.*, pp. 211–32. See also Fainsod, *op. cit.*, pp. 437–8, and Schapiro, *op. cit.*, pp. 422–6.
Much of Krivitsky's evidence was later confirmed by Khrushchev in his secret speech to the twentieth party congress. *The Anti-Stalin Campaign*, pp. 31–42.
For a detailed and horrifying personal account of interrogation and ten bouts of torture, suffered by a Red Army officer, who was later released, see A. V. Gorbatov, *Years Off My Life*, translated from the Russian by G. Clough and A. Cash (London, 1964).

20. F. Beck and W. Godin, *Russian Purge and the Extraction of Confession* (London, 1951), pp. 67–8; David J. Dallin and Boris I. Nikolaevsky, *Forced Labour in Soviet Russia* (London, 1948), p. 86; see also Fainsod, *op. cit.*, pp. 458–61.
21. The principle was not new in Russia. Peter the Great had used prison labour to man his naval galleys, to build his capital, St Petersburg, and on other projects. For over two centuries exile to Siberia and, for the most serious crimes, the severe punishment of *katorga*, or hard labour, usually served on construction work at some distant outpost, were accepted methods of colonizing and developing sparsely settled regions. But the forced labour camps of Soviet Russia were organized on a far greater scale and with a ruthlessness that tsarist methods had lacked.
22. *VKP (b) v Rezolyutsiyakh*, II, pp. 671–7; Fainsod, *op. cit.*, p. 442.
23. Beck and Godin, *op. cit.*, pp. 189–91.
24. F. Beck and W. Godin are the pseudonyms of two former prisoners of

the NKVD. Their account of the purge is remarkable for lack of bitterness, for impartiality and for its descriptions. The authenticity of their account can hardly be doubted.

Writing of the arrest of NKVD officials, they noted that:

'The behaviour of NKVD officials in the cells was quiet, modest, and comradely. The attitude of the other prisoners towards them was completely friendly and feelings of vindictiveness towards them were exceptional.

'Arrested NKVD officials were treated in the same way as other prisoners, except that their interrogation tended to be more severe. They failed to share the general optimism of others or to take part in the invention of confession . . . for they knew what lay ahead of them. . . . They expected to be executed at any moment, though they had not been convicted, and the slightest sound made them start, but their behaviour was always very reserved and quiet, and as a rule they took the greatest care never to reveal any NKVD secrets. Most of them admitted that their faith in the Soviet had never been shaken until their arrest . . .'

Beck and Godin, *op. cit.*, pp. 146–7.

25. Jack Miller, 'Soviet Planners in 1936–37' in *Soviet Planning*, edited by Jane Degras and Alec Nove (Oxford, 1964), pp. 118–19.

NOTES TO CHAPTER 17

1. Ivan Maisky, Soviet ambassador to the United Kingdom from 1932 to 1943, described Chamberlain as 'undoubtedly the most sinister figure on the political horizon of Britain at that time' and as 'a man of narrow views and small capabilities'. Ivan Maisky, *Who Helped Hitler?* translated from the Russian (London, 1964), p. 67 and *passim*. Maxim Litvinov held similar views. Both he and Maisky were well disposed towards Britain and their regret that at such a time Britain should have such a man as prime minister emerges from their writings.

Maxim Litvinov, *Notes for a Journal*, translated from the Russian, introduction by E. H. Carr (London, 1955), p. 222 and *passim*.

Chamberlain was, after Hitler and the other nazi leaders, probably the foreigner most detested by the Russians.

2. Stalin had remained convinced that Chamberlain and influential cliques in Britain and France were secretly pursuing such a policy. In his report to the eighteenth party congress on 10 March 1939 he spoke bluntly of their 'urging the Germans to march farther east, promising them easy plunder . . .'

Stalin, *Voprosy Leninizma*, 11th ed. (Moscow, 1939), p. 571.

3. *ibid.*, p. 574.

4. Degras, *op. cit.*, III, pp. 322–3.

5. Maisky, *op. cit.*, p. 102.

6. Degras, *op. cit.*, p. 324.

7. *ibid.*, p. 329; Maisky, *op. cit.*, pp. 118–19.

8. Degras, *op. cit.*, pp. 332–40.

9. *ibid.*, pp. 340–1.

10. Churchill, *op. cit.*, I, p. 346.

11. Maisky, *op. cit.*, pp. 141–2.

12. Degras, *op. cit.*, pp. 361–2.

13. *ibid.*, pp. 356–7.

14. *ibid.*, pp. 358–9.

15. The Soviet and German versions of the steps leading to the Molotov-

Ribbentrop pact vary in some details. See *Istoriya Velikoi otechestvennoi Sovietskogo Soyuza*, Vol. I (Moscow, 1960), pp. 174–6; W. R. Shirer, *The Rise and Fall of the Third Reich* (London, 1960), pp. 520–8.

In the West it was widely believed that during the spring and summer of 1939 the Soviet Union was playing the treacherous game of negotiating openly with Britain and France and at the same time seeking secretly to make a deal with nazi Germany. The evidence supporting this charge of Soviet double-dealing is set out in the official U.S. publication *Nazi–Soviet Relations 1939–41* (Washington, 1948), pp. 1–109. But see Maisky, *op. cit.*, pp. 178–95.

Winston Churchill wrote in the 1940s that 'it is not even now possible to fix the moment when Stalin definitely abandoned all intention of working with the Western democracies and of coming to terms with Hitler' (*op. cit.*, I, p. 289) and this opinion is still valid.

16. Alexander Werth, *Russia at War* (London, 1964), pp. 46–7.

17. Degras, *op. cit.*, pp. 360–71.

18. *ibid.*, p. 375.

19. Responsibility for the terrible Katyn massacre has never been established beyond all doubt. The nazis discovered the mass graves in April 1943. They invited the International Red Cross to carry out an impartial investigation which would, they claimed, establish Russian guilt. The Red Cross refused to act without Russian participation and this was refused. The Germans then carried out their own investigations and published the results, which indicted the Russians. In 1943 when the Red Army recaptured the Smolensk region, the Russians conducted their own examination of the evidence which, they asserted, established German guilt.

At the Nuremberg trial of German war criminals, one of the charges against Goering was that he had ordered the Katyn massacre. In his defence he produced the published German report on investigations at Katyn. Russians and Poles produced no counter-evidence and the charge was allowed to drop.

Werth, *op. cit.*, pp. 661–7; Churchill, *op. cit.*, IV, pp. 678–81.

20. Degras, *op. cit.*, pp. 382–4.

21. *ibid.*, pp. 396–7.

22. Douglas Clark, *Three Days to Catastrophe* (London, 1966), gives a most interesting account of the excited mood, especially of the press, in Britain and France at this time.

23. Degras, *op. cit.*, p. 442.

24. Alexander Werth in his valuable study, *Russia at War 1941–1945*, states that 'In 1945, Paasikivi and Kekkonen, both future presidents of Finland, who had favoured accommodation with the Russians, told me that they had considered the Russian proposals moderate and understandable, and maintained that the war could have been avoided had their policy prevailed.' (*op. cit.*, p. 66 note.)

25. Boris Shaposhnikov was one of the tsarist army officers taken into the Red Army, on the direction of Trotsky, during the civil war. He was an extremely able professional soldier and in some miraculous way he escaped being purged. He was chief of staff during most of the 1941–5 war, retiring finally on grounds of ill-health.

26. At this time the four marshals of the Soviet Union were Voroshilov, Timoshenko, Shaposhnikov, and Kulik. The last named was a political appointment who was to pass from the scene soon after the beginning of the war. He was to be blamed for much of the unpreparedness of the Red Army in 1941 and especially for having failed to equip it with automatic weapons.

Werth, *op. cit.*, p. 82.

27. *ibid.*, pp. 84–5.
28. *ibid.*, p. 87.
29. Degras, *op. cit.*, pp. 450–3.
30. *ibid.*, pp. 462–3.
31. The Soviet press announcement read: 'London, August 22 (TASS). London radio reports that Trotsky has died in hospital in Mexico City of a fractured skull, the result of an attempt on his life by one of the persons in his immediate entourage.'
Werth, *op. cit.*, p. 97 note.
See Deutscher, *The Prophet Outcast. Trotsky 1929–40* (London, 1963), pp. 495–509 for a very moving account of the death of Trotsky. See also L. A. S. Salazar, *Murder in Mexico* (London, 1950).
32. Werth, *op. cit.*, pp. 96–100.
33. Degras, *op. cit.*, pp. 474–5.
34. On 18 December, just over a month after Molotov's visit, Hitler reached his final decision to launch his invasion of Russia. He had had the campaign in mind for some time, but it is possible that his exasperation with Molotov's incessant questioning and his refusal to take an interest in Hitler's proposals, was a factor in bringing him to the final decision.
At the banquet given by Molotov at the Soviet embassy, from which Hitler was absent, a raid by British planes interrupted proceedings. Ribbentrop hurried Molotov to the nearby shelter of the German foreign office. There Ribbentrop took from his pocket a draft agreement which would have the effect of making the three-power pact of Germany, Japan, and Italy embrace the Soviet Union as the fourth power. Terms of the draft included a guarantee of Soviet frontiers, and a secret protocol defined each country's 'territorial aspirations'.
Molotov showed no interest and renewed his questions about German intentions in Finland and in the Balkans. Ribbentrop grew more and more exasperated. Finally he bluntly told Molotov that he was ignoring the most important question which was whether the Soviet Union would 'co-operate in the great liquidation of the British Empire'. To this Molotov replied, 'If you are so sure that Britain is finished, then why are we in this shelter?'
Churchill, *op. cit.*, III, p. 586; Werth, *op. cit.*, pp. 105–6.
Valentin Berezhkov, who accompanied Molotov as an interpreter on this visit and who in December 1940 was himself posted to the Soviet Embassy in Berlin, has written a valuable account of Molotov's talks with Hitler and Ribbentrop and of the developments in the first months of 1941 when it was clear to the Soviet Embassy that Hitler was preparing to attack Russia. See *Na Rubezhe Mire i Voiny* in *Novy Mir.*, No. 7 (Moscow, 1965).
35. Degras, *op. cit.*, pp. 479–84.
36. Werth, *op. cit.*, pp. 122–3.
37. Degras, *op. cit.*, pp. 487–90.
38. *ibid.*, p. 489.
39. Werth, *op. cit.*, p. 127.

NOTES TO CHAPTER 18

1. N. G. Kuznetsov, *Pered Voinoi* (Moscow, 1965), *Oktyabr*, Nos. 8, 9, 11.
2. Churchill, *op. cit.*, III, pp. 320–3; *The Anti-Stalin Campaign*, pp. 44–5.
3. V. Berezhkov, *Na Rubezhe Mira i Voiny* (Moscow, 1965), *Novy Mir*, No. 7.
4. F. W. Deakin and G. R. Storry, *The Case of Richard Sorge* (London, 1966), pp. 228–31.
5. Kuznetsov, *op. cit.*

6. *ibid.*

7. P. N. Pospelov and others, *Istoriya Velikoi Otechestvennoi Voiny Sovetskovo Soyuza 1941–1945* (Moscow, 1961), II, p. 11 (cited by its initials, viz. IVOVSS, in further references).

8. IVOVSS, I, p. 441.

9. *ibid.*, pp. 405, 481.

10. *ibid.*, p. 475.

11. *ibid.*, p. 476.

12. German sources maintain that the Russians had a numerical superiority in troops and tanks and aircraft. Manstein, for instance, has stated that in June 1941 the Soviet Army personnel, including rear services, etc., on the European Front numbered 4·7 million men, as compared with 3·3 million Germans; that the Soviet tanks numbered between 15,000 and 20,000 although the majority were obsolete, while German tanks numbered about 3,200. Erich von Manstein 'The Development of the Red Army 1942–1945' in *The Soviet Army* edited by B. H. Liddell Hart (London, 1956), pp. 140–1.

In his valuable study *The Soviet High Command* (London, 1962), p. 584, John Erickson maintains that, although Soviet military historians make much of German superiority in men, tanks and aircraft, the Red Army in fact enjoyed an advantage of thirty divisions more than the Germans and Finns, but excluding Rumanians and others. Soviet superiority in tanks was at least seven to one and in aircraft the Germans were outnumbered 4–5:1.

The true figures probably lie somewhere between the German under- and the Russian over-estimates of German strength.

13. IVOVSS, I, p. 476.

14. *ibid.*, pp. 470, 479.

15. IVOVSS, II, pp. 17–18.

16. Erickson, *op. cit.*, p. 587.

17. I. I. Fedyuninsky, *Podnyatie po Trevoge* (Moscow, 1961), quoted by Werth, *op. cit.*, p. 149.

18. I. Stalin, *O Velikoi Otechestvennoi Voine Sovetskovo Soyuza* (Moscow, 1943), p. 11.

19. The Germans claimed to have captured in the Smolensk fighting 348,000 prisoners, more than 3,000 tanks, and more than 3,000 guns. Soviet authorities dismissed these figures as wildly exaggerated. They put the losses at 32,000 men, 685 tanks, and 1,176 guns. The true figures may well lie between the figures claimed. IVOVSS, II, p. 77.

20. Heinz Guderian, *Panzer Leader*, translated from the German (London, 1952), pp. 185, 189–90, 198–200.

21. Stalin, too, evidently believed that Leningrad was lost. Admiral Kuznetsov describes a meeting he had with Stalin to discuss the possibility of having to abandon the city. Stalin was insistent that in this event the Baltic Fleet and all other ships must be scuttled.

Kuznetsov, *op. cit.*

22. The official Soviet *History* states that 677,085 men were on the south-western front at the beginning of the battle for Kiev and that 150,541 broke out of the encirclement. The Germans claim that they took 665,000 prisoners in the operation. Both claims seem improbable. Russian casualties were, however, extremely high both in the fighting around Kiev and in the attempts to break out of the encirclement.

Khrushchev, Budyonny, and Timoshenko escaped from Kiev by air.

Stalin, Timoshenko, and Shaposhnikov have been strongly criticized for refusing to allow Budyonny and Khrushchev to withdraw as they proposed. It is claimed that in the two to three days before the Germans closed the gap, they could have withdrawn the bulk of their forces.

Guderian and other German generals considered that, while the Kiev operation brought a tactical victory, it involved strategic disadvantage in that it delayed the plans of the German High Command to take Moscow before the winter began. This view supports Stalin's decision to stand fast at Kiev as long as possible. The Soviet *History*, having strongly criticized the decision, also claims that the German victory at Kiev completely upset Hitler's plans.

IVOVSS, II, pp. 108–11; Guderian, *op. cit.*, pp. 225–6; Werth, *op. cit.*, pp. 207–8.

23. Erickson, *op. cit.*, p. 624; Werth, op. cit., pp. 225–6.

24. The Soviet *History* makes no mention of the wave of panic which overtook the people of Moscow in mid-October; it refers only to their heroism (pp. 242–6). The best account of the *bolshoi drap* is given by Alexander Werth (*op. cit.*, pp. 232–42).

25. Stalin, *op. cit.*, pp. 27–8.

26. *ibid.*, pp. 36–7.

27. IVOVSS, II, pp. 52, 252–5; Werth, *op. cit.*, pp. 244–50.

28. Churchill, *op. cit.*, III, pp. 342-6

29. Hopkins' description of Stalin is of special interest, for it portrays the man in the midst of disaster, but in charge of himself and of the situation. Hopkins wrote:

'He welcomed me with a few swift words in Russian. He shook my hand briefly, firmly, courteously. He smiled warmly. There was no waste of word, gesture, or mannerism. It was like talking to a perfectly coordinated machine ... The questions he asked were clear, concise, direct ... His answers were ready, unequivocal, spoken as if the man had had them on his tongue for years ... He curries no favour with you. He seems to have no doubts ... He laughs often enough, but it's a short laugh, somewhat sardonic perhaps. There is no small talk in him. His humour is keen, penetrating.'

Robert E. Sherwood, *The White House Papers of Harry Hopkins* (London, 1949), I, p. 345.

30. Alexander Werth's account of Hopkins' visit (*op. cit.*, pp. 280–6).

31. *ibid.*, p. 290.

32. IVOVSS, II, p. 268.

33. *ibid.*, p. 265.

34. Guderian, *op. cit.*, pp. 248–64.

35. *ibid.*, p. 359.

36. *ibid.*, pp. 359–60.

37. *ibid.*, p. 151.

38. Werth, *op. cit.*, p. 303.

39. *ibid.*, p. 305.

40. D. V. Pavlov, *Leningrad 1941: The Blockade*, translated from the Russian (Chicago and London, 1965), pp. 12–13.

41. Zhukov subsequently claimed much of the credit for saving Leningrad. As chief of staff of the Soviet High Command, however, he must bear a great share of the responsibility for the inadequate preparation of the defences of the city before the German invasion and in June–July 1941.

42. Caught in the blockade were 2,544,000 civilians, including 400,000 children, in Leningrad proper, and 343,000 in the suburbs and other localities inside the ring of the German blockade.

In the four categories of workers, office workers, dependents and children under 12 according to which rations were distributed, the children fared badly, especially in the 12 to 14 group when they received only the 'dependents' ' ration.

Pavlov, *op. cit.*, pp. 58–60, 79–80.

43. For the criminal negligence and lack of foresight on the part of the civil and military authorities in failing to ensure basic food reserves, the explanation given after the war was that they were so taken up with the defences of Leningrad, which had been neglected, and with resisting the Germans that they had 'no time to give much thought to the problem of food'.

Pavlov, *op. cit.*, p. 64.

44. *ibid.*, p. 123.
45. *ibid.*, pp. 123–4.
46. *ibid.*, pp. 121–2.
47. *ibid.*, p. 144.
48. A. V. Karasev, *Leningradtsi v gody blokady* (Moscow, 1959), pp. 189, 227.
49. IVOVSS, II, p. 406.
50. The official Soviet *History of the Great Patriotic War* is often highly critical of the conduct of the war by the Supreme Command and generally with justice. The *History* was, however, compiled after the twentieth Congress at which Khrushchev made his anti-Stalin speech. A major defect of the *History* is that where possible it diminishes the role played by Stalin and expands that of Khrushchev. No doubt it is now being revised to diminish Khrushchev's role and with pens poised the contributors wait and wonder who next is to be extolled. It really is time that the Soviet authorities, rulers of a mighty power, abandoned this foolishness.

Before the Kharkov offensive Khrushchev, according to his speech of 25 February 1956, tried desperately to persuade Stalin to call it off, but Stalin confirmed his orders. *The Anti-Stalin Campaign*, pp. 51–2.

51. IVOVSS, II, p. 410.
52. Werth, *op. cit.*, p. 419.
53. Casualties among Red Army officers had been extremely high and many commissars who had had battle experience and had proved their worth were appointed as officers to operational commands. *Red Star*, on 11 October announced that from the ranks of ex-commissars 200 new regimental commanders and 600 new battalion commanders would shortly be appointed.

Werth, *op. cit.*, p. 427.

54. The bitter fighting as the Russians were slowly driven back and then the battle for Stalingrad have been stirringly described by General, now Marshal, V. I. Chuikov, who was appointed to command the Soviet 62nd Army on 12 September.

Soviet press and other accounts of this fighting were written in heroic style and the heroics degenerated into a jargon. Chuikov in his account *Nachalo Puti* (The Beginning of the Road) noted panic and chaos among Red troops and the inadequacy of some senior officers, but his story is one of rising morale, extraordinary courage and fortitude, and as commander of the 62nd Army which withstood German bombing and attacks inside the city until its relief, he himself was one of the foremost heroes of this desperate battle. In his account rather than in the official Soviet *History*, the heroism and the epic quality of the struggle become apparent and truly unforgettable. His book was published in Moscow in 1959 and a new edition appeared in 1962, heavily revised, no doubt because it had given offence to Yeremenko and other senior officers. The English translation, published in London in 1963, was from the revised edition of 1962.

55. V. I. Chuikov, *op. cit.*, pp. 31–3, 79.

56. *ibid.*, pp. 243–4; Werth, *op. cit.*, p. 493.
57. V. I. Chuikov, *op. cit.*, p. 277.

NOTES TO CHAPTER 19

1. IVOVSS, III, pp. 22, 26.
2. Erich von Manstein, *Lost Victories*, translated from the German (London, 1958), pp. 316–18.
3. Werth, *op. cit.*, pp. 544–62, *passim.*
4. The Volga Germans, deported as a precaution rather than as a punishment, were treated better than later deportees, but their treatment was nevertheless harsh. NKVD troops descended on the Volga German Republic, confiscated property, and gave the inhabitants a few hours in which to get ready. There followed for all of them long journeys in cattle trucks. Many died of cold and hunger and the survivors on arrival at their destinations in Kazakhstan or in Siberia were marched to uninhabited country where they were given a few agricultural tools and left to make a new life.
R. Conquest, *The Soviet Deportation of Nationalities* (London, 1960), pp. 96–7.
5. Alexander Dallin, *German Rule in Russia* (London, 1957), p. 300.
6. Khrushchev in his secret speech of 25 February 1956 to the twentieth party congress said:

'The Soviet Union is justly considered as a model of a multinational state because we have in practice assured the equality and friendship of all nations which live in our great Fatherland.

'All the more monstrous are the acts whose initiator was Stalin and which are rude violations of the basic Leninist principles of the nationalist policy of the Soviet State. We refer to the mass deportations from their native places of whole nations, together with all Communists and Komsomols without any exception; this deportation action was not dictated by any military considerations.'

After referring to the Karachai, the Balkars, the Ingushi, the Chechens, and the Kalmyks, he continued:

'Not only a Marxist–Leninist but also no man of common sense can grasp how it is possible to make whole nations responsible for inimical activity, including women, children, old people, Communists, Komsomols, to use mass repression against them and to expose them to misery and suffering for the hostile acts of individual persons.'

The Anti-Stalin Campaign, pp. 57–8.
See also Werth, *op. cit.*, p. 581; Conquest, *op. cit.*, pp. 51–71.
7. I. Stalin, *O Velikoi Otechestvennoi Voine Sovetskovo Soyuza*, 3rd ed. (Moscow, 1943), pp. 86–8.
8. IVOVSS, III, pp. 160–1.
9. *ibid.*, p. 216.
10. *ibid.*, pp. 215–17.
11. According to the official Soviet *History*, *Hurricane* and *Tomahawk* aircraft were already obsolete when received and were certainly inferior to German and Soviet fighters in many respects. The *Airocobras* and *Kittyhawks* were the best of their types, but too few were supplied. They first came into service in the Red airforce in spring 1943.
The tanks, supplied in considerable numbers by Britain and the U.S.A. in 1942 and 1943 were even more strongly criticized. The proportion of light tanks—55 per cent in 1942 and 70 per cent in 1943—was much too high; light

tanks were of such limited usefulness that Soviet industry had already stopped producing them. Moreover, in fire-power and armour the Allied tanks were said to be inferior to Soviet tanks.

IVOVSS, III, pp. 214–16.

12. Between 22 June 1941 and 30 April 1944 the U.S.A. sent to Russia 6,430 aircraft, 3,734 tanks, 10 minesweepers, 210,000 vehicles as well as vast quantities of raw materials, minerals, and 4·5 million tons of food.

Britain sent 5,800 aircraft, 4,292 tanks, 12 minesweepers and large quantities of raw materials.

The combined contributions was considerable. The vehicles, food, and raw materials in particular were valued by the Red troops. The fact remained, however, that Russians were dying in thousands on all fronts, while the Allies were suffering far less, and the Russians regarded this aid not as benevolent charity but as the least the Allies could do in their own interests, certainly until they had opened the second front.

In March 1943 the U.S. ambassador, Admiral Standley, complained at a press conference about the 'ungracious' attitude of Russians to this and other aid. This protest annoyed the Russians, but the Soviet press did something to make amends by paying tribute to Allied aid.

Werth, op. cit., pp. 625–8;

J. R. Deane, The Strange Alliance (London, 1947), pp. 93–5.

13. IVOVSS, III, p. 261.

14. ibid., p. 295.

15. Dallin, op. cit., p. 427

16. Werth, op. cit., pp. 607–8.

17. ibid., p. 693.

18. George Fischer, Soviet Opposition to Stalin (Cambridge, Mass., 1952), pp. 36–8.

19. ibid., pp. 32–3.

20. ibid., p. 53.

21. The Army of Liberation subsequently became the Committee for the Liberation of the Peoples of Russia (KONR), still nominally under Vlasov's command. The first KONR division, commanded by General Buniachenko, finally fought in the Prague resistance against the Germans and thus helped liberate the city. But most of the members of the first and second division of the KONR were seized by Soviet units or handed over to them by the U.S. authorities. Vlasov and his associates made desperate efforts to obtain U.S. sponsorship of their movement, but in vain; they too were seized by the Soviet units or handed over by the Allies.

On 2 August 1946 Pravda announced that the military board of the supreme court of the U.S.S.R. had found Vlasov and eleven others in the movement guilty of 'treason to the Motherland'. They were hanged.

Fischer, op. cit., pp. 101, 115–20.

22. The exception to this suppression of national identity as quoted by George Fischer, was the German plan to set up a Turkestan Legion, a Caucasian-Mohammedan Legion, a Georgian Legion, and an Armenian Legion. This plan did not progress far.

ibid., pp. 45, 48.

23. Werth, op. cit., p. 161.

24. I. Stalin, op. cit., p. 13.

25. Guderian, op. cit., pp. 266–7.

NOTES TO CHAPTER 20

1. Churchill, *op. cit.*, III, pp. 342–5, 420–2; IV, pp. 280–91.
2. *ibid.*, IV, pp. 297–300.
3. *ibid.*, p. 302.
4. IVOSS, II, p. 368.
5. Churchill, *op. cit.*, IV, p. 305.
6. *loc. cit.*
7. Reports were received that the *Tirpitz* had put to sea with an escort of cruisers and destroyers. The Admiralty, anxious not to expose the two British and two American cruisers of the convoy escort to such a force and to bring in the battlefleet, covering the convoy from the west, took the decision to withdraw the convoy escort and to scatter the merchantmen. Not only the cruisers, but the destroyers were withdrawn, leaving the merchantmen defenceless. Withdrawal of the cruisers was perhaps justifiable, but withdrawal of the destroyers was a tragic mistake by the Admiralty as Churchill himself later agreed.
ibid., p. 237.
8. Churchill maintained that, so far from breaking 'contractual obligations', as Stalin stated in his letter of 23 July 1942, the Russians were at fault because 'it had been particularly stipulated at the time of making the agreement that the Russians were to be responsible for conveying them [war supplies] to Russia.' But, as was well known, the Russians had no ships. They were, moreover, so desperate that they clung to the hope of a second front, despite Churchill's equivocating *aide-mémoire*.
ibid., p. 242.
9. *ibid.*, pp. 428–9.
10. *ibid.*, p. 434.
11. Churchill's fascinating account of this visit to Moscow reveals something of the veiled strength of Stalin's personality. It is a pity that no similar record by Stalin of this and subsequent meetings is available.
ibid., pp. 425–51.
12. I. Stalin, *O Velikoi Otechestvennoi Voine Sovetskovo Soyuza* (Moscow, 1943), pp. 55–6.
13. Werth, *op. cit.*, p. 487.
14. I. Stalin, *op. cit.*, pp. 62–72, 76.
15. *ibid.*, pp. 77–8.
16. Werth, *op. cit.*, pp. 638–9.
17. I. Stalin, *op. cit.*, p. 97.
18. *ibid.*, p. 90.
19. Werth, *op. cit.*, p. 674.
20. I. Stalin, *op. cit.*, p. 92.
21. In June 1943 Stalin decided that the *International* was no longer suitable as the national anthem of the Soviet Union. It proved difficult to find a new anthem. Finally in 1944 the party anthem with new patriotic wording was adopted as the national anthem. The *International* then became the party anthem.
22. I. Stalin, *op. cit.*, pp. 98–9.
23. Churchill, *op. cit.*, IV, pp. 671–2.
24. *ibid.*, p. 676.
25. Werth, *op. cit.*, p. 729.
26. Churchill made the point constantly that Russia had in 1940–1 been prepared to stand by while Britain faced Germany alone and that had Hitler not invaded Russia in June 1941 Stalin would probably have remained neutral throughout the war.

Stalin was to acknowledge and praise Britain's lone stand in 1940–1 and to state that had Britain been prepared to join in alliance with the Soviet Union in 1939 the pact with Germany would never have been signed.

Meanwhile Russians felt that Britain even in the bombing of her cities had not suffered destruction and loss comparable with Russian losses, and that Britain was now evading her responsibilities while they were saving the world from nazism. Churchill, *op. cit.*, IV, pp. 420–1.

27. *ibid.*, V, pp. 234–7.

28. Stalin was strongly opposed to any increase of British naval personnel in Russia, asserting that there were already too many in North Russia, an assertion not without some substance. But his main objection was, so Eden reported, 'that if only our [the British] people had treated his people as equals none of these difficulties would have arisen, and that if our people would treat his people as equals we could have as much personnel as we liked.' Churchill, *op. cit.*, V, p. 244.

29. *ibid.*, p. 247.

30. *ibid.*, p. 261.

31. *ibid.*, pp. 261, 266; Cordell Hull, *Memoirs* (London, 1948), II, pp. 131–2; Deane, *op. cit.*, p. 23.; Werth, *op. cit.*, pp. 748–52.

32. Churchill was undoubtedly unsettled by Roosevelt's refusal to continue their personal contacts, while in Teheran, for fear that Stalin might think that they were in collusion against him. This was surely naïve on the part of Roosevelt: Stalin knew that they had been closely associated and, indeed, that they usually concerted their correspondence with him.

33. Churchill, *op. cit.*, V, p. 335.

34. *ibid.*, p. 339.

35. Moran, Lord, *Winston Churchill. The Struggle for Survival* London, 1966), pp, 54–65, 125–44, 225–7

36. Deane, *op. cit.*, p. 43.

NOTES TO CHAPTER 21

1. In his secret speech to the twentieth party congress on 25 February 1956, Khrushchev severely criticized Stalin for his interference in military decisions and his paranoic determination 'to inculcate in the people the version that all victories gained by the Soviet nation during the Great Patriotic War were due to the courage, daring and genius of Stalin and no one else.' *The Anti-Stalin Campaign*, pp. 54–5.

Khrushchev probably went too far in his attempts to debunk Stalin's role in the conduct of the war and as leader of the nation. As supreme commander-in-chief, Stalin in Moscow directed all military operations from day to day and bore the full burden of the Soviet war effort. While he clearly made mistakes, he more than any other man was responsible for leading the Red forces and the nation finally to victory.

Admiral Kuznetsov has stated that in naval matters Stalin was highly competent, if too autocratic. But he sums up Stalin's war record as follows:

'It is only fair to say that, if Stalin showed some signs of bewilderment during the first days of the war he soon pulled himself together. He quickly understood the real nature of modern warfare and carefully listened to his generals. There is absolutely no truth in [Khrushchev's] malicious tales that he planned his campaigns on a school globe. I could quote dozens of cases when, in discussing the situation with generals, he knew where every regiment was located. He carried with him a notebook with endless details

... As the war progressed, he listened more and more to the generals, and the brilliant Stalingrad operation was the outcome of a collective decision.'
N. G. Kuznetsov, 'Pered Voinoi' in *Octyabr*, 1965.

Zhukov, who was closely associated with Stalin throughout the war and who despite his brilliant record was subsequently demoted by Stalin, nevertheless paid tribute to his leadership. He did not disregard Stalin's tendency to overrule expert opinion, but acknowledged that as war leader 'he achieved the impossible'. *Literaturnaya Gazeta* quoted by *The Times*, London, 2 December 1966.

Marshal Yeremenko's account of the defence committee meetings which he attended in the critical summer of 1942, portrays Stalin as leading a team, listening to and heeding expert advice, but taking the final decision.
A. I. Yeremenko, *Stalingrad* (Moscow, 1959), pp. 33–9.

Churchill, Hopkins, Deane, and others who had discussions with Stalin during the war were all impressed by his mastery of military problems and techniques.

2. Stalin had always resented the independent spirit of the Leningradtsi and the prestige enjoyed by the former capital. It has even been alleged that he allowed the city to suffer this siege in order to eliminate it as the rival of Moscow. (Harrison E. Salisbury in the foreword to the English translation of D. V. Pavlov, *Leningrad 1941*.) This strikes the present writer as improbable, but Leningrad was undoubtedly a casualty of the war and Moscow survived, supreme and unchallenged as the first city in Soviet Russia.

3. IVOVSS, IV, p. 94.
4. Werth, *op. cit.*, p. 843.
5. *loc. cit.*
6. *ibid.*, p. 855.
7. IVOVSS, IV, pp. 163–6.
8. *ibid.*, p. 166.
9. Guderian, *op. cit.*, p. 336.
10. The official Soviet *History* refers to the 'silent, angry Muscovites' who watched the parade. Alexander Werth, however, noted that:

'Youngsters booed and whistled, and even threw things at the Germans, only to be immediately restrained by the adults; men looked on grimly and in silence; but many women, especially elderly women, were full of commiseration (some even had tears in their eyes) as they looked at these bedraggled "Fritzes". I remember one old woman murmuring, "just like our poor boys ... *tozhe pognali na voinu* [also driven into the war]".'

IVOVSS, IV, p. 185; Werth, *op. cit.*, pp. 862–3.
11. Werth, *op. cit.*, pp. 884–98.
12. IVOVSS, IV, p. 239.
13. *ibid.*, pp. 239–40.
14. Churchill, *The Second World War*, VI, pp. 115–16.
15. *ibid.*, p. 118.
16. *loc. cit.*
17. *ibid.*, p. 127.
18. Accounts of the Warsaw rising leave much unexplained. The Soviet version, as given in the official Soviet *History* (IVOVSS, IV, pp. 237–52) omits references to unpalatable facts as, for example, the Moscow radio appeal of 29 July to the people of Warsaw to rise, and clearly states a case. Churchill was prone to listen to the London Poles and to suspect the Russians of things 'strange and sinister'. See his account of his intercession with Stalin. (Churchill, *op. cit.*, VI, pp. 113–28.)

Without doubt, however, the London Poles and Bor-Komarowski were utterly misguided in starting the uprising without reference to the Red army commanders on the right bank of the Vistula: on them falls the responsibility for exposing their compatriots in Warsaw to a massacre, which cost some 300,000 lives.

Stalin could and should have done more to help the Poles once the uprising had started, but allegations that he deliberately halted the Red Army advance so that anti-Soviet and other Poles would perish would seem untenable. The Red Army advance had undoubtedly been held up by German resistance and the Russians were unable to force the Vistula at this time.

H. Guderian, then chief of the German general staff, has recorded his impression and that of the German 9th Army on 8 August, 'that the Russian attempt to seize Warsaw by a *coup de main* (which in their hitherto uninterrupted successes they might well have believed possible) had been defeated by our defences despite the Polish uprising, and that the latter, from the enemy's point of view, had been begun too soon.' Guderian, *op. cit.*, p. 359.

The account, given by Alexander Werth, of his interview with General Rokossovsky in Lublin on 26 August 1944, is also convincing (Werth, *op. cit.* pp. 876–8).

19. IVOVSS, IV, pp. 277–8.
20. Churchill, *op. cit.*, VI, p. 181.
21. Churchill's record of his discussion was as follows:

'The moment was apt for business, so I said "Let us settle about our affairs in the Balkans. Your armies are in Rumania and Bulgaria. We have interests, missions and agents there. Don't let us get at cross-purposes in small ways. So far as Britain and Russia are concerned how would it do for you to have ninety per cent predominance in Rumania, for us to have ninety per cent of the say in Greece, and we go fifty-fifty about Yugoslavia?"

'While this was being translated I wrote out on a half sheet of paper: Rumania–Russia 90%; the others 10%; Greece–Great Britain 90% (in accord with the U.S.A.), Russia 10%; Yugoslavia 50–50%; Hungary 50–50%; Bulgaria–Russia 75%; the others 25%.

'I pushed this across to Stalin, who had by then heard the translation. There was a slight pause. Then he took his blue pencil and made a large tick upon it, and passed it back to us. It was all settled in no more time than it takes to set down ... The pencilled paper lay in the centre of the table. At length I said, "Might it not be thought rather cynical if it seemed we had disposed of these issues, so fateful to millions of people, in such an offhand manner? Let us burn the paper." "No, you keep it," said Stalin.'

Churchill, *op. cit.*, VI, p. 198.
22. *ibid.*, pp. 209–11.
23. IVOVSS, V, p. 467.
24. Churchill, *op. cit.*, VI, pp. 242–4.
25. IVOVSS, V, p. 57.
26. Churchill, *op. cit.*, VI, p. 310.
27. E. R. Stettinius, *Roosevelt and the Russians* (London, 1950), pp. 140–2, 160.
28. *ibid.*, pp. 182–7.
29. Churchill, *op. cit.*, VI, p. 314.
30. *ibid.*, p. 325.
31. *ibid.*, p. 320.
32. *ibid.*, p. 338.
33. *ibid.*, pp. 341–2.
34. *ibid.*, pp. 308–18.

S

35. According to Eisenhower, supreme commander of the Allied forces, Churchill disagreed with his plan of operation at this stage and even more strongly disapproved of the fact that Eisenhower, following normal procedure, had communicated these plans to Stalin. Eisenhower has recorded that Churchill 'was greatly disappointed and disturbed because my plan did not first throw Montgomery forward with all the strength I could give him from the American forces, in the desperate attempt to capture Berlin before the Russians could do so. He sent his views to Washington', and a large and wasteful exchange of telegrams took place as a result of which Eisenhower was vindicated.

In the context of relations with Russia, it would have been a great mistake for Allied forces to have beaten them to Berlin. Churchill the statesman probably realized this, but Churchill the warrior was thinking of the glory of final victory, and Churchill the politician was calculating short-term advantages.

D. D. Eisenhower, *Crusade in Europe* (London, 1948), pp. 436–40; Churchill, *op. cit.*, VI, pp. 402–9.
36. IVOVSS, V, p. 264.
37. *ibid.*, p. 279.
38. *ibid.*, p. 285.

NOTES TO CHAPTER 22

1. Werth, *op. cit.*, p. 1002.
2. The total Russian casualties in the war can only be estimated. Stalin in March 1946 stated that seven million Soviet citizens lost their lives in battle or as a result of the German occupation. The number wounded or taken prisoner has not been stated.

The figure of seven million is conservative. According to James W. Brackett (*Demographic Trends and Population Policy in the Soviet Union*. Prepared for the Joint Economic Committee, Congress of the U.S., Washington, 1962, pp. 509–10) 'between 1941 and 1946 the Soviet Union experienced an absolute decline of between 25 and 30 million persons . . . Some indication of the military losses can be had by comparing prewar and postwar populations by sex. There were probably about 95 million males and 105 million females in mid-1941. At the beginning of 1950 the estimates show only 78 million males and 102 million females. The net declines of 17 million males and 3 million females would suggest that male military losses may have approached 15 million.'
3. IVOVSS, V, p. 376.
4. Dobb, *op. cit.*, pp. 300–1.
5. IVOVSS, V, p. 392.
6. *ibid.*, p. 384.
7. 'In the period of the first half of 1945 the output of coal amounted to barely 77 per cent of the output of the first half of 1941, of oil 54 per cent, of electric power 77 per cent, of pig-iron 46 per cent, of steel 52 per cent, of coke 54 per cent, of ferrous metals 50 per cent, of machine tools 65 per cent, of trucks 43 per cent, of vehicle tyres 50 per cent.'
ibid., p. 384.
8. Churchill, *op. cit.*, VI, p. 308.
9. Stettinius, *op. cit.*, p. 115. Earlier in the war several prominent American industrialists, and especially Donald M. Nelson, discussed in Moscow the possibility of a large loan to Russia. Stalin expressed strong approval and even gave Nelson a list of Russian priority needs as a first step in working out a programme.

Nelson and others who favoured massive U.S. aid to Russia were anxious to ensure an expanding foreign market and saw the possibility of large-scale exports to Russia. Had Roosevelt lived he might have lent his support to such a programme which would have benefited both countries.

W. A. Williams *The Tragedy of American Diplomacy* (Cleveland and New York, 1959), pp. 156–7.

10. In the first months of 1945 responsible opinion in Washington was evidently inclined to the view that a loan to Soviet Russia should be considered. Stettinius wrote that:

'Secretary of the Treasury Morgenthau had sent a letter to the President on January 1st 1945, stating that he had discussed Soviet credits several times with Harriman. "We are not thinking of more Lend–Lease or any form of relief but rather of an arrangement that will have definite and long-range benefits for the United States as well as for Russia," he wrote. "I am convinced that if we were to come forward now and present to the Russians a concrete plan to aid them in the reconstruction period it would contribute a great deal towards ironing out many of the difficulties we have been having with respect to their problems and policies." '

Stettinius, *op. cit.*, p. 116.
11. *ibid.*, pp. 280–1.
12. Churchill, *op. cit.*, VI, pp. 386–98.
13. *ibid.*, p. 468.
14. Werth, *op. cit.*, p. 1016.
15. Williams, *op. cit.*, p. 168.
16. Churchill, *op. cit.*, VI, pp. 505–7.
17. Stettinius, *op. cit.*, pp. 281–2.
18. Churchill, *op. cit.*, VI, 498–9.
19. Stettinius, *op. cit.*, p. 314; Churchill, *op. cit.*, VI, p. 342

The official Soviet *History* maintains that even in May, that is, before the atom bomb was first exploded, U.S. governing circles were hoping for Japanese surrender before the Soviet entry into the war. Truman offered some relaxation of the demand for unconditional surrender in the hope that this would persuade the Japanese to end the war. Special American radio appeals from 8 May to 4 August, calling on the Japanese to surrender to the Americans were, it is alleged, made in the hope of forestalling the Russians.

IVOVSS, V, p. 536.
20. Churchill, *op. cit.*, VI, p. 554.
21. Churchill felt quite certain that Stalin had no prior knowledge through Russian or other intelligence reports of this atomic research and the atom bomb that resulted.

ibid., p. 580.
22. General J. R. Deane was referring to the attitude of the Americans attending the chiefs of staff meetings in Berlin. It became the attitude of both Americans and British at all levels. Deane considered that as a result of their 'tough and indifferent' approach, 'The conference marked the high point of Soviet–American military collaboration.'

Deane, *op. cit.*, p. 268.
23. James Byrnes, *Speaking Frankly* (London, 1948), p. 79.

The theory was evidently accepted by the allies that they must 'get tough', presumably on the grounds either that this would intimidate the Russians or lead to genuine understanding or both. The possibility that the Russians would develop atomic weapons of their own and themselves 'get tough' was not considered or considered to be remote, for it was generally assumed that they were too backward in technology to achieve on their own such a sophisticated and powerful weapon.

24. In conversation with Churchill at Potsdam, Truman acknowledged that 'If you had gone down like France, we might be fighting the Germans on the American coast at the present time.'
Churchill, *op. cit.*, VI, p. 547.

25. *ibid.*, p. 570.

26. Churchill was to maintain later that 'neither I nor Eden would ever have agreed to the Western Neisse being the frontier line'.
ibid., p. 581.

27. Byrnes, *op. cit.*, pp. 81–5.

28. Deliveries to Russia of the ten per cent of industrial equipment from the Western zones were stopped a few months later by the military governor of the American zone, General Lucius Clay, apparently on his personal responsibility.

29. Stettinius, *op. cit.*, pp. 313–14.

30. IVOVSS, p. 539.

31. Japan was already on the point of capitulation and would probably have capitulated within a few days even had the bombs not been dropped on Hiroshima and Nagasaki and even had Russia not entered the war.
J. F. C. Fuller, *The Second World War* (London, 1948), pp. 390–7.
Indeed an important motive in using the bomb against Japan was to impress and intimidate Russia. Secretary of state Byrnes took the line that the bomb was needed not so much against Japan as to 'make Russia manageable in Europe'.
Williams, *op. cit.*, p. 169.

32. Werth, *op. cit.*, p. 1038.

33. *Pravda*, 13 March 1946.

34. As a result of this and subsequent speeches calling for a more conciliatory and understanding attitude to Soviet Russia, Byrnes insisted on the resignation of Wallace and threatened to resign himself if Truman did not back him. Wallace resigned. Byrnes, *op. cit.*, pp. 239–43; Williams, *op. cit.*, p. 171.

35. In practice the pressure exerted by the Western powers on the Soviet Union served to entrench the regime and to make Soviet leaders tougher at home and abroad, while intensifying their efforts to catch up with the West.
In April 1957 Chester Bowles concluded that 'The harder the Soviet Union is pressed, the more vigorous her people will rally behind their leaders. If the Kremlin is forced to the wall, it will almost certainly strike out with all its very formidable nuclear capacity.' Williams, *op. cit.*, p. 187.
At the time of the proclamation of the Truman Doctrine, of course, Russia was weak and devastated and had no nuclear capacity.

36. The U.S. government was indeed soon to make this abundantly clear. In March 1948 Marshall himself bluntly warned Italy and all other countries participating in the European Recovery Programme that 'benefits under ERP will come to an abrupt end in any country that votes communism into power'.
Kenneth Ingram, *History of the Cold War* (London, 1955), p. 63.

37. Stalin was, of course, committed to the thesis that war between the socialist and capitalist camps was in the long run inevitable. He considered that the West was already threatening Russia with war and he was on the defensive. Whether he would eventually have embarked on a policy of open aggression, especially in view of the development of thermonuclear weapons is, to the present writer, doubtful.

NOTES TO CHAPTER 23

1. Dobb, *op. cit.*, p. 310.
2. *ibid.*, p. 304.
3. Production of cotton cloth was to be some 34 per cent higher in 1950 than in 1938, woollen cloth 39 per cent higher, leather footwear 12 per cent higher, rubber footwear 30 per cent higher, and the output of artificial silk was to increase to four and a half times the pre-war level. The paper and fishing industries were to increase their output by 65 per cent and 50 per cent respectively over pre-war levels. The plan also referred to production of such items as television sets, cameras, bicycles and motor cycles, radio sets, clocks and watches, and refrigerators.
ibid., pp. 307–8.
4. The extent to which the industrial centre of gravity was moving to the new centres in the Urals and Siberia was illustrated by the fact that, while Donbas coal production was to be restored to pre-war levels or slightly more, the Donbas was to contribute only 35 per cent of the nation's total coal production, compared with 60 per cent in 1937 and 78 per cent in 1928. Iron and steel production in southern Russia, although to be restored to pre-war production levels, now became a smaller part of the total production which was dominated by the new centres in the Urals, Siberia, and Central Asia.
The dramatic growth of the new centres may be gauged from the increase in electricity output in Kazakhstan from one quarter of a million kilowatt hours at the beginning of the war to a milliard kilowatt hours by the end of the war. The new plan provided that this output should be doubled by 1950.
ibid., pp. 309–10.
5. *ibid.*, p. 308.
6. Fainsod, *op. cit.*, pp. 198–200.
7. Schapiro, *op. cit.*, p. 512 note.
8. *ibid.*, p. 513.
9. *ibid.*, p. 515.
10. *The Anti-Stalin Campaign*, pp. 84–5; Fainsod, *op. cit.*, pp. 323–5.
11. Fainsod, *op. cit.*, p. 269.
12. *ibid.*, pp. 274–5.
13. Schapiro, *op. cit.*, p. 524.
14. Fainsod, *op. cit.*, p. 274.
15. *The Anti-Stalin Campaign*, p. 59.
16. *ibid.*, pp. 59–60.
17. *ibid.*, pp. 63–5.
18. *ibid.*, p. 84.

NOTES TO CHAPTER 24

1. Averell Harriman, *Peace with Russia?* (New York, 1959), pp. 102–3. Stalin's illness and death were, like his private life, shrouded in secrecy. Khrushchev's account of his death, while leaving much unsaid, nevertheless seems probable and acceptable.
2. Grey, *Ivan the Terrible*, p. 138.
3. *The Anti-Stalin Campaign*, p. 85.
4. Sukhanov, *op. cit.*, p. 230.
Trotsky, *Chto i kak proizoshlo* (Paris, 1929), p. 25.
5. Quoted in *The Times*, London, 2 December 1966.
6. In the discussions at Yalta on the United Nations organization and especially the member states and the voting, Stalin's direct approach is illustrated. See the account by James F. Byrnes (*op. cit.*, pp. 35–9).

7. Much has been made of Stalin's silence and apparent inactivity immediately after receiving news of the German invasion. George F. Kennan has written that at this time 'this man who had cried "Wolf" so long and insistently, became for the first time quite paralyzed and helpless, lost his nerve, and had to be bailed out by the men around him.' (*Russia and the West under Lenin and Stalin* (Boston, 1961), p. 252.) The source for this description of Stalin's reaction is not given.

Marshal Zhukov, who was one of the men around him at the time, has, since Stalin's death, rejected the allegations that Stalin lost his nerve. (*op. cit.*) Kuznetsov, the people's commissar for the navy, wrote that 'It is only fair to say that, if Stalin showed some signs of bewilderment during the first days of the war, he soon pulled himself together.' (*op. cit.*)

8. At the victory celebration in the Kremlin on 24 May 1945, Stalin, proposing a toast to the Russian people, said:

'Our government made not a few errors. We experienced at moments a desperate situation in 1941–42, when our army was retreating because there was no other way out. A different people could have said to the government: "You have failed to justify our expectations. Go away. We shall instal another government which will conclude peace with Germany . . ." The Russian people, however, did not take this path . . . Thanks to it, to the Russian people, for this confidence.'

Deutscher, *Stalin*, p. 465.

9. Many have written of Stalin's paranoia and of the 'Stalinolatory' which mounted in a crescendo during his reign, reaching a climax in the extravagant celebration of his seventieth birthday on 21 December 1949 when he was virtually apotheosized.

Stalin probably mounted this campaign of adulation less from vanity and more to reinforce his authority in the task of leading Russia to strength and security. Like Lenin he was to many who knew him a man without personal vanity. In all his meetings in Moscow, Yalta, Teheran, and Potsdam with Western leaders, he behaved with dignity and modesty, concentrating exclusively on the problems in hand.

Averell Harriman, who met him on numerous occasions, wrote:

'Publicly Stalin had permitted the most abject adulation of himself and accepted without hesitation every tribute and gift offered him, believing it was good propaganda. But privately he combined great dignity with an almost unpretentious modesty. In 1942 when I accompanied Churchill to Moscow to see him, we found him wearing for the first time the uniform of Marshal of the Soviet Union, a title he had just assumed. Churchill admired the uniform and congratulated Stalin on his elevation, but Stalin brushed the compliment aside with an unassuming manner. "They said I ought to accept the position of head of the armed forces in order to improve the morale of the troops", he said modestly. Just who "they" were was not made clear.'

Harriman, *op. cit.* (New York, 1959), p. 113.

10. Kennan, *op. cit.*, p. 254.

Mr Kennan is generally more concerned to pass moral judgements than to achieve understanding. His chapter on Stalin in the above book is, in the opinion of the present writer, mistaken in approach and misleading.

11. Francis B. Randall, *Stalin's Russia: An historical Reconsideration* (New York, 1965), p. 2.

NOTES TO CHAPTER 25

1. The four alternate members were N. M. Shvernik (chairman of the all-union central council of trade unions); P. K. Ponomarenko (minister of culture); L. G. Melnikov (first secretary of the Ukrainian party organization); M. D. Bagirov (first secretary of the Azerbaidjan party organization).

Among the alternate members who were now omitted completely were L. I. Brezhnev (secretary of the party central committee and former first secretary of the Moldavian party organization) and A. N. Kosygin (vice-chairman of the council of ministers and minister of light industry).

Fainsod, *op. cit.*, pp. 324–5.

2. This amnesty freed prisoners sentenced to terms of five years or less, halved the sentences of those serving longer terms, and released unconditionally all women with children under ten, pregnant women, all persons under the age of eighteen, men over fifty-five, and women over fifty years of age, and all suffering from incurable diseases.

The amnesty did not apply to those sentenced 'for counterrevolutionary crimes, large thefts of socialist property, banditry, and intentional murder'. This exemption of political prisoners from the amnesty led to a series of desperate strikes and riots in certain camps—Norilsk in mid-1953, Vorkuta in 1953 and 1955, and Kingir in mid-1954. The outbreaks were suppressed with severity. They led, however, to improvements in camp conditions and were to lead to further amnesties.

Fainsod, *op. cit.*, p. 449.

3. *Pravda*, 10 July 1953.

4. *loc. cit.*

5. The official announcements on the trials of Beria, Ryumin, Abakumov, and Bagirov are given in full in Robert Conquest, *Power and Policy in the U.S.S.R.* (London, 1961), pp. 440–53.

6. *The Anti-Stalin Campaign*, p. 69.

7. *Pravda*, 3 February 1955.

8. Harriman, *op. cit.*, p. 105.

9. *The Anti-Stalin Campaign*, p. 6.

10. *ibid.*, p. 300.

11. *ibid.*, pp. 276–308.

12. Fainsod, *op. cit.*, pp. 275–7.

13. *Pravda*, 4 July 1957.

14. Fainsod, *op. cit.*, p. 173.

15. In the course of a visit to the U.S.S.R. in 1959, Averell Harriman, who had formerly been U.S. ambassador in Moscow, dined with Khrushchev, Mikoyan, and Kozlov. During dinner Khrushchev began complaining jokingly of Mikoyan's failings. Harriman in the same spirit defended Mikoyan, suggesting that he would have been a great capitalist in another age and that, if Khrushchev ever tired of him, he should send him to America and not to Siberia. Mikoyan himself broke in at this point with the significant comment: 'Nikita can't send me to Siberia any more. He's too late. That sort of thing is ended.'

Harriman, *op. cit.*, p. 106.

NOTES TO CHAPTER 26

1. *The Anti-Stalin Campaign*, p. 285.

2. *Pravda*, 13 March 1954.

3. *Izvestiya*, 13 June 1954.

4. *Izvestiya*, 27 April 1954.

5. R. Goold-Adams, *A Time of Power, A Reappraisal of John Foster Dulles* (London, 1962), pp. 112–13, 126–7.

6. Dulles was pessimistic. His attitude to the Russians was one of belligerent mistrust. In San Francisco at the conclusion of the General Assembly, Molotov had proposed the dismantling of NATO in favour of a single system for the whole of Europe. The three Western powers had rejected the proposal for sound reasons. Dulles added gratuitously to the Russians that 'You cannot base a security system on joining forces with those whom you do not trust.'

R. Goold-Adams, *op. cit.*, pp. 186–7.

7. *Pravda*, 15 February 1956.

8. John F. Kennedy. Speech of 22 October 1962. (USIS, London.)

The Soviet government promptly protested against the President's blockade of Cuba and his other precautions as 'unprecedented acts of aggression'.

Narody SSSR i Cuba naveki vmeste. Dokumenty Sovetsko-Cubinskoi druzhby (Moscow, 1963), pp. 344–50.

9. *ibid.*, pp. 359–64.

10. Khrushchev claimed that the crisis had ended in victory for Soviet peace policy and Kennedy with statesmanlike restraint refrained from proclaiming it as an American diplomatic victory, but this was apparent to all, including the Russians.

ibid., pp. 383–99 for text of Khrushchev's report to the Supreme Soviet on 12 December 1962, concerning the Cuban crisis.

11. N. S. Khrushchev, *World without Arms—World without Wars* (Moscow, 1961), I, p. 276.

NOTES TO CHAPTER 27

1. The twenty-second congress, apart from this main task of adopting the party programme for social and economic development up to 1980, carried the de-Stalinization policy further, and even ordered the removal of Stalin's body from the mausoleum in the Red Square. Also it began, under the cover of attacks on Albania, the long and bitter polemics with the Chinese Communists.

2. *Pravda*, 2 November 1961.

3. *loc. cit.*

4. *loc. cit.*

5. The sixth plan was closed in 1958 because several of the goals specified could not be reached. The new seven-year plan replaced it, scheduled to begin in 1958 and covering the years 1958–65.

6. *Pravda*, 8 May 1957.

7. *Pravda*, 22 January 1961.

8. Fainsod, *op. cit.*, p. 551.

9. *ibid.*, p. 557.

10. *Pravda*, 14 January 1961.

11. Fainsod, *op. cit.*, p. 558.

12. D. J. I. Matko in *World Today* (Chatham House, London), July 1965.

13. Fainsod, *op. cit.*, p. 570.

14. Matko, *loc. cit.*

15. *loc. cit.*

16. *loc. cit.*

17. *Pravda*, 16 October 1964.

18. *Pravda*, 17 October 1964.

NOTES TO CHAPTER 28

1. A. Zauberman in *World Today* (Chatham House, London), April 1964.
2. Matko, *op. cit.*
3. Pressures have been developing in the Soviet Union towards breaking down the collective and state farms in favour of ownership of the land by groups of five or six peasants. The purpose would be to revive individual incentive and the personal responsibility of the peasant. This proposal would involve the admission that the collective and state farms are subject to the same criticisms as those which Stolypin levelled against the commune. See article in *The Times*, London, 7 September 1965.
4. Matko, *op. cit.*
5. *Soviet News*, London, 16 February 1967.
6. A. Zauberman, *op. cit.*
7. *Soviet News*, London, 8 March 1967.
8. *Soviet News*, London, 16 February 1967.
9. *Pravda*, 30 March 1966.
10. Neville Brown in *World Today* (Chatham House, London), September 1966; John Erickson, *ibid.*, March 1967.
11. The West German government has been a strong opponent of the non-proliferation treaty, alleging that it would severely handicap the development of the peaceful uses of nuclear energy in West Germany. Speaking in Moscow on 14 March 1967, Brezhnev said that:

'Among the ruling circles in the Federal Republic of Germany, the prospect of such a treaty being concluded seems to have been received as a real disaster and as the collapse of the most cherished aspirations and hopes ... We have stated on more than one occasion that we should like to see a considerable improvement in the relations between the Soviet Union and the Federal Republic of Germany. In order to make this possible, however, the policy of revanchism and militarism which is now being pursued by that German state must give way to a genuinely peaceful policy. This is not the case so far.'

Soviet News, London, 14 March 1967.

Bibliography

The following are the main sources on which I have drawn directly or which have contributed indirectly to this study. The notes to each chapter contain further references, especially to *Voprosy Istorii* and to British and American journals which I have found useful:

Paul B. Anderson, *People, State, and Church in Modern Russia* (London, 1944).
The Anti-Stalin Campaign and International Communism. A selection of documents edited by The Russian Institute, Columbia University (New York, 1956).
Angelica Balabanov, *My Life as a Rebel*, translated from the Russian (London, 1938).
A. Barmine, *One who Survived* (New York, 1945).
F. Beck and W. Godin, *Russian Purge and the Extraction of Confession*, translated from the German (London, 1951).
Max Beloff, *The Foreign Policy of Soviet Russia 1929–41*. Vol. I, 1929–36 (London, 1947); Vol. II, 1936–41 (London, 1949).
Nicholas Berdyaev, *The Origin of Russian Communism*, translated from the Russian (London, 1937).
Valentin Berezhkov, 'Na Rubezhe Mira i Voiny', in *Novy Mir* (Moscow, 1965).
G. Buchanan, *My Mission to Russia* (London, 1923).
Paul Bulygin, *The Murder of the Romanovs*, translated from the Russian (London, 1935).
James Bunyan and H. H. Fisher, *The Bolshevik Revolution 1917–18*. Documents and materials (Stanford, 1934).
James Bunyan, *Intervention, Civil War, and Communism in Russia. April–December 1918*. Documents and materials (Baltimore, 1936).
P. M. Bykov, *The Last Days of the Tsardom* (London, 1937).
James F. Byrnes, *Speaking Frankly* (London, 1948).
E. H. Carr, *The Soviet Impact on the Western World* (London, 1946); *The Bolshevik Revolution 1917–23*. Three vols (London, 1950–3); *The Interregnum 1923–24* (London, 1954); *Socialism in one Country 1924–26*. Three vols (London, 1958–64).
W. H. Chamberlin, *The Russian Revolution* (London, 1935); *The Soviet Planned Economic Order* (Boston, 1931).
Richard Charques, *The Twilight of Imperial Russia* (London, 1958).
V. I. Chuikov, *Nachalo Puti* (Moscow, 1959);
Winston S. Churchill, *The Second World War*. Six vols (London, 1948–54).
Douglas Clark, *Three Days to Catastrophe* (London, 1966).
R. Conquest, *The Soviet Deportation of Nationalities* (London, 1960); *Power and Policy in the U.S.S.R.* (London, 1961); *Russia after Khrushchev* (New York, 1965).
Cordell Hull, *Memoirs of* (London, 1948).
Edward Crankshaw, *Khrushchev* (London, 1966).
Alexander Dallin, *German Rule in Russia* (London, 1957).
D. J. Dallin and B. Nikolaevsky, *Forced Labour in Soviet Russia* (London, 1948).

D. J. Dallin, *The Changing World of Soviet Russia* (Yale, 1956).
Joseph E. Davies, *Mission to Moscow* (London, 1942).
F. W. Deakin and G. R. Storry, *The Case of Richard Sorge* (London, 1966).
J. F. Deane, *The Strange Alliance* (London, 1947).
Jane Degras (editor), *Soviet Documents on Foreign Policy*. Vol. I, 1917–24 (London, 1951); Vol. II (London, 1951); Vol. III (London, 1953); *The Communist International 1919–43*. Documents. Vol. I, 1919–22 (London, 1956); Vol. II, 1923–8 (London, 1960); Vol. III, 1929–43 (London, 1965).
Isaac Deutscher, *Russia after Stalin* (London, 1953);
    The Prophet Armed: Trotsky 1879–1921 (London, 1954);
    The Prophet Unarmed: Trotsky 1921–29 (London, 1959);
    The Prophet Outcast: Trotsky 1929–40 (London, 1963);
    Stalin: A Political Biography (paperback edition) (London, 1961).
Maurice Dobb, *Soviet Economic Development since 1917* (London, 1948).
L. C. Dunsterville, *Adventures of Dunsterforce* (London, 1921).
D. D. Eisenhower, *Crusade in Europe* (London, 1948).
C. H. Ellis, *The Transcaspian Episode* (London, 1963).
John Erickson, *The Soviet High Command: A Military–Political History 1918–41* (London, 1962).
Merle Fainsod, *Smolensk under Soviet Rule* (Cambridge, Mass., 1958);
    How Russia is Ruled (Revised edition) (Cambridge, Mass., 1963).
George Fischer, *Soviet Opposition to Stalin* (Harvard, 1952);
    Russian Liberalism (Harvard, 1958).
Louis Fischer, *The Life of Lenin* (London, 1965).
Peter Fleming, *The Fate of Admiral Kolchak* (London, 1963).
William C. Fletcher, *A Study in Survival: The Church in Russia 1927–43* (London, 1965).
M. T. Florinsky, *Russia* (5th edition) (New York, 1959).
David Footman, *The Civil War in Russia* (London, 1961).
Mark Frankland, *Khrushchev* (London, 1966).
Michael Futrell, *Northern Underground: Episodes of Russian Revolutionary Transport and Communications through Scandinavia and Finland 1863–1917* (London, 1963).
D. A. Gaiduk, *Istoriya Sovetskoi Konstitutsii 1917–59. Sbornik dokumentov* (Moscow, 1957).
Raymond L. Garthoff, *How Russia makes war: Soviet Military Doctrine* (London, 1954).
P. Gilliard, *Thirteen Years at the Russian Court*, translated from the French (London, 1921).
F. A. Golder, *Documents of Russian History 1914–17* (New York, 1927).
N. N. Golovin, *The Russian Army in the World War* (New Haven, 1931).
R. Goold-Adams, *A Time of Power, A Reappraisal of John Foster Dulles* (London, 1962).
A. V. Gorbatov, *Years Off My Life*, translated from the Russian (London, 1964).
Maxim Gorky, *Days with Lenin*, translated from the Russian (London, 1932).
H. Guderian, *Panzer Leader*, translated from the German (London, 1952).
Leopold H. Haimson, *The Russian Marxists and the Origins of Bolshevism* (Cambridge, Mass., 1955).
J. Hanbury-Williams, *Nicholas II as I Knew Him* (London, 1922).
Sidney Harcave, *Russia: A History* (5th edition) (Philadelphia and New York, 1964).
Averell Harriman, *Peace with Russia?* (New York, 1959).
L. E. Hubbard, *Soviet Labour and Industry* (London, 1942).

Kenneth Ingram, *History of the Cold War* (London, 1955).

Ironside, Lord, *Archangel* (London, 1953).

Ivanov-Razumnik, *Memoirs of*, translated from the Russian (London, 1965).

Naum Jasny, *The Socialized Agriculture of the U.S.S.R.* (Stanford, 1949); *Soviet Industrialization 1928–52* (Chicago, 1961).

A. V. Karasev, *Leningradtsi v gody blokady* (Moscow, 1959).

G. F. Kennan, *Russia Leaves the War. Soviet–American Relations 1917–20* (London, 1956); *Russia, the Atom, and the West* (London, 1958); *Russia and the West under Lenin and Stalin* (London, 1961).

Alexander Kerensky, *The Crucifixion of Liberty* (New York, 1934); *Russia and History's Turning Point* (London, 1966).

A. Knox, *With the Russian Army 1914–1917* (London, 1921).

V. I. Kokovtsov, *Iz moevo proshlovo* (Paris, 1933).

Walter Kolarz, *Religion in the Soviet Union* (London, 1961); *Communism and Colonialism* (London, 1964).

W. G. Krivitsky, *I was Stalin's Agent* (London, 1939).

N. K. Krupskaya, *Memories of Lenin*, translated from the Russian (London, 1930).

N. G. Kuznetsov, 'Pered Voinoi', in *Oktyabr* (Moscow, 1965).

V. I. Lenin, *Polnoe Sobranie Sochineniiya* (4th edition) (Moscow, 1941–57).

V. I. Lenin, *Letters of*, translated and edited by Elizabeth Hill and Doris Mudie (London, 1937).

W. Leonhard, *The Kremlin since Stalin* (London, 1962).

B. H. Liddell-Hart (editor), *The Soviet Army* (London, 1956).

A. A. Lipatov and others, *Istoriya Sovetskoi Konstitutsii v Dokumentakh* (Moscow, 1957).

Maxim Litvinov, *Notes for a Journal*, translated from the Russian (London, 1955).

R. H. Bruce Lockhart, *Memoirs of a British Agent* (London, 1932).

Ivan Maisky, *Who Helped Hitler?* translated from the Russian (London, 1964).

E. von Manstein, *Lost Victories*, translated from the German (London, 1958).

C. Maynard, *The Murmansk Venture* (London, 1928).

John Maynard, *The Russian Peasant and other Studies* (London, 1942); *Russia in Flux* (London, 1941).

P. Milyukov, *Ocherki po istorii Russkoi Kultury* (5th edition) (St Petersburg, 1904); *Histoire de Russie* (Paris, 1932); *Vospominaniya 1859–1917* (New York, 1956).

Boris I. Nikolaevsky, *Aseff: The Russian Judas* (London, 1934); *Power and the Soviet Elite*, edited by Janet D. Zagoria (London, 1966).

G. Paloczi-Horvath, *Khrushchev: The Road to Power* (London, 1960).

Bernard Pares, *Moscow admits a critic* (London, 1936); *The Fall of the Russian Monarchy: A Study of the Evidence* (London, 1939).

D. V. Pavlov, *Leningrad 1941: The Blockade*, translated from the Russian (London, 1965).

L. Peitromarchi, *The Soviet World*, translated from the Italian (London, 1965).

Lazar Pistrak, *The Grand Tactician: Khrushchev's Rise to Power* (New York, 1961).

P. N. Pospelov (Chairman of the Editorial Committee), *Istoriya Velikoi Otechestvennoi Voiny Sovetskovo Soyuza 1941–45.* Six volumes (Moscow, 1961–3).

Stefan T. Possony, *Lenin, The Compulsive Revolutionary* (London, 1966).

Karl Radek, *Portrety i Pamflety* (Moscow, 1933).

Georg von Rauch, *A History of Soviet Russia* (London, 1957).
John Reed, *Ten Days that Shook the World* (New York, 1922).
G. T. Robinson, *Rural Russia under the Old Regime* (London, 1932).
M. V. Rodzyanko, *The Reign of Rasputin* (London, 1927).
Leonard Schapiro, *The Communist Party of the Soviet Union* (London, 1960).
Harry Schwarz, *The Soviet Economy since Stalin* (London, 1965).
John Scott, *Behind the Urals* (New York, 1942).
H. Seton-Watson, *The Decline of Imperial Russia 1855–1914* (London, 1952).
Robert E. Sherwood, *The White House Papers of Harry Hopkins* (London, 1949).
W. R. Shirer, *The Rise and Fall of the Third Reich* (London, 1960).
David Shub, *Lenin* (New York, 1955).
V. V. Shulgin, *Dni* (Belgrade, 1925).
Marshall D. Shulman, *Stalin's Foreign Policy Reappraised* (Harvard, 1963).
Ernest J. Simmons (editor), *Continuity and Change in Russian and Soviet Thought* (London, 1956).
B. Souvarine, *Stalin* (London, n.d.).
I. Stalin, *Voprosy Leninizma* (11th edition) (Moscow, 1939);
    O Velikoi Otechestvennoi Voine Sovetskovo Soyuza (Moscow, 1943);
    Sochineniya (Moscow, 1946–9).
E. Stettinius, *Roosevelt and the Russians* (London, 1950).
N. N. Sukhanov, *The Russian Revolution 1917*, edited, abridged, and translated by Joel Carmichael (London, 1956).
B. H. Sumner, *A Survey of Russian History* (London, 1944).
N. S. Timasheff, *Religion in Soviet Russia 1917–42* (London, 1943).
A. I. Todorsky, *Marshal Tukhachevsky* (Moscow, 1965).
D. W. Treadgold, *Lenin and his Rivals* (New York, 1955);
    Twentieth Century Russia (Chicago, 1959).
L. Trotsky, *The Suppressed Testament of Lenin with two explanatory articles* (New York, 1935);
    The History of the Russian Revolution. Three volumes (London, 1932–3);
    The Revolution Betrayed (London, 1937);
    Moya Zhizn (Berlin, 1930);
    Chto i kak proizoshlo (Paris, 1929);
    Stalin (New York, 1946).
E. Varneck and H. H. Fisher, *The Testimony of Kolchak and other Siberian Materials* (London, 1935).
Franco Venturi, *Roots of Revolution*, translated from the Italian (London, 1960).
G. Vernadsky, *Lenin, The Red Dictator* (London, 1931);
    A History of Russia (Paperbound) (Yale, 1961).
Anna Vyrubova, *Memories of the Russian Court* (London, 1923).
J. Walkin, *The Rise of Democracy in Pre-revolutionary Russia* (London, 1963).
Alexander Werth, *Russia at War 1941–45* (London, 1964).
J. Wheeler-Bennett, *Brest-Litovsk: The Forgotten Peace March 1918* (London, 1938).
W. A. Williams, *The Tragedy of American Diplomacy* (New York, 1959).
Edmund Wilson, *To the Finland Station* (London, 1941).
Bertram D. Wolfe, *Three who made a Revolution* (London, 1956).
Victor A. Yakhontoff, *Russia and the Soviet Union in the Far East* (London, 1932).
Avrahm Yarmolinsky, *Road to Revolution* (London, 1957).
Felix Yusupov, *Rasputin* (London, 1927).
Z. A. B. Zeman and W. B. Scharlan, *The Merchant of Revolution: The Life of Alexander Israel Helphand [Parvus] 1867–1924* (London, 1965).

INDEX

Index

DATE DUE

Pocket Inside

SOVIET RUSSIA
FRONTIER CHANGES
1945-47

NORWAY
SWEDEN
FINLAND

Kola Inlet
Murmansk

NORTH SEA

Leningrad

Tallinn
ESTONIA

Pskov

BALTIC SEA

Riga
LATVIA

MOSCOW

LITHUANIA

Kovno

Vitebsk

Hamburg

4

Smolensk

Danzig

1

Vilna

Cologne

Berlin

3

5

Minsk

Orel

GERMANY

Breslau

Warsaw

6

Belostok

Kursk

FRANCE

CZECHOSLOVAKIA

POLAND

Cracow

Kiev

AUSTRIA

Lvov

6

7

Dnepropetrovsk

Milan

Budapest

MOLDAVIA

Venice

HUNGARY

Nikolayev

Odessa

Kherson

RUMANIA

ITALY

Belgrade

Bucharest

Sevastopol

YUGOSLAVIA

Varna

BLACK SEA

Sofia
BULGARIA
Adrianople

ALBANIA

Salonika

GREECE

TURKEY

MEDITERRANEAN SEA

0   100   200   300
Miles